The McGraw-Hill

Construction
Business
Handbook

The McGraw-Hill
Construction Business Handbook

A Practical Guide to Accounting, Credit, Finance, Insurance, and Law for the Construction Industry

Edited by

ROBERT F. CUSHMAN
of the Pennsylvania Bar

McGRAW-HILL BOOK COMPANY
New York   St. Louis   San Francisco   Auckland   Bogotá
Düsseldorf   Johannesburg   London   Madrid
Mexico   Montreal   New Delhi   Panama
Paris   São Paulo   Singapore
Sydney   Tokyo   Toronto

Library of Congress Cataloging in Publication Data
Main entry under title:

The McGraw-Hill construction business handbook.

Includes index.
1.   Construction industry—Handbooks, manuals, etc.
2.   Construction industry—Law and legislation—
Handbooks, manuals, etc.   I.   Cushman, Robert Frank,
date.
HD9715.A2M27   658′.92′4   77-13349
ISBN 0-07-014982-8

658.924
M.147

34567890   KPKP   7654321098

*The editors for this book were Jeremy Robinson and Janine Parson,
the designer was Naomi Auerbach, and the production supervisor
was Teresa F. Leaden. It was set in Baskerville
by University Graphics, Inc.
Printed and bound by The Kingsport Press.*

"We are a unique industry because everyone in it from user to designer to general contractor, subcontractor and laborer can see tangible evidence of his work on the job site every day. We labor mightily and bring forth a mountain (sometimes we labor mightily and move the mountains away) and we do it without a rigid caste structure that often limits opportunity in other industries. Each of us perceives his role differently in our industry. Each of us feels like Atlas, holding the world on his shoulders. But we all know that there are many other Atlases and without an understanding of one another, that globe we help support would topple with a crash heard throughout the universe."

SAUL HOROWITZ, JR. (1925–1975)
President, Associated General Contractors
AGC Convention, March, 1974

Contents

Preface

Everyone associated with the construction industry—contractors, subcontractors, material suppliers, developers, trade association executives—time and time again ask the same business, financial, management, and legal questions of their professional advisors. To field these recurring but complex questions is by no means an easy task, for few, if any, individuals have the training, background, and knowledge to do justice to problems of so broad a scope, and fewer still the ability to render answers clearly and practically which to those who supervise America's largest industry is an absolute prerequisite.

The conscientious businessman or for that matter the advising professional desiring to proceed with understanding and confidence has hungered for readily available and readable information and answers to these key questions in one single source. This need could only be met through concerted action—a collaboration of well-qualified specialists.

To accomplish the purpose of this volume, it first became necessary to compile a list of the problems and questions most frequently asked by the construction community. I have tried, I hope successfully, to superimpose upon my personal preference the knowledge of many prominent professionals associated with the industry to develop those most worthy of inclusion.

The 52 chapters of this *Handbook,* each representing a key question, are organized to follow the construction process from formation of the construction entity through accounting and record keeping, taxes, financing, insurance and bonding, credit reporting, contract analysis, procurement, pertinent federal regulations, contract performance and rights, special collection remedies, collection procedures, arbitration, financial difficulties and bankruptcy, and estate and retirement planning. Although some chapters within a section are interrelated, each chapter can be read and understood independently and separately.

The accountants, bankers, contractors, engineers, insurance consultants, and lawyers who have been selected to author these chapters were chosen with two criteria in mind: First, they had to be outstanding authorities within their field with proper qualifications and expertise to write their particular article and second, they had to be able to write in understandable nontechnical language.

I believe that I have chosen wisely and well, for through the generous efforts and skill of the distinguished coauthors, we have, in this *Handbook,* presented the industry with a reference work which without cooperative effort could never exist.

The compiling of this *Handbook* represents the work, advice and encouragement of many. I am indebted to each of the coauthors, whose reward is filling the void.

I do not feel that I can sufficiently express my appreciation to my colleague and friend, Penrose Wolf, Esquire, of Hartford Accident & Indemnity Company, who performed the legal editing of this handbook, or my gratitude to Philip Heller, Esquire, General Counsel of Fischbach and Moore, Inc., whose guidance and direction have been most helpful.

I shall always be indebted for the guidance and support of my father, Edward H. Cushman, Esquire—the strongest man and finest construction attorney I have ever known. He led the way.

ROBERT F. CUSHMAN
Philadelphia, Pennsylvania

Disclaimer

The McGraw-Hill Construction Business Handbook is designed to present accurate and authoritative information and to reflect the state of the law and regulations as they exist at the time of publication. Major changes may result from future action of commissions, governmental departments, Congress, state legislatures, or the courts.

The *Handbook* is written with the understanding that the publisher, the editor, and the coauthors are supplying guidelines and not attempting to render legal, accounting, or other professional services.

In recent years, the role of women in the construction industry has seen tremendous growth, and this is indeed desirable. However, our industry terminology is replete with words such as "draftsman," "workmans compensation," etc. In addition, the English language has no neuter personal pronoun. Therefore, where words such as "draftsman" or the pronoun "he" are used, we hope they will be understood to mean persons of either gender.

About the Coauthors

ALEXANDER B. ADELMAN, Esq. (chap. 50)
Partner, Adelman and Lavine, Philadelphia, Pennsylvania

Mr. Adelman received his B.S. in economics from the University of Pennsylvania in 1928 and his LL.B. from the University of Pennsylvania in 1931. He is a member of the Philadelphia, Pennsylvania, and American Bar Associations and of the American Judicature Society and is a Permanent Conferee of the 3rd Judicial Conference. His practice since graduation from Law School in 1931 has been devoted exclusively to debtor-creditor problems.

ROBERT LEE AGER, Esq. (chap. 34)
Seattle, Washington

Mr. Ager has practiced law in Seattle, Washington, since 1948, with emphasis on construction, corporation, fidelity and surety, and international law. He is a member of the American Bar Association—Section of Public Contracts Law (Vice Chairman, Construction Committee), Section of Insurance, Negligence and Compensation Law (former Chairman, Fidelity & Surety Committee; Co-Chairman, National Institute Committee)—and is also a member of the Federal Bar Association, International Bar Association, American Judicature Society, and the American Arbitration Association, serving on the Northwest Construction Advisory Counsel.

GERALD AKSEN, Esq. (chap. 43)
General Counsel, American Arbitration Association, New York,
New York

Mr. Aksen is a member of the New York Bar. He is General Counsel of the American Arbitration Association and an Adjunct Professor of Law at New York University School of Law, teaching courses on labor and commercial arbitration. He is co-editor of *Arbitrating Labor Cases* and a frequent contributor to legal periodicals.

MORGAN P. AMES, Esq. (chap. 33)
Partner, Cummings and Lockwood, Stamford, Connecticut

Mr. Ames chaired a series of seminars conducted by the Practicing Law Institute on the subject of breach of contract. He has lectured widely on a variety of other legal subjects and has been a contributor to numerous legal publications. A past chairman of the Commercial Law Section of the American Trial Lawyers Association, he is a well-known member of the Connecticut trial bar.

LOUIS AUERBACHER, Jr., Esq.   (chap. 35)
Newark, New Jersey

A graduate of Rutgers University Law School, Mr. Auerbacher is a practicing lawyer in the State of New Jersey, with offices in Newark. For many years he has been a member of the Fidelity and Surety Committee of the Insurance Section of the American Bar Association and a member of the Fidelity and Surety Committee of the International Association of Insurance Counsel.

THOMAS J. BARFIELD   (chap. 11)
Regional Financial Manager, Otis Elevator Company, Montvale, New Jersey

Mr. Barfield is responsible for supervision of fiscal operations of Otis Elevator Company in the Northeastern United States. He has been associated with Otis since 1947, following his graduation from Emory University with a B.B.A. degree. He is active in the American Subcontractors Association and has served as President of that organization's New York City chapter and as National Vice President and Chairman of its AIA Liaison Committee. He is Vice Chairman of the National Association of Credit Management's National Construction Group and Chairman of NACM's Committee for Improved Construction Practices.

TONY BERMAN, Esq.   (chap. 14)
Partner, Berman, Paley, Goldstein & Berman, New York, New York

Mr. Berman is a graduate, cum laude, of the New York University School of Law, where he also served as an Assistant Editor of the *Law Review*. Both he and his firm have specialized in matters involving heavy construction for many years and have been involved in some of the landmark litigation concerning the law affecting the construction industry. In addition, they serve as general counsel to many large heavy construction firms.

BYRNE A. BOWMAN, Esq.   (chap. 26)
Partner, Bowman & Pittman, Oklahoma City, Oklahoma

Mr. Bowman is an experienced trial lawyer practicing in Oklahoma City. His practice involves general contractors, subcontractors, surety companies, real estate development, financing, and taxation. Various law journals have published numerous scholarly articles written by him. Mr. Bowman has written Chapter 26 from the standpoint of problems encountered which may result in administrative or court litigation.

JOE F. CANTERBURY, Jr., Esq.   (chap. 19)
Partner, Smith, Smith, Dunlap & Canterbury, Dallas, Texas

Mr. Canterbury is a member of the Dallas, Texas, and American Bar Associations. His practice is primarily in the construction industry, with particular emphasis on labor law problems in the industry.

PETER A. COCKSHAW (chap. 3)

Editor, Cockshaw's Construction Labor News + Opinion,
Newtown Square, Pennsylvania

Mr. Cockshaw is a nationally known authority on construction labor-management problems. He is Founder, Editor, and Publisher of *Cockshaw's Construction Labor News + Opinion,* a widely read national newsletter published in Newtown Square, Pa. An award-winning former editor-in-chief of *Chilton's Contractor News* magazine, Mr. Cockshaw is one of the construction industry's most controversial figures because of his no-holds-barred criticism of both labor and management.

A. SAMUEL COOK, Esq. (chap. 3)

Partner, Venable, Baetjer and Howard, Baltimore, Maryland

Mr. Cook is an attorney, author, and lecturer, who has specialized in the representation of management in labor relations, both public and private sectors. He is a partner in the Baltimore law firm of Venable, Baetjer and Howard, heading up the firm's Labor Department. A graduate of Princeton and the University of Maryland Law School, Mr. Cook served on the staff of the Solicitor, U.S. Department of Labor and on the staff of the General Counsel, National Labor Relations Board in Washington, D.C.

JAMES J. CRENNER (chap. 12)

President, Dun & Bradstreet, Inc., New York, New York

Mr. Crenner began his D&B career at Pittsburgh, in 1945, following four years' service with the U.S. Marines. He was named District Manager at Chicago in 1969, Regional Vice President in 1970, and Senior Vice President in 1972. He has served as President of Dun & Bradstreet, Inc., since 1976.

RICHARD S. CRONE, Esq. (chap. 39)

Partner, Crone and Zittrain, Pittsburgh, Pennsylvania

Mr. Crone is a graduate of Yale University and the University of Pittsburgh School of Law. A major portion of his practice is devoted to the area of construction law. He is Counsel to the Associated Subcontractors of Western Pennsylvania and a member of the Legal Advisory Council of the American Subcontractors Association.

SAMUEL H. CROSSLAND (chap. 14)

Vice President, Secretary, and General Counsel, Morrison-
Knudsen Co., Inc., Boise, Idaho

Mr. Crossland is a graduate of the Law School of the University of Oklahoma. He formerly served as chief legal counsel to the Governor of Oklahoma and was in private practice in Washington, D.C. He joined Morrison-Knudsen Company in 1964. He is a member of the Oklahoma, District of Columbia, and American Bar Associations.

KENNETH M. CUSHMAN, Esq. (chap. 46)

Partner, Pepper, Hamilton & Scheetz, Philadelphia,
Pennsylvania

Mr. Cushman is a graduate of the University of Pennsylvania Wharton School of Finance and Commerce and the University of Pennsylvania Law School. He is the

Pennsylvania Chairman of the Litigation Section, Construction Committee of the American Bar Association; the Executive Vice Chairman of the Forum Committee on Construction, Claims and Disputes Procedures Subcommittee of the American Bar Association; a member of the Special Committee on Public Contract Law of the Pennsylvania Bar Association; and a member of the Fidelity and Surety Section of the American Bar Association.

ROBERT F. CUSHMAN, Esq.   (chap. 36)
Partner, Pepper, Hamilton & Scheetz, Philadelphia, Pennsylvania

Mr. Cushman is the Editor of this *Handbook* and is the Editor of the *Construction Industry Formbook* published by Shepard's Citations, Inc. He was admitted to practice in 1956. He is a recognized author and lecturer on construction and surety law. He is a member of the International Association of Insurance Counsel and the Fidelity and Surety Section of the American Bar Association and served as Regional Chairman of the Public Contract Law Section of the American Bar Association. He was an incorporator of and general counsel to the Construction Industry Foundation.

VIRGIL B. DAY, Esq.   (chap. 20)
Partner, Vedder, Price, Kaufman, Kammholz & Day, New York, New York

Mr. Day served until recently as Chairman of the Business Roundtable Construction Committee and has been long associated with efforts to improve the industrial relations posture of the construction industry. After 27 years at General Electric, where he was a Vice President, he returned to private law practice in 1974. He was active in founding the Labor Law Study Group and the Construction Users Anti-Inflation Roundtable, which later merged into the Business Roundtable. He was a member of the Phase II Pay Board and Chairman of the business members.

JOHN B. DENNISTON, Esq.   (chap. 27)
Partner, Covington & Burling, Washington, D.C.

Mr. Denniston holds a bachelor of engineering physics degree from Cornell University (1958) and a J.D. degree from Harvard Law School (1962). Mr. Denniston is a member of the American Bar Association Section of Public Contract Law and has lectured on legal topics at the Massachusetts Institute of Technology and the University of Sydney (Australia).

WALTER T. DERK   (chap. 10)
Senior Vice President, Fred S. James Agency, Inc., Chicago, Illinois

Mr. Derk is a construction insurance specialist. He currently represents several trade associations, including The National Roofing Contractors Association, Mason Contractors Association of America, and Mechanical Contractors Chicago Association, and is the author of the popular paperback *Insurance for Contractors.*

IRVING M. FOGEL, P.E.   (chap. 7)
President, Fogel & Associates, Inc., New York, New York

Mr. Fogel is a graduate of the Indiana Institute of Technology, Fort Wayne, Indiana, with a degree in Civil Engineering (1954). He is a registered professional engineer in 14 states, the District of Columbia, and the State of Israel. He has lectured and written extensively on the subject of project management, management systems for contractors, and construction claims. He is President of Fogel & Associates, Inc., a multidisciplined consulting engineering organization with its executive offices in New York City and branch offices in Cambridge, Massachusetts, and Detroit, Michigan.

THEODORE W. GEISER, Esq. (chap. 30)
Partner, McElroy, Connell, Foley & Geiser, Newark, New Jersey

Mr. Crenner began his D&B career at Pittsburgh, in 1945, following four years' College of Trial Lawyers and is a member of the American Bar Association and a Vice-Chairman of the Public Contract Law Section. He is counsel for many contracting companies, engineering and architectural firms, as well as owners of construction projects, public and private.

CHARLES A. GILMARTIN, Esq. (chap. 37)
Partner, Gilmartin, Wisner & Hallenbeck, Ltd., Chicago, Illinois

Mr. Gilmartin is a graduate of Chicago-Kent College of Law (LL.B., 1950). His practice is concentrated in the areas of fidelity and surety law. He is a member of the Fidelity and Surety Committee of the American Bar Association and the International Association of Insurance Counsel.

HOWARD G. GOLDBERG, Esq. (chap. 23)
Partner, Smith, Somerville & Case, Baltimore, Maryland

Mr. Goldberg is a graduate of Western Maryland College (A.B., 1968) and the University of Maryland (J.D., 1971).

RONALD MICHAEL GREEN, Esq. (chap. 20)
Partner, Vedder, Price, Kaufman, Kammholz & Day, New York,
New York

Mr. Green served as Associate General Counsel of the U.S. Department of Labor and had responsibility for the Department's civil rights and labor relations. He participated in the drafting of the revised Philadelphia Plan and other Labor Department regulations in the EEO area. He currently teaches EEO compliance and law at Cornell University ILR School.

MAX E. GREENBERG, Esq. (chap. 45)
Senior Partner of Max E. Greenberg, Trayman, Cantor, Reiss &
Blasky, New York, New York

Mr. Greenberg has been practicing law for over 56 years, working particularly in connection with matters relating to building and construction contracts. Referred to nationally as the "Dean" of the construction contract bar, he is well known as a lecturer and author of numerous articles relating to construction contract problems.

H. PETER GUTTMANN (chap. 5)
President, H.P.G. Associates, Washington, D.C.

Mr. Guttmann is the principal of H.P.G. Associates, consultants to the international engineering and construction industry. Formerly, he was a Vice President and principal of Stanley Consultants, Inc., of Muscatine, Iowa, and Chairman and Chief Executive Officer of Amer-Asia Consultants, Inc., a consortium of 12 U.S.

design consulting firms operating in Asia. He is the immediate past Chairman of the International Engineering Committee of American Consulting Engineers Council (1971–1976) and of the International Engineering and Construction Industries Council (1975–1977) composed of the American Consulting Engineers Council, the Associated General Contractors of America, and the National Constructors Association.

WILLIAM F. HAUG, Esq.   (chap. 31)
Partner, Jennings, Strouss & Salmon, Phoenix, Arizona

Mr. Haug is a member of the State Bar of Arizona. He is Vice-Chairman, Fidelity & Surety Committee, Section on Insurance, Negligence and Compensation Law, American Bar Association. He is a member of the International Association of Insurance Counsel.

G. CHRISTIAN HEDEMANN, Esq.   (chap. 6)
TRW, Inc., Redondo Beach, California

Mr. Hedemann is a member of the California and Hawaii Bar Associations. He is employed as Counsel in the Law Department of TRW, Inc., in Redondo Beach, principally serving as legal advisor to De Leuw, Cather & Company, engineers, a wholly owned TRW, Inc., subsidiary. He has previously worked in the Legal Departments of Bechtel Corporation and Stone & Webster Engineering Corporation.

PHILIP HELLER   (chap. 4)
Executive Vice President and General Counsel, Fischbach and Moore, Incorporated, New York, New York

Philip Heller is Executive Vice President of Fischbach and Moore, Incorporated, a leading electrical-mechanical contractor which became publicly held in 1960 and has made a number of acquisitions in the contracting field.

ALEXANDER M. HERON, Esq.   (chap. 51)
Partner, Pope, Ballard & Loos, Washington, D.C.

Mr. Heron has been a member of the District of Columbia Bar since 1927 and the Maryland Bar since 1952. He is also a member of the District of Columbia, Maryland State, and American Bar Associations. In addition to holding membership in the Fidelity and Surety Committee, the International Association of Insurance Counsel, he is former Chairman of the Fidelity and Surety Committee, Section of Insurance, Negligence and Compensation Law and Executive Vice Chairman of the Financing Committee, Forum Committee on the Construction Industry of the ABA and a Fellow American Bar Foundation.

RICHARD M. HOLLAR   (chap. 18)
Vice President of Procurement, Fluor Engineers and Constructors, Inc., Irvine, California

Mr. Hollar has been associated with Fluor for over 30 years and during this time has held procurement management positions in Los Angeles, Houston, and London. In his present capacity he is responsible for overseeing procurement operations in Fluor's worldwide network of procurement offices. He is a member of the National Association of Purchasing Management, Inc., and has been designated as Certified Purchasing Manager.

ROBERT R. HUME, Esq. (chap. 49)
Hart & Hume, New York, New York

> Mr. Hume is a partner with the firm of Hart & Hume. He served 19 years with the American Surety Company before joining the Seaboard Surety Company in 1952 as Secretary and General Counsel. A graduate of St. John's University with an LL.B. from St. Lawrence University, Mr. Hume is admitted to practice in New York, in the federal courts, in the Court of Claims, and in the Supreme Court of the United States. He holds memberships in the New York State Bar and American Bar Associations and in the International Association of Insurance Counsel. He is currently serving as Chairman of the American Bar Association's Forum Committee on the Construction Industry.

JOSEPH J. HYDE, C.P.A. (chap. 2)
Partner, Coopers & Lybrand, Dallas, Texas

> Mr. Hyde is a graduate of the University of Arizona. Having been with Coopers & Lybrand since 1946, he specializes in taxation and has been for many years the firm's specialist in construction industry taxation. He has spoken frequently on construction industry taxation, given testimony regarding proposed regulations. Mr. Hyde authored the chapter on taxation in the *Handbook of Construction Management and Organization.*

JACK A. JEFFRIES, Esq. (chap. 13)
Partner, Keck, Cushman, Mahin & Cate, Chicago, Illinois

> Mr. Jeffries holds bachelor of science, master of laws, doctor of jurisprudence, and doctor of philosophy degrees and is a graduate of the University of Stockholm. He represents many construction industry subcontractors and their national and local trade associations and in this connection has written articles and given numerous speeches on legal problems faced by contractors including mechanics' liens, wage and hour requirements, political contributions, EEOC, OSHA, contract terms, and employee stock ownership plans.

JOHN P. KELSEY, C.P.A. (chap. 1)
Price Waterhouse & Co., Philadelphia, Pennsylvania

> Mr. Kelsey is a certified public accountant in Pennsylvania and several other states and is a partner in the firm of Price Waterhouse & Co., where he is in charge of that firm's Tax Department of the Philadelphia office. A graduate of Dartmouth College, Mr. Kelsey also attended selected courses at New York University Graduate School and Georgetown Law School. He has authored several articles on taxes and has spoken on numerous occasions before business and technical groups. In addition, Mr. Kelsey is Chairman of the Mid-Atlantic Committee of the International Fiscal Association and Vice Chairman of the Advisory Board of the University of Pennsylvania Tax Conference.

R. EMMETT KERRIGAN, Esq. (chap. 22)
Partner, Deutsch, Kerrigan & Stiles, New Orleans, Louisiana

> Mr. Kerrigan is a member of the American Law Institute, American College of Trial Lawyers, International Academy of Trial Lawyers, and serves as Vice Chairman of the Fidelity and Surety Law Committee of the American Bar Association.

PAUL E. KNAG, Esq.   (chap. 33)

Associate, Cummings and Lockwood, Stamford, Connecticut

Mr. Knag is active in various committees of the American, Connecticut, and Stamford Bar Associations and has contributed to the Connecticut Bar Journal. He formerly served as Clerk to Judge Leonard P. Moore of the U.S. Court of Appeals for the Second Circuit.

MARK R. KOENIG, Esq.   (chap. 38)

Manager, Credit and Accounts Receivable, Commercial Division,
Honeywell, Inc., Minneapolis, Minnesota

Mr. Koenig is a member of the National Association of Credit Management, the American Refrigeration Institute, and the Wisconsin Bar Association.

MELVIN LASHNER, Esq.   (chap. 50)

Partner, Adelman and Lavine, Philadelphia, Pennsylvania

Mr. Lashner graduated from Temple University Law School and was admitted to the Bar in 1955. He has specialized in bankruptcy law since 1957, when he joined the firm of Adelman and Lavine, Esquires. He has been involved in insolvency proceedings in the Pennsylvania state courts and in various federal courts, primarily in Pennsylvania.

DONALD LAWRENCE, Jr., Esq.   (chap. 29)

Associate, Weller, Friedrich, Hickisch & Hazlett, Denver,
Colorado

Mr. Lawrence received his B.A. degree at Southwestern College and J.D. degree from the University of Colorado.

KENNETH E. LEWIS, Esq.   (chap. 36)

Partner, Anderson, McPharlin & Conners, Los Angeles,
California

Mr. Lewis obtained his undergraduate education at the University of Redlands and his legal education at the University of Southern California. He and his firm specialize in the practice of surety, fidelity, and insurance law, and are familiar with all phases of construction industry law. Mr. Lewis has written articles pertinent to his practice for *Forum,* the journal of the Insurance, Negligence and Compensation Law Section of the American Bar Association. He is also a member of the International Association of Insurance Counsel.

WILLIAM McCABE, Esq.   (chap. 47)

Surety Claim Counsel, American International Group, New York,
New York

Mr. McCabe is a member of the New York Bar, handling surety claims for various sureties with 10 years' experience in domestic and international bonding. Mr. McCabe attended Fordham University, Bronx, New York. He received his LL.B. from New York Law School.

J. PAUL McNAMARA, Esq.   (chap. 47)

Partner, McNamara and McNamara, Columbus, Ohio

Mr. McNamara attended Miami University in Oxford, Ohio, where he later served as a trustee from 1935 to 1975. He received his LL.B. from the College of Law of Ohio State University and received the Distinguished Alumnus Award from that college in 1974. In 1962, 1963, and 1964 he was Chairman of the American Bar Association Committee on Fidelity and Surety Law and has three times served as Chairman of the Committee on Fidelity and Surety Law of the International Association of Insurance Counsel.

RICHARD MARLINK, Esq.   (chap. 48)
President, Richard Marlink & Associates, Inc., Cherry Hill, New Jersey

Mr. Marlink is a graduate of the University of Michigan Law School and is admitted to practice in the states of Michigan and Illinois. Formerly Vice President of Reliance Insurance Company and United Pacific Insurance Company and in charge of the Bond Claim Department for the Eastern Divisions of those companies.

ROY S. MITCHELL, Esq.   (chap. 28)
Partner, Lewis, Mitchell & Moore, Washington, D.C.

Mr. Mitchell received his B.S. degree in 1957 from Cornell University and his J.D. degree with honors in 1959 from Washington University Law School. He is a member of the National Panel of Arbitrators of American Arbitration Association and Chairman (1976–1977) of the Public Contract Law Section of the American Bar Association. Mr. Mitchell is an author and lecturer on construction law for Federal Publications, Inc., and for various universities.

ROBERT D. MORAN, Esq.   (chap. 21)
Attorney at Law, Washington, D.C.

In 1970 Mr. Moran headed the government planning group which organized OSHA, and from 1971 to 1977 he served as Chairman and Member of the U.S. Occupational Safety and Health Review Commission. His numerous articles on the law have appeared in leading legal and professional journals and have been cited many times by courts throughout the country. Mr. Moran is also Editor and Publisher of *OSHA Casebook,* a twice-monthly newsletter covering current OSHA court decisions.

WILLIAM J. PALMER, C.P.A.   (chap. 2)
Partner, Coopers & Lybrand, San Francisco, California

Mr. Palmer is Chairman of the Construction Industry Accounting Division of Coopers & Lybrand, an international accounting firm, and, in that capacity, coordinates his firm's construction efforts. He is also responsible for coordinating the services for the largest engineering construction firm in the world. Mr. Palmer has been a member of the Board of Directors of the Associated General Contractors of California, is coauthor of *Construction Accounting and Financial Management* published by McGraw-Hill Book Company and is currently Vice Chairman of the American Institute of CPA's committee rewriting the *Construction Industry Accounting and Audit Guide.*

HUGH E. REYNOLDS, Jr., Esq.   (chap. 32)
Partner, Locke, Reynolds, Boyd & Weisell, Indianapolis, Indiana

Mr. Reynolds is a graduate of the University of Notre Dame (B.S., Commerce,

1950) and the University of Michigan Law School (J.D., 1953). He is a member of the Indianapolis, Indiana, and American Bar Associations; the International Association of Insurance Counsel; the Federation of Insurance Counsel and Fellow; and the American College of Trial Lawyers. He is Vice-Chairman of the Fidelity and Surety Committee, ABA, and Chairman of Surety and Public Contract Committee, FIC.

MARVIN P. SADUR, Esq.   (chap. 17)
Washington, D.C.

Mr. Sadur is principally engaged in government contract law involving the construction industry and is general counsel to several construction industry associations.

CARL M. SAPERS, Esq.   (chap. 16)
Partner, Hill & Barlow, Boston, Massachusetts

A partner in the Boston law firm of Hill & Barlow, Mr. Sapers graduated from Harvard College (1953) and Harvard Law School (1958). His practice includes the representation of over 50 architecture and engineering firms, the National Council of Architectural Registration Boards, and the Massachusetts chapters of the American Institute of Architects. Mr. Sapers is a Senior Lecturer at MIT, where he teaches a course on legal problems in the construction process. He has participated frequently in construction industry arbitration. In connection with his representation of architectural firms, his practice has involved projects throughout the United States as well as in several foreign countries. In 1975 he was awarded the Allied Professions Medal of the American Institute of Architects, being the first lawyer so honored.

PAUL SILBERBERG, J.D., C.L.U.   (chap. 52)
CMS Companies, Philadelphia, Pennsylvania

Mr. Silberberg received his juris doctorate in 1973 from the University of Pennsylvania Law School and is a member of the Pennsylvania Bar Association. He has had a number of articles published nationally and has addressed various audiences on estate planning.

MICHAEL S. SIMON, Esq.   (chap. 24)
New York, New York

The author of the *Engineering News-Record* legal column, Mr. Simon is a nationally known lecturer on construction law, contracts, and claims for universities and for construction, architectural, engineering, and bar associations. He is a member of the New York Bar and the Director of the American Institute of Constructors.

MARK I. SOLOMON, C.L.U.   (chap. 52)
Chairman of the Board, CMS Companies, Philadelphia, Pennsylvania

Mr. Solomon is Chairman of the Board of CMS Companies, a Philadelphia-based sales and consulting firm specializing in corporate insurance, employee benefits, and estate planning. Mr. Solomon is a graduate of the Wharton School of the University of Pennsylvania. He is a member of the Board of Directors of the Five Million Dollar Forum and has written and lectured widely on estate planning and insurance subjects.

WILLIAM B. SOMERVILLE, Esq.   (chap. 23)

Partner, Smith, Somerville, & Case, Baltimore, Maryland

> Mr. Somerville is a graduate of Duke University (A.B., 1938) and the University of Maryland (LL.B., 1946). He has been elected to membership in the American College of Trial Lawyers and serves on the Fidelity and Surety Section of both the American Bar Association and the International Association of Insurance Counsel.

DONALD E. SPICKARD, Esq.   (chap. 8)

Vice President, Safeco Insurance Co. of America, Seattle, Washington

> Formerly Assistant Vice President and Surety Counsel to Safeco Insurance Group, Mr. Spickard is a member of the American Bar Association Fidelity and Surety Law Committee. He has held the position of Vice President and Manager of the Surety Department of the Safeco Insurance Group since 1967.

McNEILL STOKES, Esq.   (chaps. 41 and 42)

Stokes & Shapiro, Atlanta, Georgia

> McNeill Stokes, a practicing attorney with an engineering degree and many years' experience in the construction industry, is one of the nation's leading experts on construction contracts and is the author of the engineering record book, *Construction Law in Contractors' Language* published by McGraw-Hill. He has worked extensively with construction associations, as well as with individual clients who are involved in the construction industry. He currently serves as General Counsel for the American Subcontractors Association, the National Roofing Contractors Association, and the International Association of Wall & Ceiling Contractors/Gypsum Drywall Contractors International.

IRWIN M. TAYLOR, Esq.   (chap. 15)

Partner, Kaufman, Taylor, Kimmel & Miller, New York, New York

> Mr. Taylor is Counsel to the Subcontractors Trade Association of New York and former Chairman of the Legal Advisory Committee of the American Subcontractors Association. He is Professor of Law at Brooklyn Law School and the author of *Law of Insurance.*

GIRARD R. VISCONTI, Esq.   (chap. 44)

Partner, Abedon & Visconti, Ltd., Providence, Rhode Island

> Mr. Visconti is a member of the Rhode Island and Massachusetts federal and state courts, the Panel of Arbitrators of the American Arbitration Association, and the Legal Advisory Council of the American Subcontractors Association. He is Executive Secretary and General Counsel of the Rhode Island Subcontractors Association.

DREW E. WAITLEY   (chap. 8)

Vice President and Manager of Construction and Engineering Division, Continental Illinois National Bank, Chicago, Illinois

> Mr. Waitley began his career at Continental Bank in 1952 after graduation from Dartmouth College. He has had diverse experience in the Commercial Depart-

ment of the bank and began specializing in construction financing in 1969 when he became Vice President. His present responsibilities are international as well as domestic.

BRUCE T. WALLACE (chap. 9)
Executive Vice President, National Association of Surety Bond Producers, Washington, D.C.

Previously associated with U.S. Fidelity & Guaranty Co., Royal-Globe Insurance Companies, and Ritter General Agency of Denver, Colorado, Mr. Wallace has held the position of Chief Staff Executive of the National Association of Surety Bond Producers since June 1960.

W. ROBERT WARD, Esq. (chap. 29)
Partner, Weller, Friedrich, Hickisch & Hazlett, Denver, Colorado

Mr. Ward received his B.S. degree at the University of Nebraska and LL.B. degree at the University of Denver.

H. G. WHITTON (chap. 39)
Collection Manager, Bethlehem Steel Corporation, Bethlehem, Pennsylvania

Mr. Whitton is a graduate of Springfield College, Lehigh University, and Rutgers University School of Law. He is a member of the Pennsylvania Bar.

ROY L. WILSON, P.E. (chap. 7)
Vice President, Fogel & Associates, Inc., New York, New York

Mr. Wilson is a graduate of Polytechnic Institute of Brooklyn (B.S.C.E.) and Hofstra University (M.B.A.). He has lectured and written articles on various areas of project management. In addition to being Vice President of Fogel & Associates, Inc., he is an Adjunct Professor at Columbia University.

PENROSE WOLF, Esq. (chap. 40)
Hartford Accident & Indemnity Co., Hartford, Connecticut

Mr. Wolf is an Assistant Secretary in the Claim Department of The Hartford Insurance Group. He is a graduate of The Pennsylvania State University and University of Connecticut Law School, a member of the Connecticut and American Bar Associations, and the Vice Chairman of The Fidelity and Surety Committee and The Forum Committee on the Construction Industry, ABA.

CHARLES YUMKAS, Esq. (chap. 25)
Partner, Blum, Yumkas, Mailman & Gutman, P.A., Baltimore, Maryland

Mr. Yumkas, a practicing attorney in Baltimore, Maryland, since 1958, is a partner in the law firm of Blum, Yumkas, Mailman & Gutman. He specializes in various aspects of construction law and has lectured extensively in his field, particularly on legal considerations arising from construction agreements. Mr. Yumkas is a 1957 graduate of the University of Maryland School of Law, where he was a member of the Order of the Coif for high achievements in the study of law. He is married, the father of three children, and is a member of the American, Maryland, and Baltimore City Bar Associations. From 1974 to 1976 he served as Chairman of the Legal Advisory Council of the American Subcontractors Association.

The McGraw-Hill
Construction
Business
Handbook

Part One

Organization, Accounting, Taxes, and Record Keeping

Chapter **1**

The Advantages of Incorporation: Choosing a Form for Business Organization

JOHN P. KELSEY, C.P.A.
Price Waterhouse & Co., Philadelphia, Pennsylvania

INTRODUCTION

Among the many decisions which must be made upon the formation of a business, two of the most important are: (1) selection of the form for conducting the business and (2) selection of appropriate methods of accounting for the income and expenses of the business. This chapter deals with the selection of an appropriate form for conducting the business. Another chapter in this handbook considers various alternative methods of accounting and the advantages and disadvantages of the completed-contract method of recognizing income from long-term contracts, which is of particular importance to the construction industry.

For tax purposes, decisions regarding methods of accounting may normally be deferred until the time for filing the initial tax return for the business. In contrast, the selection of the form for conducting the business must be made at the inception of the business. Sadly, this decision is often made by default. The consequences of making an ill-advised decision or no decision at all may be disastrous. The selection of an appropriate form for business organization is dependent upon an analysis of many tax and nontax factors, each of which must be critically evaluated in the light of the expectations and characteristics of the proposed venture and the personal financial status of the owners.

Important factors which usually have a significant impact on the form of a proposed venture are:

1. The amount and timing of income (or losses) which the venture is expected to generate

2. The nature and magnitude of liabilities or potential liabilities attendant to the venture

3. The necessity for borrowing or otherwise raising capital to finance the proposed venture

4. The amount and nature of other income earned by the entrepreneur

5. The number of owners of the proposed venture

6. The extent of the owners' participation in the management and control of the venture

7. The tax consequences of the various forms of organization

As indicated by the title of this chapter, the primary emphasis will be a discussion of the advantages of operating in the corporate form since in a great majority of cases the use of the corporate form is indeed the optimal alternative. However, this discussion of the advantages of incorporating is not intended to be a substitute for a thorough analysis of the factors affecting each proposed venture. A sound decision regarding the form of business organization cannot be made without knowledge of the available alternatives and an understanding of the primary tax and nontax consequences of each.

ALTERNATIVE FORMS FOR BUSINESS ORGANIZATION

Business operations are normally conducted in one of the following basic forms:

1. Sole proprietorship

2. General or limited partnership

3. Corporation[1]

---

[1]There is, in addition, the alternative of using a business or "Massachusetts" trust. This form of organization is relatively rare and is normally taxed as a corporation.

There are, of course, many variations of these basic forms—each of which has its own characteristics and tax attributes.

In reviewing the various alternatives for business operations, differences among the various forms may occur in the formality of organization, the extent of liability, the transferability and continuity of the business interest, and the taxation of income from the business.

Sole Proprietorship

The sole proprietorship is the oldest and most direct form for conducting business operations and historically has been the most prevalent form for conducting business. As of 1972 (latest data available), there were approximately 10.2 million sole proprietorships in the United States, compared to 1.8 million corporations and 1.0 million partnerships. According to the 1975 *Statistical Abstract of the United States,* U.S. Department of Commerce, the sole proprietorship is normally the form selected for small-scale business operations as evidenced by the fact that only 11 percent of the business receipts in the United States were received by sole proprietors.

Very simply, a sole proprietorship is created when an individual engages in a business activity. There are no set formalities of organization other than registration or licensing requirements which may be imposed by various state and local statutes. In addition, it may be necessary to register business names with state agencies. The continuity of the business enterprise is dependent entirely on the sole proprietor's desire or ability to continue the business, although it is normally possible to sell or otherwise transfer the business interest, subject to statutory or contractual restrictions on the transfer. For example, financing agreements or other contractual obligations may prohibit the transfer of a business interest.

Taxation of income   For tax purposes, any income or loss generated by the sole proprietor is merely reported on his personal tax returns and is taxed directly to the individual at normal individual tax rates. There is no separation of the business enterprise from the individual proprietor, except as to matters relating to the election of or requirements for certain methods of accounting for the income and expenses of the business.[2] As more fully described below, one of the primary tax differences between sole proprietorships and corporations is the method of taxation of the business income. Another major difference is that the sole proprietor is not eligible to participate in many of the tax-favored fringe-benefit plans available to employees.

Unlimited liability   The major nontax difference between a sole proprietorship and a corporation is the sole proprietor's unlimited liability for claims arising from the business. This risk is eliminated through the use of the corporate form, since a corporate shareholder is not liable for claims against the corporation. In ventures involving potential high risk, the use of the corporate form is normally recommended in order to protect the owner from personal liability related to the business.

---

[2]Treas. Reg. 1.446-1(c)(1)(iv) provides that a taxpayer using one method of accounting in computing the income and deductions of his or her trade or business may use a different method of accounting for items of income and deductions not connected to the trade or business.

General Partnership

Under the Uniform Partnership Act, a partnership is defined as "an association of two or more persons to carry on as co-owners a business for profit."[3] For tax purposes a partnership includes a syndicate, group, pool, joint venture, or other unincorporated organization by means of which any business, financial operation, or venture is carried on.[4]

The partnership as a separate entity   A partnership is recognized as a separate legal entity for purposes such as owning property, having employees, and suing or being sued. A partnership may arise informally, with no written agreement, or may (and should) be reduced to a formal written agreement. There are no statutory requirements relating to the capitalization of a partnership, and a partner may contribute property and/or services in exchange for his or her partnership interest. The performance of services for a partnership in exchange for an interest in the partnership will result in taxable income to the contributing partner.[5] However, the contribution of property to a partnership in exchange for a partnership interest can normally be accomplished without incurring any income taxes,[6] but the contribution of property which is subject to a liability in excess of the partner's basis in the property may result in taxable income to the partner. Similarly, no gain or loss will be recognized in the case of a distribution by the partnership unless money distributed exceeds the adjusted basis of the partner's interest in the partnership.[7]

Similarities with sole proprietorships   Certain partnership attributes make a partnership closely akin to a sole proprietorship. First, general partners normally are subject to unlimited personal liability with respect to claims against the partnership. Second, for tax purposes each partner must report his or her distributive share of the partnership's income and deductions.[8] The character of items of income or deduction of the partnership maintain their identity when reported on the individual partner's return.[9] This distinction can be important for items such as capital gains and losses, dividends, tax-exempt interest and charitable contributions—all of which are subject to special rules for tax purposes.

Partnership interests are normally freely transferable. However, the disposal of a partnership interest may result in ordinary income (rather than capital gain) to the transferor partner and may, under certain circumstances, result in the termination of a partnership for tax purposes.[10]

---

[3]Uniform Partnership Act, § 6.
[4]Int. Rev. Code, § 761.
[5]Treas. Reg. 1.721-1(b).
[6]Int. Rev. Code, § 721.
[7]Ibid., § 731.
[8]Ibid., § 702(a).
[9]Ibid., § 702(b).

[10]The Int. Rev. Code, § 751, provides that money or the fair-market value of any property received by a transferor partner in exchange for his partnership interest and attributable to unrealized receivables of the partnership constitutes ordinary income. Treas. Reg. 1.708-1(b)(ii) provides that the sale or exchange of 50 percent or more or the total interest in the partnership within a period of 12 consecutive months will terminate a partnership.

Limited Partnership

The characteristic of unlimited liability for general partners is probably the primary reason that the partnership form of organization is not more widely employed. It is possible to avoid unlimited liability through the use of a limited partnership. Limited partners are normally subject to partnership liability only to the extent of their capital contributions.

Avoiding unlimited liability   Each limited partnership must have at least one general partner. One technique which has been used in order to gain the potential benefits of the pass-through of partnership income and deductions and at the same time limit the liability of the individual owners is to use a limited partnership with a corporation as the general partner. In cases where the sole general partner of a proposed limited partnership is a corporation, the Internal Revenue Service will not issue an advance ruling regarding whether the entity will be treated as a partnership (rather than as a corporation) unless the corporate general partner meets certain minimum capitalization requirements. In addition, the limited partners may not own directly or indirectly more than 20 percent of the stock of the corporate general partner or its affiliates.[11]

Use of limited partnerships for tax-sheltered investments   Limited partnerships are not appropriate for many business ventures, since limited partners may not exercise management or control over the partnership without losing their limited-liability status. Because of these restrictions, the uses of the limited partnership are primarily in situations where it is necessary to attract equity capital to a partnership or in providing a vehicle for tax-sheltered investments.

Corporation

A corporation is formed under state law by a certain number of shareholders filing, with the appropriate state department, a certificate or articles of incorporation. Generally more formality and expense are involved in the formation of a corporation than is associated with other forms of business enterprise. The formation of a corporation brings into being a legal entity separate and apart from the owners of the corporation. A corporation is also treated as a separate taxable entity.

Corporate characteristics   Unincorporated entities such as associations and joint-stock companies may be considered as corporations for tax purposes. In order to determine whether an entity is deemed to be a corporation, the major characteristics which distinguish a corporation from other forms of business organization are:

1. Associates
2. An objective to carry on business and divide the gains therefrom
3. Continuity of life
4. Centralization of management
5. Liability for debts limited to corporate property
6. Free transferability of ownership interests[12]

---

[11]Rev. Proc. 72-13, 1972-1 CB 735.

[12]Treas. Reg. 301.7701-2. These principles evolved from the U.S. Supreme Court's decision in the case of *Morrissey v. Comm.* 296 U.S. 344 (1935).

A corporation pays taxes on its own income and its shareholders pay taxes on dividends distributed to them. The federal tax rate on corporations for 1975 to 1978 is 20 percent on income up to $25,000, 22 percent on income from $25,000 to $50,000, and 48 percent on income over $50,000.[13] In contrast, federal taxes on individuals range from 14 percent on income of $500 to 70 percent on income over $100,000 for a single taxpayer ($200,000 for a married taxpayer filing a joint return).[14]

State taxation of corporations may also vary significantly from state taxes imposed on individuals. For example, Pennsylvania taxes the allocable net income of corporations at 9.5 percent, and taxes the net business income of a sole proprietor or partner at 2 percent.

Limited liability   Other differences between the corporate form of organization and proprietorships (and general partnerships) include the fact that a corporate shareholder's liability is normally limited to his investment in the corporation and that the ownership and management of the corporation may be separated. Additionally, a corporation in most states may have a perpetual term of existence, and the transfer of shares of the corporation or the death of a shareholder will not terminate the corporation's existence.

Transactions between a corporation and its shareholders are normally treated the same as transactions between unrelated parties except for certain special rules deemed necessary to prevent tax avoidance. Among these special rules are the following Internal Revenue Code sections:

- Section 267, which forbids the deduction of certain losses, expenses, and interest in transactions between a corporation and certain of its shareholders
- Section 269, which disallows certain tax benefits if control of a corporation has been acquired for the principal purpose of tax avoidance
- Section 382, which reduces or eliminates net operating loss carryovers in certain cases where corporate ownership changes
- Section 482, which empowers the Internal Revenue Service to allocate or apportion income or deductions among related taxpayers in order to prevent the evasion of taxes

It is possible under certain conditions to transfer property to a corporation without recognizing any taxable gain.[15] This provision is especially useful in incorporating an existing business.

THE TAX CONSEQUENCES OF INCORPORATION— TAXATION OF INCOME

As outlined above, the tax-rate structure applicable to individuals is significantly different from that applicable to corporations.

Comparison of Individual and Corporate Tax Rates

At income of $50,000 or more, corporations are taxed at a constant 48 percent rate, while individuals are taxed at an increasing marginal rate which reaches 70

[13]Int. Rev. Code, § 11.
[14]Int. Rev. Code, § 1.
[15]Int. Rev. Code, § 351.

TABLE 1.1

Pre-tax income	Individual tax*	Corporate tax
$ 25,000	$ 4,600	$ 5,000
50,000	14,910	10,500
100,000	39,910	34,500
300,000	139,910	130,500
500,000	239,910	226,500
1,000,000	489,910	466,500
2,000,000	989,910	946,500

*Assumes a married individual filing a joint return, using the standard deduction.

percent. This difference has been reduced to a certain extent by the Tax Reform Act of 1969 which established a maximum tax rate on *earned income.* Earned income generally includes wages, salaries, or professional fees received as compensation for personal services actually rendered. The effect of this provision is to limit the maximum tax rate on income earned by an individual to 50 percent. A comparison of the total tax burden on a proprietorship as opposed to a corporation at various income levels illustrates this difference.

Table 1.1 assumes that no income has been distributed as dividends by the corporation. Significantly different results occur if it is assumed that a corporation distributes its after-tax income as a dividend to its shareholders, since the amount distributed as dividends will incur a second tax at the shareholder level. For example, the total individual and corporate taxes on a corporation earning $100,000 and distributing its after-tax income to its sole shareholder would be approximately $58,000. At pre-tax income of $300,000, the total tax burden increases to approximately $216,000 (assuming a married individual filing a joint return, using the standard deduction and ignoring the $100 dividend exclusion).

The above comparison would appear to indicate that the corporate form of business organization is extremely disadvantageous as compared to a proprietorship or a partnership. Why, then, is the corporate form often the preferred form of organization?

The answer to this question is found partly through an understanding of some of the tax advantages allowed to a corporation in computing its taxable income. In the above example, note that the taxes payable by the corporation do not consider the availability of deductions to the corporation for payment of reasonable salary to its employees. The corporation could pay a salary to its shareholder-employee and thereby reduce its own tax burden and, because of the maximum tax provisions, limit the marginal tax rate on the employee's salary to 50 percent. Indeed, if a corporation made up of one person paid out all its income to its employee, the net after-tax income to the shareholder-employee would be the same as that of the sole proprietor (assuming that the salary payments were deemed to be reasonable). In addition, a corporation is entitled to deductions for contributions to qualified pension and/or profit-sharing plans which could further reduce its tax burden without increasing current taxes payable by its employees. The advantages of qualified plans are more fully discussed below.

Special Tax Rules Applicable to Corporations

As outlined above, the use of the corporate form significantly alters the taxation of business income. Within the corporate form of organization several special tax rules are applicable to corporations.

Subchapter S corporations   Qualifying corporations may elect to be considered as a conduit, similar to the partnership form.[16] Corporations electing under these provisions are commonly referred to as Subchapter S corporations or Pseudo corporations. The special rules and restrictions of this optional tax treatment are summarized in Chapter 2.

Small business stock   Another special provision available to corporations is an election to issue a special tax-favored stock. Stock issued under these provisions is referred to as Section 1244 stock. The advantage of this stock is that any loss on its sale or worthlessness will be deductible as an ordinary loss (up to $25,000 per year, $50,000 on a joint return) rather than as a capital loss which is subject to special rules and limited to $2,000 per year for 1977 and $3,000 per year for 1978 and later years.[17] Generally, in order to qualify as small business corporation stock, the stock must be common stock issued pursuant to a written offering plan (limited to $500,000) of a corporation whose total equity including the proceeds of the offering does not exceed $1 million.[18]

Accumulated-earnings tax   Corporations are subject to certain special rules which may be disadvantageous. These provisions are the accumulated-earnings tax and the personal holding-company tax, discussed below. The accumulated-earnings tax is a penalty tax on the accumulation of earnings in a corporation for the purpose of avoiding income tax to its shareholders by permitting earnings and profits to accumulate in the corporation. If the proscribed purpose is found to exist, the corporation may be assessed a penalty tax of $27\frac{1}{2}$ percent of the first $100,000 and $38\frac{1}{2}$ percent of the accumulated taxable income in excess of $100,000. For purposes of computing whether "excess" accumulated earnings exist, corporations are permitted to accumulate the larger of $150,000 or an amount sufficient to provide for the reasonable needs of the business without penalty.[19]

For purposes of determining whether a proscribed purpose exists and also the amount of "excess" accumulated earnings, it may be necessary to determine the reasonable needs of the business. The regulations set forth guidelines which, in general, will be considered reasonable business needs. These include providing for: (1) bona fide expansion of the business or acquisition of another business, (2) the retirement of bona fide indebtedness, (3) working capital for the business, and (4) loans or investments for suppliers or customers if neces-

[16]Int. Rev. Code, § 1371–1377.
[17]Int. Rev. Code, § 1244.
[18]Ibid., § 1244(c)(2).
[19]Int. Rev. Code, § 535(c).

sary to maintain the business.[20] Particular attention should be given to the documentation of specific plans for business expansion since a vague general intention to expand the business will not be deemed to be a reasonable need of the business. Calculation of the working-capital needs of the business is normally based on a formula approach.

Personal holding-company tax   Another potential penalty tax applicable to certain corporations is the personal holding-company tax. The personal holding-company tax will apply if 60 percent or more of a corporation's adjusted ordinary gross income is personal holding-company income and at any time during the last half of the taxable year more than 50 percent in value of the corporation's outstanding stock is owned by not more than five individuals.[21] Personal holding-company income generally includes passive investment type of income—such as dividends, interest, rents, royalties, and annuities—and income from certain personal services.[22] Although this tax should not generally apply to contractors, special rules apply to rental income and income from personal services. Rental income will not be personal holding-company income if it is at least 50 percent of adjusted ordinary gross income and the undistributed personal holding-company income from other sources does not exceed 10 percent of the corporation's ordinary gross income.[23] Income from personal services will be personal holding-company income if the contract for services specifies the individual who is to perform the services or someone other than the corporation has the right to designate the individual to perform the services and that individual owns 25 percent or more in value of the corporation's outstanding stock.[24]

OTHER CONSEQUENCES OF INCORPORATION

Limited Liability

As mentioned above, a corporation is a separate legal entity, and as such, the corporation's shareholders are not legally liable for any debts or liabilities of the corporation.[25] This factor can be of paramount importance in certain high-risk ventures, such as construction of a major real estate project. In such situations, the use of the corporate form may be dictated by this factor alone, other considerations notwithstanding.

In certain situations protection from the creditors of the corporation is more illusory than real. For example, in many cases involving newly formed corporations without substantial assets or equity, the corporation will not be able to obtain financing without the personal guarantee of the shareholder. The use of the corporate form does, however, protect the shareholder from potential liabilities such as those arising out of product liability or warranty claims.

[20]Treas. Reg. 1.537-2.
[21]Int. Rev. Code, § 542(a).
[22]Ibid., § 543.
[23]Int. Rev. Code, § 543(a)(2).
[24]Ibid., § 543(a)(7).
[25]Assuming the shares issued by the corporation are nonassessable and fully paid.

Other means of insulating an entrepreneur from the risks of a proposed venture are also available. Insurance protection against a wide variety of business risks is available regardless of the form of organization. Another potential risk-limiting alternative which is commonly encountered in real estate construction and financing is the use of nonrecourse loans. A typical arrangement would be to operate a venture as a partnership in order to enable the partners to deduct start-up losses on their personal tax returns but limit their potential liability by obtaining a nonrecourse loan secured solely by real property owned by the partnership.

Centralization of Management

Another characteristic of the corporate form of organization is that it is possible to separate the management and ownership of the enterprise. For tax purposes, an organization is deemed to have centralized management if any person (or group of persons, not inclusive of all owners of the organization) has continuing authority to make the management decisions necessary to conduct the business of the organization.[26] This condition is not possible in a general partnership, since each partner legally has an equal voice in the management and control of the partnership unless otherwise agreed by all general partners.[27] Centralization of management can be achieved through the use of a limited partnership. However, the conditions under which a limited partner may be entitled to a voice in the management and control of the partnership are normally more restrictive than those applicable to the corporate form of organization.

Corporate Continuity of Existence

Under the proprietorship or partnership form of organization, existence of the venture may be terminated upon the occurrence of any of a number of events such as death, bankruptcy, or withdrawal of a partner or proprietor. In addition, for tax purposes the sale of a 50 percent or greater interest in a partnership will terminate the partnership. These problems do not occur under the corporate form of organization because of the separation of the corporate entity from its shareholders. The ownership interests in a corporation, evidenced by shares of stock, are freely transferable unless agreed otherwise. Factors such as the death or bankruptcy of a shareholder do not ordinarily have any legal or tax consequences to the corporation, although in certain circumstances, by agreement, a corporation may be liable to redeem all or a portion of the stock of a deceased shareholder.

Flexibility for Personal Tax Planning

The ease of transfer of corporate stock and securities and the wide variety of corporate debt and equity securities that may be issued by a corporation provide many personal tax planning opportunities for the corporate share-

---

[26]Treas. Reg. § 301.7701-2(c)(1).
[27]Uniform Partnership Act, § 18(e).

holder, especially in the case of a corporation owned by one or a few individuals (a closely held corporation). For income tax purposes, shares of stock may be gifted to or purchased by different family members. Various classes of stock with different dividend rates may be held by different family members in order to split the income among multiple taxpayers and direct the income to individuals in lower tax brackets. Estate tax planning alternatives may also be greatly increased through the use of the corporate form of organization because of the ability to issue various types of securities with differing preferences and redemption values. The estate tax planning area is very complex, and few rules are universally applicable. Most transactions, particularly those involving a rearrangement of the corporate structure, are subject to many pitfalls and should not be undertaken without competent professional advice.

Qualified Employee-Benefit Plans

Perhaps the most significant tax-saving opportunity derived through the use of the corporate form is the availability of qualified pension, profit-sharing, and employee stock-ownership plans. A qualified plan may be established by forming a trust to receive and invest the contributions to the plan or by means of a nontrusteed plan whereby funds may be used to purchase retirement annuities directly from an insurance company or United States retirement bonds.

Employers are entitled to tax deductions for contributions to a qualified plan; employees do not pay tax until payments are received from the plan; and any income earned by the plan is not subject to income tax.

In addition, when an employee receives pension payments upon retirement, either in a lump sum or in the form of an annuity, they are usually taxed at a lower rate than they would have been if received during employment. If the payment is received as a lump-sum distribution, the individual may elect to have it taxed according to a 10-year income-averaging provision which usually results in a lower tax.[28]

The final benefit of a qualified plan is that the payments in the form of an annuity are excluded from an individual's estate.[29]

Pension plans   A qualified pension plan is a plan established by an employer for its employees; thus a partner or sole proprietor is not entitled to participate as an employee under a qualified plan. The plan is structured so as to provide a retirement benefit to an employee which is expressed in terms of either a fixed-dollar amount or a percentage of compensation. Under the Employee Retirement Income Security Act of 1974 (ERISA), a participant's annual benefit has been limited to the lesser of $75,000 or 100 percent of the average nondeferred compensation for three consecutive years while a member of the plan.[30] Partners, sole proprietors, and owner-employees of Subchapter S corporations are subject to special restrictions, which are outlined hereinafter.

Another special feature of a pension plan is that the employer's tax-deduct-

---

[28]Int. Rev. Code, § 402(e).
[29]Int. Rev. Code, § 2039(c).
[30]Ibid., § 415(b).

ible contribution to the plan is not dependent upon the corporation's profits and must be made even if the corporation has a loss. The amount of an employee's benefit that must be funded is actuarily determined based on the age of the employee, the expected earnings of the fund, and the employee's prior service with the corporation. Under ERISA, contributions must be made so as to satisfy the minimum funding standard.[31]

In addition to the provisions already mentioned, a qualified pension plan must satisfy both the participation and vesting provisions of ERISA. In general, an employee who has completed one year of service (defined as 1,000 hours) and who has attained age 25 must be allowed to participate in the plan. As an alternative, the plan may provide for the exclusion of employees who have not completed three years of service or attained age 25 provided that upon entering the plan, they are entitled to 100 percent vesting. However, an employee within five years of the normal retirement age may be excluded from a pension plan.[32]

The vesting provisions are designed to allow employees to take a percentage of their retirement benefits with them if they should leave the corporation before attaining the normal retirement age. ERISA requires a plan to select a vesting standard at least as generous as one of three specified formulas: (1) 10-year vesting, (2) 5- to 15-year vesting, and (3) the rule of 45. The effect of these rules, generally, is that employees are entitled to 100 percent of their accrued benefit upon attaining (1) 10 years of service, (2) 15 years of service, or (3) 10 years of service and an age of 45, respectively.[33]

Profit-sharing plans   A qualified profit-sharing plan establishes an account for each employee participating. Employer contributions and investment income are allocated to the account, and upon retirement the employee is entitled to receive the balance in his account. The total annual contribution cannot exceed 15 percent of the participants' combined compensation,[34] and under ERISA an individual may not be allocated more than the lesser of $25,000 or 25 percent of his or her compensation for that year.[35]

The employer usually makes an annual tax-deductible contribution from the corporation's income according to a preestablished formula; however, unlike a pension plan, no contribution need be made if the corporation incurs a loss.

The participation and vesting rules are the same as for a pension plan except that employees may not be excluded from participation if they are within five years of normal retirement age.

Employee stock-ownership plans (ESOP)   Under ERISA a pension or profit-sharing plan is not permitted to invest in the employer corporation's stock if the fair market value of the employer corporation's stock exceeds 10 percent of the

---

[31]Int. Rev. Code, § 412, in general provides that employers must contribute annually a sufficient amount to fund the normal costs of the plan plus amortization of past service liabilities over no more than 30 years. Experience gains and losses must generally be funded over no more than 15 years.

[32]Int. Rev. Code, § 410(a).

[33]Int. Rev. Code, § 411(a).

[34]Ibid., § 404(a).

[35]Ibid., § 415.

total fair-market value of all the assets held.[36] It is, however, possible to establish an employee stock-ownership plan that will invest exclusively in the stock of the employer corporation. This type of plan is included within the general category of plans called *stock bonus plans* which are generally subject to the same requirements as profit-sharing plans. The possible uses of ESOPs are numerous, but the advantages usually cited are that they provide employee participants with the same incentives as the other stockholders of the corporation and that they can provide a means of corporate financing that can be repaid with before-tax dollars rather than after-tax dollars.

Subchapter S and owner-employee (H.R. 10) plans   If an enterprise is structured as a Subchapter S corporation, a partnership, or a sole proprietorship, retirement benefits for owner-employees may be provided, but only in reduced amounts. These types of plans are similar to profit-sharing plans in operation. Under ERISA the maximum annual contribution was increased to the lesser of $7,500 or 15 percent of the first $100,000 of a participant's compensation.[37]

Other Tax-Favored Employee-Benefit Plans

In addition to the advantages of qualified pension and profit-sharing plans discussed above, other tax-favored fringe-benefit plans may be used to increase an employee's compensation. These fringe benefits are, in most cases, fully deductible by the corporation, nontaxable to the employee, and limited to employees (not including sole proprietors or partners).

Accident-and-health insurance plans   It is possible for a corporation to set up an insured accident-and-health plan whereby employees are completely relieved of medical and dental care payments for themselves, their spouses, and their dependents. Such plans are not limited to insured plans and may be merely a plan to reimburse employees for such expenses.[38] The definition of a plan is flexible enough to allow a company to limit coverage to executives or other key employees. However, it is uncertain whether a plan could be limited to shareholder-employees.

Group-term life insurance   An employee is not taxed on premiums his employer pays up to $50,000 of life insurance under a group-term life insurance policy. The cost of any group insurance coverage exceeding $50,000 is taxable to the employee. The employer may deduct the total amount of the premiums.[39] Coverage may be limited to executives and other key employees when certain conditions are met, but it is not permissible to limit coverage to shareholder-employees.[40]

Death benefits for employee's dependents   In addition to furnishing life insurance coverage to its employees, an employer may pay tax-favored death benefits to a deceased employee's beneficiaries or estate. Where these death

[36]Employee Retirement Income Security Act, § 407.
[37]Int. Rev. Code, § 401(a)(17) and 1379.
[38]Ibid., § 105.
[39]Int. Rev. Code, § 79.
[40]Treas. Reg. 1.79-1(b).

benefits are paid as further compensation for past services of the deceased employee, they will be deductible as compensation by the employer and tax-free to the recipient up to $5,000 under a special death benefits exclusion.[41]

Qualified stock options   The special tax treatment outlined below is applicable only to options issued (pursuant to a qualified plan) prior to May 21, 1976, and exercised prior to May 21, 1981. Under a qualified stock option plan, a key employee may be given an opportunity to purchase stock at a given price. If the price the employer sets for the stock when it grants the option at least equals the stock's fair-market value at that time, the employees are not taxed when they exercise the option. If employees hold the stock for more than three years before selling it, their profit will be taxed as a long-term capital gain. The corporation, however, is not entitled to a deduction unless the employee disposes of the stock before holding it for three years.[42] These plans may favor executives or other key employees except that those owning more than 5 percent (10 percent for certain small corporations) of the company's stock may not receive stock options under a qualified plan.[43]

Nonqualified stock options   Nonqualified stock options are options which do not meet the special requirements of qualified stock options. Opportunities for capital-gain treatment are limited for nonqualified stock options, however, such arrangements are sometimes used since it is permissible to favor certain key employees regardless of stock ownership. The employer is generally permitted a deduction at the same time and for the same amount as is included in the employee's gross income.[44]

Phantom stock   Under a typical phantom-stock plan, the employer corporation awards bonuses to an employee in the form of hypothetical shares of its stock. This stock, known as phantom stock, is credited to the employee's account as well as all cash and stock dividends which are attributable to his or her phantom shares. No tax is payable by the employee at such time. Upon the termination of employment (due to retirement, death, or other cause), or at a specified future date, the employee becomes entitled to receive an amount equal to the excess (if any) of the market value of all phantom shares plus accumulated dividends on the date of such termination over the value of such shares on the date on which the shares were awarded. This amount can be paid out in installments either in cash or common stock of the company over a period of years. The cash or fair-market value of the stock is treated as ordinary income (compensation) in the year that it is transferred to the employee.

The employer corporation may deduct as compensation in the year paid all of its payments to the employee, including those attributable to hypothetical dividends on the phantom stock.

CONCLUSION

It is not possible, in one brief chapter, to consider all consequences, potential problems, and planning opportunities which may be encountered in connec-

---

[41]Int. Rev. Code, § 101.
[42]Int. Rev. Code, § 422(a).
[43]Ibid., § 422(b).
[44]Ibid., § 83.

tion with the selection of an appropriate form for conducting a business. Every proposed venture is unique in some respect, and accordingly no single, best alternative can be assumed to apply. There is no substitute for a thorough analysis of the tax and nontax consequences applicable to each business enterprise. For a new business it is essential that decisions regarding the form for conducting the business be made at the inception of the business. Such decisions should not be postponed. The assistance of competent advisors is essential in formulating plans for conducting a business. The participation of one's attorney and tax accountant in developing plans for the business can result in significant savings to the business and avoid serious tax and other consequences which may occur without such advice.

Chapter 2

Taxes and the Construction Industry

WILLIAM J. PALMER, C.P.A.
Partner, Coopers & Lybrand, San Francisco, California

JOSEPH J. HYDE, C.P.A.
Partner, Coopers & Lybrand, San Francisco, California

INTRODUCTION

As with any business, the timing and amounts of income taxes can be affected by both the form in which business is conducted and the methods of accounting used for tax purposes. Form can include sole proprietorship, partnership, corporation, or combinations of these forms. In addition to the many choices of accounting methods which are available for business generally, a construction contractor may choose among four possible methods (and some choices within these methods) in reporting taxable income from so-called long-term construction contracts. Where business is conducted through a parent corporation and its subsidiaries, consolidated income tax returns may be advantageous. When foreign business is undertaken, taxation can be seriously affected depending upon whether the business is conducted by a domestic corporation (which can be consolidated with its domestic parent) or by a foreign corporation.

This chapter will deal with these subjects in a general way—intended to highlight problem and decision areas—but necessarily cannot go into sufficient detail to solve specific problems. For the latter, the reader should enlist the help of lawyers, accountants, bankers, and others who are familiar with the tax problems of the construction industry and are familiar with the taxing rules of the countries in which business is conducted. This chapter will deal with federal income taxes and similar foreign taxes, but will not attempt to deal with state or local income taxes, licenses, sales taxes, payroll taxes, and the like.

Taxation is ever-changing so that what is said here (representing the situation at September 1, 1976) may not be accurate when read, which underscores the necessity for consulting people who specialize in tax matters as problems arise.

FORMS OF BUSINESS
Sole Proprietorships

The simplest way of conducting most any business, and the way in which many small specialty contractors and subcontractors conduct business, is through the sole proprietorship. In a sole proprietorship, the income or loss from operations is added with the owner's other income and deductions on his personal income tax return to arrive at the amount of his tax. There are no tax problems associated with starting the business, withdrawing money for personal use, or ending the business. On the other hand, all the owner's assets are at risk in the business, and if the owner's total taxable income, including income from the business, is substantial, income taxes may be paid at higher rates than would apply if the business were incorporated.

Presently there are also severe limitations on the amounts which can be set aside for retirement on a tax-deductible basis when business is conducted as a proprietorship. We might generalize by saying that a sole proprietorship is a good, easy way to get going in business but that consideration should be given to other forms after a reasonable degree of financial success is achieved.

Partnerships

Perhaps the next step in the upward evolution of a business might be the partnership form where two or more people join their capital and efforts. The tax situation is the same as the proprietorship form in that each partner includes his or her share of partnership income, loss, credits, and other tax attributes directly in his or her personal income tax return to figure the annual tax bill. The partnership has the advantage of representing a larger pool of capital and skills which can be used to carry out larger contracts but which has the practical disadvantages of exposing each partner to the liabilities of the other partners and of having to work in concert—not always an easy trick.

Unlike starting a proprietorship, there can be tax problems in the formation of a partnership, in its actual operation, and in withdrawing from or dissolving the partnership.

It is fair to say that competent professional tax advice is almost always required when the partnership form of operation is used. At a bare minimum, there should be a partnership agreement, and because of the legal, equitable, and tax problems inherent, the advice and counsel of qualified advisors is required.

Corporations

Virtually all enterprises of any great size and continuity are conducted in the form of corporations, and that will almost inevitably be the ultimate form of a successful construction business. A corporation permits limitation of liability of the owners, continuity, flexibility in ownership, attractive retirement and fringe-benefit plans for the owners, and under present law a maximum federal income tax rate of 48 percent on income in excess of $50,000 per year. This compares with a maximum rate of 48 percent on individual taxable income in excess of $40,000 which graduates to 62 percent on income in excess of $100,000 and to 70 percent on income in excess of $200,000.

A simple comparison may be helpful here. Let us assume a business owned by a married man whose income from sources outside the business is equal to his itemized deductions and personal exemptions and whose net construction-business income is $60,000 a year after taking a personal salary of $40,000. If he operates as a sole proprietor his federal income would be $42,060 on income of $100,000. If he operates as a corporation, the figures would read as shown in Table 2.1

TABLE 2.1

Individual tax on $40,000 salary	$12,140
Corporate tax on $60,000 income @ 48 percent	
less $13,500 surtax exemption	15,300
Total annual tax load	$27,440

The use of a corporation produces current tax savings of $14,620 or 15 percent of the total business taxable income involved. But, as with all seeming bonanzas, there is a catch. The money retained by the corporation has not been converted to personal possession; that is, the owner cannot use it to build a new home, take a trip to the Far East, or do any of the other good things he or she might wish to do with it. Practically speaking, if the $40,000 salary will not provide the desired standard of living, the salary should be increased even though a tax disadvantage is involved. The alternative would be to take out the additional money needed for the standard of living as a dividend taxable to the owner and not deductible by the corporation, which is even more disadvantageous in terms of tax.

Again, to generalize, it probably is not possible in most situations to balance perfectly the desire of the owner for money to live on, the needs of the business for increased capital, and the desire to minimize taxes. The best strategy usually is to take whatever amount is needed for the standard of living as salary, pay the taxes involved, and let the rest ride permanently in the corporation.

As mentioned above, one of the main advantages of the corporate form of business is limitation of legal liability for the owner or owners to whatever they have in the corporation. The construction business often requires the furnishing of bid and performance bonds, and bonding companies often will require the personal guarantees of the shareholders of closely held corporations as a condition to writing the bonds. When this is the case, the corporate form does not really serve the purpose of limiting the owners' liability to the amounts invested in the corporation. In such circumstances the long-range objective should be to retain sufficient earnings in the corporation so that its financial condition will be adequate to support the writing of bonds by insurers without personal guarantees.

Subchapter S Corporations

The United States tax law includes a peculiar entity called a Subchapter S corporation which might be advantageous in some situations. Basically it is a corporation which does not have a great deal of passive income, with 10 or fewer shareholders who are individuals, and which elects to have the income or loss and other tax attributes passed through to the shareholders in much the same manner as a partnership. In proper circumstances it could be used in lieu of the partnership form and has the advantage of limitation of liability of the owners to amounts invested in the business. This device might be particularly attractive in start-up situations where losses are expected in early years, as it would allow the shareholders to directly offset such losses against their other taxable income. In the usual corporate form of business, start-up-period losses do not currently reduce the income taxes of anyone, and are simply available, with limitations, to offset future taxable income of the corporation.

Joint Ventures

A great deal of construction is carried on by joint ventures between one or more contractors. The business reasons are typically that the project is too large and risky for a single contractor to undertake, that the combined bonding capacity is needed to obtain performance bonding, or that a variety of skills is needed which can be supplied by the venture members. At times some of the venture members will be no more than financiers. For tax purposes a joint venture is a partnership, meaning that the taxable income, loss, and other tax attributes flow out to the owners of the venture and are included with other items on their tax returns.

The important tax consideration is that a joint venture may elect its own accounting methods for tax purposes regardless of the methods used by the venture members with regard to their own contracts and other operations. This can be used effectively for tax planning as illustrated by the following simplified example. Assume that a contractor uses the completed contract method for its own contracts, that forecasts indicate losses on jobs which are completed and to be completed to the degree that such losses will not produce any tax benefit. Further assume that the company has obtained a very profitable cost-plus-fixed-fee type of contract which will take five years to complete. By assigning this contract to a joint venture in which another contractor has a minority interest and which elects the cash, accrual, or percentage of completion method of accounting, income from this contract can be recognized currently and can be offset for tax purposes against what would otherwise be wasted losses. This same scheme could be helpful in using expiring foreign tax credits or investment credits and could be used in reverse with respect to loss contracts (if someone can be found to share the loss and if deferring recognition of losses is desirable).

These remarks are intended only to scratch the surface of the subject of the different forms of doing business and to make clear that tax savings or wastes can be involved and that the problems are sufficiently complex to merit seeking professional advice and assistance. Such advice and assistance should always be obtained in advance as it is much easier to set up a proper structure than to unscramble an improper one.

Methods of Accounting

In computing taxable income from activities other than performance of so-called long-term contracts, construction contractors are like all other taxpayers in that they may use the cash receipts and disbursements method, the accrual method, or modifications of the accrual method. With respect to income or loss from performance of long-term construction contracts, which really are contracts started in one tax year and completed in a later tax year, the United States regulations provide for the use of any one of four methods:

- Cash
- Accrual
- Completed contract
- Percentage of completion

Whatever method is adopted must be used for all long-term contracts. In addition whatever devices within the methods (other than the cash method) are used for determining accrual, completion, or percentage of completion must be used with consistency throughout the life of a contract although different measuring devices may be used for different contracts.

Here a bit of background may be in order. Regulations governing long-term contracts were adopted about 55 years ago and remained substantially unchanged until January 1976 when revised regulations were adopted. The new regulations are purported to be effective for all open tax years on the theory that they merely restate and clarify the old regulations in the light of case law, rulings, and practices of the Internal Revenue Service. To a degree, this is true; but in many important respects the new regulations are, in fact, new and should not be applied to the detriment of the taxpayer to periods prior to their adoption. Although, as with all aggregations of written words, there is room for doubt as to meaning in some cases, the authors believe that on the whole the new regulations are soundly conceived, reasonably clear and consistent, and in all are an improvement over the rather brief and hoary regulations which they replaced. Incidentally, the regulations deal in detail only with the percentage of completion and completed contract methods of reporting income.

Cash Method

Under the cash method of accounting, revenue consists of amounts *received* as payments for work done, advances for work to be done, and deductions are amounts *paid* for such items as labor, supplies, subcontracts, and materials. About the only noncash item which enters into the determination of taxable income is depreciation on equipment used on a contract. This is by far the easiest method of accounting, and possibly the most accurate in that it does not involve estimates and computations. It has the unassailable advantage that tax is never payable unless sufficient cash has been received to be the source for payment, and it affords the opportunity to manage the amount of taxable income, within limits, by deferring or accelerating collections and payments.

With all its advantages it is not widely used by major contractors, although it is probably the principal accounting method of small specialty contractors and subcontractors. The drawback is that cash receipts and disbursements alone do not measure financial condition, and when a business reaches a size where reports of financial condition are important for credit, bonding, and other financial purposes, other methods must be employed in keeping the books and preparing financial statements. The authors believe that the advantages of the cash method for tax purposes are too often overlooked. It is possible that, with care, a substantial business could use the cash method for tax purposes and other methods for financial reporting and perhaps achieve the best of both worlds.

Accrual Method

The accrual method is not widely used by contractors, although the authors believe that a high percentage of companies which say they use the percentage of completion method are in fact using the accrual method. Under the accrual method, income consists of all amounts which the contractor is entitled to bill (whether or not billed) for work performed, and deductions are costs and expenses incurred, but not necessarily paid, plus depreciation on equipment used. Costs do not include materials purchased for the job for which the customer cannot yet be billed.

Having just defined the accrual method, let us modify the definition. A contract often provides that the owner will not pay a certain percentage of the progress billings but will retain that amount until satisfied with the work. Court decisions make it fairly clear that the amounts billed which will not be paid until the occurrence of some uncertain future event are not income until the future event occurs. Under this view income consists of amounts which could be billed, less amounts retained or to be retained out of such billings. Deductions would similarly be reduced for amounts retained by the contractor out of billings received from subcontractors. The unfortunate fact is that most contractors who use the accrual method have historically included total billings, including retentions, in income and such treatment constitutes the adoption of an accounting method which cannot be changed without the consent of the Commissioner of Internal Revenue.

Another problem with the accrual method results from the fairly common situation where the bid or payment schedule is skewed or unbalanced (front-loaded) in order to obtain relatively high payments for work done at the early stages of a job in relation to the cost of doing the work. Under the accrual method (as with the cash method) this causes an earlier recognition of taxable income than would result from use of the percentage of completion method. Another usual problem is that the payment schedule typically provides for final billing on completion of work so that income is recognized before the expense of demobilization and move out is incurred, meaning that, temporarily, more income may be recognized than is actually earned on the job.

Completed-Contract Method

Under the completed-contract method, as the name implies, income or loss from a contract is reported in the year in which the contract is completed. The underlying theory for this method is that the hazards of construction are often such that measurement of income or loss from a contract prior to its final completion lacks suitable precision to form the basis for taxation. Regardless, it is now reasonably clear that the method may be used for cost-reimbursement contracts even though the probability of significant errors in estimating profit or loss prior to final completion is not great.

The method has the advantage, as compared to other methods which recognize income or loss somewhat in relationship to progress of the job, of deferring recognition of profit or loss until the year of final completion of the project. If the contractor's jobs as a whole are profitable, which in the long run they must be, the method defers the time of payment of income taxes as compared generally with the other permitted methods of reporting. Certain practical disadvantages, however, should be recognized and considered:

1. If retentions are a greater percent of contract price than net profits, and if retentions are not released for some period of time after completion of the job, the taxpayer will be paying tax on money not in hand. This result can be avoided by the cash method or the accrual method if retentions are not included in income until released.

2. Management and forecasting of taxable income can be difficult because of the inherent uncertainty as to when a job will in fact be completed. (The Internal Revenue Service feels that taxpayers play games with the revenue by delaying completion of jobs, but the authors' experience is that the exigencies of business typically override these considerations.)

3. There is a considerable feeling by bonding companies, credit grantors, financial analysts, and some shareholders—not to mention the public accounting profession—that financial statements embodying the completed-contract method do not clearly reflect financial position and results of operations. As a result, the books are often kept on the percentage of completion method, which involves a certain amount of bother and expense.

When the completed-contract method is used, certain significant problems must be considered. They are:

1. What is a contract?
2. When is it in fact complete for tax reporting purposes?
3. What happens when there are disputes and claims which are unresolved during the year in which the contract is complete?
4. What overhead expenses should be considered contract costs and consequently deferred rather than being deducted as incurred?

Generally, if there is a single contractual arrangement for an integrated project, it will be treated as a contract for tax purposes, but if an integrated undertaking is covered by a number of contracts for the purpose of perhaps trying to recognize loss on the early phases, the Internal Revenue Service is likely to treat the arrangement as a single contract. On the other hand, if a number of unrelated or loosely related projects are covered by a single contractual arrangement, the result is a long delay in the time of recognition of income, and the Internal Revenue Service is likely to contend that there are a number of contracts for tax purposes—each of which must be reported separately. These provisions for segregating and aggregating contracts are now in the recently adopted regulations and will likely be used only to curb deliberate abuses. The authors speculate that, where the contractual arrangements represent reasonable business practice in the circumstances, a contract will be treated as a contract for tax purposes.

Time of completion of a contract has been a matter of controversy. The old regulations and the new ones state that a contract is complete in the year in which it is finally completed and accepted by the owner. Perhaps a simpler rule is that a contractor should consider a contract as being completed in the year when he says to the owner: "Here it is, completed in accordance with the contract; and I'm through." The regulations provide, correctly we believe, that a contractor may not deliberately drag his feet in completing a contract for the purpose of deferring time of recognition of income. As a practical business matter, the contractor is typically anxious to complete and walk away from a job so that he may get on with other work. He usually is also anxious to settle up with the owner in order to get retentions released—all of which require completion of the job.

The new regulations also deal with the time of completion of a subcontract, providing in substance that it is complete for tax purposes when the subcontractor says he is through doing whatever he was to do. This conflicts with a fairly widespread practice of subcontractors reporting completion in the year of completion of the overall project by the general contractor.

The recently adopted regulations deal with treatment of disputes and claims which are unresolved at the time of completion of a contract. Former regulations were silent on this matter and industry and administrative practices in this area were not highly developed. So the new regulations bring a degree of certainty into a formerly uncertain area.

The regulations define a dispute as an allegation by the owner that certain deficiencies in the work must be corrected at the contractor's expense or that the contract price should be reduced. The regulations provide that, if the contract is profitable *after* deducting the amount "reasonably in dispute" (which is the reasonably estimated cost to correct or the reasonably estimated downward adjustment of contract price), the profit after deducting the amount reasonably in dispute is reported in the year of completion of the contract. Any difference between the estimated effect of the dispute and the actual settlement cost is recognized in the year in which the matter is resolved. If the amount in dispute is so material that the job could result in either a profit or a loss when the dispute is finally settled, recognition of income or loss from the job is deferred until the dispute is taken care of. If there is a loss on the job regardless of the outcome of the dispute, the loss is recognized in the year in which the contract is completed, and the loss from the dispute is recognized in the subsequent year or years in which the amount is determined.

Although on the surface these rules seem complex, and the regulations manage to state them in their usual murky manner, they are in fact sensible and not difficult to apply. Where the job is profitable despite the outcome of dispute, taxpayers will be well-advised to carefully document the computation of the amount reasonably in dispute as agents will be inclined to doubt these numbers and perhaps take a "cheap shot" at them.

A claim is defined in the regulations as an allegation by the contractor that he is entitled to additional compensation because of extra work, changed circumstances, or other conditions not agreed upon during the year in which the contract was completed. Here the regulations provide that the contract is reported as complete in the year of completion. Additional income from claims is recognized in the later year or years in which the amounts are agreed upon.

Where there are both disputes and claims, which is probably the usual business situation, disputes are handled under the dispute rules and claims under the claims rules. The point is that for tax purposes these countervailing contentions do not offset one another or merge.

The new regulations probably advance the time of recognition of contract results as compared with past industry practice, which was to treat a contract as incomplete as long as claims and disputes were unresolved. The new regulations also make it clear that expenses under warranties are to be treated separately from the basic contract, that is, recognized for tax purposes as incurred and not as a part of contract costs.

The prior regulations did not deal with the manner of allocation of indirect costs to contracts when the completed contract method of accounting was used, nor were administrative practices or industry practices highly developed. As a generalization, most contractors included costs incurred at the jobsite in job costs, currently deducted everything else. The new regulations provide that certain enumerated types of indirect expenses must be allocated to contract costs. They provide for latitude in determining the manner in which such expenses are allocated among contracts so long as the resulting allocations are reasonable. Although the regulations are silent on this point, we would expect that consistency of application of the allocation methods might be necessary in order for the results to be considered reasonable.

Percentage of Completion

The percentage of completion method is one of the most frequent methods used for reporting income from long-term construction contracts. It certainly is the method which most accountants and financial analysts believe most clearly reflects income and financial position for financial reporting purposes.

Under this method, income is contract price, multiplied by the percentage of the contract which is complete. Deductions are costs incurred excluding costs for materials not in place which are not considered in determining percent complete.

The regulations provide that any reasonable basis may be used in arriving at percent complete so long as the same method is used each year with respect to a contract. Different methods may be used for different contracts.

Public accountants tend to believe that the best measure of percentage of completion is cost incurred to date divided by estimated total contract cost, which is by no means always accurate although it is one of the acceptable ways of measurement. Other methods in use by many contractors are hours of effort divided by forecasted total hours of effort and physical observation of architects and or engineers.

Many contractors assume, probably incorrectly, that the amount billed or billable as a percentage of total contract price represents percent complete and report on that basis. This more nearly resembles the accrual method than the percentage of completion method.

Methods Contrasted

Table 2.2 presents a simplified example demonstrating the differences in the amount of taxable income recognized under the four different methods of accounting. The assumptions are that at the end of its first tax year a new construction company has partially completed a single contract.

TABLE 2.2

Contract price		$4,000,000
Estimated cost		3,600,000
Estimated profit		$ 400,000
Total billed		$2,000,000
Retainages		$ 300,000
Cash received		$1,400,000
Direct contract costs incurred:		
Paid for	$1,400,000	
Unpaid	200,000	
		$1,600,000
Overhead, all paid for:		
Allocable to contract on completed contract method	$ 30,000	
Not allocable to contract	20,000	
		$ 50,000

In the example, it is assumed that the contract is completed in year 2 at its original contract amount of $4 million and at the original estimated cost of $3.6 million, all of which is paid by the end of year, and that overhead for year 2 is the same as in year 1. However, total retainages amounting to $600,000 are not released until year 3. For simplicity, overhead in year 3 is treated as being zero.

Table 2.3 compares taxable income which would be reported in each of the years under the four basic methods, and with respect to the accrual method under the two possible treatments of retainages.

TABLE 2.3

	Year			
	1	2	3	Total
Cash method:				
Contract receipts	$1,400,000	$2,000,000	$600,000	$4,000,000
Contract costs paid	(1,400,000)	(2,200,000)		(3,600,000)
Overhead paid	(50,000)	(50,000)		(100,000)
Taxable income or (loss)	$ (50,000)	$ (250,000)	$600,000	$ 300,000
Cash flow in or (out)	$ (50,000)	$ (250,000)	$600,000	$ 300,000
Accrual method excluding retainages from income until released:				
Contract billings	$2,000,000	$2,000,000		$4,000,000
Less retainages	(300,000)	(300,000)	$600,000	
Revenue	1,700,000	1,700,000	600,000	4,000,000
Contract costs incurred	1,600,000	(2,000,000)		(3,600,000)
Overhead	(50,000)	(50,000)		(100,000)
Taxable income or (loss)	$ 50,000	$ (350,000)	$600,000	$ 300,000
Accrual method including retainages in income:				
Contract billings	$2,000,000	$2,000,000		$4,000,000
Contract costs incurred	(1,600,000)	(2,000,000)		(3,600,000)
Overhead	(50,000)	(50,000)		(100,000)
Taxable income or (loss)	$ 350,000	$ (50,000)	—	$ 300,000
Completed-contract method:				
Income		$4,000,000		$4,000,000
Contract costs		(3,660,000)		(3,660,000)
Nonallocable overhead	(20,000)	(20,000)		(40,000)
Taxable income or (loss)	$ (20,000)	$ 320,000	—	$ 300,000
Percentage of completion method:				
Contract revenue*	$1,776,000	$2,224,000		$4,000,000
Contract costs incurred	(1,600,000)	(2,000,000)		(3,600,000)
Overhead	(50,000)	(50,000)		(100,000)
Taxable income	$ 126,000	$ 174,000	—	$ 300,000

*Here it is assumed that the ratio of costs incurred to estimated total costs (44.4 percent) represents percent complete.

What this model tells us is that only the cash method matches taxable income with cash flow, the accrual method excluding retainages comes next closest to doing so, and that the accrual method including retainages and the percentage-of-completion method are both disastrous if the objective is to avoid paying income taxes from sources other than net revenues received in cash. Other assumptions of fact will change these results, but the essential lesson is that on the percentage of completion method and the accrual method (if retainages are included in income when billed) tax may be paid on income before it has been realized in cash.

OTHER TAX STRUCTURING—AFFILIATED COMPANIES

Equipment Partnerships

The seemingly natural thing for a construction company to do is to directly acquire the equipment which it regularly needs for its operations, and that in fact is the way it is usually done. In the case of a successful closely held construction company, tax savings may be gleaned through the use of a separate partnership of trust to own equipment. The key to these savings is having ownership of the partnership or trust vested in the children and grandchildren of the principal owners. Ordinarily such children or grandchildren will not have a great deal of taxable income from other sources so that the taxable income generated will be taxed at comparatively low rates. Financing of such an arrangement is not particularly difficult because the rents received will typically more than amortize the purchase cost of the equipment.

This device can also be advantageous from the nontax standpoint in that ownership of equipment outside the operating business can remove assets from exposure to the hazards inherent in the business.

Brother-Sister Companies

For a number of years there have been tax advantages in conducting business by establishing several corporations—either parent and subsidiaries or corporations owned substantially by the same shareholders—because each corporation enjoyed a reduced rate of tax on the first $25,000 or $50,000 of its taxable income. Changes in the Internal Revenue Code in recent years have fairly well eliminated these tax savings opportunities, although it is still possible (although by no means easy) for corporations owned substantially by the same families each to enjoy a reduction in the tax rate on the first $50,000 of taxable income. The authors do not greatly favor efforts in this direction because they have found that those who go to a lot of trouble to obtain a fairly minor tax savings eventually lose sight of the primary purpose of making money in the first place.

Holding Companies

There may be a number of good nontax reasons for conducting business through the medium of a number of corporations, and most large construction operations end up as a parent corporation or holding companies which own the stock in a number of operating subsidiaries. Where this is the case, the best structure is probably a parent corporation which owns 80 percent or more of the voting stock of one or more subsidiary companies organized in the United States. In this situation it is possible to file a consolidated income tax return in which the income and loss and other tax attributes of all the companies are combined. In the construction business losses—sometimes substantial in amount—occur, and the consolidated return permits the loss of one company to be offset against the income of the others in arriving at the tax payable. When a consolidated return is filed for a group, money can be moved around the group as desired without attracting tax, and no particular tax significance results from the way in which expenses or income are allocated among the members of the group.

International Structuring

A great deal of heavy construction is done by United States companies outside the United States, and such activity (particularly in the Middle East) will likely increase. This brings into play a bewildering assortment of new tax problems, such as foreign income taxes and foreign tax credit.

The first lesson to learn about foreign taxes is that most countries, particularly the developing countries where the big potential market for construction appears to be, do not have highly developed, codified systems of taxation which are widely and accurately reported upon by tax services and commentators. The optimum strategy is to negotiate income taxation with the government of the country involved at the time the contract is negotiated or let. Failing to nail down the ground rules in this way, the next best thing is to obtain the advice of local tax practitioners who know how the tax rules actually work, for there is often a material difference between what the laws and regulations seem to say and what actually happens in practice.

Our laws allow a foreign tax credit, which is a direct subtraction of foreign income taxes from the United States tax otherwise payable, subject to limitation. In substance, the limitation is that the amount of creditable foreign tax cannot exceed the amount of foreign source taxable income included in the taxpayer's return divided by total taxable income in the return, multiplied by the amount of United States tax before the foreign tax credit.

In the example shown in Table 2.4, the allowable foreign tax credit would be 50 percent of $40,000, or $20,000. As a general rule, where foreign income and foreign income taxes are involved, a United States taxpayer will pay the higher of the effective foreign or United States tax rate.

TABLE 2.4

Foreign source income	$50,000
Domestic income	$50,000
Foreign tax	$30,000
United States tax before credit	$40,000

For the purpose of computing the limitation on the foreign tax credit, the income and taxes from all foreign countries may be aggregated. This is usually a good idea since it allows income and tax from countries having an effective rate lower than the United States rate to offset taxes levied at effective rates higher than the United States rate.

A critical element in determining the foreign tax credit is the amount of foreign source income. Examining agents are inclined to allocate all sorts of deductions against foreign source income in order to reduce its amount and the allowable foreign tax credit. The taxpayer's best defense here is a rational and well-documented system for determining net foreign-source income.

As long as the effective rate of foreign tax is less than the United States effective rate, no advantage will be gained (assuming for the moment that a foreign corporation will not be used to carry out the work) by splitting the contract into several pieces. However, if the foreign tax rate is effectively higher than the United States rate, and the taxpayer does not have the good fortune to have other lowly taxed foreign source income, the overall tax load can be reduced by limiting or reducing the amount of income which the foreign jurisdiction will tax. This can be done by having separate contracts for work such as engineering and procurement done offsite and the actual construction and other activities conducted in the foreign country.

At one time the use of foreign corporations to carry on foreign construction had some material tax advantages. For the most part those advantages have been erased by the increase in taxes levied by foreign governments and by changes in the United States tax laws. Some very limited opportunities still exist to reduce overall taxation by use of foreign corporations which operate in so-called less-developed countries with effective tax rates lower than the United States rate. In these instances the potential saving is somewhere in the area of 18 percent of the taxable income involved, but a ten-year wait is required in the repatriation of earnings to the United States. Use of foreign corporations also facilitates timing of recognition of foreign source income and foreign taxes paid in the United States return of the parent company, which can be advantageous in some circumstances.

On the other hand, the operating losses of foreign corporations cannot be used currently to reduce United States taxable income of the parent corporation, which can be a severe tax disadvantage. On balance, the authors believe that it is usually preferable from a tax standpoint to carry out worldwide activities through the use of corporations formed in the United States which can join in the filing of consolidated income tax returns. If a foreign corporation is to be used, its creation and structure require careful advance consideration.

Employee Incentive Plans

Since most construction companies are closely held, the usual stock option and stock purchase plans used by public companies are not useful. It quite often is desirable for key employees to have a stake in the success of the business, and this can be done by means of cash bonus plans, qualified profit-sharing and retirement plans, and by the stock purchase and sale plan described next.

Ownership of a minority interest in the stock of a closely held company is usually of little use to the owner because dividends typically are not regularly paid, and there is no real market where shares can be sold. One device which provides employee incentive and in which the ultimate gain is taxed at favorable long-term capital-gains rates is a stock purchase plan under which stock is bought at a formula price geared to book value, and the corporation is obligated to repurchase the stock upon retirement, death, or other termination of service at a price determined by the same formula. In this way the employee participates, eventually, in the increase in net worth of the enterprise which takes place while he or she is a shareholder, and presumably has incentive to work toward contributing to that increase.

SUMMARY

In evaluating the tax cost of the various methods of accounting, certain basic economic principles should be considered. From inception to ultimate termination or liquidation of the business, the taxable income will be the same no matter what form of business or what method of accounting is employed. While the taxable income in the aggregate will be the same, how it is reflected during each tax year of business life can vary significantly. Taxes deferred to subsequent tax periods are worth at a minimum the cost of capital, that is, the cost to borrow money or the return which can be earned on the cash retained by tax deferrals. Careful selection of the method of accounting for long-term contract can result in tax deferral for every year of the business' existence except the year of termination.

Because of the advantages and disadvantages of the various methods of accounting for long-term contracts discussed in this chapter and the resulting improvements in cash flow that can result from selecting the most appropriate method, the original selection must be carefully studied, and the advice of lawyers, CPAs, bankers, and other experts must be carefully considered.

Chapter **3**

Pros and Cons of Operating Dual Union and Nonunion Shops

PETER A. COCKSHAW

Editor, *Cockshaw's Construction Labor News + Opinion,* Newtown Square, Pennsylvania

A. SAMUEL COOK, ESQ.

Partner, Venable, Baetjer and Howard, Baltimore, Maryland

INTRODUCTION

The building and construction trades unions are in a bind. They have priced themselves right out of the competitive marketplace and their unemployment lines range from 15 percent to 50 percent of their membership.

Construction's customers—smarting under the burden of soaring prices, shrinking profits, a loss of public confidence, and uncertainty over the econ-

Note: The authors acknowledge the able assistance of N. Peter Lareau, Esq., of Venable, Baetjer and Howard, Baltimore, Maryland.

omy—have developed strong feelings of anxiety over where building costs are going.

After studying recent inflation figures and disturbing projections for the future, these cost-sensitive users are focusing attention anew on merit shop and nonunion contractors throughout the country. Currently, such operations garner more than half of the owner-users' business nationwide, up from only a 20 percent share of the market in the fifties.

This trend toward unorganized employers has come about because they can deliver impressive savings. Depending on the project, they can work for 15 to 40 percent less than unionized operations—unhindered by labor agreements which provide restrictions on labor-saving devices and systems, add costly featherbedding work rules and practices, inflated wages and fringe benefits, job foremen controlled by the unions, forced use of skilled personnel to perform unskilled work, interunion jurisdictional disputes, restrictive apprenticeship training ratios, and other productivity-inhibiting practices.

Lately, with so many construction users building open shop, unionized employers have begun exploring ways to recapture some of their lost market. Two methods are frequently considered:

ALTERNATIVE NO. 1—CONFRONTATION FOR SURVIVAL

One procedure is for the contractor to offer the unions representing its employees two alternatives: either negotiate moderate wage scales and operating efficiencies through collective bargaining or take the consequences of an all-out confrontation for survival. If a company determines to do this, it is of course necessary that it be able to negotiate on its own behalf and not be required to abide by the terms and conditions which may be negotiated jointly by a group of employers. Therefore, if the contractor has previously delegated its bargaining rights to an employer association, it must rescind the authority previously given to that association and give timely notice thereof to the union and the association.

Once an employer has achieved this needed independence in negotiations, it may bargain for whatever terms and conditions it in good faith believes are necessary to operate its business competitively. The mere fact that this may entail a decrease in wages and fringe benefits and a modification of featherbedding work practices does not make s ich demands unlawful. Of course, in most cases union representatives will not agree to such a revised contract. Therefore, any contractor determined to embark on this course of action should be aware that in all probability the company will be facing a *strike*.

Concomitant with the union's right to strike, however, is the contractor's right to permanently replace the striking employees with new hires. If this should occur, the union may decide to abandon the workers, conceding defeat. Alternatively, once the contract has expired, the newly hired employees are free to petition the National Labor Relations Board (NLRB) to conduct an election to decertify the union as the workers' bargaining agent. It should be noted that, if any such election were conducted, both the new employees and the replaced strikers would be eligible to vote.[1]

ALTERNATIVE NO. 2—THE DUAL-SHOP APPROACH

The second and more popular method of competing with the open-shop contractor is to adopt what is commonly referred to as the "dual-shop" or "double-breasted" approach. This concept basically refers to two distinct companies, one of which is party to a collective bargaining agreement and one which is not. To accomplish this, stringent legal guidelines imposed by the National Labor Relations Board and the courts must be followed.

This chapter discusses legal and practical issues in establishing such an operation. Before taking any action, contractors must examine a number of factors, including construction user attitudes, availability of manpower, union strength, and law enforcement. However, suggested courses of action should never be implemented without first consulting *legal counsel* familiar with the construction industry and labor law.

Regardless of the nature of the second company, when the employees of the first company are represented by a labor organization, the question often arises whether, under the federal Taft-Hartley Act, recognition of that labor union and application of the terms and conditions of the collective bargaining agreement between the parties is required by the second company. The ultimate resolution of this issue turns on the degree of "separation" versus the degree of "integration" of operation of the two businesses, as evidenced by the facts and circumstances of each situation and the applicable law.

In the construction industry, it is not uncommon for the same enterprise to have two separate organizations, one to handle contracts performed under union conditions and the other to handle those performed under nonunion conditions. Of major concern to the contractor is the immediate financial risk of

---

[1]Two recent cases are worth noting by the unionized contractor who is considering modification of its collective bargaining agreement: *R. J. Smith Construction Company,* 208 NLRB 615 (1974), *rev'd,* 156 U.S. App. D.C. 294, 480 F.2d 1186 (D.C. Cir. 1973); and *Higdon Contracting Co.,* 216 NLRB 5, 88 LRRM 1067 (1975), *rev'd,* 535 F.2d 87 (D.C. Cir. 1976), petition for *cert.* filed. In both these cases, a contractor entered into an agreement with a union at a time when the union did not represent a majority of the contractor's employees. Further, during the term of these agreements the union was never able to obtain majority status. In both cases, the contractors unilaterally determined not to abide by the terms and provisions of the contract and the unions filed charges with the National Labor Relations Board. The NLRB held for the contractors in both instances but the United States Court of Appeals for the District of Columbia reversed the Board, holding that the unilateral abrogation of a collective bargaining agreement, even where the union had never achieved majority status, constituted an unfair labor practice. A petition for *certiorari* has been filed with the United States Supreme Court in the *Higdon* case, and if the Court determines to hear that case, this particular question may be decided in the near future. However, even if the Supreme Court agrees with the Board, a word of caution is necessary. Assuming the Court rules that it is not an unfair labor practice to unilaterally breach a contract under such circumstances, the question would still remain as to whether the union could enforce the agreement by suing in federal or state court for breach of the contract.

setting up a dual shop. If it is established improperly, the second firm could be held jointly liable retroactively for "underpaid" wages and "delinquent" payments to various labor union pension, health-and-welfare, and other fringe-benefit funds under the parent company's collective bargaining agreement. The second firm could also face a National Labor Relations Board order merging the employees of the second firm into the original company's labor contract and all of its costly and restrictive work-rules provisions.

Most decisions by the NLRB as to whether two enterprises will be treated as a single one have been made in the context of determining the Board's jurisdiction over such related businesses:

> In applying the present jurisdictional standards, the Board early reaffirmed the long-established practice of treating separate concerns which are closely related as being a single employer for the purpose of determining whether to assert jurisdiction. The question in such cases is whether the enterprises are sufficiently integrated to consider the business of both together in applying the jurisdictional standards.
>
> The principal factors which the Board weighs in deciding whether sufficient integration exists include the extent of:
>
> 1. Interrelation of operations;
> 2. Centralized control of labor relations;
> 3. Common management; and
> 4. Common ownership or financial control.
>
> No one of these factors has been held to be controlling, but the Board opinions have stressed the first three factors, which go to show "operational integration," particularly centralized control of labor relations. The Board has declined in several cases to find integration merely upon the basis of common ownership or financial control.[2]

The Board also applied these four criteria when determining whether to order a company which had a union contract to recognize the union and abide by the contract's terms if it started a new and separate firm. The union might claim that the employer was unlawfully refusing to bargain and request the NLRB to order the employer to recognize it as representative of employees in the new company, since the new business was really not a separate employer. If the Board agreed, it would order the new company to obey the terms of the collective bargaining agreement signed with the first firm.

The Board's use of these four factors has been given approval by the federal Circuit Courts of Appeal and by the Supreme Court of the United States. In the most commonly cited cases, *Sakrete of Northern California, Inc. v. NLRB*,[3] and *Radio Union v. Broadcast Service of Mobile*,[4] the courts have approved the four-prong test and have enforced Board orders which relied on it. The Supreme Court has agreed with the Board that:

---

[2]Twenty-first Annual Report of the NLRB (1956), pp. 14–15.
[3]332 F.2d 902 (9th Cir. 1964), *cert. denied*, 379 U.S. 961 (1965).
[4]380 U.S. 255 (1965).

The controlling criteria, set out and elaborated in Board decisions, are interrelation of operations, common management, centralized control of labor relations and common ownership.[5]

Years of litigation have led the Board and courts to place greater stress on certain of these factors and less emphasis on others. As the NLRB noted 20 years ago in its annual report, it has emphasized those factors showing operational integration, with special consideration of control of labor relations.

The Board's current position on common ownership reflects the view that, unless there are other indications of common control, the same corporation, person, or group can maintain 100 percent financial control of two companies engaging in the same general type of business in the same locality, *without* subjecting the second company to the terms of a collective bargaining agreement entered into by the first. Thus, as a general rule, the Board finds that common ownership is of lesser importance in comparison with the other factors, while centralized control of labor relations is the most important. What must be constantly remembered, however, is that no case is ever presented to the Board or a court in a vacuum or on identical facts. Each instance in which several firms are alleged to constitute a "single employer" requires the Board to look at the totality of the circumstances.

Common ownership, therefore, will normally not be sufficient to support a single employer finding. While the Board, moreover, has focused on common control of labor relations as strong evidence of operational integration, it has sometimes minimized even this factor when other evidence appeared more convincing. In one case, the Board refused to accord controlling significance to the fact that the two related companies had separate and distinct labor policies, holding that "the presence or absence of a common labor relations policy is not conclusive in determining whether separate legal entities constitute a 'single employer.'"[6]

Almost every case decided by the Board and courts follows a pattern of considering the four criteria for finding single-employer legal status. Since the decision is ultimately based on the *totality of all the circumstances,* it would be virtually impossible to list every fact the Board has considered relevant in applying the four general tests. There are, however, some general guidelines which will now be discussed in detail.

FOUR MAIN FACTORS WEIGHED BY THE NLRB

1. Common Ownership

The question of a dual shop will seldom arise unless a person or group owns a substantial portion of one company and also has a similar interest in another separate firm. If there is no common ownership, it is unlikely that there will be

---

[5]*Supra* note 4.
[6]*Canton Carp's, Inc.,* 125 NLRB 483, 484 (1959).

such other evidence of the operational integration of several firms as to warrant a single-employer finding.

It is possible, however, as previously stated, for the same corporation, person, or group to maintain a 100 percent financial control over two companies in the same locality and same type of business without having the two firms considered to be a single employer. This will be true, provided there is no further substantial evidence of integration between the two companies. As the NLRB noted in its twenty-first annual report, the degree of common ownership or financial control is rarely absolutely controlling in decisions of whether to overlook corporate form to find that two or more nominally separate companies are a single legal entity.

Many kinds of common ownership structures have been considered by the Board and courts. Yet their decisions on the single-employer issue do not seem readily classifiable on the basis of *how* common ownership is actually carried out. Thus, the fact that two companies may be wholly owned subsidiaries of a parent company demonstrates common ownership no less significantly than where a single individual owns all or substantially all outstanding stock in two companies.

Common ownership is not easily hidden, and questions that usually arise concern the degree of the ownership interrelation. In closely held businesses, family-owned or otherwise, it may be difficult to avoid the type of common ownership the Board has found sufficient to meet its threshold test to determine whether there is a single-employer relationship.

2. Common Management

How and by whom top-level and intermediate management decisions are made in firms alleged to be a single employer is a factor which may demonstrate interrelationship of operations. Since this factor is stressed in decisions characterizing multiple-company operations, the NLRB and courts have particularly examined management relationships in the construction industry as to how the decision was made over what *type* of construction the second company performs. Common management has been inferred, despite an employer's claim that two businesses were separately managed, on evidence that a unionized contractor established a second company to do business nonunion, continued to solicit jobs as he had before forming a second company, and simply apportioned the work between the two companies as cost requirements dictated. Exercise of such control over these two companies was held to be incompatible with nonintegrated and separately managed enterprises.

It is not enough, however, that the *potential* for common management exist. In almost every instance in which an individual or group has substantial financial interests in two companies, they could choose to exercise their financial control to influence management decisions. But it is the *actual* exercise of common management which is controlling and not the potential to do so. In other words, the possibility of financial interests exerting pressure on day-to-day management decisions will not, without other indicators of operational integration, lead to a finding that several businesses constitute a single employer.

Normally, proof as to active exercise of common management is found in the day-to-day operation of the business. Thus, if supervisors from one company perform similar functions for a second enterprise; or if the chief managing officials are identical or possibly rearranged (the president of one company is vice president of the other, and vice versa); or if officials of one company ordinarily lack authority to undertake jobs and make major capital expenditures without permission from officials of another firm, active common management will be found to exist.

3. Common Control of Labor Relations

The NLRB has characterized this third factor—common control of labor relations—as "critical . . . in determining whether separate legal entities operate as a single employing enterprise."[7] Unfortunately, however, evidence that the Board considers relevant in a decision as to whether there is a common labor relations policy has not been firmly established.

The Board's concern has sometimes centered on the actual, active control of day-to-day labor problems as well as the creation of overall personnel policies. As is true with the test for common management, proof that the same individuals have the potential, by virtue of their financial interests in two companies, to enforce a common labor relations policy has not normally been given significance. The control of labor matters, also, must be active rather than potential.

Thus, a company whose supervisors lack the power to hire, fire, and discipline without permission from officers or supervisors of another business entity is unlikely to be seen as anything other than a single employer, joined with the related firm. A majority owner of two companies who insists that he be consulted on such daily, routine labor relations decisions also gives strong evidence that his several businesses have a common labor relations policy controlled by him.

Another, much broader view of what constitutes common control over labor relations policy has been expressed recently. In the *Kiewit* case, a federal appellate court has gone so far as to espouse dictum that a contractor's mere choice to establish a second business as initially nonunion constitutes per se the common control of labor relations requisite to a finding of "single employer."[8]

In this case, a holding company with two wholly owned construction company subsidiaries—one union and one nonunion—decided to activate the nonunion company in a geographical location in which, theretofore, only the union company had operated. Both subsidiaries engaged in the same type of construction. The appellate court stated that the very decision by the parent to have the second firm operate on a nonunion basis in a particular locality

[7]*Gerace Construction Co.,* 193 NLRB 645 (1971).

[8]*Local 627, Int'l Union of Operating Eng., AFL-CIO v. NLRB,* 96 Sup. Ct. 1842 (May 24, 1976), *rev'g in part,* 518 F.2d 1040 (D.C. Cir. 1975), *rev'g Peter Kiewit Sons' Co.,* 206 N.L.R.B. 562 (1973).

demonstrated the required common labor relations policy. It reasoned that the parent company's establishment of a nonunion framework within which the second company was to operate constituted the touchstone for day-to-day decisions as to wages, hours, and working conditions, and was therefore significant to the single-employer issue. In reviewing the case, the United States Supreme Court did not comment on this point.

It is doubtful that this *Kiewit* decision will affect the well-established rule that owners of a business have the legal right to own more than one firm without automatically and universally applying a collective bargaining agreement to every commonly owned enterprise. This is especially true in the construction industry where it is a recognized practice for the same enterprise to have separate union and nonunion organizations.

Under the great weight of legal authority, it is the amount of control over day-to-day decisions on such matters as hires, discharges, transfers, wages, hours, and working conditions which the Board reviews. A shareholder's direct involvement in these labor relations decisions of two firms in which he owns majority interests, going beyond a general concern for the companies' financial conditions, will likely cause the two firms to be viewed as possessing a common labor relations policy.

But avoiding a common labor relations policy between two companies will not guarantee that the firms will be held to constitute separate employers. The Board's "total circumstances" test allows it to minimize the importance of any one factor when it believes a single-employer finding is otherwise appropriate. Even though there is no doubt that two companies possess distinctly separate labor policies and practices, but they otherwise meet the criteria for operational integration, the Board has stated that failure to find a single employer where there is "close control through common ownership and management" would "ignore the realities of commercial organization."[9] Thus, although the existence of a common labor policy may be said to be critical, it is ultimately no more than one of the four general factors which are weighed on a case-by-case basis.

4. Interrelation of Operations

The NLRB and courts have found that several companies constitute a single employer when the facts demonstrate that their operations are so dependent on one another as to operate, in effect, as one single and continuous production or sales organization. Thus, outside the construction industry, if one firm performed the first four steps in a production process and then sold all of its partially completed goods to a commonly owned second firm for the completion of the manufacturing process, single-employer status will almost certainly be found. For example, a clothing manufacturing company which performs only cutting functions and sells all its completed piece goods to a commonly owned second company for completion of the clothing will demonstrate such integration of operations as has been required by the Board.

---

[9] *Canton Carp's, Inc., supra* note 6.

In the construction industry, the NLRB will test for common management in the same manner as it tests for integration of operations. Where commonly owned contracting companies engage in similar types of construction, the method of operation and decision as to which jobs each company will bid may demonstrate operational integration. Thus, the fact that one company—operating under a union contract—chooses to seek only those types of jobs for which there is no significant nonunion competition, or that the common management has a policy that one firm will bid for contracts of a small maximum amount while the other firm will bid on larger jobs, demonstrates some degree of interrelation of operations. Where one person sets these policies for both companies, there is a chance that they will be found to constitute a single legal entity.

Seemingly minor indicators of day-to-day operating integration may also become significant. Two companies' use of a single or adjoining office facility, sharing the same group of office clerical personnel, or the use of one bookkeeper for both firms, have been cited by the Board as evidence of interrelation of operations. In construction industry cases, the Board has also said that the use of one company's tools by another company, without proportional reimbursement, supports operation integration. These and similar facts might most appropriately be labeled secondary, since they are not conclusive and do not normally point unerringly to integration. But they will almost always be thrown into the balance as "bootstrap" evidence supporting a Board decision. Although they demonstrate integration only by inference, the Board may rule that such extensive, though minor, relationships would not exist in nonintegrated businesses.

On the other hand, interchange between companies of employees in the bargaining unit is a *major* indication of interrelationship of operations. If employees of one company with a union contract are ordered to perform work for another commonly owned company but continue to be paid by their own company, the Board may find an operational integration significant enough to partially support a single-employer finding. On the other hand, the impact of such employee interchange and transfer will be somewhat blunted if each company pays a proportionate share of the salary of any employee of the related enterprise who performs work for it. Even then, however, if workers for two companies are frequently or routinely transferred back and forth, the inference of integration will be certain. Where, on the other hand, there is only a one-time transfer of some workers from one company to another at the time of the establishment of the second company, and there is no further employee interchange, a single-employer finding is unlikely.

In a recent case decided by the NLRB, for example, the owners of Company 1 decided to set up a second firm. When Company 2 was initially staffed, there was a transfer of employees of Company 1 to Company 2. Although a continual transfer of employees back and forth between the two firms might have persuaded the Board to make a single-employer finding, it declined on the facts of the case to hold that the initial transfer of employees, standing alone, demonstrated the degree of integration required to make the two companies legally a single entity.[10]

As has been noted, these various factors are never reviewed in a vacuum. They will interrelate, and the *totality* of the particular facts of each case will prompt the Board or courts to give varying weight to their four overall tests. Several discussions by the Board on double-breasted operations may be helpful for their reasoning and illustrative of the types of evidence which tip the balance in a dual-shop case.

In the 1971 *Gerace Construction Co.*[11] case, for example, the Board considered union charges that a unionized contractor, Gerace Company, unlawfully refused to apply its labor contract to Helger, a separately incorporated non-union firm.

Helger had been established with the majority owner of Gerace and his wife owning similar controlling stock. It was not disputed that three-fourths of the capital required to establish Helger originated with Gerace Company directors, but Helger had never borrowed any money from Gerace.

During the first five months of Helger's existence, it operated under Mr. Gerace's close supervision and control, and he and a Gerace Company official constituted two of the three Helger directors. Although he and his wife started with majority ownership of Helger stock, he began severing his ties with Helger within a few months. He resigned from his positions with Helger and transferred his stock holdings to Helger's principal management officer. Following this transfer, he neither possessed nor exercised any further authority over Helger's operations.

When Helger was incorporated to operate nonunion, it was set up as a separate legal entity, with separate bank and payroll accounts. Mr. Gerace testified that the prime reason for the decision to have Helger refrain from signing a prehire agreement with a union was his desire to obtain a particular construction job, for which a prerequisite was the giving of a guarantee that there would be no work stoppages. Additionally, Mr. Gerace testified that for several years Gerace Company had been unable to win construction contracts for jobs smaller than $100,000 because of rising costs associated with union jurisdictional requirements. Since it was intended that Helger would compete for smaller jobs than Gerace normally undertook, it was understandable that Helger's average job was normally less than $50,000, while Gerace's was usually over $250,000. While Helger's top employment was 16 employees, Gerace employed 95 persons at its peak. Helger never hired any of Gerace's employees, and there was no other evidence of employee interchange.

The two companies had only rarely submitted joint job bids and normally did not bid on the same jobs. It appeared that Helger's manager and Mr. Gerace did consult on approximately one of every ten bids submitted by Helger. Although Helger had used a trailer owned by Gerace for its temporary office and had used tools and equipment owned by Gerace, it paid proportionate rent

---

[10]*Gerace Construction Co., supra* note 7.
[11]*Supra* note 7.

for such use. Its offices were later moved to a location a mile and one-half from Gerace's. The companies maintained separate health-and-welfare and workmen's compensation insurance contracts.

The NLRB, reversing its administrative law judge, held that the two contractors did *not* constitute a single employer. It ruled that while the common ownership of the two firms had established the potential for common control, actual exercise—particularly as to labor relations—had never been established. In addition, the Board was persuaded that Mr. Gerace's *gradual relinquishment of control* over Helger's operations to a separate manager was a significant indication that the two firms were now separate, even if they had not been separate at their founding.

One month after it decided the *Gerace Construction Co.* case, the NLRB again held that two construction companies with some degree of common ownership constituted separate employers. In *Frank N. Smith Associates, Inc.,*[12] the Board affirmed a decision by its administrative law judge that the unionized company—Frank N. Smith Associates—was not a single employer with a second nonunion company—Keuka—in both of which Frank N. Smith had 70 to 75 percent ownership interest and served as president. The remaining stock in both companies was owned by the same three persons, who held all corporate offices in both companies. There was thus complete common ownership and interrelation of corporate officeholders, although Keuka reimbursed Smith Associates for the salaries of the directors in proportion to the time they spent on Keuka business. Keuka had been in operation from 1966 to 1969, when it was dissolved. In 1970, it was reincorporated to acquire a contract on a specific job.

The four owners of Frank N. Smith Associates, Inc., did not, however, participate in the day-to-day management of either business. The control of business decisions, and particularly of labor relations, was vested in separate people at both high and low levels in each company. There had been minimal employee interchange, either at the managerial or rank-and-file level. Employees of the two companies had never worked side by side at a job site. There was evidence that Keuka had never serviced any of Smith Associates' customers nor had Keuka ever taken any business away from Smith Associates which would deprive bargaining unit employees of work. It was undisputed, however, that after Keuka's reactivation, it steadily expanded its nonunion work force, while Smith Associates was contemporaneously laying off union members.

Smith Associates was organized along strict trade union craft lines, while each Keuka employee normally did the work of several different crafts. The Carpenters' Union sought to have its contract apply to Keuka's employees, claiming its employees constituted an "accretion" to the Smith Associates unit. The Board's administrative law judge noted, however, that it would be inappropriate to include all of Keuka's employees in a unit of carpenters since they performed many jobs that carpenters normally did not. Using the framework of the tests for finding an appropriate bargaining unit, the judge first rejected the attempt

[12]194 NLRB 212 (1971).

to classify Keuka's employees as an "accretion" to the Smith Associates bargaining unit.

In examining the four primary single-employer factors, the Board decided that the evidence did not point to a single-employer relationship. It noted that the companies shared office space and clerical help, but that Keuka paid a proportionate share for both; that although paychecks for both companies were prepared by the same employee, separate payroll lists were maintained; that although the same accountant was retained by both firms, they paid him separately; that while Smith Associates always obtained work through bidding, Keuka never did; that the two firms maintained separate telephone lines; that they advertised separately and never referred customers to one another. These facts, combined with the separation of day-to-day management and labor relations decisions, convinced the Board that common ownership did not require the application of Smith Associates' union contracts to Keuka.

Another decision involving a contractor's attempt to go dual shop was *J. J. Cook Construction Co.*[13] Once again, the Board considered the four main factors of common ownership, common management, interrelation of operations, and centralized control over labor relations. In this case, though, the Board found that the two construction companies *did* constitute a single employer.

The two firms, one union and the other nonunion, were owned in the same proportion by the same three people. There could be no doubt of common ownership. The two men who jointly held 98 to 100 percent of the stock of each company also jointly directed each company's operations. Together, they determined whether a particular job would be bid by the union or the nonunion company. Water and sewer contracts and residential work were normally bid by the nonunion company, while schools, churches, and other industrial buildings were normally bid by the union company. The owners freely testified to the NLRB that this arrangement was used because of the structure of the construction industry. They noted that in those types of work which were typically done by "open-shop" contractors, a company forced to pay higher, union-scale wages would be unable to compete.

In addition to this evidence of an interrelationship of operations, the Board noted that the two companies occupied adjoining office suites in a building held by their majority owner. Although the Board found little evidence that one company's clerical staff performed work for the other firm, it pointed out that these employees were paid by checks prepared by one computer located in the nonunion firm's offices. All the supervisors were interchanged between the two companies and under an apparently arbitrary decision, three-fourths were listed on the union company's rolls, while the others were carried on the rolls of the nonunion company.

The totality of this evidence was found sufficient to pierce the corporate veil which indicated that two firms existed, and the Board found that the two majority owners had a "multicompany operation though they did business requiring union conditions and employees under the name Cook Co., while doing the non-union or open-shop business under the name of Empire."

[13]203 NLRB 41 (1973).

One of the most recent cases illustrating the Board's treatment of contractors' efforts to meet competition by operating dual shop is *Peter Kiewit Sons' Co.,*[14] previously noted. There, a holding company called "Kiewit, Inc." wholly owned two subsidiaries named "Kiewit" and "South Prairie," both of which were separately incorporated, distinct legal entities. Both subsidiaries performed general construction and highway construction. Kiewit had operated for many years as the only union contractor doing highway construction in Oklahoma. South Prairie had operated nonunion for many years in states other than Oklahoma. When Kiewit, Inc. saw that Kiewit's costs would prevent it from continuing to be competitive in bidding for Oklahoma jobs, it decided to activate South Prairie in Oklahoma. It was believed that this would allow it to compete on an even basis in that state with the dominant nonunion contractors.

The union filed unfair labor practice charges with the NLRB, seeking to have its contract with Kiewit apply to South Prairie.

The Board held, despite the common ownership of the two subsidiaries, that they constituted separate entities. It found no significant interrelation of operations. The companies maintained separate Oklahoma offices, separate bank accounts, separate telephone numbers, and separate supervisory and office clerical staffs. They avoided competing against each other in bids for jobs, submitting separate job bids. The Board was not convinced that there was any common labor relations policy because there was sufficiently separate control of labor relations on a day-to-day basis. South Prairie's policies were set by its president, while Kiewit, Inc., officials determined Kiewit's labor policies.

The case could have been merely a reaffirmation of the NLRB's frequently stated view that "it is not uncommon in the construction industry for the same interests to have two separate organizations, one to handle contracts performed under union conditions and the other under non-union conditions." However, the union successfully petitioned the Court of Appeals for the District of Columbia to reverse the Board. In a split decision, two of the judges stated that they were persuaded that the two companies were a single employer by certain facts whose significance the Board had minimized.

There was, of course, common ownership. The court majority also found evidence of the most important factor: centralized control over labor relations. In so holding, however, the Court adopted the novel theory that Kiewit, Inc.'s original establishment of a nonunion "framework" for South Prairie in itself "constituted a very substantial qualitative degree of centralized control of labor relations." As noted previously, the court surprisingly equated this initial and potential "framework" of overall labor relations with the day-to-day decisions on labor matters which had heretofore formed the touchstone of the test for a common labor relations policy. The court stated simply that the relationship between the two firms' frameworks would not be found in the arm's length relationship existing among nonintegrated companies.

In addition, the court disagreed with the Board's implicit holding that there was no common management or interrelation of operations. The court's interpretation of these two latter factors focused on a shift of numerous manage-

[14] *Supra* note 8.

ment personnel from Kiewit to South Prairie's Oklahoma management and supervisory staff, in addition to some evidence of rank-and-file interchange. These personnel changes were viewed as demonstrating "a reasonable likelihood" that Kiewit's employees would lose work at the expense of South Prairie. As further support for this position, the court pointed to the fact that after South Prairie's activation in Oklahoma, Kiewit's bidding activity—and its success rate—declined.

Both the employer and the NLRB petitioned the United States Supreme Court for review of the case. The Board not only argued that the single-employer finding was erroneous but also alleged that even if the two firms were a single enterprise for purposes of the act, the court below had usurped the role of the Board to ascertain whether the employees of both Kiewit and South Prairie possessed a sufficient community of interest to constitute an appropriate collective bargaining unit.

In its petition to the Supreme Court, the Board wrote as to the single-employer issue:

> Wholly-owned subsidiaries are always subject to control by the parent corporation. The court's reliance upon potential control—which the Board properly discounted—ignores the settled principle that the test "is not whether an unexercised power to control exists" [*American Federation of Television & Radio Artists v. National Labor Relations Board*, 462 F.2d 887, 892 (C.A.D.C.)]; rather there must be something more in the form of common control . . . denoting an actual, as distinct from merely a potential integration of operations and management policies. *Miami Newspaper Pressmen's Local No. 46 v. National Labor Relations Board, supra*, 322 F.2d at 409. Here there is little evidence of an "actual . . . integration of operations and management policies," and certainly not enough to justify the court in rejecting the Board's determination that Kiewit and South Prairie are separate employers. "What the court of appeals has done in this case was to draw its own inferences from the facts the Board found, even though the Board's inferences were reasonable, and to substitute its own evaluation for the agency's of the weight to be given the various factors for determining single rather than multiple employer status. In so doing, the court exceeded the proper boundaries of judicial review.[15]

On May 24, 1976, the Supreme Court rendered a short opinion, without allowing extensive briefs or argument, in which it reversed part of the Court of Appeals' holding but left intact that portion relating to the single-employer issue.[16]

The Court of Appeals majority opinion in *Kiewit* may still indicate how at least two members of that lower court will treat the dual-shop issue. Even they, fortunately, did not base their decision solely on their novel "potential control of labor relations" theory, but rather on a detailed review of "all the [factual] circumstances of the case," including their disagreement with the Board's implicit holding that there was no common management or interrelation of operations.

In reversing the Court of Appeals in *Kiewit*, the Supreme Court unanimously

[15]Petitioner's Brief for *Certiorari* at p. 16, *Local 627, International Union of Operating Engineers, AFL-CIO v. NLRB, supra* note 8.

[16] *Supra* note 8.

held that the lower court improperly reached and ruled upon the issue of whether employees of both firms should be included in one collective bargaining unit. This decision, stated the Court, should always be made by the Board in the first instance. The opinion observed that a determination that two firms constitute a single employer "in the construction industry . . . 'does not necessarily establish that an employer-wide unit is appropriate, as the factors which are relevant in identifying the breadth of an employer's operation are not conclusively determinative of the scope of an appropriate unit.'" [17]

Thus, the Supreme Court's opinion emphasizes the existence of *two* prongs to the test to determine whether related companies may operate double-breasted. Even if the NLRB determines that two firms are, in fact, a "single employer," it must still further determine whether the employees of the firms share a sufficient community of interest for the Board to include all of them in a single collective bargaining unit. It is possible, therefore, that although a unionized operation and an open-shop operation are found to constitute a single employer, the Board nonetheless will not require the open-shop operation to adhere to the union contract.

Over the years, the Board has developed a set of criteria it routinely applies to determine the size and scope of appropriate bargaining units. In double-breasted operations in the construction industry, these criteria will likely include not only the four major factors applicable to the single-employer issue but also those criteria which have been applied to the general issue of collective-bargaining-unit size and scope. The Board's normal rule would be not to join employees into one collective bargaining unit when it found among them:

> [A] difference in method of wages or compensation; different employment benefits; separate supervision; the degree of dissimilar qualifications, training and skills; differences in job functions and amount of working time spent away from the employment or plant situs . . . ; the infrequency or lack of contact with other employees; lack of integration with the work functions of other employees or interchange with them; and the history of collective bargaining. [18]

Therefore, the teaching of the Supreme Court in *Kiewit* is that even if two construction firms have sufficient ownership and management relationships to be considered a single employer, the Board must further consider these "unit appropriateness" tests to determine whether to require the one company to apply the other company's labor union contract. Upon remand of *Kiewit* to the NLRB, the Board applied these tests to hold that employees of the two companies involved (one unionized and one nonunion) constituted two "distinct and separate" appropriate units. The Board therefore dismissed the union's complaint in its entirety. [19]

The apparent significance of the Supreme Court's emphasizing the appropriate bargaining unit question is to add another defense by a construction firm

---

[17] 96 Sup. Ct. 1842, 1844 (1976), citing *Central New Mexico Chapter, Nat'l Elect. Contractors Ass'n, Inc.*, 152 NLRB 1604, 1608 (1965).

[18] *Kalamazoo Paper Box Corp.*, 136 NLRB 134, 137 (1962).

[19] *Peter Kiewit Sons Co. and South Prairie Construction Co.* and *Int'l Union of Operating Engineers, Local 627*, 231 NLRB 13 (1977).

which is operating dual shops. One set of facts could be held to fall on the single-employer side of the line, but the Board could still conclude that employees of the two enterprises do not constitute an appropriate collective bargaining unit. The resolution of each case will depend on the factual variations, that is, the "totality of the circumstances." Until the Board or the courts develop more definitive guidelines, contractors who contemplate double-breasted operations must face these kinds of risks, which should be minimized through careful planning.

In addition to these aspects of the decision to go double-breasted, a contractor also faces uncertainty over how certain secondary factors relating to the single-employer issue will be applied, since the Board and the courts frequently find them probative of the four basic factors previously discussed. Some of these secondary factors might also impact upon determination of the size of the bargaining unit.

ADDITIONAL GUIDELINES EVERY EMPLOYER SHOULD CONSIDER

The following checklist, though not exhaustive, should provide a guide to a contractor's initial decision whether to proceed to establish dual shops:

1. Act on Lawful Motivation

This first and most important caution to any contractor's efforts to go double-breasted should be considered carefully. An employer who has signed a collective bargaining contract with a labor union will be found to commit an *unfair labor practice* if it establishes or purchases a new business intending to evade its legal obligation to bargain with that union or avoid the terms and conditions of its contract with that union.

Any action which could be viewed by the National Labor Relations Board as an effort to establish a nonunion company to siphon business away from a unionized construction company thus is vulnerable to a Board order requiring not only that the new firm recognize the union as the collective bargaining agent of its employees, but that the new firm also adhere to the terms and conditions of the collective bargaining agreement with the union company, including retroactive payment of union-scale wages and contributions to fringe-benefit funds (such as pension or health-and-welfare funds).

The corporate minutes of the organizational meetings relating to creation of the new firm should express a "neutral" policy and a lack of anti-union "animus" if factually true.

Where a second company is established, there is nothing to prevent a union from seeking to negotiate with the contractor concerning the wages and conditions of employment of workers of that second firm. While the contractor is under no legal obligation to bargain with the union until such time as it can demonstrate that a majority of the second company's employees desire it to represent them, the contractor may nevertheless have an open mind on working out a realistic and practical agreement with the union. If such negotiations are undertaken, there is nothing that requires the contractor to capitulate to the union's excessive demands. In fact, the contractor may legally insist on signing a contract only if the union is willing to agree to the more moderate and less restrictive terms and conditions which the contractor proposes. Again, due to the union's desire that all its members receive uniform wages and benefits, it is extremely unlikely that a union would agree to any contract which deviated from the "standard agreement" which it had executed with other area contractors, including its "favored nations" clause. However, the mere fact that the contractor was willing to negotiate with that union could be significant evidence of a lack of anti-union animus on the part of the contractor.

2. Make an Audit of Local Construction Conditions and Labor Climate

Before going double-breasted, one should survey all business and economic conditions in the locality where the new firm will do business. Some of the questions that need to be answered include:

- Are the local unions in the area powerful and aggressive?
- Will the public attitude be friendly or hostile?
- Are the construction users prepared to award jobs to open-shop contractors?
- Is there adequate law enforcement against labor union coercion and violence?
- Is there an ample supply of skilled nonunion craftsmen and apprenticeship training programs?

3. Review the Geographical Jurisdiction of Your Current Collective Bargaining Agreements

In most cases, collective bargaining agreements in the construction industry relate to a limited geographical area covered by the local union's territorial jurisdiction. As such, the terms and conditions of a specific agreement are only applicable to employees working within that area. It may well be possible for a contractor to commence operations outside of the geographical area covered by its collective bargaining agreements. In such a case, the contractor would not be bound by those agreements unless it specifically contracted with the respective labor organizations to extend their current agreements to cover another geographical area.

4. Purchase an Active, Ongoing Business

As noted, financial ownership or control of a second business is not alone sufficient cause for the Board to find that separate business entities are actually a single employer. Frequently, the greatest degree of separation in management, operations, and labor policies may be obtained by purchasing an existing ongoing nonunion construction company in the desired type of construction, allowing its executives to retain their positions and to make all day-to-day decisions on the newly acquired firm's operations. In such ideal circumstances, the only major interrelationship between the companies would be financial.

5. Determine whether Your Union Contracts Contain Restrictive "Anti–Dual Shop" Clauses

Some unions include a provision in their standard labor agreements designed to prevent unionized employers from going dual shop. One version of the clause reads as follows:

> If any Employer covered by this Agreement controls, operates, or has any financial interest in any other business within the trade and territorial jurisdiction of the Union, such other business entity shall either have a signed agreement with the Union or this Agreement shall be interpreted as including such business entity under the term Employer in this Agreement.

A more sophisticated sample is the following language, extracted from a mechanical trades union contract with a mechanical contractors association:

> 1. In the event that the Employer, a stockholder or stockholders of the Employer whose stock constitutes a controlling interest of the stock of said Employer, or an owner or owners of the Employer who own a controlling interest in said Employer in any form other than stock, own, on the effective date of this Agreement, or acquire, at any time thereafter during the term of this Agreement, a controlling interest in any other Company engaged in the performance of all or any of the types of construction work covered by this Agreement within the territorial jurisdiction covered by this Agreement, whether said controlling interest is owned directly or indirectly, then said other Company shall be bound and covered by and subject to each and every provision of this Agreement as if already a signatory hereto, and said other Company shall sign and adopt this Agreement as its own collective bargaining agreement with the Union immediately upon being requested to do so by the Union.
>
> 2. The purpose of this Article is to terminate, once and for all, the growing practice of Employers subject to this Agreement attempting to operate two companies, one subject to this Agreement and one not subject to this Agreement, for the obvious purpose of attempting to circumvent and escape from the obligations of this Agreement, thereby jeopardizing the wages, hours and other terms and conditions of employment of the employees covered by this Agreement and making a mockery of collective bargaining relations between the Union and the Employers in the construction industry.
>
> 3. Under no circumstances shall this article be applied or enforced in a manner which, or be applied to circumstances which, would constitute an unfair labor practice by the Employer or Union under any provision of the National Labor Relations Act, as amended.

The restraint-of-trade aspects of such contractual provisions apparently have not been legally tested. In 1975, however, the Supreme Court of the United States rendered a decision in *Connell Construction Co. v. Plumbers & Steamfitters Local 100*[20] in which the Court passed on the basic issue of a labor union's exemption from the antitrust laws. The Court's decision has a profound effect on the legality of agreements, particularly subcontracting agreements, between organized labor and employers where there is no existing collective bargaining relationship and where such agreements will have a substantial effect upon the access to a product market. Moreover, the opinion in *Connell* reflects the Supreme Court's current attitude toward a labor union's antitrust liability and might be a preview to other rulings by the Court on this topic of vital interest to both labor and management in the private industrial sector of our economy.

[20]421 U.S. 616, 95 Sup. Ct. 1830 (1975).

In short, the Supreme Court will now scrutinize such agreements for antitrust violations by focusing on such factors as whether the union has created a sheltered market for itself, the impact of such agreements on nonunion competitors, and the power of the union to control access to its product market. However, the Court's decision in *Connell* does not clearly define the boundaries of organized labor's exemption from the antitrust laws. Only time and further legal testing of these restrictive agreements will provide the answer, but it is safe to say that their enforceability is now subject to serious legal question and challenge.[21]

Moreover, a dispute over interpretation of these restrictive clauses may be initially resolved through binding arbitration, provided the collective bargaining agreement at issue contains any sort of broad arbitration provisions. An arbitrator is not bound by the tests developed in the context of Board jurisdictional and unfair labor practice questions or by antitrust law, and his decision will almost surely be immune from any collateral attack in a federal court. It is also true, however, that the NLRB has not been reluctant to render its own evaluation of the single-employer issue, even if it conflicts with a prior determination by an arbitrator on the same facts.

In summary, there are few legal decisions on this question, and as yet there appears to be no established precedent. Obviously, any contractor contemplating dual-shop operation should attempt to avoid entering into or remaining under a labor contract containing one of these restrictive clauses.

6. Ascertain whether at the Time the Union Was Originally Recognized or at Any Time Thereafter It Ever Represented a Majority of the Contractor's Employees in the Bargaining Unit

As noted previously, although it has been reversed on both occasions by a court of appeals, the National Labor Relations Board has twice held that where a union has never represented a majority of the contractor's employees in an appropriate bargaining unit, it is not an unfair labor practice for a contractor to fail to abide by any agreement it may have signed with the union. Consideration of this option should be approached with extreme caution and only after thorough review with legal counsel, even if the Supreme Court ultimately upholds the NLRB's position. Moreover, even if the Supreme Court does uphold the Board, the unions may well adopt a different tack and attempt to enforce their agreement with the contractor by suing for breach of contract in federal or state court.

7. Vest Overall Policy as well as Day-to-Day Control of Labor Relations in the Second Firm's Management

No recommendation can be more strongly emphasized. The Board, as noted, has viewed the existence of a common labor relations policy as a critical factor to finding a single employer. If there is to be an ownership connection between

---

[21] For a discussion of the parameters of labor antitrust law, see Richard J. Reibstein, Esq., *After Connell Construction Company*, FEDERAL BAR JOURNAL, vol. 35, no. 2, Spring 1976, p. 133 *et seq.*

two firms, any major stockholder or the officers should select separate managers in whom they have sufficient confidence to delegate authority for fixing and administering separate labor relations policies and practices on a day-to-day basis. The more an owner involves himself in the daily labor relations of a second firm, the greater the risk that the Board will find the two firms as a single employer.

8. Delegate Absolute Control over Day-to-Day Operations to a General Manager or Superintendent Who Has No Connection with the Original Business

Since the NLRB and courts consider evidence of integration of operations as a critical indication of single-employer status, it is vital that the day-to-day operation of any construction company under common ownership with a unionized firm be as separate and distinct as possible. If one person or family owns majority holdings in the two companies, there may be strong practical considerations favoring the installation of a member of the family as manager of the daily affairs of the second business. Nevertheless, the better-advised owner will seek an independent outsider, to whom he or she should delegate complete authority to make all normal business decisions. Extensive involvement of family members in a group of family-owned businesses has been viewed as evidence upon which to base a finding of a single employer. If such an intra-family arrangement is chosen for a second company, notwithstanding the risks, every effort should be made to ensure that any family member not responsible for the second business displays no more than an expected financial interest in how the business is doing in the long run.

9. Avoid Interchange of Rank-and-File Employees

The easiest method of staffing a second, commonly owned construction company may appear to be to hire or transfer workers from the first company. But such a practice should be avoided! Employee interchange, as has been noted, is one of the critical factors considered by the NLRB in determining whether several nominally separate enterprises constitute a single employer. Since the unionized contractor will likely obtain his workers through a hiring hall, while the nonunion company may use newspaper advertisements or word-of-mouth, there should be no need to interchange construction workers from one company to another. Even a one-time, one-person interchange has been viewed as some evidence that two companies should legally be viewed as one. Ideally, if it is possible, no employee on a unionized company's payroll should be employed by another enterprise for which there may even be a question of the existence of single-employer status.

10. Engage in a Different Type of Construction

The establishment of a second nonunion company to engage in identical types of construction and in the same locality as a commonly owned unionized company runs a higher risk that the union will successfully charge that the second company's creation was a subterfuge to draw business away from its bargaining-unit union members employed by the first company. If there exists a particular segment of the construction market which the unionized contractor has never attempted to penetrate, it would be wise for the second company to commence dual-shop operations in this new market.

11. Avoid Interlocking Officers and Boards; Use Strict Accounting for Salaries of Officials Who Serve Both Companies

When two or more firms are closely held, the owners may wish to use the same personnel in similar official capacities for each company. For instance, the president of Company 1 might serve as vice president of Company 2, while the same person might be treasurer of both firms; and the vice president of Company 1 might serve as president of Company 2 or as a member of its board of directors. These interlocking officerships and boards should be avoided if possible. Where no acceptable alternative is found, however, care should be taken to ensure that each of the officers or board members is paid separately by the two firms, in direct proportion to the work performed for each company. For example, if the person who serves as president of one company and vice president of another spends 75 percent of the time working as president and 25 percent of the time working as vice president, his or her compensation from the two companies should reflect this ratio.

12. Avoid Interchange of Supervision

Using a unionized company's supervisors or bid estimators to staff any new or newly acquired company has been cited by the NLRB as a factor supporting a finding of a single employer. If it can be avoided, supervisors should never be transferred directly from a unionized contractor to a prospective nonunion firm. If, after consulting counsel, it is decided that no practical alternative exists, a solution might be to *temporarily* transfer the supervisors to the new firm but return them to the original firm's employ as soon as possible. Of course, during the time of the transfer, the supervisors should be carried on the new company's payroll and removed from their former company's payroll.

13. Use Separate Office Facilities

If a contractor controls one company which is already established with office space, there is a temptation to operate a second company out of the same location. If possible, this should be avoided. Geographic separation of offices is more costly, but it will serve to further demonstrate the separateness of the two firms. Where it is not feasible to establish offices in separate spaces or a separate building, the second enterprise should at least pay its proportionate share of the rent (as well as rent on furniture, office machines, and other fixtures) to the original company. Once the second firm establishes itself financially, however, the move to a separate location should be made promptly.

14. Use Separate Office Clerical Personnel

Sharing of clerical personnel should also be avoided. If the two companies share clerical personnel at the same office location, however, billing and payroll records of all employees, including clericals, should be maintained separately for each firm. If the same clerical personnel are used, they should be proportionately compensated by each company for the time spent on that company's business.

15. Share Tools and Equipment, If Any, on an Arms-Length, Businesslike Basis

When a contractor starts a second business, he will understandably try to economize on his initial capital investment by allowing the new business to use the expensive tools and equipment of the unionized company without cost. This should be avoided. Each construction company should ideally own all its tools and equipment. If the dual company must rent tools and equipment, however, it would be preferable to lease them from an unrelated business. If this is not economically practical or advantageous, the equipment should be leased by the related company from the first firm on an as-needed-and-as-available basis. Any such transaction should demonstrate arms-length negotiations, and the rental rates should be at or near market rates. The Board has noted the prevalence of this practice in the construction industry, and has implied that this one indication of operational integration may be less "damaging" than other facts.

16. Use Separate Payrolls

Some business people attempt to set up a second, dual-shop enterprise but continue to pay employees of the new firm from the payroll of the old. The payrolls should be separated in as many ways and as much as possible. For example, use different banks and have different personnel sign the checks for the two companies. If computerized accounting is employed, use different companies for the different businesses; pay on different days. If using the same bookkeeper or accountant cannot be avoided, ensure that this employee is compensated by the two firms in direct proportion to the time spent on the two payrolls.

17. Do Not Refer Customers from One Business to the Other

Some evidence of common management may be found in one firm's consistent referral of customers to its sister company. The unionized company's management ideally should avoid any referral of customers to the nonunion company in which the construction user is told the reason is to obtain a lower price on similar work. Such actions may be held to imply that the two firms are linked more closely than by ordinary business dealings.

18. Submit Separate Job Bids

Even if a new business has been created which engages in a completely different type of construction or contracting, it is not advisable for two commonly owned companies owned by legally separate enterprises to submit joint bids covering work to be done by the two firms. This could be viewed as evidence of integration of operations and less than an "arms-length relationship" between the companies.

19. Employ Different Job Estimators

The effect of submitting separate bids on projects may be diminished if the same persons estimate work for both firms. Independent employer status may be more difficult to establish if there is an overlap in use of even these personnel.

20. Use Competitive Bidding to Award Subcontracting Work

Many union contracts prevent a contractor from subcontracting job-site work to nonunion firms. However, where such contractual limitations are not in force, a contractor may wish to create or purchase a new company to perform work formerly done by tradesmen working either directly for the unionized company or for subcontractors. The Board will consider the companies less interrelated if work is not normally—and without economic justification—subcontracted to a company sharing some form of common ownership with the subcontracting firm. Use of competitive bids for all work will ensure that, regardless of ownership of the companies, any decision to award subcontracting jobs will not be subject to the charge that it was based solely on family ties or common ownership.

21. Establish an Independent Line of Credit for the New Company; Avoid Interchange Guarantees of Performance Bonds

In small, closely held businesses, establishing a line of credit for the new business has proven to be a troublesome problem for firms seeking to establish a dual shop. Any employer who is the sole or majority owner of a unionized business would be well-advised to avoid personally guaranteeing the credit of or securing a performance bond for a second company which he or she also owns or controls. If possible, the new enterprise should obtain any financing (after the initial capitalization) from established financial institutions in its own right. In any event, this separate credit line should be established as soon as possible.

22. Use Separate Bank Accounts

Integration of management is implied by the undifferentiated use of one bank account by two companies.

23. Avoid Insuring the Two Companies under a Single Policy

Even the use of the same insurance policy for accident, workmen's compensation or health insurance, or pension benefits could be used as evidence toward finding a single-employer status. If the two companies are separated and do not share common management, it would be reasonable to expect the new firm to shop around for its insurance rather than to rely on the same policy—and possibly even the same company—which had insured the original business. This type of reasoning will be applied against the decisions of allegedly nonintegrated companies.

24. Use Different Time Clocks

Where time clocks are used and two companies share offices or job sites, each company should provide its own clock for its personnel.

25. Use Separate Advertising

If one firm advertises to attract business, the other should not combine its advertising if they claim to be nonintegrated businesses.

26. Differentiate Vacation Policy

Two companies' policies on vacations should not be coordinated in any manner. It would be preferable to delegate decision-making authority on this as far down the line as possible. In no case should there be a policy of timing vacations granted employees of one firm to coordinate with those granted employees of the other firm.

27. Use Different Telephone Lines

Where a new company maintains its offices in a different location from the established firm, there normally would not be a problem about telephones. Where two or more companies share office spaces or use adjoining offices, however, different telephone numbers and a different switchboard should be maintained. This is an easily apparent fact which has been frequently cited by the Board.

IS A DUAL SHOP WORTH THE RISK?—THE PRACTICAL SIDE

While the preceding discussion dealt with broad legal guidelines for dual-shop operation, contractors must also look at the harsh reality of things: If a local union hears about a new double-breasted setup, how will it react? Will there be slowdowns, work stoppages or other forms of intimidation, coercion or violence? To be sure, different unions will behave differently.

Some owners of dual shops have endured threats, property damage, and other harassment. Other contractors who have gone double-breasted report that the building trade unions have not bothered them at all. The union reaction in any particular situation may well depend, among other facts, upon the character and personalities of the particular union representatives involved, upon the number of union tradesmen out of work, and upon the strength of the open-shop movement in the area where the companies operate.

Obviously, a dual shop is not a sure bet for all. Those who have made the switch, however, observe that the increased business and versatility such an operation gives them is well worth the risk, which for the most part has been minimal.

These same contractors also warn against making a spur-of-the-moment decision and forming a dual shop too hastily. Without proper planning, effective implementation, and competent legal counsel, a dual shop is doomed to costly failure. Set up properly, however, a double-breasted operation might well be the key to many unionized contractors' survival.

The decision whether to go dual shop ultimately is for each employer to make based on the particular facts and circumstances of his situation. For the informed and competently advised contractor who wants to remain competitive, the words of Supreme Court Justices Stewart, Douglas, and Harlan in their concurring opinion in the *Fibreboard Paper Products Corp.* case are apt:

> It is possible that . . . Congress may eventually decide to give organized labor or government a far heavier hand in controlling what until now have been considered the prerogatives of private business management. That path would mark a sharp departure from the traditional principles of a free enterprise economy. Whether we should follow it is, within constitutional limitations, for Congress to choose. But it is a path which Congress certainly did not choose when it enacted the Taft-Hartley Act.[22]

---

[22]*Fibreboard Paper Products Corp. v. NLRB,* 379 U.S. 203, 225–26 (1964).

Chapter **4**

Advantages and Disadvantages of Going Public

PHILIP HELLER

**Executive Vice President, Fischbach and Moore, Incorporated,
New York, New York**

INTRODUCTION

"Going public" is often a very emotional change. The thought arouses in the owner of a privately held business some of the emotions with which a seasoned bachelor views marriage. Each fears the unknown status and is concerned over the possible loss of freedom, independence, and control, with perhaps a diminution of the benefits and perquisites of single status.

The business owner should recognize the emotional accompaniment for what it is and make a decision only on a clear understanding of individual wishes and alternatives, personal needs and the needs of the business. Hence this article is written merely to help the owner to make this weighty decision.

Take, for example, John Smith, a young entrepreneur who started out by rejecting the freedom from responsibility offered by an ordinary job and opened his own business—primarily with the thought of growth and independence. Now, years later, his business has prospered, his earnings have risen, the "perks" are sweet, and public recognition is satisfying. In recent years, however, any number of factors beyond his control are troubling his contentment. He may be young but impatient with his growth. Or he may be older, more concerned about succession and security, or troubled by the fact that his children have no interest in the business. In either case, prospective jobs vital for growth may be too large for safety or financing or bonding; or estate problems and the uncertain future of the business without him have been suggested; or the Internal Revenue Service has noted his success and threatens a tax on undistributed income. Perhaps, to put it gently, he is approaching middle age; he can still render years of good service, but would like to avoid the consequences of illness, death, or changing economic conditions. He desires to preserve the nest egg he has accumulated, while ensuring continued employment, at least for a reasonable time, with more security and peace of mind. For whatever the reason, he feels that going public may be the answer to his problem; but as a prudent entrepreneur, he knows that he should examine the pros and cons.

Most owners of a privately held business are aware of, and the introduction to this article suggests, the more obvious advantages to them of going public—security for the owner and his family, with an opportunity for continued activity if desired, and perhaps even cash in his pocket. The disadvantages are usually not as obvious. Similarly, certain advantages are not immediately apparent.

In some respects, the advantages and disadvantages of going public will vary, if only in degree, with the method or procedure used. An understanding of the methods of going public is helpful at this point. Of course, the principal's lawyers and accountant should be consulted about every aspect of the problem, and the comments made in this article should be subject to their advice.

HOW A PRIVATELY OWNED BUSINESS BECOMES PUBLICLY OWNED

A privately owned business generally becomes publicly owned in one of three ways.

Direct Sale of Stock

It may become publicly owned by selling stock directly to the public—that is, by registering the stock with the Securities and Exchange Commission (*registration*) and issuing a detailed prospectus describing the offering. The stock to be sold may be previously unissued stock of the corporation (a *primary sale*) or issued stock held by existing stockholders (a *secondary sale*), or both. In a primary sale, the corporation receives the cash proceeds; in a secondary sale, the selling stockholders receive the cash applicable to the shares sold by them. Preliminarily, the principal should understand that a primary sale will be utilized if the corporation needs cash for working capital, repayment of loans, future acquisitions, or any other corporate purposes and that a secondary sale will be utilized if the existing stockholders want some cash. In either case, the principal will end up with a reduced share of the outstanding stock, but in a richer corporation after a primary sale, and with the consolation of cash if a secondary sale is included. An underwriter, usually a stockbroker or investment firm, will be selected by the sellers to distribute the shares to the public and in turn the underwriter may guarantee that the stock will be sold at an agreed price. When all preliminary matters, including SEC approval of the registration statement and prospectus, have been accomplished, the stock is offered to the public as a *new issue*. There are many variations of the basic transaction, and the principal will have to consider the ideas which may be suggested by his attorneys and accountants. He will also have to decide whether he wants a primary or secondary sale, or both, how much cash is needed or desired, and what percentage of issued stock will be retained by management. Timing is important since the market for new issues is sometimes very good and at other times, very bad.

Acquisition: "Stock-for-Stock" Exchange

A privately owned business may become publicly owned by acquisition, in which the stock of the private company is exchanged for stock of a publicly held company. This process comes about when, in lieu of selling stock to the public, the principal decides to merge with or be acquired by a publicly held company which is usually larger and richer or offers more promise for future growth. All terms are negotiated between the parties, usually without the involvement of the Securities and Exchange Commission unless a new stock issue or stock sale is contemplated or the company going public has more than a few stockholders, or some other factor makes it advisable to secure SEC approval. In the usual transaction of this type, the principal receives only common stock of the parent, although in many situations he receives shares of an existing or new class of preferred stock. Occasionally, there will be an *earn-out provision* under which he may receive additional shares at a later date, the number or amount of which will depend on future earnings. Of course, an exchange of stock is possible only when an acceptable and willing acquiring company has been found, and sometimes—as with an older bachelor—finding the right partner takes longer than the ceremony. Other than that, an exchange of stock is generally much simpler and less expensive than a sale of stock to the public and can be closed more quickly once the parties agree on the basic terms of the exchange.

Acquisition: Other than for stock

The third method of "going public" is a variation of the stock-for-stock exchange discussed previously. Instead of receiving only stock of the acquiring company, the owner of the privately held company may receive cash, bonds, debentures, or notes, with or without stock. As will be discussed further in this article, the differences between the second and third methods are primarily in tax treatment and liquidity.

Some other methods of going public are more unusual for the average business, but the advantages and disadvantages are substantially the same; and an enumeration of these other methods would not add much to this article, except length.

With this understanding, the pros and cons of going public can then be weighed with respect to each separate factor or purpose in the transaction, and with respect to the importance to the principal or to his company of each such factor or purpose.

TAXES

To some individuals, taxes—capital gain taxes in this instance—may be the most important factor in the transaction, assuming as we do that the current value of the individual's shares is in excess of his cost for tax purposes. The advice of the principal's lawyers and accountant will be required, and every statement made in this article should be taken subject to their advice on the specific facts involved.

The privately held company can go public without tax consequences to itself or its stockholders in one of two ways:

1. By a direct primary sale *by the corporation* to the public in a formally registered offering of newly issued stock.

2. By being acquired by a publicly owned company, with at least 80 percent of the outstanding stock of the private company being exchanged for only voting common stock, and nothing else, of the public company. The cost basis to each stockholder of his old stock will be carried over as the cost basis of his new stock.

Any other method may introduce a taxable element into the transaction. If, in the public sale, any shareholder sells any of his own shares, then his gain will be taxable. If, in an acquisition, any of the shareholders of the privately held company receive any bonds, debentures, notes, or cash (regardless of amount and irrespective of whether he also received stock in the publicly held company), then the entire transaction will generally be taxable immediately, and the taxable gain will be computed on the excess of the total value of all assets received by each stockholder over the cost basis. This general rule is subject to a broad exception involving mergers and other situations in which property received in addition to voting stock would be taxable while the voting stock would not be. The publicly owned company may enter into employment contracts with the principals of the acquired company to ensure that top management will continue at least for a while.

The principal may, of course, take the position that cash is beautiful and is the only secure asset, in which case he can sell for cash, or some cash, pay his taxes, and carry on without any problems other than in deciding where to invest the balance of the cash received. However, this method presents a further disadvantage for the older principal under the current law in that on his death the remaining proceeds will be subject to estate tax treatment, which may result in double taxation.

CONTROL OF COMPANY

Following a public sale, the issued stock is usually widely held by stockholders who have had no experience in the business of the company. Irrespective of employment contracts, stockholders are generally in favor of continuing experienced management and would not have bought the stock if the principal were no longer in office. If the business is honestly and capably run, the principal should remain in control and in the top position even though he owns far less than 50 percent of the outstanding shares. In fact, the former owner or owners will usually remain in firm control after a public sale, even with 20 to 30 percent of the stock, because of the stockholder support. However, management can expect to be reminded from time to time that stockholders who bought shares have a right to ask questions and even to criticize management.

Similarly, when a company is acquired by a publicly held corporation in an exchange of stock, both sides will usually agree, as noted below under Employment Contracts, that the principal of the acquired company shall remain as its top officer and that he will manage the company. However, the acquiring company owns all or most of the acquired company's shares and can be expected to ask for conformity with its overall corporate policies, as well as financial return on its investment. The parent which acquired the company has the right, and its executives the duty, to ask questions, insist on reports, give advice, and in some areas to require that its policies or directives be followed as the will of the sole stockholder which the parent in fact is.

The principal's feeling with respect to giving up some of the absolute control which he enjoyed as an individual proprietor may be purely emotional, or it may be a matter of personality—which may be the same thing. Some owners— for reasons of habit or pride, or even quirks of character—are extremely autocratic in their relations with partners, associates, and employees; others may merely resent any suggestion of criticism, or request for explanation. Some will never admit an error or mistake of judgment, or automatically oppose any suggestion or order to change an act or direction. Some of these traits may in fact have made the principal the success that he is, and can be found in men whose superior vision and ability prevailed only because they were prideful and stubborn. However, when dealing with stockholders, or a board of directors, or a parent, one is confronted by people whose power is great, even if their abilities and vision are considered by management to be less. And if the top executive, after fully presenting his views and opinions, does not have the ability to yield with understanding and grace to the wishes of his stockholders or directors, his unhappiness may become more important to him than all the benefits derived from going public. Since this article is addressed to the individual who contemplates public ownership of a business and is not directed to the acquiring public, we suggest that if the principal is like the proud, autocratic person discussed above, it may well be that going public is not advantageous, particularly if he contemplates being acquired by a larger company. However, in the usual situation, the executive who sold or exchanged stock control recognizes the interest and concern of the acquiring stockholders and extends to them the understanding cooperation which is the basic desire of these new stockholders, and finds that they appreciate and reward his efforts and ability, are anxious that he continue in his office, and in general, encourage him to exercise full control of the business with a minimum of interference by them or their representatives, particularly if the operations of the acquired business are successful.

EMPLOYMENT CONTRACTS

The principal whose company is going public will usually be interested in continuing his activities in the business, at least for a time. Prospective buyers of the stock, or an acquiring company, as the case may be, will probably also require the principal to execute an employment contract with his corporation in order to preserve the leadership and direction which made the purchase or exchange attractive to them. The employment contract may be important to preserve the tax-free status for an exchange of stock, if this method is used, to establish that "solely voting common stock" of the acquiring company was received in exchange for the stock of the acquired company. The absence of such an employment agreement increases the likelihood that cash paid to the selling shareholder may be attacked by the IRS as additional payments with respect to the stock rather than as employment compensation. In any event, a contract for a specific number of years at a fixed or minimum salary, if salary is tied to earnings, is usually satisfactory to the principal and represents an advantage to him, since the contract will be negotiated prior to the public sale or exchange of stock.

After the expiration of the term of the initial employment contract, the question of the principal's continuation will depend on the management's decision. If the stock was sold to the public, the principal usually will be the controlling stockholder, if not the largest stockholder, and will be in a position to control his continuation in office, assuming his capability, competence, and behavior are satisfactory. In the case of an acquisition and exchange of stock, the acquiring company may be assumed to have the same interest as any individual stockholder in preserving for the company the continued employment of its top officer or officers, even after the expiration of the initial employment contract. However, if for any reason the management of the acquiring company does not desire to continue or renew the principal's employment, then he will be out of a job. And, frequently the acquisition or employment contract will restrict the principal's ability to establish or accept employment with a competing concern.

FRINGE BENEFITS

Many privately owned companies hold a tighter rein on fringe benefits for staff and office personnel than publicly owned companies, which usually have more understanding and expertise in this field and realize the need for such benefits to attract and retain personnel. As a result, employees, including the principal, may fare better after going public. Important fringe benefits, such as pension and life-and-health insurance, may be set up or implemented prior to going public, if not already in effect. If going public is to be accomplished by exchange of stock, the principal can discuss and negotiate these benefits (and his perquisites, as well) with the acquiring company, as part of the acquisition agreements. In any event, the aggregate of employee benefits should be as good or better after going public than before.

Certain other benefits are either not practical or possible in a privately held company but are common in a public company. Stock options, incentive plans, and many other sophisticated programs to encourage and reward employees, in amounts which relate in some degree to the position and salary of the recipient, are important adjuncts to salary programs of most public companies but are rarely found in privately held companies.

LIQUIDITY

Liquidity refers to the ease and freedom with which one can convert one's property into cash. The advantage of being able from time to time to sell one's listed shares (or other securities) in a public market, even in minor quantities, is obvious when compared with the difficulty and danger involved in disposing of minor interests in a privately owned business. Liquidity also involves the ability to use property in lieu of cash. Giving shares of stock to relatives or friends is simple when the donor can nicely calculate the size of the gift from publicly listed stock prices and avoid disputes with taxing authorities over the value of the gift for tax purposes. Donating shares instead of cash to charitable, educational, religious, or other tax-exempt organizations has the advantage that an income tax deduction may be taken at the current price without capital-gains tax liability for the appreciation in value.

These advantages have some limitations. Under current federal regulations, shares acquired by the principal in a nonpublic offering cannot publicly be sold within two years after the closing of the transaction in which the company went public, unless a new registration is filed with the SEC, and even after the two-year period, the number of shares which can be sold at any time or within a six-month period may be limited by SEC regulations or by the availability of interested buyers. The lack of sufficient buyers at a particular time for a particular stock is not infrequent in the stock market, and although the principal should and probably will do everything possible to set up or pick a company which will be and will remain attractive to the public, these limitations are present. However, if the two-year-period limitation is not a factor in the principal's plans, then the advantage seems strongly with the holding of shares having a public market for purposes of liquidity.

ESTATE CONSIDERATIONS

Often, a strong motivation toward going public is the owner's concern with the future of his business in the hands of his executors or trustees or family, in the event of his death or serious illness. The publicly held company, *usually* larger and with a stronger board of directors which includes experienced outside members, is expected to have made some preparation for succession and, in any event, will be able to take quick, positive action so as to minimize the effect of the death of a top officer.

One of the benefits to the estate itself is the ease with which the value of the shares held by the estate can be determined from listed market prices without appraisal and without disputes over valuation for estate and estate tax purposes such as would arise if the stock were in a privately owned company at the death of the owner. A further advantage is that a public market exists for the sale of shares, to raise the cash needed for payment of taxes and legacies and for diversification of investments for the benefit of the family. However, the existence of a public market may turn out to be a mixed blessing, if the market price is excessively high on the estate valuation date, or low on the day when the executor or trustee wants to sell.

Sometimes other plans or options besides going public are available to the concerned principal, and each plan has certain advantages and disadvantages. But if there are no children or family members who would be able to carry on the business, co-owners who will buy out, or any other acceptable plan, then being public on the date of death should be an advantage to the estate as the best safeguard against forced dissolution or liquidation.

PERSONAL RESPONSIBILITY

The owner of a privately held business may expect to be relieved of some items of personal financial responsibility on going public. For example, he may have been required by the company's bank to personally endorse or co-sign the business' obligations to the bank. Such requirements are comparatively rare in the case of public companies because of the larger, more financially sound state of the public company or because the individual officer does not see or is not willing to see the need to add his personal guaranty.

On the other hand, the same principal should expect to assume certain additional responsibilities on going public. As a top officer and director, he is responsible to the public to be diligent in matters involving securities transactions, to make proper and timely disclosures about the company, and to refrain from trading in shares of the company with knowledge of material information which has not been made public; and he is responsible to his stockholders for his misconduct or negligence. However, this additional responsibility extends mainly to his misdeeds or neglect and does not require his assurance of success or profit, and for that reason must be considered not as a disadvantage but as a reminder of his fiduciary obligations to the public who have been invited to invest in his business.

Certain other statutory requirements are designed to prevent corporate officers and directors and large stockholders (over 10 percent) of companies which must register with the SEC from benefiting from "insider information." These requirements are technical but are based on the need to avoid the appearance as well as the fact of insider trading. For example, any such officer or director or large stockholder must promptly report any changes in his holdings of stock or other securities of the company, so that the public may always know what those people who are close to corporate information are doing with their securities. In fact, as a general rule if any such officer, director, or large stockholder buys and sells or sells and buys the corporation's equity securities within a six-month period, any profit on the transaction must be paid into the corporation, even though the transactions may have been entirely innocent.

Certain other statutory requirements may affect the corporate executive, but in general these acts or regulations were drawn in a fair-minded attempt to preserve public confidence in public companies, and an informed officer should not find them onerous or consider them a disadvantage of being public.

CORPORATE ADVANTAGES AND DISADVANTAGES

Apart from the personal stake of the owner and his family and the benefits accruing to them when their company goes public, certain advantages and disadvantages apply more directly to the company and its employees. And it is to be expected that in making his decision whether or not to go public, the principal will—out of pride in founding or furthering the company which bears his name or the imprint of his leadership—be strongly affected by the possible effect on the company itself. A number of these advantages are obvious:

1. *Growth potential*—which may be the sum total of all the other advantages listed below

2. *Additional capital*—supplied by the new stockholders in the public sale or by the backing of the new parent in an acquisition, which should result in an increase in bonding capacity, bank lines of credit, and bidding capacity

3. The *public status*—particularly if accompanied by successful operations, may enable the company to obtain additional public financing by issuing new stock or other securities

4. *Acquisitions*—a means of growth peculiarly fitted for the public company, which can use publicly traded stock to acquire other companies

5. *Succession*—particularly in top management, usually a matter given more attention in a public company, because of pressure by directors, analysts, and stockholders

6. *Employee relations*—improved by the prospect of quicker promotion and succession, as well as by various forms of fringe benefits and not least by the employee's pride in his participation in the growth and prestige of his employer

Some items may or may not be deemed disadvantages but add administrative duties or expense, such as the following:

1. Public disclosure of volume, profits, top salaries, loans to officers, contracts with top officers, and various other matters of which stockholders and the public have a right to know

2. Compliance with various SEC requirements, not difficult or oppressive, but new and unfamiliar to a privately held company

3. Additional recurring administrative expenses for handling SEC matters, for stock transfer agent and registrar fees, stockholders' relations, outside directors' fees, increased legal and accounting fees, and preparation and printing of interim and annual reports

4. Executive time spent with stockholders, stockbroker analysts, and market researchers

Obviously, the "advantages" tend toward improving corporate operations, whereas the "disadvantages" add to administrative functions and expense.

CONCLUSION

The weight to be given to each advantage and disadvantage by the owner who contemplates going public will, of course, depend on its relative appreciation or importance to him. In general, it can be expected that the owner who decides in favor of going public as a means of satisfying his company will then decide whether to take this step through direct public sale of stock or through acquisition by a public company. In the latter case, the choice of the proper company with which to associate himself becomes the most significant decision, and then having made his choice, he will enter into the necessary negotiations. In each of these steps, the owner will be helped in making his decision after a consideration of the advantages and disadvantages attending each factor.

Chapter **5**

Foreign Subsidiary or International Division

H. PETER GUTTMANN
President, HPG Associates, Washington, D.C.

The accomplishments of United States engineers and builders are a legendary part of American history. Early industrial development enabled the young Republic to successfully counter foreign embargos and provided logistical support for the battles of independence. The construction industry, the country's largest, was born when continental railroads opened the vast lands of the West, telegraph and telephone installations accelerated communications, electricity came to supply light and power, and highways and bridges stimulated transport. The completion of the Panama Canal early in the twentieth century demonstrated American ingenuity to the world.

Today, the American engineering and construction industry is prominently involved in foreign work. United States design firms billed a total of $360 million, and American contractors invoiced $11.6 billion for their overseas engagements during 1974.[1,2] Design professionals (in private, independent practice), general contractors, and design-construct firms follow developments in the international marketplace with the greatest of interest. Foreign work is not only challenging and exciting: for industrious and creative engineers and builders it holds the promise of profit, growth, diversity, and prestige.

Competitive conditions within the United States have historically demanded that successful builders be efficiently managed and professionally competent. Abroad, the international engineering and construction industry is in an ever-increasing technical and price competition for overseas work. Although planning and design can occasionally be performed in the United States, construc-

[1]*Engineering News Record,* Apr. 10, 1975.
[2]*Engineering News Record,* May 15, 1975.

tion must be done on location. Thus it has become very important to give most careful consideration to the corporate domicile as well as to business structures and practices for all enterprises that become involved in the international markets.

As design and construction managers have a natural tendency to specify materials, goods, and services with which they are most familiar, governments of many industrial countries are providing incentives for their nationals and corporations in an effort to step up exports and increase foreign income. Similarly, a number of the lesser-developed and emerging nations have developed legislation to attract foreign investment and in some instances actually oblige the builders of large projects to incorporate locally. Thus, international contracts nowadays are frequently won only by those firms which, in addition to their professional experience and proven record of performance, take advantage of tax concessions, governmental subsidies, and other available direct and indirect host-country support. The existence of a subsidiary in an acceptable location to a prospective client can be decisive in the final selection process and award of a contract.

Foreign subsidiaries of American engineering and construction companies have sometimes been established for tax savings alone. So-called tax havens, such as those in the Bahamas or Panama, attracted considerable attention in years past and provided a flag of convenience for financial shelter. Today, however, still other important reasons explain why American builders have been obliged to become multinationals and their international subsidiaries are frequently incorporated in more than just one foreign country.

In order to obtain new business, successful bidders require low-cost financing, acceptable bonds and guarantees at reasonable premiums, and at times the image of—if not the full support of—a friendly and cooperative host government. For the execution of an engagement and during the performance of a job, engineers and constructors must comply with local labor laws which vary substantially from country to country, observe social obligations which particularly in the emerging countries contain stipulations that may not be compatible with legislation in the United States, and assume general responsibilities alien to United States industry practices. The multinational, or transnational approach, as it is sometimes called, has provided some of the basic facilities to operate efficiently and profitably without improper risk exposure.

Generally, foreign-based subsidiaries of United States engineering and construction firms are permanently registered and fully operative with local nationals and third-country interests; they serve as headquarters for international undertakings and joint ventures in a particular geographic area. Occasionally foreign subsidiaries are also established as temporary corporate shells for the execution of a series of important local engagements or for just one large specific job.

Where the major emphasis in the past has been on operations economy, marketing considerations are now equally important in the choice of a location for a foreign subsidiary. The creation of economic blocs, such as the European Market Community and the Andean Group in Latin America, have attracted many firms to incorporate therein, as the simple advantages of "belonging" easily outweigh the extra legal and administrative work that is necessary for regional or local integration.

Ever-changing conditions in the world's markets continuously oblige international executives to be alert to exchange rate fluctuations, insurance and guarantee costs, bond availability, rising or falling discount rates, shipping facilities and costs, in addition to political developments of national and international importance. There is no doubt that foreign subsidiaries strongly support corporate flexibility and have proven to be invaluable channels for the purpose of obtaining and conducting engineering and construction activities abroad.

A review of specific foreign government incentives will demonstrate why American engineering and construction firms have found it advantageous to establish overseas subsidiaries and incorporate abroad:

France France has been a leader offering highly effective export credit support programs. Currency fluctuation and inflation insurance is provided to French companies along with attractive financial packages for clients within France's vast sphere of industrial commercial interests. Tax exemptions in general, tax rebates on exports, partial and total tax exemptions on foreign branch income can be applied. Deferral of export income is legal and protection against export losses is available. French diplomatic posts take an active part in obtaining foreign business for her nationals throughout the world.

Germany The Bonn government has efficiently supported a generous export credit program. The Ausfuhrkredit Gesellschaft (AKA) charges German commercial banks attractive discount loans on medium- and long-term transactions. Insurance against currency fluctuations, export losses, and guarantees are provided by the Hermes Kreditversicherungsgesellschaft (HERMES) at nominal rates. The Kreditanstalt fuer Wiederaufbau (KFW) is dedicated to long-term credits to developing countries. Tax rebates on exports and deferral of export income is authorized. German banks closely interlocked with many of Germany's prosperous industries constitute a powerful element in the international market.

Italy Hampered by a lack of funds, the Italian credit support system has lost some of its attraction in recent years. Nevertheless, Italian engineering and construction firms are formidable competitors, particularly on very large projects. Mediocredito Centrale (MC) finances commercial credits for Italian firms; the Instituto Nazionale Delle Assicurazioni (INA) covers export insurance for a wide range of risks. A new inflation indemnity program introduced in 1974 is close to implementation. Tax exemptions and rebates are legal, and indirect tax incentives assist Italian corporations in their quest for overseas work.

Japan Unquestionably one of the most aggressive and successful trading nations, Japan offers her exporters a number of highly competitive credit terms, guarantees, and insurance and general incentives. The Ministry of International Trade and Industry (MITI) and the Export-Import Bank of Japan are specifically charged by the Diet to ensure active participation of Japanese firms in international projects. The Japan International Cooperation Agency (JICA) finances feasibility studies for large-scale projects where developing countries have requested assistance. The studies amount to technical assistance grants with no provision for reimbursement either by the recipient government or by the Japanese firm, which naturally is favored to win subsequently related export contracts. Powerful trading corporations enjoy practically unlimited government support along with Japanese industries and their banks. All business expenses are fully tax deductible. Tax rebates and exemptions are a well-established part of the official export incentives. Noteworthy for the engineering and construction industry is the availability of government-to-government guarantees in lieu of commercial performance bonds or bank guarantees.

The United Kingdom   Seasoned as an exporter of goods and services, the United Kingdom frequently changes rules and regulations to offer commercial and financial advantages to her industries. The Exports Credit Guarantee Department (ECGD) underwrites liberal insurance and guarantee programs. Recently ECGD introduced a plan to insure members of a consortium which contracts overseas against losses incurred through insolvency of a consortium member. An inflation indemnity program gives additional flexibility to British exporters. Tax rebates and concessions are available, as is generous new business support to British firms by the United Kingdom's respected foreign service officers.

The examples of France, Germany, Italy, Japan, and the United Kingdom are given to illustrate why American engineers and constructors may be well-advised to establish subsidiaries abroad, if they have not done so already. Nor are these five major competitors of the United States the only ones offering positive incentives. Canada has extremely effective aids, as do Ireland, Spain, Portugal, several Scandinavian countries, and to a lesser extent, Brazil, Israel, Mexico, New Zealand, Venezuela, and others.

When additional factors are taken into consideration, such as the labor market, regionalism, nationalism, restrictive import and work practices, and the emergence of regional blocs, it becomes evident that a truly international design and/or construction firm may also need operating subsidiaries in the areas where major work can be expected to be performed. Thus, it is not at all uncommon to find some of the industrial world's major capitals listed alongside little-known and still exotic-sounding names on the letterheads of American builders.

Foreign subsidiaries, in short, are fully justified and necessary for the United States engineering and construction industry.

Engineering and construction firms incorporated in the United States generally operate overseas through an export department or an international division. Design consultants in high-technology disciplines and builders with only occasional overseas exposure do not always find it necessary to establish foreign subsidiaries; as a matter of fact, even large corporations profit occasionally from some of the export incentives which the United States government provides for American business interests.

Some international divisions may be fully staffed by overseas specialists and at times constitute a separate corporate entity under the umbrella of a domestic company; others maintain a skeleton force of knowledgeable international pros, who then draw on domestic personnel to execute work in the world's markets. For large international engagements, international divisions of an American parent company increasingly team up nowadays with their own foreign subsidiaries in order to propose the best-possible terms to overseas clients by combining the most attractive available support and conditions.

The best-known and probably most frequently used United States export incentive for American builders is the Western Hemisphere Trade Corporation (WHTC). Originally devised to improve the competitive position of United States business which made direct investments in Latin America, it has been forged by court decision into valuable aid for the export of goods and services within the geographical limits of North, Central, or South America and the West Indies. The Internal Revenue Code permits qualified domestic corporations to pay tax on only about 70 percent of its profits.[3]

Another incentive to United States companies is the Domestic International Sales Corporation (DISC), effective since January 1, 1972, which permits exporters to generate a pool of tax-deferred earnings and can be utilized to expand and modernize export production facilities, intensify or initiate export efforts, or provide more favorable credit terms to export customers. The DISC is a sophisticated instrument particularly valuable for exporters of capital goods but also of worthwhile benefit to engineers and constructors.[4]

International divisions are exposed somewhat more than foreign subsidiaries to large cartels of international competitors. As early as 1918, the United States Congress provided qualified exemptions for export trade associations from the prohibitions of the Sherman Antitrust Act of 1890 and the Federal Trade Commission and Clayton Acts of 1914. Unfortunately, despite repeated efforts by the U.S. Departments of Commerce, Treasury, and Justice, the Export Trade Associations continue to be limited to the export of materials and goods and not to services. Thus, the Webb-Pomerene Act, as it is known, is currently of no practical assistance to the United States engineering and construction industry.

Certain other aids, however, favor international divisions. The Export-Import Bank of the United States (EXIM), established in 1945, maintains a number of programs to finance and facilitate the export of American goods and services. While EXIM's direct and discount loan policies are neither fully comparable nor competitive in scope or size with some of the facilities available to the French, Japanese, and British, these as well as insurance and guarantee programs have proven to be useful to the American engineering and construction industry. Commercial and political risk insurance offered jointly by EXIM and the Foreign Credit Insurance Association (FCIA) are widely used by American firms.

Another source of support for international divisions is the Overseas Private Investment Corporation (OPIC), which was established as a United States government corporation to help make more effective the investment of Ameri-

---

[3]WHTC Revenue Act (1942) § 921, Internal Revenue Act, 1954.

[4]Internal Revenue Act, 1954, § 991, as amended.

can private capital and know-how in friendly developing countries. OPIC issues insurance policies against loss due to specific political risks, currency inconvertibility, expropriation, war, and revolution. OPIC also offers financial assistance through guarantees against loss from commercial or political risks and direct loans in United States dollars or local foreign currencies.

Finally, there is the Agency for International Development (AID), which spends substantial amounts of the American taxpayer's money in overseas development programs. With but a few exceptions, only United States and host-country firms can obtain AID contracts. However, capital development programs involving engineering and construction have lately given way to AID activities in the area of humanitarian assistance, and American builders can no longer use AID as a convenient vehicle to obtain overseas jobs.

Company executives reviewing the advantages and disadvantages of foreign subsidiaries versus international divisions should also consider the implications of the Internal Revenue Act of 1954, as amended, Section 911: Personal Income Exclusion; Section 901: Foreign Tax Credits; and Section 951: Taxation of Undistributed Profits of Foreign Corporations.

Since World War II, innumerable worldwide conferences and discussions have taken place between the industrial and emerging nations to study—among other matters—the transfer of technology, the brain-drain, patent rights, tax responsibilities, and international codes of conduct of multinational corporations. Currently, important international negotiations are under way to reach an understanding limiting international competition by official export credit agencies. However, as long as governments are concerned with prosperity, employment, and favorable trade balances and as long as private enterprise is motivated by profits, there will always be changes favoring the establishment of certain foreign subsidiaries over international divisions and vice versa.

Not many years ago, the reconstruction of Europe and Japan and a generous United States program to assist the newly independent nations brought about an unprecedented demand for American engineers and constructors. Many of today's foreign subsidiaries of United States firms had their origin in the international divisions during the years of the Marshall Plan, Point Four, and the Alliance for Progress. The current trend in industry is to cover foreign and United States bases with sufficient flexibility to be prepared for all eventualities.

Where America's major foreign competitors can count on aggressive and well-coordinated government-supported programs, the United States export community in general and the engineering and construction industry in particular depend largely upon their own ingenuity and initiative and enjoy comparatively little official support. Tax reform, currently a subject of considerable congressional activity, is seriously threatening the very few existent United States government export incentives. If Western Hemisphere trading corporations, domestic international sales corporations, personal income exclusion, foreign tax credits, and deferred taxation of undistributed profits of foreign corporations should be abolished, American engineers and builders will be forced to emigrate, abandon their international divisions, and incorporate abroad in order to remain competitive. On the other hand, should concern by the U.S. Departments of Commerce, State, and Treasury bring about increased export support for such substantial contributors to the United States balance of payments as the American engineering and construction industry, then there will be a continuation of the current mix of domestic and foreign operations.

Successful international operations demand careful attention to ever-present changes. Foreign subsidiaries and/or international divisions are both appropriate and desirable, alone or in combination, according to the particular circumstances of opportunity and time.

Chapter **6**

Joint Ventures and Consortiums

G. CHRISTIAN HEDEMANN, ESQ.
Counsel, TRW, Inc., Redondo Beach, California

Joint ventures and consortiums have always played an important role in the engineering and construction industry, and their use as convenient, flexible vehicles to achieve varied objectives in diverse contexts, both in the United States and internationally, is becoming increasingly common.

Because of the diversity of the forms which joint ventures and consortiums take in modern practice, this section will broadly use the term "joint venture" to mean a business alliance of limited duration formed by two or more unrelated business or professional entities for the purpose of furnishing engineering, consulting, procurement, construction, and construction management services by consolidating the skills and resources of the participants.[1] This definition also includes the joint venture of a longer duration formed with the purpose of developing expertise or sales in a prospective, attractive market without being tied to a specific project.

REASONS TO FORM JOINT VENTURES

Although engineering and construction companies decide to form joint ventures with one another for reasons which are often unique, some factors recurringly bear on this decision.

Need to Pool Expertise and Financial Resources and to Share Risks

One common reason is the need to bring together the individual technical and manpower resources of the participants to enable them to furnish a kind and magnitude of services which they are not able to provide individually. It also allows the participants to share and allocate among themselves extraordinary risks which may be involved.[2] A notable example is the consortium of companies formed several decades ago to build the Hoover Dam.

Legal Requirements

Many countries have enacted laws which require engineering and construction companies (among others) to form joint ventures which might not otherwise be necessary on the basis of strictly technological or business judgment. The regulations recently put forward by the United States government which require contractors on federally funded highway projects to make affirmative good faith efforts to find minority contractors with whom to form joint ventures in performing such services appear to fall into this category. The laws of several Latin American and Middle Eastern countries (and, in some respects, Canada) which require foreign engineering and construction companies to enter into associations with one or more local firms have similar economic objectives, that is, to maximize utilization of local talent (or some protected class) and, in developing countries, to provide an incentive (or compulsion) for

---

[1]The word "participant" is used in this section to refer to companies planning to form joint ventures,

[2]See Segal, "Joint Adventures—The Sharing of Losses Dilemma," 181 U. MIAMI L. REV. 429 (1963–1964).

foreign firms to impart their technology and know-how to local firms in order to decrease the country's dependence on foreign expertise in the future.[3]

Business or Political Judgment

Aside from the need to form a joint venture to consolidate technical or financial resources, or to comply with applicable laws, engineering and construction companies may decide, on the basis of business or political judgment, that it would be advantageous from a marketing standpoint to form an association of some sort. For instance, one of the participants may be a sales representative, a licensee, or a source of supply of knowledge of local business and political conditions.

Financing and Materials Supply

With the increasing need for creative packaging of project services and the significant role which financing plays in many major projects, joint-venture proposals frequently offer a substantive financing component. However, financing institutions are ordinarily constrained by banking regulations and business risk factors to avoid being deemed as a joint venturer with either the borrower or the engineer-contractor. Laws such as those in the United States which govern investment advisors may prohibit companies from offering financing advice without registration and compliance with regulatory strictures. Where the proposal calls for the manufacture and supply of materials for incorporation into the project, a manufacturer of some of the materials may be a member of the joint venture offering a turnkey package. In fact, such a manufacturer of materials may also be instrumental in obtaining financing for the project.[4]

SOME THRESHOLD CRITERIA IN DECIDING TO FORM A JOINT VENTURE

Form of the Joint Venture

Partnership In the United States and some other countries, joint ventures often legally consist of a written partnership agreement between separate entities which sets forth the terms upon which they agree to work together, including their respective obligations, rights, and liabilities. Unlike the often cumbersome formality of the corporation, the partnership agreement offers considerable flexibility and may be amended quite simply to accommodate the developing needs of the participants and to reflect changes in the project or the client's wishes.

---

[3]Franko, "International Joint Ventures in Developing Countries: Mystique and Reality," 6 LAW & POL. INT. BUS. 315 (1974); "Contractors Fight Forced Joint Ventures," *Engineering News Record,* Feb. 12, 1976, p. 49.

[4]*United States v, Penn-Olin Chem. Co.,* 378 U.S. 158 (1964), on remand 246 F. Supp. 917 (D. Del. 1965); *aff'd per curiam* 389 U.S. 308 (1967), for further reasons for which joint ventures are formed.

Liability considerations   In recent years, as the magnitude of projects has increased and the associated legal liability has reached menacing proportions, companies in the engineering and construction industry have attempted to limit this liability and minimize the risks to which they are exposed. Since each of the participants in a joint venture may be exposed not only to its own liability but to liability for the acts of other participants, and since one or more of the participants may be companies with substantial assets and significant other activities unrelated to the joint venture, this concern is very real and bears upon the choice of the legal form of the joint venture. The partnership form is particularly troublesome in this regard because unlike shareholders in a corporation, each of the participants in a partnership is personally exposed to liability for the acts of the joint venture.

Subsidiary corporation as partner   One response to the liability problems inherent in a partnership is the formation of subsidiary corporations whose sole purpose is to carry out the participants' activities in the partnership. In such a case, the joint venture would be operated by the subsidiaries according to the terms of the joint-venture agreement as though the parents had been the participants, although the subsidiaries would protect the parents from liability.

Joint-venture corporation   The participants may conclude for liability and tax considerations that it is best to form a corporation, the stock of which is held by the participants, which would have the effect of isolating the stockholders from liability arising out of the project. As a further insulation, the newly formed corporation, possessing minimal assets and capabilities, might subcontract substantially all of its project services to the individual participants, who would accordingly be shielded from the activities of the other participant subcontractors.

Shareholders agrement   Where a corporation or its equivalent is used, a shareholders' agreement is often executed which defines the rights and obligations of the participant-shareholders and sets forth the basis upon which the company will be operated and the project managed. Such an agreement would be in addition to, but should complement, the legal mechanisms built into the articles of incorporation and bylaws of the company, and would contain project-related details similar to those usually found in partnership joint-venture agreements.

Restrictions on use of shareholders agreements   Many countries and states have laws which restrict the extent to which such shareholders' agreements may be legally used, particularly where the agreement confers upon one of the shareholders a degree of control and management which is disproportionate to its actual ownership of the corporation, or dispossesses some of the shareholders of their rights at law. And some jurisdictions have laws which render unenforceable any agreements which attempt to give management irrevocable authority of any corporation to persons other than officers.

This may be problematic where management and control of the project is important to the participant's providing most of the expertise, reputation, or financial resources to the joint venture and where that participant does not or cannot legally own a controlling interest of the stock. Such a participant may wish to maintain final authority with respect to project management decisions, and in such cases the provisions of the shareholders' agreement must be drafted with a view toward these laws. In some countries, there may be potential restrictions on the enforceability of some control provisions set forth in partnership-type agreements as well.

Tax Considerations

The form selected for a joint venture often depends upon the particular tax needs of the participants and, specifically, the method by which the joint venture itself will be taxed. The scope of this section does not permit an extensive treatment of this subject, except to note briefly some of the principles often applicable in this area.[5]

Partnership not taxable in United States   In the United States, a partnership ordinarily does not constitute a taxable entity separate and apart from the participants. Accordingly, profits and losses directly pass through to the individual participants and, subject to certain limitations, must be declared for tax purposes immediately whether or not the profits are distributed or losses are covered by contributions. This is often thought to benefit some firms in the United States but may not if one of the participants is a non-United States entity. The benefits of passing through profits and losses without double taxation may under some circumstances be obtained by having a subsidiary corporation declare taxes on a consolidated return with its parent.[6]

Partnership may be taxable outside the United States   In many countries other than the United States, the partnership is a taxable entity thus giving rise to double taxation on the partnership as well as the partners. In such situations, the participants may decide that the limited liability aspects of a corporation are sufficiently important to mandate the use of a corporate vehicle rather than the traditional (in the United States) partnership form.

Characterization for United States tax purposes   It is important to keep in mind in selecting an appropriate form for a joint venture formed outside of the United States that there are innumerable foreign variants of business entities other than the corporation or partnership and that the United States will characterize these entities for tax purposes according to its own criteria, not according to the law of the place in which the entity is formed. For instance, the *limitada* in Argentina and Colombia (and in other countries in which this form is used) will be taxable in the United States as a corporation notwithstanding its partnership attributes in the countries of its formation.[7]

[5]For a more complete treatment, see Int. Rev. Code of 1954, § 701 *et seq.*, and Treas. Reg. § 301.7701-1(a) *et seq.;* Wigner, "Joint Venture with Corporate Participants Including Questions on Characterization as an Association," 22 N.Y.U. Tax. Inst. 611 (1964); Pugh and Thomas, *Income Tax Aspects of Joint Ventures Abroad,* "Private Investors Abroad—Problems and Solutions in International Business in 1975," p. 275 (Matthew Bender, New York, 1976).

[6]Int. Rev. Code of 1954, 1501, Bittker and Eustice, *Federal Income Taxation of Corporations and Shareholders,* § 15.20 *et seq.* (Warren, Gorham & Lamont, 1971).

[7]*Abbott Laboratories Int'l Co. v. United States,* 160 F. Supp. 321 (1958); aff'd per curiam, 267 F.2d 940 (7th Cir., 1959). See also, *Aramo-Stiftung v. Comm'r,* 172 F.2d 896 (2d Cir., 1949).

Foreign taxation checklist The following is a checklist of some of the tax issues which may be involved in the selection of a joint-venture form outside of the United States:

1. The possible differences in tax rates applicable to locally formed companies and those applicable to domestically qualified branches of foreign corporations

2. The possible differences in tax rates on dividends payable by a local company to its foreign parent (often withheld by the payor subsidiary and sometimes exigible whether or not payment is actually made or legally permissible) and the tax rates on remittances of profits by branches to the home office

3. The percentage of participation and other factors of a United States participant in a domestic joint-venture corporation doing business abroad might require the earnings of the subsidiary to be included on the parent's consolidated tax return

4. The effect of any applicable tax treaties on the rate of taxation of the joint venture

5. The creditability of foreign taxes paid by the participants; the individual needs of the participants regarding the timing of the use of foreign tax credits[8]

6. The "controlled foreign corporation" and subpart F provisions of the Internal Revenue Code[9]

7. Some countries disallow deduction for purposes of calculating net taxable income of certain kinds of expenses which could have a debilitating effect on the joint venture's profitability[10]

8. Tax holidays or incentives may be available

9. A withholding tax may be levied on payments made by the joint venture to the individual participants for subcontracted services, and whether this is an expense to be borne by the joint venture or the participant should be determined.

Antitrust Considerations

Any company contemplating entering a joint venture should consider the potential antitrust impact of the laws of any country with which the contemplated joint venture is connected.

In the United States, it has been clear for many years that joint ventures fall

---

[8]Pugh and Thomas, op. cit. *supra* note 5. See also, the foreign-tax-credit election requirements in Treas. Reg. § 1.703-(b) (1).

[9]Int. Rev. Code of 1954, §§ 951-972 and Pugh and Thomas, op. cit. *supra* note 5, 289–296.

[10]For instance, Brazil disallows any payments made abroad by a Brazilian company for technical services to a company which is related to the payor, Decree 178 (1975); Saudi Arabia disallows deductions for payments for overhead charges incurred abroad, Circular no. 3 of 1389; and Venezuela disallows any payments whatsoever for technical services performed abroad, Income Tax Law, Article 3.

within the purview of the antitrust laws,[11] and the engineering and construction industry has come under the scrutiny of antitrust enforcement agencies in a number of contexts.[12] This complex subject is further complicated by the fact that the scope of United States laws governing anticompetitive abuses often extends into international transactions.[13]

Without attempting to be comprehensive in this area, the following are a number of preliminary antitrust checkpoints potentially applicable to joint ventures.

Eliminating potential competitors   In the engineering and construction industry, joint ventures are often formed by agreements between competitors, thus potentially restraining competition. One operative factor in determining the legality of a joint venture is whether or not the participants would have been able or willing to perform the object of the joint venture alone.[14] If they might have individually competed for the project, it may be argued that competition is restrained by the fact that a competitive factor in the market has been eliminated.

Discouraging new entrants   It has been suggested that another factor used in determining illegality is whether or not the size of one or more of the joint-venture participants in the relevant geographical and/or product market is such that the combination of these participants might discourage other potential competitors from entering that relevant market.

Territorial divisions   It may be important for the participants in a joint venture to contractually agree that they will not compete with the joint venture in the area in which the joint venture will operate. Antitrust laws generally prohibit any contractual prohibition against competing in a specific area, and depending on the details of the prohibition, such a provision in a joint-venture agreement could be illegal.[15]

---

[11] *Timkin Roller Bearing Co. v. United States,* 341 U.S. 593 (1951); *United States v. Penn-Olin Chemical Co.,* 378 U.S. 158 (1954) on remand 246 F. Supp. 917 (D. Del. 1965) *aff'd per curiam* 389 U.S. 308 (1967); Handler, "Emerging Anti-Trust Issues: Reciprocity and Joint Ventures," 49 VA. L. REV. 433 (1963); Pitofsky, "Joint Ventures Under the Antitrust Laws: Some Reflections on the Significance of Penn-Olin," 82 HARV. L. REV. 1007 (1969); Backman, "Joint Ventures and the Anti-Trust Laws," 40 N.Y.U. L. REV. 651 (1965). See generally, Von Kalinowski, *10 Antitrust Laws and Trade Regulation,* § 74.05 *et seq.* (Matthew Bender, New York, 1975).

[12] *United States v. Halliburton Corp.,* Civil No. 73-1806, Dist. Ct. S.D. N.Y., and *United States v. Bechtel,* Civil No. C-76-99, Dist. Ct. N.D. Cal. The Halliburton consent decree is set forth in 1976 CCH Trade Regulation Reports § 50,260. United States Justice Department Antitrust Division *Antitrust Guide for International Operations* "Case C: Joint Building," 1977.

[13] *Timkin Roller Bearing Co. v. United States,* op. cit.; Kellison, "Joint Ventures Abroad and Per Se Antitrust Violations," 1 CAL. WEST. INTL. L.J. 95 (1970); Joelson and Griffin, "Multinational Joint Ventures and the U.S. Antitrust Laws," 15 VIR. J. INTL. L. 487 (1975).

[14] *United States v. Penn-Olin Chem. Co., supra* note 4. See also, *United States v. Nat'l Elec. Contractors Assn.,* 1956 CCH Trade Cases § 68,534; and *Commonwealth Edison v. Federal Pacific Elec Co.,* 1962 CCH Trade Cases § 70,488; *United Nuclear Corp. v. Combustion Eng., Inc.,* 302 F. Supp. 539, 555 (E.D. Pa. 1969).

[15] *United States v. Arnold Schwinn & Co.,* 388 U.S. 365 (1967); *White Motor Co. v. United States,* 372 U.S. 253 (1963); *Timkin Roller Bearing Co., supra* note 11.

Illegal tying   United States antitrust law prohibits the practice of conditioning the sale of one product, over which the seller has a distinct competitive advantage, to the concurrent sale of another product, over which the seller has no advantage, thereby giving the seller an unfair competitive advantage in the market for the second product.[16] This might arise in the situation where one of the participants is furnishing financing, patented process technology or materials for the project, which are either unavailable in the open market, or which are offered at terms which are substantially better than those available in the open market; and the purchase of these services is tied to the sale of the nonunique services offered by the joint venture.

Business review letters   Potential participants may decide to request the Justice Department to review a proposed joint venture in advance, and to render an opinion with respect to its compliance with the United States antitrust laws.[17]

SUGGESTIONS FOR DRAFTING JOINT-VENTURE AGREEMENTS

The foregoing discussion touches upon a number of threshold areas of potential concern regarding joint ventures. Obviously, each situation will be unique, and the resolution of these issues and the formal structure established will in each case be based upon the particular variables involved, including the country or state in which the project is located or the work is to be performed.

In any event, it will probably be necessary to draft at least one agreement setting forth the participants' expectations regarding the joint venture, and the methods by which the project itself will be managed, including the obligations and rights of each of the participants. However, it is often convenient to execute a brief statement of intent when submitting a proposal, containing the basic outline of understanding, and wait until the proposal is accepted before executing a more extensive agreement. As noted, if the corporate form, or its equivalent, is used, the participant-shareholders' agreement should relate directly to the formal mechanisms built into the articles of incorporation and bylaws. If services are to be performed in more than one country, for example, home office engineering and on-site construction work, it may be advisable to have two or more separate agreements or entities. And if the services provided by the individual participants are to be functionally isolated from those of the others, it may be helpful to have a master agreement containing general provisions, with subsidiary agreements with individual participants.

In any case, the following are some of the features often found in joint-venture agreements.[18]

---

[16]*Fortner Enterprises, Inc. v. United States Steel Corp.*, 394 U.S. 495 (1969).

[17]See, e.g., Business Review Letter Number 57 (1972), Chicago Bridge & Iron and General Electric Company, joint venture to fabricate nuclear reactor pressure vessels, 1976 CCH Trade Regulation Reports, § 50,194.

[18]See generally, Note, "Joint Venture Corporations: Drafting the Corporate Papers," 78 HARV. L. REV. 393 (1964); Birrell, *International Joint Ventures,* "Private Investors Abroad—Problems and Solutions in International Business," p. 241 (Matthew Bender, New York, 1976).

Name of the Joint Venture

The agreement may provide that the right to use the name of the participants is limited to the joint venture, and upon termination of the joint venture that right also terminates. This provision may be fortified by a provision by which each party indemnifies the other against damages caused by unauthorized use of the individual participant's names. In countries where trade-name protection is not adequate, consideration might be given to the execution of a separate license agreement with the joint venture which would govern use of the name.

Purposes

The agreement should specify the purpose for which the joint venture is being formed. It is usually prudent to specify with some precision the parameters of the effort to distinguish the joint-venture activities from other activities of the participants on their own behalf.

Obligations of the Participants

The obligations of the participants should be clearly set forth. In this regard, the proposal or contract for the project may in some cases be made a part of the joint-venture agreement. The agreement should also clarify whether the joint venture itself will hire personnel to perform the services or whether instead the participants will be required to furnish such personnel, either by way of a seconding agreement or subcontract. Any special contributions of the participants such as patents or secret processes should be spelled out.

Restrictions on Use of Joint-Venture Assets

The agreement should generally restrict the joint venture's use of joint-venture assets to the specified purposes of the joint venture. Similar restrictions might be placed upon the ability of the participants to individually use the assets of the other participants other than as authorized in the joint-venture agreement.

Control of the Joint Venture

One of the most important and potentially controversial features of a joint-venture agreement is the mechanism for management and control of the joint venture and of the project in which the joint venture is involved. It is dealt with in many different ways but often involves the following pattern.

Board decides policy   A board or managing committee composed of representatives of the participants may be given responsibility for policy and broad-based management decisions and this board will in turn appoint management personnel of the joint venture. The procedures by which the board will meet and decide issues should be set forth, including the place, time, and notice requirements of the meetings and, in a multinational setting, the language of deliberation. The number and importance of the matters which must be submitted to the board, and which require unanimous consent, generally depend upon the degree of responsibility and authority which the participants are willing to confer on the executive personnel carrying out the board's decisions.

Sponsoring participant   One of the participants may be designated "sponsor" of the joint venture for purposes of maintaining overall project direction and implementing the decisions of the board. In order to ensure a mechanism for comprehensive project management and coordination, the agreement may refer in general terms to the methods by which decisions regarding staffing the project team will be made. These matters can be specifically delegated to the sponsoring participant or left to the decision of the board. In some cases, a second-level management board may be created, again with representation by all concerned.

Impasse breaking   The agreement may provide that in the event of a dispute regarding a decision affecting the projects, one of the participants may act without the consent of the other in certain specified areas. For instance, the sponsor could be authorized to take certain actions relating to the project without the consent of the board in the interests of continuity.

Interests and Contributions of the Participants

The percentage of the participation interests in and contributions to the joint venture by each of the participants should be stated. This statement should include the methods by which working capital, including funds to cover losses, will be originally and subsequently required to be contributed by the participants and the fact that profits and losses will be shared in proportion to the participation percentages or upon some other basis, if so agreed. The participants may wish to place some limit upon the amount of working capital which they may be obligated to contribute. In cases where more than one currency is involved, this should be clarified in the agreement, and if the participants agree that non-cash capital contributions may be made, such as the value of services, a limitation (for instance, a minimum cash requirement) might be placed upon this right.

Basis of Compensation

If one of the participants will individually perform services for the joint venture or furnish some of its employees to the joint venture, or if contributions to the capital of the joint venture are to be made in part by the value of the services of one of the participants, then the commercial basis upon which such services will be performed should be specified in the agreement.[19] Where one of the participants will perform services to the joint venture by way of a subcontract, on a cost basis, it is necessary to clarify whether part of the fee, as contrasted to reimbursable costs, will be passed along to that participant. Considerable detail should be included in this section, including all the customary charges for overhead and special rates and surcharges. In long-term arrangements, percentages and rates should be subject to adjustment on a showing of increased costs.

---

[19]See Int. Rev. Code of 1954, §§ 61 and 721 *et seq.*, and Treas. Reg. § 1.721-1(b)(i), regarding the tax treatment of such services.

Limitation of Liability between the Participants

Joint-venture agreements usually set forth provisions limiting liability between the participants similar to those contained in agreements with clients. Frequently, a joint-venture agreement will provide that each of the participants indemnify the other for any liability arising out of activities of the participants which are unrelated to the joint venture (for example, floating liens against one of the participants which encumber joint-venture assets). Where one of the participants brings specialized services to the joint venture, such as patented-process technology or materials or financing services, it may be appropriate, on the one hand, for the participant supplying the specialized service or product to limit its liability to the other participants and, on the other hand, for the other participants to require that the participant furnishing such services hold them harmless against liability arising out of these special activities.[20]

Right to Follow-Up Business and the Right to Compete

Participants in a joint venture often feel that they each should be prohibited from individually competing against the joint venture or the other participants with respect to the project or projects which are the object of the joint venture, or at least that some sort of right of first refusal should exist in the agreement. In this respect, however, consideration should be given to the antitrust issues mentioned above.

The obvious practical disadvantage with such a restriction is that a particular client may find one of the participants unacceptable for some reason, thus foreclosing the project involved to all of the other participants. But in another context, if one of the participants has proprietary data or processes which are disclosed to the other participants on the joint-venture project, it may be unfair to allow the other participants to thereafter individually bid on other jobs which utilize these data or processes.

A provision restricting follow-up business can sometimes cut both ways. For instance, during the course of construction, the client may perceive that one of the participants is making a more significant contribution to the project than the others and may ask the participant to bid individually on follow-up work closely allied to the original project without the other participants. If a contractual provision forbidding such activity exists, the participant of superior skill and industry may be unable to free itself from the association of a participant which does not positively contribute to the joint venture; but the participant who does in fact contribute to the success of the project, and who may have played a role in developing new techniques, but whose role may not be known to the client, would have protection of its rights in the business opportunity which developed in part as a result of its efforts. Even in the absence of such a contractual provision, a fiduciary obligation may be imposed by law on each of the participants which may include a prohibition against individually participat-

[20]See Int. Rev. Code of 1954, §§ 752(a) & (b), 722, 733, and Treas. Reg. § 1.752-1(b).

ing in business opportunities which were developed through the efforts of the joint venture.[21]

Inventions and Secrecy

It is frequently important to determine which participant has the right to inventions developed during the course of performing the project services. This is a matter of negotiation, and unless one of the participants has a strong proprietary position in information to which the invention relates, this may be resolved by sharing ownership according to the participation percentages of the participants or by giving each a royalty-free license. Additionally, participants often wish to provide that each will keep the proprietary information of the others confidential.

Timing, Place, and Currency of Payments

The agreement should specify the time at which payment of profits to the participants will be made. If several contingent liabilities are involved, the participants may wish to defer paying profits until these liabilities are discharged. If one of the participants has a unique need with regard to the timing or place of payment for tax purposes, or if potential currency-conversion problems exist, it may be advisable to specify the place and currency of payment as well.

Methods of Calculating Profit

Problems in defining profit may arise over the appropriateness of special deductions, including contingency reserves, allocation for business development expenses, insurance premiums, employee benefits and programs to be individually maintained by the participants, project support services such as data processing and soils analyses, in-house economic analysis, and the services of the legal, insurance and finance departments. Losses from prior years should naturally be recouped before any profit in the current year is deemed to exist; and if the applicable tax laws allow special accounting methods which cause a different definition of profit than would result using generally accepted accounting principles, then the selected method should be stated.

Methods of Conduct

Where legal or ethical conflicts may exist, there may be some benefit in stating that certain specified norms will be observed, particularly regarding such matters as public disclosure of policies and payments to agents. Also, labor relations policies on the project should be clarified.

Contracting Methods

The participants may have different contractual policies which potentially conflict. For instance, one of the participants may be willing to accept more liability for a project than the other participant. Or one participant may require

[21]*Meinhard v. Salmon,* 249 N.Y. 458, 164 N.E. 545 (1928)

the client to provide advance funds and mobilization payments while the other participant may be willing to use its own funds until payment is received from the client. In short, contractual policies differ among companies as do business policies, and in the interest of good client relations, it is often advisable to decide in advance on certain fundamental contractual issues so that the joint venture may deal with the client with a consistent approach.

In an international joint venture, services related to a project are frequently performed in more than one country, but the joint venture will participate in only one country. This may be the case where a project is located in a less-developed country and one of the participants is a national of the country. If it is anticipated that a participant will individually perform services directly for the client such as worldwide procurement or home office engineering without the participation of the other participants, this fact should be set forth.

Duration and Termination

The joint venture ordinarily exists for the term of the project unless otherwise terminated by mutual agreement. If one of the participants becomes insolvent, or breaches the joint-venture agreement, the other participants may have the right to take action necessary to ensure the continued success of the project in the name of the joint venture without the insolvent or breaching participant's consent. Such action may include replacing the insolvent or breaching partici-pant with another capable substitute, and ceasing all further payments.

Preformation Expenses

The participants will likely incur expenses in advance of or collateral to the formation of the joint venture, such as costs for business development and legal efforts. The participants will either agree to bear these expenses themselves— even though they may directly contribute to the fortunes of the joint venture— or agree that they will form a part of the capital contribution of the participants if the project is awarded.

Accounting and Auditing

Each participant should have the right to audit the records of the joint venture, as well as the records of the participants as they relate to services performed for the joint venture. It may be agreed that a certified public accountant firm unrelated to the participants will prepare and audit the books and records, or one of the participants may perform that function. In any case, the agreement should determine where the joint-venture bank accounts will be located, who will be authorized to receive and disburse funds, where the books of account will be stored, and, in the multinational situation, the currencies to be main-tained in the account.

Governing Law and Arbitration

It is increasingly common for multinational joint-venture agreements to specify a law governing dispute and to agree to submit all disputes to arbitration.

Chapter **7**

Contract Record Administration

IRVING M. FOGEL, P.E.
President, Fogel & Associates, Inc., New York, New York

ROY L. WILSON, P.E.
Vice President, Fogel & Associates, Inc., New York, New York

INTRODUCTION TO MANAGEMENT OF CONSTRUCTION PAPERWORK

The required paperwork for a modern construction project is greater than ever before. The organization of this paperwork is critical in determining whether the paperwork will aid in managing the project or hinder efficient management.

The current increase in paperwork can be found in all segments of the construction industry. The home builder is faced with a variety of environmental and consumer protection documents, while the atomic engineer for a nuclear power plant is faced with "controlling" documents numbered in the tens of millions.

Proper management of construction paperwork will increase effectiveness of the overall project by:

1. Opening up channels of communication and keeping all parties aware of job progress

2. Filing documents in such a way that they can be easily retrieved for future reference

3. Allowing for movement of personnel between various projects without long periods of orientation

4. Providing a history of the project for future planning of similar projects

5. Aiding in resolution of future construction claims and disputes

This chapter will outline how to design systems or procedures to manage paperwork, how to implement these systems or procedures, and how to review new or existing procedures to determine their usefulness.

Finally, the chapter includes a series of sample procedures and forms designed to improve the flow of paperwork in a construction organization. Although these procedures were designed to meet the particular needs of a particular construction company, they should serve as a "how-to" guideline for developing procedures for any construction-related organization.

DESIGNING THE SYSTEM

The development of systems or procedures to improve the management of paperwork should not simply evolve from the practices of a number of individuals. These systems or procedures should be carefully designed to fit the organization's needs as well as the organization's abilities.

Too many construction companies operate by having each project manager, engineer, or superintendent "do his own thing." The records kept on one project in no way resemble the records kept on another project. This is a result of the mobility and independence that exist in the construction industry. This haphazard system greatly increases the difficulty of moving personnel from one project to another.

The first step in developing a paperwork system is to define the need for the system. This may sound pretty basic, but it is difficult for in-house personnel to clearly see the need for a new or improved system. As a company grows, paperwork systems tend to evolve and are accepted by in-house personnel. However, here are a number of clues which can point out the need for an improved system:

1. Great difficulty in determining the status of a particular shop drawing

2. Inability to find correspondence for a specified date

3. Inability to develop even the most basic history of how a job progressed

4. Inability to produce the necessary documentation to support or defend a construction claim

Many other situations can alert a good manager to recognize the need for a better system. In many cases an independent review of existing paperwork systems by an outsider, a fellow contractor or management consultant, will highlight the areas where new systems are needed. The first step, however, is to recognize the need for a new or improved system. If there is no valid need for a change, there is absolutely no reason to take the next step in developing the new system.

The next step is to define the scope of the particular system. The scope of a system includes such factors as what it will do, what it will not do, personnel involved, extra cost, and interfacing with existing systems and procedures.

The scope of the system should be prepared in a written format and be thoroughly reviewed with all parties who will be involved with the eventual system. If the system is limited in size (such as one of the procedures at the conclusion of the chapter), the written scope may simply be a draft of the procedure which is to be implemented. If the system is more complicated, such as a computer system to control shop drawings on a billion-dollar project, then the written scope will be more in the format of a proposal to management.

Once the scope has been committed to writing, it should be reviewed by all levels of personnel that will be involved in making the system operate, from file clerk to executive. This review will turn up better ways to accomplish the end results and will gain "grass-roots" support for implementing the system.

Unless the system is one that can be designed and implemented within a period of a few days, a schedule and a budget should be prepared to show the cost and time required to design and implement the system. Even a relatively simple system to control equipment deliveries can require a series of proposed formats and reviews that can consume excessive dollars and time unless a schedule and budget have been established to control the development.

Written procedures that explain what each individual must do to make the system operate must be clear and explicit. Very few areas should require "special interpretation." When an instruction is not clear, the question on procedure should be referred back to the author, and the procedure should be changed to clarify the questionable area.

IMPLEMENTING THE SYSTEM

Implementation of the new system may be the most important step in the success or failure of having the system successfully meet the need for which it was originally intended. Too often the system is carefully designed, forms are carefully drawn, and computer programs (if there are any) debugged; but the introduction of the system is carried out with a duplicated copy of a "memo-to-staff."

The memo-to-staff is greeted with an assortment of grunts and groans by individuals who see the new system as an increase in their work load with no corresponding benefits. No wonder that this type of introduction can lead to total failure of the system in a very short period of time.

The key to effective implementation of a new system is education. This education should include explicit information regarding the benefits to be derived by both the individual and the organization, and what is expected of the individual. If possible, the new system should be introduced by a top company executive. It should be made clear that this executive is interested in the success of the system and will be monitoring the implementation of the system.

REVIEWING THE SYSTEM

All too frequently, systems for managing paperwork are well designed and properly implemented, but then forgotten. The system which was designed for a company doing $X amount of annual sales and having Y employees may have never been updated to reflect company growth in sales, employees, or market conditions. All existing company procedures and systems should be reviewed periodically.

This review is especially important with new systems. During the design phase of a new system it is almost impossible to consider all the conditions under which the system will have to operate and all the individual needs that it will have to meet. Rather than constantly change the design of the system before implementation, it is better to put the system into operation after a reasonable period of design and then review the operation of the system after a set period of time. Based on this review, the system can then be "fine-tuned" to make it fully compatible with the company's requirements.

A regular review period should be set for each system. The operation of a new system should be reviewed six months after the initial operation. For existing systems, a more meaningful review period would be every year or two.

The review of the system, if it is to be effective, should be comprehensive in nature. Every individual involved with the system, or at least a representative of each group, should be requested to offer comments on the strengths and weaknesses of the system as it currently operates. A discussion period among the individuals who use the system is one of the more effective methods for eliciting comments that will improve the system.

If changes are made to the system as a result of an individual's comments, these changes should be publicized and credit given to the individual who initiated the change. This will encourage other individuals to come forth with future changes.

Changes in an existing system should be implemented with the same care that would be given to the installation of a new system. All individuals should be educated as to the importance of the changes and the benefits that the changes will bring to the company and the individual.

Conclusions

The paperwork associated with the modern construction project can be either an aid to improved management control or a dead weight which simply burdens the project. The development of *effective* formalized systems to manage the flow of construction documentation is the major factor in making record keeping an integral part of overall project management.

INTRODUCTION TO THE STANDARD PROCEDURES

The standard procedures which follow were developed for one particular contractor. They were intended to improve communications between all project management levels, provide a history for each project, and serve as an aid in pursuing or defending against construction claims. Although these procedures were developed to meet the particular need of a particular company, they may fit the needs of your own organization or serve as a model from which to fashion a set of procedures suitable to your needs.

The importance of developing a "project history" as an aid in supporting or defending against construction claims cannot be overemphasized. The old construction adage about "putting it in writing" is more important today than ever before. In addition, the ability to retrieve information is of vital importance. Very often the information is there in the form of a memo or minutes but cannot be located at the critical point in the preparation of a claim. Development of adequate distribution and filing procedures goes a long way toward ensuring the availability of key documentation in a timely manner.

Many construction disputes involve project delays and require development of as-built schedules to determine the causes and fault of delay and resulting damages. The proper recording of key chronological information (such as submission dates or approval dates) is invaluable in supporting and defending against construction delay claims.

Properly formalized documentation methods and systems will:
1. Improve communications within an organization
2. Improve communications with outside agencies
3. Formalize the history of a project
4. Serve as a source of facts for the prosecution of claims for extras
5. Serve as an information base for the defense against claims by others

STANDARD PROCEDURE: INCOMING CORRESPONDENCE

DISTRIBUTION
    OFFICE: Executives, Engineers, Office Staff
    JOB SITE: Superintendents, Engineers, General Foreman
        1. *PURPOSE AND SCOPE OF PROCEDURE*
The purpose of having a standard procedure for incoming correspondence is to ensure proper distribution of information and ensure a permanent file record.

    2. *PROCEDURE*

The Secretary

Will stamp and hole-punch each letter with the distribution stamp and make one copy of each letter. The copy will be filed in the master incoming-correspondence file in chronological order. The original will be forwarded to the president's office.

The President

If absent, designated personnel will initial and indicate on the distribution stamp who is to receive copies. The original is then returned to the secretary.

The Secretary

Will make copies and forward them to personnel indicated on the distribution stamp. On correspondence with job numbers, if the project engineer is indicated on the distribution stamp, the original and three copies will be forwarded to the engineer. On correspondence with estimate numbers, if the chief estimator is indicated on the distribution stamp, two copies will be forwarded to the chief estimator.

The Project Engineer

Will file the original in the master job file. One copy will be circulated to the staff indicated on the distribution stamp if required. After circulation, this copy will be filed in the subject file. If necessary, one copy will be filed in the come-up file. When action is complete, this copy will be filed in the subject file. (Two copies of the same letter in the subject file will indicate that the concerned staff have seen the letter and that the necessary action has been completed.) The last copy will be forwarded to the job site.

The Chief Estimator

Will circulate one copy, if required, to the staff indicated on the distribution stamp. After circulation, this copy will be filed in the estimate file. If necessary, one copy will be filed in the come-up file. When action is complete, this copy will be filed in the estimate file. Two copies of the same letter in the estimate file will indicate that the concerned staff have seen the letter and that the necessary action has been completed.

3. *RESPONSIBILITIES*

Secretary

Distribution-stamp and hole-punch each piece of incoming correspondence. File copy in master incoming-correspondence file and forward original to the president's office. Make necessary number of copies and forward to indicated personnel.

Project Engineer

File original in master job file.
Check distribution stamp on the copy and circulate to indicated personnel. After circulation, file this copy in the subject file.
If necessary, file one copy in the come-up file and take appropriate action. When action is complete, file this copy in the subject file.

Chief Estimator

Check distribution stamp on one copy and circulate to indicated personnel to be initialed. After circulation, file this copy in the estimate file.
If necessary, file one copy in the come-up file and take appropriate action. When action is complete, file this copy in the estimate file.

STANDARD PROCEDURE: MEETING NOTES

DISTRIBUTION
OFFICE: Executives and Engineers
JOB SITE: Superintendents, Engineers, General Foreman
  1. *PURPOSE AND SCOPE OF PROCEDURE*
The purpose of keeping notes is to provide a written record of what happens on the job. Meeting notes are used to keep all job personnel up to date on information

about the job. A secondary use of written notes is to provide a record in case of future differences of opinion, or as evidence in case of legal actions. Procedures and responsibilities will be set up for the following types of meetings: (1) pre-bid, post-bid, and contract-signing meetings; (2) job progress meetings; and (3) informal job meetings.

   2. *PROCEDURE: GENERAL*

Notes will be kept in books having tear-out copy sheet.

The senior representative at each meeting will designate the notetaker.

Notes will list name, title, and company affiliation of all persons at the meeting.

Notes will cover all points that affect the job.

Notes will be concise. They will not cover all discussions, but will be a statement of the final resolution of each point.

If agreement is not reached, the position of each party will be noted.

All representatives attending a meeting will read and initial notes at the conclusion of the meeting. If there is any nonconcurrence with the notes, the notes will show the differences of opinion.

   3. *PROCEDURES: PRE-BID, POST-BID, CONTRACT-SIGNING MEETINGS*

Notebooks for pre-bid, post-bid, and contract-signing meetings will be kept by each employee who attends such meetings.

Notebooks will be used on more than one job and are chronological records of meetings.

Tear-out copy sheets will be filed with the bid documents.

Estimating engineers assigned to bid preparation on any job will read and initial the tear-out copy in the bid document file for that job.

   4. *PROCEDURE: JOB PROGRESS MEETINGS*

When a job is manned, a meeting notebook will be set up for the job.

The notebook will be kept at the job site.

Superintendent, job-site engineers, and general foreman will read and initial the notes after each meeting.

Tear-out copy sheets will be filed in the meeting file maintained in the office by the project engineer, after he has read and initialed the notes.

When the job-progress-meeting minutes arrive, the project engineer will compare them with the meeting notes.

If there are discrepancies between the notes and the job-progress-meeting minutes, a letter will be written immediately to the author of the minutes. The letter will point out the discrepancy. If the minutes are not amended by the date of the next meeting, the letter will be taken to the meeting and the discrepancy resolved at the meeting.

   5. *PROCEDURE: INFORMAL JOB MEETINGS*

Notes of informal job meetings will be kept in pocket job logs, or meeting notebooks if they are available.

Noncompany personnel involved in these meetings will be asked to give their name and company for these notes.

After any meeting, noncompany personnel may be asked to initial the notes, but do not make an issue of it if they refuse. Project engineer will write a letter to the company concerned, specifying the agreement, problem, or action.

Tear-out copy will be read and initialed by general foreman, superintendent, and job-site engineers and then delivered to the main office by the superintendent.

Tear-out copy will be filed in the job file by the project engineer after he has read and initialed the page and taken any necessary action.

   6. *RESPONSIBILITIES*

General Foreman

Make notes of informal meetings in pocket job logs, or meeting notebooks.
Make notes in meeting notebook at job-progress meetings if designated by the senior supervisor.
Read and initial notes of job progress whether or not you attended the meeting.
Discuss notes with superintendent and take appropriate action.
Subforeman are not to have informal meetings in which decisions are made, without the presence of the general foreman or superintendent.

Superintendents

Make notes of informal meetings in pocket job logs or meeting notebooks.
Make notes in meeting notebook at job-progress meetings, or designate foremen or engineer to take notes.
Read and initial notes of all meetings.
Discuss meeting notes of all meetings with project engineer and take appropriate action.

Job-Site Engineers

Make notes of informal meetings in pocket job logs or meeting notebooks.
Make notes of job-progress meetings if designated by senior supervisor.
Read and initial notes of all job-progress meetings and informal meetings.
Discuss notes with project engineer or superintendent and take appropriate action.

Project Engineer

Make notes of informal job meetings in pocket job logs.
Make notes or designate a notetaker for the progress meetings.
Make notes of off-job site meetings in personal meeting notebook. The tear-out sheet will be duplicated before filing, and the copy will be sent to the job site and stapled in the job-site meeting notebook.
Read and initial notes of all meetings.
Discuss notes with superintendent or job-site engineer and decide on appropriate action.
Write all letters to owner, architect, other contractors or suppliers as necessary from information obtained from meeting notes.
The project engineer will have notes of all meetings typed. Unless a member of another organization at the meeting has been designated to record and distribute minutes of the meeting, the project engineer will transmit notes of all meetings to the general contractor and any other organization involved with the project.

STANDARD PROCEDURE: POCKET JOB LOGS

DISTRIBUTION
   OFFICE: Executives and Engineers
   JOB SITE: Superintendents, Engineers, Foreman
      1. *PURPOSE AND SCOPE OF PROCEDURE*
The purpose of the pocket job log is to provide a convenient means of recording important information about the job.
Recorded information has two important uses:
Office and supervisory personnel are kept up to date on job progress and made aware of job problems.

Written records are valuable in settling claims and differences of opinion that may arise in the future.

Pocket Job Logs will contain information on the following subjects:

Crew size (daily).

Major job activities (daily).

Problems (as they occur).

Delays of any kind.

Areas not available for work.

Difficulties in getting material to work area.

Delayed material deliveries.

Discrepancies in drawings and specifications.

Interference with job progress by other trades.

Prints and drawings not available when area is ready for work.

Informal job meeting notes (as they occur).

Oral instructions (as they occur).

   2. *PROCEDURE*

All superintendents, job-site engineers, and foreman will carry pocket job logs.

Personnel working more than one job will keep a separate pocket job log for each job.

Dates and crew sizes will be recorded daily by all foremen.

Job-site engineers will not list crew sizes in pocket job logs.

The superintendent will not list crew sizes in pocket job logs.

Major activities will be listed each day and be specified as work on contract (use job number), work on change orders (use change-order number), and work on field orders (use field-order number).

Work areas will be described by floor and rooms.

Problems will be noted as they occur. Solutions to the problems will be noted if the problems are solved on the spot. If there is no immediate solution, note the name of the supervisor to whom you reported the problem. Make certain that the problem is transferred into the daily job log and that it remains on the active problem list until solved.

Pocket job logs will also be used to record notes of informal job meetings with representatives of owner, architect, suppliers, and other contractors.

Verbal instructions from supervisors will be briefly noted along with the name of the person giving the instructions. Noncompany personnel must give *all* instructions in writing except in case of emergencies. In case of emergency, if instructions are accepted from noncompany personnel, the instructions will be recorded as well as the name and company of the person involved. The record will be made as soon as possible after the emergency. Ask the person who gave the instructions to sign your record of the incident but do not make an issue of signing.

As many pages as necessary will be used each day. Each page will be dated.

Pocket job logs will be signed each day, and the copy delivered to the job-site office for attachment to the daily job log copy. After the superintendent and job-site engineer read and initial copies, the copies will be delivered to the project engineer.

   3. *RESPONSIBILITIES*

General Foreman

General foremen will fill out pocket job logs daily.

Signed copies of pocket-job-log sheets will be turned in at job-site office at the end of each workday.

Unsolved problems noted in the general foreman's and subforeman's log, and the site engineer's pocket job log, will be entered in the daily job log by the general foreman and kept on the active list until solved.

Subforeman

Subforeman will fill out pocket job logs daily.

Signed copies will be turned in at the job-site office each day.

Problems entered in the pocket job log will be discussed with the general foreman as soon as possible after the problem occurs.

Subforeman will not make agreements with noncompany personnel. All problems with noncompany personnel will be taken to the general foreman for resolution.

Superintendent

Superintendent will fill out pocket job logs daily, for each job under his supervision. Copies of pocket-job-log sheets will be turned in to project engineer.

Superintendent will read and initial all foreman's and job-site engineer's pocket-job-log copies each visit to the job and deliver all copies to the project engineer.

Superintendent will check that *all* unresolved problems are entered in the daily job logs and kept active until resolved. Superintendent is responsible for problem solutions in cooperation with the project engineer.

Job-Site Engineers

Job-site engineers will keep a daily pocket job log.

Signed copies will be turned in at the office each day.

Engineers will read and initial foremens', superintendents', and other on-site engineers' pocket-job-log copies for information purposes.

Unsolved problems will be noted in the daily job log and kept on active status until resolved.

Project Engineer

Project engineer will read, initial, and take action on all pocket-job-log notes before filing in the daily-job-log file.

Letters based on pocket-job-log information will be written as needed by the project engineer.

The project engineer is responsible for seeing that pocket job logs are properly filled out.

STANDARD PROCEDURE: CONTRACT DRAWING REVISION CHART

DISTRIBUTION

   OFFICE: Executive, Project Engineer, Engineer

  JOB SITE: Superintendent, Designers, General Foremen

     1. *PURPOSE AND SCOPE OF PROCEDURE*

The purpose of the contract drawing revision chart is to provide a complete and up-to-date record of each contract drawing associated with a project. The chart will be maintained during the life of the project.

This procedure is to be used for every project. If necessary, two or more projects can be combined on one chart.

     2. *PROCEDURE*

The contract drawing revision chart will be prepared at the start of the project (letter of intent, contract, signing, etc.).

CONTRACT DRAWING REVISION CHART

PROJECT NAME: _____
PROJECT NUMBER _____
OWNER _____
CONTRACTOR _____
ENGINEER _____

PAGE Nº _____

STATUS DATE: _____

DRAWING Nº	DRAWING TITLE	ORIGINAL ISSUE DATE	DRAWING CHANGE INFORMATION					
			REV Nº	REV DATE	DATE REC'D	DATE TO JOB	CH EST REQ	CHANGE DESCRIPTION

Figure 7.1

The contract drawing revision chart will be maintained in the office for the life of the project. Updated copy will be sent to the field office at the end of each month.

The following information is to be included on the chart:

Drawing number.

Drawing title—Include a description of the work if required.

Original-issue date—If the contract drawing has been revised prior to start of the project, indicate the revision number and date of the revision.

Drawing change information—Space is allowed for eight contract revisions.

Revision number.

Revision date—Date shown on drawing.

Date received—Date revised drawing was received in office.

Date to job—Date revised drawing was sent to field office.

Change estimate required—Indicate "yes" or "no" if revised drawing required a change estimate.

Change description—Location and type of work involved with the change.

3. *RESPONSIBILITIES*

Project Engineer

Prepare chart and continually update.

Send updated chart to field office at end of each month.

Check with field office to verify correctness of drawing status shown on chart and to ensure that all work is being done from current drawings.

Assistant Superintendent/General Foremen

At the end of each month verify chart against their records and notify project engineer of any discrepancies.

STANDARD PROCEDURE: MATERIAL AND EQUIPMENT STATUS CHART

DISTRIBUTION:

OFFICE: Executive, Project Engineers, Engineers

JOB SITE: Superintendent, Designers, General Foremen

1. *PURPOSE AND SCOPE OF PROCEDURE*

The purpose of the material and equipment status chart is to provide a complete and up-to-date record of every item to be purchased for a particular project. It will be used to monitor and record every phase of the purchasing and approval cycle.

This procedure is to be used for every job where material and equipment are to be purchased. If necessary, two or more jobs can be combined on one chart.

2. *PROCEDURE*

The material and equipment status chart will be maintained continuously in the office. An updated copy will be sent to the field office at the end of each month.

At the start of each job (letter of intent, contract signing, etc.), the chart will be filled out, listing every item which is to be purchased over the life of the job.

The following information is to be included during the initial preparation:

Description of material equipment—A basic description of the item to be ordered. Each item and size should be shown.

Quantity—The estimated quantity should be shown.

Spec/drawing reference—Indicate the part of the specification or drawing which calls for the item.

MATERIAL & EQUIPMENT STATUS CHART

PROJECT NAME:_____

PROJECT NUMBER _____

OWNER:_____

CONTRACTOR:_____

PAGE Nº _____

STATUS DATE:_____

DESCRIPTION OF MATERIAL / EQUIPMENT	QUANTITY	SPEC / DWG REFERENCE	DATE REQUIRED AT SITE	VENDOR	PURCHASE ORDER NUMBER	PURCHASE ORDER DATE	VENDOR'S PROMISED DELIVERY	NUMBER OF SHOP DRAWINGS	SHOP DRAWING APPROVALS			APPROVAL TO FABRICATE	CONFIRMED DELIVERY DATE	ACTUAL DELIVERY DATE	COMMENTS
									SUBMIT	RETURN	ACTION				

Figure 7.2

Date required at site—The date should be shown as well as the source of the date. Acceptance of earlier or later delivery should be indicated.

Vendor—The name of the vendor should be shown if it is known at this time.

The following information is to be included after a purchase order has been placed.

Vendor—The name of the vendor

Purchase order number

Purchase order date

Vendor's promised delivery date—If other than date required at site, it should be highlighted.

Number of shop drawings—Indicate the number of shop drawings required for the item.

The following information is to be entered for each submission of shop drawings or samples:

Submission date

Return date

Action—This indicates the submission was rejected, accepted as noted, accepted, etc.

The following information is to be entered as it becomes known:

Date of approval to fabricate—Enter here the date the manufacturer was given approval to ship or start fabricating the item

Confirmed delivery date—Date that vendor promised delivery, based on fabrication approval date

Actual delivery date—Date that material or equipment arrived on site

If an approval has not been received by the required date as shown on the chart, a form letter will be sent to the organization responsible for the approval. This will be repeated every week until the approval has been received.

3. *RESPONSIBILITIES*

Project Engineer

Prepare chart at the start of each job.

Keep chart up to date.

Send updated chart to field at end of each month.

Maintain schedule of submissions.

Superintendent/General Foremen

Review updated chart each month to ensure status is in line with his field information.

Inform project engineer of any changes relating to date required at site.

STANDARD PROCEDURE: FIELD ORDER STATUS CHART

DISTRIBUTION

OFFICE: Executive, Project Engineer, Engineer

JOB SITE: Superintendent, Designers, General Foremen

1. *PURPOSE AND SCOPE OF PROCEDURE*

The purpose of the field order status chart is to provide a complete and up-to-date record of every field order received during the life of a project.

This procedure is to be used for every project where the owner-contractor issues field orders. If necessary, two or more projects can be combined on one chart.

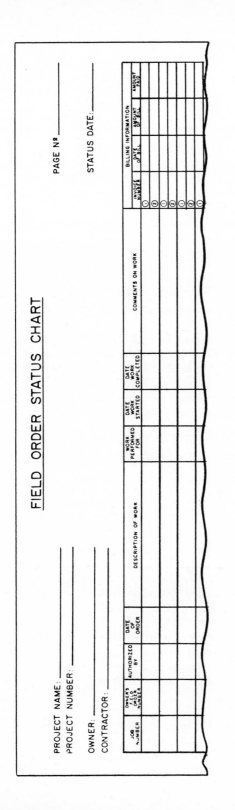

FIELD ORDER STATUS CHART

PROJECT NAME: _____

PROJECT NUMBER: _____

OWNER: _____

CONTRACTOR: _____

PAGE N°: _____

STATUS DATE: _____

JOB NUMBER	OWNER'S FIELD ORDER NUMBER	AUTHORIZED BY	DATE OF ORDER	DESCRIPTION OF WORK	WORK PERFORMED FOR	DATE WORK STARTED	DATE WORK COMPLETED	COMMENTS ON WORK	BILLING INFORMATION			
									INVOICE NUMBER	DATE OF BILL	AMOUNT OF BILL	AMOUNT PAID

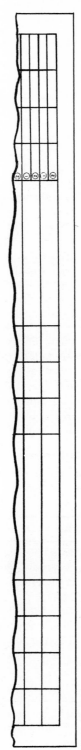

Figure 7.3

7-15

2. *PROCEDURE*

The field order status chart will be prepared for each project at the time the first field order is received. On major projects, the chart should be prepared at the start of the project (letter of intent, contract signing, etc.).

The field order status chart will be maintained in the office for the life of the project. An updated copy will be sent to the field office at the end of each month.

The following information is to be included on the chart:

Job number—The number assigned the work in question

Owner's field order number

Authorized by—Name of individual, company, affiliation, and title

Date of order—The date that oral or written instructions were first received to perform the work

Description of work—Location and type of work to be performed under the field order

Work performed for—Name of owner-contractor-subcontractor for whom work was performed

Date work started

Date work completed—Indicate if work was continuous or intermittent

Comments on work—Any note of general interest relating to the work performed under the field order

Billing Information—Space is allowed for information relating to two invoices

At the end of each month, an updated copy of the field order status chart will be sent to the field office where it will be verified against the records in the field office.

3. *RESPONSIBILITIES*

Project Engineer

Prepare chart and continually update.

Send updated copy to field office at end of each month.

Check with field office to verify correctness of chart.

Assistant Superintendent/General Foreman

At end of each month verify chart against their records and notify project engineer if any discrepancies.

STANDARD PROCEDURE: CHANGE ORDER STATUS CHART

DISTRIBUTION

OFFICE: Executive, Project Engineer, Engineer

JOB SITE: Superintendent, Designers, General Foreman

1. *PURPOSE AND SCOPE OF PROCEDURE*

The purpose of the change order status chart is to provide a complete and up-to-date record of every proposed change order during the life of a project.

This procedure is to be used for every project where the owner-contractor issues proposed change orders. If necessary, two or more projects can be combined on one chart.

2. *PROCEDURE*

The change order status chart will be prepared for each project at the time the first proposed change order is received. On major projects, the chart should be prepared at the start of the project (letter of intent, contract signing, etc.).

The change order status chart will be maintained in the office for the life of the

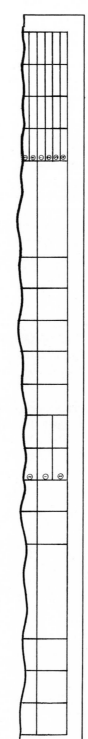

CHANGE ORDER STATUS CHART

PROJECT NAME: _____

PROJECT NUMBER: _____

OWNER: _____

CONTRACTOR: _____

PAGE Nº _____

STATUS DATE: _____

PROPOSAL NUMBER	OWNER'S PROPOSAL NUMBER	DATE RECEIVED	DESCRIPTION OF CHANGE	REFERENCE DRAWINGS OR SPECS	DATE PROPOSAL REQUIRED	DATE PROPOSAL SUBMITTED	AMOUNT OF PROPOSAL	DATE PROPOSAL APPROVED	OWNER'S CHANGE ORDER NUMBER	JOB NUMBER	DATE WORK STARTED	DATE WORK COMPLETED	COMMENTS ON WORK	BILLING INFORMATION			
														INVOICE NUMBER	DATE OF BILL	AMOUNT OF BILL	AMOUNT PAID

Figure 7.4

7-17

project. For each proposed change, information will be added to the chart as it becomes available. An updated copy of the chart will be sent to the field office at the end of each month.

The following information is to be included on the chart:

Proposed number—Numbers will be assigned sequentially to each required proposal.

Owner's proposal number

Date received—The date owner's request for proposal was received in office

Description of change—Location and type of work to be performed under the change

Reference drawings on specs—Indicate if proposed change is shown on a contract drawing, rough sketch, written instruction, etc.

Date proposal required—Indicate date established by owner or others

Date proposal submitted—Space allowed for two submissions

Amount of proposal—Space allowed for two submissions

Date proposal approved—Indicate date proposal approved, by whom, and how (orally, written, etc.)

Owner change order number

Job number

Date work started

Date work completed—Indicate if work was continuous or intermittent

Comments on work—Any note of general interest relating to the work performed under the change order

Billing information—Space is allowed for information relating to four invoices

3. *RESPONSIBILITIES*

Project Engineer

Prepare chart and continually update.

Send updated copy to field office at end of each month.

Check with field office to verify correctness of chart.

Assistant Superintendent/General Foreman

At end of month, verify chart against their records and notify project engineer of any discrepancies.

Part Two

Financing, Insurance, and Bonding

Chapter 8

Obtaining Bank Financing

DREW E. WAITLEY
Vice President and Head of Construction and Engineering Division, Continental Illinois National Bank, Chicago, Illinois

There is absolutely no reason why a viable construction company should not be able to obtain adequate and appropriate credit from its bank. Almost every article I have ever read on the subject starts off by describing how risky loans to contractors are, how high the bankruptcy rates are in the construction industry, how difficult it is for contractors to control their costs, and so forth, *ad nauseam*. Admittedly there are difficulties, some of which we shall go over in detail. Despite the problems, nevertheless, the construction industry is huge, and for banks that intelligently accept the challenge, the industry can be a source of lucrative deposit balances, high-quality short-term seasonal working capital loans, profitable equipment financing, project loans, and other auxiliary banking business, such as trust accounts and the like. Beyond this, there are a few psychic benefits for the banker, because contractor customers by and large are enjoyable people to deal with, as they tend to be a red-blooded breed, independent and entrepreneurial. The key goals for the contractor are to develop a strong relationship with a good bank, to establish a reputation for meeting his obligations, and to maintain a creditworthy business.

For the purpose of defining the term "construction company," we mean construction contractors, including general contractors, subcontractors of every type, design-build contractors, and construction engineering firms. Excluded from this discussion are real estate developers, whose credit needs are based primarily upon real estate values, and building supply companies, which generally utilize rather conventional financing techniques.

It is perhaps unfortunate that, aside from banks, most contractors have few alternative sources of financing, either short-term or long-term. Contractors are generally shut out of the public equity and out of public and private long-term debt markets because of their earnings volatility, their relatively small size, the risk nature of the industry, the lack of a marketable product, and the unorthodox accounting practices typically followed by many in the industry. Commercial finance companies, which normally relish the financing of a company's accounts receivable and inventory, tend to avoid financing a contractor because of the nature of its receivables. Among the reasons for this refusal, finance companies cite the many state mechanic's lien laws that frequently give to suppliers lien rights that are superior to a finance company's. In addition, they do not like the contractual nature of a contractor's receivable, which makes its collectibility conditional upon the performance by the contractor. Finally, finance companies cite the possible intervening rights of a bonding company on contracts that are bonded by virtue of the bonding company's rights of subrogation.

A banker faces these same problems when he advances money to a contractor. Because of the nature of the receivables, they are typically not acceptable collateral, and therefore most bank loans—except for equipment loans—are made on an unsecured basis. I confess that it is worrisome knowing that, if a loan gets into trouble, we cannot look to having a finance company bail us out, as is often the case with our loans to manufacturing companies or other conventional borrowers.

I hope it is obvious from the above discussion that contractors are uniquely difficult for bankers to finance. So much so that, in a recent survey conducted by the Robert Morris Association of Bank Credit, it was found that 48 percent of the banks polled had a *policy* against making loans to contractors.

This makes it critically important for such a firm to select its bank carefully, avoiding banks that have such a policy, and seeking a strong bank large enough to handle its needs. Even more desirable would be a situation where a contractor would select a bank that actually specializes in financing contractors. Such a bank would have a number of experienced lending officers who understand the operations of their contractor customers and thus can handle their financing needs in a responsible and knowledgeable way.

TYPES OF BANK CREDIT

Many types of bank credit are available. In this chapter they are rather arbitrarily broken down into transaction loans, lines of credit, loan commitments, and letters of credit.

Transaction loans are generally advanced for a specific transaction and are not made under a prearranged line of credit or other type of credit arrangement. Examples of transaction loans would be a bid check loan, which is used by a contractor when it borrows money to purchase a bid deposit check at the time the contractor is submitting his bid to the owner, usually a public body. The check is returned to the contractor if he is not low bidder; or if he is the low bidder, the check is returned at the time that he provides the owner with a performance bond. Transaction loans for working capital might be used to meet the construction company's payrolls or pay taxes, and are generally short-term loans, that is, they mature in 60 to 90 days and are normally expected to be paid off completely from receivable collections within a one-year period. Equipment loans are generally used to purchase new equipment, thus allowing the contractor to increase or modernize his equipment and improve his efficiency in performing the field work. The latter type of financing is long-term, that is, three to five years, and rests upon the borrower's ability to generate sufficient cash flow—that is, net earnings plus depreciation—to service the debt. Interest rates on short-term loans range between prime and perhaps 2 percent over prime. Rates on equipment loans are somewhat higher, ranging between prime plus $\frac{1}{2}$ percent to prime plus 3 percent.

A line of credit is an arrangement whereby the bank expresses its willingness to extend credit for various purposes up to the amount of the line at a certain rate of interest and based upon certain levels of compensating balances. It is generally used for short-term working-capital purposes and is normally established annually, based upon the borrower's year-end audited financial statements along with supporting documents. A line of credit is not generally considered as legally binding because certain events could cause the bank to cancel the line, the principal reason being a deterioration in the borrower's financial condition. Generally, no cost is involved in establishing a line of credit other than that the bank customer is expected to maintain a certain compensating balance requirement.

A loan commitment is normally a formal and legally binding loan agreement setting forth the exact conditions of any borrowings thereunder, and the various covenants that the borrower must conform to during the life of the agreement. Commitments can be either revolving, in which case borrowings can go up and down flexibly without disturbing the original committed amount, or they can be nonrevolving, in which case borrowings are generally taken down in stages and a loan reduction reduces the amount of the available credit. Generally, there is a commitment fee involved, most commonly $\frac{1}{2}$ of 1 percent of the unused portion of the available credit.

Letters of credit, in laymen's language, are credit instruments whereby the issuing bank substitutes its name and its credit for the customer's. The issuing bank is irrevocably obligated to make payment when the beneficiary meets the requirements as outlined in the letter-of-credit agreement. Letters of credit can be either documentary or standby. Documentary letters of credit involve the sale of goods or services and are often used when the seller wants assurance of payment by a third party, that is, the bank issuing the letter of credit. Typically, once the buyer has established a letter of credit, the seller ships the goods and sends a draft and the required documents through his bank to the issuing bank, which then inspects them to be sure they conform to the terms of the letter. If satisfied, the issuing bank remits to the seller's bank for his credit. A standby letter of credit does not normally involve the physical transfer of goods or services and is often equivalent to a guarantee of the applicant's financial responsibility for performance of a contract. Standby letters of credit can have an expiry from several weeks to several years. They are commonly used in international construction work when foreign governments require a bank performance guarantee equal to a certain percentage—usually 5 percent of the contract price—or require such a guarantee to ensure return of an advance payment should the contractor fail to perform. These advance payments are usually equal to 20 percent of the contract price and decline as the contract is actually performed by the contractor. The bank uses special care in approving such credits; although the construction work may be well within the contractor's capabilities to perform domestically, the work may be impossible to perform under the difficult conditions existing in some foreign countries. Standby letters of credit are included as an extension of credit when the bank computes its legal limit to any one customer.

BASIC INGREDIENTS IN OBTAINING CREDIT

After certain very fundamental points are emphasized a construction company will find it easier to obtain a fair hearing and elicit a positive attitude from the bank.

First and foremost, the contractor must be a financially sound, viable company with a reasonably large working capital, net worth, and profitable operations in order to make the banker feel comfortable in lending money to it. Ordinarily, no amount of talking, pleasant personality, entertainment, or "good moves" by the contractor will convince the banker if the credit is shaky. The financial condition must be presented in believable terms, that is, by a certified public accountant who is experienced in the construction business. The source of repayment of the loan should be clearly explained, should be logical, and should be supported by the facts.

The second basic factor is the credibility of the borrower. Obviously, nothing is more important in developing a strong relationship than that the banker have deep trust in the contractor's revealing *all* the facts, both good and bad. The contractor should be sure to live up to every commitment, keep his word, and be scrupulously honest in his dealings at all times.

Next, the construction firm should try to be important to the bank, that is, the firm should be a customer that is profitable to the bank and one that the bank would hate to lose to a competitor. Typically, a bank's analysis of customer profitability focuses almost exclusively upon the level of collected demand deposit balances carried. These balances should earn the bank enough to profitably cover the costs of check processing and other operating costs associated with the account. In addition, to the extent that there is credit involved, these balances should be fully compensating, that is, they should average some agreed-upon percentage of the credit. At the time a credit facility is negotiated, the borrower and the bank usually reach such an understanding as to the level of compensating balances. Typically, they would be "ten and ten," that is, the borrower would be expected to maintain over one year an average collected balance equal to 10 percent of the line of credit plus 10 percent of borrowings under that line. To the extent that the customer is deficient in meeting his obligation on both credit-related compensating balances and balances to cover activity costs, the bank will frequently charge a fee. It is entirely appropriate for a bank customer to request an analysis of his account relationship from the bank, and he should study this analysis to determine just how profitable he is to his bank. It is just possible that he may have more leverage with the bank than he thinks.

Once the contractor has met these criteria, he is well on his way to obtaining bank financing. The banker, if not actually eager to lend him money, is at least receptive to any reasonable request from a good customer whom he trusts and whose banking business he would hate to lose to a competitor. The next step for the contractor is to sit down with his banker and review his financing needs, cite the expected source of repayment, and for him to lay out in sufficient detail the financial condition of the company. In making his credit analysis, the banker will focus his attention primarily upon the *capital adequacy* of the borrower, both the sufficiency of his working capital and of his equity capital. As the banker reviews the financial statements, he will make an overall judgment as to the amount of capital available to cushion against a possible setback from operating losses or from unexpected deterioration in some of the assets on the balance sheet—either of which could jeopardize the ultimate collection of his loan.

FINANCIAL INFORMATION REQUIRED

Obviously, the banker's primary source of information is the financial statements of the borrowing entity. The contractor should routinely furnish the bank with a year-end audited financial statement, bearing an unqualified opinion from a certified public accountant fully conversant with the construction industry. Many bankers—including the writer—like to meet the accountant personally to make sure that such is the case. During the times that borrowings are outstanding, the contractor should furnish quarterly financial statements which normally are internally prepared. At the heart of any financial analysis is a careful and thorough review of the contractor's schedule of contracts in progress which, to be meaningful, *must be dated the same date as the financial statement and must tie in to the statement.* Figure 8.1 is a sample schedule used by many banks to assist in their analysis.

Beyond this, the bank will often require agings of accounts receivable and accounts payable, a complete schedule of equipment along with a current appraisal, and a cash-flow projection.

CONTRACTOR'S SUPPLEMENTAL STATEMENT

CONTRACTS IN PROCESS OR TO BE CLOSED OUT IN CURRENT FISCAL YEAR

NAME _____

SUBMITTED TO _____

DATE _____

| CONTRACT
INDICATE WITH WHOM, WHETHER LUMP SUM, FEE, ETC. ON PERCENTAGE OF RETENTION, AND BRIEF DESCRIPTION OF JOB | TOTAL CONTRACT AMOUNT, INCLUDING EXTRAS | AMOUNT BEING SUBCONTRACTED | PER CENT COMPLETED | ESTIMATED COMPLETION DATE | COST OF WORK PERFORMED | TOTAL AMOUNT BILLED | RECEIVABLES | | ESTIMATED JOB PROFIT TO DATE | ANTICIPATED TOTAL PROFIT ON COMPLETION |
							AMOUNT BILLED AND NOW OWING, EXCLUSIVE OF RETAINER	AMOUNT OF RETAINER		
	$	$			$	$	$	$	$	$

This interim form is submitted for the purpose of providing supplemental information in connection with establishing or maintaining credit with the above named bank. The information contained herein is true and correct to the best of my knowledge and belief.

_____ Signature

_____ Title

Robert Morris Associates, Form C-137
Carried in Stock by Cadwallader & Johnson, Inc., 5170 Northwest Highway, Chicago, Illinois 60630

Figure 8.1 Robert Morris Associates, form C-127. Carried in stock by Cadwallader & Johnson, Inc., 5170 Northwest Highway, Chicago, Illinois 60630.

BANKER'S ANALYTICAL TECHNIQUES

The financial information submitted allows the banker to start his analysis of the borrower's capital adequacy. Basic to this analysis is the need for the banker to understand the accounting method being used, normally either the completed-contract basis of accounting, under which no income is recognized on a contract until it is completed, or the percentage-of-completion method, which allows recognition of income as the contract is being performed. Many companies advantageously combine the two methods by reporting income on a percentage-of-completion basis and by paying taxes on a completed-contract basis, thus utilizing the advantages of both. Proper accounting requires immediate reporting of any losses when they are known, regardless of the accounting method being used. The banker's initial review of the company's operating history will indicate how successfully management has performed, and thus how profitable the business is likely to be in the future. At this point, the contractor should be able to intelligently and realistically explain to the banker exactly what happened in past years and how it was reflected on the financial statements. Next, the banker will quickly check the balance sheet to get in mind the size of the company's net worth, its debt-to-worth ratio, and its working-capital position in order to get a "feel" for its general size, capital adequacy, and its debt burden. The next step is for him to review the schedule of contracts in progress, which is a very important document and which really tells the most critical facts about the financial condition and about the ability of the contractor to service present and future debts. The banker will pay particular attention to individual jobs where costs exceed billings in order to satisfy himself that these costs are truly reimbursable and not actually losses in disguise. He will carefully review the anticipated profit or loss on each job and will compare the anticipated gross profits with the company's general corporate overhead to determine the outlook for net annual profit or loss. As the future unfolds, the banker will monitor these *actual* results and compare them to *projected* results, thus gaining insight into the accuracy of the contractor's past forecasts. At this point, the banker will often look long and hard at the company's level of overhead expenses and form a general opinion of whether they are too high in relation to, first, his ability to obtain enough volume at sufficiently high profit margins to cover this overhead and, secondly, whether with the company's present capital, it can comfortably cover the debts involved in handling the required amount of volume.

Assuming the banker is still interested in pursuing the possibilities of a loan, we know that he will turn back to the balance sheet and critically review each individual asset. For example, how much of the *cash* shown is under the control of a bonding company to prevent its diversion to an unbonded job? Or how much is pledged as cash collateral to a bank for a loan or for a letter of credit and is thus unavailable for general corporate use? The banker will study the *accounts receivable* to assure himself that they are current and due from financially responsible entities. *Retained percentages* may be carried as a current asset even though they may be due only upon completion of jobs that may have two or three years to run and, therefore, do not truly represent cash available to the contractor to pay its current debts. *Claims* for extra compensation, unless approved in writing by the owner or his authorized agent, may be severely discounted or never paid at all. In today's inflationary economy, construction *equipment* is likely to hold its value rather well and be worth more than its carrying value, but management may have an inflated opinion of what it would bring on the open market after the costs of repair, painting, and sales commissions. To the extent that the company is carrying *investments* in nonoperating assets, the banker will analyze the values involved and, on any significant *joint-venture* investments or advances, he will want to review the terms of the joint-venture agreement, its financial statement, and projections for profits or losses. On the liability side of the balance sheet, the banker will look at the *accounts payable* to satisfy himself they are not materially past due. If it is a general contractor's statement he is reviewing, the banker will check to be sure that the *amounts due subcontractors,* both progress billings and retentions, are not larger than the progress billings and retentions due to the general contractor, thus satisfying himself that his customer is not taking money due his subcontractors and using it for other purposes. The liability known as *billings in excess of costs* on uncompleted contracts is usually carried as a current debt. Generally, this liability arises when a contractor unbalances his bid to accelerate his cash flow early in the job, or it represents unrecognized earnings. Thus, the item is not truly a debt, even though in the former case, the contractor must be aware that he will need to have some cash to finance the less profitable phases of the unbalanced-bid job. Even though it is a liability on the balance sheet, most knowledgeable bankers are pleased to see a large "deferred-income" item, as this is sometimes called, because it represents intelligent cash-flow planning by the construction company, or unrecognized earnings, or both. *Deferred taxes* can be a significant liability when a contractor is on a percentage-of-completion basis of accounting for reporting and a completed-contract basis for payment of taxes. Deferred-tax liability is an attractive source of non-interest-bearing financing from the United States government, a rare commodity indeed. In order to understand the contractor's cash requirements to make these tax payments in future years, however, the banker must review the composition of this item and also the contractor's estimated completion schedule of present work on the books.

The analysis of the financial statement is important, but it is perhaps just as important for the banker to obtain a clear idea of what the contractor's reputation is in the trade. He learns this from his contacts in the industry, from general views that he may have picked up in social conversations with owners, architects, subcontractors, suppliers, and competitors. This will be a very important ingredient in his decision of whether to finance his customer.

SOME PROBLEMS COMMONLY EXPERIENCED BY CONTRACTORS

Many events can negatively impact the capital adequacy and thus the borrowing capacity of a contractor.

Loss jobs.   Probably very few contractors have not had at least one loss job, whether from poor bidding, poor field supervision, bad labor conditions, inclement weather, cost escalations, poor material deliveries, subcontractor performance failures, difficult relationships with owners or architects, or combinations of these problems.

Inadequate construction volume.   This can result in inadequate gross profits to cover overhead and can create operating losses. It can also cause the contractor to start bidding more closely, shaving his bid prices to get sorely needed volume and thus increase the risk of taking on unprofitable contract work.

Too much volume.   This can spread supervisory management too thin, in which case the construction company may lose control of its field work and can result in profit erosion or actual losses. It can further create financial stress as the company's capital may be inadequate to finance the higher levels of work in progress, receivables, and retentions required to carry the higher work load. Bank loans may be inadequate to make up the difference, especially if the bank should get nervous about the level of debts being carried and possible loss of control on the field work.

Overhead expenses too high.   An inordinately high overhead creates a need to take on volume and can result in the problems outlined above.

Slow or poor-quality receivables.   Probably the largest asset on the balance sheet of most contractors is accounts receivable. The contractor should select his customers carefully to avoid the possibility of an uncollectible receivable. On most private construction he should know the source of the owner's financing and should not hesitate to verify this independently, either directly or through his own bank. Beyond this, he should be careful how he handles his lien waivers, as these may end up being the ultimate source of collection of his receivables, no matter how carefully he screens his customers. Finally, he should use strong and persistent collection efforts because, as we all know, "the squeaky wheel gets the grease."

Overinvestment in fixed assets.   Some contractors carry too large an investment in equipment or in other fixed assets such as their office building, leasehold improvements, or the equipment yard. Rental options should constantly be considered to reduce the potential long-term risks of ownership, such as servicing the debt involved, reduction of working capital, and possible capital loss on ultimate disposal of the fixed assets.

The wrong kind of joint ventures.   Joint ventures can be helpful in spreading risk, in having another source to check estimates, and possibly in eliminating a potential competitor for the job involved. On the other hand, joint ventures are essentially partnerships and they can be a source of severe problems if (1) the contractor's joint-venture partner is weak financially and cannot make his cash or equipment contributions; (2) the partners do not have a clear understanding of their individual rights and duties; or (3) there is poor communication between the partners leading to a lack of control and direction.

Investments in outside ventures.   The business should not have any important portion of its capital tied up in an outside and unrelated activity. This simply reduces the company's working capital—often reducing the cash flow and the credit availability—and, furthermore, makes it more difficult for the banker to fully comprehend the business and thus take care of his financial needs.

Entering into a new line of construction with inadequate knowledge. The bankruptcy courts are replete with instances of contractors going into bankruptcy after failing at a type of construction they knew nothing about. Excavators have lost money in paving work, road builders have dropped millions on sewage-treatment work, high-rise builders have lost money on hospitals, and so forth. Diversification is fine, but only after rigorous examination of the new business, its problems and hazards, and only if based on experience gleaned from handling smaller jobs which would not create serious problems if unsuccessful.

Entering new geographical areas without adequate knowledge. This can occur domestically and internationally and can result in some tragic losses because of unfamiliarity with local customs, labor relations, labor productivity, etc.

SOME MEANINGFUL FINANCIAL RATIOS

Lenders and creditors have historically used certain financial ratios as shortcuts to analyzing the debt-paying ability of their customers. Obviously, these are only general guidelines and not necessarily applicable to any specific situation. Inasmuch as construction firms have somewhat different characteristics than normal, the ratios are also somewhat different.

Current ratio, that is, the ratio of current assets to current liabilities, is often targeted at 2:1, but for a contractor it is normally less than this and could easily be 1.75:1 without indicating any liquidity problems.

The quick ratio, that is, the ratio of cash-plus receivables to current debt, is usually targeted at 1:1, but for a contractor should normally be at least 1.25:1.

Debt-to-worth ratio, that is, the ratio of total debts to equity, is often targeted at 1:1 as a goal, but for contractors can reach much higher levels, sometimes as much as 20:1, and still not indicate trouble. Its comfort-level depends upon the composition of the debts, and how rapidly they must be paid. If, for example, debts are composed primarily of subcontractor obligations due only upon payment to the general by the owner, then the subcontractors cannot legally press for payment. This ignores the problem that sometimes arises in such cases when a financially weak subcontractor, who may not be able to continue working indefinitely without getting paid, might require cash advances from the general to meet his payrolls.

The gross-profit ratio, that is, the ratio of gross profit to total revenues, is normally rather low in the construction industry, as is the net-profit ratio. For general contractors the former is seldom about 10 percent and often around 5 percent, and the latter is generally 1 to 2 percent net after taxes. For subcontractors, the ratios are often higher, approximating 15 percent gross and 2 to 3 percent net.

More important in judging the true value of a business is the percentage return on equity, that is, the ratio of net income to average net worth. Here a contractor should measure up to any other company in any other industry, in fact, it should theoretically exceed returns available in other industries because of the heavy risks involved in construction. An acceptable return is perhaps 10 percent per year, but some contractors earn 15 to 25 percent on their equity without taking inordinate business risks. If the average return on invested capital is less than 5 percent, thought should be given to liquidating the company and simply investing the capital in risk-free government securities or other high-grade investments.

HOW MUCH MONEY WILL THE BANK LEND?

As we conclude our discussion of bank loans, I hope it has become apparent that there is more "art" than "science" involved in a banker's credit judgment. We have tried to explain how a contractor can get to a position where he will get a fair hearing from his bank. This is by being a valued customer, by living up to his word, by providing the banker with understandable current financial statements, by maintaining his financial affairs in reasonably good shape, and by maintaining a good general reputation. The banker can do the most penetrating financial analysis, but the analyzing amounts to nothing if the owner of the business is dishonest or if he panics when adversity strikes.

In responding to a request for credit, the banker will have certain guidelines in mind. He will not be particularly anxious to lend the contractor more than the amount of his working capital, nor will he be likely to make a loan which is larger than the contractor's net worth. He may make these advances, however, if he is convinced that there are overriding considerations, the most important being that he sees a reasonably certain source of ultimate repayment. Another possible reason for advancing larger sums would be that the banker is trapped into lending more money to a company that already owes the bank a lot of money and the banker feels that it is necessary to make further advances to recover his original loan. Obviously, there are limits to such arrangements.

On equipment loans, he will be looking for a collateral margin of at least 20 percent and for cash-flow coverage—that is, earnings plus depreciation—of at least double the debt service requirement.

INTERNATIONAL FINANCING

Recently, there has been a tremendous construction boom in the Middle East, which has been fueled by the quadrupling of crude-oil prices. As the Opec countries emerge from various stages of poverty, they must build their basic infrastructure such as ports, roads, sewage-treatment plants, communications systems, new cities, and the like. Contractors from all over the world are seeking this work, which is most often awarded on a lump-sum-contract basis and is normally awarded in very large amounts—frequently $100 million or more.

Normally, this type of work involves the large, internationally oriented construction companies, often in joint ventures.

This phenomenon has created a vast need for bank credit to contractors. The new need is not so much for loans, because the owners usually make large cash advances, but more often the credit is in the form of bank guarantees (letters of credit for American banks).

The bank guarantees are for performance, normally 5 percent of the contract price, and for the advance payment, generally 20 percent of the contract price. These bank letters of credit or guarantees can be drawn down if the contractor fails to perform properly. There are many techniques used to establish nonperformance, but many Middle Eastern countries insist upon having the sole unqualified right to draw against the letters of credit without having to prove nonperformance, making them demand instruments subject to arbitrary call by the owner. The construction contract will contain the vehicles for resolution of disputes, but here again these may favor the owner as they often involve local jurisdiction under local law.

The amounts of credit are so immense that they frequently require international bank syndications, and the international banking system has been coping with the problem for several years, particularly the matter of the possibility of arbitrary drawdowns. Various governments have devised schemes to insure their contractors against arbitrary drawdowns, but so far the United States has—to the writer's knowledge—no operative government-sponsored program; and although private insurance is available, its coverage is sometimes inadequate for the large risks involved. Other countries, such as the Netherlands, the United Kingdom, and South Korea have government-supported insurance programs that do give some protection to the contractors and to the banks. Fortunately, so far, there have been few instances of arbitrary drawdowns, so the banking system appears to be gaining confidence that drawdowns will be made only for cause, that is, such drawdowns will be made only where the contractor fails to perform the contract satisfactorily.

In establishing guidelines for our issuance of letters of credit for performance and advance-payment guarantees, we must analyze the contractor just as if these facilities were direct loans. Indeed, the irrevocable nature of the letter of credit and the potential for arbitrary drawdown make the extension of this type of credit more risky in some respects than a loan. Usually, it involves work in foreign countries where the contractor may not have experience, adding another dimension of risk.

It is easy for the bank to imagine a scenario which would scare it so badly it would establish a *policy* of declining such credit. Let us assume that a contractor-engineer with a $20-million net worth and a $10-million working capital takes on a large contract from a Middle Eastern government totaling $100 million, and the bank establishes a $5-million performance guarantee and a $20-million advance-payment guarantee. Let us say, for example, that at the time the job is 50 percent completed, the owner arbitrarily calls the letters of credit, which at that moment would stand at $15 million ($5 million performance and $10 million advance payment). The bank must pay out the $15 million and must seek reimbursement either by charging the contractor's account, by demanding that the contractor pay the bank from other sources, or by lending the customer sufficient money to cover any deficiency.

The accounting treatment of this drawdown, under the worst conditions where there is no reimbursement from the owner for the drawdown, involves an immediate charge of $5 million against the company's net worth equal to the performance portion of the guarantee, and a charge against the company's working capital for the advance-payment portion, to the extent that the advance-payment money had been reinvested in noncurrent assets. An example of the latter would be that if the $10 million remaining balance of the advance payment were invested by the company in fixed assets, such as construction equipment or a housing compound, then the full $10 million would be deducted from the company's working capital. Under these conditions, the company's net worth would be immediately reduced from $20 to $15 million and its working capital from $10 million to 0. But this is not the end of the scenario. If we assume a drawdown, it is logical also to assume that the contractor would either pull off the job or would be removed from the job, thus jeopardizing the contract assets—such as the work in progress, progress billings, and retentions. At the same time, the contractor would still have to meet his debt obligations to his suppliers and subcontractors, so he would get no relief from this source. Therefore, if for example the receivables on this job were $2 million and the work in progress totaled $3 million, then the contractor would have to charge off an additional $5 million, which in this case would reduce his net worth to $10 million and his working capital to a minus $5 million.

Many of the substantial international banks are accepting these potential dangers, so far with good experience. The banks are making a basic judgment as to the contractor's financial condition, its ability to survive a drawdown, its ability to perform; and they are relying on the absence to date of any substantial arbitrary drawdowns. It is true that the amounts of credit are huge and certainly represent a potential problem for both contractors and banks.

To establish a program for handling these risks, many banks have developed the following informational requirements to be included under various types of loan agreements:

1. The contractor will furnish the bank with the estimated dollar amount of the letter of credit.

2. The text of the letter of credit will be provided if the contract calls for specific language.

3. The bank must approve the country in which the job is to be performed.

4. The type of work will be fully described.

5. The contract will be adequately described in terms of dollar amount, duration of the contract, payment terms, subcontracts, etc.

6. The bank will be furnished with an explanation of the arbitration provisions in the contract, including a statement of where any arbitration proceedings would take place.

7. The bank will be informed as to the ultimate owner of the facility to be constructed, and if the owner is not to be the central government of the country, a brief résumé of the owner, its background, and its financial capabilities.

8. If the project will be performed by a joint venture, information will be submitted regarding the other partner or partners and a description of the joint-venture agreement will be provided.

9. A cash-flow analysis of the project will be provided on a monthly or quarterly basis.

This basic information would normally be included as a part of a loan agreement. The agreement would contemplate inspections by the bank to ensure that the project is being completed according to its plans and its schedules, and the agreement would also include various covenants that would trigger collateralization of the credit if they were breached. These covenants would generally include a working-capital minimum, debt limitations, and other covenants common to any loan agreement; they might also include a requirement for collateralization if the actual cash flow varied significantly and adversely from the cash-flow projections. The rationale for this would be that a slowdown in collections or an unusual buildup in unbilled costs could easily be a prelude to a drawdown and removal of the contractor from the job.

Chapter **9**

Contract Surety Bonding

DONALD E. SPICKARD, ESQ.
Vice President, Safeco Insurance Co. of America, Seattle, Washington

BRUCE T. WALLACE
Executive Vice President, National Association of Surety Bond Producers, Washington, D.C.

Perhaps the least understood and yet one of the most important facets of the contract construction process is that of contract surety bonding. No one would like more to dispel the mystery and misunderstanding surrounding surety bonding than the bonding companies and agents themselves.

WHAT IS A CONTRACT BOND?

Stated in the simplest terms, a contract bond is a guarantee of contractor performance and is the instrument by which a corporate surety company (the *guarantor*) guarantees the owner of a construction project (the *obligee*) that the contractor to whom a construction contract has been awarded (the *principal*) will fulfill the contract in accordance with the plans and specifications and with all attendant financial obligations (such as wages, materials, and subcontracts) having been paid in full. The contract-bond form, as a rule, is a short, concise instrument, referring to the terms of the contract itself and stating that failure of the contractor (principal) to properly fulfill all obligations under the contract will cause the surety (guarantor) to intervene in response to the principal's default, nonperformance, or debt to protect the contractual interests of the owner (obligee) and to indemnify the owner in the event of loss, not to exceed the face amount, called the *penalty* of the bond.

Many people tend to think of surety bonds as a form of insurance, perhaps in part due to the fact that most surety companies are so-called *multiple-line* companies, that is, they are in the business of underwriting property and casualty insurance as well as surety bonds. Surety bonds, however, are *not* insurance: a surety bond is a credit guarantee, actually more akin to a guaranteed or irrevocable bank line of credit than to a policy of insurance.

BENEFITS TO THE OWNER

Perhaps the single, most important facet of contract bonding, from an owner's vantage point, is that by issuance of contract performance and payment bonds, the surety has prequalified, in effect guaranteed, the contractor's ability to complete the contract successfully. Put another way, the surety has informed the owner that it has thoroughly investigated the contractor's ability to complete the contract successfully, and has determined that the contractor is capable of successful contract completion. Further, the surety guarantees the owner that should its contractor prequalification decision prove to be wrong, it will indemnify the owner for contractor nonperformance, default, or unpaid bills.

COST OF PERFORMANCE AND PAYMENT BONDS

The *premium* for performance and payment bonds is not a premium in the sense that one pays a premium when purchasing an insurance policy; rather, the cost of performance-payment bonding is a fee charged by the bonding company for prequalifying the contractor to whom the contract is awarded and for lending its credit, in effect, to that contractor. The premium or fee charged is a percentage of the amount of the contract to be bonded. A surety bond premium, although considerably less costly, is very similar in nature to the fee charged by a bank for extending a line of bank credit to a customer. Performance-payment bond premiums, or fees, generally cost less than 1 percent of the contract price, dependent upon the size of the contract and the type of construction involved. The larger the contract size, the smaller the percentage of contract price charged as the surety's fee or premium. For example, the cost of performance-payment bonds charged by a so-called *manual rate* surety company on a $100,000 office building or hospital construction contract would be $1,200; the cost of the bonds for a $900,000 building would be only $8,900; and so on. Bonds on contracts for construction of highways, bridges, airport runways, and parks cost only $9.00 per $1,000 of the contract price or less, again, dependent on contract size. Banks charge from 3 to 5 percent of the amount of their letter of credit for issuing a line of credit.

In theory, although certainly not in recent practice, no losses should be paid by sureties, because the contractors for whom bonds have been executed have been prequalified by the sureties and found to be fully capable of completing their contracts. Surety bond rates, or fees, do not contemplate losses, or contractor defaults. Rather, surety fees are more in the nature of a service charge for contractor prequalification services, plus the lending of surety credit to the contractor for the protection of the owner.

Surety companies assuredly do have losses on contract bonds, however, due to contractor default, nonperformance, or nonpayment of bills; and these losses, particularly in the years 1974 and 1975, have been little short of disastrous for many United States surety companies.

CANCELLATION OF CONTRACT BONDS

Contract bonds and performance and payment bonds cannot be canceled by the contractor or the surety once they have been executed in connection with a contract award. This is true irrespective of fraud or even nonpayment of the premium to the surety company. The reason for this is fairly basic: the bond is a three-party contract with the contractor and the surety joining in a guarantee to protect a third party, the owner. The law is very clear that regardless of what relationship exists between the contractor and the surety, no penalty or damage can be permitted against the innocent third party, the owner, who is the beneficiary of the bond.

REQUIREMENTS TO OBTAIN BONDS

Now that we have covered some of the basics about contract bonding, what it is and how it operates, let us look at what is required of a contractor in order to obtain surety bonding or a line of surety credit. The surety's requirements and information needed are basically the same whether application is being made for a *bid bond,* the bid guarantee required of a contractor in order to submit a bid on most public construction projects and many private projects, or for performance and payment bonds required at the time of contract award by the owner.

Generally, a contractor must start out in business performing work on which bonds are not required, at least until a "track record" has been established of several successfully completed jobs, created a record of owner satisfaction with his work, and established a record of prompt payment of labor and material bills and subcontractors.

Before a surety will extend surety credit or issue bid or performance-payment bonds to a contractor, the contractor must be able to convince the surety that he is *qualified* to successfully undertake the construction contract or work program which he is seeking. The traditional "three C's" requirement of sureties that are asked to issue bonds or extend surety credit are:

- Character—Does the contractor's past overall record indicate good character and responsibility in fulfilling all obligations and contracts?

- Capacity—Do the contractor and his organization have the skills, experience, knowledge, and equipment essential to perform the work in question?
- Capital—Does the contractor have the necessary cash, or *assured* access to the necessary cash, to finance the project or work program and, if needed, to be able to absorb a reasonable loss on one or more projects if unexpected difficulty in performance is encountered or if a subcontractor fails to perform?

A contractor, or a construction company, is not qualified simply by reason of having money in the bank, or owning construction equipment, or having previously constructed a building, or having a crew of skilled workers, or having a good record of payment to subcontractors and material suppliers. Certainly, all these are very important factors in persuading the surety that the contractor *is* qualified for surety credit, but there is much more involved.

Contractors must demonstrate to the surety that they and their organizations are fully trained to the point of full understanding of what is involved in entering into the contract, and to the extent that they are capable of performing the type and size of construction involved. Further, they must have a record of demonstrated responsibility in fulfillment of contracts and promises, and must be able to show the surety that they have the financial cushion or reserves necessary to withstand the kind of financial loss that can and does occur from time to time in the construction process.

In considering what amount of working capital is adequate for a contractor in order to undertake a particular construction contract, or work program, we must remember that not only can and will there be an occasional bad or losing job for which a cash cushion must be available to absorb the loss, but the contractor's cash flow must be adequate to finance the project up to receipt of the first estimate, and between estimates thereafter. We must remember, in determining the amount of working capital necessary to finance a job, that normally all estimates paid to a contractor for work performed are paid *after* withholding by the owner of a retainage amount (until job acceptance), usually 5 to 10 percent of the amount of each estimate submitted by the contractor. There is also a growing number of public and private owners who are not prompt in the payment of monthly or periodic estimates to contractors. In many cases, actual receipt of monthly estimate checks by contractors is as much as 30 to 60 days late, which means that the contractor must have adequate cash to finance the job for as long as three or four months at a time in the event of late payment of estimates by the owner.

The first step for the contractor who needs a bond is to demonstrate to the surety that he is qualified in all three respects, capital, capacity, and character, to perform the job successfully. He should first contact a knowledgeable and experienced bonding agent, one who knows what information is needed in order to properly submit a bonding case to a surety and who represents several surety companies. The reason for this is that the agent must determine which of the surety companies that he represents is the most likely market for the contractor or bond being applied for, considering the size of the contract, the type of construction involved, the geographical location of the construction to be performed, and the size and experience of the contractor. Different surety companies have different underwriting policies and preferences in regard to bonding certain types of construction, certain types and sizes of contractors, and construction in different geographical areas.

The agent will need to know what type and size of construction the contractor has previously performed, either on his own or as a superintendent or project manager for another construction company; what other jobs he now has on hand and uncompleted, whether bonded or not; what his future development plans are, and many other things including his detailed financial condition, usually as determined, audited, and reported by a certified public accountant.

After presenting all the necessary information to the professional bonding agent, the agent can then decide if, in his opinion, the contractor is in fact qualified for the project or work program on which he wants to bid. If he is found to be qualified, the agent then decides which of the surety companies he represents is the most likely market for bonds on construction of the type and size to be bid on by the contractor, and the case is submitted to that surety company for its consideration.

An experienced professional surety agent will never submit a bond case to a surety, unless and until the agent has first satisfied himself that the contractor *is* qualified to perform the project in question. It should be kept in mind, however, that a good bonding agent, and a good bonding company, do not make their livelihood by declining bonds. Rather, they are in business to—and want to— provide bonds to qualified contractors, including contractors who can be made qualified by means of arranging for additional financing or whatever else the contractor may need in order to ensure successful performance of the contract. After the agent has satisfied himself that the contractor is qualified for the project, he then prepares a complete and detailed submission of the case for presentation to the surety company selected.

This submission *must* include all details relative to the contractor's finances, including bank credit available; the names of the officers or principal owners of the construction company along with their construction experience; the amount of construction the company has performed previously, including type and size of project, location of previous projects, and owner satisfaction with previous projects; the nature of the job or work program the contractor wants to bid on at this time, including the type of construction, the size of project(s), and the number of projects to be under way concurrently; the kind of reputation the contractor has with material suppliers, subcontractors, architects, and other contractors and owners for whom he has previously performed work; his past credit or payment record to suppliers and subcontractors; and a statement declaring whether the contractor seeks, and heeds, advice from his accountant, banker, attorney, and bonding agent.

Most bonding agents, and surety companies, will want to see, and in most cases require, the contractor's last three years' fiscal year-end financial statements, including balance sheets and profit-and-loss statements, along with all explanatory notes and schedules needed to understand and verify the statements. If the contractor or construction company has not been in business for three years, detailed financial statements will be required for whatever length of time he has been in business. Generally, most contractors have a certified public accountant audit their records and prepare annual financial statements, and many sureties will require CPA statements, at least at fiscal year-end.

The surety company and bonding agent will also need full information about the contractor's accounting methods and system, what cost controls are used, and whether the contractor's accounting is done on a cash basis, a percentage of completion basis, or a completed-contract accounting system. Many contractors will use a completed-contract accounting method for tax purposes, which in many—or perhaps even most—cases is wise, but generally a percentage of completion accounting systems is preferred for bonding and bank credit purposes and for the benefit of the contractor as well; this method of accounting gives a truer or more accurate picture of the contractor's actual financial condition as of statement date than the other methods.

When all the foregoing information is furnished to the bonding agent, he can make a determination as to whether the contractor appears to be qualified to bid or perform the job in question, after which the surety company receives its agent's submission and makes the final determination: Is the contractor qualified or not, and if not, can any steps be taken in order to qualify the contractor for the job? For example, one of the most common means of assisting a contractor to become qualified for a project that might otherwise be too large for him to undertake on his own is by means of a joint venture or a combination with one or more other contractors having similar or complementary skills, none of whom, alone, is large enough or has the necessary organization, equipment, or financial resources to perform the project.

INDEMNITY

Another means of making an otherwise marginally unqualified contractor (who may be qualified in all respects other than adequate financing) qualified for a particular job is by obtaining the *indemnity* or personal guarantee of a financial backer, a person or entity having substantial or adequate financial reserves, to be able to assist the contractor if financial assistance is needed. Normally, this *outside indemnity* would be in addition to the *personal indemnity* of the contractor or that of the officers (in the case of a privately held corporation) and in many cases their wives as well, depending upon the nature of the contracting organization and the extent of the assets *in* the construction company or corporation. Obtaining the personal indemnity of the contractor, or of the officers if a private corporation, is usually a requirement, as it is evidence to the surety of the contractor's faith and belief in his organization and in its ability to successfully complete the contract.

Additional factors to be considered by the surety, and information needed by the surety, include: (1) Does the owner have all the necessary construction funds on hand or are they guaranteed to be available to him by a lending institution? Are these funds in an escrow account? It is very important for the contractor, and his surety, that assurance is obtained *beforehand* of the owner's ability to pay for the construction project. (2) Is guaranteed bank credit available to the contractor if needed? This bank credit must be available, if needed, for the entire length of the job, rather than for a shorter period of time. (3) Will the job require the purchase of additional equipment by the contractor? Would it be more practical to lease or rent additional equipment needed for the job? (4) Will the contractor be able to "front-load" the job, i.e., will he be able to include in his first estimate a "mobilization" cost or a similar charge which will permit payment to the contractor of a first estimate which is in excess of his actual costs to date? It is common practice for a contractor to *front-load* or overbill as an offset against retainage withheld by the owner, and as a supplementary source of working capital. A contract that enables a contractor to front-load can substantially lessen the amount of cash or working capital necessary to finance the job successfully.

Only after all the foregoing information has been made available to the contractor's bonding agent—and to the surety selected by the agent as being the best market for him—can the surety determine that the contractor is qualified for the job in question or not.

We emphasize the importance of a contractor's applying for a bond, or for surety credit, *well in advance* of the time he actually needs his first bond. It takes a surety agent, and the surety company selected, considerable time to verify the contractor's financial statements and to determine whether or not the contractor is qualified for the job or work program in which he is interested. Most sureties will decline to consider a new case wherein their decision must be made within a period of time which does not allow sufficient time to make a full investigation of the contractor applicant.

After a contractor has established a track record of successful performance and has applied to a surety agent and bonding company for a bond, or a line of surety credit, and after he has been qualified for his first bonded job, the bonding agent and company will want to work with him continuously to ensure success. For example, if a contractor submits a bid on a job, accompanied by a bid bond, and finds that, when the bids are opened, his bid is low by a margin of more than 10 percent below that of the second bidder, he may have a serious problem. His bid may have an arithmetical error, he may have left out a price for an item, or he may have simply underestimated what his costs will be. When this happens, a surety will normally want to review the contractor's entire bid to determine if there is an error or if the bid is sound, despite its being considerably lower than the second and successive bidders.

A surety will not permit issuance of performance and payment bonds unless and until the contractor can demonstrate that his bid price is not too low and that he is capable of handling the contract successfully at his bid price. Normally, an owner will not hold a contractor to a bid price that is obviously in error or that would cause him to default on the job. If the owner chooses to exercise his right to force the contractor to enter into a contract or forfeit his bid guarantee, the contractor, or his surety if the contractor is unable to, normally will have to pay the difference between his bid and the price submitted by the second bidder, not to exceed the penalty of the bid bond.

It is obvious that a great many factors must be weighed and considered before a bonding agent and company will consider a contractor qualified for a job. Many contractors consider bonds and bonding companies a necessary evil, and yet a great many very successful contractors in America today attained their success in part due to the advice, counsel, and support of a good, experienced bonding agent and company. Like an experienced accountant, banker, and attorney, a capable bonding agent and surety company should be considered a contractor's partners in business.

The business of construction contracting is one of the most hazardous of businesses. At the same time, it is potentially one of the most lucrative fields a person can enter if one has the skill, good judgment, resources, imagination, and willingness to work that are necessary for success in contracting. As previously pointed out, bonding agents and companies are not in business to find ways of declining to write bonds, but rather to help contractors to become qualified for bonding or surety credit.

Fortunately, even in very difficult economic times, which may be particularly difficult for the construction industry, a great many contractors in the United States can continue their pattern of success due to experienced and sound management, not attempting to overextend their capabilities and financial resources and having the necessary foresight to anticipate the potential pitfalls ahead.

We must remember, however, that every year many contracting companies, large and small, old and new, fail for a variety of reasons and cause their sureties to pay out many millions of dollars in losses. For every successful new contractor or contracting company, there are *ten* or more failures. The smaller the company and the less experience it has, the more likely it is to fail.

Bonding agents and companies seek to assist and work with those contractors who have sound construction skills, good management and judgment, a willingness to work, and a recognition that growing too fast too soon can be disastrous. These are the seeds of a successful construction venture.

BONDING FOREIGN CONTRACTS

Increasingly, American contractors are looking abroad for construction opportunities. This is especially true at the present time in the Middle East, particularly in Saudi Arabia, Kuwait, and some of the other major nations of the Organization of Petroleum Exporting Countries (OPEC) which are undertaking major construction programs involving billions of dollars worth of construction—almost all of which will be performed by non-Arabic contractors.

Many construction opportunities are also becoming available to American contractors in Europe, Africa, and in other parts of the world as well.

Bonding of foreign construction projects is too diverse a subject for an exhaustive analysis country by country. Certain characteristics, however, affect what a contractor must expect when entering into a construction contract outside the United States.

Nationalism   Few foreign governments will accept bonds issued by United States surety companies on public construction work in those countries. Many will not permit a U.S. surety company to furnish a bond on any construction contract, public or private. Even Canada requires that a Canadian surety company must write any bond which runs in favor of the Canadian government or any department of the government.

Forfeiture bonds   The wording of most bonds required in foreign countries is similar to the wording in a bank letter of credit. In fact, much of the bonding throughout the world is done by bank letters of credit, rather than the usual surety bond with which we in the United States are familiar. These guarantees call for demand by the owner and immediate payment (often within three to seven days) by the surety (or bank) without the right of the contractor, surety, or bank to contest whether the owner has the right to make a claim or not. The effect is to place the contractor in the position of bringing a lawsuit to recover the money paid out by the surety (or bank) on his behalf. Such a suit must be brought in the foreign court. Frequently such suits may be brought only if the ruler of the country gives permission to bring suit.

Bond amount   Few performance bonds in foreign countries are for more than 5 or 10 percent of the contract amount. Bonds required where advance payment is made to the contractor are normally in the amount of the advance payment. They are not reduced in amount as work progresses unless that provision is bargained for. This may result in a duplication in liability for nonperformance. In some cases where several advance payments are made in succession as the work progresses, the bond amount can approximate 100 percent of the contract price. The terms of such bonds are seldom statutory but rather are matters for negotiation between the contractor and the owner. Bonds guaranteeing payment to subcontractors and material suppliers are seldom required.

What must a contractor do to obtain a bond upon a foreign project? There are basically three alternatives:

Foreign Surety Specialists, such as the American International Underwriters Corporation (AIU)[1] and the AFIA (formerly the American Foreign Insurance Association[2]), each have affiliated or subsidiary companies located in many foreign countries that can handle bonds in those countries. They are experts in local law, customs, and language. The contractor's regular (United States) insurance and surety agent or broker can present an application for the bond needed on a foreign contract. The contractor and agent must be aware, however, that such bonds cannot be arranged overnight. A minimum of 30 days from the time of application for the bond should be allowed. The application will require a complete submission of all relevant underwriting information concerning the construction company, its organization, personnel, financial and credit history. Both the AIU and AFIA are exacting underwriters. If they conclude that the project is beyond the contractor's capacity or involves some unusual hazard, they are likely to decline the application. They will charge a premium customary to the country where the bond is required plus necessary underwriting fees.

[1]102 Maiden Lane, New York, New York 10005.
[2]110 William Street, New York, New York 10038.

Fronting The contractor's regular United States surety company may be able to arrange to have a bond issued by a surety company (or bank) in the country where the contract is to be performed. The ability to do this depends upon the contacts the United States surety company has in the particular country, whether the contractor has a knowledgeable representative there who can assist in arranging the bond, and the willingness of the surety (or bank) in that country to accept the guarantee of the American surety. The latter may be aided by reinsurance or banking contacts common to both sureties. In any event, such bonds also require time for communication and exchange of formal guarantees transferring the risk to the American surety. Both sureties will charge a premium according to the rates in their respective countries.

Fronting may also be accomplished through the contractor's regular American surety by arranging for a bank guarantee in lieu of a bond. The guarantee is usually made by a subsidiary or foreign correspondent of an international banking institution—such as First National City Bank, New York; Chase Manhattan; or Bank of America—through its foreign department. This arrangement requires a guarantee by the American surety to the bank to cover its guarantee of the construction contractor. Although such guarantees can usually be arranged on relatively short notice, they are not readily available from many United States surety companies, and are not available except to the largest and most experienced contractors, due to company policies and reinsurance considerations.

Use of foreign sureties For contractors who have established an office or subsidiary corporation for doing business in a foreign country, or who will joint-venture the contracts there with a local contractor, the bond may be arranged locally with a domestic surety or bank. This may be the simplest and quickest method of arranging the guarantee needed. The foreign surety or bank will need underwriting and financial information and references from the contractor's bank and surety in the United States. It will require in most cases counterguarantees, probably in the form of collateral. Fulfilling this requirement may lead to a fronting situation by the contractor's United States surety or bank.

American contractors first venturing outside the United States are likely to be struck by the contrast between the ease of obtaining surety bonds at home and the formality and difficulty of arranging for similar guarantees abroad. These differences in the foreign contract are inherent in many other aspects, some of which may be less apparent. Hence a contractor on his first venture abroad should proceed with commensurate caution.

Chapter **10**

Insurance for the Construction Industry

WALTER T. DERK
Senior Vice President, Fred. S. James Agency, Inc., Chicago, Illinois

INTRODUCTION

Insurance has always been a major consideration in the construction trades simply because the stakes are so high. Solvency, including corporate and sometimes personal assets, goes on the line with every contract. It is the job of insurance to protect those assets at a time when a claim-minded public pushes to recover from somebody whenever something goes wrong.

There is no question about it: the subject is complex. Each contract is, to some extent, a whole new ball game, while the law is continually being interpreted anew.

Although it is not possible to cover the subject completely here, we can shed some light on practical ways to manage major insurable risks. That is the purpose of this chapter.

LIABILITY TO EMPLOYEES

An employer is required by law to provide for prompt payment of statutory worker's compensation and occupational disease benefits applicable in its state(s) of operations. This is most readily and commonly met by the purchase of a worker's compensation insurance policy from a private insurance carrier or one of several state insurance funds. Monopolistic state funds exist in Nevada, North Dakota, Ohio, Washington, West Virginia, and Wyoming—states which do not permit issuance of private insurance policies for this purpose.

In certain cases the requirement to provide statutory benefits is arranged through a filed and approved self-insurance program, which in itself is something of a misnomer, because it necessarily includes strong elements of insurance, as well as the furnishing of a surety bond guaranteeing that enough dollars will be available to take care of all future claims. This subject is discussed further in the pages to follow.

Individual proprietors and co-partners often do not themselves receive protection under the applicable worker's compensation laws, since they may be considered employers rather than employees. In those states separate accident and health insurance must be arranged to properly compensate them for work-related injuries. In corporations, officers are usually eligible for the same benefits as are all other employees. There is no substitute for a specific examination of current laws in each state of operation, however, since they change with some regularity.

Limits of Liability

Coverage A, which provides for payment of statutory benefits to injured employees, carries no specific policy limit. Whatever the state law provides in the way of medical care rehabilitation, lost time, permanent disability, or other condition will be paid on behalf of the employer.

Coverage B, employers' liability, carries a standard limit of $100,000 per accident except for the State of California, where the coverage-B provision is also unlimited.

Coverage B of the worker's compensation policy provides for defense of common-law action against the employer as a result of employee injuries.

Coverage Extensions Available

Two forms of all-states endorsement are available to provide insurance in additional states not listed in the policy declarations, the broader of which is unquestionably recommended at a very nominal premium charge.

We think this particularly important in view of the trend to permit employees to seek recovery under the worker's compensation laws of the state where the contract of hire was made, where the principal operations are conducted, or where the accident occurred.

Increased limits of liability under coverage B are currently available as shown in Table 10.1.

Longshoremen's and harborworker's coverage, maritime coverage, and federal employer's liability insurance are normally available by endorsement of the policy to provide coverage which may be applicable in lieu of a state worker's compensation act where the exposure involves operations at or on waterways, vessels, or railroad operations.

TABLE 10.1

Limit per accident	Additional premium	Minimum annual premium
$ 500,000	1%	$50
$1,000,000	2%	$75

Additional medical payments beyond those provided for by statute are still technically available in a few states for payment of additional premium. This has application where these states may limit the amount of medical benefits payable, either in terms of time, or dollars, or both. Because of the nationwide trend toward liberalization of benefits, it is likely only a matter of time until such limitations are abolished or greatly minimized, making the purchase of such additional extra-legal medical benefits unnecessary.

LIABILITY TO THE PUBLIC

Comprehensive General Liability

Unquestionably, and with some justification, most contractors and material suppliers find this particular policy form the least comprehensible. Our purpose here will be to make the fine print more legible and better understood.

Having covered the matter of injury to employees in the course of their employment, and coming next to automobile hazards which are fairly easy to grasp, this section essentially deals with virtually all other kinds of bodily injury or damage to the property of others. In dealing with construction trades, such injury or damage frequently involves another contractor or his employees, but the point is that to the contractor they are the public, and this is the place to seek defense—possibly payment—of such injury or damage claims.

The Policy Format

The standard comprehensive-general-liability policy form used by most companies is published by the Insurance Services Office and consists of several self-contained "coverage parts," some automatic, some not.

Operations-premises liability   This section is really quite simple in that it covers legal liability for bodily injury or property damage resulting from an occurrence (as defined) arising from buildings or premises owned or leased, as well as business operations in progress there and elsewhere. The rating basis for this coverage is normally per $100 of payroll.

Protective liability   A shade more subtle, this section defends against allegations of bodily injury or property damage which may arise from operations sublet to others.

For example, a general contractor who sublets excavation work retains some contingent or secondary liability by virtue of his contract with the owner even where the operation is performed fully by another contractor. Assuming that the subcontractor has adequate insurance, this section may involve nothing more than an initial court appearance.

The premium rates per $100 of sublet contract cost reflect the relative modesty of the exposure in such circumstances.

Completed operations and products liability   An essential part of any contractor's or supplier's insurance program, this section covers legal liability for bodily injury or property damage after completion of work or sale of a product.

Operations-premises liability protects against injury or damage sustained while operations are under way. This extends it further, when the work is done or the product has been sold and relinquished to others.

The rating basis is usually per $1,000 of gross receipts.

Reflecting a major increase in the number and severity of claims presented by the public, premiums have begun to climb in recent years, depending upon the specific trade or product involved. The important point is that no contractor, no supplier can afford to be without this protection. If the cost seems too high, ask about the savings at various deductibles.

Contractual liability   The important thing to remember here is that the basic comprehensive-general-liability format affords very little in the way of automatic coverage for the liability of others which you may assume by agreement. Principally, such automatic coverage is confined to leases of premises or railroad sidetrack agreements.

To be insured for the liability of others contractually assumed in a construction agreement, purchase order, or other manner requires an extra step, the purchase of blanket-contractual-liability insurance.

This is a very big subject indeed. The point, however, is that each and every contractor or material supplier needs to arrange for the purchase of blanket-contractual-liability insurance automatically applicable to any agreement signed in the course of business operations. A significant number of states now limit the validity of certain very broad forms of contract; this can be and should be reflected in the premium rates charged for the coverage in your state. The most complete form of insurance protection should be purchased in this respect, namely broad-form blanket-contractual-liability coverage.

To better understand and weigh the relative degree of someone else's liability which one may be called upon to assume under contract, we indicate here the three basic divisions of such responsibility as considered by the insurance company underwriting the exposure and calculating premium rates.

There exists a considerable inclination to limit the use of hold-harmless agreements, if not to outlaw them entirely. Proposed future editions of AIA contract forms may succeed in taking it step by step, until that wondrous day when such passing-the-buck may be stopped entirely, to the point where each interest's own insurance coverage will be relied upon to protect his own legal liability under common law. Certainly we endorse that utopian concept.

Limited-Form Indemnification—Negligence. A limited form holds someone harmless against claims due to operations, negligence, or that of subcontractors. For example:

> The Contractor agrees to defend, indemnify and save harmless the Owner, Architect and Engineer, their agents and employees, from and against all loss or expense (including costs and attorney's fees) by reason of liability imposed by law upon the Owner, Architect or Engineer for damages because of bodily injury, including death at any time resulting therefrom, sustained by any person or persons or on account of damage to property, including loss of use thereof, arising out of or in consequence of the performance of this work, provided such injury to persons or damage to property is due or claimed to be due to negligence of the Contractor, his Subcontractors, employees or agents.

This is not giving them much; you were already responsible for your own negligent acts or omissions as well as those of your subcontractors. Essentially, a limited-form contract agrees to defend others if they are sued or incur expense because of something you did or should have done. If both you and your subcontractors are adequately insured, this may mean payment of some legal fees.

Intermediate-Form Indemnification—Joint Negligence. An intermediate form adds agreement to defend and pay where both parties to the contract may be contributorily negligent and therefore legally liable for a loss. For example:

> The Contractor agrees to defend, indemnify and save harmless the Owner, Architect and Engineer, their agents or employees, from and against all loss or expense (including costs and attorneys' fees) by reason of liability imposed by law upon the Owner, Architect or Engineer for damages because of bodily injury, including death at any time resulting therefrom sustained by any person or persons or on account of damage to property, including loss of use thereof, arising out of or in consequence of the performance of this work, whether such injuries to persons or damage to property is due or claimed to be due to the negligence of the Contractor, his Subcontractors, the Owner, Architect or Engineer, their agents and employees, except only such injury or damage as shall have been occasioned by the sole negligence of the Owner, Architect or Engineer.

Here, instead of splitting the bill for jointly caused injury or damage, you agree to waive the defense of contributory negligence and pay as if only you were responsible.

Broad-Form Indemnification—Sole Negligence of Someone Else. A broad-form indemnifies the other party even where he may be solely responsible for a loss. For example:

> The Contractor agrees to defend, indemnify and save harmless the Owner, Architect and Engineer, their agents and employees, from and against all loss or expense (including costs and attorneys' fees) by reason of liability imposed by law

upon the Owner, Architect or Engineer for damages because of bodily injury including death at any time resulting therefrom, sustained by any person or persons or on account of damage to property, including loss of use thereof, whether caused by or contributed to by said Owner, Architect or Engineer, their agents, employees or others.

You agree here to pick up the bill for everything, including injury or damage in no way caused or contributed to by your employees or subcontractors.

Broad-form contracts are not rare. They crop up every day, agreeing in any number of ways to defend everybody against everything, with the shortest, most innocent-looking clause often being the most dangerous.

Insertion of the phrase, "except that caused by sole negligence of the indemnitee" at the proper place in a contract before accepting it for signature may cut the exposure to loss in half. However, it is most important to keep in mind, even where coverage does exist, that it is still another's liability which is assumed. If there is a loss, it will be charged against your claim experience record.

By signing a hold-harmless agreement, you may find yourself in the position of (1) paying full worker's compensation benefits, (2) paying a common-law judgment to the same employee, and (3) losing your right of subrogation; that is, your right to be reimbursed by the responsible party for compensation benefits paid.

A loss for which you might have been 100 percent reimbursed, therefore, could cost you or your insurance company double, and probably more, because there is no statutory limit to jury awards (as there is to most compensation benefits)—for an injury caused by someone else.

Regardless of what a particular contract says, one cannot buy insurance to protect against the assumption of professional liability on the part of an architect or engineer for such diverse obligations as the preparation or approval of maps, drawings, opinions, reports, surveys, change orders, designs, or specifications, or for the giving or the failure to give directions or instructions by the architect or engineer, their agents, or their employees. If you encounter an agreement which requires you to do so, by all means strike those words before signing it.

Limits of Liability

The standard policy provides for separate limits of liability applicable to bodily injury and property damage. There is a limit per occurrence and a limit which represents an annual aggregate for all claims under that division of coverage.

Policy Extensions

Books can be and have been written on the extensive range of specific policy definitions, limitations, and exclusions, offset by myriad coverage extensions available to fill the gaps created. We shall confine ourselves here to a brief resume of coverage extensions commonly available at reasonable premium levels:

Blanket contractual liability   Blanket-contractual-liability insurance automatically covering all written agreements is commonly available; premium rates per $100 of contract cost are negotiated. Because there is little uniformity in indemnifying clauses, as well as a wide divergence of opinion about their seriousness, this is a job for the insurance representative, whether the coverage is blanket or specific.

Broad-form property damage   This endorsement is designed to help answer at least one major question concerning the care, custody, or control exclusion: just *how much* of the property being worked on is subject to the exclusion?

Intended primarily for contractors, the rider modifies this troublesome exclusion by using different and more specific language to do so, thereby covering more situations involving damage. For example, while continuing to exclude liability for damage to property being worked on, the endorsement deletes coverage only for that particular part, provided the accident occurs away from the insured's premises.

The extension covers more claims without the necessity of going to court for a decision. Additional premiums required are subject to negotiation. It is recommended, so long as the contractor understands that it does not completely eliminate the care, custody, or control exclusion itself.

While discussions concerning this endorsement sometimes tend to become fairly esoteric, we have seen enough losses defended and paid solely because it was there to prove its value many times over. Any contractor can rest more easily once it is added to his policy.

Explosion, collapse, or underground damage   When applicable under the basic comprehensive policy because work being performed involves classifications subject to one, two, or all three such exclusions, they may be removed either on a blanket basis or for specific projects. The additional premium, normally a surcharge per $100 of payroll or a negotiated flat charge, is dependent upon the physical hazards of the job.

To keep the cost down, the insurance representative should be told everything about the site to be worked on, the steps to be taken to prevent cutting into a telephone cable, gas main, or other underground facility, the adequacy of blueprints to be followed, and so on. Then, everything possible should be done to prevent such damage.

In some cases removal of the x, c, or u exclusion is fairly expensive, and the added cost should be determined before bidding on any contract which requires their removal.

Host liquor liability   In those states having strict dram-shop laws, coverage is available by endorsement or separate policy to insure against statutory liability arising from the giving or dispensing of liquor as a host.

Fire legal liability   This endorsement bypasses the exclusion of property in the care, custody, or control of the insured only as respects buildings, or portions thereof, rented to or occupied by the insured and designated in the endorsement, covering the insured's legal liability for such property accidentally damaged by fire. The practical purpose here is to insure the tenant against subrogation claims brought by the owner or his fire insurance carrier for fire damage caused by the tenant's negligence.

The same thing can be accomplished by (1) eliminating the subrogation clause as respects the tenant, or (2) issuing a fire policy in his name, or (3) amending the lease itself.

One prominent client employs this clause to accomplish the latter:

> The lessor hereby waives on behalf of each and every insuror under any insurance policies relating to the demised premises, the building on which said premises are located, the contents thereof, or any personal property of the lessor, all lessors' rights of recovery from or claims against lessee, its beneficiaries, if any employees, agents and agents employees the means of any loss, damage or injury to said building, contents, leasehold improvements, or personal property whether by way of subrogation, assignment of claims or otherwise.

Vendor's liability   The manufacturer of a material or product purchases products liability insurance to protect against bodily injury or property damage claims resulting from its use after sale. He may also endorse his policy to protect those vendors who sell his manufactured product, either individually or on a blanket basis from contingent liability claims arising from such sale.

Professional liability   Anyone employing a physician or nurse is open to claims alleging professional malpractice. Coverage may be provided by endorsement or separate policy, the premium charge being dependent upon the number of such persons employed and the facilities available for the treatment of injured employees.

Personal injury—bodily injury and intangible harm   The first insuring agreement in the policy refers to bodily injury, which implies tangible physical injury. An extension is available to include personal injury liability; that is, intangible harm. Commonly written in three divisions, these include:

1. False arrest
   Malicious prosecution
   Willful detention or imprisonment
2. Libel
   Slander
   Defamation of character
3. Wrongful eviction
   Invasion of privacy
   Wrongful entry

The endorsement often excludes claims brought by employees, advertising activities, and such liability assumed under contract. The premium charged is variable.

Employees as additional insureds   In the case of a corporate entity, the standard comprehensive-general-liability policy defines "persons insured" as "the organization so designated and any executive officer, director or stockholder thereof while acting within the scope of his duties as such."

If a claim should be filed individually naming, say, a supervisory employee outside one of these groups, there would be no primary defense coverage available to such individual employee. Umbrella-excess-liability coverage could fill the gap, subject to the substantial self-insured retention.

Certainly, the ultimate decision must always rest with the insured, but we very much favor giving a choice whether to buy certain coverage extensions, higher limits of liability, or new policy forms—in advance of loss, of course.

Comprehensive Automobile Liability

Owned automobiles—automobiles under long-term lease Covers legal liability for bodily injury or property damage caused by an occurrence (as defined) and arising from the ownership, maintenance, or use of owned automobiles anywhere in the United States, its territories, possessions, or Canada. This same section permits coverage for vehicles operated by the named insured under long-term lease, where the lessee provides primary insurance and the lessor is named as additional insured. The rating basis is usually per vehicle insured.

Hired automobiles Covers the named insured—and in this case *not* the lessor—for bodily injury or property damage caused by an occurrence and arising from use of a hired vehicle. Charge per $100 cost of hire, subject to adjustment at audit. Short-term-lease agreements automatically come under this division, as do those long-term-leased cars not specifically covered in division I of the policy.

Employers' nonownership liability Covers the named insured for business use of automobiles individually owned by employees or firm members, but not normally partners, resulting in bodily injury or property damage caused by an occurrence. This instance, which is excess over any applicable primary coverage the owner may have, protects the employer if the employee has no insurance on his car or where his limits prove to be inadequate. Note that it affords no protection at all to the owner of the automobile; he retains an obligation to insure the automobile he owns.

For premium purposes, all employees of the insured are grouped into two classes: (1) those whose duties involve regular use of personally owned automobiles for business purposes and who receive some sort of reimbursement for such use and (2) all other employees. Class-one premiums amount to several dollars per employee; the class-two rate is several cents per employee.

Purchase of nonownership coverage does not mean that certificates of insurance are unnecessary, but rather that such evidence of coverage from the employee-owner is not required before the employer is protected. Continuing efforts should be made to confirm that all class-one employees are adequately insured and stay insured.

Limits of liability The comprehensive-automobile-liability policy provides for one bodily-injury limit per person, another per occurrence. Property damage liability is subject to one limit per occurrence.

Policy extensions
Medical-Payments Coverage. Medical-payments coverage provides for reimbursement of reasonable medical expenses incurred by occupants of an insured automobile. The insurance is not applicable to employees eligible for worker's compensation benefits; therefore, it is commonly omitted on trucks.

Use of other Automobiles. Specific individuals may be named by endorsement to protect against bodily-injury, property-damage, and medical-payments losses arising from use of a nonowned automobile, whether for business or pleasure purposes. This is ordinarily not required where that individual has in force a separate family-automobile policy which names him (or his spouse) as insured. Each child of driving age must be separately named, however. There is enough variance in personal-automobile-liability policies to make close examination of this subject mandatory.

Foreign Coverage. Use of any automobile outside the United States, its territories, possessions, or Canada requires special foreign coverage.

Statutory No-Fault Benefits. These are in essence designed to modify or restrict tort liability in favor of first-party benefits payable under the insured's own policy, regardless of fault, in an effort to speed claim settlements, avoid long court delays, and perhaps reduce automobile premiums.

Automobile Physical Damage

Physical damage to owned vehicles, as well as those under long-term lease, is normally covered as part of the automobile-liability contract, but may be insured in an entirely separate policy form. Insured hazards may include:

Comprehensive coverage For a single premium the hazards of fire, theft, glass breakage, malicious mischief, vandalism, and accidental damage to the vehicle other than that caused by collision may be insured on an actual cash value or stated amount of insurance bases. Note that in either case, the amount recovered in the event of total loss is the current market value of the vehicle at the time of loss. The coverage may be written with a deductible.

Fire, theft, and combined additional coverage As an alternative, the specific perils of fire, theft, windstorm, hail, earthquake, explosion, flood or rising waters, riot, civil commotion, malicious mischief, and vandalism may be insured at a premium savings over comprehensive coverage, particularly where the glass breakage exposure is negligible and may be written with a deductible.

Collision Damage to owned or long-term–leased automobiles is available at deductibles ranging from $50 to $1,000 or more.

Coverage extensions

Fleet Automatic Coverage. A fleet consists of five or more insured units and if automatic coverage is desired, a fleet automatic endorsement is available without additional charge to pick up changes and additions to the automotive schedule without the need to endorse midterm. It is recommended.

Umbrella Excess Liability

As excess over existing primary insurance Existing liability insurance policies become the underlying layer, above which umbrella provides excess limits for the same hazards insured under primary policies, subject to a high limit per occurrence and in the aggregate.

As excess over self-insured hazards For hazards omitted or excluded in existing liability insurance policies, umbrella provides coverage in excess of a self-insured retention or deductible, usually $10,000 or $25,000 per occurrence.

Following-form excess liability By way of specific policy conditions or endorsement, umbrella underwriters commonly restrict their policies so that umbrella coverage applies to certain hazards only to the same extent that they are covered by underlying policies.

This is pure following-form excess liability insurance as respects those specified hazards.

Such restrictions are most often concerned with: (1) contractual liability, (2) damage to property of others in your care, custody, or control, and/or (3) explosion, collapse, or underground damage. Where such restrictions are in force, the broadest possible underlying comprehensive-general-liability insurance should be secured.

Maintenance of underlying insurance Umbrella policies normally schedule underlying primary liability insurance coverages maintained by the insured, and the insured contractor warrants to keep such underlying insurance in force during the umbrella policy term. Failure to comply may jeopardize coverage. The deductible may become $100,000, $300,000, or more in such circumstances. Do not drop or reduce such underlying policies without approval of the umbrella carrier.

Every contractor, regardless of size, owes it to himself to secure a quotation for this broad coverage. It is often available for less cost than would be charged for equivalent limits under basic policies affording far less protection.

HOW TO DEAL WITH INSURANCE OVERHEAD

The adoption of sweeping worker's compensation reforms coupled with a major increase in the number and cost of liability claims presented by the public makes it absolutely mandatory that any contractor or supplier stay on top of insurance costs, some of which may become fully evident only upon completion of the final audit, after expiration of the policies themselves.

For example, when a midterm increase in compensation benefits is granted, the rating authorities customarily grant a corresponding increase in premium rate effective that date, normally with very little warning. It is important to build into long-term contracts an adequate cushion against these factors.

The most effective way of doing that is for contractors to establish a close working relationship with their insurance representatives, charging them with responsibility for overall business insurance risks and asking to be kept closely advised of any developments of consequence as they occur. This should be done at least annually, more often if required, to discuss what the insurance companies are going to bill, when, and how. Once the list is complete, a little arithmetic will permit an accurate measure of insurance overhead geared to payroll or gross receipts. This is important, because payroll audit rules are changing all the time, and some of the previous limitations which were applicable across the country are being changed along with the specific rates themselves. Ask about any other changes which might affect operations midterm, and insist upon prompt notification of those which do occur.

As part of the previously mentioned, close working relationship, we feel that the insurance representative should be shown or sent things to read: the insurance specifications you are called upon to meet, special limit requirements which might be stated in a contract you are about to bid, certificates of insurance received from suppliers and subcontractors, certificate requests you have to meet from your own contractual relationships, copies of the hold-harmless agreements you are asked to sign, and copies of claim reports if the injury or damage is either severe or concerns you in a way that you would like some special attention given to such cases. All in addition to the legal counsel you may wish from your attorney.

The last thing in the world a contractor wants is another salesperson calling upon him. What he needs is someone able to help determine his exposure to loss, discuss with him what is available, and go out into the marketplace *to buy* in his behalf what is required.

SELF-INSURANCE PROGRAMS

We are all in favor of self-insurance wherever the concept fits and circumstances point to its logical adoption. A good many of our clients have elected to institute such programs after a full investigation of the advantages and disadvantages to their specific operations.

It would be wrong, however, to look upon the spectre of ever-rising insurance costs and conclude that self-insurance is *the* answer. The major factor affecting insurance premiums is, of course, losses. With rare exceptions, the loss content cannot be expected to change dramatically, simply because you chose to perform—or pay someone else to perform—some of the duties which are built into insured programs.

In our view, some conservatism is in order when moving away from purchase of an insurance policy without limit, as in the case of worker's compensation insurance, to assumption of such unlimited liability yourself. First, the respective states will require evidence of ability to pay losses in timely fashion by means of a surety bond. Presumably, claim and safety engineering services will have to be bought and paid for to cover prevention, investigation, and defense of claims which do occur.

Now, most importantly, a limited amount of specific excess-liability insurance and/or aggregate excess insurance must be purchased to stop individual losses or losses in the aggregate at some point. Such insurance, which is written for a specific maximum amount, naturally tends to cost a good deal more in an age where benefit levels and claim settlement costs are rising. The top limit selected had better be way up there.

In short, self-insurance is surely not a panacea and probably not worth consideration by the average contracting risk performing work at a significant number of job sites every year.

MAKING THE MOST OF INSURANCE OVERHEAD

In the following illustration we will not be talking about ways to reduce costs per se, but rather about getting the most mileage out of the annual insurance budget, whatever that may be.

Our cast of characters consists of two contractors, NQR Building, Inc., and MB Enterprises, Inc. They are astoundingly similar; both do about the same amount of work in Indiana and neighboring states, devote time to detailed consideration of insurance matters at least annually, genuinely care about safety, and do business with reputable firms. Further, they spend about the same amount of money on insurance, including deductibles and self-insured losses. NQR and MB are friendly competitors who generally see eye to eye on matters of importance, but one has a superior program for managing its business risks. The differences are best discussed after examining Table 10.2, which shows how they spend their premium dollar:

TABLE 10.2

NQR Builders, Inc.	Hazard	MB Enterprises, Inc.
Conventional statutory insurance	Worker's compensation	Conventional statutory insurance
$1 million limit per accident	Employers' liability	Standard $100,000 limit per accident
Coverage extensions:		*Coverage extensions:*
All-states endorsement— standard form		All states endorsement—broad form
$10,000 additional medical insurance where applicable		U.S. Longshoremen's and Harbor Workers' Act coverage; federal employers' liability coverage
	Comprehensive general liability	
Bodily injury:		*Bodily injury:*
$500,000 per occurrence		$250,000 per occurrence
$1 million aggregate		$500,000 aggregate
Property damage:		*Property damage:*
$500,000 per occurrence		$100,000 per occurrence
$1 million aggregate		$100,000 aggregate
Coverage extensions:		*Coverage extensions:*
Blanket contractual liability— intermediate form		Blanket contractual liability— broad form
Completed-operations liability		Completed-operations liability
"Care, custody, or control" exclusions removed		Broad-form property damage coverage
Incidental malpractice liability		Incidental malpractice liability
Fire liability		
Employee benefit liability— $1,000 deductible		
Personal injury liability		Personal injury liability
Additional insureds— employees		
	Comprehensive automobile liability	
Auto bodily injury:		*Auto bodily injury:*
$300,000 per person		$250,000 per person
$500,000 per occurrence		$250,000 per occurrence
Auto property damage:		*Auto property damage:*
$500,000 per occurrence		$100,000 per occurrence

TABLE 10.2 *(Continued)*

NQR Builders, Inc.	Hazard	MB Enterprises, Inc.

Coverage extensions:
Medical payments coverage—
  all units
Compulsory uninsured
  motorists and/or no-fault
  coverage
Use of other automobiles
  coverage
		Coverage extensions:
		Medical payments coverage—
		  passenger cars
		Compulsory uninsured motorists
		  and/or no-fault coverage
		
		Use of other automobiles
		  coverage

	Automobile physical damage	

Comprehensive coverage:
Actual cash value—all units
  including trailers and other
  contractor's mobile
  equipment
		Comprehensive coverage:
		Stated amounts—$50 deductible
		  all automobiles and trucks,
		  excluding any valued at $500
		  or less
		Fire, theft, combined additional
		  coverage, including vandalism
		  and malicious mischief cover-
		  age—$100 deductible all
		  trailers

Collision coverage:
Actual cash value—$50
  deductible all passenger
  cars; $100 deductible all
  other vehicles
		Collision coverage:
		Actual cash value—$100 deduct-
		  ible all passenger cars; $250
		  deductible all commercial
		  vehicles, excluding any valued
		  at $1,000 or less

Towing coverage: $25 per loss, all passenger cars		
	Umbrella excess liability	

$1 million per occurrence and
  aggregate, $10,000 self-
  insured retention on
  otherwise uninsured perils
		$3 million per occurrence and
		  aggregate, $10,000 self-
		  insured retention on otherwise
		  uninsured perils

	Contractor's equipment floater	

		"All-risk" perils, subject to
		  deductibles ranging from $100
		  to $500 or more, depending
		  upon value
		Coverage extensions:
		Automatic coverage, rented
		  equipment

	Installation floater	

		"All-risk" perils, subject to $1,000
		  deductible, excess of any appli-
		  cable builders' risk coverage
		  which operates as primary
		  insurance

How they compare   NQR (Not Quite Right) certainly started off with a bang, buying consistently higher limits and broader primary coverage than his Hoosier counterpart, MB (Much Better). The latter more than made up for any early deficiencies in carrying higher-limit catastrophic coverage and forms of protection not purchased by NQR at all. Apart from this fairly obvious difference in corporate philosophy, let us look at how they compare: NQR elected to increase his Coverage B (employers' liability) limit to $1 million for 2 percent additional premium (minimum $75). He also chose to increase the statutory medical benefits payable (in his state) by $10,000 per claim, paying another 1 percent for that noble extension.

Somewhat more miserly, MB paid a flat $25 annual charge for a relatively new broad-form all-states endorsement to comply with compensation filing requirements in states not listed in the policy at inception. Then he added automatic marine-and-railroad-liability coverage should he ever undertake work near waterways or trains. Vitally necessary, abnormally expensive by audit, but should that day never come, the extensions are free if not used.

So far, then, MB has saved only 3 percent of his worker's compensation premium, but he is on his way to better risk management.

General liability   Both contractors bought broad comprehensive-liability policy forms, NQR the more so. He liked the symmetry of $½ to 1 million limits across the board, above which his umbrella policy provided another million dollars, enough to meet most, but not all, job specifications he encountered. When short, he simply advised his agent of his need for higher limits, which were provided by endorsement for that particular job.

More importantly, NQR had attended enough meetings where insurance was discussed to be concerned about "care, custody, or control" exclusions present in most insurance policies. After some searching, he found an insurance carrier willing to delete these exclusions entirely for a significant additional premium. Not particularly welcome, but at least predictable.

Since he leased his building, he added fire-legal-liability insurance to protect against the owner's fire insurance company coming to him for any damage his employees might negligently cause, as permitted by the lease. This added 25 percent of the building fire rate to NQR's general-liability policy premium—a necessary evil, he thought.

Wanting an optimum program, NQR added an endorsement naming all employees as additional insureds to protect against their being sued as individuals, then bought another rider to extend employee-benefit-liability coverage, in case someone in personnel erred in the administration of employee benefit insurance programs.

It would be pure conjecture here to establish what these coverage differences amounted to in terms of dollars or percentage of premium, but a good guess might be 100 percent more than MB, also a thoughtful man, paid for his policy.

How MB handled it   Taking the advice of his insurance counsel, MB bought the lowest primary limits which would satisfy the underlying coverage requirements of those umbrella excess carriers most likely to offer a broad policy, good service, and a competitive price. That number was once $100/300,000, but has climbed in recent years along with everything else. This move alone saved MB 10 percent on his bodily-injury premium, almost 50 percent on property damage.

He chose to deal with the "care, custody, or control" exclusions by adding a broad-form property damage endorsement available at fairly nominal cost from almost any insurance company. Not the same as removal of the exclusions in their entirety—but a great deal less expensive. Importantly, this precluded the need, otherwise created, to do business with only one of a handful of companies willing to delete the "care, custody, or control" exclusions at any price. We do not mean to imply that anything is wrong with the imaginative companies willing to do so, but the choice is so limited that the buyer's options then tend to become minimal. That price, a severely restricted market, is our primary objection to NQR's handling of the problem.

Next, MB handled the leased-building matter by modifying his lease to waive the fire insurance company's right of subrogation against MB, should the premises be negligently damaged. It worked free.

Knowing that the comprehensive-general-liability policy form covered the corporation (plus its officers and directors while acting in that capacity), MB chose to rely upon his umbrella policy to defend suits directed against one of his superintendents or foremen as individuals. In that event, his particular umbrella policy would provide primary legal defense, but could require him to pay up to $10,000 in case of an eventual verdict against that employee who was acting as his agent.

Similarly, MB arranged for his employee-benefit-liability coverage via endorsement of the umbrella policy, subject to the same $1,000 deductible applicable to NQR. The difference is that the umbrella carrier included the coverage extension when negotiating premiums at the $3 million limit level; some make a modest extra charge.

Automobile hazards   Both contractors found their respective umbrella carriers willing to accept somewhat lower primary automobile liability limits. MB's were already lower, and he remembered that his automobile- and general-liability limits should ideally be identical to obviate quarrels over which may apply to mobile equipment, loading or unloading claims, and so on.

NQR made the classic mistake of insuring too much under automobile physical damage. By agreeing to insure up to depreciated stated amounts in lieu of "actual cash value" as shown in insurance company manuals, MB saved premium. By accepting a deductible for such noncollision losses, a considerable additional reduction was possible. Instead of trying to cover all manner of contractor's mobile equipment under the automobile policy, MB listed his major items in a separate contractor's-equipment-floater policy, achieving broader "all-risk" coverage for less premium, subject to selected deductibles.

Instead of paying for glass coverage on trailers which have no glass, MB insured them for combined additional coverage at $100 deductible.

NQR continued to insure too much under collision at expensive premium levels, actually paying more than $50 premium annually on some cars for the privilege of having $50 instead of $100 deductible collision. Implausible? We see it happen again and again. MB displayed good business acumen in deciding to self-insure more. As units became older, they were dropped from physical-damage coverage entirely.

Towing coverage, offering a maximum insurance recovery of $25 per claim, appealed to NQR because the premium was so reasonable. It never even occurred to MB, because a $25 loss was clearly a petty-cash-drawer transaction.

Umbrella Excess Liability

Both saw the advantage to this broad policy form, MB more so than NQR, who at times had to endorse his primary liability limits upward on a job-to-job basis, incurring certain inherent premium penalties in the process. MB's limits were there to be certified immediately as needed. His certificates of insurance conveyed a better sense of optimum coverage, a subtle selling point.

Installation floater Both firms knew that many job specifications require some form of builder's risk insurance. MB's broker dealt with imaginative inland marine underwriters who knew that, too, and therefore were willing to write a policy form which would fill any gap in coverage on an "all-risk" basis, subject to a negotiated deductible of $1,000 and excess of any applicable builder's risk insurance. More peace of mind at a price MB could live with, likely to cost less if not used to pay losses often.

Summing up To our knowledge, the sages have never had a word to say about insurance, good or bad. If they had, it probably would have been something like: "A smart insurance company wants more than one dollar for each dollar of routine loss it pays out."

All contractors can benefit from that, as MB Enterprises did so admirably in our purely hypothetical examples here.

CONCLUSION

Hopefully, the foregoing pages have provided food for thought and made the subject a bit more understandable. There is no substitute, however, for an effective, working, day-to-day relationship with an experienced insurance professional—someone representing the buyer's interests in what is today decidedly a seller's market. More than ever before, that kind of individual is earning his keep!

Part Three

Credit Reporting

Chapter **11**

Extending Credit in the Construction Industry

THOMAS J. BARFIELD
Regional Financial Manager, Otis Elevator Company,
Montvale, New Jersey

BASIC CRITERIA FOR USE IN CREDIT EVALUATION

Up to a point, the decision to extend credit in the construction industry involves much of the same logic required for extension of credit in any line of business. Even though the peculiarities of the industry tend to make construction credit evaluations more difficult than most, it is important to concentrate first on the general considerations important to any sound credit decision.

The three C's of credit The time-tested criteria of character, capital, and capacity should be among the first considered. Of these, perhaps the most important is character. Without a willingness to pay, the necessary ingredient of confidence is missing. That is why past history, personal knowledge, and exchange of information about payment practices are so vital. Generally a pattern develops that shows how a company and its principals treat creditors when the chips are down. What we are looking for are demonstrations of good faith and integrity in the past.

Capital is another vital element in the decision to extend credit. Many of the bad debts charged off during recent years resulted from the fact that a contractor or subcontractor had an inadequate supply of capital to withstand the drain of a major cost overrun or to pay off debts in the event of owner default. Remember that the net worth of the prospective customer should not only be adequate to sustain a setback, but also be convertible into cash in case of trouble.

Capacity needs close evaluation to be sure the customer is not overextending. This necessarily involves the total volume of all projects being undertaken by the customer. It can be evaluated to some extent by past performance, but when a company takes on substantially more work than normal, a personal contact is in order to ascertain whether customer personnel will not be stretched too thin.

Common sense   Each decision to extend credit should be approached on the basis that one is, in fact, going into business with one's customer. No single technique or yardstick will suffice unless it is accompanied by a close knowledge of the marketplace and as much information about the customer as can be obtained if the decision is a difficult one. As we move along to describe the various pieces of information available, bear in mind that not all of these will have equal weight in each credit evaluation. That is where common sense comes into play. The emphasis placed on each conflicting factor will often determine the soundness of the decision reached. Common sense, by its very nature, is subjective. Hence, it is necessary not to let feelings unjustifiably hold sway over the weight of contrary objective evidence.

Statistics and ratios   Within the construction industry there is a limit to the value of ratios that are used generally in other industries. Of the fourteen basic ratios included in trade publications, many involve inventory values that are frequently not a major part of contractor and subcontractor operations. Still, it is important that use be made of those ratios which do apply. Some of these are:

1. *Current Assets to Current Debts*—This provides a basis for judging the liquidity of a customer. It is calculated by dividing current assets by current liabilities. The results should be two (2) or more with the higher, the better.

2. *Debt to Equity*—It is obtained by dividing total liabilities (long-term plus short-term) by net worth. If total debt is approaching the net worth, questions should be asked about future plans for additional financing.

Some large companies use a point system for general evaluation of credit potential. These can be valuable adjuncts in making the decision to extend credit, but of necessity are too arbitrary to serve as a full substitute for a reasoned decision that takes into account all known factors. Smaller firms in the construction industry would have difficulty in justifying the time needed to set up and maintain such systems. Generally, these are most successul when they are used in conjunction with computer analysis of accounts, and they apply best to decisions concerning material sales rather than labor and material contracts with developers and general contractors.

Practical considerations   The decision to extend credit should never be made in a vacuum. Due consideration must be given to such important factors as the profit expected from the contract or order being considered, the need for the business it affords, retainage and other contract terms, general economic conditions, and the prospective duration of the project. It might seem obvious to say that none of these should override the weight of credit data received. However, all too often a need has been felt to increase volume at any price with resulting collection headaches. On the other hand, many companies have grown and prospered through their judicious care and feeding of the marginal accounts.

How can the odds for a favorable result be improved? One good way is to treat the credit operation, large or small, as a profit center and measure its effectiveness on the basis of income from sales approved and collected less the sum of bad debts and anticipated profits lost from sales declined where a competitor collected in full.

Mutual respect and confidence between the party responsible for credit and his counterpart in sales can go a long way toward achieving overall company goals. By working together, the two of them are often able to get better contract terms or additional security from a customer in order to allow approval of a sale. On the other hand, they may agree that the expected margin is not worth a credit gamble. Together, they can make their boss look good through correct joint decisions that also go a long way toward meeting their individual responsibilities.

Danger signals In reviewing an application for credit, one should not hesitate to ask for a current financial statement from a prospective customer. One may not always get all the information needed in the preferred form. However, it is rare that the statement is not helpful at least to some degree, and refusal to furnish the statement is a red flag that signals the need for more information than usual from other sources.

What are some of the danger signs to be considered?

1. *Liquidity Problems*—Evidence may show that the owner, contractor, or subcontractor being evaluated has let his receivables get out of hand or that he owes more on a current basis than he has coming to him. Construction companies, particularly in labor intensive lines, need either to show an obviously liquid position or else to stand ready to demonstrate the availability of additional investment capital.

2. *Diversion of Contract Funds*—The primary symptom here is a general slowness in paying amounts owed on one slender pretext or another until funds from another project are received. At that time, the reports of past-due amounts outstanding drop off substantially. If the contractor or subcontractor has several uncompleted projects, the potential problem may be only slow pay. However, a larger danger arises if the customer's business has declined sharply, since that may signal a substantial chance of loss as well.

3. *General Payment Slowness*—Continuing slowness, particularly if accompanied by notations of unauthorized backcharges, disputes and similar practices, obviously spells trouble. What is surprising is that so many extend credit in the face of this adverse experience. The common notion that others failed because of lack of effort or improper performance is almost always wishful thinking. A good precaution is to talk directly with those who have had unfavorable experience before making a decision to extend credit.

4. *Lien Notices and Delinquency Recordings*—The mere fact that there

are notices on record does not necessarily preclude normal extension of credit. However, such filings are a major signal of potential trouble that warrants particular attention including some frank talk with the customer and those making the recordings.

Vulnerability study   A warning at this point is necessary. This part of the overall credit evaluation will hurt. It involves an analysis of common traits among accounts that have proven troublesome during recent years. Specifically, the study consists of pulling out the contracts and orders that resulted in the need to charge off bad debts and those which were collected only after referral to an attorney or collection agency.

To determine what the contracts have in common, a check sheet should be used that includes such items as the following:

- Geographical location
- Amount of contract
- Relative profitability of job
- Unusual contract terms (if any) and whether signed on contract forms, A.I.A. forms, or the customer's contract documents
- Product line
- Number of years customer in business
- Type of owner
- Credit rating and general credit reputation at time of sale
- Security (if any)

The list is not intended to be all-inclusive and the study should not be a highly structured one. Instead, the emphasis should be on discovering common denominators. Oddly enough, there are almost always some surprises in comparison with anticipated results. Once a recurring pattern shows itself, particular attention can be paid to future orders showing similar traits. In the process, most of us will find ourselves thinking through what we might have done to spot the trouble before initialing approval for credit.

This type of study has one other beneficial effect. It develops an extra degree of caution on the part of the person reviewing future contracts. It should also turn up basic trends that cause trouble spots to develop.

Once the initial study has been completed and the results have been evaluated and acted upon, it can then serve as a good standard to use in identifying the type and extent of future changes in the trend of problems. It is to be hoped that by concentrating on the cumulative factors involved, the list will not only become shorter but also indicate those new areas on which to concentrate before the problems become serious.

Staying out of the banking business   In the construction industry, if a customer asks for extended terms of payment, frequently this means that ordinary banking channels are not open to him. Either he is trying to save interest or else he cannot qualify for as large a loan as he needs. Under either circumstance, one is placed in the position of trying to decide if one is a better judge of the customer's worth and security than those institutions in business for that specific purpose.

Credit in the construction industry divides itself into two parts—first, the construction loan and, later, the takeout or permanent financing. For a venture to be viable, an owner or developer should have enough funds to add to what he can borrow from a bank to pay the cost of construction. Part of his investment may be in the form of land or, in some cases, services. Bankers will practically never lend 100 percent of the anticipated construction costs. The specific percentage of their investment is based on the degree of risk they foresee and the rate of interest charged. Since the loan extends only for the duration of the construction period, it is essentially a short-term credit decision for the bankers.

Permanent financing is normally provided by insurance companies or other institutional investors. It comes into play upon completion of construction and represents a long-term investment. For office buildings and apartment houses, commitments may be made for permanent financing that are contingent on agreed-upon interim rental results. For example, the permanent financing may involve payments on a progressive basis when 50 percent occupancy has been achieved, with further monies payable for each additional 10 percent of occupancy up to, say, 80 or 90 percent of capacity.

Contractors may be asked to participate directly in financing the construction phase. Before agreeing to do so, it is obvious that an unusually intense investigation of all facets of the venture would be necessary. It is equally obvious that contingency clauses in permanent financing commitments and also in cost overruns during construction could tie up money for extended periods of time.

Indirect financing of projects by contractors and subcontractors can come about where there is failure of an owner or contractor to pay promptly for work performed. The main protection to guard against this in advance is evidence of adequate overall project financing and contract terms that allow one to protect one's interests if payments are not made on schedule.

Finally, we should be aware that there are secondary sources of construction financing. These credit corporations charge higher rates of interest than normal since their security is not as good as that of the primary construction lender. Still, it is more appropriate for an owner or developer to use this method of obtaining additional capital than for contractors to use their precious funds in a way that will, for all intents and purposes, put them in the banking business.

Credit extension options   At first glance, the decision to extend the credit is frequently viewed as one of "yes" or "no," as simple as that. However, in actual practice, we usually determine the basis on which credit can be extended. In other words, an outright yes nearly always means that credit will be extended as long as payments are made as agreed during construction and that final payment will follow within a reasonable time after acceptance of your work. On the other hand, if the customer's credit worthiness seems more doubtful, it is much more likely that he will get a conditional yes than an outright no.

It is the marginal customer that poses the biggest problem for anyone extending credit. But, at the same time, such customers often provide a good opportunity to work out arrangements of benefit to one's company. The marginal customer is often willing to pay a better price and also to appreciate consideration received in time of need.

A conditional yes may involve the obtaining of guarantees from a parent company, the principals themselves, or from a bank. One strategy to be considered is an understanding that additional security will be provided in the event payments are not made as scheduled. That is effective so long as one has the ability to stop work until the guarantee is received in case slowness of pay develops. However, it offers little protection for a contractor whose work could be readily completed by others if he pulled off the job.

The main thing to bear in mind about corporations established for a single project or similar reason is that these are organized for the express purpose of limiting liability. The good names and reputations of the principals must be viewed in light of the fact that these parties did not have enough confidence to put the full weight of their resources behind the project. In such cases, it is particularly important to examine the viability of the project and not hesitate to ask for specific security.

In the case of material suppliers and small subcontractors, there is the alternative of doing business on a c.o.d. basis. Even this qualifies as a conditional yes since one must assemble and deliver the material in expectation that payment will be made upon arrival. Down payments are common in other parts of the world and certainly are not out of the question as another alternative consideration.

Long-duration projects Special dangers are inherent in the extension of credit for jobs that will not be completed for many years. First of all, a customer's worth can change substantially with the passage of time. In addition, periods of severe inflation can produce cost overruns that negate basic presumptions originally used to justify the project financially. Similarly, overbuilding of office buildings or apartment houses can occur and adversely affect the owner's ability to qualify for full permanent financing monies.

One less obvious consideration is that lengthy projects are not as consistently predictable in terms of profit. Hence, if tempted to extend credit on a marginal risk account mainly because of a large expected return, it is usually well to look again when a long, drawnout job is involved. In doing so, care should be taken to discount for the prospective effects of inflation.

The rule of thumb to remember here is that lengthy projects multiply the credit risk and should be evaluated accordingly.

PECULIARITIES OF CONSTRUCTION INDUSTRY CREDIT EXTENSION

Contingent-payment terms Often construction contracts include a "pay-when-paid" provision whereby a contractor is not obligated to pay his subcontractors until he has been paid by the owner. This practice may be extended to lower tiers as well. When subcontractors, sub-subcontractors, and material suppliers allow themselves to be bound by these contingent-payment terms, they are in effect extending credit as well to the owner and higher tier contractors. This spells trouble since we have privity of contract with only one party. In other words, a subcontractor can suffer grievous delays in receiving his money because of default or slowness of pay by an owner in spite of the fact that the subcontractor has no contractual rights for enforcing owner payment. He is dependent on his customer, the general contractor, to protect his interests with the owner. That can prove to be a thin reed if the general contractor is owed little or nothing on his own account by the owner. The problem is often worse for a sub-subcontractor or lower tier material supplier.

To be successful, the party responsible for credit review should work closely with others who may be reviewing contract documents for legal, technical, and other conditions. Often, with better contract language, a tough credit decision can become a far easier one. It cannot be emphasized too strongly that adverse clauses should be renegotiated for satisfactory changes or total elimination to the full extent possible.

A number of court decisions have held that contingent-payment provisions do not excuse payment by a contractor for an unlimited period of time. Instead, the "pay-when-paid" practice has been held to apply for only a reasonable time.[1] The problem is that court action is often required to enforce the reasonable-time doctrine. Accordingly, subcontractors may find themselves not only waiting for unreasonable times, but also incurring legal fees in order to obtain their monies through court actions.

Some recent court decisions have held that a bonding company cannot avoid its obligations for payment of proper claims simply on the theory that its bond covered a contractor whose subcontractors signed contracts with contingent payment terms.[2] However, there are prior cases holding that the bonding companies are protected in such instances.

Other problems caused by contingent-payment terms involve lien rights, bond filings, and establishment of valid receivables. Liens must be filed within a specific period after last performance of work or delivery of material. If that period passes prior to the time an owner pays the general contractor, a subcontractor may well find he has no lien rights to enforce. Similarly, bond notices must be filed on a timely basis, and the failure of the owner to pay allows bonding companies to challenge claims that otherwise would be accepted without question. To make matters worse, a subcontractor wishing to borrow against its receivables may find that the contingent-payment clause has precluded his doing so since the unpaid amount is not necessarily considered as due even though the subcontractor has completed his work to the satisfaction of all concerned.

Many subcontractors help their credit effort by clarifying in their contract

---

[1] *Thomas J. Dyer Co. v. Bishop International Engineering Co.*, 303 F.2d 661 (6th Cir. 1962). *Byler v. Great American Insurance Co.*, 395 F.2d 273 (10th Cir. 1968). *Moore v. Continental Casualty Co.*, 366 F Supp. 954 (W. D. Okla. 1973). *Howard-Green Electrical, Inc. v. Chaney & James Construction Co., Inc.*, 12 N.C. App. 63 (1971). *A. J. Wolfe Co. v. Baltimore Contractors, Inc.*, 355 Mass. 361 (1969).

[2] *Schuler-Haas Electric Corp. v. Aetna Casualty & Surety Co.*, 49 App. Div. 2d 60 (4th Dept. 1975), affirmed, 40 N.Y. 2d 883 (1976).

acceptance that the contingent payment provision applies only for a specific period of time, such as 60 or 90 days following proper submission of invoice and documentation.

In any event, the thoughtful subcontractor will check out the overall project financing as well as the credit standing of the general contractor since it is obvious that owner delays in payment can cause problems all down the line even under the best of contract conditions.

Replevin considerations and lien rights   In most industries, those extending credit rely on their ability to repossess as a form of at least partial security. The construction industry offers relatively little opportunity for replevin (recovery of goods) since much of the work becomes part of a structure making it difficult to remove without substantial damage to the freehold. Even after removal, such material often has limited value for reuse, and the value of labor to install and remove is difficult to recover. That general rule does not apply in all cases, however, inasmuch as elevators and other specific items have successfully been reclaimed on the basis that title is retained until payment is made. A number of court decisions in recent years have considered what constitutes proper notice to a creditor before repossession is allowed. Presently, the rules vary from state to state, so it is wise to know exactly what the replevin laws say for those states in which credit is extended.

Because of this limited opportunity for repossession of construction work, the law provides lien rights to protect the interests of those improving real property. The recording of a lien gives a measure of security, but practically all state laws allow a higher priority to the claims of mortgage lenders. From a credit standpoint, lien rights should be treated as a definite plus but not a substitute for credit worthiness. One should also take into account the fact that lien rights do not always apply on public projects.

Surety bonds   Surety bonds are commonly used in the construction industry to ensure the performance of contract work and the payment of obligations by a contractor or subcontractor. These are almost always required on public projects and provide good ultimate security inasmuch as the surety company stands in the shoes of the company it has bonded in the event of default by that company. However, when extending credit, bonds are a much better protection against bad-debt vulnerability than a means of ensuring prompt payment. Bond claims usually involve lengthy periods before eventual payment since the surety does not have an obligation to pay until it is demonstrated that the bonded party is unable to do so. Bond requirements call for precise steps to be followed on a timely basis in order for a claim to be valid. Even technical failure to follow notice provisions can result in either nonpayment or slow down the process. Once again, we have a plus factor but no panacea from a credit viewpoint.

Problems of general and prime contractors   The construction industry is unlike most others in that there are relatively few jobs, but each of those jobs usually involves a large amount of money. Thus, it is not usually possible to start out selling on a small basis and build up to larger-sized orders. Credit must often be evaluated for developers with little personal investment beyond some mortgaged real estate and a loan commitment that might suffice to build the project if all goes well.

We can see from the unfortunate experience of banks and real estate investment trusts that many projects were commenced in recent years with unbounded optimism that favorable economic conditions would continue indefinitely. In most cases, the money that was available gave out before contractors had been paid their last 10 to 20 percent. Since demand for construction is highly cyclical, contractors need to be extra watchful for signs of overbuilding.

Even in the case of public work, care must be taken to ensure that the contract does not unduly restrict payment liability. Some state and city projects have been stopped in mid-construction and payments deferred indefinitely for material fabricated and delivered but not in place. The person passing on credit need not become overly concerned about this in normal times, but it is a major consideration when bond markets dry up.

The current trend of general terms and conditions for construction contracts is to require that an owner supply evidence of financial adequacy prior to commencement of a project. This provides a good basis for a contractor insisting upon solid information as to the total anticipated cost and the source of funds to be used. For projects that seem the least bit marginal, this information should be sought even though the general conditions do not make it an obligation for the owner to furnish the data.

Changing role of general contractors   At one time general contractors performed much of their own work and supplemented that by subcontracting out specialized portions of projects. Some still follow that practice, but there has been an increasing trend during recent years for the general contractor to serve more in the role of manager or coordinator of a project and to subcontract practically all of the work called for in the technical specifications. Estimates of work being subcontracted vary from 50 to 80 percent, but all agree that the trend is toward even more subcontract work on general building construction projects.

This trend has had a major impact on the credit decision. First, it limits the amount of working capital required by a general contractor under normal conditions. This allows operators to set up in business with relatively little in the way of financial resources and without a major line of bank credit. Similarly, even well-established contractors have accustomed themselves to operating with limited cash and are not in a position to arrange readily for prompt payment to subcontractors if trouble develops.

It is not surprising, under the circumstances, that the failure rate in the construction industry is high. Because of this failure rate, subcontractors and material men must look particularly hard at the payment practices and worth of the general contractor even though the project as a whole is obviously well-funded. Remember that a contractor can suffer losses on other projects that would result in his default on all jobs.

There is no assurance of fair treatment by an owner to subcontractors when a general contractor fails. The owner may cite the fact that he has no direct contractual relationship with the subcontractors and may even be able to show that he made payments to the general contractor that were diverted.

This all boils down to the need for subcontractors to either satisfy themselves that the general contractor can be trusted to pay per contract terms or else to line up a system of joint or direct payments by the owner in the event of contractor default. Bear in mind that such arrangements can be made only with the acquiescence of the contractor as long as he remains solvent.

Retainage   The practice of retainage is unique to the construction industry. It consists of holding back a stated percentage from each progress payment to be paid upon completion of either the contractor's work or completion of the entire project, depending on contract terms in each instance. Many years ago, it was normal to retain 15 percent. Presently, it is rare to find retainage exceeding 10 percent. The trend now is for contracts to call for 10 percent retainage during the first half of a job with no further retainage thereafter. Many public jobs require only 5 percent, and several federal agencies, including the General Services Administration and Veterans Administration, have adopted no retainage policies.

What does this mean to the credit evaluators? Simply stated, it says that the higher the percentage of retainage, the more closely she or he needs to check out the credit worthiness of the customer and the project. The payment of retainage falls due after all work is complete and when collection leverage is at a minimum.

What can be done to improve the odds of collecting promptly? One of the best ways is to reach an understanding with the customer that all retainage will be paid no later than a specified time after substantial completion of work, that any reductions in percent of retainage to higher tiers will be reflected in progress payments and that issuance of change orders will not delay release of retainage under the base contract.

Contract and credit terms   Most construction firms think of their terms of payment as being relatively simple, such as net 30 days less retainage which is payable upon completion. However, we have already observed that various terms of payment are actually determined by the contract wording on an individual basis. Thus, while the person evaluating credit does not need to be expert in overall contract review, he or she should participate actively in the review of those provisions dealing with payments and terms that might limit the ability to collect promptly.

A checklist should be used to record credit terms included in each contract. This serves both as a reference tool in the credit evaluation process and also as a handy guide later on when reviewing billing and collection results. The list should include:

- Basis of retainage
- Contingent payment provision
- Payment for material delivered but not installed
- Deferral of final payment to completion of entire project
- Waiver of any lien rights
- Performance and payment bond requirements
- Any limitations related to public funding

In many instances, changes and clarifications can be arranged prior to execution of the contract for improvement of these terms and result in a more favorable credit evaluation.

Scarcity of reliable credit information   The peculiarities of the construction industry are nowhere more apparent than in the difficulty of securing meaningful credit experience and consistent financial statements.

Credit reports showing the payment experience are spotty at best and often fail to include retainage data or a comparison of the contractor's receipts versus payments on individual projects. If work progresses slowly, the delay is often glossed over by attributing it to disputes. Because construction work does not normally involve cash discounts and because conditional payment terms are common, a simple trade listing of experience reported is of limited value. It is also difficult to identify through credit reports which contractors make it a routine practice to hold back some of the monies paid to them covering subcontracted work for, say, 30 days' time after receipt of their checks from owners.

Financial statements in the construction industry must be reviewed with a full understanding of the reporting basis being used. Some contractors report their income on a completed-contract basis while others record their profit or loss progressively during the course of a construction job.

The completed-contract basis provides a more exact method for computing income since it relates actual cost to actual revenues for each job. The main distortion to watch for is in assessing year-by-year activity and profit. That is because a job might be sold in 1975, performed during 1976, 1977, and very early 1978, but the entire results will appear on the 1978 report.

On the other hand, contractors who record profit or loss progressively during the course of a job run the risk of over- or underestimating the amount of progress on the job as related to the cost incurred at any particular point. That can result in large income adjustments at the time of completion of the job if not done properly. Still, it does provide a generally good reading on the year-to-year activity.

Another consideration to keep in mind when reviewing contractors' financial statements is that unpaid retainage is not treated the same by all companies. Some do not count retainage as a receivable until the contract is complete. Others record retainage as a current asset throughout an entire project. Thus, one needs to know the accounting basis used by a contractor before being in a position to evaluate his statement. Certainly, retainage that is due and payable well in the future should not be considered as a strictly current asset, particularly if there is concern about the contractor's ready ability to pay in case the owner delays payment.

Even concerning accounts payable, one needs to know how much a contractor or owner owes for retainage as part of this figure in order to make a meaningful evaluation of his current obligations.

Similarly, net worth for a specific year may tell relatively little about profits taken during a given year. If the contractor is on a completed-contract basis, his income is deferred for the period necessary to complete all work. For those on a percentage-of-completion basis, errors can be made in estimating the extent of progress which can distort the profit that is taken periodically throughout the job. Thus, regardless of the accounting method a contractor uses, the primary evaluation of the customer's net worth should focus on long-range trends.

Many contractors generate working capital by billing more than the amount of their total costs during a project. This is most apparent during early stages of a job when opportunities for this front-end loading are usually available. The credit evaluator should never mistake this excess of billing over cost as being profit and should be wary of a big differential if the customer's volume of business is declining since it could foretell a coming squeeze on his working capital.

Difficulty in applying credit limits   Aside from those in the construction industry selling through distributors and agents, there is very little way of setting up a screening process whereby orders below a certain point are automatically passed for credit. We have observed earlier that credit terms will often vary from job to job, and we must also consider that the same general contractor working for a well-funded owner, such as a bank or major corporation, often has an entirely different payment pattern and general attitude toward his subcontractors and material suppliers than he does on a contract with a speculative developer.

Those companies using a system which involves a credit value or limit for a customer generally consider it to be simply a reference point to trigger special action rather than a point beyond which credit would be refused.

There is a practical question about what to do when one's company is bidding to many contractors, including a few who could not qualify for credit except by providing special security and/or favorable payment terms. The generally accepted practice is to bid to all and deal with the credit basis later on an individual basis if one of the marginal contractors gets the job.

Role of bankers   Some bankers have had a far better knowledge of how to finance and control their loans for automobiles, residences, and personal purposes than for the huge sums of money being invested by them in construction projects. Bank officials were often concerned more with theoretical rates of return on construction loans than on the critical need to ensure a pass-through of monies from themselves through the owner, then through the prime and general contractors on down to the lowest sub-subcontractor and material supplier on each job. As a result, staggering losses resulted from diversion of funds, and the banks frequently found themselves negotiating to complete projects by paying, in effect, twice for many portions of the work.

Bankers have learned a number of valuable lessons as a result of these experiences. Tighter controls now exist to prevent diversion of funds by owners, contractors, or subcontractors. At the same time banks have developed more expertise in evaluating the extent of job progress and in keeping their payments keyed to actual results. Many have opened lines of communication with members of the construction industry and are monitoring day-to-day operations to a much greater extent than ever before.

This is a healthy sign for the person responsible for credit extension in a construction company. It means that he or she can expect a more cooperative attitude on the part of bankers when payment problems arise on construction jobs. However, it would be too much to hope that all bankers will have changed their ways or that each of their loan officers now has a complete understanding of the vagaries of the construction industry. As a consequence, credit personnel in the construction industry should evaluate not only the adequacy of funds being loaned but also the controls that will be used to ensure that the funds will reach the company promptly each month and upon substantial completion. This is of particular importance on major projects where slowness of pay could have disastrous effects on cash flow.

Extras and change orders   It is important that signed orders be obtained for each extra or change order covering work performed beyond the scope of basic construction contract. The collectibility of charges for extras authorized only on a verbal basis is notoriously poor. All too often, attempts are made by contractors to set off extras with backcharges at the conclusion of a project. Hence, the better the evidence of agreement on extra work, the basis for payment and other conditions, the easier collection will be. Many contracts specifically state that all change orders must be signed by authorized representatives, so you should verify the authority of the signing party if you have any doubts.

OBTAINING CREDIT INFORMATION

No single source for credit information will suffice in each instance. As we shall see, there are limitations as to what can be obtained from any one party. Consequently, the credit investigation process is really an information-gathering effort that involves a blending of all information into a sufficiently meaningful picture to permit a reasoned decision. The decision-making process really begins as the information is being compiled, and by asking the right questions during investigation, the person evaluating the credit can often shorten the process by following through on loose ends or questionable items as soon as possible during the investigation stage.

Customer statements   One should not hesitate to ask searching questions of the customer about either his own finances or the funds that are to be borrowed from banks for the project. Customers recognize that they must give up their secrecy as a price for doing business on a credit basis. Since outside financing rarely, if ever, covers all the anticipated costs of a project, one must be assured that the owner, developer, contractor, and all parties through whom the funds must pass have adequate resources to pay. That must include a sufficient reserve to cover cost overruns and the effects of inflation.

Whether a contingency payment clause is involved or not, the failure of an owner or developer inevitably places major pressure on general and prime contractors. Thus, on those occasions when working as a subcontractor, discussions with the customer should include all aspects of financing the job and his own ability to honor commitments.

The key to obtaining adequate credit information lies in the matter-of-fact asking of the right questions. In effect, one is actually going into business with one's customers, and therefore it is necessary to know as much as possible about their financial resources. Questions will obviously vary according to the amount at stake and the track record of each customer. For all major projects, the questions should certainly include an identification of the customer's banking relations, any peculiarities in his financial statements, the ready availability of those funds he will be investing in the project, his contingency plans in case cost overruns are encountered, what restrictions—if any—are imposed on the drawing down of funds under his construction loans and conditions that must be met before his permanent financing takes effect. Follow-up questions need to be asked each time a potential problem arises or there is an area of doubt. These questions should center on what contingency plans have been developed.

The financial statements of customers in the construction industry must be reviewed with extreme caution. Often a developer will present a financial statement showing the bulk of his investment in real estate. It is all too easy for him to obtain several appraisals of value, but use only the highest to substantiate his equity. As a result, real estate may be valued far in excess of the price it would bring if sold under any but the most favorable conditions.

Naturally, it is helpful if a financial statement has been audited by a certified public accountant and includes an accountant's statement that it conforms to generally accepted accounting principles. However, the mere fact that a C.P.A. has certified the statement does not substitute for a searching analysis of the figures if there are any doubts about credit worthiness.

Also, be wary of the operator who insists on hand delivering his financial statement. He may be more concerned about avoiding a charge of using the mails to defraud than in expediting receipt of the information.

More information than usual is necessary if a special or dummy corporation is being set up for a particular project. Quite often, in such cases, an operator will place heavy emphasis on his personal credit record and that of his various operations. However, we need to keep constantly in mind that the very reason most such corporations are established is to limit liability in case the project fails. Thus, if the operator is sufficiently concerned to take this step, the person extending credit must be unusually cautious. It is altogether appropriate to explore the possibility of guarantees by the operator himself or one of his stronger business enterprises. These can be set up to apply automatically to all debts or can be of the delayed variety whereby the guarantee is conditional on failure to pay within an agreed time after such monies are scheduled according to contract terms.

As mentioned earlier in this chapter, financial statements of contractors are particularly difficult to evaluate without a good understanding of the methods used in recording contract profits as each job progresses. It is not necessary to be an accountant in order to see that certain items seem unusual on the year-by-year statements of a marginal customer, and questioning the customer about these items often leads to a much better understanding about his true financial condition.

Dun & Bradstreet and other credit information agencies The information received in most cases from these agencies varies. Reporters for the agencies vary greatly in their ability to ferret out meaningful information, ask penetrating questions, and follow up on loose ends. Still, there are certain areas where the information is helpful and others where there is a general weakness.

The reports are good for use in identifying the names and backgrounds of the principals, how long they have been in business, the number of employees, lien and uniform commercial code filings, any suits instituted against the business, prior bankruptcies of the principals, and certain general payment trends. In certain cases, particularly reports on large companies, there is enough information in support of net worth to be helpful.

On the other hand, agency reports for construction companies are generally short on meaningful data about payment practices related to release of retainage, backcharges, or other transactions peculiar to the construction industry. There is also a tendency in many cases for the reporter to accept the word of a construction operator for his worth and excuses for slow pay without any evidence of verification. In many cases, the payment experience reported is too sparse to be of real value in forming a reasoned opinion of the customer's paying habits.

One way to make these reports as meaningful and current as possible is to report one's experience to the agencies promptly so that agency representatives can investigate without delay.

For small orders, Dun & Bradstreet ratings will often suffice to allow one to ship material or perform a moderate amount of labor without further investigation. The record for reliability of these ratings is well-enough established that one should not hesitate to use them as a quick, inexpensive way of qualifying customers who seem to have more than enough worth for the size of the order involved. However, it is obviously not sufficient for any situation where the slightest doubt exists about the credit worthiness of a customer.

Increasingly, credit agencies are utilizing computers to speed up reports. For those construction companies who maintain computerized accounts receivable data, T.R.W. has inaugurated a National Credit Information System (NACIS) that offers excellent reports of recent payment experience.

Banks　Increasingly the single most important source of construction credit information is a banker. For that reason, it is vital to establish a good working relationship with one's banker for obtaining the specific financing information needed concerning a customer or a project. An important point to bear in mind is that the banker can often obtain more information than an individual because bankers are usually less reluctant to speak freely with others in the banking fraternity than with outsiders. Also, a banker can readily work through a system of correspondent banks to get the information quickly.

Once again, a key element is asking the right questions. Unless one insists upon specific answers about financing for a specific project, one may get a fast shuffle in the form of vague generalities such as "maintains account averaging balance in low five figures—relations satisfactory."

If you wish to ask the right questions, but do not have any specific potential problem in mind, there are forms available for this purpose. One of the best is that developed jointly by the National Association of Credit Management and Robert Morris Associates (Appendix A to this section). Personalizing the approach by direct contact or through inquiry by letter is possible.

Writing in *Credit and Financial Management* magazine, William Dornburgh suggested the following good questions: "Is the company profitable? What is the sales trend? Profit trend? What is the debt to worth ratio? Current ratio? What is the trend of balances carried with the bank? If it is a borrowing account, is it secured, and if so, what is the collateral? Have there been cleanups?"[3]

Another important question is one to determine if the credit relationship is supported by endorsements or guarantees.

In order to retain the trust and respect of one's banker, it is important to keep the information received strictly confidential and not to discuss it with the customer or others outside one's company.

For small companies, banks are often willing to help train an employee in credit analysis work and to set up special procedures for getting needed information on an expedited basis. Of course, the extent of bank services expected usually depends on the extent of bank relations with them. In most cases these relations will be adequate for reasonable bank help without specific cost.

In some instances, one may wish to contact the customer's bank directly. One should not hesitate to do this since it is in the customer's interest to demonstrate his financial status promptly through the bank he has given as his credit reference. In doing so, one should expect to share one's information and experience with the bank.

A word of caution is necessary about bank opinions of their customers. They are far from infallible, and one should not give undue emphasis to the data and experience they provide if it conflicts with reports from other sources. When doubts arise, even more specific questions to the bank can often provide the facts needed for a credit decision.

In writing to banks, enclose a stamped, self-addressed envelope, a clear identification of the project, the amount of credit involved, and a list of any parent companies involved. Also, we should help to avoid the complaints of banks that inquiries are received on well-established companies for small credit decisions.

A Code of Ethics for the Exchange of Information has been established by the Robert Morris Associates (see Appendix B) which spells out mutual obligations involved in a productive arrangement for the obtaining and supplying of credit information. All those concerned with inquiries to banks should be familiar with and follow its provisions.

Trade associations

National Association of Credit Management.   This association maintains an active system of credit interchange for its participating members with emphasis on ledger experience with respect to payment practices. There is active cooperation between local chapters which results in nationwide credit experience availability for companies dealing in many locations. Increasingly, NACM credit reports are being coordinated with the computerized NACIS system mentioned earlier. These written reports are supplemented by direct inter-

---

[3] "Approaching a Bank for Credit Information," *Credit and Financial Management,* September 1975.

change of past credit experience at various industrial trade meetings. That is particularly helpful in evaluating the credit worthiness of new accounts.

Besides local construction credit groups established in various localities, there is a National Construction Group which is composed of larger companies doing business in the construction industry. Its Improved Construction Practices Committee is most active in working toward more favorable contract terms, lien provisions, surety relationships, and laws governing credit. The committee issues periodic newsletters containing summaries of recent legislation, court decisions, and related developments affecting credit which are quite helpful to those making credit decisions for projects in many states.

American Subcontractors Association. Most local chapters of ASA have active credit interchange programs. While the formats vary by location, interchange procedures are similar and involve exchange of specific credit experience in the recent past. During these sessions, good as well as bad credit practices are reported. Participants are free to draw their own conclusions based on the facts. These sessions are almost always conducted with an attorney present who often provides advice to help avoid problem situations that come up during discussions of accounts.

Another helpful program offered by several ASA chapters is a credit referral service. The chapter maintains a file of subcontractors having had recent credit experience with each of the general contractors in the area. When an inquiry is received, the chapter refers the party to those having credit information. The actual exchange of past credit experience is then made directly between the two subcontractors.

Legal implications   Recent changes in the law require disclosure of sources of certain credit information if demanded by a party who has been refused credit. For that reason and to avoid any inference of concerted action, it is important that the giving and receiving of credit information be on a completely factual basis and limited to specific personal experience. The party providing the information should be particularly careful not to draw conclusions or impute motives. It is a case of sticking strictly to the facts. Naturally, there should be no discussion about credit attitudes relating to pending or future projects.

EFFECT OF SECURITY ON THE DECISION TO EXTEND CREDIT

We have seen that evaluating a customer for credit is often a matter of deciding the *basis* on which credit can be extended rather than being a simple yes or no choice. Thus, it is important to examine the various forms of special security that may be available when needed on a selected basis.

Guarantees   These become particularly important considerations in dealing with limited partnerships, dummy corporations, and other organizations established by individuals or firms having more worth than the business entity created. Until a new corporation has had time to establish a good payment record, there is every reason to expect the principals either to demonstrate that ample funding of a project exists or to guarantee to make good on contractual debts.

For those contractors, subcontractors, and suppliers who are in a position to stop work in the event of nonpayment on a project and thereby exert extreme pressure, the decision to extend credit might involve no more additional security than an understanding with an owner or parent company that a guarantee would be forthcoming if any payment problems developed. It is best to get this guarantee on an unequivocal basis at the time the contract is signed. A natural approach is to point out that the owner or parent company has the closest knowledge of the situation, and if no problem is foreseen, the guarantee should be given without any reluctance.

In dealing with personal guarantees, it is important to be sure that these would be enforceable in case of need. In this time of sheltered assets, the cosignature of a spouse may well be required to provide good security.

Payment bonds   A measure of security is provided by a surety bond obtained by the customer for a given project. For one thing, it means that the customer has passed certain bonding-company standards. Thus, in most cases he has convinced the surety of his basic worth and capacity since the bonding company would have to step into his shoes in the event of default by him. One word of caution, though. If the customer's bond has been guaranteed by the Small Business Administration, the requirement standards used by the surety company are understandably lower.

Credit evaluators should look upon payment bonds as a backstop rather than a substitute for good credit worthiness. At best, bond claims involve delays in payment and, at worst, losses due to failure to follow all the notice and claim requirements. Also, bonds are only as good as the sureties themselves; and there have been notable failures of bonding companies in recent years.

In case of doubt, the credit evaluator should request a copy of the bond to confirm the stature of the bonding company and identify the claim requirements and restrictions that are involved.

Credit insurance   The ability of a creditor to pass along all or part of his credit risk is an asset available to him in many forms through credit insurance. The common denominators involved here are avoidance of catastrophies and utilization of professional specialists.

Credit insurance is a reasonable consideration for a small operator who finds himself spending a disproportionate amount of time on credit and collections whereas his strong suits are sales and construction operations. Naturally, it can relieve him of credit decisions or limit these to sales under a set amount.

One consideration is that a contractor can easily get out of touch with many facets of the business. Similarly, a false sense of confidence can develop when only a portion of credit losses is insured. One last point is that the cost of credit insurance is, over the long haul, influenced heavily by loss experience, so the contractor must continue to be concerned about the quality of credit risk taken.

Bank guarantees   With the consent of a customer, banks and other lending institutions are often agreeable to a set-aside of the contract amount in exchange for payment of a 1-percent fee. This has the obvious advantage of substituting the net worth of the bank for that of the customer. However, the payment of a fee represents an unnecessary cost if a fully creditworthy customer is involved.

One very practical consideration must also be taken into account before deciding to go the route of a bank guarantee in lieu of the normal extension of credit. That is the later problem of obtaining timely release of payments. Usually, the bank insists upon contractor approval before making progress or final payments. Since the bank benefits from delay of payment, the contractor can take advantage of the situation to get favors in exchange for his approval of a requisition.

All in all, this is a solution of limited value, but one that might just fit the bill where the selling price is especially favorable and the decision to extend credit is a particularly tough one.

Notes   The acceptance of notes should be considered with great care. Ordinarily, a decision about notes does not arise until collection problems have already occurred. However, notes can occasionally be utilized to provide added security throughout the job. The notes often apply only to a portion of the job where payment is being deferred beyond normal due dates.

The primary advantage of a note is that additional parties can be made responsible for payment of the note amount, and interest can be obtained.

There are some practical problems. The party or parties may have practically no assets that can be attached in case that becomes necessary. Also, the note represents satisfaction of the debt until it becomes payable. Thus if the job starts to go sour, one may find that one has no leverage such as stopping work or filing liens until the note matures.

This solution should be limited to those situations where the credit worthiness of the customer is unmistakably and markedly improved by the acceptance of notes.

Assignments and joint check arrangements   At times a contractor or owner can be persuaded to authorize either assignments or joint check arrangements whereby one can receive protection against diversion of the funds advanced by the source of financing for a project. Because of the obvious administrative problems imposed on lending institutions, these practices are not common, but they do provide a positive means for a lender to ensure that the proper flowthrough of funds is taking place.

IMPORTANT CHARACTERISTICS NEEDED BY CONSTRUCTION CREDIT DECISION MAKERS

Characteristics of contractors   Generally, successful contractors tend to be hard-nosed business people, optimistic about the risks they take, having strong desires to run their own businesses and maintain full control of projects. They are normally frank in discussing differences and quite knowledgeable about construction operations. Most are far more comfortable dealing with operating problems than financial and contract matters. However, they are usually quite able to negotiate appropriate terms.

Contractors have had to adapt to severe gyrations in construction volume, the risks inherent in job delays due to weather, shortages, or strikes, and the difficulty of estimating costs accurately. It is an industry where one large losing job can wipe out a business, and many undercapitalized contractors are tempted to venture over their heads.

Attributes needed by persons involved in extending credit   Against this backdrop of tough characteristics, it is apparent that the party who is responsible for credit evaluation must have a thorough knowledge of both his particular business and the construction industry generally.

The person responsible for approving credit needs a reasonable knowledge of finance in order to interpret figures from statements, plus the tact to ask the right questions, and persuasion to sell customers on terms that are fair to both parties. In making judgments, the difference between unique circumstances and temporary expedients must be recognized and acted upon positively. For the obvious reason, the person approving credit should have responsibility as well for later results in attempts at collection and bad-debt costs.

While tact is needed in obtaining credit information and arranging for special payment terms, it is vital that credit personnel have the courage of their convictions and be at their best during forthright discussions with customers. Contractors are accustomed to vigorous exchanges and are quick to seize upon any lack of sincerity or goodwill during negotiations. Time is usually limited during meetings with customers. Credit representatives therefore should be able to make their points directly and gain respect by demonstrating a good grasp of industry practices and an awareness of any peculiarities of the job in question and the needs and problems of the customer himself.

These attributes apply whether the task is performed by a highly professional credit manager or one who must wear many hats in a smaller contracting company. Irrespective of organization, credit policies must evolve based on each individual company's own credit experience. A big determinant of long-term profitability will be success in arriving at credit policies and practices which strike a necessary balance between the potential profit from sales as against money lost through bad debts or tied up by slow payments.

The key is to select and train persons willing to take reasonable risks, who will understand the vagaries of the construction industry, have demonstrated the courage of their convictions, speak and write effectively, and who have acquired the resourcefulness so necessary for working in an industry having few pat answers.

Long Form

REQUEST FOR BANK CREDIT INFORMATION

FORM 19

rma

(This form approved by the Robert Morris Associates and the National Association of Credit Management. Published by the National Association of Credit Management.)

TO:

Bank _____

Address _____

City/State/Zip _____

ACCOUNT

Name _____

Address _____

City/State/Zip _____

Will you please provide bank credit information on this account as requested below? Our inquiry has been prepared in accordance with the principles in the exchange of credit information adopted by Robert Morris Associates and the National Association of Credit Management. Information is requested for use in the extension of credit for *business purposes only* and will be held in strict confidence.

Very truly yours,

Company _____   Signed By _____

Address _____   Title _____

City/State/Zip _____   Date _____

Purpose
- ☐ Initial order $ _____ , anticipated requirements $ _____
- ☐ Established customer, increased requirements to $ _____
- ☐ Change in payment experience from _____ to _____
- ☐ Other: _____

Reference
- ☐ Banks with _____
- ☐ Your bank has been given as a reference.
- ☐ We are checking with other area banks and information from your file only will suffice.
- ☐ Bank unknown.

Our Experience

Sold Since _____   Amount Owing $ _____

Last Sale $ _____   Past Due $ _____

High Credit $ _____   Terms _____

Our File
- ☐ Current NACM and/or mercantile agency reports ☐ Trade clearances
- ☐ Financial statement dated _____
- ☐ Other _____

Comment: _____

Information Requested

☐ Loans:	Amount	security	endorsements	pay experience
	$ _____	_____	_____	_____
	$ _____	_____	_____	_____
	$ _____	_____	_____	_____

- ☐ Financial Statement Information: Balance sheet and operating figures for year ended _____ or interim _____ .
- ☐ Deposits: Average balances, how handled _____

- ☐ Other: _____
_____

Bank signature _____

Date _____   Title _____

(BANK COPY)

APPENDIX B

ESTABLISHED 1914

ROBERT MORRIS ASSOCIATES

The National Association of Bank Loan Officers and Credit Men

CODE OF ETHICS
FOR THE EXCHANGE OF INFORMATION

Preamble

The Robert Morris Associates, recognizing the importance and value of the interchange of credit information in the conduct of business, adopted (1916) the following code of credit ethics and urges its use in order to maintain the exchange of credit information on the confidential and ethical basis that this phase of credit activity warrants and requires.

The Code

1. The first and cardinal principle in credit investigation is to respect the confidential nature of the information received.

2. The name of the inquirer, in whose behalf the inquiry is made, should not be disclosed without permission.

3. In answering inquiries, the source of the information should not be disclosed without permission.

4. Any betrayal of confidence stamps the offender unworthy of future consideration.

5. Each letter of inquiry should indicate specifically the object and scope of the inquiry.

6. When more than one inquiry on the same subject is sent simultaneously to banks it should be indicated that information from their own files is sufficient as other checkings are being made.

7. All letters, including form letters, should bear the manual signature of the inquirer to establish responsibility.

8. The recipient of a credit inquiry is negligent in his duty if he does not read carefully each letter of inquiry and answer frankly, to the best of his ability, its specific questions.

9. In answering inquiries, it is advisable to disclose all material facts bearing on the credit standing of the subject, including the basis upon which credit is extended.

10. Indiscriminate revision of files, when there is no real need for information, is wasteful and undesirable.

11. Where periodic revision of file information is made, it may be desirable to give your own experience in the letter of inquiry, in order that duplication and unnecessary correspondence may be kept to a minimum.

12. In soliciting accounts, it is not permissible nor the part of good faith for the soliciting bank to make inquiries from a competitor without frankly disclosing the nature and object of the inquiry.

This code was originally adopted in 1916, revised in 1921, 1948 and again in 1954.
Copyrighted: Free use is permitted with proper credit.

Chapter **12**

Maintaining Favorable
Credit Ratings

JAMES J. CRENNER
President, Dun & Bradstreet, Inc., New York, New York

THE CONSTRUCTION INDUSTRY AND THE CREDIT WORLD

Open the *Dun & Bradstreet Reference Book* and columns of ratings greet the eye: 5A1, 1A3, DC4, GG2,--. Subscribe to the D&B's Change Notification Service and discover that *Reference Book* notations change fast in the workaday world. For every 1,000 businesses, D&B records seven major changes (rating changes, discontinuances, changes in ownership or control) every week.

Examine Key Business Ratios and find that the median ratio of net profits (after taxes) on net sales for general building contractors in 1975 was 1.18. That means that for every $100 of construction revenue, the contractor realizes $1.18 profit. However, accompany any of D&B's 2,000 reporters on their rounds (together, reporters make 20,000 interviews each day; on average 2,000 will be with business people in the construction industry) and quickly, you will become acquainted with the endless variety of people, personalities, and problems that lie behind the figures.

The world of credit holds the world of business in its grasp. Compare short-term bank loans outstanding in 1974 of $130 billion to accounts and notes payable of $276.6 billion in 1976. Remember that there is not enough cash in the world to cover daily business transactions now handled on credit. Finally, when you consider that the construction industry, unlike 95 percent of America's 5 million businesses, touches every other business operation, the importance of maintaining a favorable credit rating—and the healthy business that rating presupposes—has paramount importance for all of us.

Failures in the Construction Industry

Given the influence of the construction industry on the national economy and countless suppliers across the country, the trend in construction failures causes considerable concern.

Number of construction failures   Construction failures climbed in 1975 to 2,262, an eight-year high. Total business failures also hit an eight-year high of 11,432. However, the construction upswing was steeper, 23 percent, as opposed to 15 percent in all types of operation. Casualties of construction contractors comprised 19.8 percent of total failures in 1975, up from 15.2 percent in 1974, and the largest portion in two decades.

Construction failure liabilities   Continuing to break records for the sixth straight year, the dollar amount of liabilities for all business failures surged 43 percent to a new peak of $4.4 billion. In contrast, the rise in liabilities incurred in construction failures was considerably milder, 22 percent, but did lift construction losses to $640.8 million, a new high for the industry. Construction accounted for 14.6 percent of total failure liabilities, appreciably less than the 25.6 percent slice in 1967. These comparisons were influenced greatly by the largest single bankruptcy in a nonconstruction entity featuring liabilities of $1.03 billion or 23.5 percent of total failure dollars for the year. Excluding this big bankruptcy from total liabilities in the United States construction accounted for 19.1 percent of the liabilities, still less than 1967's 25.6 percent.

Breakdown of construction failures   Subcontractors generally comprise a little over one-half of construction failures: It was 53 percent in both 1975 and 1965. However, the subcontractors appear to have been less severely affected by the recession than the general builders. In 1975, their casualties increased by 17 percent over 1974's figures, whereas the total among general builders swelled at almost twice that rate, 32 percent. While subcontractor failures in 1975 were running one-fifth lower than their record of 1,520 set in 1961, general builder failures came within 3 percent of equalling their peak of 847 in 1965.

Large construction failures   In 1965, more than one-third of the construction failures had liabilities under $25,000; the segment owing $100,000 or more amounted to one-fifth. By 1975, the tables had turned. The $100,000-plus group was up to 36.7 percent and the $25,000-or-less group was down to 21.7 percent.

Risk, Ratings, and Dun & Bradstreet

Obviously, suppliers selling the building trades run risks because the construction industry itself runs risks—risks associated with all business enterprises as well as hazards more peculiar to contracting than to any other line of business endeavor. These hazards are that:

1. Contracting is cyclical and seasonal.
2. Contracting is subject to the direct hazards of weather and performance of other contractor trades.
3. Contracting is subject to low profit margins—about the lowest of all industries except, perhaps, the food industry.
4. In contracting, frequently the entire capital of the business is risked on one big job.
5. In contracting, money is sometimes tied up through no fault of the contractor.

Wise suppliers anticipate risks and plan accordingly. Others, like a certain tile contractor, can be caught short. The tile contractor had been going along for years with no appreciable losses and then, suddenly, two doubtful accounts turned up with an aggregate loss possibility of $15,000. A representative of this contractor, in telling what happened, acted as though nothing like this had ever taken place before—anywhere.

However, unexpected losses can always occur. Take the case of a New Jersey builder who filed a petition in bankruptcy. He was an established builder, putting up houses for fifteen years. Although the latest financial details were not available, outwardly the company seemed in pretty good shape.

At least creditors were reporting the account "prompt pay," almost to the time the petition was filed. The business ran into a series of problems. There were lengthy construction delays. Lumber costs proved to be well above his original estimates. The housing market hit bottom by the time the homes were finished and only a few were sold. Construction loans and some other temporary borrowings helped him pay promptly for a while. But the big factor was that the three largest suppliers either reported the account "prompt" or did not furnish paying experience. The business was "delinquent" with all of them, but they were not telling each other about the slowness, let alone anyone else.

Of more concern are those situations where the credit risk is not weighed carefully. The contractor is not investigated properly in advance, and losses result. Such cases, and they are not rare at all, point out an important truth: Sellers are geared to sell. Buyers are geared to buy. Neither group is impartial; neither has a full ability to act without emotion. Only an impartial agency, with no financial involvement in sales transactions, can accumulate relevant information, appraise it impartially and communicate it with discretion to concerns having a legitimate need to know.

In the case of the construction industry, Dun & Bradstreet functions as this impartial agency, providing information to building trades suppliers, general contractors, subcontractors, banks, and insurance and bonding companies. The information Dun & Bradstreet provides, as well as the ratings which sum it up, is simply what this group of subscribers desire in those reports.

The Dun & Bradstreet business information report   In Figure 12.1, a sample D&B report on a construction company illustrates the six major sections of a typical report.

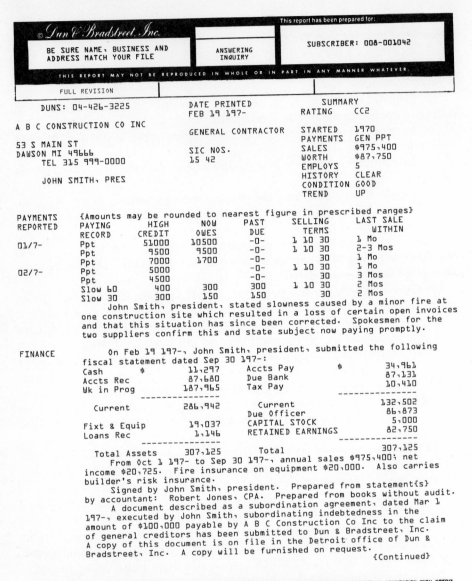

Fig. 12.1 Sample Dun & Bradstreet Business Information Report. This fictionalized report was prepared by Dun & Bradstreet, Inc. for purposes of illustration only. Used with permission.

Summary.   The Summary which introduces the report provides a concise analysis, with basic identification of the business, the business' U.S. Standard Industrial Classification code for product line and function, D-U-N-S Number (unique for every establishment in the D&B files), principal executive, line of business, year business started or came under present control, and Dun &

		This report has been prepared for:
BE SURE NAME, BUSINESS AND ADDRESS MATCH YOUR FILE	ANSWERING INQUIRY	SUBSCRIBER: 008-001042

FULL REVISION	
	PAGE 2

WORK IN PROGRESS: CONTR AMOUNT   % COMP   COMP DATE   TYPE OF BOND
Cumberland Farms $ 250,000   50   4/7-   None
Inc. Dawson MI
    Business is trading actively on the equity invested but use of long-term bank loans and subordinated long-term loans from an officer provides adequate funds for prompt retirement of obligations. Trade comments are generally favorable with slowness explained by a temporary problem. Subject is an established concern run by experienced management and has shown a progressive trend.

BANKING
02/7-
    Bank reports account opened Feb 197-. Balances average high five figures. Loans granted on an unsecured basis with medium five figures outstanding. Account is satisfactory. A second bank reports account opened Jan 197-. Balances average high three figures. Account is routine, non-borrowing and satisfactory.

HISTORY
JOHN SMITH, PRES   JANE SMITH, SEC
ROBERT JONES, TREAS
DIRECTORS: The officers
    Incorporated Michigan Jan 10 1970. Authorized capital consists of 200 shares common stock, no par value. Starting capital $5000 derived from $5000 savings.
    Each of the three officers holds 1/3 of the outstanding capital stock.
    SMITH born 1930 married. 1951-1960 was employed by New York Construction Co., 10 Myrtle St. Brooklyn NY as assistant superintendent. 1960-1970 was employed by Dawson Construction Corp., 230 E 40th St. Dawson MI as job superintendent. 1970 started subject concern.
    JANE SMITH born 1935. Is the wife of the president and not active in subject concern.
    JONES born 1933 married. Is a certified public accountant with offices at 2 Main St. Dawson MI and is not active in day-to-day activities of subject.
PERFORMANCE RECORD   LOCATION   VALUE   COMP DATE
Broadway Toy Co   3500 Broadway $ 725,000   197-
1300 1st Ave Realty Inc.   1300 1st Ave.   750,000   197-
Dawson 9th St. Realty Inc.   300 9th St.   665,000   197-
    FIRE RECORD: Sustained loss as result of a minor fire in October 197- at a job site office.

OPERATION
    Contractor specializing in commercial construction. Construction financed through short-term bank loans and subordinated long-term loans. Subject contracts 75% of work to others. Contracts are obtained through bidding 100%. Terms are progress payments 50%. Retainages, if any, generally 10%.
EMPLOYEES: 5 including officers. Number of employees varies widely according to work on hand.
FACILITIES: Rents on 1st floor of 3 story office building in good condition.
LOCATION: Central business section on side street.
10/12-353   /62   39524/01   0000 1 001   F
Dawson National Bank, Main St., First National Bank, Promenade St.

Bradstreet's capital and credit rating. This section summarizes all information obtained, usually including payments, sales, worth, number of employees, history, condition, and trend. Briefly, the summary condenses relevant facts for the credit or sales executive and highlights for review much of the important information detailed in the narrative that follows.

Payments.   Obtained via computer tapes from companies with automated accounts receivable systems (as well as manually from those hundreds of thousands of companies without computerized systems), payments show how the business pays its bills, as reported by suppliers. This section includes payments as of a given month and year, paying record, high credit, amounts owing and past due (if any), selling terms, and period of last sale.

From this section, a supplier intending to open a new account receives an historical indication of the contractor's previous paying habits based on the financial condition prevalent at the time the obligations were paid.

Finance.   Finance includes essential facts for determining the financial condition and trend of a business. Most reports contain financial information which may represent audited figures prepared by a certified public accountant (with or without qualification in the accountant's opinion); unaudited figures from the books of account (not prepared by an outside accountant); or management's own estimate of assets, liabilities, sales, expense, and profit. In any event, no audit is conducted by Dun & Bradstreet, Inc. Principals of some concerns decline to furnish detailed figures, and financial figures may therefore be based on bank and supplier comment, investigation of public records or the D&B business analysts' estimates of certain balance-sheet items.

Of key importance in reports on the building trades is the Work in Progress section. Here, D&B provides the name of the job, the contract amount, the percent completed, scheduled completion date, and type of bond.

Although it is virtually impossible to provide coverage of all public record information, an effort is made in the finance section to provide information regarding suits, judgments (or releases from same), Uniform Commercial Code filings and rulings of regulatory agencies. Financial information is also frequently supplemented with information regarding leases, insurance coverage, and other pertinent details. Comment in this section is devoted to further necessary explanation of the figures and a description of sales and profit trends. The D&B rating is based to a large extent upon the degree of financial stability and the trend as reflected in this section.

Banking.   In this section, information concerning banking relations may include indication of average balances, previous and current loan experience, whether loans are secured or unsecured, length of time the bank has had the account, and whether or not the bank considers the account satisfactory. In some instances, names of some or all banks of account are provided, though not necessarily in order of importance.

History.   The names, ages, and past business experience of the principals or owners of a concern are provided in the history section. This information is obtained from management of the business on which the report is written. Past business experience and outside affiliations of principals are important considerations in evaluating management. In the case of prior business affiliations, D&B files are utilized where feasible to verify and augment the information provided by management. Other background information is sometimes verified but that is not usually the case. Criminal proceedings of which D&B learns are reported. Those resulting in convictions are reported indefinitely, but in other instances, the information is ultimately eliminated from reports when the span of time dilutes its significance and relevancy.

There are a number of important uses for this history section including verifying ownerships; identifying owners, partners, or officers; and revealing outside interests of the principals.

Of particular interest to building trades suppliers is the Performance Record of those reported upon. D&B reports the name of the job, location, value, and completion date.

Operation.   For contractors, the operation section describes the type of construction in which the firm is engaged as well as the method of financing. Subcontracting arrangements are reported. In addition to other details, D&B provides the number of employees, facilities, and location.

By describing the machinery of production and other operation information, this section helps give the reader of the report a better understanding of the balance sheet and of the profit and loss figures. Knowing the principal operating features, the reader is better able to judge whether capital is adequate or debt excessive.

The Dun & Bradstreet rating   D&B business analysts, or reporters, have the responsibility of assembling all available information regarding the subject and of evaluating and summarizing it in the form of a D&B rating. As can be seen in Figure 12.2, the rating is divided into two sections: the Estimated Financial Strength rating (running from HH, up to $4,999, to 5A, over $50 million) describes the financial stability of the firm as evidenced by its financial figures, particularly tangible net worth. The Composite Credit Appraisal rating, running from 1 (high) to 4 (limited), represents the reporter's judgment as to the company's commitment and ability to pay its trade bills within terms. This latter half of the D&B rating raises most questions as to how a high rating can be maintained. In this connection, the criteria for establishing this rating will be of interest.

Criteria Considered in Assigning Ratings.   In general—but there are always exceptions and unusual cases—reporters consider the following when determining the composite credit appraisal of a subject:

1. *Sound legal constituency of organization, with adequate evidence of ownership.* Legal structure, of course, determines the resources open to creditors in the case of financial embarrassment. Personal resources of partners (in a partnership) or a proprietor (in a sole proprietorship) are available unless otherwise attached.

Ownership becomes a vital concern in that only the owners of a business are legally responsible for paying the debts of the firm. If the supplier cannot establish who the owners are, he cannot establish their ability to pay their bills or their commitment to paying bills as demonstrated by past performance. Ownership, moreover, is not as obvious as it might seem. Is Johnson's Hardware owned by old Joe Johnson? Not at all. It is owned by the A-1 Corporation. First Street Lumber Yard may be owned by First Street Realty Corp., the subsidiary of a company with headquarters thousands of miles away.

Joint ventures offer particular hazards to the building trades. Legal responsi-

Key to Ratings

ESTIMATED FINANCIAL STRENGTH			COMPOSITE CREDIT APPRAISAL			
			HIGH	GOOD	FAIR	LIMITED
5A	Over	$50,000,000	1	2	3	4
4A	$10,000,000 to	50,000,000	1	2	3	4
3A	1,000,000 to	9,999,999	1	2	3	4
2A	750,000 to	999,999	1	2	3	4
1A	500,000 to	749,999	1	2	3	4
BA	300,000 to	499,999	1	2	3	4
BB	200,000 to	299,999	1	2	3	4
CB	125,000 to	199,999	1	2	3	4
CC	75,000 to	124,999	1	2	3	4
DC	50,000 to	74,999	1	2	3	4
DD	35,000 to	49,999	1	2	3	4
EE	20,000 to	34,999	1	2	3	4
FF	10,000 to	19,999	1	2	3	4
GG	5,000 to	9,999	1	2	3	4
HH	Up to	4,999	1	2	3	4

CLASSIFICATION BASED ON BOTH ESTIMATED FINANCIAL STRENGTH AND COMPOSITE CREDIT APPRAISAL

FINANCIAL STRENGTH BRACKET

1 Over $125,000

2 20,000 to 125,000

EXPLANATION

When only the numeral (1 or 2) appears, it is an indication that the estimated financial strength, while not definitely classified, is presumed to be within the range of the ($) figures in the corresponding bracket and while the composite credit appraisal cannot be judged precisely, it is believed to be "High" or "Good."

"INV." shown in place of a rating indicates that the report was under investigation at the time of going to press. It has no other significance.

"FB" (Foreign Branch). Indicates that the headquarters of this company is located in a foreign country (including Canada). The written report contains the location and rating of the headquarters.

ABSENCE OF RATING DESIGNATION FOLLOWING NAMES LISTED IN THE REFERENCE BOOK

The absence of a rating, expressed by two hyphens (--), is not to be construed as unfavorable but signifies circumstances difficult to classify within condensed rating symbols. It suggests the advisability of obtaining a report for additional information.

ABSENCE OF A LISTING IN THE REFERENCE BOOK

The absence of a listing is not to be construed as meaning a concern is non-existent, has discontinued business, nor does it have any other meaning. The letters "NQ" on any written report mean "not listed in the Reference Book." The letters "FBN" on any written report also mean that the business is not listed in the Reference Book and that the headquarters is located in a foreign country.

EMPLOYEE RANGE DESIGNATIONS IN REPORTS ON NAMES NOT LISTED IN THE REFERENCE BOOK

Certain businesses do not lend themselves to a Dun & Bradstreet rating and are not listed in the Reference Book. Information on these names, however, continues to be stored and updated in the D&B Business Information File. Reports are available on these businesses but instead of a rating they carry an Employee Range Designation (ER) which is indicative of size in terms of number of employees. No other significance should be attached.

KEY TO EMPLOYEE RANGE DESIGNATIONS

ER 1	Over 1000 Employees
ER 2	500-1000 Employees
ER 3	100 - 499 Employees
ER 4	50 - 99 Employees
ER 5	20 - 49 Employees
ER 6	10 - 19 Employees
ER 7	5 - 9 Employees
ER 8	1 - 4 Employees
ER N	Not Available

Fig. 12.2 Copyrighted © 1977 by Dun & Bradstreet, Inc. Used with permission.

bility is similar to that of partnerships and, in most court decisions, the law of partnerships is applied. The contract of joint venture should show the intent of the contractors and will use appropriate words to bind the promisors to complete the whole of the obligation—either together or separately, if one or the other fails to perform. The fact that joint venturers often do not realize they have actually formed a joint venture, subject to special laws, makes careful investigation of such a situation essential.

2. *Seasoning and maturity of business management experience.* For business in general—and the construction industry is no exception—the greatest single cause of failure is incompetence. Unbalanced experience (experience not well rounded in sales, finance, purchasing, and production) accounts for the second highest percentage of failures, followed by lack of experience in the line or lack of experience in management. Table 12.1 shows how these factors, and others, affected the construction industry compared with all other industries in 1975.

It takes time, moreover, to acquire proper management attributes. One-half of the construction businesses failing in 1975 were only in their first five years of operation (exactly the same percentage as in 1965). Neophyte contractors had somewhat easier going in 1970 when they comprised 44 percent of the total and the construction boom was getting under way. Construction firms active for ten or more years at time of failing lightened slightly, in 1975, to 21.8 percent (from 25.9 percent in 1970) indicating their years in management may have toughened them to survive the severe slump in building.

3. *A record of reasonably profitable operations and growth in retained earnings, reflected, at least to some degree, in working capital.* No company can earn a supplier's confidence if it is not operating profitably or has not operated profitably in the past. Earnings retained in the business provide protection to creditors. Increased working capital assists the means for prompt payment of bills as they come due.

4. *Proper balances in the condition of liquid assets and position of debts in relation to business equity.* The typical ratio of current debt to tangible net worth for general building contractors was 133.8 in 1975. (See Table 12.7.) One-fourth had a ratio higher than that; another fourth had a lower ratio. Ordinarily, a business begins to pile up trouble when this relationship exceeds 80 percent.

As for total debt to tangible net worth, the typical 1975 ratio for general building contractors was 234.0. Again one-fourth of the contractors surveyed had a higher ratio; another fourth had a lower one. However, since the equity of creditors in the assets of the business exceeds that of owners when this relationship exceeds 100 percent, the construction industry as a whole shows a high degree of creditor risk. Moreover, general building contractors rarely display the 2-to-1 ratio of current assets to current debt, a relationship considered most desirable in most industries. The median is 1.43; the upper quartile is 1.77 and the lower quartile is 1.23.

5. *A management record clear of past business blemishes in the form of frequent suits, judgments, former bankruptcies.* A clear public record indicates in a broad way the likelihood of integrity and capability in everyday business dealings.

TABLE 12.1 Causes of 11,432 Business Failures in 1975

Percent (underlying)						Underlying causes	Due to†	Apparent causes†	Percent (apparent)					
Manufac-turers	Whole-salers	Retailers	Construc-tion	Commercial services	All				Manufac-turers	Whole-salers	Retailers	Construc-tion	Commercial services	All
0.8	0.8	1.2	1.0	1.0	1.1	Neglect	Due to	Bad habits	0.3	0.3	0.5	0.4	0.3	0.4
								Poor health	0.3	0.3	0.2	0.4	0.2	0.3
								Marital difficulties	—	—	0.1	0.1	0.2	0.1
								Other	0.2	0.2	0.4	0.1	0.3	0.3
0.6	1.2	0.5	0.3	0.4	0.5	Fraud	On the part of the principals, reflected by	Misleading name	0.1	—	—	—	—	0.0
								False financial statement	0.1	0.4	0.2	0.1	—	0.1
								Premeditated overbuy	0.1	0.3	0.1	—	—	0.1
								Irregular disposal of assets	0.2	0.5	0.2	0.2	0.2	0.2
								Other	0.1	—	0.0	—	0.2	0.1
14.2	14.0	20.4	12.7	17.1	16.9	Lack of experience in the line	Evidenced by inability to avoid conditions which resulted in	Inadequate sales	56.0	54.8	52.4	45.7	48.8	51.3
11.5	12.2	13.9	15.7	13.3	13.7	Lack of managerial experience		Heavy operating expenses	17.4	16.3	14.7	16.6	16.4	15.9
19.9	21.2	21.9	21.1	19.9	21.1	Unbalanced experience*		Receivables difficulties	17.5	18.1	3.8	13.4	6.9	9.5
48.5	47.0	37.7	42.4	38.7	41.2	Incompetence		Inventory difficulties	8.8	12.9	12.3	1.7	1.8	8.3
								Excessive fixed assets	4.6	1.0	2.0	1.9	3.7	2.5
								Poor location	1.0	1.6	5.9	0.8	2.9	3.4
								Competitive weakness	16.9	18.1	23.3	26.5	21.6	22.3
								Other	2.1	2.0	1.2	3.1	1.4	1.8
2.1	0.9	0.9	1.1	0.3	1.0	Disaster	Some of these occurrences could have been provided against through insurance	Fire	0.5	0.3	0.5	0.1	0.1	0.4
								Flood	—	—	0.0	0.1	0.1	0.0
								Burglary	—	—	0.1	—	—	0.0
								Employees' fraud	—	0.1	—	—	—	0.0
								Strike	—	0.1	—	0.1	—	0.0
								Other	1.6	0.4	0.3	0.8	0.1	0.6
2.4	2.7	3.5	5.7	9.3	4.5	Reason unknown		Reason unknown						
100.0	100.0	100.0	100.0	100.0	100.0	Total								
1,645	1,089	4,799	2,262	1,637	11,432	Number of failures		Percent of total failures	14.4	9.5	42.0	19.8	14.3	100.0
$620,431	$370,034	$382,561	$283,307	$290,461	$383,150	Average liabilities per failure								

*Experience not well rounded in sales, finance, purchasing, and production on the part of the individual in case of a proprietorship, or of two or more partners or officers constituting a management unit.

†Because some failures are attributed to a combination of apparent causes, the totals of these columns exceed the totals of the corresponding columns on the left.

NOTE: Classification failures based on opinion of informed creditors and information in Dun & Bradstreet reports.

SOURCE: Compiled by the Business Economics Division, Dun & Bradstreet, Inc. Copyrighted © 1976 and used with permission.

6. *A uniform and up-to-date record of meeting obligations in accordance with preagreed terms* is indicative of a contractor's desire to pay promptly provided the financial position so permits.

Weighing the Criteria.   A business that meets all the above criteria would certainly earn a high composite credit appraisal rating. A business might be slightly deficient in some—though not all—of the foregoing standards and still be assigned a rating of "high credit." Generally, however, reporters do not deviate from the requirement that management be clear of relatively recent entanglement with the law or business failure. There have been notable exceptions demonstrating the ability of contractors to prosper anew after experiencing setbacks. For example, two companies which grew into highly respected and successful multimillion-dollar enterprises from humble beginnings were founded by men who launched their careers after serving prison terms. Ultimately, the companies were acquired in mergers. Each carried a high credit rating at the time of the merger.

Where a moderate deficiency in one standard or slight deficiency in several standards occurs, placing the overall appraisal just below the highest relative credit standing, the composite credit appraisal would be in the second, or "good credit" column.

Where there is *substantial* deficiency in one or more of the criteria described, the composite credit appraisal will be in the third, or "fair credit" column or fourth, "limited credit" column.

Insufficient Information.   Whatever the strengths or weaknesses of the contractor, there is no surer route to a blank rating (symbolized by two hyphens: --) than failure to provide adequate information, particularly financial information, for analysis. Compare the complete information shown in the report in Figure 12.1 with the lack of details in the report in Figure 12.3. In the former, a rating of CC2 has been assigned, and credit executives and other business people reviewing the report can proceed quickly to a sound decision. In the case of the latter, additional effort will have to be expended by report readers, if they are so inclined, before a decision can be reached. That means additional work for ABC Construction as well: supplying individual financial statements to every supplier, bonding and insurance company, and bank; answering numerous questions about past performance and payment record; explaining operating details over the telephone and in personal interviews. Blank ratings are not to be construed as unfavorable but signify circumstances "difficult to classify" within condensed rating symbols. They suggest the advisability of obtaining a report for additional information. Dun & Bradstreet and its 80,000 subscribers urge contractors and their accountants to provide D&B with the latest information available, particularly financial statements, thus facilitating assignment of the highest possible rating.

MAINTAINING FAVORABLE CREDIT BALANCES
Financial Statements and Ratings

The foregoing illustrates that the financial health of a construction business, as indicated by its figures, plays a major role in determining its Dun & Bradstreet

Fig. 12.3 Sample Dun & Bradstreet Business Information Report. This fictionalized report was prepared by Dun & Bradstreet, Inc. for the purposes of illustration only. Used with permission.

rating. Every industry has its own characteristics, so D&B business analysts compare individual company figures against industry standards before arriving at a fair evaluation. Moreover, business analysts consider the following financial characteristics of contractors when examining the figures:

1. Annual statement closing generally falls on December 31. Liquid position for most companies is shown in least-active months: winter. Cash position

at that time should be high, receivables low. The reverse is true during the peak summer season.

2. Working capital needs rise in peak seasons. Financing can be expected through commercial banks on both a secured and unsecured basis. Officer loans are also used for this purpose. D&B finds it not unusual for contractors to be performing contracts exceeding working capital twelve times.

3. Receivables include current billings and retained percentages. Work in progress will be included in receivables at times. A breakdown should be determined as it may represent a job considerably in the red even though it is carried as an asset.

Cost of doing business in the construction industry   Dun & Bradstreet's Business Economics Division has calculated certain important financial measurements for the construction industry. Those for corporations are shown in Table 12.2. (Similar data for partnerships are in Table 12.3; those for proprietorships in Table 12.4.) Further, for corporate operations, an industry profile of the profit and loss statement (Table 12.5) and balance sheet (Table 12.6) are reproduced in percentage format. These figures were developed from U.S. Treasury Department records of 52,647 general building contractors for 1972–73, the latest information available.

Finally, Table 12.7 shows key business ratios for the general contracting line based on 1975 financial statements. Each ratio is quoted in upper, median, and lower quartile figures, in that order. These ratios give analysts a focal point from which to evaluate individual construction businesses. The more favorable the ratio, compared with industry standards, the greater the possibility for a higher rating. But two ratios, as well as certain balance sheet items, require special comment.

Net Profits on Revenue. Since technically, construction is regarded as a function separate from manufacturing (though it involves people, money, materials, and management in the assembly of a finished product), it could be considered a type of manufacturing. As such, it would operate with some of the lowest gross margins of all manufacturers.

Statistical evidence is not available to support this assumption completely, but data are available as to net-profit performance after taxes in relation to contract revenue.

Annual samplings made by Dun & Bradstreet among 125 lines of business corporations (manufacturing, construction, retailing, wholesaling) yield an interesting array of figures. In 1975, only 2 of the 71 manufacturing/construction industries showed lower median net profits on net sales ratios than the 1.18 percent reported for general contractors.

Over the last fifteen years, the profit rates of general contractors have fluctuated over a relatively narrow range. From a peak of 1.82 in 1972, net profits on revenues plunged to a low of 1.07 in 1973, edged up slightly to 1.18 in 1975. But it should be noted that this was the second lowest level in the last decade and a half.

Net Profits on Tangible Net Worth.   In the past fifteen years, general contractors' net profits on tangible net worth hit their lowest ebb in 1962 and their highest level in 1971. Then, a downslide occurred in 1972 and 1973,

TABLE 12.2 Cost of Doing Business Ratios—Corporations

Industry	Total number of returns filed	Cost of goods sold %	Gross margin %	Compensation of officers %	Rent paid on business property %	Repairs %	Bad debts %	Interest paid %	Taxes paid* %	Amortization depreciation depletion %	Advertising %	Pension and other employee benefit plans %
										Selected operating expenses		
All industrial groups	1,812,760	70.37	29.63	2.06	1.46	0.83	0.41	3.63	2.99	3.57	1.06	1.36
Contract construction	154,418	82.02	17.98	3.54	0.61	0.53	0.17	0.88	2.12	1.92	0.21	0.90
Building construction	52,647	88.28	11.72	2.57	0.42	0.25	0.09	1.09	1.37	1.04	0.18	0.50
General contractors, except building construction	14,935	79.92	20.08	2.40	0.70	1.13	0.15	1.00	2.20	4.03	0.13	0.90
Special trade contractors		76.91	23.09		0.75	0.50	0.27	0.61	2.82	1.72	0.27	1.29

SOURCE: Prepared by the Business Economics Division of Dun & Bradstreet, Inc. Copyrighted © 1976 and used with permission, from *Book of Statistics of Income*, U.S. Treasury Department, Internal Revenue Service, Statistics Division, 1972–73.

TABLE 12.3 Cost of Doing Business—Partnerships

Industry	Total number of returns filed	Selected costs				Salaries and wages	Payments to partners	Selected operating expenses					Depreciation amortization depletion	Profits on business receipts
		Cost of goods sold	Merchandise purchased	Labor, supplies	Gross margin			Rent	Interest	Taxes	Bad debts	Repairs		
		%	%	%	%	%	%	%	%	%	%	%	%	%
All industries	992,012	48.25	33.26	5.89	51.75	9.25	2.05	2.73	6.42	3.91	0.16	1.45	5.70	9.22
Construction	60,945	70.92	13.51	27.62	29.08	3.83	2.04	1.39	0.89	1.52	0.09	0.97	1.89	9.60
General contractors	22,570	78.24	9.47	27.28	21.76	2.49	1.27	1.49	1.08	1.08	0.05	0.88	1.61	6.42
Special trade contractors	37,869	57.39	20.79	28.35	42.61	6.31	3.48	1.21	0.53	2.34	0.15	1.12	2.36	15.51
Masonry, stonework and plastering	6,142	57.88	12.50	38.25	42.12	6.68	2.52	0.53	0.34	2.63	0.45	0.41	1.47	19.54
Painting, paperhanging, and decorating	4,731	47.27	11.54	28.08	52.73	7.91	3.59	0.92	0.42	2.65	0.11	0.52	2.03	21.73
Plumbing, heating, and air conditioning	5,446	71.24	36.47	28.07	28.76	2.73	2.92	1.00	0.63	2.20	0.11	0.48	1.50	9.69

SOURCE: Prepared by the Business Economics Division of Dun & Bradstreet, Inc. Copyrighted © 1976 and used with permission, from *Book of Statistics of Income*, U.S. Treasury Department, Internal Revenue Service, Statistics Division, 1972.

TABLE 12.4 Cost of Doing Business—Proprietorships

Industry	Total number of returns filed	Selected costs Cost of goods sold %	Merchandise purchased %	Labor %	Materials and supplies %	Gross margin %	Salaries and wages %	Selected operating expenses Rent %	Interest %	Taxes %	Bad debts %	Repairs %	Depreciation amortization depletion %	Profits on business receipts %
All industries	10,172,792	55.68	38.58	3.87	3.10	44.32	6.14	2.45	1.69	2.25	0.13	1.82	4.21	14.17
Construction	804,528	57.25	16.73	11.44	15.20	42.75	7.51	0.98	0.89	1.88	0.13	1.26	2.77	15.03
Building construction	155,587	68.85	14.36	10.45	18.83	31.15	5.04	0.92	1.22	1.54	0.10	1.09	2.19	8.65
Special trade contractors	609,021	48.81	18.57	12.35	12.68	51.19	9.23	1.04	0.63	2.16	0.14	1.36	3.15	19.93
Carpentering and flooring	185,764	42.86	12.43	11.16	12.22	57.14	6.53	0.72	0.43	1.34	0.25	0.62	2.20	30.95
Electrical work	44,592	59.89	28.50	14.44	14.48	40.11	7.45	0.58	0.48	2.40	0.16	0.54	2.01	16.84
Masonry, stonework, and plastering	63,693	48.87	11.31	16.66	14.93	51.13	13.04	0.72	0.42	2.34	0.05	0.66	2.12	18.71
Painting, paperhanging, and decorating	109,058	38.60	6.01	16.49	10.50	61.40	10.32	0.92	0.38	2.45	0.08	0.72	2.16	28.47
Plumbing, heating, and air conditioning	77,369	57.42	33.00	8.71	11.44	42.58	8.72	0.88	0.47	2.13	0.17	0.72	2.21	15.62

SOURCE: Prepared by the Business Economics Division of Dun & Bradstreet, Inc. Copyrighted 1976 and used with permission, from Book of Statistics of Income, U.S. Treasury Department, Internal Revenue Service, Statistics Division, 1972.

TABLE 12.5 Profit and Loss Statement

Sales	100.0%
Cost of goods sold	88.3
Gross margin	11.7
Compensation of officers	2.6
Rent	0.4
Repairs	0.3
Bad debts	0.1
Interest	1.1
Taxes	1.4
Amortization, depletion, and depreciation	1.0
Advertising	0.2
Pension and benefit plan	0.5
All other expenses	2.4
Net profit before taxes	1.2
Net profit	0.5

NOTE: The above model was constructed by the Business Economics Division of Dun & Bradstreet, Inc., from *Statistics of Income,* U.S. Treasury Department Internal Revenue Service, Statistics Division, 1972–73.

followed by a moderate rebound in 1974. However, of the 71 manufacturing and construction businesses surveyed for 1975, general contractors with a net profit on tangible net worth ratio of 11.30 stood twenty-eighth from the top, a marked contrast with 1971 when they stood third from the top.

Components of the satisfactory financial condition In most instances, the financial condition of a general contractor may be analyzed only in terms of the extent of profitability plus ability to realize a sufficient cash flow from work in progress and accounts receivable so that payables to subcontractors and material people may be met with invariable promptness. In peak periods, a satisfactory condition will exist if:

TABLE 12.6 Balance Sheet

Cash	8.3%		
Notes and accounts receivable	28.5	Accounts payable	23.8
Inventory	19.9	Bonds, notes and mort-	
Investments	0.7	gages under 1 year	16.7
Other current assets	11.8	Other current liabilities	11.2
Total current assets	69.2	Loans from stockholders	2.3
Loans to stockholders	0.9	Total current liabilities	54.1
Mortgage and real estate loans	1.3	Bonds, notes, and mort-	
Other investments	6.7	gates over 1 year	15.7
Depreciable and depletable assets	13.0	Other liabilities	12.5
Land	4.7	Capital stock	5.2
Other assets	4.2	Surplus	12.5
Total assets	100.0%	Total liabilities and capital	100.0%

NOTE: The above model was constructed by the Business Economics Division of Dun & Bradstreet, Inc., from *Statistics of Income,* U.S. Treasury Department, Internal Revenue Service, Statistics Division, 1972–73.

TABLE 12.7 Key Business Ratios

Line of business (and number of concerns reporting)	Current assets to current debt	Net profits on net sales	Net profits on tangible net worth	Net profits on net working capital	Net sales to tangible net worth	Net sales to net working capital	Collection period	Net sales to inventory	Fixed assets to tangible net worth	Current debt to tangible net worth	Total debt to tangible net worth	Inventory to net working capital	Current debt to inventory	Funded debts to net working capital
	Times	Percent	Percent	Percent	Times	Times	Days	Times	Percent	Percent	Percent	Percent	Percent	Percent
1541-42 General Building contractors (103)	1.77	2.96	21.52	42.16	14.54	24.43	*	*	11.2	73.5	123.9	*	*	19.0
	1.43	1.18	11.30	16.67	7.32	15.02	*	*	22.9	133.8	234.0	*	*	48.3
	1.23	0.44	4.07	7.07	4.43	8.19	*	*	46.7	235.6	388.9	*	*	120.9

*Not computed. Building trades contractors have no inventories in the credit sense of the term. As a general rule, such contractors have no customary selling terms, each contract being a special job for which individual terms are arranged.

NOTE: Dun & Bradstreet's Business Economics Division compiled these ratios from year-end financial statements of concerns in the survey (almost exclusively corporations with a tangible net worth over $100,000).

SOURCE: Copyrighted © 1976 by Dun & Bradstreet, Inc.

1. There is a margin of profit in work under way, without likelihood of unusual hazards which may wipe out the profit margin before contracts are completed.

2. A modest investment is reflected by work in progress, most of which will be billed to the client in the near future.

3. Accounts receivable indicate that billings are being collected within short periods and no undue accumulation is indicated by retainages receivable.

4. A strong margin of coverage for the debt is afforded by the total of cash and receivables.

Chapter **13**

Legal Hazards in the Distribution of Market Information by Construction Industry Trade Associations

JACK A. JEFFRIES, ESQ.
Partner, Keck, Cushman, Mahin & Cate, Chicago, Illinois

INTRODUCTION

Construction industry trade associations often serve their members and the general public by collecting and disseminating marketing information such as costs of doing business and credit information. Such activities must be very carefully controlled to avoid the legal liability under federal and state antitrust laws.

Criminal convictions under these laws can result in prison terms of three years and fines of $100,000 for individuals and $1 million for corporations. Private treble damage antitrust actions are being brought with greater frequency and success. The costs of defending such actions are substantial burdens with or without the possible damages that may be established.

Trade associations, because their members are often competitors, are especially vulnerable to attack under antitrust laws. In many areas the exchange of market information, although apparently innocent in purpose, has the effect of restraining trade and, hence, is in violation of these laws.

The purpose of antitrust laws is to prevent only unreasonable restraints of commerce. Thus, it is possible that decisions made by individual association members based upon proper statistical market information may tend to affect market conditions. The guiding principle here can best be summarized by a public statement of a senior Department of Justice attorney:

> An information exchange program, which allows a seller to make intelligent decisions for the future on the basis of an *informed guess* as to what his competition *might* do in the future, arouses our suspicion far less than one which enables him to make such decisions on the basis of *certainty* as to what his competitors *will* do in the future, whether based on the competitors' reports as to what his future action *will* be or on a report on his past performance so detailed that his future conduct becomes predictable with certainty.[1]

STATISTICAL INFORMATION

Inventory, shipment, production, and sales information as to past transactions from which to judge the market is a valid business activity.

The Wrong Way

The hazards of gathering general statistical information are demonstrated by two reporting programs condemned by the United States Supreme Court. In one program,[2] association members were required to make daily reports on sales and shipping with exact copies of invoices, monthly production and inventory reports, price lists, and inspection reports on product grading. The disseminated information was a monthly production summary, a weekly sales report identifying purchaser and price, a weekly report of shipments, a monthly stock report, and a price list summary. Deviations from the price list were immediately communicated to the association and distributed to the members. An expert analyzed the statistics and published a market forecast. Monthly meetings were held to discuss the statistics, and members completed questionnaires on estimated production and condition of the market.

This program was held to be illegal since such detailed reporting between competitors indicated their intent to control production and price. The Court cited the interpretation of the reports and the estimate of production as indicative of a tacit agreement to restrain trade. The Court also objected to the nonavailability of information to customers and the public.

The second reporting system[3] which was condemned by the United States Supreme Court was even more restrictive and detailed than the first. Here, trade association members contracted with an independent agency to gather information. Members were required to give detailed price information, includ-

---

[1]John J. Galgay, "Antitrust Consideration in the Exchange of Price Information among Competitors," 8 *Antitrust Bulletin 617,* 620–621 (1963).

[2]*American Column & Lumber Co. v. United States,* 257 U.S. 377, 66 L.Ed. 284, 42 Sup. Ct. 114 (1921).

[3]*United States v. American Linseed Oil Co.,* 262 U.S. 371, 67 L.Ed. 1035, 43 Sup. Ct. 607 (1923).

ing price quotations, any special prices given, and the buyer's or prospective buyer's name and address. Audit reports were given to all members. Penalties were imposed for failure to comply with terms of the agreement. The information compiled was available only to subscribing members.

The Court did not in either of the above two cases condemn the propriety of general statistical reporting. It did object to the abuses of such reporting which resulted in curtailing production and fixing prices.

The Right Way

The following is a description of two Supreme Court decisions which approved exchange of statistical reports showing details about quantity, prices, freight costs, and commissions. The reports related only to *past* transactions. In one case,[4] a trade association compiled and disseminated the information by showing average figures without identifying either the buyer or the seller. The information was made available to the public. At meetings of the association, general statistics rather than the individual transactions were discussed. In approving the program, the United States Supreme Court stated that there was no proof of an agreement to restrain commerce.

In the second case,[5] which is the leading case upholding information exchanges justified by a legitimate business purpose, the data distributed were more detailed and were not available to the public.[6]

The trade association was composed of cement manufacturers who sold to builders. Pursuant to industry custom, builders were not obligated to use cement ordered. Builders abused the system by ordering cement from several manufacturers. When prices rose, the builders accepted all of the orders, diverting cement to other jobs. In order to prevent these fraudulent practices, the trade association members exchanged detailed information on specific job contracts. No agreements were made to act in a concerted fashion. The plan was upheld despite the detailed and confidential nature of the information since its purpose was to prevent fraud.

The Federal Trade Commission (FTC) has approved an industry reporting program with the following information and averages being disseminated:

1. Percent return on total investment
2. Percent net profits after taxes to total sales
3. Percent advertising costs to gross sales
4. Percent labor cost to gross sales
5. Ratio of current assets to current liabilities
6. Ratio of net sales to inventory
7. Ratio of net sales to working capital[7]

The Federal Trade Commission has also approved a reporting program

[4] *Maple Flooring Mfrs. Ass'n v. United States,* 268 U.S. 563, 69 L.Ed. 1093, 45 Sup. Ct. 578 (1925).

[5] *Cement Mfrs. Protective Ass'n v. United States,* 268 U.S. 588, 69 L.Ed. 1104, 45 Sup. Ct. 586 (1925).

[6] In *United States v. Citizens and Southern National Bank,* 422 U.S. 86, 113 (1975) the Supreme Court reaffirmed this fifty-year-old principle, stating that "dissemination of price information is not itself a *per se* violation of the Sherman Act," and held that agreements to exchange information which result in the "lack of significant price competition" are nonetheless lawful when done for a "permissible reason."

[7] F.T.C. Advisory Opinion 359, 76 F.T.C. 1099 (1969).

which collects average profit-and-loss statements for 15 companies.[8] The FTC advised that only average figures should be used. It is desirable to use certified public accountants to collect the individual member's reports and to compile averages to ensure confidentiality of individual company reports.

CREDIT INFORMATION

Collecting and distributing information for the purpose of enabling trade association members to evaluate the credit risk of their customers can be a legitimate activity. These programs must also be carefully monitored.

The United States Supreme Court in the *Cement* case previously referred to upheld the legality of an association program for providing its members with monthly reports on delinquent customer accounts. The reports contained the following information:

1. Name and address of the delinquent debtor
2. Amount of overdue account and ledger balance
3. Statement of accounts placed with attorneys for collection
4. Explanation of any reason for nonpayment or reasons why account was being disputed by debtor
5. Total of delinquent accounts compared with those for the preceding 12 months
6. Reports of payment of account placed with attorneys for collection

The Court in approving this arrangement noted the absence of certain conduct as follows:

> There were never any comments concerning names appearing on the list of delinquent debtors. The Government neither charged nor proved that there was an agreement with respect to the use of this information, or with respect to the person to whom or conditions under which credit should be extended. The evidence fell far short of establishing any understanding on the basis of which credit was to be extended to customers or that any co-operation resulted from the distribution of this information, or that there were any consequences from it other than such as would naturally ensue from the exercise from the individual judgment of manufacturers in determining, on the basis of available information, whether to extend credit or to require cash or security from any given customer.[9]

Disseminated information should be limited to accurate and objective data concerning delinquent accounts. The information should be relevant to an individual association member's determination of a credit risk. The information should be given only to those who have a legitimate interest in it. This is important to reduce the risk of defamation action by an irate creditor.

Comments, recommendations, and interpretation of the information must be avoided. Blacklisting delinquent creditors or white listing any approved customers is illegal per se as a boycott.

[8]F.T.C. Advisory Opinion 486, 83 F.T.C. 1844 (1974).
[9]*Supra* note 5, at 599, 600.

Members should not be compelled to report their dealings with delinquent creditors. Listing detailed information concerning transactions with individual customers in order to give them credit ratings is not advisable. All agreements, regulations, and understanding on credit terms must be avoided since all agreements with respect to price or elements of price are illegal per se.

Limiting the exchange of credit information to delinquent accounts will help to avoid an inference that the information exchanged is to be used for improper purposes. A Federal Trade Commission Advisory Opinion supports this conclusion and states in part:[10]

> (1) The members of the association are left free to determine on the basis of their individual judgment whether or not to sell to delinquent debtors and on what terms; (2) there is no agreement among members in regard to credit terms, prices, or any other joint action which illegally restrains trade; (3) that the reporting member indicate that a debt turned over to a collection agency was treated by the debtor as offset or was otherwise disputed, where that is the case; (4) the association furnishes to the debtor the same credit information reported by a member at the same time the request is answered; and (5) in order for the debtor to have the opportunity to correct his credit record, if he believes it needs correcting, the association must pass on to the inquiring member any explanatory statements which the debtor may submit; the identity of the inquiring member need not be revealed to the debtor.

If the guidelines contained in the above opinion are followed, risk of violating antitrust laws will be minimized.

PRICE INFORMATION

The exchange of price information is an extremely hazardous reporting activity. Any agreement among competitors as to pricing is illegal per se without consideration of whether the actions in a reporting scheme were reasonable. Thus, price reporting can easily be attacked as a basis for price fixing, price stabilization, or other tampering. A conviction can be obtained solely on circumstantial evidence.

If prices are shown to be at an artificial level following price reporting, the exchange of price information can be cited as the cause. The agreement to tamper with the price can be inferred from the exchange of information.

In the Supreme Court case of *United States v. Container Corp. of America,*[11] the extreme dangers of exchanging price information were demonstrated. Competitors voluntarily exchanged information on the most recent price charged or quoted to a particular customer. Reciprocal information was expected. The Supreme Court concluded that the exchange stabilized industry prices and thus held it illegal in spite of the fact that the stabilization of prices resulted from individual pricing decisions rather than an explicit agreement between compet-

---

[10]F.T.C. Advisory Opinion 361, 76 F.T.C. 1100 (1969).
[11]393 U.S. 333, 216 Ed.2d 526, 89 Sup. Ct. 510 (1969).

itors. The case did not condemn all price stabilization resulting from price reporting. It is, however, fair warning that exchange of any price information either directly among competitors or through the structure of a trade association is an extremely dangerous undertaking.

CONCLUSIONS AND RECOMMENDED ACTION

The following recommendations are made to associations to avoid violating any antitrust law:

1. The exchange of past or closed transactions of production, inventory, or other market data is allowed. Reporting current transactions may be permitted if not used as the basis for an agreement to restrain trade. Use of a forecast of future prices contains the extremely high prospect of being construed as a manipulation of price or production. Distribution of suggested price lists is subject to the same extreme dangers.

2. Composite or average figures in which neither the buyer nor the seller in the transactions is identified is the recommended procedure for disseminating all information by trade associations. It is not clear whether identifying the parties to the transaction is fatal to the reporting scheme, but it is suspect. Where credit reporting for the purpose of fraud prevention is intended, identification of the parties may be allowed.

3. An information exchange using coercion of association members by means of fines, expulsions, required submission to audits, or other penal sanction is illegal. Compelling members to act in a certain way, to report deviation from a standard policy, or to adopt a standard policy is also forbidden.

4. Information collected should be made available to nonmember competitors, buyers, and the general public. A possible exception to this is where the information is exchanged to prevent fraud as in the *Cement* case previously cited. If the information is withheld from nonmember competitors or buyers, an inference is raised that trade association members might be acting as a group against other competitors or against buyers. It is recognized that nonmember competitors should not be able to obtain the information collected by an association without a charge. A reasonable condition would be that the nonmember competitors be able to join the association and to participate in the exchange of information at a reasonable price or that the price charged for the information without joining the association is directly related to the costs of obtaining that information.

5. Statistics and information should not be interpreted or otherwise commented upon. This will tend to ensure that data are being independently acted upon by association members. Meetings should not be held to discuss the information since this increases the risk of violation. Opportunities to discuss legitimate topics present the temptation to discuss price, production, and other dangerous topics which can result in allegations that there was the opportunity and actual conspiracy to restrain trade.

Association programs for exchanging economic information for the purpose of serving their membership and allowing them to better evaluate the market and credit risk of customers and to arrive individually at independent decisions are valid association activities. On the other hand, agreements as to pricing or sales, blacklists, or agreements not to deal with delinquent customers, agreements on terms and conditions of sale or credit, including discounts, maximum credit periods, cash-only requirements, freight allowances, or lien waivers are subject to attack under the antitrust laws and should be avoided.

It is essential that any trade association program for the exchange of market information be evaluated by an experienced antitrust attorney who is cognizant of current legal developments. The exposure to legal liability from such programs is great, and the civil and criminal penalties are extreme.

Part Four

Contract Analysis and Procurement

Chapter **14**

Selecting the Appropriate Construction Contract

TONY BERMAN, ESQ.
Partner, Berman, Paley, Goldstein & Berman, New York, New York

SAMUEL H. CROSSLAND
Vice President, Secretary and General Counsel, Morrison-Knudsen Co., Inc., Boise, Idaho

INTRODUCTION

The selection of the appropriate construction contract, both as to its form and content, is one of the most important factors in the entire construction process. Indeed, the selection of the contract—like the selection of a mate—is something that if done hurriedly or lightly can result in painful and unseemly conflict, protracted litigation, and possible disaster.

To begin with, there are obviously a number of situations where a prospective contractor has little or nothing to say about the form or the content of the contract. In heavy construction in particular (such as roads, tunnels, or bridges) the owner is generally a governmental body or authority that advertises and takes bids for the project. In those cases the bidders are given a set of plans, specifications, and a form of contract all prepared by the owner, and its consultants, and the contractor has literally nothing to say as to the terms of the contract. The attitude often expressed by owners in that situation—as well, unfortunately, as by many courts faced with conflicts arising out of such contracts—is "if you don't like it, don't bid it." To someone in the heavy construction business that is an answer that is of no practical meaning or value, since almost all governmental authorities (federal, state, and local) have made a practice of including extremely onerous and one-sided provisions in their contracts and since it is hard to find a private enterprise, in present times, that is about to undertake the construction of a major highway, bridge, or tunnel. Since the government is, in such a case, "the only game in town," the contractor has no option but to accept the contract and to try to make the best of it. There is, however, one thing that the contractor can and must do to protect himself in such a situation and that is to thoroughly familiarize himself with the contract provisions (including the usually extensive and involved general conditions or general specifications) and to take particular note of such things as the notice provisions, requiring prompt notice to the owner in the event of a dispute or claim, and of all the other technical provisions that may be used by the owner in an attempt to defeat an otherwise equitable right to additional payment.

Since many of these public contracts contain a series of extremely involved, often ambiguous and generally onerous provisions, the importance of prompt and regular consultation with an attorney knowledgeable in the contracting field cannot be overstated. Such a course runs counter to many deep-seated prejudices in this industry, where the word "lawyer" is often preceded by an adjective not printable here, but it is a course that most experienced contractors will grudgingly admit has become increasingly necessary. Obviously, a contractor having full knowledge of his rights, and what is necessary to protect them, is in a much better position to protect himself against both the badly worded and unfair provisions of such a contract as well as the arbitrary use of those provisions that governmental representatives may attempt.

In a situation where the contract is really the product of the exchange of ideas, and of arms' length bargaining, then the contractor obviously can have much to say about both the form and the content of the agreement. We turn now to a consideration of that type of situation, beginning first with the various types of construction contracts and the basic concerns in selecting the appropriate type of agreement.

THE TYPE OF CONTRACT

In general, there really are only three basic types of construction contracts. They are normally referred to as the lump-sum agreement, the unit-price contract and the cost-plus contract. The separation of the type of contract into three broad categories is useful for purposes of analysis. It is necessary to point out, however, at the outset, that in practice each of these three different categories has a number of possible variations.

In addition, a single agreement may well contain elements of two or even of all three categories. Thus it is not unusual to have a unit-price contract that contains, in addition, both lump-sum items as well as cost-plus provisions.

Nevertheless, a knowledge of the three basic categories and of the various conditions that affect them should be of material help in the selection of the appropriate contract.

The Lump-Sum Agreement

This is, perhaps, the simplest (in theory at least) of construction contracts. As its name implies, the contractor agrees that he will be paid a lump sum in return for the work that he performs. The amount is, of course, fixed by the agreement and is meant to cover all the work that the contractor will perform.

Although simple, in concept, this type of agreement is one which perhaps requires the greatest attention and concern by the contractor. That is true, in fact, both in the precontracting stages as well as in the consideration of what provisions are to go into the agreement itself. Here, of course, when we refer to bargaining as to the terms of the agreement, we necessarily refer primarily to private work, not to public work where such bargaining is simply not possible. An owner, once a lump-sum contract has been signed, will almost invariably assume and strenuously defend the position that the contract price is meant to cover everything required—no matter what happens—to accomplish the work. Accordingly, the contractor must carefully examine the work to be performed and must satisfy himself to the full extent possible that the plans and specifications are clear and complete in the description of exactly what the contractor is required to do. This obviously includes such things as the materials or equipment to be incorporated in the work and all similar consideration. All of this must obviously be done prior to establishing a price for the work. Too often have contractors found themselves with a lump-sum contract with incomplete plans and specifications; with a general clause somewhere in the extensive specifications providing that the contractor must do "everything necessary" to accomplish the work and with an owner insisting that expensive and really unanticipated work must be performed at no additional cost to him.

In addition, since a lump-sum contract, without more, usually does not depend upon the quantities of work to be performed, that question too must be considered. What if, in excavating the foundation for a building, say, the contractor finds that he must remove ten times as much rock as everyone thought? Here, of course, the question of a changed-conditions clause, as later discussed in this chapter, is both relevant and important.

What if a much larger quantity of general excavation is encountered than what was anticipated? One solution to this type of problem is to spell out in the contract, in some way, the basis for the price. In other words, provisions can be made for additional payment if the quantities of work, such as excavation or concrete, exceed a fixed quantity. One way to cover this is by adding unit prices to cover additional quantities of work beyond the stated amount. The idea here is not to suggest a fixed or detailed solution for particular problems but, rather, to indicate general areas of concern which must be given thought in entering into this type of contract.

The essential here, in summary, is to make sure that the precontracting consideration and the agreement covers plainly and as fully as possible exactly what work is to be covered by the contract price.

A second matter that must be carefully considered in the lump-sum agreement is how payment is to be made. Obviously, in any sizable job a contractor must receive partial or progress payments as the work proceeds. It is neither customary nor usual to expect that the contractor will finance an entire job by himself and await payment until completion.

As we have previously indicated, the contract must provide some method for determining how and when progress payments are to be made. It is not unusual, in a lump-sum contract, for the owner to require the contractor to furnish a payment breakdown allocating specific amounts to specific categories of work for payment purposes (e.g., so much for excavation and so much for concrete). The contractor is then paid periodically, often monthly, for the work accomplished during the prior period.

Again, as we previously indicated, with this particular type of contract a far better method is to have the payment breakdown agreed upon in advance and incorporated in the contract.

Finally, the terms of this type of agreement must be comprehensive, and the matters outlined previously in this chapter must be considered by the contractor and covered by appropriate provisions in the agreement.

The Unit-Price Contract

This type of agreement divides the work into various quantities, such as excavation, concrete, structural steel, etc., and fixes a price per unit of work for each classification. Thus the excavation will be paid for by the cubic yard, the structural steel by the erected pound, the concrete by the cubic yard placed, and so on.

The theory behind this particular type of agreement is that it is best-suited for the type of job where the quantities of work to be performed may vary substantially.

In that case, payment will be made for the work actually performed since the unit-price contract does not contemplate the payment of any fixed sum. Rather, the ultimate contract amount will depend upon the amount of work that is actually performed during the course of the job.

The unit-price contract is generally the type of agreement that is used by public authorities in their heavy construction projects. (Heavy construction, in the sense used here, is generally the building of highways, bridges, tunnels, and similar type work.)

The unit-price agreement is less frequently found in the private sector of the industry, but there are many occasions when it is selected by private parties.

As we have indicated, the basic theory behind this type of contract is that it is flexible enough to take care of variations in the quantities of work. Indeed, a typical provision in this type of contract warns the contractor that the quantities shown in the plans and specifications are approximate only. The agreement will go on to expressly provide that the unit prices agreed upon will apply to the work actually performed no matter what quantity is actually found during the course of the work and no matter what the reason for the variation.

It takes but a moment's thought to realize that, taken literally, such an agreement can be extremely hazardous as far as the contractor is concerned.

Driving 20 piles is obviously much more expensive *per unit* than driving 200 piles; placing 1,000 yards of concrete is plainly more expensive per cubic yard than placing 100,000 cubic yards of the same type of concrete, and so it goes.

To add to this problem, this type of agreement (particularly those tendered by public authorities) will usually contain a clause purporting to give the owner the unlimited power to add work to, or to delete work from, the contract, at any time, and to pay for that work at the unit prices specified in the agreement. Here too, like large variations in quantities caused by unanticipated conditions, the possibility of abuse by the owner and of resulting damage to the contractor is a formidable risk.

Courts faced with such situations have limited the seemingly boundless scope of these provisions. To do so, however, they have had to devise a whole series of complicated and, at times, conflicting rationales. For example, the courts of some jurisdictions purport to apply a "quantitative" versus a "qualitative" test. If the change ordered by the owner is simply "quantitative" (simply a change in quantity), then, so the theory goes, the contractor is not entitled to additional compensation beyond the agreed-upon unit price. A change that alters the nature or "quality" of the work (a "qualitative" change) does, it is held, entitle the contractor to the additional costs he incurs as a result of the change.

This distinction, "quantitative" versus "qualitative," is all very well when discussed in theory. Indeed, what can be more logical than to base a distinction upon the very nature of the work that is actually being performed. In practice, however, it is not so simple. Almost every single change that one can think of is, in some ways, *both* quantitative and qualitative, and experience has shown that it is not a simple matter to determine in particular instances which change is simply one of adding quantities or one which basically alters the work being performed under the particular item. The results of such a distinction can, at times, be confusing and, possibly unjust. One case held that a 400-percent variation in rock excavation was simply a *quantitative* change. That decision involved a general excavation item, with a unit price per yard that covered all excavation, regardless of whether it was earth or rock. It is hard to conceive of a situation where such a change in the expensive portion of the excavation can only be "quantitative."

To state the problem is, as always, much simpler than to offer a reasonable solution. In publicly let contracts there is little that the contractor can do about this type of problem since he must either accept the provisions of the agreement or forget about the contract. He must, however, be aware of the particular type of problems that this type of agreement can give rise to both in formulating his bid as well as in performing the work.

Notice to the owner of substantial variations encountered during the performance of the work, or of the additional expense flowing from any proposed change, is essential and extremely valuable: essential, since most of these contracts require such notice as a prerequisite to any additional payment; valuable, since the very fact that a contractor indicates *at the inception* that a change will affect his costs is often given considerable weight by a court in the event of a dispute.

The contractor can try to include a provision for the renegotiation of a unit price if the quantity of the work actually performed for that item varies from the estimated quantity by a fixed percentage (say, 15 percent). This type of provision is often found in contracts with federal agencies and authorities. To complicate matters, however, such a provision may not always prove to be advantageous to the contractor, since it is not unreasonable to assume that the provision will give the right to renegotiate to *both parties*. In the event of a large overrun in quantity, such renegotiation is clearly not always desirable from the contractor's standpoint.

What is definitely desirable from the contractor's point of view is to make sure that the agreement limits and restricts the owner's right to add work to the contract at the unit price. The contractor should be sure that there is no unlimited right expressed in the agreement that gives the owner the apparent right to add whatever work he chooses, at any stage of the job, and to pay for that work at the unit prices.

The limitations in that connection must, of course, be worked out in the context of each individual job. Nevertheless, the importance to a contractor of being aware of and of providing for this type of situation in a unit-price agreement cannot be overstated. Indeed, the countless number of reported cases throughout the courts of this country that involve this very type of dispute is ample evidence of just how important this question is.

Many unit-price contracts also contain various lump-sum items. There, it is particularly important that the agreement clearly specify what work is covered by the lump-sum item and what work, associated with that item, will be paid for under the unit prices. For example, certain pipe work, or a junction chamber, may be included as a lump-sum item in a basic unit-price contract. Disputes have often arisen, where the contract is unclear, as to whether the excavation necessary for that work is included in the lump-sum price or is to be paid for separately under the unit prices. The point is that whatever the parties intend should be specifically stated in the agreement.

The unit-price contract also requires that particular attention be given to the payment provisions. The agreement must not only cover when the progress payments are to be made and how they are to be certified, but it also must specify *how* the quantities are to be measured.

If material, such as fill, is to be brought to the job, is the pay quantity to be based on what is excavated at the pit, or is it to be paid for on a cubic-yard-in-place basis? Is concrete to be measured based upon theoretical neat lines, or upon the quantity of concrete actually incorporated in the work?

Again, the method selected is less important than the fact that the parties each have a firm understanding as to how the measuring is to be done, and that that understanding is clearly expressed in the agreement.

In addition, the inclusion in the contract of the provisions outlined later in this chapter concerning such things as the scope of the work, the time of performance, payment, and all other necessary matters is, of course, essential.

Finally, the preparation of a proper bid for a unit-price contract—particularly one that is publicly let—is a consummate art. We could not possibly deal adequately with that subject within the confines of this chapter. All that we can say, in that connection, is that a thorough knowledge both of the contracting business, as well as of the more important legal considerations, is critical in the submission of such a bid.

Cost-Plus Arrangements

The cost-plus contract is one which, as its name implies, provides for payment to the contractor of the *cost* of the work, *plus* something to cover the contractor's overhead and profit. In general, this type of agreement is particularly appropriate where, for one reason or another, the contract work is not or cannot be clearly defined at the time of contracting. Thus, in a situation where an owner wants the work on his project to start before the plans and specifications are substantially completed, a cost-plus agreement may be the only practical solution.

Similarly, where it is not really possible to tell just what work must be performed because of the nature of the job, paying the contractor the actual cost that he incurs, plus overhead and profit, is probably the fairest arrangement. This type of situation often occurs where a contractor is taking over, for whatever reason, a partially completed job. In that case it is often literally impossible to accurately tell just how much of the work remains to be done, how much of what is done is satisfactory, and what the final cost will be.

The "cost" provisions of the contract The basic concern with such an agreement, from the contractor's point of view, is that he must make sure that the written agreement clearly defines and includes all the costs of doing the work.

Obviously, the cost of all labor, fringe benefits, materials, equipment, and everything else incorporated in the work, should be reimbursed to the contractor. That, of course, most contractors need not be told. In addition, however, the contractor must concern himself with the question of what taxes, permit fees, insurance provisions, engineering costs, and any other unusual expenses may be encountered during the performance of the work. These, too, the payment provisions of the agreement must cover.

Another question that the contractor must concern himself with is to how he is to be reimbursed for his own equipment. Where the equipment is rented from others, payment is usually based on the rentals actually paid by the contractor. Where the equipment is owned by the contractor, the agreement should establish a fair rental rate—whether based upon the Associated Equipment Dealers' book or some other criterion—and it should expressly spell out whether fueling and maintenance of the equipment is included in the rate or is to be paid for separately.

Another area often overlooked in this type of agreement is the question of who bears the risk of loss during the performance of the work. Since the basic theory behind this type of agreement is that the contractor is to be reimbursed for all costs incurred in the performance of the contract, the agreement generally should provide that any damage to the completed work—whether by fire, flood, or other cause—is the owner's and not the contractor's risk. Suitable insurance to cover this risk should, of course, be obtained on behalf of whoever bears the risk.

If, however, something happens to or is wrong with the work because of the contractor's fault, then the agreement will generally provide that the faulty work must be replaced at no additional expense to the owner.

Finally, a question will often arise in this type of contract as to just what supervisory or administrative expense is reimbursable to the contractor. Generally, the cost of all supervisory or administrative forces employed on the job site on a regular basis should be reimbursed as part of the labor cost. The questionable area will include such things as a general superintendent, who may cover this and four other jobs during the course of a week. Or a field engineer who might divide his time between two jobs. The question here is as to whether a prorated portion of the salaries of such personnel is reimbursable as labor, or is to be covered by the overhead provisions of the agreement. Here, as we have so often indicated, the important thing is that the problem be recognized by the parties at the outset, be resolved by agreement, and the agreement incorporated in the contract.

The "plus" provisions of the contract   These provisions of the agreement are of great importance to the contractor since, literally, they are what he is working for. The basic purpose of these additive provisions is to cover the contractor's overhead attributable to the job and to provide him with a profit for performing the work.

The overhead referred to is basically the contractor's home office costs, such as his rent, executive personnel, office expense, legal and accounting costs, and all the other general expense that goes into doing business in today's world. Obviously, in theory at least, each job that a contractor takes must bear its share of his overhead cost, or the contractor would soon be out of business.

Since the question of what is a fair share of that cost is not really very definite and since this is an area where there are many possible variations (such as how many jobs a contractor may have at a particular time), the overhead factor generally must be fixed by negotiation, often by simply agreeing upon some simple method of calculation. The parties may, for example, simply fix a percentage of the cost of the work, say 10 percent, as the way in which the contractor will be reimbursed for overhead.

It is also possible, but less likely, for an agreement to provide that the contractor will be reimbursed for a fixed percentage of his actual home office expense. The trouble with such a method is that it would require extensive accounting and a clear definition of what the contractor's home office actually is in order to be viable. Yet another way to cover this particular problem is to agree upon an amount, known as a "fixed fee," that will generally cover both the contractor's overhead and some profit.

Obviously, the profit that a contractor is to receive must also be fixed by the agreement. Here too, the method of fixing that profit can vary. As indicated, the "fixed fee" is one method that is often used.

The problem with this method is that it may turn out to be entirely inequitable from the contractor's standpoint if there is a large variation in cost between what is anticipated and what is actually spent on a contract.

If the scope of the job doubles or triples, it would generally be unfair for the contractor to be confined to a fixed fee negotiated in the context of a much smaller and more limited job. Basing profit, as well as overhead, upon a percentage of the cost of the work may lessen that danger to the contractor, depending upon the circumstances.

Another factor often not considered in this type of agreement is the possibility of substantial delay in the performance of the contract. The parties generally contract for a construction project with at least some type of scheduling in mind. Since, more often than not, cost-plus contracts involve situations either where the full extent of the work is not definitely known or where the plans are not yet completed, the time factor in such a job is often less definite than in others.

Nevertheless, the time that the contractor will have to spend on a job is of great importance to him. An agreed-upon fee, or even a fixed percentage of cost, may be perfectly adequate to cover the contractor's overhead and profit if the job lasts for a year or two. If, however, the job extends for a substantial period of time beyond that reasonably expected by the contractor when the agreement was negotiated, through no fault of his own, then even a cost-plus contract can turn into an unfair and losing arrangement. Thought must be given to and provision made for this possibility in entering into such an agreement. Here, in addition, the question of when the work is to start, as well as when it is to finish, should be covered.

In addition to the basic ingredients ("cost" and the "plus"), this type of contract may have provisions added to it that very much change the basic nature of the agreement. Two relatively common provisions that are of great importance involve the *upset* or guaranteed price and the provisions for a share in any savings in accomplishing the work.

The Guaranteed Maximum Cost

Just as a contractor approaches a lump-sum agreement with many misgivings, so too will most owners contemplate any cost-plus arrangement.

Indeed, many owners feel, perhaps not entirely unreasonably, that an unlimited cost-plus agreement destroys any real incentive to hold costs down and usually results in a large increase in the cost of construction. The issue can, of course, be debated, but the fact that this feeling is prevalent cannot be denied.

To combat this threat, owners will often insist that the contractor agree to a guaranteed maximum price. Typically, this type of provision will fix a maximum amount, often referred to as an upset price. The contractor agrees that he is to be reimbursed by the owner for all the costs of the work up to a fixed amount, and the contractor further agrees that any cost of the work beyond that fixed amount will be his responsibility.

Such a provision naturally increases the contractor's risk of performing the work and requires extremely careful consideration. To begin with, the contractor must make sure that the extent of the work for which he is guaranteeing a price is carefully defined. The agreement should specifically provide for an adjustment in the maximum price in the event that the work is changed or altered to any significant degree.

Similarly, the duration of the job, to which the upset price applies, must be spelled out. Escalating costs, in inflationary times, are of particular importance and cannot be ignored. Furthermore, where particular equipment or large quantities of materials must be purchased from others, some protection must be afforded the contractor in the event that the suppliers insist, as they have recently, upon large increases in price before they will deliver.

It is also essential that the guaranteed price have sufficient contingencies built into it, so that it really is a "maximum" price. Otherwise, one is simply converting this agreement into a lump-sum contract, which is generally not what is intended by the parties.

Then, too, the agreement must plainly define what costs are to go into the computation to determine whether the maximum price has been exceeded or not. A similar consideration, that really applies to every type of contract that has been mentioned, is whether the provisions outlined in the latter part of this chapter are to be included in the agreement. A changed-conditions clause, for example, is generally not thought to be necessary in a true cost-plus agreement, since the owner is to pay *all* costs. This is entirely separate and apart from the question of time and its relation to the cost of overhead and profit in a cost-plus contract. Where the contractor is guaranteeing a maximum price, however, such a clause may be extremely important from the contractor's standpoint.

Finally, the amount of overhead and profit to be incorporated in the contract should, ideally, be related to the inclusion of a guaranteed maximum price.

In the context of a no-risk (or at least extremely low risk) contract, the amount of overhead and profit that a contractor may expect is one factor. Where the risk to the contractor is greatly increased, by his guaranteeing a particular price, then the contractor's corresponding benefits should be considerably greater—at least in theory. Obviously, all the elements of the marketplace will really determine the amount of overhead and profit included in each particular contract.

The Shared-Savings Provisions

This type of agreement is, in one way, the reverse of the maximum price provision. Here, an amount is fixed by the agreement, often referred to as the "target" price; and if the contractor brings the job in under the fixed price, then he shares the savings with the owner. Thus, the agreement may provide that any such saving is to be divided equally (or in any other agreed proportion) between the owner and the contractor.

This provision requires, as well, a plain definition of the costs that are to be included in the determination of any savings. Similarly, if the owner makes major changes that raise the cost of the work, the agreement, to protect the contractor, must provide for appropriate *upward* adjustments of the target figure. Suffice it to say that this type of agreement, like everything that goes into the construction contract, must be carefully thought out and clearly set forth in the context of the particular project being covered.

To this point we have been dealing with the various types of construction contracts and the basic concerns in selecting the appropriate agreement. We will now consider the major provisions to be included in construction contracts.

THE PROVISIONS OF THE AGREEMENT

Whether the contract is, in its type, a unit-price, lump-sum, or cost-plus agreement, or some other variation of all three, certain critically important areas must be covered in order to ensure an adequate agreement. In fact, one way to eliminate most conflict between owner and contractor is to have the respective rights and obligations of each clearly and fully set forth and defined by the contract. The following is a brief outline of the major provisions that should be included in a construction contract.

Scope of the work   Of primary importance, obviously, is a clear and complete description of what the work includes and what it does not include.

Needless litigation often has resulted from an incomplete description of what work is *not* to be performed by the contractor and of what conditions are *not* to be considered the contractor's responsibility.

A full description of both what is to be included in the contract, and what is not, as well as a thorough tabulation and incorporation of the plans and specifications that show the work to be performed will go a long way toward the formation of a satisfactory contract.

Similarly, where a particular type of material or equipment (such as heating, ventilating, and air-conditioning equipment in a building) is to be incorporated in the work, the specifications should plainly define precisely what type and quality is required. Too often the agreement has been vague as to exactly what major items of material or equipment are to be incorporated in the work and has simply provided that they are to be of "first-class quality." Too often the parties entering into such an agreement have found that once the work has started there is a large difference of opinion between the owner and the contractor as to what satisfies such a requirement. Simply put, the contract must clearly define the major items that are to be incorporated in the work.

Payment   To the contractor, perhaps no provision is of greater interest. He must know how, when, and where he is to be paid; and those terms must be clearly set forth in the agreement. The type of contract—whether unit-price, lump-sum or cost-plus—will dictate the way in which payment is to be measured. The contract must also provide how the amount of the payments to be made during the progress of the work (the *progress payments*) are to be determined, when they are to be made, and what—if anything—is to be withheld as *retainage*.

How the amount of each of the progress payments is to be fixed must be given thought. Generally, the owner will have either an architect, a consulting engineer or some other representative involved with the job as it progresses. Many agreements provide that the owner's representative will certify the quantities and amounts involved for each of the progress payments. Here the contractor must try to provide some way of protecting himself from arbitrary or unreasonable action by the owner's representative. With a lump-sum contract, a previously agreed upon breakdown for payment purposes of the major items in the contract is a help. The breakdown should be agreed upon at the time of entering into the contract and, if possible, annexed to the agreement itself. This will not, of course, protect the contractor in the event of a disagreement as to how much of a particular item has been accomplished at a particular time period. It will, however, help materially to eliminate disputes in putting a value on the work.

Retainage provisions are often a source of controversy, since many contractors do not think of negotiating for a provision that the owner will stop deducting retainage at a particular point in the job. If asked, it is not unusual for an owner to agree that at some stage of completion (say 50 percent) no further retainage will be deducted. Indeed many public contracts contain such a provision.

Final payment also gives rise to difficulties, since the question of when the project is complete may be a source of dispute. The time when final payment is to be made and how that time is to be determined must be covered. Similarly, any failure by the owner to make timely payments should be covered by a provision which affords the contractor a proper remedy.

The question of final payment, and when it is to be made, is of even greater importance to a subcontractor, or to a prime contractor doing only a portion of a particular project. There, the contractor should attempt to have the contract provide that the final payment is to become due when his portion of the work (as opposed to the entire project) has been completed. Failing that, some time limit as to when the final payment will be made should be established. A number of recent decisions in New York State, each not entirely consistent with the others, have dealt with the provisions in contracts that provide that a subcontractor is to be paid "when" the contractor receives a corresponding payment from the owner. A number of these cases have held that notwithstanding such a provision, final payment must be made to the subcontractor by the contractor even though the contractor had not yet received a corresponding payment from the owner. The cases in question generally arose in a situation where the failure of the contractor to receive payment from the owner was the result of a lengthy claim or some other uncontemplated condition.

Time of performance   A construction contract will normally provide that the work must be completed by a fixed date.

Many contractors, in agreeing to such a provision, are entirely unaware of a serious and usually unintended risk that results from such an agreement. Courts in many jurisdictions throughout the country have held that a contractor, agreeing *without limitation* to complete the work by a fixed date, may render himself liable for any delay in performance even if that delay is the result of a strike, material shortage, or other matter beyond the contractor's control.

It is essential that the contract contain a clause providing that should the work be delayed by reason of a strike, act of God, major material shortage, or—preferably from the contractor's standpoint—any other cause beyond his reasonable control, then the time of completion will be extended for a comparable period of time.

The contractor must also be wary of owner-supplied contract forms that contain extension provisions. To begin with, they generally are too narrowly drawn and should be expanded for reasonable and proper protection. In addition, such agreements often contain technical notice requirements that if ignored may defeat the right to an otherwise suitable extension of time. It is not unusual for such a provision to require written notice of any condition causing a delay within a few days after the condition first arises. Indeed, the typical provision in such a contract will then go on to provide that failure to furnish such written notice is a complete waiver of any right to an extension of time. Although many courts have found one reason or another not to enforce these harsh provisions, knowledge of and compliance with the technical requirements of the contract is by far the better way to sleep at night. Better still, delete or modify such harsh provisions.

A contractor, faced with a delay, must also be extremely careful to preserve whatever right he may feel he has to be reimbursed for the resulting additional costs. Many owner-supplied contracts provide that, regardless of cause, a contractor's sole right in the event of a delay is to an extension of time. Most courts that have dealt with such a cause have held that it does not preclude the contractor's right to be reimbursed for the additional cost of a delay that has been caused by the owner's interference or breach of contract.[1] A contractor should make it clear to the owner, in such a case, that he expects not only an extension of time, but also to be paid for the additional costs incurred as a result of the delay.

Another major concern, often overlooked by contractors, is the question of when the work is to start. Where construction is not to begin until the owner either directs that it start or until some precedent work, such as the foundation of a building, has been completed, the contractor would be well advised to make sure that his obligations are limited in time. Obviously, the pricing and other essential considerations of most jobs are directly related to the time of performance, including the period when the work is to proceed. Any protracted delay in starting the project will often have severely adverse effects, particularly in inflationary times, upon the contractor's cost of doing the work. To cover this contingency, the contract might provide that if the work is not actually begun by a fixed date then the contractor may, at his option, cancel the agreement. Alternatively, the contract may provide for the payment of escalation or of other added expense resulting from any delay in commencing the project.

Extra work   The contract should, insofar as practicable, define and limit the extent to which the owner may order extra work. The agreement should also set forth the method by which such work is to be directed and how it is to be paid for.

Payment for additional work should obviously include something for the contractor's overhead and profit, and it is customary to agree on some percentage to be added to the direct cost of the work to cover those items. It is not uncommon for such an agreement to provide for 10 percent for overhead and 10 percent for profit on such extra work. Here too, the contractor must carefully examine any owner-supplied contract, since it is usual for the extra work provisions in such an agreement to require a *written* direction by a designated individual, or individuals, as a condition to the recognition of any work as being additional to the contract.

[1]*Cauldwell Wingate Co. v. State,* 276 N.Y. 365.

Another thing that a contractor must be wary of is preserving his right, when extra work is ordered, to an extension of time, if that is necessary, as well as to reimbursement for any additional costs over and above the direct cost of the added work.

A change to a contract, if major, may result in both added cost for the work itself *and* in a costly delay in the completion of the contract. To many owners, the cost of delay is a factor that they do not choose to recognize. The execution of a change order covering only the direct cost of the additional work may ultimately result in a contention by the owner that any delay or other added cost has been liquidated by the agreement. This is another situation where the courts may ultimately reject such a contention but where a simple and timely reservation will make it clear just what is covered by the change order as well as what is not.

Disputes   The mere mention of this word, in the warm afterglow of a newly attained contract, is enough to send chills down the spine of the most intrepid contractor. The attitude here is basically that it is not nice—or possibly inviting trouble and ultimate difficulty—to talk about this subject during the initial contracting stages. In fact, the reverse is often the case.

A provision that clearly outlines the procedures to be used to determine disputes between the owner and the contractor, should they arise, is often a step in itself to the resolution of such a dispute. An agreed-upon procedure as to how, when, and in what forum a dispute is to be settled at least narrows the controversy to its basic merits, rather than leaving open the possibility of procedural jockeying by either side for some real or imagined advantage.

A disputes clause in a contract should include, at a minimum, an agreement as to what law is to apply (generally the law of the state where the work is to be performed) and the court or tribunal to which the dispute is to be submitted. Thus, the parties might agree to arbitrate their disputes and in such a case must spell out what association, entity, or individual is to select the arbitrators and the locale where the arbitration will take place. It is not unusual for construction contracts to provide for arbitration in accordance with the American Arbitration Association. It is helpful, in such a case, to specify in the agreement exactly where such an arbitration will be held. Conversely, the parties may agree to litigate any disputes, and here it is helpful to have an agreement as to the court in which such litigation will take place. For example a contract may specifically provide that any dispute will be determined by a particular court in a particular location. The contract may also provide that the parties waive their right to a jury in any such case, and in complicated cases in the construction industry, such a waiver may be preferable. These questions obviously involve complicated legal considerations that must be thought out and determined in the context of each particular job. The question of whether arbitration or litigation is more satisfactory in resolving disputes is one, for example, about which there is substantial difference of opinion.

Insurance   The insurance requirements of the contract must be clearly defined and must cover at least the type of coverage required and the limits in respect to policies.

The contractor must make sure that *he is adequately covered* for all the risks involved, and he cannot simply assume that the insurance required by the contract provisions is adequate for his purposes. Thus, a contractor will often obtain supplementary or umbrella policies to cover any occurrences that might exceed the basic coverage required by the contract.

Wrap-up policies, provided by the owner, have become increasingly popular. In this situation, the owner purchases an insurance policy covering himself and various contractors for a premium that is supposedly substantially less than the premiums that would be paid if everyone purchased insurance separately. In the case of such a policy it is doubly important for the contractor to make absolutely certain as to the nature and extent of the coverage that is being provided by the owner, and to supplement that coverage if necessary. This is an area where many usually sophisticated contractors have no idea, until too late, about the nature of the coverage included in the so-called wrap-up policy and, indeed, never even bother to look at that policy.

Another thing that must be considered by the contractor is any possible contractual liability created by the terms of the agreement. In other words, if the agreement itself may create some liability (such as an indemnity provision), a special endorsement is usually required to cover that risk. Here the contractor must work with a knowledgeable broker and his counsel, to make sure that he is properly protected.

The furnishing of a bond or other security   It is not unusual for the owner to require the contractor to furnish a surety bond, or bonds, that guarantee both payment to the contractor's laborers, materialmen, and suppliers as well as the contractor's performance of the project.

The contractor's first concern, in such a situation, is to make sure that the cost of the bond is somehow included in his price. That can be easily accomplished by including either the bond's cost in the payments to be made for the work or by providing that the owner will make direct payment for the cost of the bond.

A prime consideration from the contractor's standpoint, often completely ignored, is how to secure *his* right to payment. Shockingly, little attention is generally given by contractors to the question of just what protection he will have if the owner finds himself in financial difficulty. In the present day, when things that were previously unthinkable happen with increasing regularity (such as the near bankruptcy of the nation's largest city), such considerations cannot be safely ignored. A contractor must generally invest a substantial sum of money in a job before recovering corresponding payments and must be concerned with the protection that he will have in the event of the owner's default.

It has not been the custom for owners to furnish contractors with surety bonds guaranteeing payment of the contract price. Notwithstanding, there is no reason why a contractor cannot bargain for such protection. Short of that, the contractor can try to protect himself in the following ways:

He can make certain exactly with whom he is dealing. Owners often attempt to contract in the name of a shell or subsidiary corporation that has no real net worth. When dealing with a substantial entity, make sure it is that entity, and not some undercapitalized subsidiary that is responsible for the payments to be made under the contract.

Similarly, the contractor must be aware of the situation where a party is ostensibly contracting *as agent* for someone else. These agreements typically provide that the agent has no responsibility for the payments under the contract. If it is the so-called agent whose credit the contractor is relying on, such a provision is obviously completely unacceptable. Furthermore, if the credit of the principal is critical to the contractor, he obviously must make sure (preferably in a writing) that the agent has authority to sign for the principal.

A contractor can try to arrange for an initial payment, whether for mobilization or otherwise, to make sure that he is not so heavily invested in a job from the start that in the event of default he will be faced with an absolute disaster. This is often referred to as *front loading.*

He can try to structure the contract and to exercise such tight control over the administration of the contract that he never permits the owner to fall increasingly behind in progress payments for the work that has been performed.

The foregoing are, of course, much easier to say (or write) than to do. Nevertheless, a shocking number of contractors have found themselves in desperate trouble because they have continued to pour their resources into a job long past the time when, in retrospect, they should have called a halt. In today's market the risks of the contracting business, normally very large, have been increased enormously because of the added risk of financial default by the owner. Only determined and, at times, drastic action by the contractor can help to lessen such risks.

Changed conditions   A changed-conditions clause is one which provides that if, during the course of the work, the contractor encounters conditions materially different from those represented by the plans and specifications, or from those reasonably anticipated by the contractor, any additional costs of performing the work as a result of those different conditions will be added to the contract price. Such clauses generally, by their terms, refer to subsurface conditions. The theory behind such a provision is that the contract was entered into on the assumption, by both contractor and owner, of a certain set of conditions that would affect the work. Had both parties known of the conditions actually to be encountered, the cost of performing the work that is the natural result of those conditions would have been included in the contract price. Thus, it is equitable for the owner to bear the cost, in such a situation, that is actually necessary to perform the desired work.

Conversely, it is clearly not fair to try to throw the entire risk of such conditions on the contractor. This type of clause is generally limited to subsurface conditions since that is the type of risk that a contractor cannot generally protect himself against. It is simply not reasonable to expect a contractor to make extensive subsurface borings, or other investigations, prior to entering into a contract. The cost of such a program, as well as the time necessary to carry it out, all make such a detailed investigation almost impossible.

A contractor must carefully examine any contract tendered by an owner to see what risks, in this connection, the literal words of the contract attempt to place on him. Cases are legion which involve disputes concerning *whose* risk a possible occurrence or condition is, and it is not possible to generalize as to how courts will treat particular provisions. Some of the provisions are one-sided and unfair from a contractor's standpoint.

In recent years a trend has slowly but clearly been developing in public construction contracts to include changed-conditions clauses. For example, various agencies of the City of New York, such as the Transit Authority and the Environmental Protection Authority, have been including such clauses in their contracts with some regularity. This is a somewhat surprising and rather refreshing exception to the otherwise one-sided and extremely onerous provisions that generally find their way into such contracts.

It is also surprising, given the importance of this type of clause in the event of real subsurface problems, how infrequently a contractor will attempt to bargain for a changed-conditions clause in a private contract. It appears that the vast majority of contractors either do not consider the possibility of asking (or insisting) that such a clause be included in their contract, or start with the assumption that the owner will simply refuse to consider such a clause. Like anything else in the give and take of contractual bargaining, there is certainly no reason why this subject should not be discussed and, hopefully, successfully resolved.

Lien rights   This is one subject on which, from the contractor's standpoint, literally the less said, the better.

Since the law of most jurisdictions accords a contractor the statutory right, if unpaid, to file a lien against the job or against the premises being improved, no provision conferring such a right is generally required in the agreement. A contractor must, of course, check with counsel as to just what his lien rights are and how they must be perfected, in the jurisdiction where he is working.

More often than not, however, a contract tendered to a contractor by a private owner will contain a clause purporting to have the contractor waive, both for himself and for his subcontractors and suppliers, any right to file a lien. Such a provision will often be legally sufficient to preclude the contractor's right to lien, and such a waiver should be carefully considered by a contractor. The right to file a lien may, in some instances, be very important in securing the contractor's payments. Accordingly, a contractor faced with a request to waive his right to lien must weigh all the financial considerations, including the solvency of the owner, in deciding just how strenuously he will object to such a provision.

In some jurisdictions—notably New York State—the legislature has declared the prospective waiver by a contractor of his right to lien a job to be contrary to public policy and thus void.[2] Such legislation, of course, obviates any pressure on the contractor to waive his lien rights in the process of negotiating for a job.

Guarantee provisions   It is not unusual for an owner to insist that a contractor guarantee his work for some period of time after completion. Here too, the important thing, from the contractor's standpoint, is to be sure that the risks

[2]New York Lien Law §34.

that he undertakes are reasonable ones that are, in general, related to the performance of his work. In other words, if the contractor is to guarantee anything it should be the adequacy and sufficiency of his work and the quality of the material supplied by him. Damage caused by factors beyond his control—such as acts of God, normal wear and tear, or other accident—generally should not be guaranteed by the contractor beyond the completion of the work.

Here, like almost everything else mentioned, concern must be given in advance to the provisions in the contract so as to prevent the type of broad language and all-inclusive terms that, after the fact, may be argued to have placed unintended responsibility on the contractor.

The foregoing is a necessarily brief outline of some of the major areas which must be considered and covered in the formation of a construction contract. It is only a beginning; it is only an alert. Many special conditions and circumstances must be recognized and provided for in relation to each specific project. Indeed, the variations are as extensive and different as are the jobs themselves.

So alerted, the contractor, with competent and experienced counsel, consulted in the initial stages of negotiation, can help to ensure a complete and clear agreement. Such an agreement will not, in itself, ensure either a profitable or a litigation-free project, but will materially increase the chances that the venture will not turn into the disaster feared by the contractor and—at times— hoped for by his competitors.

Chapter **15**

Pitfalls of Subcontracts: From the Subcontractor's Point of View

IRWIN M. TAYLOR, ESQ.
Partner, Kaufman, Taylor, Kimmel & Miller, New York, New York

INTRODUCTION

In the construction process, the subcontractor is commonly regarded as "the low man on the totem pole." Although he and his fellow subcontractors provide by far the bulk of the work and materials, historically he has often been victimized by onerous provisions in the subcontracts he has signed. These provisions have often resulted in the impairment of his rights to recover payment, in costly litigation and generally in inadequate legal remedies. The multitiered levels of construction responsibility place the owner and the architect at the top of the construction process. Collaterally at their side is to be found the institutional or private lender who provides the funding. Below that level is the general contractor who assumes the overall responsibility for the erection and completion of the building or structure. These two tiers of principals have made it their usual practice to engage and utilize the services of highly skilled counsel. The subcontracts which will be presented to the subcontractors emanate from the owners or the general contractors and their respective counsel. Too often subcontractors fail to read subcontracts carefully, or if they do read them, they fail to appreciate fully the implications and consequences of much of the language. This has become increasingly so as subcontracts have become more and more lengthy, complicated, and deliberately devised in many instances to protect the interests of general contractors and owner-builders at the expense of subcontractors.

The subcontractor's desire to get a particular job frequently overrides any other consideration so that his usual sound judgment is blunted by the vision of dollars dancing in his eyes. More often than not, he fails to have his attorney examine a subcontract *before* he signs it. Experience has now shown him beyond a doubt that, in order to avoid unnecessary financial risks and burdensome legal involvement, the subcontractor and his attorney must read every subcontract carefully in advance. Such review and reasonable negotiation may result in the deletion of oppressive provisions and the insertion of other provisions that are protective of the subcontractor's legitimate interests.

Of course, litigation is always a possibility despite the best intentions of all parties to the construction process. If the subcontractor is to fight his battle in the law courts or before arbitration panels on equal terms with general contractors and owner-builders, he must maintain full and complete records of (1) his costs of labor and materials, (2) extra work orders, additional work orders and change orders—all properly authorized, (3) job minutes, (4) daily logs and the daily reports of foremen, (5) shop drawing logs, (6) partial payment requisitions, and (7) correspondence files—including answers to claims of general contractors which, if left unanswered, may constitute legal admissions.

The maintenance of the records indicated above may go a long way to mitigate the effects of onerous provisions in subcontracts but, obviously, if those provisions are in the subcontract to begin with, the subcontractor is at a considerable disadvantage in any legal battle with his general contractor or with an owner-builder. It is to the analysis and possible correction of those provisions that this chapter is addressed.

SUBCONTRACT FORMS

There is a multiplicity of subcontract forms employed in the construction industry. Major builder-owners, general contractors and some construction managers have developed their own forms of subcontracts. They differ widely in comprehensiveness, complexity, and fairness insofar as the interests of subcontractors are involved. Some of these subcontracts constitute not only legal challenges but also a test of the eyesight and patience of subcontractors and their counsel. The attempt to make such subcontracts reasonably equitable by the deletion of offensive provisions and the insertion of more favorable ones calls for courage, firmness, bargaining skill and a thorough understanding of the risks involved in the prospective work.

A more effective method of establishing a greater degree of parity between the builder-owner and the general contractor, on the one hand, and the subcontractor, on the other hand, has been through the use of such standard forms of subcontracts as those sponsored by the American Institute of Architects (AIA Form A-401) and by the Associated General Contractors of America (AGC). Even these recommended subcontract forms require intelligent modification and supplementation to fit the needs of a particular job, special circumstances, or a particular trade or subcontractor.

Necessarily, this chapter is directed at subcontract provisions in general and not at provisions in any specific subcontract. At the risk of repetition, every subcontractor is well advised to seek the guidance of competent legal counsel before signing any subcontract.

SCOPE OF THE WORK

Ideally, the work and materials to be provided by the subcontractor should be precisely and concisely described. In bidding a job, the usual practice is for the subcontractor to direct his attention only to plans and specifications which directly relate to his particular trade. He bases his price upon those documents, but if he neglects to observe or appreciate certain expansive terms of his subcontract, he may unwillingly have agreed to perform other work and possibly furnish materials not expressly set forth in the plans and specifications.

Article 2 of the AIA subcontract Form A-401 states "The Subcontractor shall furnish. . . . " and then the form contains the instruction that there be inserted "a precise description of the Work covered by this Subcontract and refer to numbers of Drawings and pages of Specifications including Addenda and accepted Alternates." The best way to eliminate controversy and unanticipated expenses is for both parties to a subcontract to follow the practice—which has become quite common—of specifying the page number, section number, paragraph number, and line number of the portion of the plans and specifications or other documents that the subcontractor intends to furnish.

Despite the intended delimitation of the scope of the work as suggested above, some subcontracts will contain further provisions which may have the effect of expanding the work beyond that contemplated by the subcontractor. Thus, a widely used subcontract contains the following language:

> All of the above work shall be performed agreeably to all the contract drawings and specifications and any addenda and modifications thereof made by the said architect and to the dimensions and explanations thereon, therein and herein contained and any detailed drawings of said architect hereafter furnished, subject to all general and special clauses and conditions contained in said contract, specifications, addenda and modifications, according to the true intent and meaning thereof and of these presents including all labor, engineering services for lines, grades, elevations, etc. and materials, incident thereto or as are usually performed or furnished in connection with such work, and regardless of whether the labor or

material hereby sublet are referred to as under one or more headings in the specifications, it being the intention that all work usually performed by the trades covered by this agreement and required by the general contract, shall be performed by the second party. All such labor and material shall be the best of their respective kinds and the second party shall provide at his own expense all tools, scaffolding, hoisting facilities for materials, elevator service for employees, implements, water, heat, light, power, electric service, cartage, storage space, shop drawings, tests, molds, photographs, models, guarantees, samples and permits necessary for the due and proper performance of this contract and pay all inspection fees, royalties and license fees and save the first party harmless from loss or annoyance on account of claims or suits of any kind for infringement of patents in connection with the work. If drawings or specifications conflict, the decision of the said architect must be obtained before proceeding with the work, otherwise the second party will be held liable to make any change necessary to correct any such conflict without expense to the first party. Any work or material shown on the plans and not mentioned in the specifications, or vice-versa, shall be taken as shown and mentioned in both. The approval by the architect of drawings submitted by the second party shall not relieve the second party from changes or deviations not specifically called to the architect's attention in writing nor for errors therein. It is the intention that in so far as the portion of the general contract being performed by the second party is concerned, the second party assumes all the obligations of the first party under the general contract.

Invariably this type of provision is in small type and is alone sufficient to discourage a careful and thoughtful reading. Despite the pinpointing and specification of the exact work and materials to be furnished by the subcontractor, the all-embracing language quoted above, if taken literally, would require the subcontractor to do "all work usually performed by the trades covered by this agreement and required by the general contract." Very often, the subcontractor is never presented with a copy of the general contract nor does he request a copy. Usually the subcontract, in some other provision, will contain a representation by the subcontractor that he has examined the general contract or that he has been given a copy when, in fact, he has never seen one at all.

The same quoted provision would require the subcontractor to provide, among other things, the best material although it was his intention in his bidding to provide good or average quality material. In most instances, moreover, the subcontractor does not intend to provide at his own expense such services as hoisting facilities, elevator service, water, heat, light, power, or electric service, unless otherwise expressly set forth in the subcontract as a specific obligation of his particular trade. There are, of course, in the same quoted paragraph other objectionable features which the individual subcontractor will recognize. One of them, in particular, warrants special attention. That is the one which requires the subcontractor to assume all the obligations of the general contractor under his general contract with the owner. Conceivably, a subcontractor might be persuaded, to his detriment, during the course of construction that he did have a legal obligation to perform some additional work which the general contractor obligated himself to do under his general contract with the owner but which was not specifically described in the subcontract between the general contractor and the subcontractor. If the subcontractor refused to do such work, he might find himself in a controversy with the general contractor which would result in the withholding of payment to him of his progress-payment requisitions and in mutual claims for delay. Needless to say, this would be productive of considerable financial expense to the subcontractor who might thereafter have to face also the uncertainties of costly litigation or arbitration. Consequently, it is of vital importance to a subcontractor that he and his attorney delete, modify, or otherwise amend the quoted language with a strict regard for confining the subcontractor's obligations to precisely the extent, character, and quality of the work contemplated by him.

It would appear that it is the responsibility of the subcontractor, not that of his attorney, to thoroughly study and analyze the scope of the work he plans to perform by reference to the plans, specifications, drawings, and other related documentation. The lawyer is unlikely to be a construction "expert" insofar as the technical aspects of the work are concerned.

Besides agreeing to furnish all labor, materials, equipment, supplies, and other things necessary to perform and complete the job in accordance with his contract, the subcontractor must comply with the requirements of applicable building codes. In addition, he agrees to abide by the terms of the general contract between the general contractor and the owner (provided, of course, he does not at the same time accept language which expands his obligations beyond the scope of the work contemplated by him, as indicated above). If governmental financing or assistance is involved, the subcontractor should be familiar with the requirements of that specific public agency before he signs his subcontract.

An examination of the general contract, general conditions, and special conditions of the various contract documents may reveal that there are other duties and liabilities imposed upon the subcontractor's work which may not be expressly set forth in the specific trade sections relating to his work. There may be time schedules which will be impossible for the subcontractor to comply with unless he intends to incur extensive overtime expenses. If he is unaware of these time schedules at the time of his bid and the signing of his subcontract, he will have subjected himself to financial burdens that will threaten the profitability of his subcontract.

In some instances, there is the possibility that architectural and engineering services will be deemed to constitute part of the term "work." Where such an interpretation may possibly be applied, it would obviously be best to expressly exclude such services. From state to state, there is considerable variation on the definition of architectural or engineering services. In some states the definition may be so broad as to encompass the performance of such work by a non-professional, even a nonprofessional subcontracting corporation.

A subcontract will usually contain a statement that the subcontractor has examined the work site and, through his independent investigation, is familiar with all conditions affecting the work to be done and the material to be furnished. If the subcontractor's work will be vitally affected by the nature of the site and work conditions, he will be bound by this provision and will not be entitled to extras occasioned by conditions and circumstances that he did not anticipate. Further, if despite reasonable inspection, unusual site conditions or subsurface conditions should develop not within the reasonable contemplation of the parties, the subcontractor may be entitled to an extra for the additional costs attributable to those conditions. Test borings are often furnished to an excavator on an "information-only" basis. The general contractor will then expressly disclaim any warranty and shift the responsibility to the subcontractor. Under those circumstances, the test borings are a guide and the subcontractor must be prepared for possible surprises that may appear during the performance of his work.

TERMS OF PAYMENT

During the course of construction, the subcontractor will be paid so-called "progress payments" against requisitions furnished by him to the general contractor and thereafter approved by the owner and/or architect. The payment requisitions are usually submitted on a monthly basis and actual payment will follow within 20 or 30 days of the time of the submission of the requisition. The subcontract will usually contain the so-called "contingent-payment" provision whereby payment of the monthly requisition (or final payment) will be made only after payment therefor has been received by the general contractor from the owner.

Some subcontractors may enjoy sufficiently strong bargaining positions so that their subcontracts will make the monthly payment (or final payment) unconditional and not dependent upon whether the general contractor has been paid by the owner. Particularly where the performance of the work will span a lengthy period of time, the subcontractor has some leverage in enforcing payment of his monthly requisitions because delay in payment over an unreasonable period of time will be deemed to be a material breach of the subcontract and permit the subcontractor to leave the job. Ultimately, however, the extent to which he is willing to countenance delinquencies in payment of his monthly requisitions will depend on his business judgment, whether the delay be attributable to the owner's failure to make timely payments to the general contractor or whether the delinquency represents an accrual of unpaid balances stemming from the refusal of the owner, the architect, or the general contractor to agree with the amount claimed by the subcontractor as the fair value of the work performed to date.

The subcontract will usually provide that the estimate of the architect as to the value of the work performed will be binding on the subcontractor for the purpose of computing the amount of the monthly progress payment to be made. Deducted from that estimate, however, will be "retainage" or "retention," a percentage of the completed work which is withheld to ensure the quality and complete performance of the work by the subcontractor. The amount of such retainage will vary. No subcontractor should agree to permit retainage to exceed 10 percent at any time. It is a widespread practice that, once the subcontractor has completed 50 percent of his work, no further retainage is withheld from his subsequent progress payments. The result is that the percentage of the retainage on his work is gradually reduced to no more than 5 percent.

The concept of retainage is engraved in the construction business, but the validity of this concept has more recently been subjected to serious challenge by aggressive and militant subcontractor organizations, such as The American Subcontractors Association. Particularly where a subcontractor posts a performance bond, there would appear to be no persuasive reason for the subcontractor to have to be subjected to the retainage provision. The existence of the retainage practice itself is a cost factor to the subcontractor. This has been recognized by the Federal General Services Administration and by other federal construction agencies. They have experimented with the elimination of retainage provisions and have found that bids for work have come in at comparatively lower prices than in those situations where the general contractors will impose retainage provisions on subcontractors.

Whatever the retainage, a reasonable time limit should be provided. If the subcontract provides that the retainage be withheld until completion of the entire project, it is especially unfair to such subcontractors as the excavator and the steel erector whose work is completed early in the course of construction. Such a provision may even be unfair if the project consists of several buildings and the retainage is to be held on one building until after completion of the other buildings constituting "the entire project." Obviously, provisions of this kind create very severe hardships, particularly in the case of complex construction projects.

If no trade breakdown is made as to the progress payments received by the general contractor from the owner as the work proceeds, it is virtually impossible to determine how the payments are to be fairly allocated to the various trades. The general contractor is in a position to use his own discretion to pick and choose the subcontractors he will favor or discriminate against. In some instances, the general contractor will be doing some of the work himself and will be inclined to "front-load" his requisitions and his payments so as to favor himself or dummy corporations controlled by or affiliated with him. It thus becomes of paramount importance that the subcontractor ascertain, in advance of signing his subcontract, whether the contract documents require the owner or the architect to break down the monthly progress payments according to trade.

In some instances, a dispute may arise between a general contractor and an owner about a portion of the work involving only one subcontractor. If the owner now stops all payments to the general contractor, the other subcontractors whose work is not involved in the dispute are left without payment. Where subcontractors accept—without restriction or limitation—payment provisions of this type, the financial burden for the construction has, in effect, shifted from the general contractor to the subcontractors. This type of subcontract provision, therefore, should be modified to limit the number of days within which the general contractor must pay the subcontractor, irrespective of whether the general contractor has been paid by the owner.

The burdens of adequate funding and financial responsibility should lie most heavily on the owner and on the general contractor. The contingent-payment provision becomes the vehicle for shifting these burdens to the shoulders of the subcontractors. More and more, subcontractors have been insisting that their responsibility in the hierarchy of construction is to do the work and supply the materials; and having done so, they should be paid within a reasonable period of time, irrespective of whether the general contractor has been paid by the owner and irrespective of any dispute which may have arisen between them not involving work for which a particular subcontractor is responsible.

If a subcontractor's progress requisitions are not paid to him, whatever leverage he may have in his right to cease work is entirely gone when he has completed his work and is awaiting final payment. If the final payment, like the earlier progress payments, is made contingent upon the general contractor being paid by the owner, the subcontractor runs the actual risk that he will never be paid his final payment. A common form of final-payment provision states that "the balance shall be payable thirty days after the General Contract is completed and accepted and the last payment received from the owner." The owner may be financially incapable of meeting his obligations to the general contractor; or he may be delayed for other reasons in doing so; or there may be a dispute, as between the owner and the general contractor; or there may be other vexing problems involving delays in institutional funding or governmental financing, licenses or permits, community pressures and interferences, or other circumstances that impede the flow of final-payment funds to the general contractor. If the literal language is followed, then the fact of payment to the general contractor by the owner becomes a condition which must be satisfied before the subcontractor may insist upon payment from the general contractor.

An increasing number of courts, however, have taken the view that the literal language of the so-called contingent-payment clause is not to be strictly followed in that the parties intended something else by that language, namely, that the subcontractor intended to wait only a reasonable period of time for the general contractor to be paid by the owner. Once, therefore, such a reasonable time has elapsed, the subcontractor is entitled to receive his final payment in full.[1]

Although the courts now tend to interpret the contingent-payment clause as one which only fixes a reasonable time within which the subcontractor may be expected to wait for payment from the general contractor rather than making payment by the owner to the general contractor a condition of payment by the general contractor to the subcontractor, nevertheless the mere existence of such a provision in a subcontract is a risk which the subcontractor should not take. Where the contingent-payment provision does appear, it should be qualified by the subcontractor by the addition of such language as "but in no event shall payment to the subcontractor be made more than (30, 60) days after substantial completion of the work by the subcontractor."

---

[1]*Schuler-Haas Elec. Corp. v. Aetna Cas. & Sur. Co.*, 49 A.D. 2d 60, 371 N.Y.S. 2d 207, aff'd 40 N.Y. 2d 883, 389 N.Y.S. 2d 348, 357 NE 2d 1003; *Thomas J. Dyer Co. v. Bishop Int'l Eng. Co.*, 303 F.2d 655 (6th Cir., 1962).

The AIA and AGC standard forms of subcontract do not contain the contingent-payment provision, but they do contain a provision which makes progress payments and final payments contingent upon payment certificates issued by the architect. This type of provision also has an objectionable aspect in view of the fact that the architect may refuse to certify the job because the work of another subcontractor or the work of the general contractor is improper, incomplete, or otherwise defective. Thus, a subcontractor who has performed his work completely and satisfactorily may not get paid even though his work is not the cause of the refusal of the architect to issue the necessary certificates. Therefore, the clause which makes payment to the subcontractor contingent upon the issuance of a certificate for payment by the architect should be modified by annexing a provision which, in substance, requires the general contractor to pay the subcontractor on demand for his work at the time when payment is otherwise due the subcontractor if refusal or failure of the architect to issue the certificate for payment is based on any cause not the fault of the subcontractor.

An owner may willfully delay payment to the general contractor because he has other uses for those monies. The same may be true of the general contractor. The effect of contingent-payment clauses generally is to enable the owner and/or the general contractor to shift the financial burdens for the construction to the subcontractors who invariably have obligations of their own to pay for their labor and material on a far more current basis. In addition to modifying or limiting the application of contingent provisions, as indicated above, the subcontractors should insert other language which will have the effect of making the unjustified use of their funds costly to the owner and to the general contractor. Where a subcontractor has sufficient bargaining power, his subcontract could provide that he will be entitled to receive interest if progress payments, retainage, or final payment are not promptly made, together with reasonable counsel fees, should legal services be required to effect collection.

TEMPORARY SITE FACILITIES

Many forms of subcontracts impose responsibility for temporary site facilities on all the subcontractors even though, obviously, some of those facilities may have no application or, at best, minimum application to particular subcontractors. In the quoted provision on pages 15-3 to 15-4, every subcontractor is required to provide scaffolding, hoisting facilities for materials, elevator service for employees, water, heat, light, power, electric service, and storage space. This type of provision should be stricken so that responsibility for such temporary facilities will rest upon the general contractor except that ordinarily the electrical subcontractor will provide the temporary electrical service while the plumbing subcontractor will see to the supply of water and temporary heat.

Removal of trash and debris is usually a term of every subcontract also. Each subcontractor is required to remove his trash and debris to a common site provided by the general contractor. The provision is a reasonable one, but it frequently becomes a source for the assertion of substantial backcharges by the general contractor. Close scrutiny of such backcharge claims will often reveal that a general contractor has pyramided his claims by repetitious and fictitious charges against many subcontractors where their actual contribution of trash and debris during the course of the performance of their work is relatively minor or far less than claimed. Having accepted the responsibility for trash and debris removal, the prudent subcontractor will police such removal and maintain adequate records and, in appropriate cases, suitable photographs.

MECHANIC'S LIENS

In every jurisdiction, subcontractors are granted by statute the right to file a mechanic's lien against the realty being improved to the extent of the work and labor performed and materials furnished. This right may even extend to materials fabricated but not yet delivered and even to equipment that is leased for use by others at the site where the work is proceeding. The extent and nature of a mechanic's lien will vary from state to state as will the circumstances under which the notice of mechanic's lien may be filed. Some states may require a preliminary notice of intention to file a lien. Similarly, the time within which a notice of mechanic's lien may validly be filed will vary widely from state to state. Thus, it is possible for a subcontractor to lose his right to file a mechanic's lien with respect to all or part of his claim simply because of his own failure to comply with statutory requirements.

When a subcontractor impairs his statutory rights through his own neglect, he has, of course, only himself to blame. It is another thing, however, when his rights are impaired by reason of his having been compelled by an unreasonable general contractor to waive his rights to file his notice of mechanic's lien. New York and Massachusetts have protective legislation which expressly makes the waiver of a mechanic's lien void as against public policy. Such statutes recognize that the purpose of mechanic's liens is to encourage construction of improvements to realty by ensuring those who contribute to a project that they will be compensated for their efforts. This principle has been long ingrained in this country's history. The first mechanic's lien law was enacted by the Maryland General Assembly in 1791 and the drafting is attributed to Thomas Jefferson.

Whether or not the right to file a mechanic's lien came from the same brilliant and inspired mind as that which fashioned the Declaration of Independence, the fact is that subcontractors have treasured that right. A dilution or impairment of that right is not likely or casually to be accepted by subcontractors. If that right is not expressly protected against waiver by statutory enactment, its surrender in a contract should not be made by a subcontractor unless some other reasonable and equivalent guaranty of payment is afforded. Thus, if a payment bond is furnished by a general contractor, the subcontractor may very well consider such a waiver appropriate. He should realize, however, that his right to sue on the payment bond may not have the immediate remedial effect in obtaining payment that his right to file a mechanic's lien would obtain for him.

Even where there is no waiver, the benefits of the filing of a mechanic's lien may be of dubious value in some instances. Thus, where the owner has a relatively minor equity in a property subject to a large outstanding mortgage, a default in the construction loan and its subsequent foreclosure by the lender is likely to wipe out all or substantially all of the claim of the subcontractor.

The states vary widely as to the extent to which advances under construction loans will have priority over the claims of subcontractors. In some states, the construction lender is protected, once he has filed his construction loan document, not only to the extent of advances made prior to the inception of the subcontractor's work or prior to the filing of the subcontractor's lien, but also to the extent of advances made thereafter. Where the construction lender does not have this advantage by statute, a subcontractor may be required by his subcontract to subordinate his right to file a mechanic's lien to all advances thereafter made by the construction lender even to the extent of advances made after the effective date of the filing of the mechanic's lien. The wisdom of agreeing to such subordination is something which each individual subcontractor should carefully consider in the light of the circumstances affecting his particular work and the credit risks he is assuming in dealing with the particular general contractor and owner.

Once a subcontractor has agreed to waive his lien, the subsequent default of the general contractor, including even nonpayment, will not permit the subcontractor to file his lien. The subcontractor should also not be misled by a provision in his subcontract under which he agrees not to file a lien until his claim has been arbitrated. If he binds himself to such provision, in all likelihood the matter would not have been arbitrated within the statutory time permitting him to file his lien. The practical effect of such provision is to cause the contractor to effectively waive his lien.

CHANGES IN THE WORK

Although the parties to a subcontract may by the very terms of the subcontract define the entire scope of the work and accurately define and limit the obligations of the subcontractor (as set forth above under Subcontract Forms), most subcontracts contain provisions permitting the general contractor to make changes which may increase or diminish the work. Such terms as "extra work" and "additional work" are frequently used as interchangeable terms. Some courts have found the distinction between these terms and look upon extra work as that which arises entirely outside of and independently of the subcontract while additional work is regarded as that which is required for the performance of the subcontract even though it is not included within the description of the work.

The foregoing legal distinction is very difficult to make, understand, or apply. Some subcontracts will require the subcontractor to perform both additional work and extra work while other forms will simply refer to "changes" in the work.

The presence of a provision in a subcontract which permits the general contractor to require the subcontractor to perform either or both additional work and extra work imposes certain risks upon the subcontractor. Thus, the additional or extra work may be required to be performed on a cost-plus basis where the "plus" factor may be as little as 5 or 10 percent for overhead and a similar percentage for profit. Consequently, the overall profitability of the job may be significantly decreased where the subcontractor is required to perform substantial work on such a basis where his anticipated profit margin was considerably larger. Moreover, should the subcontractor be given numerous change orders which compel him to defer the completion of this work, the subcontractor may be adversely affected by being unable to transfer his work force to other more profitable jobs or he may be caught by noncompensable rising prices. Even the manner of performing the changed work may be so inefficient for the subcontractor that his costs in performing the changes may exceed those which were connected with the original basic work of the subcontract.

As much flexibility as possible in the pricing of the changes should be made part of the terms in the subcontract for the performance of extra work or additional work. If that work is to be done on a cost-plus basis, the plus factor should anticipate as far as possible the extra work which the subcontractor may be expected to perform. A unit price schedule may be included which recognizes or anticipates the extra costs, and it may be prudent also to have an escalation formula as well.

Where the subcontract permits the general contractor to require changed work, a frequent provision—in place of the cost-plus basis—is that of a negotiated price. Of course, if the price cannot be negotiated and the work must, nevertheless, be done, some other formula must be found which will permit the work to proceed and yet protect the subcontractor from having to perform the work at a loss or on an unprofitable basis. This can be accomplished by providing for a speedy arbitration proceeding.

Most subcontracts provide that a subcontractor will not be entitled to be paid for extra work or additional work unless it was authorized in writing prior to its performance. In the field, it is a common experience for subcontractors to find that the work is demanded by the general contractor's field superintendent even though the subcontract may limit the authorization of such work to an officer of the general contractor. On these occasions, it often appears to the subcontractor and his field force that the only realistic, practical, and economical thing to do is to perform the work and hope that the general contractor will pay at least its reasonable value. Such disregard of the express terms of the subcontract frequently results in a dispute wherein the general contractor will, in fact, refuse to pay the amount demanded by the subcontractor or reject the claim altogether on the ground that it was never authorized.

If the subcontract expressly provides that the subcontractor will be paid for extra work or additional work only if it is authorized in writing prior to its performance, then the subcontractor should make it a field rule that he will not perform such work unless there is appropriate authorization in writing. For a subcontractor to proceed to do extra or additional work without proper written authorization is to assume a serious risk. Not only is it a source of likely controversy with the general contractor which may end up with the subcontractor having to accept a much lesser amount than the value of his work, but he may have to incur further costs by resorting to litigation or arbitration. Some courts will strictly apply the provision and will deny recovery to a subcontractor where he proceeded to do the work without written authorization. In many cases, however, if there is adequate proof that there was an oral direction for the work to be done, and the general contractor or the owner-builder has knowingly received and accepted the benefits of the work, the subcontractor is likely to be awarded the reasonable value of his work, notwithstanding the subcontract provision requiring written authorization.

On occasion, the subcontract provides that the subcontractor will be paid for extra or additional work only to the extent that the general contractor is paid for such work as extra or in addition to his own contract. This is a dangerous provision because, frequently, the work involved was originally the responsibility of the general contractor under his own contract with the owner and was not covered by any of the subcontracts. Accordingly, the owner would have no obligation to pay the general contractor who, in turn, would then contend he had no obligation to pay the subcontractor.

WARRANTIES

A common provision in a subcontract is one which requires a subcontractor to warrant his work for one year from the date of final acceptance of the entire project. However, with formal acceptance so often subject to inordinate delays, this provision can be a source of trouble. Moreover, the work of a subcontractor frequently affects only one part of a large project on which work may proceed for several years, and a long time may elapse before final acceptance is given to the entire project. Nevertheless, the time of the warranty by the individual subcontractor will not have commenced despite the fact that he has long since completed his work and the premises may even be occupied. The effect of such a warranty is to put the subcontractor into the position of maintaining the premises, rather than simply acting as a guarantor for a reasonable period of time. In many instances, of course, the subcontractor has recourse to the manufacturer of the product he has installed, but the time period of that guarantee is likewise limited. Unless the subcontractor is careful, he may find himself in the position of guaranteeing the installation far beyond the period of the manufacturer's guarantee.

Subcontractors should insist that their warranties commence from the date of completion of their portion of the work—building by building, section by section, floor by floor—if this is possible. The last date for commencement of the warranty period should certainly be no later than the date the owner obtains the beneficial use of the subcontractor's work product.

Aside from considerations of the time period of a warranty, the subcontract will usually require the subcontractor to warrant that he has used all new materials and equipment, that his work complies with the plans and specifications, and that the work is free of any defects due to faulty materials or workmanship. The subcontractor will also warrant that his work and materials are of good quality. Some warranties may state that the materials used are to be of the *best* quality. Unless the subcontractor has taken this latter requirement into consideration in fixing his price, he should change the word "best" to "good" or "average."

If a subcontractor is essentially a vendor of equipment or materials or fixtures, he is really engaged in a sales transaction, and as such, his transactions are subject to the Uniform Commercial Code. The Uniform Commercial Code has been adopted by all states except Louisiana. The Uniform Commercial Code imposes on vendors so-called "implied warranties," which are not expressly set forth in the subcontract. Such a vendor should be aware that these implied warranties mean that the vendor impliedly warrants (1) that the fixtures or equipment or the materials are merchantable in that what is supplied is at least of average or medium quality and (2) that the equipment or fixtures or materials supplied are fit for the particular use for which they are required providing the customer relied on the vendor's skill or judgment in selecting or furnishing the specific equipment, fixtures, or materials supplied.

Some subcontract provisions call for the subcontractor to warrant that his performance of the work will be to the satisfaction of the general contractor or the owner or the architect. Depending upon the circumstances, the subcontractor should avoid a situation where his work will be dependent for approval upon a third party who may be arbitrary and unreasonable in his judgment. Even where that occurs, a court may still be disposed to consider the warranty as having been satisfactorily performed if the work done and/or the materials supplied by the subcontractor operate in a reasonably satisfactory way. Of course, if the subcontractor has warranted that his work will be to the satisfaction of a third party and the approval of that party involves his artistic or esthetic sense or his unique or expert judgment, then the subcontractor will be bound by the warranty that he has made. Consequently, a warranty provision in a subcontract must be thoughtfully considered by a subcontractor, and, in an appropriate case, part or all of the proposed provision should be deleted.

A warranty provision in a subcontract is frequently tied in with an inspection provision whereby the work is made subject to inspection and test by the owner or general contractor. The inspection clause may specifically define the time and method of inspection as well as the consequences of an unsatisfactory inspection. The financial consequences of the inspection clause as well as the feasibility of the inspection method should be carefully weighed by the subcontractor.

"HOLD-HARMLESS" AND INDEMNITY CLAUSES

It is reasonable to expect that a subcontractor should agree to "hold harmless" and indemnify a general contractor and/or the owner against any claims, damages, or other liability caused by the subcontractor's negligence or from the performance of his subcontract. It is unreasonable, unfair, and costly, however, to require the subcontractor to hold the general contractor and/or the owner harmless even from their own negligence. Some hold-harmless provisions are so broad in scope as to cover not only the general contractor and the owner but the architect as well and also their agents and employees.

These broad forms of hold-harmless and indemnity provisions subject the subcontractor to substantial potential liability. The subcontractor's insurance policies may not cover him against such liability. It would be well for a subcontractor who accepts a broad form of hold-harmless and indemnity provision as part of his subcontract to ascertain whether his own insurance policy covers him against this type of exposure. Such coverage necessarily entails additional premiums.

Without such insurance protection, a subcontractor who is subject to a broad form of hold-harmless and indemnity provision assumes obligations to pay for damages for which he would otherwise not be responsible. What he is doing, in effect, is to assume a contractual obligation, as distinguished from a liability imposed by law, and is responsible for his own negligence or the breach of his obligation to perform the subcontract work. Should some accident or event occur for which he does not have insurance protection, the contractual obligation he has assumed may be so large as to deal his business an irreparable blow. For this reason, the subcontractor must be extraordinarily vigilant against accepting a broad form of hold-harmless and indemnity provision in his subcontract.

The preferable form of hold-harmless and indemnity is that which limits the subcontractor's liability solely to claims or damage arising out of the act or omission of the subcontractor. The AIA form of hold-harmless and indemnity provisions establishes a middle ground between the limited form and the broad form in that the subcontractor is required to indemnify and hold harmless the general contractor from damages caused in whole *or in part* by any negligent act or omission of the subcontractor.

An increasing number of states have adopted legislation which declares the broad form of hold-harmless and indemnity provision void as against public policy.[2] Nevertheless, the intermediate form which is embodied in the AIA subcontract would be considered to be valid and effective in the instance where, in addition to the subcontractor himself, the general contractor is partly to blame. Consequently, even in those states where the broad form of hold-harmless and indemnity provision is invalid, the subcontractor should still ascertain from his insurance broker and verify with his insurance carrier that his liability insurance policy fully protects him as against the operation of any intermediate form of hold-harmless and indemnity provision.

INSURANCE

Every precaution should be taken by a subcontractor to make certain that all risks which he has agreed to insure are, or can be, covered by insurance. In

[2]California, Delaware, Florida, Georgia, Hawaii, Idaho, Illinois, Indiana, Maryland, Michigan, Mississippi, Nevada, New Hampshire, New Mexico, New York, North Dakota, Ohio, Oregon, Pennsylvania, South Dakota, Tennessee, Texas, Utah, Virginia, Washington, West Virginia.

addition to having his lawyer review the subcontract, the subcontractor should have a knowledgeable insurance broker give special attention to the insurance provisions. Moreover, the cost of the insurance should not be overlooked in figuring the subcontractor's bid price.

The usual coverages include workmen's compensation, comprehensive automobile liability, comprehensive general liability, and contractual liability insurance for the benefit of the general contractor whereby the general contractor is insured for claims resulting from any or all liabilities assumed by the subcontractor under the subcontract. The subcontract usually provides that this insurance is to be obtained and paid for by the subcontractor. In some states, a practice has developed of having the subcontract provide that the subcontractor is to place all his insurance through a master policy obtained by the general contractor. In some instances, where there is this method of placement of insurance, the general contractor may agree to pay all the premiums. These arrangements may be variously known as "wrap-up" and "designated carrier" insurance.

While wrap-up and designated carrier insurance may have some advantages for the general contractor, there are serious objections so far as the subcontractor is concerned. These objections may include: (1) increased clerical work because the subcontractor must have separate policies and audits for each job; (2) loss of premium discounts and, thus, higher net insurance premiums; (3) excess-limits charges on each separate job instead of one single charge by his own insurance carrier for public liability coverage; (4) no control over claim investigations and their handling, with the result that the subcontractor may be saddled with higher loss ratios and premiums, and (5) the insurance company would appear to be more responsive to and concerned with the general contractor than with the subcontractor.

In addition to the possible objections set forth above, a loss will be applied against a subcontractor's rating even in the circumstance where a lawsuit is settled without the consent of the subcontractor and even where he has substantial proof that he was not liable.

Vigorous objection on the part of a subcontractor to participation in a wrap-up or in a designated carrier insurance program will very often result in its elimination from a subcontract.

Some subcontracts may require a subcontractor to furnish a performance bond by whose terms the subcontractor agrees to indemnify an owner against loss resulting from his failure to perform the subcontract work in accordance with plans and specifications. If such requirement is imposed upon the subcontractor at the very outset, the subcontractor obviously must ascertain whether his company is bondable and what the cost of the premium will be. If he cannot furnish the bond, the general contractor will not accept him as a subcontractor unless, of course, he chooses to waive that requirement.

Another provision which is capable of creating a problem for a subcontractor is one where initially the subcontractor is not required to furnish a performance bond but may be required to do so at a later time during the course of the performance of his work. If it should then be required, he may find himself unable to provide such a performance bond, and at that time he will be deemed to be in breach of his subcontract. Consequently, the subcontractor should seek to delete from the subcontract any provision which subjects him to the risk that he may be called upon at a later date, during the course of construction, to furnish a performance bond.

By contrast with the performance bond which runs to the benefit of the general contractor, a subcontract may provide that the subcontractor furnish a labor and material payment bond which will guaranty payment by the subcontractor to those furnishing labor, material, and supplies to him in the performance of the work on the subcontract.

Of particular importance to the subcontractor is the presence of a labor and material payment bond furnished by the general contractor for the subcontractor's benefit. Such bonds are required by federal and state laws with respect to work performed on governmental construction projects. Under the federal Miller Act, where a subcontractor has not been paid within 90 days after he last provided labor or material, he may sue on the bond furnished by the general contractor. If the subcontractor is a second-tier subcontractor who does not have a direct contractual relationship with the general contractor, he must give written notice to the general contractor within 90 days after the labor and/or material was furnished. If a lawsuit is to be commenced upon a Miller Act bond, then it must be brought within one year after the last of the labor was performed or the last of the materials supplied.

Most states have statutes similar to—but not identical with—the Miller Act.

In many instances of private construction, an owner may require a general contractor to furnish a payment bond for the benefit of the subcontractor. Whether there is a labor and material payment bond as the result of governmental requirement or because a private owner has insisted upon one, the subcontractor should routinely request that he be furnished with a copy of the particular bond. In private construction payment bonds, there may be considerable variation with respect to the notification procedures and the time limitations within which a lawsuit may be begun. If a subcontractor is not in possession of the bond, he may find his rights with respect to notification or timeliness of suit jeopardized by his inability to obtain a copy of the bond quickly and thereby ascertain what he must do to come within its terms.

DELAYS

A subcontract may state that "time is of the essence" in completion of the job. The subcontract may even fix a specific date for completion and subject the subcontractor to damages for any delay beyond the contemplated date of completion. The damages to be determined will be those which can reasonably be shown to be the consequence of the acts of delay on the part of the subcontractor, or a fixed amount may be set forth as "liquidated damages." A liquidated-damage clause may fix such a sum as $2,000 for each calendar day of delay in completing certain specified work. If it is evident that the amount fixed is not a reasonable measure of the actual damages but is intended to operate as a penalty, a court will not enforce such a liquidated-damage provision and declare it to be void as a penalty.

Where the subcontract provides for damages for delay, the subcontractor should insist that he will not be liable where the delay is caused by strikes, insurrection, civil disorder, embargoes, acts of God, or other causes and circumstances beyond his control.

Even without an express provision in the subcontract imposing on the subcontractor liability for liquidated damages, he may, nevertheless, be responsible for such liquidated damages by reason of a common provision in subcontracts whereby the subcontractor is bound to the general contractor in the same manner in which the general contractor is bound to the owner. Thus, if the general contractor becomes liable to the owner for liquidated damages by reason of his delay in performance of the contractor's work, the subcontractor would be bound to the general contractor for liquidated damages also. This could result from the circumstance where a general contractor has lost time in the early phases of the performance of his work and now seeks to make up that lost time by subjecting his subcontractors to accelerated and unrealistic time schedules. Subcontracts will often provide that the subcontractor will comply with the time schedules of the general contractor. Consequently, if the general contractor now requires performance by the subcontractor within an unrealistic time frame and the subcontractor cannot comply, then the subcontractor will become liable for the resulting damages within the subcontract provision which provides that the subcontractor is bound to the general contractor in the same way that the general contractor is bound to the owner.

In the exercise of prudence, a subcontractor should have included in his subcontract a provision whereby he is allowed a specific period of time, measured in terms of days, within which to perform his work for any delays arising from circumstances beyond his control, and he should not agree to perform the delayed work in overtime periods unless there is appropriate compensation for such overtime. He should be alert also to avoid the performance of such work on a staggered scheduling basis which might result in substantially more cost to him resulting from interruption of performance and out-of-sequence performance.

Inasmuch as it is the general contractor, not the subcontractor, who has control over coordinating and progressing the work, the subcontractor should reject any liquidated damage provisions in his subcontract unless it is expressly and specifically tied to delays caused by the subcontractor. For this purpose, the subcontractor should consider the protective language of the AIA and AGC subcontract forms which bar the general contractor from assessing subcontractors with liquidated damages unless there is an express provision to that effect in the subcontract itself. Both the AIA and AGC subcontracts contain the following language:

> The Contractor shall make no demand for liquidated damages or penalty for delay in any sum in excess of such amount as may be specifically named in this Subcontract, and no liquidated damages shall be assessed against this Subcontractor for delays or causes attributed to other Subcontractors or arising outside the scope of this Subcontract.

The inequity of many delay provisions in subcontracts is emphasized by the fact that the subcontractor may be held liable to the general contractor and/or the owner for delay damages, and the same subcontract will usually excuse the general contractor from any liability to the subcontractor even though the delays are the fault of the general contractor or the owner. Inasmuch as delays can result in very substantial damages to the subcontractor in terms of increased wages, higher prices for materials, protracted central office overhead, extended insurance, extended equipment costs, and loss of efficiency, the subcontractor should vigorously resist waiving his rights to recover damages for delays against the general contractor and/or the owner. He will not be sufficiently protected if he confines his remedies for delay merely to receiving an extension of time within which to perform his contract work.

Even where a subcontract does permit either the questionable remedy of an extension of time or the right to recover damages attributable to the fault of the general contractor, the subcontract will frequently provide that the subcontractor can assert these rights only if written notice of the delay is made to the contractor within as little as 48 hours from the commencement of the delay. In most circumstances, this type of notice provision is much too short and should be modified by the subcontractor so that he has at least one week or more within which to provide the general contractor with appropriate notice. The notification provisions may contain other language which will require the subcontractor simultaneously to specify or itemize the damages sustained by him by reason of the delay. It may be virtually impossible for the subcontractor to provide these particulars within such a brief period and any provision for such notification should be stricken from the subcontract.

Of course, if the subcontractor is concerned at the very inception of the subcontract about the provisions therein affecting his rights in case of delay, he should be prepared to maintain accurate records against the day when he may be called upon in litigation or in arbitration to prove his actual damages. Necessarily, the subcontractor should have given timely notice of his claim but, in addition, his files should include all pertinent correspondence, daily logs, job minutes, partial-payment requisitions, the foreman's daily reports, shop drawing logs, and cost records and reports.

In reviewing the delay provisions of a subcontract prior to its signing, the subcontractor should realize that not all delays are compensable. Generally speaking, if the delay is caused by circumstances or forces beyond the control of a party to a subcontract, that party will not be liable for the resulting damages. Thus, in addition to such factors as strikes, fires, war, civil disorder, acts of God, and the like which would ordinarily excuse a general contractor for damages for delay, he is likely to be excused also if the delay is attributable to another subcontractor unless the delay on the part of this other subcontractor is itself traceable to lack of coordination of the job by the general contractor himself. The subcontractor should understand the significance of the concept of non-compensable or excusable delays. So far as his general contractor is concerned, it means that the owner will not be able to assess liquidated damages against the general contractor (in which the subcontractor may possibly be called upon to participate); the owner will not be able to demand that the general contractor adhere to the original progress schedule by requiring the general contractor and the subcontractor to accelerate the work at possibly increased cost; and the owner will not be able to default the general contractor and thereby the subcontractors as well. As far as the subcontractor himself is concerned, if there is delay which has been caused by factors beyond the subcontractor's control, he will not be liable in damages, and he must be granted time extensions within which he may reasonably be expected to perform the work which was delayed.

The subcontractor should be alert to any provision in the subcontract which may permit the general contractor to disrupt the normal work schedule. Thus, a provision which permits the general contractor to order a change in the accepted normal sequence of work or accelerate the completion of the work within a significantly shorter period of time may result in additional cost to the subcontractor. Provisions of this kind are distinguishable from delay provisions, but they may be equally costly to a subcontractor who has permitted such provisions to be inserted in his subcontract. If the subcontract does give the general contractor some latitude in ordering changes in the sequence of work or ordering acceleration of the work, some protective language should be inserted which will provide for compensating the subcontractor for his additional costs.

The bargaining position of the subcontractor, in a particular case, may be so weak that in essence he agrees to be liable to the general contractor for damages for delay while he agrees that he will not look to the general contractor for damages for delays caused by the general contractor. He will have some comfort, nevertheless, in knowing that provisions of this type will not always be enforced by the courts. Certainly, if the subcontractor has been delayed by the general contractor, he will at least be given the remedy of an extension of time within which to perform his subcontract work. Beyond that extension, however, the courts will frequently refuse to excuse the general contractor for the damages he has caused the subcontractor where there has been (1) fraud, bad faith, or malice on the part of the general contractor or (2) acts of interference by the general contractor or (3) delays of such a character as not having come within the contemplation of the parties when they signed the subcontract. It appears also that New York and Iowa courts have held the general contractor liable in damages to the subcontractor where the delays have been so unreasonable and so lengthy as to constitute an abandonment of the subcontract. In most circumstances, despite the provision excusing a general contractor or an owner from liability to a subcontractor for delay, willful conduct on the part of that general contractor or owner or failure on their part to coordinate the work will provide the subcontractor with a justifiable claim for damages for delay.

TERMINATION

Many contracts authorize cancellation of the agreement should the owner, general contractor, or architect determine that the subcontractor's performance of the work is unsatisfactory or, in some cases, if the owner chooses not to continue the project.

Particularly because the basis for the exercise of this option is so vague, it is important for the contract to include provisions that ensure that the subcontractor is fairly compensated.

A common provision provides that the subcontractor shall be compensated only for damage resulting directly from the cancellation, but that he shall not be entitled to compensation for prospective profits or materials not furnished. This is not sufficient.

The subcontractor should be paid fairly for work already performed. He is also entitled to a share of his loss of profits sustained by reason of the cancellation and adequate reimbursement for materials not furnished but which he has fabricated or for which he is contractually liable to a third party.

Of course, if the subcontractor is in clear breach of his agreement and there is an objective standard for establishing such breach, he should not be entitled to this protection. If the termination or cancellation provision is retained in the subcontract, the subcontractor should be alert to have appropriate language inserted to make certain that he is compensated fairly for his work to date, with due consideration being given to the possibility of liability to third parties.

THE SETTLEMENT OF DISPUTES

Despite the best intentions of both parties to a subcontract, disputes may arise which ultimately require recourse to the courts or to arbitration. Some subcontracts expressly require the parties to submit their controversies to arbitration and other subcontracts do not. In the absence of an agreement to arbitrate, neither party may compel the other party to submit to arbitration, in which event, the only road to follow will be that of litigation.

Which is the more desirable tribunal for a subcontractor? There is no easy answer and the attitude of subcontractors and their lawyers will vary widely depending upon the experiences they have had.

In theory, at least, an arbitrator will bring to a construction dispute more knowledge and practical experience than will be found in a court of law. Moreover, in many instances, the arbitration proceeding can be speedily initiated and concluded within a few months as contrasted with litigation in the courts where calendar congestion and procedural formalities can bring about lengthy delays. Legal fees are likely to be much more reasonable as well.

Despite these apparent advantages, complex arbitration proceedings often result in protracted hearings that are adjourned for lengthy intervals to suit the convenience of the parties, their counsel, and the arbitrators with the result that the proceedings may go on, in a few instances, for several years. Moreover, inasmuch as the arbitrators are paid for their time, extended hearings may result in the parties incurring very substantial fees for the arbitrators. A frequent objection made to arbitration is the belief that arbitrators tend to compromise a dispute and find a middle ground between the parties.

When a subcontractor is confronted with the choice of having an arbitration provision in his subcontract, he would do well to review with his counsel the desirability of agreeing that this should be the method of resolving disputes with the general contractor and/or the owner.

The subcontractor and his counsel should be alert also to a jurisdictional provision that is found in many subcontracts, particularly those employed by some major general contractors. If the construction site, for example, is in Bergen County, New Jersey, one might reasonably expect that in most instances the litigation or arbitration should proceed in Bergen County or conveniently elsewhere in New Jersey. However, the subcontract form of a major general contractor, whose home office is in Chicago, Illinois, may contain a provision to the effect that the subcontract is to be interpreted by the laws of the State of Illinois and that the place for the litigation or arbitration should, likewise, be in that State. Obviously, such a provision would impose a great burden upon a New Jersey subcontractor and, therefore, such a provision should be firmly resisted by the subcontractor.

Chapter **16**

Harsh Contract Language Regularly Enforced Against Contractors

CARL M. SAPERS, ESQ.
Partner, Hill & Barlow, Boston, Massachusetts

TOUGH CONTRACT LANGUAGE IS GENERALLY ENFORCEABLE

The American Institute of Architects (AIA) statement of *General Conditions* sets out the basic provisions of a construction contract in terms which are reasonably fair to all parties concerned.[1] It is possible, however, to draft an enforceable contract which favors the owner to the disadvantage of the contractor.

Will such contracts be enforced by the courts? An English commentator[2] has concluded that in England a contractor will be bound to perform in accordance

---

[1] Note that each edition of the AIA *General Conditions* is the result of intense review and negotiation by both the American Institute of Architects and the Associated General Contractors. Both trade organizations have historically resolved their differences prior to the issuance of a new edition. But we should observe that the agreement is between *owner* and contractor (not architect and contractor), and no one represented the owner's interest during the development of the form.

[2] *Hudson's Building and Engineering Contracts,* Sweet & Maxwell (10th ed. 1970), chap. 5.

with his bargain unless performance is impossible. The English courts do not mean hard, arduous, or unfair—they mean impossible. A contractor may be made to replace a nearly finished bridge with no extra payment if the bridge was washed away by an extraordinary flood; to replace a seawall when an extraordinary storm swept away the nearly completed wall; and to complete a housing project at the original price notwithstanding the unavailability of labor and materials due to a national emergency.

Although (as discussed below) American courts have, on occasion, relieved contractors of burdensome commitments, it is a fatal error for contractors to assume—as many often do—that tough language is unenforceable. It is a basic principle of our economic system that private citizens may, through the instrument of a negotiated contract, establish *private law* which will govern their affairs together, and that our judicial system will uphold and enforce that private law. In general, American courts will not substitute for an agreement reached by two parties the court's view of what that agreement should have been.

There are exceptions. If liquidated damages are exorbitant, courts may construe them as punitive and therefore unenforceable.[3] If there is enormous disparity in the bargaining power of the parties, courts (or legislatures) may intervene on behalf of the unsophisticated or downtrodden party; but contractors do not notably fit into either category and hardly need the intervention of the state to counterbalance the power of owners.[4] But the fact that everybody in the construction industry believes a harsh clause is unenforceable *is not one of those exceptions.* It may be careless of an owner on a large project to treat the legal language of his contract documents as casually as he often does, but it is nonetheless language which he is entitled to enforce when a dispute arises. He is not expected to live by the private-code language which may (or may not) exist among engineers, architects, and contractors. An excellent illustration is the case of *Citizens National Bank v. L. L. Glascock, Inc.*[5] Glascock removed an existing foundation and claimed the work was an "extra." Notwithstanding the explicit AIA *General Conditions* language that extra work should only be undertaken with the owner's authorization, Glascock said he was ordered to do the work by the structural engineer, and it is customary within the construction industry for a contractor to comply with the request of the owner's representative. The court's holding against the contractor's claim is instructive:

> We can only conclude in comparing [the plain language of the *General Conditions*] to the vague assumption of the contractor that custom of the trade would imple-

---

[3]See 13 Am. Jur. 2d *Building and Construction Contracts* § 84–86 (1964).

[4]There are, of course, many examples of legislation which intercede on behalf of a class of promisors to free them from the effect of their promise. Much consumer legislation does precisely that. In the past decade, contractors did declare themselves downtrodden and went in great numbers to state legislatures to free themselves of the provisions of ¶4.18 of the AIA *General Conditions* (the indemnification clause). In some states (for example, California) they won passage of statutes rendering such provisions void and unenforceable as against public policy. In those states, ¶ 4.18 would not thereafter be enforced by the courts.

[5]*Citizens Nat'l Bank v. L. L. Glascock, Inc.*, 243 So.2d 67 (Miss. 1971).

ment the written document in his behalf, that the [*General Conditions* language] prevails. The written contract anticipated every contingency upon which this suit was based. Its very purpose was to forestall imposition of vague claims derivative of custom within the trade with which laymen are often unfamiliar. The owner, being desirous of limiting its financial obligation, should not have its pocketbook exposed to the custom of architects and contractors unless it agrees thereto. In this instance, the owner agreed to pay for extra work only if it was authorized in writing prior to its execution. Having contracted directly upon the point, there was no leeway for an award [to the contractor].

We now turn to four specific examples of harsh contract conditions which are regularly enforced against contractors.

SUBSURFACE CONDITIONS: YOU BOUGHT WHAT YOU GOT

One much-litigated provision is the requirement that bidders satisfy themselves by personal examination of the location, conditions, and requirements of the work, and the accuracy of information furnished for bidding purposes. The provision may contain a clause in which the owner disclaims any warranty or guarantee that boring samples or other information furnished to the contractor accurately represents the actual materials or conditions which the contractor may encounter during construction. (Neither AIA Doc. A701 *Instructions to Bidders* nor AIA Doc. A201 *General Conditions* contains a disclaimer clause, but such clauses are common in government contracts and in many supplementary general conditions used in private work.) The following is an example of such a disclaimer quoted in *Fanning & Doorley Construction Co. v. Geigy Chemical Corp.*:[6]

> All information given on the drawings or in the contract documents relating to borings, materials encountered, groundwater, subsurface conditions, and existing pipes and other structures is from the best sources at present available to the Owner. All such information and the drawings of existing construction are furnished only for the information and convenience of bidders.
>
> It is agreed and understood that the Owner does not warrant or guarantee that the materials, conditions, and pipes or other structures encountered during construction will be the same as those indicated by the boring samples or by the information given on the drawings or in the contract documents. The bidder must satisfy himself regarding the character, quantities, and conditions of the various materials and the work to be done.
>
> It further is agreed and understood that the bidder or the Contractor will not use any of the information made available to him or obtained in any examination made by him in any manner as a basis or ground of claim or demand of any nature, against the Owner or the Engineer, arising from or by reason of any variance which may exist between the information offered and the actual materials or structures encountered during the construction work, except as may otherwise be provided for in the contract documents.

The so-called *Spearin Doctrine* is responsible for this effort on the part of

---

[6]*Fanning & Doorley Constr. Co. v. Geigy Chem. Corp.*, 305 F. Supp. 650, 653 (1969).

owners to disclaim responsibility for the accuracy of boring samples, plans, and specifications. In *United States v. Spearin*,[7] the Supreme Court held that an owner warrants the accuracy of information furnished to bidders and that contractual provisions requiring contractors to visit the site, check the plans, and verify work requirements will not relieve the owner of liability under the warranty. Massachusetts recently followed this view in *Alpert v. Commonwealth*.[8] Alpert sued the Department of Public Works for breach of an earth excavation contract. Although bidders had been informed that there would be 17 cubic yards of suitable material for every 1 cubic yard of unsuitable material, there proved to be almost 400 percent more unsuitable material than had been anticipated in the contract documents. Despite a contractual provision which disclaimed in the clearest possible manner all responsibility for the accuracy of information furnished to bidders, the court permitted Alpert to recover. It is interesting to note that the court did not mention another recent Massachusetts opinion in which the opposite result was reached—*Daniel O'Connell's Sons v. Commonwealth*.[9] In the O'Connell case, the contractor relied on geological data furnished by the Commonwealth. The contract contained an express disclaimer of the owner's responsibility for the accuracy of the data. The court upheld the disclaimer and said that the contractor was not entitled to damages for extra excavation required when a solid ledge proved to be deeper than indicated on the data.

Some explanation for the conflict in decisions may be found in the case of *Wunderlich v. State*,[10] where the court said,

> We have heretofore recognized liability based on a theory of breach of an implied warranty when a governmental agency represents as a fact what in fact does not exist, and the claimant is damaged by its reliance on the assertion. . . . A contractor of public works who, acting reasonably, is misled by incorrect plans and specifications issued by the public authorities as the basis for bids and who, as a result, submits a bid which is lower than he would have otherwise made, may recover in a contract action for extra work or expenses necessitated by the conditions being other than as represented. . . . On the other hand, if one agrees to do a thing possible of performance, "he will not be excused or become entitled to additional compensation, because unforeseen difficulties are encountered."

The court held that where there is no misrepresentation of factual matters or withholding of material information, and when both parties have equal access to information, the contractor cannot contend, in the face of an express disclaimer, that he relied on the owner's representation.

WORK HELD REASONABLY INFERABLE

Construction contracts often cover the situation where the agreement, drawings, and specifications either omit information or contain conflicting instruc-

[7] *United States v. Spearin*, 248 U.S. 132, 39 S.Ct. 59, 63 L. Ed. 166 (1918).

[8] *Alpert v. Commonwealth*, 357 Mass. 306, 258 N.E.2d 755 (1970).

[9] *Daniel O'Connell's Sons v. Commonwealth*, 349 Mass. 642, 212 N.E.2d 219 (1965).

[10] *Wunderlich v. State*, 65 Cal.2d 777, 56 Cal. Rptr. 473, 423 P.2d 545, 548 (1967).

tions. The AIA *General Conditions* provide that the contract documents should be treated as complementing one another and that the requirements of one should be considered the requirements of all. The *General Conditions* oblige the contractor to do work not specifically required by the contract documents but which is reasonably inferable from them.

In *Watson Lumber Co. v. Guennewig,*[11] the court said that, "in order for the contractor to recover for items as 'extras' they must be shown to be items not required to be furnished under plaintiff's original promise as stated in the contract, including the items that the plans and specifications *reasonably implied* even though not mentioned" (emphasis supplied). In *Granberry v. Perlmutter,*[12] the parties had signed a written contract to construct a house, which contained no mention of bathroom tile, although the contractor earlier indicated to the owner that the walls and floor would be covered with ceramic tile. The court concluded that the tile was included in the contract, pointing out that "when parties contract for a substantial addition, including a bathroom, it is fair to assume that appropriate walls and flooring are to be included." In *Shields v. City of New York,*[13] the court defined *extra work* as "work arising outside and entirely independent of the contract—something not required in its performance" and for which a contractor would be entitled to extra payment. The court distinguished extra work from *additional work,* the latter being something "necessarily required in the performance of the contract, and without which it could not be carried out." The contractor would not be entitled to additional compensation for doing additional work.

INDEMNITY FOR PERSONAL INJURY OR PROPERTY DAMAGE

Construction contracts often contain a provision which makes the contractor an indemnitor for personal injury or property damage claims occurring during the construction period. At one end of the spectrum are contracts which limit such liability to damage caused by the contractor's negligence or the negligence of someone for whom he is responsible. At the other end of the spectrum are contract provisions requiring the contractor to indemnify the owner against the owner's own negligence. Compare AIA Doc. A201, ¶ 4.18, with the clause quoted in *Fanning & Doorley Construction Co. v. Geigy Chemical Corp:*[14]

> The Contractor shall take all responsibility for the work done under this contract, for the protection of the work, and for preventing injuries to persons and damage to property and utilities on or about the work. He shall in no way be relieved of his responsibility by any right of the Engineer to give permission or issue orders relating to any part of the work, by any such permission given or orders issued, or by failure of the Engineer to give such permission or issue such order. The Contractor shall bear all losses resulting to him or to the Owner on account of the

[11]*Watson Lumber Co. v. Guennewig,* 79 Ill. App.2d 377, 226 N.E.2d 270 (1967).
[12]*Granberry v. Perlmutter,* 147 Col. 474, 364 P.2d 211, 212 (1961).
[13]*Shields v. City of New York,* 82 N.Y.S. 1020, 1021, 84 App. Div. 502 (1903).
[14]*Fanning & Doorley Constr. Co. v. Geigy Chem. Corp.,* 305 F. Supp. 650, 653 (1969).

quantity or character of the work, because the nature of the land in or on which the work is done is different from what was estimated or expected, or on account of the weather, elements, or other causes. The Contractor shall assume the defense of all claims of whatsoever character against the Contractor or the Owner, its officers, or agents against all claims for injury or damage to persons, corporations, or property arising out of the work done under this contract whether said claims arise out of negligence or not, or whether said claims are groundless, false, or fraudulent or not, and from all claims relating to labor and material furnished for the work. The Contractor shall not be required to indemnify the Owner against damage or claims occasioned solely by acts or omissions of the Owner other than supervisory acts or omissions of the Owner in connection with the work performed by the Contractor for the Owner, except as otherwise provided in the article relative to patents.

In *George A. Fuller Co. v. Fischbach & Moore,*[15] the court construed a provision requiring a subcontractor to indemnify both the owner and the contractor for claims resulting from their negligence. The contractor sued the subcontractor for indemnity and the court said,

> The language is clear and unambiguous and must be given its ordinary meaning. [The subcontractor] undertook to indemnify [the contractor] for the consequences of [the contractor's] own negligence. The language "arising out of or in consequence of the performance of this work" when used in this context, refers to the scope of the employment of the person injured and the site of the occurrence. Both are met here. Moreover, the parties presumably dealt at arm's length, and the provision for indemnity is not illegal or void as against public policy.

In *Buscaglia v. Owens-Corning Fiberglas,*[16] the court said,

> The present-day judicial view [is] that indemnity clauses of construction contracts are to be viewed realistically as efforts by businessmen to allocate as between them the cost or expense of the risk of accidents apt to arise out of construction projects on a fairly predictable basis, rather than upon the generally debatable and indeterminate criteria as to whose negligence, if any, the accident was caused by, and to what degree.

The court in *Titan Steel Corp. v. Walton*[17] held that the Utah contract before it had been entered into freely and without the exercise of superior bargaining power, and that it clearly and unequivocally expressed the intention of the parties that the subcontractor would indemnify the owner and the contractor for their negligence. In response to the subcontractor's contention that it was unconscionable and against public policy to impose full tort liability for a huge construction project on one who had agreed to perform only a very small part of it, the court said,

> Much has been said concerning the enforceability of so-called release-from-negligence contracts whereby one possessed of superior bargaining power is enabled to contract against liability for his own negligence. . . . The general rule,

[15]*George A. Fuller Co. v. Fischbach & Moore,* 180 N.Y.S.2d 589, 592 (1958). Leave to appeal denied 182 N.Y.S.2d 331 (1959).

[16]*Buscaglia v. Owens-Corning Fiberglas,* 68 N.J. Super. 508, 172 A.2d 703, 707 (1961). Affirmed 178 A.2d 208 (1961).

[17]*Titan Steel Corp. v. Walton,* 365 F.2d 542, 548 (10th Cir. 1966).

however, seems to be that while private contracts of this type are not favorites of the law, they are enforceable provided they are made at arm's length without disparity of bargaining power, and the intent of the parties is manifestly plain and unequivocal.

DAMAGE FOR DELAY

In construction, delay is expensive. Particularly in a period of rapidly escalating costs, the time for completion is critical. While ¶ 8.3.4 of the AIA *General Conditions* permits either side to recover delay damages, some contracts recite that no extension of time will be given to the contractor for ordinary delays and that no damages—only an extension of time—will be granted to the contractor even if the delay was caused by the owner. An example of such a harsh provision is quoted in the *Fanning & Doorley* case,

> Art. XV. The Owner may delay the beginning of the work or any part thereof if it is deemed in the Owner's interest so to do. The Contractor shall have no claim for damages on account of such delay, but shall be entitled to so much additional time wherein to perform and complete this contract on his part as the Engineer shall certify in writing to be just.
>
> Art. XVI. It is agreed that the rate of progress herein required has been purposely made low enough to allow for the ordinary delays incident to construction work of this character. No extension of time will be made for ordinary delays, inclement weather, and accidents, and the occurrence of such will not relieve the Contractor from the necessity of maintaining this rate of progress.
>
> The time in which this contract is to be performed and completed is of the essence of this agreement.

In *Psaty & Fuhrman, Inc. v. Housing Authority of the City of Providence*,[18] the contract contained a *no-damage* clause, and the court ruled, as a matter of law, that only acts of bad faith by the owner would permit the contractor to circumvent the clause. When the owner, in furtherance of its own interest, knowingly delayed the contractor's progress, the owner was not liable for damages. The court cited cases from a multitude of jurisdictions upholding *no-damage* clauses except in circumstances where the owner acts with malicious intent to damage the contractor.

Although decided nearly 30 years ago, *Psaty & Fuhrman* is still good law, and a contractor who signs an agreement containing a no-damage clause should expect little sympathy from a court when he complains that the delay was induced by the owner's dilatory behavior. For a more recent case, see *W. C. James, Inc. v. Phillips Petroleum Co.*[19] Psaty & Fuhrman and W. C. James each made similar last-ditch arguments that they were being badly abused by the small print in their contracts. Courts have rejected these arguments out-of-hand, with the U.S. Supreme Court observing that, "men who take million-dollar contracts for government buildings are neither unsophisticated nor careless."[20]

---

[18]*Psaty & Fuhrman, Inc. v. Housing Authority of the City of Providence*, 76 R.I. 87, 68 A.2d 32 (1949).
[19]*W. C. James, Inc. v. Phillips Petroleum Co.*, 485 F.2d 22 (10th Cir. 1973).
[20]*Wells Bros. Co. v. U.S.*, 254 U.S. 83, 87 (1920).

JUDICIAL CIRCUMVENTION OF HARSH CONTRACT LANGUAGE

The foregoing four examples make the point that tough conditions are commonly enforced against contractors. To the list might be added clauses requiring notice of claims within short time periods,[21] compliance with difficult-but-not-impossible technical specifications[22] and more. But it is here appropriate to indicate that there are limits to enforcement, also recognized by our courts.

The observant reader will have noticed that many of the illustrations of tough contract language have been taken from the case of *Fanning & Doorley Construction Co. v. Geigy Chemical Corp.*[23] The general conditions drafted for Geigy's contract with Fanning & Doorley are a veritable catalog of horrors for the general contractor. Not only are each of the tough conditions discussed above included, a fair reading of the general conditions compelled Fanning & Doorley to produce a satisfactory underground piping system whether or not the engineer's design would produce a satisfactory system. When it was obvious to the court that the design could not produce a satisfactory system, the court gagged over this last requirement.

The court circumvented the language of the general conditions by employing what may, to the layman, appear as judicial sleights-of-hand. First, the contractor's performance of corrective work with the owner's approbation amounted to either a waiver of the owner's right to enforce or an agreement to amend (manifested by the parties' conduct) the clauses which stood in the way of the contractor's recovery. Second, the requirement that the contractor produce a satisfactory result was in conflict with the requirement that the contractor faithfully follow the plans and specifications (which were defective) and the court resolved the conflict against the owner. Finally, the court declared that the owner impliedly warranted that the plans and specifications were fit for their intended purpose, citing *United States v. Spearin.*[24]

That last is a transcendent piece of judicial legerdemain. Simply stated, when all else fails, one claims that the owner has breached his implied warranty that the design works and that the owner is therefore not entitled to the benefits of the harsh contract language. What the contractor then claims are his damages for breach of contract rather than simply the extra compensation which the contract provisions would permit.[25] Recent court decisions have, however, retreated from the excesses perpetrated in the name of *Spearin.*[26]

These judicial circumventions of harsh contract language may offer some comfort to the contractor in trouble, but they should also instruct the contractor negotiating the conditions of his contract. For they are proof of the weight and deference which courts will give to contract language and the length to which a court must go to avoid enforcing that language.

---

[21]*Practical Constr. Co. v. Granite City Housing Authority,* 416 F.2d 540 (1969).

[22]*Blount Brothers Corp. v. Reliance Ins. Co.,* 370 F.2d 733 (1967).

[23]*Fanning & Doorley Constr. Co. v. Geigy Chem. Corp.,* 305 F. Supp. 650, 653 (1969).

[24]*United States v. Spearin,* 248 U.S. 132, 39 S.Ct. 59, 63 L. Ed. 166 (1918).

[25]See, *e.g., Luria Bros. & Co., Inc. v. United States,* 369 F.2d 701 (Ct. Cl., 1966).

[26]See, *e.g., Jefferson Constr. Co. v. United States,* 392 F.2d 1006, Cert. den. 393 U.S. 842 (1968).

Chapter **17**

Interpretation of Working Conditions

MARVIN P. SADUR, ESQ.
Washington, D.C.

A construction contractor enters a contract for the purpose of making a profit, either short-term or long-term. Achieving that purpose requires sound understanding and evaluation of the working conditions for each contract, that is, the context, both physical and by agreement, within which the contract must be performed.

A working condition is anything which influences the performance of the contract between the contractor and the owner. The method in which the technical requirements are stated, the contract conditions which fix responsibility or obligations, the physical site in which the work is to be performed, statutes, ordinances, regulations, and building codes which restrict building performance, and local custom—all create working conditions under which a construction contract is performed.

IMPLICATIONS OF THE TECHNICAL REQUIREMENTS FOR THE WORK

The plans and specifications state the technical requirements for the work. The method by which and the extent to which the technical requirements are set forth establishes by implication the working conditions under which the work is performed.

Design versus Performance Specification

The starting point in interpreting working conditions under which a construction contract must be performed is the plans and specifications; particularly, how they set forth the design and technical requirements for the work. Expression of technical requirements in the plans and specifications ranges across a spectrum from pure design statement to pure performance statement.

A pure design statement provides a cookbook recipe. The plans and specifications spell out in explicit terms what must be done and how it must be done in order to accomplish the desired end result. The end result may or may not be articulated; it flows naturally from the recipe specification. The design specification includes the exact dimensions, the exact materials to be utilized, the specific type of services to be furnished, and all structural and engineering design. The contractor has little discretion. He must perform in accordance with good workmanship, and he must perform and construct *exactly* to the design and dimensions which are spelled out in the technical requirements of the contract.

Performance specification substantially enlarges the contractor's discretion. The focus of performance specification is upon the end result desired. The contractor's obligation is to achieve the end result. While the design specification spells out in a recipe the path to take and the materials and equipment to use to achieve the end result, the pure performance specification merely states the end result and leaves to the contractor's discretion and expertise the appropriate steps and the materials and equipment needed to produce the end result.

When an owner adopts design specification as his mode of stating technical requirements, he assumes the responsibility that such design statement is suitable for and capable of obtaining the desired end result. If the owner adopts a performance type of specification, he places the responsibility for end result upon the contractor.

As a practical matter, very few construction contracts are entered into which are based upon either pure design or pure performance specification, nor do the contracts make a clear-cut division of responsibility for the end result. The majority of construction contracts contain a mix of design and performance specifications and a confusion as to responsibility for the end result. Generally speaking, the technical specification will be explicit with regard to the structural elements of the work, leaving the contractor with limited discretion, if any, in selection of material or method of construction. Assuming that the contractor complies with the detail of the structural design, he will not be responsible for the end result. In contrast, the specification for mechanical and electrical services to be incorporated in a building frequently enlarge the contractor's discretion and responsibility by utilizing performance specification for selected elements.

The manner in which electrical services may be specified offers an illustration of the distinction between design and performance specification, as well as a combination of both. The pure design specification will specify and locate the source of power to the space, identify and locate the switchgear for such power, specify the type of conduit to carry the specified service (in size and number of wires) to the panel board; identify and specify the number and size of breakers in the board; identify and locate the number and type of fixtures required, method of installation, method of connection; and identify and locate any necessary switching.

In contrast, a pure performance specification for lighting the same space may spell out the intended use of the space and demand a minimum lighting for it. An alternative (and far more common) expression of performance specification would be to state the amount of candlepower required for distribution within the space. Such a specification leaves the contractor with full discretion and responsibility for the selection of the proper number and type of fixtures, locations, circuitry, proper materials to be incorporated in the circuitry, and selection and location of suitable power source. Under such an obligation, the contractor is solely responsible for obtaining the end result specified.

An example of a combination of performance and design specification for lighting the same space would include a statement of the candlepower required which would leave the contractor with discretion in selection of the type, number and locations of fixtures, and responsibility for their satisfactory function. However, the specification might also specify the circuitry to be contained in rigid conduit of a designated type, located in a designated space, carrying a designated number and size of conductors, connecting with a designated panel limiting the number of circuits, which would place the responsibility for their adequacy on the owner.

When an owner attempts to combine both design and performance obligations in the specification, the contractor should be alert to whether the limitations of design will affect his ability to obtain the performance requirement. As long as the performance specification and design specification elements are complementary, both are binding on the contractor. The contractor should recognize, however, that where both types of specification are utilized, in the event of conflict, *design-specification obligation is paramount,*[1] and the performance obligation may be negated. For example, if the owner, after having specified the candlepower in a given space as the desired end result, then limits the

---

[1]*J. L. Simmons Co. v. United States,* 188 Ct.Cl. 684, 412, F.2d 1360 (1969); *Aerodex, Inc.,* ASBCA #7121, 1962 BCA 3491.

number, type, and location of fixtures, he may frustrate the ability to obtain the performance standard required. The contractor cannot be obligated, without contract adjustment, to modify the design-specification elements to comply with the performance-specification obligation.

If the contractor recognizes the obligation of the specification, whether design or performance, he will then be in a position to ascertain for pricing purposes where he has discretion to utilize different modes of accomplishing a task, and the extent to which he has such discretion as compared to circumstances where he is tied to a particular and specific mode of accomplishing a task or purpose. The contractor, further, is in a position to ascertain, subsequent to contract award, when and where he is being called upon to provide something in excess of his contract obligation. Thus, in the electrical illustrations in the first example noted above, the contractor has no discretion. In the second example, the contractor has absolute discretion. In the third example, the contractor has no discretion in circuitry or circuitry components; however, he is free to select type, number, and location of fixtures in the most economic combination which will produce the desired lighting result. In the fourth example, the contractor, in fact, has no discretion. He is bound by the definitive design statement both with regard to circuitry and lighting without regard to the superfluous performance requirement. After following the design statement for lighting, if the intended lighting result is not achieved, the contractor is not obligated without appropriate price adjustment to supplement or otherwise modify the design lighting statement.

Implied Warranties

Certain implied obligations or warranties have arisen in construction contracting by operation of law. These are obligations or duties which are not articulated in the contract but are created by law. They affect performance and therefore become an element of working conditions.

Adequacy of design   The design furnished by the owner to the contractor is assumed to be accurate and adequate to accomplish the end result intended. Even though it is not stated in the contract, the contractor has a right to rely upon the accuracy and adequacy of the plans and specifications. Unless the contract expressly provides otherwise, the contractor is not obligated to review and verify the design for consistency, accuracy, or adequacy.

Examples of how the lack of accuracy or adequacy of the plans and specifications affects performance are as fol'ows.

1. The contract may include a structural design that calls for two steel beams spanning an open area upon which a heavy machine will sit. The beams are identified by size, shape, and weight in the plans and specifications and are installed in accordance therewith. After the machine is in place, it is discovered that while the beams clearly provide the necessary structural support, the structure is not sufficiently stiff or stable to prevent excess vibration when the heavy machine which it supports is started or running. Under the assumption of adequacy of design, the contractor is not responsible for this condition.

2. The contract may include a complete statement of the mechanical distribution systems for a building reflecting installation in chases, utility closets, ceiling spaces, or imbedded in slabs. The piping, duct, insulation, equipment, and the number and type of incremental units, vents, and diffusers are identified by size, shape, and area of location. The contract information also includes a complete detailed statement of the architectural and structural design of the building. If, in fact, the mechanical systems physically do not fit into the spaces provided in the structural design of the building, or elements of the architectural or structural design interfere with the mechanical system, under the assumption of accuracy of design for the purpose intended, the owner will be responsible for the error and adjustments necessitated thereby.[2] It should be noted that the typical contract obligation of the contractor to coordinate the installation of the work among the various trades is not to be confused with verifying the accuracy or adequacy of the design. These two activities are independent, and the coordination task does not include the obligation to verify accuracy of design. In fact, the contractor has the right to rely upon the adequacy of the design in the belief that work can be coordinated among the various trades.

3. A contract for installation of a major sanitary or storm sewer may specify the size of pipe; the depth at which the sewer pipe is to be laid; the type, class, and depth of the bedding for the pipe; the type of joint connecting lengths of pipe; and the harnessing or other control of thrust pressure and backfill. Under the assumption of adequacy of design, the contractor has a right to believe that the installation of the pipe in accordance with the statement will fulfill the obligation of the contract. If, in fact, the pipe moves or the joints open up, the owner will be responsible.

The general rule regarding owner's responsibility for design defect is subject to an important exception. Procurement law recognizes two kinds of design defects. The defects are either patent or latent, i.e., apparent or hidden. The examples given above are of latent defects and are not the contractor's responsibility. However, if the defect is patent or apparent, the contractor is under a duty to bring the defect to the attention of the owner for correction *prior to bid*. Otherwise, the contractor will be responsible for the result and the cost of overcoming the apparent discrepancy.

Consider the following example of a patent defect. The contract specifies a low-pressure air distribution system but also includes a high-pressure mixing box in the ductwork. The language of the specification redundantly advises that the static pressure of the duct system will be less than 1.5 psi and that the mixing box will not operate with less than 2+ psi. The contractor should recognize that the two elements of the design are incompatible and that the design is defective to that extent. (Some contractors would call this condition an ambiguity.) The

---

[2]*United States v. Spearin,* 348 U.S. 132, 39 S.Ct. 59, 63 L.Ed. 166 (1918); *Warren Bros. Roads Co. v. United States,* 105 F.Supp. 826, 123 Ct.Cl. 48 (1952); *Laburnum Const. Corp. v. United States,* 163 Ct.Cl. 339, 325 F.2d 451 (1963); *J. D. Hedin Const. Co. v. United States,* 171 Ct.Cl. 70, 347 F.2d 235 (1965).

contractor cannot ignore an apparent defect in the plans and specifications. The apparent conflict of the two conditions requires the contractor to seek correction before bid. Otherwise, he will suffer the responsibility to correct the resulting condition in accordance with the owner's reasonable direction.

Whether the defect is patent is not dependent upon whether the contractor actually recognizes it as such. The nature of defect is determined by an objective standard, what a reasonably prudent and experienced contractor under similar circumstances would recognize in the plans and specifications.[3]

Duty to cooperate   There is an unwritten obligation between the parties not to hinder, harass, improperly interfere with, or make more expensive the performance of the other party. This is sometimes referred to as the *implied duty of cooperation*. This implied duty does not require a party affirmatively to assist the other in his performance. The obligation of the implied duty is not to hinder performance, to refrain from action detrimental to the other's performance. This implied duty to cooperate often comes into play where a contractor completes the performance of a project in a greater time than he contemplated and could have accomplished but for the owner's act or omission which delayed the contractor's performance. The contractor would be entitled to recovery of any additional cost he incurred as a result. This is true even if the contractor's contemplated time of completion which he, in fact, could have accomplished was a shorter interval of time than provided for in the contract. The duty to cooperate contemplates the party's control over his conduct.

Examples of how the owner can detrimentally interfere with the contractor's performance are as follows: Making changes in the plans and specifications which require changes in the sequence of performance as the work progresses; failing to approve shop drawings either within the time allocated in the contract for such approval or within a reasonable time so as to allow the approved product to be manufactured and delivered to the project for installation within the time allocated in the schedule; failing to furnish equipment on time which the owner has agreed to furnish; failing to provide access if such is an element or condition of performance; and failing to make timely arrangements for electrical outages if outages are necessary in existing utility services and they are the owner's responsibility.

Implied Site Conditions

Situations can arise where the statement of technical requirements is such as to imply a site condition upon which the contractor may reasonably rely despite the lack of any express reflection of subsurface conditions. Thus, where a pipe trench specification calls for the contractor to provide straight vertical cuts, prohibits overexcavation, limits the side banks to no more than 8 inches outside the pipe width on each side, requires hand shaping of the trench bottom to fit the contour of the pipe and the bell, and calls for the pipe to rest directly on undisturbed soil at every point along its entire length, the contractor may

---

[3]*J. A. Jones Constr. Co. v. United States,* 184 Ct.Cl. 1, 395 F.2d 783 (1968); see also extensive analysis of Court of Claims decisions on this point in *Pathman Constr. Co.,* ASBCA #13911, 70-2 BCA 8557.

reasonably infer a site condition suitable to accomplish the design require-ments. The design statement implies a stable subsoil, material of sufficient plasticity to retain shaping, and sufficient bearing capacity to support the pipe structure satisfactorily. Standard-form provisions regarding dewatering responsibility or contingent procedures for removal of isolated pockets of unstable material will not negate the implication naturally flowing from the detailed technical requirements. This implication is, of course, premised on the supposition that there is no definitive information regarding the quality of the subsoil in the area of the pipe installation. If, in fact, there were borings or other subsoil information indicating a prevailing water condition or unstable material inconsistent with the design-requirements statement, there arises a circumstance of patent ambiguity, and the contractor must make a timely inquiry of the owner or suffer the consequences. If the contractor from his experience working in the specific locale has *actual* knowledge, not merely imputed knowledge, that the site conditions are other than as implied by the design, the contractor cannot reasonably rely upon the implied site condition. He should notify the owner prior to bid concerning the discrepancy.

EXPRESS PROVISIONS OF THE CONTRACT

General and special conditions of the construction contract create express obligations and conditions which affect performance of the work and thus create working conditions.

Differing Site Conditions

There is a distribution of responsibility between the parties which flows from the method and manner of statement of the technical requirements as well as the status of the parties to the transaction. By the same token, there is express distribution of responsibility between the parties which is created by agreement stated in the general and special conditions. An example of an express alloca-tion of responsibility in the contract is the differing site conditions or changed-conditions clause that is contained in most construction contracts. *The exact language of the differing-site conditions type of clause in any particular contract must be considered to determine the specific risk allocation between the parties.* This discussion will consider the differing-site-conditions clause contained in the federal stan-dard construction contract for purposes of general example. We emphasize, however, that each clause must be considered individually to determine the operative elements of establishing responsibility or rights.

The federal differing-site-conditions clause is as follows:

> Differing Site Conditions
> (a) The Contractor shall promptly, and before such conditions are disturbed, notify the Contracting Officer in writing of: (1) Subsurface or latent physical conditions at the site differing materially from those indicated in this contract, or (2) unknown physical conditions at the site, of an unusual nature, differing materi-ally from those ordinarily encountered and generally recognized as inhering in work of the character provided for in this contract. The Contracting Officer shall

promptly investigate the conditions, and if he finds that such conditions do materially so differ and cause an increase or decrease in the Contractor's cost of, or the time required for, performance of any part of the work under this contract, whether or not changed as a result of such conditions, an equitable adjustment shall be made and the contract modified in writing accordingly.

(b) No claim of the Contractor under this clause shall be allowed unless the Contractor has given the notice required in (a) above; provided, however, the time prescribed therefor may be extended by the Government.

(c) No claim by the Contractor for an equitable adjustment hereunder shall be allowed if asserted after final payment under this contract.[4]

Under this clause, the owner assumes two distinct risks: (1) the risk that a subsurface or latent physical condition may be encountered by the contractor which differs materially from that reflected in the plans and specifications; and (2) insofar as the plans and specifications are silent with regard to a physical condition, the risk that a physical condition may be encountered which is unusual and differs materially from that ordinarily encountered in work of that type.

The first class of risk applies when the contract contains some indication of physical condition. This indication need not be express but may be implied. Consider again the pipe trench example of the preceding section requiring a series of operations indicative of stable subsoil. Notwithstanding the absence of any boring log data or express representation of subsoil characteristics in the region of pipeline installation, there is sufficient information in the plans and specifications to place the risk upon the owner in the event unstable subsoil material is encountered.

Application of the provision does not require any "fault" on the part of the owner in the sense of intentional misrepresentation or negligent assembly of data. The clause simply shifts the risk of occurrence of the physical condition described to the owner as part of the bargain. The rationale is simply one of economy: to reduce the contingencies a contractor must include in his bid and thus the price to the owner.

The second class of risk depends upon encountering an unknown physical condition which a prudent contractor would not reasonably anticipate as a result of his examination of the site and experience in work of that type. With no information in the contract documents regarding subsoil conditions, encountering an underground stream during foundation installation would result in application of the second part of the differing-site-conditions provision.

The physical condition under either of the two risk allocations need not relate only to subsurface ground conditions. The clause applies to any physical condition. Thus, in a remodeling contract where the drawings indicate existing utility lines in certain walls and utility lines (not shown) are encountered in the walls, the first risk allocation of the differing-site-conditions clause would apply. Similarly, where a contractor encounters an existing double roof not disclosed

[4]ASPR F-100.23-A, Standard Form 23-A: General Provisions.

by the contract documents, during performance of a reroofing contract, the second risk allocation provision would provide relief (encountering an unforeseen condition where the contract documents are silent on physical condition).

The purpose of the differing-site-conditions clause is to eliminate contingency from the contract price for unknown and unforeseeable conditions which may affect the work. This clause, however, does not excuse the contractor from taking reasonable and necessary steps to ascertain the nature and location of the work and the general and local conditions which can affect the work. Most contracts include provisions for prebid site investigation. A condition of the contractor's bid is that he make such an investigation and determine the character, quality, and quantity of surface and subsurface materials or obstacles to be encountered insofar as this information is reasonably ascertainable from an inspection of the site. In other words, the contractor will be excused from unforeseen conditions or conditions which are materially different from that shown in the plans and specifications only if the nature of the discrepancy is so well hidden as to prevent discovery by *reasonable* prebid site investigation and examination of available contract information. "Reasonable" is simply a matter of common sense. Thus, if a structure to be rehabilitated and remodeled contains a myriad of exposed pipes, one of which is not shown on the contract documents, the owner cannot contend a reasonable prebid site investigation would have disclosed the existence of the pipe merely because it is exposed. Mere exposure does not equal "reasonably apparent" when there is a large number of exposed pipes running through the area and their number and grouping serves to mask the existence of the additional pipe. Similarly, the prebid site investigation does not contemplate disturbing existing conditions, such as cutting an observation panel in a ceiling or exhaust duct system to ascertain the condition hidden from view. However, if such access is readily available at the time of prebid investigation, the contractor will be held to have taken the opportunity to observe the otherwise concealed condition to the extent allowed by such access.

Since the owner contractually assumes the risk for conditions which differ materially from those indicated in the contract or are unknown, unusual and differing materially from those ordinarily encountered and generally recognized as inherent in the work required by the contract, he may be entitled to associated benefit under the operation of the clause. The relief provided for under the federal differing-site-conditions clause obligates the owner to make an equitable adjustment in the contract price and time of performance if the condition causes an increase or decrease in a contractor's cost or time required for performance of the work. While it would be rare to find a differing site condition which would lessen the obligation of the contract, nevertheless that is a contingency which is covered in the clause. The owner may be entitled to a reduction in price consistent with the reduction in cost if, in fact, the amount of work was less as a result of encountering differing site conditions. Consider a situation where the contract calls for removal of existing piping which lies 9 feet beneath an existing pavement which also must be removed. Upon removal of the pavement, the contractor discovers the existing pipeline in the gravel base immediately below the pavement, thereby eliminating the necessity of excavating an additional 9 feet in depth to remove the line as shown in the contract. This change in situation would be a differing site condition which conceivably could have the effect of decreasing the contractor's cost or time of performance. Under the equitable adjustment requirement of the clause, the owner would be entitled to a credit.

Shop Drawings

All contractors are familiar with the class of technical data termed *shop drawings*. These typically include any descriptive technical submission required of the contractor to show the compliance with contract requirements of specific items the contractor intends to include in the work, as well as how the items interface with other elements of the work. The phrase "shop drawings" may also on occasion be used to include "working drawings," i.e., technical representations not submitted to the owner, used entirely in-house by a contractor in accomplishing the work. For purposes of this discussion, we limit the meaning of the phrase to contractually required submissions to the owner. The shop drawings reflect greater detail than the contract drawings and are usually necessary to actually execute the contract work. As a supplement, enlargement, and clarification to the contract design, they also can become an important factor in working conditions.

Most contract shop-drawing provisions state that approval of a contractor's submission does not negate the contractor's overriding obligation to conform strictly with the contract documents (that is, the plans and specifications). Thus, if the shop drawings contain a deviation from the contract requirements, approval of the shop drawings will not constitute an acceptance of the deviation. However, if the deviation is expressly brought to the attention of the approving agent, then approval of the submission will have binding effect with respect to the deviation.

To appreciate how shop drawings create a working condition, the contractor must recognize the primary function of shop drawings, that is, to communicate his interpretation of contract requirements. As long as there is no explicit contradiction between shop-drawings statement and contract requirement, owner approval reflects agreement with the contractor's contract interpretation and will be binding on the owner in the event of a subsequent dispute over requirements in a design specification. The importance of this principle is self-evident where the contract is silent or ambiguous on a particular feature of a system. Consider, for example, a contract which calls for installation of manual balancing valves and flowmeter venturi tubes as part of a hydronic system associated with a mechanical installation. The contract drawings and specifications fully delineate the system including number and location of valves. This contract also includes an option to install automatic flow-control valves in lieu of manual balancing valves and venturi tubes. The specifications fully describe the requirements for installation of an automatic flow-control-valve system, but the drawings do not contain a schematic diagram for such installation. The contractor elects the automatic flow-control-valve alternative and submits shop drawings including schematic diagrams of the system which are approved by the owner. The total number of automatic flow-control valves he uses is substantially less than the number of manual balancing valves required under the first alternative. Subsequent to installation, the owner cannot seek a credit because a lesser number of valves is incorporated in the system than indicated on the drawings.

As long as the system as installed conforms to the approved shop drawings, the contractor has complied with his contract obligation and has not provided the owner with less than contractually required. In approving the shop drawings, the owner has indicated his contemporaneous agreement with the contractor's interpretation prior to any dispute that automatic flow-control valves are included in the system on a performance determination and not on a pure one-for-one substitution with the manual balancing valves.[5] The owner cannot subsequently change his position and demand a credit based on fewer valves provided.

The responsibility for performance of work required under a contract is generally divided among specialty firms. The scope of their responsibility includes the obligation to prepare and furnish shop drawings reflecting their intended compliance with the prime contract plans and specifications. Where the contract allows for selection of product or method, there is a need to coordinate and check the shop drawings submitted by the several specialty interests to ensure their proper interfacing and compatibility. The responsibility for checking the shop drawings of all trades and verifying their compatibility is an obligation of the prime contractor. Conceivably, without such coordination, the electrician could submit shop drawings of the control system which are not compatible with the requirements of the specific air-handling equipment selected by the mechanical contractor. Both submittals could be approved as independently complying with the standard of the specifications even though they do not work together. The contractor cannot rely upon such approval to excuse himself for the failure to coordinate the shop drawings.[6]

"Or-Equal" Provisions

Another general provision found in many construction contracts provides that the designation in the technical specification of a particular brand name shall not be considered as a limitation on the contractor but rather as establishing a standard of quality. A product may be substituted for the brand-name item, provided it is equal or superior thereto. The contractor, of course, must submit technical data on the item he proposes to use for the owner's evaluation of its quality. This contract provision which provides for use of a product other than brand name recited in the technical specification is frequently referred to as an *or-equal* provision.

The purpose of an or-equal provision is to maximize available procurement alternatives without detrimentally affecting quality. This, in turn, allows an owner to realize the full economic benefit of competitive bidding and contract

---

[5]*J. A. Jones Constr. Co.,* VACAB #929, 70-1 BCA 8267; *Ray M. Lee Co.,* ASBCA #5103, 59-2 BCA 2457; *Electronics & Missile Facilities, Inc.,* ASBCA #9971 and #10262, 65-2 BCA 5122.
[6]*Wexler Constr. Co.* ASBCA #12508, 68-1 BCA 6987.

experience and expertise. Utilizing the brand-name item as a quality standard, the contractor is free to explore alternative sources to find the least-cost choice which will satisfy the quality standard. The owner's benefit from an or-equal specification in a competitive procurement environment is reflected in price. It allows equal products to compete for purchase and prevents artificial price inflation from the named source because he has a lock on the procurement.

The primary problem which arises in the or-equal area is simply what constitutes "or equal." It is unusual for items of different manufacturers to be identical in *all* respects. Frequently, two brand-name items of a class, equally suitable for some particular application, will differ in certain design respects.

Or equal does not mean that the item tendered by the contractor must be identical with the brand-name product designated in the specifications. It does not mean that the proferred product must perform its function in precisely the same manner as does the brand-name item. The or-equal provision requires only that the item tendered by the contractor must function as well as the named product and provide all necessary functional features. For example, Ford, Chevrolet, and Plymouth may be considered of a class equally suitable for the purpose intended, notwithstanding their difference in design features.

A contractor, of course, cannot ignore technical specifications which identify essential functional features of the item in issue as part of the procurement. However, these features must be distinguished from mere design features. The proper concern in determining "equals" is equality of end result and not the mechanism by which the end result is achieved. This is the distinction between functional and design features. For example, a specification may call for a particular name-brand plywood siding for a building. This name-brand plywood may include and the specification require a factory-applied polyvinyl fluoride coating. The functional purpose of the coating is to enhance the weather resistance of the panel. An or-equal selection of a plywood siding material with an acrylic coating for weather resistance would be acceptable under the standard of the specification as an or equal, provided the acrylic coating offered the same degree of weather resistance as the polyvinyl fluoride. The use of different types of coating to achieve weather resistance is a matter of design feature.

An exception to the functional-versus-design feature standard occurs when an owner desires to elevate a design feature of a particular brand product to an essential functional requirement. The owner may do so by reciting the functional reason for such design feature. In such a case, the contractor would be limited to selecting a product which accomplishes the recited functional feature. If the owner in our previous example needed a coated plywood which could withstand certain chemical attack as well as weather, and chemical resistance was spelled out which only the polyvinyl fluoride coating would meet, then the product utilizing the acrylic coating would not qualify.

Finally, the contractor should recognize that or equal may apply to other than a circumstance of brand-name recital in the technical specifications. In federal construction contracts, where or-equal provisions are included by statutory direction, the owner may not avoid application of the clause by simply omitting the brand-name recital from the technical specification and writing the specification around the various proprietary features of that item. In such a case, the specification will be treated as if the brand name were recited and the or-equal factor will apply. Again, utilizing the plywood example, if the brand name of the product were not recited in the specification but the unique properties of that product were included without designation of functional reason, then the technical specification would be treated as stating the brand-name item around which the specifications were written and, as such, only establishing the standard of quality.

The or-equal specification is associated with competitive bidding and as stated is usually included as a general provision of the contract. However, the contractor should carefully review the language of the or-equal condition to be certain he has that right to select a competitive product after award of a contract in determining his competitive price. Many contracts insist upon the specified product but give the contractor the right to offer a different product as an alternate in his bid proposal. In order to perfect that right, the contractor must identify the product he intends to submit (other than specified) and the price benefit to the owner if he chooses the alternative product. This type of provision is not a true or-equal condition in the contract. The inclusion of the right to make a substitution in the bid will not carry over as a right to provide an or-equal product in the performance of the project after award of contract. If the owner requires identification of the substitution prior to bid, and the contractor fails to offer a substitute product, he will be bound to furnish that product named in the specification.

Performance Time

Most contracts contain a stipulation limiting the time interval for performance of the work, either requiring construction completion within a specific number of calendar days or by a specific date. The reason for this is to allow for finance programming, business, and use planning, and to ensure an appropriate performance effort and standard therefor.

Failure to complete within the stipulated time constitutes a breach of contract which would make the contractor liable for the owner's actual damages resulting from such failure. Because the actual damages an owner would incur upon late completion are typically difficult to ascertain with any reasonable degree of accuracy, a provision for liquidated damages is commonly associated with the contractual performance time. The stipulated liquidated-damages rate constitutes an "agreement" by the parties as to the reasonable and probable damages which the owner would suffer.

Many things could happen independent of proper contractor planning and execution which would result in a delay in completion. Hence, contracts also typically include a provision defining *excusable delay* and providing for an adjustment in the performance time.

The performance time requirement is binding upon the contractor. The contractor cannot avoid assessment of liquidated damages for late completion with the excuse that the time interval agreed upon in the contract is unreasonably short. If, in fact, the work can be performed within the stipulated time period in accordance with the terms of the contract, capability of performance is not limited necessarily by standard practices or by the most economical means of performance. Capability of performance includes the need for commercially feasible extraordinary measures as part of the contract obligation, such as employment of reasonable extra or overtime labor and equipment and premium payment for expedited material delivery. Only if there is a practical *impossibility* of performance may the contractor be relieved of the obligation of a too-short performance time interval. The definition of practical impossibility of performance embraces not only those acts which simply cannot be done but also those acts which can be done but require such extreme or unreasonably difficult measures to accomplish so as to make it commercially impossible. Relief from the obligation of time of performance because of practical impossibility is rare and unusual and can only be evaluated on a case-by-case basis. Most frequently, the failure to complete is the result of intervening circumstances which may or may not entitle the contractor to a performance time adjustment under the contract.

Where too short a performance time is stated in the contract, the contractor should be cautious in planning on late completion and including an allowance for liquidated damages in his cost estimate for bidding purposes. Most contracts include an owner right to terminate the contract for default if the contractor fails to make sufficient progress to ensure timely completion or if he fails to complete on time. Even without such a clause, the contractor is in breach of contract if the project is not completed within the stipulated completion date, and he has no absolute right to continue performance. The liquidated-damages agreement operates for the benefit of the owner and constitutes an alternate or supplemental remedy to terminating performance. The contractor cannot and should not rely upon a liquidated-damages provision as a means of purchasing additional performance time to accomplish the work.

Just as actual damages are not always susceptible to accurate computation, so also project completion is not always susceptible to precise determination. Since the completion date determines the rights of the contractor and the owner with regard to assessment of liquidated damages, it is necessary to set standards by which the completion date is established. Seldom is a contract completed in its entirety within the contract completion date. However, the contract may be sufficiently completed within the contract time interval to allow beneficial use for the purpose intended. When that degree of completion is achieved, the project is considered substantially complete. A two-fold standard is applied in determining when a project is substantially completed for beneficial occupancy. The project is examined to determine whether any single unfinished element of work prevents the beneficial occupancy for the purpose intended or—alternatively, if no single item prevents beneficial use—whether the aggregate of all unfinished elements, each of which may be insignificant, collectively prevents beneficial occupancy for the use intended. Percentage of completion value is not per se determinative of substantial completion. One project may be 92 percent complete and be deemed substantially complete; another project could be 99.9 percent complete and not be substantially complete. For example, a general purpose building including site development with summer recreational facilities, lacking completion of the recreational facilities of the value of 8 percent would be considered substantially complete in the middle of winter in that the building can be occupied and used. Alternatively, a structure intended to house a complex computer facility lacking a critical switch in the control portion of the air-conditioning system would not be considered complete in that a proper environment could not be established and regulated within which to operate the sensitive computer equipment.

Particular attention should be given to the provisions in the contract which define excusable delay and provide for adjustment in the contract performance time. These provisions can vary substantially from contract to contract and are covered more extensively in other chapters of this *Handbook.* It is important that the contractor recognize who has responsibility for the delay. The contractor's responsibility to complete within the stipulated time interval may be excused if the owner does anything to interfere with performance, or the cause of delay is unforeseeable and occurs beyond the control of the contractor. The contractor's control includes his responsibility to take reasonable measures to adjust to or overcome an unforeseeable cause of delay.

Since time is money, timely completion is critical to the profitability of the contract. The contractor must be alert to all conditions which may delay completion of the project. Excusable delay will entitle the contractor to adjustment of the performance time but will not entitle him to reimbursement of the cost of the additional time. By the same token, the owner will have to absorb his damages flowing from the delay.

Disclaimers

We have stated that the method the owner chooses in describing his requirements will define the degree of responsibility the contractor assumes for the end result. Regardless of the method selected, whether it incorporates the "cookbook recipe" design or performance specification, or combination thereof, the owner must include information and conditions which the contractor may rely upon in determining his price and degree of responsibility. Because the information which may be included is not precise, an owner generally seeks to limit the responsibility for the information included. Language included in the contract which denies responsibility is called a *disclaimer.*

The contract may include disclaimers for information concerning subsoil, site, environment, access, and regulatory information contained therein. It may also attempt to deny responsibility on the part of the owner for accuracy of dimensions, coordination of the various segments of the drawings and completeness of direction with regard to method. The contract may also incorporate contractor responsibility for omissions and misdescriptions in the plans and specifications which, in effect, would be a disclaimer of responsibility for the accuracy of the design. The tendency at law is for courts to avoid strictly enforcing disclaimers which, by their terms, are general and tend to avoid owner responsibility for any of the information contained in the contract. The rationale is that the bidding contractor has a paramount right to consider the information definitive and the predicate upon which he has estimated his price and bid. However, disclaimers are enforced which are expressed clearly and with reasonable limitations.

An example of an unenforceable disclaimer would be a provision in the contract that denies the accuracy of subsoil information incorporated in the contract when such information is critical to the performance of the work. Similarly, a disclaimer of the accuracy of dimensions contained in the plans would not be enforceable when the accuracy of dimension is necessary to determine the value of the work or the method by which it is to be accomplished.

An example of an enforceable disclaimer would be a statement that the dimensions shown on the drawings are the best information available to the owner but are not necessarily currently valid, coupled with the right and ability of the contractor prior to bid to examine and verify by reasonable investigation the actual conditions.

Other chapters of this *Handbook* discuss specific disclaimers. In context with the discussions in those chapters, the contractor should be wary of any statement contained in the contract which tends to avoid, modify, or limit any other statement of the work which is necessary to determine the price, quality, or time of performance of the contract.

EXTERNAL INFLUENCES ON PERFORMANCE OF THE WORK

The two previous sections of this chapter considered working conditions which arise out of the construction contract, by express statement and by implication. External influences upon the performance of the contract can affect price and time of performance. Codes or regulations will establish standards or limitations by which and within which the work must be performed. Awareness of these external influences is essential to the contractor's quest for profit.

Local building codes are examples of external factors which may materially affect the performance of the work. Whether the contractor is constructing a project in accordance with a design or performance specification, the contractor must accomplish the work in accordance with applicable local building codes (unless the work is being performed on a federal reservation which is beyond the jurisdiction of the local code under a contract which fails to incorporate said code by reference).

The statement of obligation which the contract imposes upon the contractor presumes that the obligation can be fulfilled in compliance with building codes. If the work statement is principally accomplished by design specification, the contractor may assume that the design meets the code requirements. If the work statement is presented by performance specification, the contractor may assume that the end result desired is lawful and may be accomplished in accordance with building codes.

In either case, the contractor's assumption of responsibility to conform to code is limited to method and performance. He must construct, install, attach, complete, test, isolate, shield, and do all other things that the codes require for compliance, unless the contractual statement expressly contradicts building code requirements. If such a contradiction is included in the design or performance specification, it creates other problems for the contractor. The contractor is not obligated to review and evaluate express design statement for conformance with code prior to bid, but he must be alert to patent conflicts between the design statement and applicable code.

Building codes, in effect, establish additional standards and restraints upon contractor discretion, particularly where the contract is silent with respect to technical requirements.

Other external influences may affect performance, not as a standard but as a limitation. Many contractors fail to consider local working conditions which affect their performance. The nature of the site and geographic location in which the work is to be performed are examples. A construction located in the heart of a city may be complicated by traffic regulation which does not allow on-street parking or loading and unloading. Traffic patterns may restrict access. Neighborhood conduct may interfere with the performance of the work or the construction of the project. The need to provide protection against such interference may be critical to the successful performance of the work and should be taken into account in the contractor's estimate of cost. Limitation of storage space for construction machinery, tools, and material will affect how the sequence of work must be planned. The same construction, if located in a rural area, may be relatively free of traffic, community interference, or storage problems, but instead may suffer problems of availability and cost of labor force as well as communication. Safety and employment standards established by code or regulation outside the contract affect performance. Application of such standards will be governed by local custom.

CONCLUSION

Working conditions are not simply a matter of looking at the construction site and determining whether it is wet or dry. Restrictions and limitations upon performance arise not only from physical limitations of the work site but also from direct expression and agreement in the contract, and the legal implications from the substance and form of contractual statement.

Full appreciation and understanding by owners, architects, specifiers, contractors, and suppliers of "working conditions" under which a potential contract must be performed benefits the construction process both in efficiency and economy. Pricing is more reflective of cost of construction. The number of disputes decreases and, thus, the expenditure of project-related funds for other than the construction is reduced. Reduced costs lead to increased profits, and that's the name of the game.

Chapter **18**

Procurement in the Construction Industry

RICHARD M. HOLLAR
Vice President, Procurement, Fluor Engineers and Constructors, Inc.,
Irvine, California

INTRODUCTION

Historically, purchased materials and services reflect approximately 50 to 60 percent of the total cost of a construction project. Depending on the individual

Acknowledgment: I express my gratitude to M. R. DeSilva, Associate Counsel, Fluor Corporation, and J. W. Drenker, Administrator, Procurement, Fluor Engineers and Constructors, Inc., who have given generously of their time in assisting me in the preparation of this chapter.

project size, this can easily range from $3 to $5 million (or less) for a small project to more than $1 billion for the larger ones.

The magnitude of such expenditures obviously deserves more than a casual look. Sound purchasing practices can often spell the difference between profit and loss on any particular job, especially if the contractor is doing work on a lump-sum basis. Any savings accrued by means of professional purchasing will be for the benefit of the contractor. Where work is on a cost-reimbursable basis, the savings will benefit both the client and the contractor.

Today's purchasing department is a vital arm of the contractor's organizational makeup. Whether it utilizes the "pro" who wears many hats in the purchasing department of the small contractor or the purchasing specialist of the large international contractor, purchasing is the operation which keeps the supply lines filled with goods enroute to the construction job site to ensure that the right material is received at the right place and the right time.

In the past, the stereotype of a buyer was a person who sat at a desk 8 hours a day and who flipped through pages of catalogs, mechanically and routinely ordering materials by phone. Today, purchasing is a different world. Although the typical contractor does have catalogs and does order a certain number of off-the-shelf items, many of the materials needed to build modern-day structures are both complex and sophisticated, involving special designs and often coming in large sizes. Such equipment might require fabrication by selected suppliers, thereby greatly increasing the scope of work for buyers far beyond the old stereotypes.

Buyers in the construction industry must get out of the office and meet with a variety of people including clients, suppliers, attorneys, engineers, and construction people working on the project. They have to communicate on a professional level. In addition, they must keep abreast of developments in the business world, such as the price of steel in Germany or Japan and not just the price in the United States.

It was previously pointed out that a contractor's purchasing department keeps the supply lines filled with the flow of goods for timely arrival at the job site. This statement conveys a "portal-to-portal" concept which, when applied to the construction industry, introduces the concept of procurement. What is procurement? Although the definition may vary from contractor to contractor, procurement, in concept, entails the obtainment of materials, equipment, supplies, and services in such a way that construction will progress in a timely, efficient, and programmed manner.

For example, prefabricated structural steel may be required for the framework of a building. The purchasing department receives the basic requisition from engineering (or possibly the contractor's client) which, in addition to providing all the technical data and drawings, also provides a *field need date*. The material must then be purchased, expedited, inspected, and shipped. With the possible exception of inspection, these functions, in a small organization, may very well be effectively handled by the purchasing person of many "hats." Of necessity, this person very often becomes knowledgeable in and conversant with the needs and techniques of expediting and shipping. However, the large internationally oriented contractor requires the services of specialists in the various procurement disciplines and the person-of-many-hats concept generally falls by the wayside. The problems associated with expediting, inspection, and shipping by such contractors are sufficiently complex to justify specialization into several procurement disciplines, such as purchasing, inspection, expediting, and shipping (traffic).

In the preceding example, it might also have been desirable (or necessary) to have the foundation and erection work done by contractors specializing in such work. This subcontracting activity could be for labor only (e.g., actual steel erection work) or labor and materials (e.g., the foundation work) and serves as the basis for another procurement discipline—subcontracting.

In summary, procurement in the construction industry encompasses the disciplines of purchasing, expediting, inspection, shipping (traffic), and subcontracting. It could be defined as follows:

Procurement is the utilization of efficient management and inventories in the functions of purchasing, expediting, inspection, shipping, and subcontracting of goods and/or services of all types (including construction work) from financially sound, reputable, and capable sources which afford the most economical cost, taking into consideration quality, price, delivery, reliability, and service.

PROCUREMENT ORGANIZATION

For effective day-to-day execution of the procurement functions, it is necessary that the organizational makeup of a procurement department (irrespective of size) be so structured as to enable it to discharge its assigned duties in an atmosphere free from the constraints and encumbrances which may be imposed upon it by other departments.

An effective procurement department should meet the following criteria:

1. The top procurement officer will report directly to the president or other senior executive.

2. The top procurement officer will have complete responsibility and authority for all procurement functions.

3. Procurement will have a set of well-defined policies and procedures which clearly define assigned duties, functions, and responsibilities of the procurement operation.

4. Procurement will be adequately staffed with professional (and support) personnel to perform its assigned duties.

PURCHASING

Purchasing activity on a project generally does not start until engineering has established the technical parameters of the equipment and materials needed at the job site. The resulting technical requisitions for such goods are provided to purchasing for conversion into viable commercial-technical packages suitable for the development of bids and eventual purchase. The purchasing arm of procurement is the first step in the procurement cycle. Although the terms "buying," "purchasing," and "procurement" are often considered synonymous, they may mean different things in modern business.

Historically, *buying* represents the simple exchange of a commodity or thing for an agreed price. *Purchasing,* as an extension of buying, generally involves a certain amount of sophisticated negotiation. *Procurement* is more inclusive and can be considered the ultimate in buying, for it adds certain steps to purchasing both before and after a purchase order is issued to the supplier. Procurement in the construction industry involves the development of supply sources, negotiation with suppliers, issuance of inquiries for purchase orders, analysis of quotations, selection of suppliers, inspection of equipment and/or materials during and after manufacture, expediting of orders, and shipment of finished products to the job site.

SUBCONTRACTS

Although this chapter concerns itself primarily with purchasing and its role in the construction industry, it should be pointed out that more and more emphasis is being placed on the subcontracting arm of the total procurement operation of the engineering and construction contractor. Both purchasing and subcontracting are empowered to commit the contractor's (or client's) monies. Since subcontracting activities are essentially an extension of the purchasing operation by virtue of the introduction of the "purchase" of labor, it is axiomatic that sound purchasing principles which have evolved over the years apply equally as well to the subcontract operation.

SELECTION OF BIDDERS

Competitive bidding is the cornerstone of the whole cycle of events leading up to and including the actual placement of the purchase order/subcontract. The purchaser should exercise his purchasing professionalism by using sound commercial judgment in the selection of bidders.

The purchasing profession does not uniformly set the number of bids which should be solicited; however, unless otherwise dictated by factors outside of purchasing's control (e.g., government requirements or requests of contractor's client), it is good practice to solicit at least three bids from financially sound, reputable, and capable firms. It is important to remember that today's purchasing professional evaluates more than price alone. He can and does help in reducing costs by analyzing and balancing values. In other words, he is participating in a value analysis. If the quality of a commodity is superior to the actual need, for instance, he will be buying a "gold-plated" piece of equipment, and the cost will be unnecessarily high. If the quality is inferior, any initial savings will be reduced or offset by increased maintenance and/or replacement costs, and a possible loss or reduction of productivity.

Modern professional purchasing techniques (e.g., careful selection of bidders and skillful negotiations) can cut as much as 5 to 10 percent from the total cost of goods purchased, without sacrifice in quality. Such savings, especially on larger jobs, can and do have a significant impact on the contractor's profit margin.

TERMS AND CONDITIONS OF PURCHASE

Many years ago, in a more simplistic society, a buyer-seller agreement was generally consummated by little more than a handshake. This is just about impossible in the current sophisticated and complex business environment. Today, the purchaser wants to buy on his "standard" terms and the supplier/subcontractor wants to sell on its "standard" terms. Each seeks maximum protection. The purchase order/subcontract is an agreement which contains the terms and conditions of purchase. When a supplier/subcontractor is satisfied that negotiated terms and conditions are generally acceptable, it will accept the purchase order/subcontract. Acceptance is best evidenced by its signing the purchase order/subcontract copy and returning it to the purchaser, thus consummating the contract between the two parties.

Depending on the type and amount of activity (and degree of risk exposure) on the part of the contractor, terms and conditions of purchase may cover (in the simplest format) only such basic areas as invoices, payment, shipping, and warranties. For more complex situations purchasers must be familiar with areas such as warranties, consequential damages, indemnification, insurance, liquidated damages, time-of-the-essence, applicable law, special statutes, the Uniform Commercial Code, and other considerations.

Warranties

An area which is often the subject of discussion and negotiations is warranty. The supplier/subcontractor would like to limit its liability and the contractor's remedies as much as possible, and the contractor wants to obtain the most for the money. Warranties are generally of two types—express and implied. The Uniform Commercial Code imposes on suppliers the implied warranties of merchantability (UCC § 2-314), fitness for an intended purpose (UCC § 2-315), and title and noninfringement (UCC § 2-312). Many suppliers attempt either to completely disclaim some of such implied warranties or to disclaim such to the extent not expressly warranted under the purchase order/subcontract. In addition to the implied warranties in the Uniform Commercial Code, there are other implied warranties normally of concern to suppliers and subcontractors, such as selection of materials, corrosion and erosion, and operating conditions in excess of those specified. Depending on the subject matter of the purchase order/subcontract, the bargaining position of the parties, and the practice in the particular area of the construction industry, the supplier/subcontractor may insist on a disclaimer of or limitation on implied warranties. This is subject to negotiation and the purchaser should ensure that the prime contract does not preclude whatever disclaimer is ultimately included in the purchase order/subcontract.

Express warranties are more varied as to their scope, duration, and remedies. The duration of such warranties is often fixed by the quote and price of the seller/subcontractor and would require a price increase for any extension of the warranty periods. The purchaser should be careful to identify the beginning of the warranty period. For example, on purchase orders "from date of shipment" might better read "from date of final shipment" or "from date of shipment of each respective unit"; and "from first use" should be further clarified "from commercial operation" or "from first use other than for testing purposes" or "from being placed in regular use."

The actual scope of the warranties of a supplier/subcontractor is normally not a major item of negotiation, except in situations where suppliers/subcontractors attempt to "pass through" (not be obligated for or not underwrite) warranties of lower-tier suppliers. In such situations purchasers are justified in their concern with respect to possible uncertainties as to scope and duration of such warranties, assignability of such warranties, whether such component equipment has been sufficiently earmarked to be tied to such warranties, loss of negotiation leverage in enforcing such warranties (the contractor will not normally be a customer of such lower-tier suppliers), and establishing precisely what is the cause of the defect or equipment failure. Purchasers should point out that the suppliers/subcontractors are making a profit on the component items of equipment and should therefore assume some responsibility under warranty for same.

In addition to the scope of the warranty of the supplier/subcontractor the question of warranty remedies in the event of breach often entails considerable discussion, especially in purchase orders. Whether a supplier disclaims packing/transportation costs and/or dismantling or erection costs will depend on the relative bargaining positions, price, location of the plant, tax, and other commercial considerations. Often the contractor is bound by either (1) express obligations in his prime contract to obtain specified warranty provisions or (2) responsibilities in the prime contract which the purchaser must "cover" in the purchase order/subcontract. The nature of the contractor's contractual obligations to his client [i.e., whether purchaser's warranty is (a) wholly independent of what the contractor is able to negotiate with supplier/subcontractor; (b) is limited to the warranties and remedies he is able to negotiate with suppliers/subcontractors; or (c) is a "pass-through" being nonexistent with respect to equipment, materials, and services provided by suppliers/subcontractors with the client looking only to the suppliers/subcontractors] will be a consideration in the purchaser's negotiations. In the pass-through situation, the purchaser will often need the client's approval or at least concurrence with the warranty.

Although the purchaser may have previously dealt many times with a supplier/subcontractor, the purchaser should remember that in each purchase order/subcontract there may be a different setting and different considerations.

Consequential Damages

In the event of a breach of contract, damages will be measured by those which naturally arise from the breach or which are reasonable within the contemplation of the parties as a probable result of the breach. Since the landmark case of *Hadley v. Baxendale*,[1] courts have made it increasingly clear that victims of contract breaches can recover damages peculiar to their special circumstances. Although judicial interpretation may vary somewhat, it appears that for such consequential damages to be recoverable, most courts require a supplier to have only had reason to know of the purchaser's particular circumstances or requirements at the time of contracting. In general, it can be said that if the losses were reasonably foreseeable (not necessarily foreseen) at the time of contracting, recovery could be obtained. For example, suppliers can be held to foresee that defective equipment will disrupt production.[2]

In the construction industry, suppliers and subcontractors are naturally concerned with their liability exposure to consequential damages such as business interruption, loss of anticipated profit, loss of use, cost of capital, and increased cost of production. These damages can consist of large dollar amounts. As a result of such concern, suppliers and subcontractors often attempt to obtain a release from such consequential damages. However, problems arise because of the fact that the boundaries of the term "consequential damages" are not clearly defined. Suppliers/subcontractors often attempt to include in their releases both indirect and special damages together with consequential damages and to include such catchall phrases as "including but not limited to" or "including but not by way of limitation" when listing consequential damages. What may be a consequential damage to the plant owner may be special damage to the contractor. Even though a contractor chooses to release the supplier/subcontractor from such a special damage, the contractor might not intend to forego his recourse for other special damages, such as medical expenses for personal injuries caused by the supplier/subcontractor. Such would defeat much of the purpose of any indemnification provision in the purchase order/subcontract. Also, the supplier/subcontractor may try to word the release in such a manner that it may be operative for negligence as well as breach of contract actions.

In view of ambiguities as to what damages are to be considered consequential, and because of provisions of the Uniform Commercial Code [§ 2-715(2)] which define consequential damages to include injury to person or property, the purchaser should consider whether to expressly word the release so that it does not include injury to persons or tangible property or is applicable for only breach of contract actions. In the alternative, the purchaser could consider limiting the types of consequential damages to be included in the release to certain specified types. Purchasers might also consider whether to make releases for consequential damages reciprocal in nature.

This area of the purchase order/subcontract is one assumed by many purchasing veterans to be unimportant, possibly as a result of the familiarity with the comments of a supplier/subcontractor to such area. A word of caution is in order here as is in any area where the liability of a supplier/subcontractor is

[1]156 Eng. Rep. 145 (Ex. 1854).
[2]*Lewis v. Mobil Oil Corp.*, 438 F.2d 500 (8th Cir. 1971).

being limited or defined. A little extra effort could make the difference between possible recovery of damages or not, or even more realistically, a successful settlement with the insurance carrier of the supplier/subcontractor or an unsuccessful settlement. Inasmuch as many suppliers/subcontractors utilize legal counsel in negotiating such areas, it is advisable for the purchaser to follow suit, or at least obtain legal reviews prior to the final agreement on such wording. As in other areas, the provisions of the purchaser's prime contract should always be considered when negotiating consequential damage provisions.

Indemnification

Purchase orders/subcontracts often contain indemnification provisions whereby the seller/subcontractor agrees to indemnify (or assume the liability of) the contractor for liability incurred by the contractor as a result of certain contingencies, such as: (1) failure of seller/subcontractor to comply with applicable laws; (2) negligence or fault of seller/subcontractor in the performance of the purchase order/subcontract; (3) infringement of patents (and sometimes copyright, or trade secrets) resulting from equipment or services provided by seller/subcontractor; (4) mechanics liens; or (5) other specific areas of concern for which contractor wants to minimize risk.

These indemnifications may be very complex in wording and are often subject to considerable negotiation. Purchasers, in considering such indemnification provisions, should realize that the statutes in some states might either prohibit or limit enforcement of such provisions.[3]

Also, in view of the judicial disfavor of indemnification, the wording may be narrowly construed in favor of the indemnitor. Thus, in certain jurisdictions, if the contractor desires the indemnity to cover the concurrent negligence and/or strict liability of the contractor (and possibly the plant owner), and the indemnity is not otherwise against public policy, then it must be expressly stated in order to do so.[4]

Among areas often covered by indemnification provisions, patent infringement is an area which may involve considerable negotiation. For the most part the subject of patent infringement is little understood by purchasers. United States patents generally run 17 years from the day of grant and give the patent owner the right to prevent others from making, using, or selling the patented invention. In addition, a United States patent owner under certain circumstances may be able to prevent the import into the United States of goods produced (by practicing an invention claimed by the United States patent) in foreign countries.

[3]Del. Code Ann. 6 § 2704; F.S.A. § 725.06 (Florida); Ga. Code Ann. § 20-504; Hawaii Rev. Stat. § 431-453; Idaho Code 29-114; S.H.A. ch. 29 § 61 *et seq.* (Illinois); M.S.A. § 26.1146(1) (Mich.); Miss. Code § 31-5-41; N.H. RSA 338-A:1; N.M. Stat. 28-2-1; N.Y. Gen. Ob. Law § 5-332.1 and 2 5-324; N.D. Century Code § 9-08-02.1; 68 P.S. § 491 (Penna.); SDCL 1967 56-3-16 (S. Dak.); Tenn. Code § 62-623; Vernon's Ann. Civ. St. art. 249d (Texas); Utah Code § 13-8-1; and Rev. Wash. Code § 4.24.115.
[4]*Price v. Shell Oil Co.*, 2 Cal. 3d 245, 466 P.2d 722 (1970).

If an owner of a United States patent—whether it be for equipment, process, or construction method—feels that his patent is being violated by a supplier or subcontractor, he can initiate an infringement action. The contractor and the plant owner might well find themselves named as defendants in such action. Such infringement action would in all probability involve discovery, which would be both expensive and time-consuming. Under certain circumstances, an injunction could even be granted. The plant owner and the contractor would look to the indemnity of the supplier/subcontractor for any damages awarded and defense costs, including attorney's fees.

As a result of potential expenses associated with infringement suits, purchasers often have patent counsel who assist them in negotiating the patent indemnification provisions. Contractors might feel it advisable to require the supplier/subcontractor to contractually assume the defense of the lawsuit. However, the contractor's interests might be best served if the contractor retained the right to at least participate (usually at his own expense) in the defense of the suit for tactical reasons. The contractor might wish to cover the contingency of an injunction being granted by providing in the indemnity clause that the supplier/subcontractor will (with contractor's consent) obtain for contractor and the plant owner a fully paid up, irrevocable, royalty-free license to practice the patented invention or, in the alternative, to substitute a noninfringing equipment or process.

The area of patent infringement is extremely complicated and should always be cleared with patent counsel. A foreign setting complicates the picture further and, as in other areas (such as taxation), may be fraught with uncertainty.

Insurance

Insurance provisions should be included in both purchase orders under which the supplier will provide supervisory erection or installation labor at the job site, and subcontracts. Normally the provisions will include the type of insurance (workmen's compensation and employer's liability, comprehensive general liability, and where appropriate, automobile liability) and the minimum limits of such insurance. Often it is advisable to require that certificates of insurance include provisions providing for notification in the event of termination of such coverage or material change in coverage. Also, to avoid suits by the insurance carrier of the supplier/subcontractor, a waiver of subrogation on behalf of the contractor and plant owner is recommended. This waiver will preclude subrogation—that is, the insurance carrier's "stepping into the shoes" of the insured and asserting whatever rights the insured has against third parties to recover loss of money which the insurance company has paid for its insured. These waivers of subrogation are usually available. However, to the extent the carrier cannot subrogate, the loss record of the insured will not receive the otherwise available credit of subrogation recoveries. Consequently, the insured's premiums could in the long run be adversely affected and suppliers/subcontractors may be very reluctant to provide such waivers of subrogation. In situations where the plant owner or purchaser provides *builder's all-risk installation insurance,* and subcontractors are normally additional insured thereon, there is a possibility that the carrier can still subrogate against an insured subcontractor if the loss occurs in a portion of the plant where the subcontractor has no insurable interest.[5] Consequently, the contractor might consider requiring all insureds under such policy to provide reciprocal waivers of subrogation (or releases).

Comments on insurance in today's procurement activities would not be complete without a few words concerning the *owner-controlled* or *wrap-up insurance* programs. In general these are programs wherein the owner (or possibly the prime contractor) provides certain insurances for all the parties performing services at the job site with specified exceptions (such as subcontracts under a certain contract value or subcontractors who perform services at the job site for periods of less than 24 consecutive hours). Such insurances usually include workmen's compensation and employer's liability, comprehensive general liability (excluding automobile), and builder's all-risk installation insurance. These owner-controlled or wrap-up insurance programs, if properly implemented, can decrease costs to the owner and eliminate questions as to which insurance carrier should respond for a given loss. Normally subcontractors are expected to reduce their prices to the extent their insurance premiums are no longer required. The contractor should endeavor, through proper timing and coordination with the plant owner, to maintain a negotiating posture which will allow such a reduction. However, if the owner-controlled or wrap-up insurance program is not implemented within a reasonable time with respect to subcontract awards and negotiations, the contractor's ability to do so may be somewhat impaired.

Liquidated Damages: Time-of-the-Essence

Occasionally purchase orders or subcontracts contain a liquidated damage provision. The liquidated damage provision is an agreement between the parties at the time of contracting as to what damages are to be paid in the event of a breach. These damages are estimated with a view toward the extent of injury which the breach would cause. The actual damages must be uncertain in nature or amount, or difficult to ascertain at the time of contracting. In addition, the amount agreed upon must not be unreasonably disproportionate to damages that could actually result from a breach. The agreed-to amount must therefore be a good faith estimate. If the primary purpose of the liquidated damage provision is to secure performance (as opposed to the good faith estimation of damages in the event of nonperformance), then courts will treat such provision as a penalty which would be unenforceable.

Often the liquidated damage provision is triggered by late performance. If the parties agree that the time of performance is very essential, they may include a "time-of-the-essence" provision. Such a provision makes even a short delay a major default and would entitle the supplier/subcontractor to full

[5] *Paul Tishman Co., Inc. v. Carney & Del Giudice, Inc.,* 320 N.Y.S., 2d 396, 36 A.D. 2d 273 (1971).

compensation only if it performs the purchase order/subcontract in time (unless otherwise legally excused or the delay has been waived). If the supplier subcontractor performed after the specified time and the work is accepted, the supplier/subcontractor could sue only for *quantum meruit,* or reasonable value to the purchaser, and not include any added costs incurred by its late performance. If time were *not* of the essence, the supplier/subcontractor would be able to sue for full payment subject to the right of the purchaser to recoup damages for failure to complete work in time. As a result of the legal position in which time-of-the-essence clauses place suppliers/subcontractors, such clauses are not favored by them. However, they are occasionally used, often with a liquidated damage provision for late performance. This limits the legal recourse of the contractor for late performance to such agreed-to liquidated damages. Sometimes where respective bargaining position demands or schedule considerations allow, the liquidated damages provision will be accompanied with a bonus-completion provision where the supplier/subcontractor gets paid an extra amount for early performance.

The subject of liquidated damages is codified in many states and purchasers should therefore coordinate with legal counsel to ensure that the purchase order/subcontract provision complies with applicable statutes. Since the purchaser needs to consider the specific objective in making time-of-the-essence, the use of *force majeure* (excusable delays) clauses should be carefully thought through when considering the use of time-of-the-essence clauses.

Applicable Law

In the United States, if the purchase order/subcontract specifies which state law is to apply with regard to the interpretation of such purchase order/subcontract and performance thereunder, such law will normally be used for such interpretation. Exceptions to this general rule are situations in which (1) there is no reasonable basis for the parties' choice; (2) the parties did not act in good faith; or (3) the application of such law would be contrary to a fundamental policy of the state whose laws would otherwise be applicable, provided such other state has a materially greater interest in the determination of an issue than the chosen state.

If the purchase order/subcontract does not specify which state law is to be applicable, the applicable law may depend upon the jurisdiction and which conflict-of-law or choice-of-law theory it follows. The older and more rigid theory (First Restatement of Conflict of Laws) is that the contract will be interpreted under the law applicable at the place of contracting for questions as to validity, and under the law applicable at the place of performance for questions as to performance. These rigid rules have given way to more liberal and modern approaches in many jurisdictions in which the law of the state with the most significant relationship to the transaction and parties or the state with most substantial interest will be applicable. The court under such theories will consider many factors, including the place of contracting, the place of negotiations, place of performance, location and subject matter of the contract, domicile, residence, nationality, place of incorporation and place of business of the parties, relevant policies of its legal system, relevant policies of the legal system of other interested states, protection of the parties' justified expectations, the desirability of predictability and uniformity of results, and the basic policies underlying a particular field of law.

The contractor, in choosing applicable law, should—where possible—select the applicable law in his prime contract so as to minimize the possibility of inconsistent judgments in litigation or arbitration between the contractor and his supplier/subcontractor.

In foreign countries the treatment as to applicable law by foreign tribunals or courts will differ from place to place. Regardless of the parties having specified the law to be applicable, the contractor might find the local law being imposed. Often the contractor will receive satisfaction, however, in knowing the prime contract contains arbitration provisions under which selection of law by the parties will be honored by some impartial arbitration tribunal. The purchaser may experience reluctance of suppliers or subcontractors to accept foreign laws; however, there remains the need to maintain consistency with the contractor's prime contract. In foreign countries the degree of development and certainty of commercial law and ability to establish such law could play a determinative role as to whether a particular law should be chosen. The purchaser may often find it necessary to include legal counsel in resolving exceptions to provisions of supplier/subcontractor concerning applicable law.

Special Statutes

There are certain statutes with which the contractor should have some degree of familiarity for the proper performance of his profession. A summary of these statutes is as follows:

Sherman Anti-Trust Act[6]   This 1890 act condemns "contracts, combinations or conspiracies" in restraint of trade (including import and export trade and interstate commerce) of the United States. The act also condemns monopolization, attempts to monopolize, and combinations or conspiracies to monopolize. For example, if competitive pump manufacturers have a meeting and decide that each will market his pumps only in certain states, competition between such manufacturers would be restrained and such an arrangement would be a violation of the act. An agreement by such pump manufacturers as to the prices they will charge for certain types of pumps would also restrain competition and be a violation of the act. The act is enforced by the U.S. Department of Justice, and violation of the act may be prosecuted either by civil or criminal action. Treble (triple) damages and attorney's fees are authorized by section 4 of the Clayton act (see below) for any person injured in his business or property by reason of the act.

Clayton Anti-Trust Act[7]   This act was enacted in 1914 and condemns both "exclusive dealing arrangements" (i.e., arrangements which preclude a purchaser from handling the goods of a competitor of the supplier) if such

[6]15 U.S.C. 1 *et seq.*
[7]15 U.S.C. 14 *et seq.*

arrangement may have an adverse impact on competition, and "tying" arrangements (i.e., where goods are sold or leased on the condition that the purchaser use certain other goods of the supplier and not those which are marketed by competitors of the supplier). The act is enforced in a civil proceeding by the U.S. Department of Justice or the Federal Trade Commission, or in treble (triple) damages proceedings by persons injured in their business or property as a result of a violation of the act.

Robinson-Patman Act[8]   This is a 1936 statute which prohibits certain differentials in price of commodities to different purchasers where the price differential may injure competition with the person granting the differential, the person receiving the benefit of the lower price, or customers of either. Price differentials are proper where granted in order to meet (and not beat) lower prices of competitors or to reflect cost savings realized out of different methods or quantities of sale or delivery. The act also prohibits the granting or receiving of discounts or allowances (kickbacks) in lieu of brokerage in connection with the sale or purchase of commodities. In addition, discrimination in making allowances (such as advertising or promotion) available to persons competing in the further distribution of commodities is prohibited, as is discrimination in the furnishing of services or facilities to persons competing in the further distribution of such commodities. The Federal Trade Commission normally enforces the act by way of civil proceedings, often coordinating with the U.S. Department of Justice. However, a private treble (triple) damage action is available to aggrieved persons. The act makes sales "below cost" for the purpose of destroying competition or eliminating a competitor a crime and is enforced by the Department of Justice.

Federal Trade Commission Act[9]   This act prohibits uniform methods of competition. It is enforced by civil proceeding brought by the Federal Trade Commission. Treble (triple) damages are not recoverable for a violation of this act.

Occupational Safety and Health Act[10]   The Occupational Safety and Health Act (OSHA) was enacted in 1970 and is applicable to most United States employers. The act requires employers to provide places of employment for their employees which are free from recognized safety hazards and further requires the employer to comply with regulations and standards promulgated under the act. Purchasers will find that suppliers frequently object to the requirement that equipment furnished by the supplier comply with OSHA. Suppliers usually object on the basis that they have no control over the manner in which the equipment is physically placed in the plant or is maintained or operated. They further object on the basis that the obligations to comply with OSHA is upon employers and not upon suppliers of equipment. Purchasers should be aware that guidelines were proposed on April 27, 1976, which would allow citations to be issued to (1) employers who created or caused hazardous

[8]15 U.S.C. 13 *et seq.*
[9]15 U.S.C. 45 *et seq.*
[10]29 U.S.C. 651 *et seq.*

conditions to which employers of others are exposed; (2) employers who had the ability to abate the hazardous condition regardless of whether such employer caused such hazard in the first instance; and (3) employers who permit their employees to be exposed to hazardous conditions, regardless of whether such employer created the hazard or had the power to abate it. The contractor and his client need to be assured that the purchased equipment complies with OSHA. If a supplier continues its objection, the purchaser will find the supplier normally will accept the obligation if such obligation expressly does not cover noncompliance resulting from the particular manner of installation or placement of the equipment or misoperation of the equipment. This act is the subject of detailed review elsewhere in this book.

Fair Labor Standards Act[11]   This 1938 statute is applicable to most United States suppliers. It prohibits child labor, specifies minimum pay and maximum hours, and prohibits wage discrimination on the basis of sex or age. With respect to the prohibition against the use of child labor, the act subjects purchasers to possible penalties and provides that goods produced by child labor in violation of the act are subject to seizure by the government. However, there is an exception for a good faith purchaser of such goods who buys the goods in reliance on a certification by the supplier that the equipment was manufactured in accordance with the applicable section of the act.

Equal Employment Opportunity Act[12]   This act was enacted to provide equal opportunity to qualified persons and to prohibit discrimination because of race, creed, color, or national origin. The act is the subject of detailed review elsewhere in this book.

Buy American Act[13]   This act was enacted in 1933. It is applicable to both government supply and service contracts. It requires that government purchases of materials and equipment for use in the United States be of American origin, unless it is determined that the cost of domestic-source end products would be unreasonable or that their acquisition would be inconsistent with public interest, or unless the government has determined that certain articles, materials, or supplies are not mined, produced, or manufactured in the United States in sufficient and reasonably available commercial quantities and of a satisfactory quality.

Davis-Bacon Act[14]   This act was enacted in 1931. It provides that a government construction contract for the construction of buildings in the United States must state the wages and benefits for craft labor that the contractor and his subcontractors are going to pay, and these wages and fringe benefits must be not less than those prevailing in the locality, as determined by the secretary of labor.

Walsh-Healy Public Contracts Act[15]   This act was enacted in 1936. It covers situations in which the government is purchasing materials (as distinguished from a government construction contract). It states that a government contract

[11]29 U.S.C. 201 *et seq.*
[12]42 U.S.C. 2000e *et seq.*
[13]41 U.S.C. 10 *et seq.*
[14]40 U.S.C. 276a *et seq.*
[15]41 U.S.C. 35 *et seq.*

for the purchase of materials must require certain basic wages and working conditions on the part of the contractor furnishing these materials and that this contractor must pay at least the prevailing minimum wages in the area, observe a 40-hour week, not employ child or convict labor, and provide safe working conditions.

Service Contract Act[16]   This act also concerns wages and working conditions on government contracts. It was designed to cover any gaps that might exist between the Walsh-Healy Act (which involves the purchase of materials) and the Davis-Bacon Act (which covers construction contracts). The act provides that in government contracts for craft services other than contracts for the purchase of materials, the contract must specify the hours, wages, and fringe benefits to be paid by the contractor and subcontractors and that these benefits must not be less than those prevailing in the locality.

The Uniform Commercial Code

The Uniform Commercial Code (UCC), which does not apply to subcontracts, is a set of rules applicable to the sale of goods. It was originally written by a nationwide committee with the idea that each state could review and decide whether or not to adopt it. At the present time the UCC has been adopted (with minor modifications) by every state except Louisiana.

The UCC had its origins in the early marketplaces of Europe. The merchants in these marketplaces developed certain customs and practices which served as practical rules for dealing in goods. These rules became known as the *law merchant* and gradually acquired the force of law in the sixteenth century when incorporated into English common law. The United States adopted the *law merchant* as the Uniform Sales Act around the turn of the century. The Uniform Sales Act was the precursor of and served as the basis for the Uniform Commercial Code.

Most of the provisions of the UCC are practical in nature. They cover the legal formalities required for a contract, details of performance, guarantees, and remedies for nonperformance. Most, but not all, of the provisions can be varied by agreement of the parties. Serving as a backdrop against which contracts for the sale of goods are made, the UCC fills in gaps which may have been left out by the parties. Also, it is important to remember that the UCC is practically complete in itself, requiring only identification of the goods, price, and some signed writing to form a complete sale of goods transaction.

Purchasers should become familiar with article 2 of the Uniform Commercial Code as it applies to sales transactions, keeping in mind that under certain circumstances they might be obligated to expressly reject supplier's proposed changes to the contractor's terms and conditions of sale or improper confirmations of transactions.

Additional Considerations

The purchaser must determine whether the contractor is purchasing as an agent for the client or as an independent contractor. If the purchasing effort is

[16]41 U.S.C. 351 *et seq.*

as an agent, the purchaser must implement a system through which he will always be identified "as agent for" the client. Failure to do this could result in adverse legal complications.

The purchaser should always consider whether the supplier/subcontractor is financially able to perform the work. For example, for tax or other business considerations, the supplier/subcontractor might wish to perform the purchase order/subcontract through a subsidiary. In such event the purchaser might wish to obtain a guarantee from a parent or affiliate corporation which in turn does have a satisfactory financial condition. In the event the purchaser is not satisfied with the financial condition, or if prior dealing has indicated that it is difficult to work with a certain supplier/subcontractor and that such a selection was nevertheless required for other reasons, the purchaser should then consider whether a performance bond or payment bond should be required. Such a bond would be written by a surety and would provide that, if the supplier/subcontractor does not perform its work or pay its materialmen and suppliers, the surety would pay or itself remedy the default by completing the contract or making such payment (up to the limit of the bond). In the event that a bond is obtained, however, the purchaser should ensure that the bond contains clauses which waive notice of any modification of the purchase order/subcontract and which waive extensions of time thereunder. If the bond does not include such provisions, the purchaser will need to obtain the surety concurrence with all such major modifications or extensions; otherwise, the surety may be released from its obligations.

For foreign projects, the bond may be replaced with a bank guarantee or letter of credit. Purchasers should, however, be aware of the reluctance on the part of many suppliers/subcontractors to provide such letters of credit or bank guarantees, or bonds in domestic settings. Inasmuch as the contingent liability under such documents would reduce the available credit which the supplier/subcontractor otherwise would have, it would reduce borrowing power and could interfere somewhat with the business operations of the supplier/subcontractor. In addition there is a premium associated with any such documents and the client would usually end up paying from $\frac{1}{2}$ to $1\frac{1}{2}$ percent of the amount guaranteed. Sometimes a requirement that the supplier/subcontractor produce lien releases from all of its materialmen and subcontractors before specified payments are made will be an acceptable compromise where payment bonds are considered. However, in certain circumstances payment or performance bonds, letters of credit, and bank guarantees are appropriate and should be used.

The purchaser for foreign projects should always be especially conscious of tax and insurance implications. For example, the contractor should make sure that title passes at the proper location to minimize tax consequences to and insurance protection for the client and the contractor. The contractor might under certain circumstances consider split or separate contracts.

Another phase of procurement worthy of comment is the area of escalation of prices. Often suppliers will quote on the basis that their prices are subject to escalation. If the contractor accepts escalation, he must make sure to identify the basis of escalation (i.e., both the identity of the index and the base month index), applicability of escalation (i.e., on unpaid amounts as opposed to the full price, even though progress payments have already been made), and duration of escalation (i.e., through date of shipment, date of invoice, or date of payment).

FINANCING THE OVERSEAS PROJECT: ITS EFFECT ON PROCUREMENT

In contrast to bidding for construction work in the United States where owner-clients can usually obtain all or most of their financing by borrowing in private capital markets, bidding for overseas projects is often conditioned on owner-clients obtaining funds through the international banking community. This often takes the form of governmental (or quasi-governmental) institutions, such as (in the United States) the Export-Import (Ex-Im) Bank, the Agency for International Development (AID), which is a branch of the U.S. Department of State, and (internationally) The International Bank for Reconstruction and Development (World Bank).

Private financing as a rule allows for freedom of development of quotations, either domestic or international. However, contractors whose clients obtain loans from the Ex-Im Bank will generally be required to restrict their inquiries to United States firms. In contrast, contractors whose clients have secured funds from the World Bank will generally be required to solicit bids from any and all suppliers located in those nations which are members of the bank and which have expressed an interest in bidding.

CURRENCY FLUCTUATIONS

In recent years an increasing number of foreign suppliers have been able to bid competitively on goods and services for both domestic and foreign projects. This trend will undoubtedly continue as foreign competitors improve their technology and business methods to meet ever-changing market requirements. Since purchasing on a worldwide basis is essentially the extension or broadening of a domestic operation beyond one's own borders, it follows that the techniques and philosophies guiding a successful domestic purchasing program will similarly provide the foundation for good purchasing on a global basis.

However, purchasing on the international market incorporates some financial risks and therefore requires knowledge of a number of specialized disciplines. One of these concerns currency rates of exchange. When goods or services are purchased abroad, the currency used for payment may be in United States dollars, the currency of the supplier's home country, or the currency of a third country. This is usually determined by the client's financial arrangements for a particular project.

Success in buying internationally demands close attention in a world market where currencies often fluctuate. A typical example might be where a revaluation (appreciation) of a country's currency (in terms of the United States dollar) occurs, which will then increase the cost of goods it exports. If this happens during the life of a purchase order on a supplier in that country, the price at delivery will increase accordingly, unless this contingency is clearly spelled out in the purchase order.

BUSINESS ETHICS

Purchasing, perhaps more than any other profession, is engaged in activities which come under continuing public and private scrutiny of management, suppliers, clients, and the press. In their contacts with individuals and suppliers, all purchasing agents should always exercise and adhere to strict rules of personal conduct to ensure that business dealings of a compromising nature, or even the appearance of such dealings, be avoided. Buyers must always remain mindful of the impressions made on the public, for it is the public which passes judgment on the purchasing profession. Hard-and-fast rules applicable to every conceivable incident and situation which may confront purchasing cannot be laid down.

If procurement is being performed as an agency, the purchaser must realize that agency entails a fiduciary duty of trust, loyalty, and full disclosure towards the client. The purchaser should avoid any possible conflicts of interest. For example, if the client (principal) requests the purchaser (agent) to deal in a certain manner with suppliers/subcontractors with which the purchaser frequently does business, the purchaser must not fail to do so because of future business considerations. The purchaser must always make full disclosure to the client (principal) and not be self-serving.

It should be remembered that policies concerning business ethics can be written and still be ineffective; ethical policy derives its strength not from the written word but from the actions of people. Ethics has been defined as the application of man's conscience liberally assisted by common sense and judgment. A buyer will always be answerable to his or her own conscience.

Part Five

Federal Government Regulations

Chapter **19**

Antitrust Aspects
of Collective Bargaining
and Project Agreements

JOE F. CANTERBURY, JR., ESQ.
Partner, Smith, Smith, Dunlap & Canterbury, Dallas, Texas

COLLECTIVE BARGAINING AND PROJECT
AGREEMENTS HAVE ANTITRUST IMPLICATIONS

Contractors, like other people in business, are subject to federal antitrust laws. The basic federal antitrust statute is the Sherman Act, 15 U.S.C., section 1, which prohibits, "Every contract, combination . . . or conspiracy, in restraint of trade or commerce among the several states." Although the methods of trade restraint in the construction industry are varied, contractors must be aware that their participation in any scheme to restrain trade can result in severe economic liability and even criminal penalties. Arrangements controlling the price of construction at any level of the competitive bidding process should be avoided. Any arrangement between contractors to control the price of a construction project, to divide customers or markets, or to force competing contractors out of business is likely to cause antitrust problems.

Although most contractors are aware that their participation in antitrust plans, agreements, or conspiracies can result in civil or criminal liabilities, many people involved in the industry are not aware of the potential liabilities they may incur as a result of collective bargaining agreements containing subcontracting restrictions. Also construction owners or users may incur extensive antitrust liabilities by being parties to project agreements with trade unions that prohibit the use of nonunion contractors. Many contractors and owners are of the opinion that any restrictions on their right to do business with open-shop or nonunion companies are exempt from federal antitrust laws because of the exemptions labor unions enjoy from antitrust laws.

Construction trade unions have been eliminating subcontracting to nonunion subcontractors for many years by getting contractors to agree to refrain from subcontracting to nonunion firms. The same result has been obtained by project agreements between owners and unions. However, the extent of antitrust immunity to contractors, owners, and unions must be reexamined in view of a recent Supreme Court decision.[1]

LEGAL BACKGROUND OF SUBCONTRACTOR AGREEMENTS

Agreements by which an employer agrees with a labor union to cease doing business with another company are commonly called *hot-cargo* agreements. In 1959 Congress enacted section 8(e) of the National Labor Relations Act (NLRA) to prohibit hot-cargo agreements; however, as a result of legislative compromise, a limited exemption was added for the construction industry which reads as follows:[2]

> *Provided,* that nothing in this subsection shall apply to an agreement between a labor organization and an employer in the construction industry relating to the contracting or subcontracting of work to be done at the site of the construction, alteration, painting, or repair of a building, structure, or other work.

With this proviso and the statutory exemptions previously afforded labor unions by provisions of the Norris-LaGuardia Act[3] and the Clayton Anti-Trust Act,[4] construction trade unions bargained for and obtained, in many cases by strikes, restrictions on, or complete elimination of, a contractor's right to subcontract work to any company that did not have a collective bargaining agreement with the union obtaining the agreement. Many contractors entered into agreements which eliminated their right to subcontract not only the work of those crafts they employed but also those they never employed. These agreements are commonly called subcontractor agreements.

The first time the National Labor Relations Board (NLRB) considered the construction industry proviso, it was of the unanimous opinion that picketing

---

[1]*Connell Constr. Co. v. Plumbers and Steamfitters, Local 100,* 421 U.S. 616 (1975).
[2]29 U.S.C. §158e.
[3]29 U.S.C. 101 *et seq.*
[4]15 U.S.C. 17 and 29 U.S.C. 52.

and other forms of coercion were not permissible for the purpose of obtaining a hot-cargo clause.[5] The NLRB later reversed its position and held that picketing was permissible to obtain a hot-cargo clause[6] and, although these clauses could not be legally enforced by picketing after they were obtained, they were legally enforced by court action. Contractors have routinely agreed with unions not to subcontract any job-site work. Also, in order to avoid labor problems, many owners have entered into project agreements which guaranteed that only union contractors would be given work on a particular project.

BASIC FACTS OF THE CONNELL CASE

Connell Construction Company, Inc., is a general contractor in Dallas, Texas. Although Connell was a party to collective bargaining agreements covering the employees it hired directly, it had no agreements with unions representing employees it did not hire and who performed the types of work the company uniformly subcontracted. Local 100, representing employees in the plumbing and mechanical crafts, was a party to a multiemployer agreement covering approximately 75 mechanical contractors. This multiemployer agreement had a *favored-nations clause,* which prohibited the union from granting any employer any better terms than contained in the multiemployer agreement. Local 100, along with other specialty craft unions, had been trying to prevent general contractors from subcontracting work to open-shop firms for several years by obtaining, through picketing, the general contractors' written agreement not to subcontract to any nonunion firm. As a part of these efforts, Local 100 requested that Connell sign the following agreement:

> WHEREAS, the contractor and the union are engaged in the construction industry; and
> WHEREAS, the contractor and the union desire to make an agreement applying in the event of subcontracting in accordance with Section 8(e) of the Labor-Management Relations Act; and
> WHEREAS, it is understood that by this agreement the contractor does not grant, nor does the union seek, recognition as the collective bargaining representative of any employees of the signatory contractor; and
> WHEREAS, it is further understood that the subcontracting limitation provided herein applies only to mechanical work which the contractor does not perform with its own employees but uniformly subcontracts to other firms;
> THEREFORE, the contractor and the union mutually agree with respect to work falling within the scope of this agreement that it is to be done at the site of the construction, alteration, painting or repair of any building, structure, or any other works, that if the contractor should contract or subcontract any of the aforesaid work falling within the normal trade jurisdiction of the union, said contractor shall perform or subcontract such work only to firms that are parties to an executed, current collective bargaining agreement with Local Union 100 of the United Association of Journeymen and Apprentices of the Plumbing and Pipefitting Industry.

[5]*Colson & Stevens Constr. Co.,* 137 N.L.R.B, 1650 (1962).
[6]*Centlivre Village Apts.,* 148 N.L.R.B. 854 (1964).

When Connell refused to sign the agreement, Local 100 established a picket line at one of the company's construction projects. The particular project selected had a union mechanical contractor on it and the union stated it had no interest in representing any employees of Connell, but only wanted the company to refrain from subcontracting mechanical work in the future to open-shop firms. The key distinction from other cases was the total absence of an employer-employee relationship, for Connell had never hired any plumbers. Over the years Connell had subcontracted plumbing and mechanical work to both union and nonunion firms without prejudice. Although the picketing was obviously a form of secondary boycott, no relief could be obtained from the NLRB because the General Counsel of the Board had refused to issue a complaint in a similar case.[7] (The General Counsel remained adamant in similar situations throughout the case even though the Court of Appeals for the Fifth Circuit strongly criticized the NLRB for not deciding the labor law questions of the case.)[8]

Connell filed suit in a Texas district court alleging that the subcontracting agreement was in violation of the antitrust laws of Texas and obtained a restraining order against the picketing. Local 100 removed the case to federal court, and Connell then signed the agreement under protest. Connell then began its antitrust attack on the agreement by amending its complaint to allege that the agreement violated sections 1 and 2 of the Sherman Act. The antitrust theory was based on the fact that the union was simply restricting competition in the construction industry while not furthering any legitimate labor interests since the union did not represent, nor seek representation, of a single employee of Connell. In response to the defense of Local 100, Connell alleged that the construction industry proviso to section 8(e) of the NLRA did not protect the agreement because the legislative history strongly indicated that the proviso applied only to collective bargaining or an employer-employee relationship. Connell did not allege a conspiracy between the unionized mechanical contractors and Local 100 but relied on the favored-nations clause to show the antitrust effects of the subcontractor agreement obtained from it by Local 100.

The federal district court held that unions were exempt from the antitrust laws and that section 8(e) of the act protected the agreement. Faced with no relief from the NLRB or the federal court, Connell appealed the case to the United States Court of Appeals for the Fifth Circuit. That court affirmed the lower court on different grounds and held the actions of the union exempt from the federal antitrust laws because, in the opinion of the majority of the panel of judges who heard the case, the union was pursuing a legitimate labor interest in organizing an entire industry. A dissenting opinion stated that the actions of Local 100 were not exempt from the antitrust laws.

---

[7]*KAS Constr. Co.* N.L.R.B. Case 16-CC-363, Complaint denied by General Counsel in 1970.

[8]*Ponsford Bros.,* N.L.R.B. Cases 28-CC-417, 28-CE-12, 28-CC-431; *Hagler Constr. Co.,* 16-CC-447; *Howard U. Freeman, Inc.,* 16-CC-472; and *Columbus Building and Construction Trades Council,* 9-CC-706-1-20.

HOLDING OF THE SUPREME COURT IN CONNELL

The Supreme Court reversed the holding of the court of appeals, holding that Local 100's actions against Connell were not exempt from the federal antitrust laws. The Supreme Court, in a 5 to 4 decision, found the following:

1. The subcontractor agreement which Local 100 forced on Connell is not entitled to antitrust immunity.

2. Local 100's picketing to obtain the agreement is not exempt from the federal antitrust laws.

3. The proviso to section 8(e) of the NLRA does not shelter the agreement from antitrust laws since the proviso was not intended to authorize subcontracting agreements that are neither within the context of a collective bargaining relationship nor limited to a particular job site.

4. The agreement is a hot-cargo agreement prohibited by 8(e) of the NLRA.

5. The picketing to obtain the agreement constituted a secondary boycott. in violation of 8(b) (4) of the NLRA.

6. Labor law remedies are not the only remedies available to contractors and federal courts should decide antitrust questions within the context of a labor case.

7. State antitrust laws do not apply since federal law preempts state remedies that interfere with federal labor policy or with provisions of NLRA.

8. The majority opinion, while not specifically so stating, indicates that a subcontracting restriction arising in an employer-employee relationship, i.e., the employer has employees covered by the collective bargaining agreement, must be limited to a particular project to be protected by the 8(e) proviso.

The dissenting members of the Supreme Court were of the opinion that Connell's exclusive remedies were under the NLRA and that the antitrust laws did not apply. Although the dissenting opinion gives a good review of the labor law remedies available to a contractor in Connell's position, those remedies were useless because the General Counsel of the NLRB would not issue a complaint under the identical agreement in other cases. If the General Counsel of the NLRB refuses to issue a complaint, there is no appeal from that refusal.[9]

EFFECTS OF THE CONNELL CASE

As stated previously, union contractors have been parties to collective bargaining agreements restricting subcontracting for many years. Even prior to *Connell,* if employers conspired with unions to restrict competition, no antitrust immunity would be granted to the conspiracy.[10]

Any agreement by which an owner or contractor agrees with a union to refrain from subcontracting to open-shop companies constitutes an agreement

---

[9]*Vaca v. Sipes,* 386 U.S. 171, 182 (1967).

[10]*Allen Bradley Co. v. Local 3, IBEW,* 325 U.S. 797 (1945); *United Mine Workers v. Pennington,* 381 U.S. 647 (1965), and *Ramsey v. United Workers,* 401 U.S. 203 (1971).

in restraint of trade and, unless exempt from the antitrust laws, could form the basis of antitrust liability to the open-shop firms excluded from the relevant construction market on account of the subcontracting agreements or clauses. If there is no immunity, the owner or contractor could be liable with the union for treble damages. Subcontracting is a mandatory subject of collective bargaining, but how far can a contractor go in restricting subcontracting at the bargaining table without risking an antitrust violation? When do subcontracting clauses become illegal hot-cargo clauses, unprotected by the 8(e) proviso? If an owner is not engaged in the construction industry, can subcontracting restrictions contained in his project agreement with trade unions be protected by the construction industry proviso to section 8(e) of the NLRA? If the subcontracting restrictions are not protected by the 8(e) proviso and/or outside of an employer-employee relationship, are the contractor and union open to antitrust suits by open-shop subcontractors?

These are some of the issues that must be considered by owners, contractors, and construction unions. This book is not intended to be a substitute for legal advice from the reader's attorney; therefore, an answer to all the antitrust questions implicit in the *Connell* case is not attempted. Further, particular subcontracting clauses must be examined in detail along with the particular facts of each situation. However, some general principles are obvious from the *Connell* case and other cases involving the balance of labor and antitrust liability. The mere fact that a subcontractor agreement is contained in a collective bargaining agreement gives no assurance of the legality of the agreement. Even prior to *Connell,* a United States district court found an antitrust violation against a union because of subcontracting restrictions contained in a collective bargaining agreement.[11] Since *Connell,* another United States district court found a subcontractor clause contained in a collective bargaining agreement to be a violation of the Sherman Act[12] because the clause restrained trade and was not limited to a particular job site. If a subcontracting clause were protected by the 8(e) proviso, the insulation from antitrust laws—without a conspiracy with intent to force competing companies out of business—would be much more certain than an agreement not protected by the proviso. To be so protected, the subcontracting agreements must arise out of a collective bargaining or employer-employee relationship. Further, the restrictions should be limited to a particular job site covering only work actually performed at the job site. The 8(e) proviso has never covered off-site work.

Agreements between an owner and trade unions are prime targets for antitrust attack if the owner has no employees represented by the unions. Further, if the owner is not in the construction business, the 8(e) proviso would not cover the agreement.

---

[11]*Morse Bros. v. Int'l Union of Operating Eng'rs., Local 701,* CCH Labor Cases ¶10,525 (U.S. Dist. Ct. Ore. 1974).

[12]*Int'l Union of Operating Eng'rs., Local 370, v. Neilson & Co.,* 4-75-19 (U.S. Dist. Ct. Idaho, 1975), presently pending before U.S. Court of Appeals for the Ninth Circuit on appeal by the unions (No. 3545).

Subcontracting prohibitions agreed to by a general contractor outside of an employer-employee relationship are subject to antitrust attacks against both the contractors and the unions.

PROTECTING YOUR COMPANY FROM ANTITRUST LIABILITY

The contractor should have his collective bargaining, or other agreements with trade unions, examined by his attorney or counsel for the trade association or multiemployer group of which he is a member. Some general guidelines for consideration are as follows:

1. Never agree to subcontracting restrictions outside of an employer-employee relationship.

2. Even within an employer-employee relationship contractors would be wise to resist subcontracting restrictions. If the right to subcontract is conceded, make certain that the clause is protected by the 8(e) proviso.

3. Contractors should explain their antitrust fears at the bargaining table and remind the unions that they will be a primary target of the open-shop companies forced out of the construction market.

4. If clauses in current collective bargaining agreements are found by legal counsel to pose an antitrust threat and/or violation of section 8(e) of the NLRA, there is a chance that the trade unions may agree to revise or delete them. Although little success could be expected with most business agents, competent union attorneys will not want to risk their clients' involvement in treble damage lawsuits. They will advise their clients to give up clearly illegal clauses or to revise them.

5. Another possibility is for multiemployer associations to advise the unions in writing that they will not comply with an illegal 8(e) agreement and then file charges with the NLRB or file a suit for declaratory judgment to have the federal district court pass on the clauses under the antitrust laws.

6. As previously mentioned, if there is no employer-employee relationship, the subcontractor agreement is illegal. The existence of this relationship may be difficult to determine in some cases, especially when the contractor is a member of a multiemployer bargaining association. If there is a collective bargaining relationship and the contractor, or the multiemployer group, is willing to give up the right to subcontract to open-shop subcontractors or, perhaps to subcontractors whose employees are represented by another union, the clauses should be structured so they can be applied to specific job sites. One method would be to limit the subcontracting clause to specific jobs listed in an attachment to the contract; another method would be to provide a method of adding the particular jobs. For example, after the clause is stated, the following language might be inserted:

> This Paragraph No. ___, restricting subcontracting by Employer, shall be of no force or effect and the same shall be unenforceable unless Employer and Union agree by an instrument in writing, signed by the duly authorized representative of

each, that it applies to a particular job site, defined by location and project name, prior to the time Employer commences work on the particular project.

7. Another suggestion to those contractors who give in to union demands for a subcontractor clause is to obtain a hold-harmless and indemnification clause from the union for any damages suffered by the contractor as a result of lawsuits by third parties over the agreement. A sample indemnification clause would read:

> Union hereby agrees to protect, indemnify, save and hold harmless the contractor from any and all damages, costs, and expenses, including reasonable attorneys' fees, from any demands, claims, and all causes of action asserted by any person, company, or governmental agency on account of contractor's agreeing to and complying with the subcontracting restrictions contained in Article ____ of this collective bargaining agreement.

However, it must be understood that a hold-harmless clause is a poor substitute for a legal clause and that it is only as good as the assets of a union that could be reached by a court process.

The owner who enters into a project agreement with trade unions must consider the same points as the contractor; however, if the owner is not in the construction business and has no employees represented by the unions, he is wide open to a suit from the companies he excludes from his project.

SUMMARY

If a contractor is a party to subcontractor agreements or collective bargaining agreements, he should have them reviewed by his attorney for compliance with labor and antitrust laws. The general guidelines for subcontractor agreements with unions which would not be violative of either federal labor or antitrust laws under the *Connell* decision may be summarized as follows:

1. There must an employer-employee relationship between the contractor and the employees represented by the union obtaining the agreement restricting the contractor's right to subcontract.

2. The subcontracting restrictions should only apply to work performed at the construction site. Work performed away from the construction site is not covered by the construction industry proviso to section 8(e).

3. The restrictions should be contained in a collective bargaining agreement.

4. The subcontracting restrictions should only apply to particular job sites that are reasonably defined.

5. It is certainly preferable that the subcontracting rights of the contractor not be limited to the extent of requiring all subcontractors to be signatories to a union agreement, but to require only that a subcontractor's employees receive the same benefits as employees of the contractor.

Antitrust laws are presently receiving high priority in Congress. At this time legislation is pending that would give the Department of Justice vastly increased powers in civil antitrust investigations.[13] Defending against antitrust allegations is both time-consuming and expensive; therefore, construction users and contractors must avoid an inadvertent violation by agreements with labor unions with the same degree of care that violations are avoided by agreements, oral or written, with nonlabor parties.

[13]S. 1284 and H.R. 13489, 94th Cong., 2d Sess.

Chapter **20**

Equal-Employment-Opportunity Compliance

VIRGIL B. DAY, ESQ.
Partner, Vedder, Price, Kaufman, Kammholz & Day, New York,
New York

RONALD MICHAEL GREEN, ESQ.
Partner, Vedder, Price, Kaufman, Kammholz & Day, New York,
New York

THE NEW EEO CHALLENGE

As many construction contractors and unions have become painfully aware, the equal-employment-opportunity issues and problems which exist in the construction industry are uniquely difficult to resolve; they require the development of special personnel policies in order to avoid or minimize extensive legal liability. Although government enforcement has been sporadic in the past, new and aggressive efforts can now be expected from the Department of Labor.[1] Further, the possibility of private class-action suits which could result in court imposition of employment quotas (not merely "goals") and heavy back-pay awards makes this a dangerously expensive area to ignore.

Most nonunion contractors will find it comparatively easy to have proper equal employment *policies* that will avoid the massive costs that improper policies may engender. It is more difficult, however, to maintain hiring *practices* that will ensure selection of a qualified work force without being accused of illegal discrimination in terms of minorities represented in applicant flow. The government guidelines and the law are currently in confusion and transition in this respect.

For union contractors, and for unions in the construction trades, the solutions are more complex and usually will require changes in both policies and practices involving apprenticeship programs, union membership requirements, hiring-hall involvement, and the realities on the job site. But penalties can be heavy in loss of union or management control of job manning and in heavy money damages if prudent decisions are not made.

Employment in the construction industry as contrasted with most service and supply industry employment is characterized by the highly transient, often nomadic, nature of the employees' life-styles and employment arrangements with general and specialty contractors. Not unlike the longshore industry's shape-up employment phenomenon, the manner in which one finds work in this industry places the employer and, more significantly, the *organized* employer less in the role of a traditional employer than the union. Indeed, this is the chief reason why the building trades unions and the employers with whom they maintained collective bargaining agreements—particularly those which utilized exclusive hiring-hall arrangements—were the earliest and most significant targets of equal-employment-opportunity law enforcement efforts.

The major cities and industrial centers of our nation host the largest share of minority and, particularly, black residents. It is also in these areas that the construction industry is most frequently and heavily unionized, controlling the supply and the price of labor. It is here that the use of the exclusive hiring hall was first born and where its use is most prevalent. Of course, the National Labor Relations Act does expressly sanction the use of the exclusive hiring hall in the construction industry by virtue of proviso 8b (7) of the act, provided its use is nondiscriminatory with respect to union affiliation or nonaffiliation. However, this nondiscrimination proviso applicable to nonunion employees has only rarely been enforced.[2]

---

[1]The Department of Labor's efforts are carried on in several ways: Equal employment opportunity in apprentice programs is under the Bureau of Apprenticeship and Training; equal employment opportunity with respect to journeymen and apprentices working on federally funded contracts is administered by the OFCCP (Office of Federal Contract Compliance Programs).

[2]*NLRB v. Mountain Pacific Chapter of Associated General Contractors, Inc.,* 119 N.L.R.B. 883, 41 LRRM 1460 (1957), *enf. denied and remanded,* 270 F.2d 425, 44 LRRM 2802 (9th Cir. 1959), *on remand,* 127 N.L.R.B. 1393, 46 LRRM 1200 (1960), *enf'd as modified,* 306 F.2d 34, 50 LRRM 2855 (9th Cir. 1962).

The use of the hiring hall coupled with the legally permissible requirement of compulsory union membership (seven days after employment) in proviso 8b (7) have combined to construct a dominant and often omnipotent status for unions in the employment environment existing in the areas of their jurisdiction, subject only to the competition of the open-shop employer who generally achieves his higher productivity and lower costs through retained control of both management functions and utilization of employees. Pursuant to these restrictions on the rights of employers to hire and otherwise establish the terms and conditions of their employment of others, the unions control the distribution of employment opportunities. Measured against the historical backdrop of racial discrimination in the building trades and most notably in the most highly skilled and better-paying crafts, including apprenticeship programs overtly or subtly closed to minorities and rampant nepotism perpetuating the all-white complexion of these crafts, the EEO issue surfaces into perspective.

Contractors bidding on federally involved construction contracts should carefully review the general requirements relative to affirmative action and nondiscrimination stipulated in the required equal-employment-opportunity (EEO) clause and the federal EEO bid conditions which incorporate the provisions of so-called hometown plans for voluntary minority and female utilization and/or impose minority and (in the future) female utilization goals and timetables on contractors.

Upon award of the federally involved construction contract, the contractor will be bound by the requirements of the EEO clause and applicable federal bid conditions and must be able to demonstrate compliance with those requirements including the designation of a high-level company official to assume the responsibility for the contractor's EEO program. As a relatively new development, female utilization goals will now receive serious attention.

APPRENTICESHIP PROGRAMS

Any analysis of the EEO issue requires an awareness of the practice of continued use of the apprenticeship-program route of exclusive entry into the building trades, serving the dual purpose of preserving the availability of work at inflated wage rates for the controlled labor supply. To a large extent it operates as the narrow end of a funnel through which only selected persons may enter after satisfying often *unvalidated* test requirements, *unrealistic* entrance standards, *de facto* nepotism, or other limitations on job access.

A focal point of EEO attacks is often the apprenticeship programs, whether union or joint union-management in nature. Although numerous attacks have been launched against the operation of discriminatory apprenticeship programs, they have been for the most part highly successful in the court with less meaningful practical and realized results.[3] The apprenticeship program as an

---

[3]*EEOC v. Local 638, Local 28, Sheet Metal Workers Int'l Ass'n,* 175 N.Y.L.J. No. 65 at 1 (2nd Cir. 3/8/76; *United States v. Ironworkers, Local 86,* 315 F. Supp. 1202, 2 FEP Cases 741 (W.D. Wash. 1970), *aff'd.,* 443 F.2d 544, 3 FEP Cases 496 (9th Cir. 1971), *cert. denied,* 404 U.S. 984, 4 FEP Cases 37 (1971).

institution has had its "integrity" preserved through the extensive and effective political and legal efforts of the AFL-CIO building trades department on the necessity for the continued validity of the union apprenticeship concept. Contractors have often joined in support, although employers and major associations have attempted to set up independent programs, many of which have operated successfully.

The full panoply of federal laws prohibiting discrimination in apprenticeship, specifically, and in construction employment, generally, include Title VII of the Civil Rights Act of 1964 as amended, Executive Order 11246 as amended, and U.S. Department of Labor regulations concerning the EEO requirements.[4]

Thus, if an apprenticeship program is not run in a nondiscriminatory manner, the sponsors (i.e., a Joint Apprenticeship Committee, union, and/or employer) may be sued for damages—declaratory and injunctive relief under Title VII; federally assisted construction contractors and subcontractors may have their contracts canceled and be ineligible for such further work or unions enjoined from interfering with that contractor's attempts to provide equal employment opportunity; and apprenticeship programs may be de-registered, thus losing the exceptions removing apprentices from the otherwise applicable prevailing wage rate for journeymen (laborers and mechanics) under the Davis-Bacon Act.[5]

AFFIRMATIVE ACTION, GOVERNMENT-ENFORCED

The first meaningful effort at affirmative action in the construction industry was attempted by the federal government in 1969, impatient with the slow and measured progress in the EEO area by voluntary action of unions and contractors or by *ad hoc* litigation against local unions across the nation.

Thus, the U.S. Department of Labor, led by former Secretary George Schultz, Assistant Secretary Arthur Fletcher, and OFCC Director John Wilkes proposed the controversial Philadelphia Plan for Affirmative Action in selected building trades crafts in a five-county Philadelphia area. The plan, as first devised, required that those seeking to work as federally assisted or direct federal construction contractors agree to the negotiation of minority manning tables on securing the contract award. Attacked by the Comptroller General of the United States as impermissibly vague and unspecific under federal competitive bidding principles, the plan was revised by the issuance of two orders in June and September 1969 following public hearings into the question of employment discrimination in the Philadelphia area building trades. The plan as revised required (and still requires) that bidders on federal or federally

[4]The Department of Labor asserts upon a tenuous legal premise that construction contractors with 50 or more nonconstruction employees and a federal contract or subcontract of any kind valued at $50,000 or more must comply with the requirements of its Revised Order No. 4 with respect to their nonconstruction work force.

[5]See 29 CFR, parts 5 and 5a.

assisted construction contracts in excess of $10,000 which relate to projects valued at $500,000 or more, submit with their bids or in any event prior to the closing date for receipt of bids, a signed and completed form which accompanied the Invitation for Bids committing the bidder and the subcontractors to the achievement of annual numerical goals or quotas which the bidder has written in on the form and which are at least equal to or greater than the minimum goals or quota ranges set forth by the Office of Federal Contract Compliance (OFCC) in the Invitation-for-Bids specification. This commitment also included the taking of specific steps to achieve the goals or quotas constituting a requisite "good faith effort."

The plan incurred the wrath of all concerned, both contractors and unions, but the theory that success and progress in labor relations is best made when all are equally unhappy did not hold fully true.

The unions, unable to supply minority craftsmen from among their ranks, were outraged by the plan's directive that collective bargaining agreements had to be adjusted if they prevented achievement of contractor goals; contractors were incensed at being placed between Scylla and Charybdis as a consequence of discriminatory practices they were not responsible for and could do little about, facing union strife or the loss of government contracts as equally unpleasant alternatives. And the so-called minority community was upset over what they considered to be too little, too late.

Litigation of the plan ensued in the case of *Contractors Association v. Secretary of Labor* resulting in both the United States District Court and a Circuit Court of Appeals upholding the plan as constitutional and consistent with applicable procurement, civil rights, and labor statutes.[6]

The Department of Labor also staved off attacks on the plan as an illegal quota device by the comptroller general as well as congressional efforts to thwart implementation of the plan and its proliferation.

However, responding largely to political pressures from all quarters, the Department of Labor announced that it would "impose" a Philadelphia Plan only where the parties (unions, contractors, and—a newly introduced third party to collective bargaining—the minority community) failed to negotiate a voluntary affirmative-action program for their "hometown."

At about this time, the Department of Labor made another unpublicized change in policy. In the imposed plans it issued, it would include a proviso indicating that contractors would be in compliance with their EEO commitments notwithstanding their failure to reach a stated goal or quota if the unions they were under contract with and through whose hiring halls they recruited had among their members a percentage of minorities equivalent to the contractors percentage goal or quota for employment or, in some plans, if the union was making a good faith effort to increase their membership to that point. Nonetheless the Department of Labor continued to press for the development of hometown plans which now outnumber imposed plans by a ratio of approxi-

---

[6]*Contractors Ass'n v. Secretary of Labor,* 311 F.Supp. 1002, 2 FEP Cases 472 (E. Dist. Pa. 1970), 442 F.2d 159, 3 FEP Cases 395 (3rd Cir. 1971), *cert. denied,* 404 U.S. 854, 3 FEP Cases 1030.

mately 10 to 1 and continues to extol the virtues of such a course of action, which are in some respects significant. Under an imposed plan a contractor's obligation is an individual one—to achieve a percentage of minority man-hours of employment in specified crafts on each job site even as to nonfederal construction and is excused from reaching a job site goal or quota only if that percentage is reached in its entire work force in the aggregate. Under a hometown plan in which generally only organized contractors may participate and where contractors and their unions have signed on and agreed to reach a goal or quota negotiated by the parties and approved by the Department of Labor, the obligation is a trade-wide, not individual contractor, responsibility.

Thus, as long as the agreed-upon number of minorities to be hired, trained, or brought into signatory craft unions (not percentage of man-hours worked), depending upon the plan, is met or a proven good-faith effort is made to reach it, signatory contractors have no measurable, quantified obligation: they need only cooperate with the committee organized by the parties to the plan and assume their fair share of the plan's total commitment.

Mechanically, the hometown plan requires the submission, with affected bids or prior to the closing date for the receipt of bids, of a short-form certification of compliance with the plan's provisions if the certifying party is a signatory of the plan together with the appropriate union. Nonsignatories and nonunion contractors, with few exceptions, may not avail themselves of the benefits and work-force flexibility of a hometown plan and must accept the imposition of individual goals or quotas for percentages of minority man-hours of employment which correspond to the negotiated percentages of trade- or craft-wide goals or quotas agreed to by plan negotiators.

A HOMETOWN AFFIRMATIVE-ACTION PLAN

Plan Development

A hometown affirmative-action plan is often developed with the active participation of a representative of the Office of Federal Contract Compliance Programs (OFCCP), but such representation is not a prerequisite to the successful development and ultimate approval of such a plan by the OFCCP. The essential ingredients in an acceptable voluntary hometown affirmative-action program are: (1) participation by unionized contractors, (2) participation by local unions, and (3) participation by ostensible representatives of the affected minority community. To date, the OFCCP has generally not permitted voluntary hometown plans to be accepted for participation by nonunionized contractors. The OFCCP theory is that the hometown plans are designed for the achievement of permanency with respect to minorities entering the construction trades and targeted for those areas where minority underutilization in the construction industry has been most acute, that is, the areas where unions tend to predominate. So, if you are not an organized contractor there is little hope for presently being permitted participation in a voluntary hometown plan. If you are an organized contractor, the first step is to enlist the cooperation of those local unions who act as collective bargaining representatives for your employees and seek out the ostensible representative for the local minority community. A voluntary hometown plan is to be generally a tripartite agreement among these three parties, albeit a two-party format including the indispensable minority community representative has been approved for limited use. As a threshold consideration, you must determine what it is you hope to achieve, that is: immediate employment at the journeyman level for minorities, the entrance of minorities into on-the-job training, and federally funded or other approved apprenticeship programs—or both. The OFCCP will accept training on the job, apprenticeship entrance, and journeyman employment, provided, however—whatever the objectives of the program may be—that they are consistent with the wishes of the three parties to the agreement and, most especially, that the so-called minority utilization for determined trades is established. (The goal, quota, or quantified objective should be negotiated.) This figure should not be an inflated one, but should be one which is considered reachable, achievable, and reasonable in light of the number of contractors and local unions who have expressed commitments to participation in the program.

The next step would be the establishment of an administrative or executive committee to monitor compliance with the plan, to gather reports periodically from all those participating under it and to furnish the required reports to the OFCCP periodically. The administrative committee should elect an executive director whose responsibility should be to obtain approval of the voluntary hometown affirmative-action plan and also to serve as liaison between the appropriate compliance agency, the plan's administrative committee, and the participating contractors, unions, and minority community representatives.

A hometown plan "model agreement" can be found in Appendix A.

Approval Procedures

A proposed hometown plan is submitted to the OFCCP regional office serving the geographical area for which the plan is designed. At that point the regional office is to submit the plan to the OFCCP national office, and a synopsis of the plan including consideration of the following items which should be anticipated, of course, by the draftsmen of the plan: (1) The signatories to the plan as to labor, management and minority community representatives. (2) The geographical area to be served by the plan including all counties, and an explanation as to whether there is a problem with overlapping labor union and plan jurisdictions. (3) The plan's overall placement, employment, and/or training goals and timetables. Note that the use of the term "quota" will be considered grounds for rejecting a plan as will reference to "proportional representation." (4) The individual composition of the administrative committee and the head of that committee. (5) The composition of any subsidiary committee, such as operations or executive committees. Many hometown plans have operations committees also known as craft committees to oversee compliance by individual craft unions and progress within a craft. These so-called operations committees would report back to the administrative committee. (6) A list of all contractor associations who may be signatory to the plan and a membership directory for each such signatory association. (7) A list of all signatory labor unions giving the name, local number, address, phone number, and the name of the business agent and all officers of the local building trades council. (8) For every local union which is signatory to the plan full membership data including the total number of active journeymen, the total number of active minority journeymen, the total number of active female journeymen, the total number of active apprentices, the total number of active minority apprentices, and the total number of female apprentices. Also, the names, addresses, phone numbers, social security numbers, classification, and union status must be provided for every minority and female listed. (9) A list of crafts which did not provide the data required by the OFCCP to evaluate the plan. The refusal of a craft union to provide necessary data will be considered grounds for rejecting the craft represented by that local signatory from participation in the voluntary home-town plan. (10) The numerical goal for every craft signatory to the plan. (11) The duration of the plan. (12) A list of those crafts seeking an exemption from having to reach goals or timetables based on their present minority and female membership. (13) A list of all recognized avenues of entry for minorities into the crafts concerned, for example, journeymen, apprentice, trainee, advanced trainee, transfers, and reinstatements. (14) The plan's requirements with respect to the resolution of disputes in the administrative committee. (15) Provisions in the plan with respect to equal opportunity and affirmative action for females. (16) Provisions in the plan with respect to the "fair-share" obligation of every participating contractor with respect to its making efforts to achieve the plan's overall objectives.

Audits

Hometown plans are audited by OFCCP representatives no later than three months after the plan's approval date anniversary and annually thereafter. The OFCCP representatives use a hometown-plan audit form entitled "OCCO-101" (Appendix B). As the form indicates, for every minority employee working pursuant to the plan, the following information will be required by the government and therefore must be obtainable by the administrative committee: age, residence status, length of time in area, craft, classification, work status and hourly rate of pay, date of original placement, date placed on current job, total time worked since original placement, source of referral, union status, minority group, and whether the plan is claiming credit for the placement of the individual.

In reviewing this and other forms, the OFCCP representatives will determine whether the administrative committee and the participating contractors and unions have made the requisite good-faith efforts to reach the numerical objectives should they have fallen short of those objectives. In determining whether the requisite good-faith efforts have been met, at least the following areas will be examined by the OFCCP: (1) the current goal and its achievement by craft for the plan year; (2) the cumulative goal and its total achievement up to and including the date of the last audit by craft; (3) the total dollar volume of construction in the plan area during the plan year and the previous three years; (4) the current total union membership by craft by journeyman, apprentice, trainee and other status for minorities, females and minority females; (5) for the current plan year the total number of new journeymen, apprentices, trainees and others who are minority, female and minority female; (6) the total number of qualified minority and female persons available for employment in the craft; (7) the number of additional craftsmen that could be absorbed into the craft considering present employee shortages, projected growth of the craft, and projected employee turnover; (8) the number of signatory contractors utilizing the craft; (9) the number of signatory contractors utilizing the craft who employed new minority, female, and minority female workers; (10) a narrative as to the individual crafts cooperation with the plan's administrative committee focusing on cooperation by the local unions, signatory contractors and minority community representatives as separate issues; (11) the extent to which labor strikes and material shortages affected employment opportunities in the craft; (12) the extent to which weather conditions affected employment opportunities in a craft; (13) the extent to which any community or legal action such as court-issued injunctions affected construction and employment opportunities in a craft, and finally the extent to which new technology has affected employment opportunities in the craft.

The administrative committee of each hometown plan is required to file a report entitled "OCCO-104" for each preceding month with the national office of the OFCCP and the regional office of the OFCCP by the fifteenth of each month. Monthly reports must include an account of the previous month's activity as well as a cumulative report to date. To complete this report the administrative committee must maintain records for every individual placement which shall include at least the following information:

Name of placement
Address
Telephone number
Age
Initial date of placement
Trade or craft
Employment records as to employer's dates of employment
Reasons for leaving employment
Date of acceptance as journeyman or apprentice
Explanation for any departure from the program

Enforcement

Enforcement of obligations under federal EEO clauses and applicable bid conditions is illustrated by the flow chart in Figure 20.1.

Enforcement in general includes the following steps:

Compliance review   Contractors, failing to meet the minimum utilization goals specified in the bid conditions, or, having allegations of discrimination in violation of the EEO clause made against them, will be subjected to, (1) a thorough review of their implementation of the affirmative-action program specified in the bid conditions and (2) where required, a thorough review of their compliance with the EEO clause.

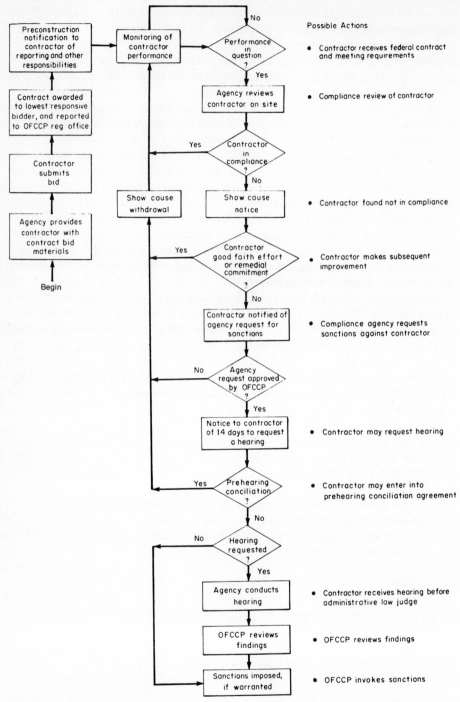

Fig. 20.1 Enforcement of Obligations under Federal EEO Clauses and Applicable Bid Conditions.

A compliance review conducted by the compliance agency (or OFCCP) will cover the following:

1. A thorough review of the contractor's books, records, and accounts including payroll records, ledgers, certified payroll summaries, and other valid payroll documents and a review of any other relevant documentary evidence. (If a contractor has met the specified minimum utilization goals for the aggregate work force, the contractor will be presumed to be in compliance with the requirement of the bid conditions and the review concluded, unless an allegation of discrimination violation of the EEO clause has been made.)

2. Validation of the materials will be made through on-site visits of a sample of all the contractor's projects to determine whether the contractor has made a good-faith effort to implement *all* the affirmative-action steps specified in the bid conditions and has not violated the EEO clause.

Remedial commitments   In the event that a contractor has failed to meet the minimum utilization goals *or* has failed to provide adequate *documentary* evidence of its good-faith efforts to implement the minimum affirmative-action program as specified in the bid conditions, the compliance agency will issue a notice to the contractor to come forward with additional evidence of its efforts to comply or to demonstrate that it has not, in fact, violated the EEO clause. The contractor will have the opportunity at the conclusion of the compliance review to make specific written commitments embodied in conciliation agreements to be signed by an officer of the company, to remedy all deficient good-faith-effort steps identified during the review.

If such commitments are made by the contractor and approved by the compliance agency, the agency will find the contractor in compliance and initiate monitoring of the specific remedial commitments.

Initiation of actions leading to sanctions   If during the 30-day period provided the contractor (a) fails to document adequate good-faith efforts to implement the minimum required affirmative-action steps or fails to make adequate commitments to correct all deficiencies or (b) fails to demonstrate that the EEO clause has not been violated, the compliance agency will initiate actions leading to the imposition of sanctions against the contractor by issuance of an administrative complaint.

Upon initiation of such actions by the compliance agency and approval by the OFCCP, the contractor will be notified that actions leading to sanctions have been initiated. The complaint will state the reasons for the action and provide 20 calendar days for the contractor to answer and request a hearing relative to the imposition of sanctions.

If no request for hearing is received within the 20-day period, the compliance agency and/or OFCCP will impose such sanctions as are deemed appropriate, including cancellation, termination, or suspension of contracts and declaration of ineligibility for further federally involved contracts.

Upon receipt of a request for a hearing, the compliance agency and/or OFCCP will arrange for and conduct a hearing on the issues.[7] During the

---

[7]Pursuant to the procedures set forth in 41 CFR 60–1 and 41 CFR 60–30.

pendency of any request for hearing, a contractor's federally involved contracts may be suspended in whole or in part.[8] However, no formal sanctions or penalties may be imposed without the approval of the director of the OFCCP.

The hearing procedures[9] provide that any conciliation agreement or consent decree proposed as a settlement of the issues must be approved by the Secretary of Labor or the Director of the OFCCP and that the Secretary of Labor or the Director shall make the final decision relative to the imposition of sanctions.

CIVIL SUITS, BACK-PAY AWARDS, DEBARMENT FROM GOVERNMENT CONTRACTS

In the decade of the sixties equal employment was not a major concern of the construction industry. However, in the last several years government involvement in mandating affirmative action in the construction industry has heightened dramatically. It can clearly be expected to accelerate even further (construction offers the best opportunity for minorities with low skills to be employed at high pay) as the construction industry regains momentum. A recent reorganization of the Department of Labor, including the Office of Federal Contract Compliance Programs, is intended to increase the thrust of equal-opportunity enforcement in the industry.

More significant may be the increase in private suits seeking to enforce equal-opportunity results. A series of multimillion-dollar awards, out-of-court settlements, and related agreements setting new patterns for future employment, training, and promotion have made EEO considerations a major factor for contractors and unions alike. To date a number of contractors have been debarred from government contracting opportunities, including work on federally funded construction. Many others have been passed over for contract awards *prior to hearing* on the strength of allegations of noncompliance with their EEO clause by compliance agencies.

CONCLUSION

Outside of the applicability of an imposed Philadelphia type of plan or a hometown affirmative-action program (AAP), there has been virtually no enforcement to date of the OFCCP regulations requiring AAP's by construction contractors,[10] and there is likely to be little until such time as appropriate guidelines for their voluntary development are promulgated.[11] However, keeping a close watch on federal and state EEO law-enforcement activities, private lawsuits, and court decisions is a must for the construction contractor endeavoring to be responsible in meeting its EEO obligations. The organized employer

[8]Pursuant to the provisions of 41 CFR 60–1.26.
[9]41 CFR 60–30.
[10]41 CFR § 60–1.40.
[11]See, e.g., 41 CFR part 60–2 which appears to apply to nonconstruction contractors only and note 4, *supra*, as to nonconstruction employees of construction contractors.

may have to answer for the sins of the union, and so should stay alert to obviously discriminatory hiring-hall and local union referral procedures and measure the representation of minorities on job sites with their general availability in the trades and the area labor force generally and the local population.

To the extent that a construction contractor or subcontractor is subject to the requirements of an "imposed" or "hometown" affirmative-action program, it must make every good-faith effort to reach whatever its employment goal or quota may be individually or by trade. This good-faith effort is rather loosely defined in the appropriate affirmative-action plan but probably requires that the contractor have an organizational plan in the nature of an individual company affirmative-action program to outline its proposed good-faith efforts and monitor what it does in that regard. In this connection such a program or plan should deal with at least the following:

1. A review of applicable collective bargaining agreements to ensure that they are nondiscriminatory as written and implemented and to effect any appropriate and necessary changes in their terms.

2. A review of the hiring process including applicant selection, use of apprenticeship programs and the selection of apprentices, compensation, restrooms and other terms and conditions of employment to ensure that they are equally applied to members of all races and to both sexes as well.

3. Review employee retention procedures and policies to ensure that they are not nepotistic or discriminatory, especially with respect to race or sex.

4. Establish a procedure for receiving EEO investigators, compliance personnel, and the development of a system for ensuring the adequacy of documentation supporting all employment decisions.

It should be noted that more contractor debarments and contract cancellations have been imposed against federal and federally assisted construction contractors pursuant to E.O. 11246, as amended, than all nonconstruction governmental contractors and subcontractors combined.

The construction industry remains nobody's darling.

FURTHER DEVELOPMENTS

The authors wish to caution that at the time this article went to press, the OFCCP had announced *published* changes in the contract compliance program for the construction industry. Those proposed changes would, if finally implemented, substantially change the procedures and requirements for EEO compliance by federal and federally assisted construction contractors covered by E.O. 11246. Among the major changes would be the requirement for goals and timetables regarding the employment of women in the construction industry and the simplification of bidding procedures. These requirements as well as the proposed discontinuance of voluntary hometown and imposed plans are strongly opposed by both unions and management in the construction industry.

APPENDIX A: Hometown Plan Model Agreement

Purpose

The objective of this agreement is to increase minority group employment in all phases of the construction industry in the __(city)__ area. This agreement establishes a comprehensive program to encourage and facilitate employment of minority group persons in the building construction trades and to encourage and facilitate the admission of such persons to membership in unions representing employees in those trades. The program is designed to ensure that all interested parties—labor, management, and the minority community—share in the authority and responsibility for its administration. All parties to this agreement shall make every good-faith effort to achieve the objectives outlined herein and all provisions of this agreement shall be interpreted to further this objective.

Scope

This agreement shall be applicable to all work on demolition, repair, alteration, rehabilitation, and construction in the residential, commercial-industrial, and institutional phases in the construction in the __(city)__ area performed by the contractors and unions signatory hereto, regardless of whether said work is federally financed, federally assisted, state or local government, state or local government assisted, or privately financed.

Duration of Agreement

This agreement shall be in full force and effect for __(number)__ years from the date of signing by the constructors, unions, and the coalition and thereafter shall automatically renew itself from year to year for successive periods of one (1) year up to a maximum of __(number)__ years. If any party wishes to terminate or modify this agreement, he must give the other parties written notice of this intent not less than 60, nor more than 90 days prior to the annual renewal date hereof.

Each year for the duration of this agreement the committee shall review the effectiveness of the procedures and specific goals established herein. This review shall have as its objective the determination of whether these procedures are achieving the result of improving employment opportunity for minority persons in the construction industry. The review of the specific goals established herein shall lead to a determination whether the specific goals adequately reflect the construction labor market situation at the time.

Parties

This agreement shall be binding upon the local building trades council and all local building trades unions which are signatory hereto, hereinafter referred to severally and collectively as the "unions"; the local general contractors association, the associations of subcontractors or specialty contractors signatory hereto, all of which are hereinafter referred to severally and collectively as the "contractors"; the individual minority group organizations in the local area signatory hereto which are hereinafter referred to severally and collectively as the "coalition."

Administration

There is hereby established the __(area)__ Construction Opportunity Policy Committee (the committee) which shall generally oversee the implementation of this agreement.

Section A—Membership:

The committee shall consist of *nine* members, *two* of whom shall be representative of the union, and *four* of whom shall be representative of the coalition. The ninth member shall be selected as follows:

1. The eight members of the committee shall first endeavor to agree on the ninth member.

2. In the event they are unable to agree, they may request that the ninth member be designated (from a list prepared by the unions, contractors, and coalition) by:

    a. The Dispute Settlement Center, American Arbitration Association, or

    b. The Community Relations Service, Department of Justice, or

    c. Any court, agency, or institution or person on whom the parties can agree

Section B—Quorum and Voting:

Five members of the committee shall constitute a quorum for the purpose of transacting business. Decisions shall be made on the basis of votes by a majority of those present.

Section C—Powers and Responsibilities:

The committee shall be empowered to enter into contracts with federal, state, and local governments and other organizations in cooperation with contractors, unions, the coalition, individuals, or community organization or organizations for the purpose of recruiting, counseling, training, and orienting persons for employment in the _____ construction industry. It shall adopt rules of procedure. It shall review all activities of the executive director, his staff, the ad hoc panels, and reports of the program. It shall be empowered to make changes in the procedures for implementation of this agreement except that the section entitled special goals shall be changed only by a vote of two-thirds of the membership of the committee.

Section D—Executive Director:

There shall be an executive director who shall have responsibility for the implementation of the programs established pursuant to this agreement. The executive director shall be selected by a majority vote of the committee on the basis of suggestions by the coalition of a person or persons sufficiently sensitive to the problems of the minority community, sufficiently knowledgeable of the construction industry and sufficiently skilled to administer a journeyman training program.

No person shall serve as executive director who is a member of the committee. The executive director shall be empowered to employ and discharge such professional and clerical personnel as are necessary for the performance of his duties in accordance with the budget allotted for that purpose by the committee. The primary responsibility of the executive director and his staff shall be the implementation of recruitment, training, preapprenticeship, orientation, and counseling, and safety programs established pursuant to this agreement. The executive director shall report and be responsible directly to the committee. He shall attend all committee meetings. The executive director may be removed by a two-thirds ($\frac{2}{3}$) vote of the membership of the committee.

Recruitment

There shall be established a program to recruit minority persons in the ___(city)___ area and to acquaint them with employment, training, and apprenticeship opportunities in the construction industry. This program shall be administered by the executive director and shall include but not be limited to:

1. Taking appropriate steps to create an image in the ___(city)___ minority community that the contractors and unions do not discriminate against minority

groups in their employment and referral practices, including, but not necessarily limited to, publicizing through advertising in the communications media serving the ___(city)___ area the contractors' and unions' commitment to an affirmative program in the construction industry.

2. Establishing a counseling program for the purpose of making personal contact and holding meetings with interested students in all secondary technical, and vocational school and colleges in the ___(city)___ area with substantial minority group enrollment. All staff counselors shall provide specific information and guidance relative to the kinds of training and apprenticeship programs open to minority persons, the types of jobs available to minority persons, methods of entering the trades, requirements of union membership, length of apprenticeship programs open to minority persons, wages paid in the construction industry, and such other information which may be pertinent to the programs established pursuant to this agreement.

3. Contacting and maintaining continuing relationships with likely sources of minority group persons available for employment and training (including apprenticeship training) in the construction industry. Counselors shall establish such relations with signatory members of the coalition and any other groups which are or hereafter may be organized to facilitate the objectives of this agreement.

Operations Committee
Section A—Panel on Experience Equivalency:

All minority group persons seeking employment and training in the construction industry shall be classified by an ad hoc Panel on Experience Equivalency. The panel shall consist of persons having expertise in manpower needs of the construction industry with one (1) representative chosen by the contractors and unions and one (1) representative to be chosen by the coalition and one (1) representative chosen by the other two. In the event they are unable to agree, the third representative will be selected by the committee. If the committee cannot agree, then he will be selected in the same manner as is provided for the selection of the ninth member of the committee.

Section B—Classifications:
The panel shall, with the approval of the committee, determine the experience equivalency necessary for the classification of minority persons seeking employment or training in the construction industry as follows:

Journeymen
Apprentice
Advanced trainee
Trainee

Section C—Journeymen:
All minority group persons who are classified by the Panel on Experience Equivalency as journeymen for the designated trades shall be referred for employment. All minority group persons shall be classified as journeymen who:

1. Are licensed by any public authority to perform the functions of said trade; or

2. Have in fact functioned as a journeymen in the trade regardless of union membership or nonmembership, or;

3. Have performed at a level of skill which is equivalent to that required of a journeyman, or;

4. Are otherwise deemed qualified to function as journeymen, in that they meet the qualifications of the least-qualified journeyman in a specific trade.

All persons classified as journeymen shall be advised of their classification in writing, shall be paid the wage and fringe benefits for journeymen as provided in the applicable collective bargaining agreement between the contractors and the unions, and shall be admitted to full membership as a journeyman in the appropriate union signatory hereto.

Section D—Apprentices:

All minority persons who possess the established experience equivalency or who meet the valid, established qualifications for apprenticeship programs and who desire to become apprentices shall be classified by the Panel on Experience Equivalency as apprentices. Such persons shall be admitted into the apprenticeship program of the trade for which they have been determined to be qualified at the rates of pay established for apprentices at the particular level of skill which has been determined by the Panel on Experience Equivalency. Employment of minority persons in the apprenticeship program of the trade for which they have been determined to be qualified at the rates of pay established for apprentices at the particular level of skill which has been determined by the Panel on Experience Equivalency. Employment of minority persons in the apprenticeship programs for the designated trades shall count toward fulfillment of the goals for minority group nonjourneyman employment for each calendar year.

Section E—Advanced Trainees:

All minority persons who are not classified as journeymen, who have had some construction work experience or its equivalent and who in the judgment of the panel require one year or less of job-related training to qualify as journeymen, but who do not meet the requirements or do not seek admission to apprenticeship programs, shall be classified by the panel as advanced trainees. Advanced trainees shall be placed in job-related training programs in accordance with the goals for minority group nonjourneyman employment.

The objective of the training program shall be to prepare advanced trainees for entry into the construction industry as journeymen. Advanced trainees shall remain in this classification for no more than one year after which they shall be entitled to certification by the panel as journeymen. For the first six months of this year, advanced trainees shall be paid not less than _____% of the journeyman rate and for the last six months, not less than _____% of said rate.

At any time during the year, a contractor may conclude that an advanced trainee has reached journeyman status, pay him accordingly and notify the executive director of the action taken. Such advanced trainee shall thereupon be certified as a journeyman by the Panel on Experience Equivalency, and shall be entitled to all the benefits which relate to that status. Persons requiring job-related training as advanced trainees for a period of longer than one (1) year shall be dealt with on a case by case basis. Employment of minority persons as advanced trainees for the designated trades shall count toward fulfillment to the additional minority group nonjourneyman employment for each calendar year.

Section F—Trainees:

Minority group persons who do not possess the qualifications for classification as journeymen or advanced trainee and who do not desire to be apprentices shall be classified by the panel as trainees. Trainees shall be placed in job-related training programs in accordance with the goals for minority group nonjourneyman employment.

The objective of the training program shall be to provide such persons with counseling, and skills necessary to become an advanced trainee, looking to journeyman status in the construction trades. No person shall remain in this classification for more than one year, after which period they shall be entitled to be certified by the Panel on Experience Equivalency.

Specific Goals

In order to ensure the prompt realization of equal-employment opportunity in the construction industry, there are hereby established specific goals for minority manpower utilization in all construction (federal, federally assisted, state or local government, state- or local-government-assisted, and private). This includes, but is not limited to demolition, repair, alteration, rehabilitation, and construction of residential, commercial, industrial, institutional buildings and other structures including roads in the geographic area covered by this agreement performed by contractors and their employees who are members of the unions which are signatory hereto either directly or through their associations, and by the agents and subcontractors of said contractors, unions, and union members.

Section A—Journeymen:

All minority group persons who are determined to be journeymen in accordance with this agreement and who so desire shall:

1. Be placed at work in their trade without delay;

2. Be assigned work in the trade by the respective unions and employers in such a way that they are not penalized for periods of time when they were not members of the union nor employed in the trade in the area, in comparison with those persons who have been members of the union and/or have previously worked in the area; and,

3. Be admitted to union membership.

Section B—Nonjourneymen:

Option 1

In each year of this agreement, there shall be a goal of minority persons, as set forth herein below, employed and in training to become journeymen in the construction trades covered by this agreement. The specific assignment of individual minority group persons to trades and to employers shall be performed by the executive director in accordance with this agreement.

Schedule

Years	*Number of Minority Persons*
First year (19__)	_____ persons employed
Second year (19__)	_____ persons employed
Third year (19__)	_____ persons employed
Fourth year (19__)	_____ persons employed
Fifth year (19__)	_____ persons employed

Option 2

For all construction work in the ___(city)___ area in which the signatory contractors and unions shall participate, there shall be a goal of minority personnel trained and employed during the first year of this agreement and for successive years thereafter in each of the designated trades as follows:

Schedule for 1970

Identification of Trades	*Goals for Minority Group Nonjourneymen Employment*
Electrical workers	_____ persons employed
Plumbers	_____ persons employed

Sheet-metal workers   _____ persons employed
(etc.)   _____ persons employed

Schedule for 1971

                                                        Goals for Minority Group
Identification of Trades   *Nonjourneymen Employment*
Electrical workers   _____ persons employed
Plumbers   _____ persons employed
Sheet-metal workers   _____ persons employed
(etc.)   _____ persons employed

(Schedules for other years would follow)

Section C—No Discrimination:

The purpose of the contractors' and unions' commitment to specific goals is to provide equal-employment opportunity for minority group persons in the construction industry in the ___(city)___ area and is not intended and shall not be used to discriminate against any qualified applicant or employee.

Record Keeping and Reporting

The executive director and his staff shall keep complete records relating to the operation and complementation of the programs outlined in this agreement. Such records shall be available for inspection by all parties and any federal, state or local agency of government concerned with the operation of the program.

Section A—What the Records Shall Include:

Records shall include likely sources for minority group recruits, journeymen, apprentices, and trainees; names, addresses, and disposition (including complete follow-up) of minority persons availing themselves of the programs established herein, and such other information and reference files as may be necessary for the efficient and effective operation of this agreement.

The executive director shall compile a comprehensive quarterly report of the operation of this agreement on the form attached hereto as Appendix B, which shall be available to the parties and for inspection on request of any person, group, federal, state, or local agency of government concerned with operation of the program.

Section B—Work Stoppages:

There shall be no work stoppages, slowdowns, picketing, lockouts, or other interference as to projects within the scope of this agreement over the terms, application, or interpretation of this agreement.

APPENDIX B: Auditor's Worksheet

Hometown Plan Audit

_____ **(Name of Area)**

Date _____

OCCO-101

_____
_____
Auditors   Office

1	2	3	4	5	6	7	8	9	10	11	12	13		14
Name	Age	Residence status, length of time in area	Craft	Classification	Work status and hourly rate of pay	Date of original placement	Date placed on current job	Total time worked since original placement	Referral source	Union status	Minority group	Credit		Remarks
												Yes	No	

Chapter **21**

OSHA Compliance

ROBERT D. MORAN, ESQ.
Former Chairman, U.S. Occupational Safety and Health Review
Commission, Washington, D.C.

BRIEF DESCRIPTION OF EMPLOYER'S OBLIGATION

OSHA coverage   The Occupational Safety and Health Act of 1970 provides for the issuance of occupational safety and health standards by the Department of Labor, enforces these standards through the federal government, and establishes very severe penalties for violations of these standards.[1] The contractor's obligation to comply began on April 28, 1971, the law's effective date. To define that obligation precisely would require hundreds of thousands of words. However, it falls generally into three categories:

1. *General Duty Requirement.* Furnish each employee with employment and a place of employment which is free from recognized hazards that are causing or are likely to cause serious physical harm or death to those employees.[2]

---

[1]Williams-Steiger Occupational Safety and Health Act of 1970, Pub. L. 91-596 December 29, 1970, 84 Stat. 1590, 29 U.S.C. 651 *et seq.*
[2]29 U.S.C. 654 (a) (1)

2. *OSHA Standards.* Comply with occupational safety and health standards promulgated by the Secretary of Labor.[3]

3. *Record Keeping and Notice Posting.* Maintain accurate records of (a) work-related deaths, injuries, and illnesses and (b) employee exposures to potentially toxic materials or harmful physical agents.[4] Display OSHA-supplied posters designed to keep employees informed of their protections and obligations under the act, and post annual summaries of work-related deaths, injuries, and illnesses so that employees may keep informed of the job safety and health situation at their work place.

All contractors must comply   Any employer who has one or more employees and who is "engaged in a business affecting commerce" must comply with the act.[5] Use of long-distance telephone lines, the postal service, or supplies and equipment from a different state or country is enough to establish that you are "engaged in a business affecting commerce."

OSHA not directly applicable in some states   The act permits the Secretary of Labor to turn over OSHA enforcement to any state which can satisfy the Secretary that it can handle enforcement in a manner which is "at least as effective" as federal enforcement.[6] The Secretary can grant this authority, and he or she can take it away. At one time nearly half the states had OSHA-approved plans, but this was the high point, and the current trend is away from state enforcement. It matters little, anyhow, for the contractor's obligations are virtually the same whether or not the state where he is working has its own little OSHA law. The only obvious difference is that in states with their own OSHA plan most job-site inspections are conducted by state rather than federal OSHA inspectors, and the reports which must be filed go to a state agency rather than to the U.S. Department of Labor. Any contractor who is uncertain of the applicable OSHA enforcement agency in a particular state or territory would be well-advised to request this information from the U.S. Department of Labor either directly or through a trade association or a representative in Congress.

OSHA COMPLIANCE AT MULTIEMPLOYER JOB SITES

In enacting this law, Congress apparently gave little thought to the unique relationships which arise when employees of a number of different employers work in and around the same job site and are subject to the hazards which may exist at that site—hazards which may or may not have been created by their own employer, or someone else's, or by employees of a totally unrelated and unknown employer, as is typically the case on a construction job site.

In conceiving job safety legislation, Congress seemed to be focusing on the typical industrial or commercial work place where a single employer has one or

[3]29 U.S.C. 654 (a) (2).
[4]29 U.S.C. 657 (c).
[5]29 U.S.C. 652 (5).
[6]29 U.S.C. 667.

more workers under his sole supervisory control engaged in furthering his business purposes. They, therefore, framed the act so that such an employer has the responsibility and duty of providing for the safety and health of his own employees. This responsibility is a requirement of the act and is, therefore, nondelegable. Generally, an employer cannot disencumber himself from it or assume it for another employer simply by writing a clause purporting to do so in a contract.

The general duty requirement says each employer shall provide *his* employees with a hazard-free work place. That seems clear enough, and little more will be written here about that part of the law since nearly all contractor or subcontractor problems arise under the special duty clause. That provision requires that employers comply with OSHA standards issued under the act.

The standards are written generally to prevent hazards that may exist at a work place. If these standards stood by themselves, complications arising from control of the work premises might be far fewer. But they are promulgated to implement the law—a law enacted in order to compel an employer to watch out for the job safety and health of his employees, not for the general public or, for that matter, for any other employer's workers. The standards therefore must be read together with the law. For example, if no employee is exposed to hazard even though OSHA standards are not being observed at the job site, it is unlikely that a violation of the act could be established, The act is *not* a building code. Its purpose is to protect employees from harm, not to force employers to adhere woodenly to physical safety requirements even when no harm could result from his failure to do so. Consequently, a violation of the act generally requires the presence of these two conditions: (1) noncompliance with an OSHA standard and (2) exposure of one or more employees of the cited employer to hazard as a result of such noncompliance.

The other side of this coin is that each employer is obligated to protect the safety and health of his workers, regardless of who "owns" a hazard to which they might be exposed or who created it. Thus, a single hazard, such as excessive noise or absence of perimeter guarding, to which employees of a hundred different employers are exposed *could* mean a hundred separate violations, if the man from OSHA shows up and discovers it. The word "could" has been emphasized because the law is undergoing changes in this area as a result of court decisions.

For four years, the OSHA rule at multiple-contractor work sites was very simple: you were in violation of the act if one or more of your employees were exposed to the hazard resulting from noncompliance with an OSHA standard. It did not matter who had created the hazard. If, for example, the carpenter subcontractor had failed to build proper railings on the stairs, any other contractor whose employees used those stairs was in violation of the act. OSHA frequently issued citations to *all* employers at the work site when a situation such as this existed. OSHA insisted that it was each contractor's duty to keep his employees away from hazardous conditions even if the only way to accomplish this was to stop the work.

The first successful challenge to this rule was made by the Anning-Johnson

Company, a building subcontractor. Its employees were working at a job site where the general contractor had not placed guardrails around floor openings. Anning-Johnson's employees were doing some plastering work near these openings and were therefore exposed to the hazard of falling. The OSHA citation was contested before the Occupational Safety and Health Review Commission which held Anning-Johnson in violation because it exposed its employees to this hazard (the general contractor was also cited but did not contest that citation).[7] The company then appealed this decision to a U.S. Court of Appeals in Chicago which reversed the commission.[8]

The court ruled that—regardless of exposure—subcontractors should not be held in violation for nonserious violations which they "neither created nor were responsible for pursuant to their contractual duties." The court reasoned that "in relation to non-serious violations we do not believe that Congress intended to subvert the well established craft jurisdiction concept or to impose burdensome expenses on subcontractors which do not have the appropriate employees to abate certain hazards."

The court criticized the OSHA rule holding that all employers must keep their employees away from hazards even by shutting down the job if necessary: "To the extent that . . . [that rule] will lead to the removal of workers from construction sites because of non-serious violations we find that policy inconsistent with the act. Correcting the hazard, not shutting down construction sites, is the desired result."

However, calling its determination a "narrow holding," the court specifically noted that "we have not held that the . . . policy of imposing liability on employers for exposure to conditions that are serious violations of promulgated standards is invalid. Nor have we held that exposure by a subcontractor's employees to a nonserious standard violation which he created or is otherwise responsible for is impermissible."

Thus, for *serious* violations, the OSHA employee-exposure-to-hazard rule remains the touchstone for determining whether or not the act has been violated. At least for now.

Contractors at multiple-employer job sites should be acquainted with the *Anning-Johnson* decision, as well as the OSHA rule the court rejected in that case, when considering their responsibility for OSHA compliance at such sites. The following points are made to assist you in this:

1. The *Anning-Johnson* decision applies only to "nonserious" citations. Although currently more than 95 percent of all OSHA citations fall into this category, a contractor who receives a citation alleging that he has committed a *serious* or a *willful* violation cannot rely on this decision. A good argument can be made, however, that the logic of this ruling applies equally to *all* alleged violations, and a subsequent decision may so hold; but at present this decision's application is limited.

2. The decision does not legally apply nationwide. The jurisdiction of the

[7]Workinger Electric, Inc., 1 OSHC 3331 (1974).
[8]*Anning-Johnson Co. v. OSAHRC,* 3 OSHC 1166, 516 F.2d 1081 (7th Cir. 1975).

Court of Appeals for the Seventh Circuit is limited to three states: Illinois, Indiana, and Wisconsin. Nevertheless, other courts usually follow circuit court opinions even when not legally bound to do so. If another circuit court (there are ten others) takes a contrary view, a nationwide ruling could come only if the U.S. Supreme Court decided to resolve the issue. In this connection it should be noted that one of the three judges who participated in the *Anning-Johnson* decision was John Paul Stevens, subsequently a Justice of the Supreme Court.

3. Under a somewhat different fact situation a subcontractor was found in violation even though none of its employees was shown to be directly exposed to the hazard resulting from noncompliance with the OSHA standard. That decision by the Second Circuit Court of Appeals (New York, Vermont, and Connecticut) ruled that proof of a violation can be shown if a hazard has existed, and the area where the hazard existed is "accessible" to the cited employer's employees "or those of other employers engaged in a common undertaking."[9] This March 1975 decision, involving Dic-Underhill, a joint enterprise, emphasized that "it is not insignificant that it was Dic-Underhill that created the hazards and maintained the area in which they were located. . . . It had control over the areas in which the hazards were located and the duty to maintain those areas. Necessarily it must be responsible for creation of a hazard."

4. This simplified rule of thumb will be helpful to a contractor on a multiple-employer job who is cited for not complying with an OSHA standard: Do I have the power to abate the violation? If the answer is "no" either because your employees are of the wrong craft, it is beyond your expertise, or you are barred by your contract from doing so, then you have a pretty good defense to the citation. For, as the *Anning-Johnson* decision states, "we do not believe that Congress intended to subvert the well established craft jurisdiction concept or to impose burdensome expenses on subcontractors which do not have the appropriate employees to abate certain hazards." Even though such a situation exists, you would still be well-advised to call the hazardous condition to the attention of the responsible contractor when the hazard is readily apparent to you. The fact that you do this ought to be helpful to your defense in case OSHA does cite you. On the other hand, if the answer is "yes," the citation is probably valid unless some of the defenses discussed later in this chapter are present.

LIABILITY OF THE CONTRACTOR FOR EMPLOYEE NEGLIGENCE OR MISCONDUCT

Experienced contractors maintain that most job injuries result from employee neglect or refusal to observe safety requirements rather than from the absence of safe conditions at the job site. Nevertheless, the entire thrust of OSHA to date has been directed at reducing injuries by requiring the observance of safety and health standards regulating working conditions. Although the act provides that employees "shall comply" with applicable OSHA standards and

---

[9] *Brennan v. OSAHRC and Underhill Constr. Corp.*, 2 OSHC 1641, 513 F.2d 1032 (2d Cir. 1975).

states that "employers and employees have separate but dependent responsibilities," there is no penalty provision applicable to employees.

The burden of ensuring the safety of the work place has been placed squarely upon the employer by this act. The Senate committee which reported the legislation put it this way: "Final responsibility for compliance with the requirements of this act remains with the employer."

Numerous court decisions have held, however, that an employer cannot be liable for a safety infraction by one of his employees if there was no feasible way the employer could have prevented it. The landmark case on this point was decided by the United States Court of Appeals for the District of Columbia Circuit in December 1973. It involved an Arlington, Virginia, motel construction site operated by National Realty and Construction Company, Inc. This decision is far and away the most cited OSHA case to date.

The case arose when OSHA investigated the death of a foreman who was killed when a piece of construction equipment rolled over on him. He was riding as a passenger on the running board of a front-end loader which was traveling across the site when the accident happened. OSHA cited National Realty for violating the act's general duty requirement—failure to keep a work place free of recognized hazards likely to cause death. The company contested the citation but the Occupational Safety and Health Review Commission sustained the violation because of inadequate implementation by the company of its safety policy prohibiting employees from riding as passengers on construction equipment.[10] This decision was reversed on appeal.[11] The court ruled that National Realty could not be found in violation because it could not have prevented the accident. The decision stated further that:

> Congress intended to require elimination only of preventable hazards. It follows, we think, that Congress did not intend unpreventable hazards to be considered "recognized" under the clause. Though a generic form of hazardous conduct, such as equipment riding, may be "recognized," unpreventable instances of it are not, and thus the possibility of their occurrence at a workplace is not inconsistent with the workplace being "free" of recognized hazards.
>
> Though resistant to precise definition, the criterion of preventability draws content from the informed judgement of safety experts. Hazardous conduct is not preventable if it is so idiosyncratic and implausible in motive or means that conscientious experts, familiar with the industry, would not take it into account in prescribing a safety program. Nor is misconduct preventable if its elimination would require methods of hiring, training, monitoring, or sanctioning workers which are either so untested or so expensive that safety experts would substantially concur in thinking the methods infeasible.

DEFENSES TO OSHA CITATIONS

Many legal defenses are available to a contractor who receives an OSHA citation, just as there are many different defenses to a lawsuit. Three of them

[10]National Realty and Construction Co., Inc., 1 OSHC 1049 (1972).
[11]*National Realty and Construction Co. v. OSAHRC*, 1 OSHC 1422, 489 F.2d 1257 (D.C. Cir. 1973).

which may be particularly pertinent to a construction contractor will be discussed here:

1. *Impossibility.* The work could not be done if the requirements of the standard were observed.

2. *Greater Hazard.* Compliance with the standard would create a greater hazard to employee safety than would the employer's normal work practices.

3. *Lack of Knowledge.* The employer had no knowledge that the OSHA standard (for which he is cited) was not being complied with at the job site.

Impossibility   A 1973 Review Commission case involving La Sala Contracting Company, a Yonkers, New York, mason contractor, is typical of many cases where this defense has been applied. Two of La Sala's bricklayers were putting in the first course of bricks around an open elevator shaft on the seventh floor of a building under construction. OSHA cited the company for failure to guard the opening with standard railings. The company admitted noncompliance with that safety standard but maintained that "railings would interfere with the work in progress." The judge agreed and dismissed the OSHA citation with this statement: "I find here that the absence of railings from the elevator shaft opening was for a proper reason—to allow the work to be accomplished—and conclude as a matter of law that respondent was not in violation."[12]

Greater hazard   Employers should not be required to comply with an OSHA standard which requires them to follow a course of conduct that is less safe than an existing work practice. That rule was laid down in a 1974 Review Commission case involving Industrial Steel Erectors of Birmingham, Alabama; and it has been followed many times since that date. The firm was cited because of its failure to require its employees who were engaging in dismantling a steel structure to wear safety lanyards. The employees had not tied off the safety lines while removing the last four bolts and pins holding a truss in place because the truss was likely to spring free when the tension holding it in place was removed. The employer's defense was that it was much more hazardous for its employees to tie off than to remain unfettered so they could dodge an out-of-control truss. This defense was upheld because, said the commission, "the purpose of the statute is to augment and not to reduce the safety of working conditions."[13]

Lack of knowledge   In order to sustain a citation, OSHA must prove that the employer had knowledge of the condition alleged to be a violation. This, then, is not technically a *defense* which a cited employer must raise since proof of employer knowledge is an affirmative obligation upon OSHA. The U.S. Court of Appeals for the Ninth Circuit made this clear in a 1975 decision involving Raymond Hendrix, operator of an Alsea, Oregon, lumber company. Hendrix was cited for several violations because OSHA observed some of his employees working when they were not wearing the required protective equipment and because another was improperly operating a buck saw. The court, however, dismissed the citation because it found that OSHA failed to prove "that the

---

[12]La Sala Contracting Co., Inc., 1 OSHC 3027 (1973).
[13]Industrial Steel Erectors, Inc., 1 OSHC 1497 (1974).

employer had any knowledge respecting these instances of employee disobedience of its established instructions."[14] In doing so the court laid down this principle: "Fundamental fairness would require that one charged with and penalized for violation be shown to have caused, or at least to have knowingly acquiesced in, that violation. Under our legal system, to date at least, no man is held accountable, or subject to fine, for the totally independent act of another."

OSHA STANDARDS

The official source for locating the job safety and health standards with which employers must comply is the *Federal Register*. At least once a year all regulations contained in the *Federal Register* are republished in the *Code of Federal Regulations* (CFR). OSHA standards appear in Volume 29 CFR, a paperback book of one thousand pages. The Construction Safety and Health Standards appear at part 1926 (29 CFR 1926.1-1926.1051).

It is important to keep in mind that OSHA standards can change even though the act remains the same. The Secretary of Labor may add new standards or revoke or modify existing standards at any time, as long as he gives at least a 30-day advance notice in the *Federal Register* and follows the procedures set out in Section 6b of the act.[15] These procedures permit "any interested person" to file written objections to the proposed standard and to demand (and get) a public hearing on the proposal as long as the demand is filed within the 30-day advance-notice period. When the Secretary does issue the new standard in final form, any person adversely affected by the change has 60 days in which to challenge the validity of such standard in the United States Court of Appeals.

OSHA Booklet 2202, a handy booklet digesting the basic standards applicable to the construction industry, will be furnished on request by any local OSHA office.

Variances from standards   The act permits an employer to obtain a variance from the requirements of a standard.[16] An application for a variance must be made to OSHA and must follow a rather elaborate procedure set out in OSHA regulations. Basically an employer who seeks a variance must demonstrate that the conditions, practices, means, methods, operations, or processes used or proposed to be used by an employer will provide employment and places of employment to his employees which are as safe and healthful as those which would prevail if he complied with the standard.

ENFORCEMENT PROCEDURE

Inspections   More than a thousand OSHA inspectors are located at a number of different communities throughout the country. Ordinarily their inspections are conducted without advance notification.[17] Although you will almost

---

[14]*Brennan v. OSAHRC and Alsea Lumber Co.,* 2 OSHC 1646, 511 F.2d 1139 (9th Cir. 1975).
[15]29 U.S.C. 655 (b).
[16]29 U.S.C. 655 (b) (6) (A) (B) and (C).
[17]29 U.S.C. 657 and 666 (f).

certainly be inspected if an employee or union files a complaint with OSHA or if there is a serious accident at the job site, a substantial percentage of inspections are conducted which are *not* triggered by either complaints or accidents. It is impossible to predict your chances of being inspected; it may happen simply because an inspector happens to be in the neighborhood.

Each OSHA inspector carries identifying credentials which must be shown to the employer before the inspection begins. A representative of the employer as well as a representative of the employees is given an opportunity to accompany the inspector on his tour of the job site. The inspector will also discuss his inspection with the employer prior to leaving the premises.

Citations   If the inspector believes a citation should be issued, he generally must get his area director's approval prior to serving it on the employer. Citations usually arrive within two weeks of the inspection by certified mail and are ordinarily accompanied by a notification of proposed penalty.[18] Citations must be posted at the job site. They should be read carefully because they specify a period of time for correcting the conditions which allegedly do not comply with the law.

Contesting the citation   Within 15 working days of receipt of the certified letter containing the notification of proposed penalty, the citation or the penalty proposal or both may be contested by mailing a letter stating the objection to the OSHA office which issued the citation.[19] No particular form is necessary. A letter in your own handwriting sent regular mail will suffice. Be sure to make clear, however, exactly what you wish to contest. If you object to the citation, say so. A letter simply objecting to a proposed penalty may foreclose you from arguing the validity of the citation, and vice versa.

When you contest a citation within the 15-day time period, its mandates are suspended. Neither the abatement (correction) date nor the penalty applies. You will be notified at a later date of the hearing procedures. Generally certain papers are exchanged between you and an OSHA lawyer prior to the date a hearing is conducted. The hearing is conducted locally by a review commission judge who has no association or connection whatsoever with OSHA. The burden of proving the violations listed on contested citations is on OSHA. You are presumed to be innocent. If the judge finds in your favor there, of course, will be no penalty. If he finds against you the judge will decide what penalty, if any, is appropriate. He is not bound to accept the OSHA penalty proposal. Review commission decisions may be appealed to the United States courts of appeal.[20]

Citations not contested   If you decide not to contest a citation or if the 15-day period expires before you act, the citation and the penalty proposal (unless separately contested) become final.[21] You are then bound to comply with the abatement period specified on the citation and pay the penalty. Failure to abate within the time prescribed will subject you to a new action in which penalties as

---

[18]29 U.S.C. 658.
[19]29 U.S.C. 659 (c).
[20]29 U.S.C. 660 (a).
[21]29 U.S.C. 659 (a).

high as $1,000 per day may be proposed. (This new action, however, may itself be contested.) If you find yourself unable to meet the abatement deadline of an uncontested citation, you may write to OSHA requesting an extension.[22] These requests are generally granted if you are unable to abate because of factors beyond your reasonable control and your request is filed before the time for abatement has expired.

RECORD-KEEPING REQUIREMENTS

In the past, one of the major difficulties in the government's effort to reduce work-place injuries and diseases was lack of knowledge. It was very difficult to know the full size, scope, or nature of the problem. Records were not kept of all injuries and even where records were kept they were not uniform. The 1970 act attempted to correct these deficiencies by defining exactly what injuries and diseases had to be recorded and by requiring that all employers maintain such records.[23] (This latter requirement was later changed in order to exclude small employers—those with fewer than 11 employees.)

Minor injuries requiring only first aid treatment need not be recorded, but a record must be made if it involves medical treatment, loss of consciousness, restriction of work or motion, transfer to another job, or time lost from work.[24]

OSHA supplies forms for this purpose which include accompanying instructions on these requirements. In 1971, an OSHA booklet containing the record-keeping requirements was mailed to every employer with a social security account number. This booklet also contained the necessary forms as well as a poster informing employees of their rights under the act which was to be displayed at every job site.

The OSHA record-keeping and poster-display requirements must be observed at each job site or other place where employees report for work.[25] Each supervisor at such sites should make sure that these requirements are being observed. If you do not have the appropriate forms and the OSHA poster, request copies of the OSHA booket *Recordkeeping Requirements* from your local OSHA office.

---

[22]29 U.S.C. 659 (c).
[23]29 U.S.C. 657 (c) (1), 673 (a).
[24]29 U.S.C. 657 (c) (2).
[25]29 U.S.C. 657 (c) (1).

Part Six

Contract Performance

Chapter **22**

Errors in Bids

R. EMMETT KERRIGAN, ESQ.
Partner, Deutsch, Kerrigan & Stiles, New Orleans, Louisiana

INTRODUCTION

Construction contracts are awarded in two ways. One is by competitive bidding. The other by negotiation between the owner and a contractor who has been chosen by the owner. The latter method is usually used when the owner has had experience with a particular contractor and believes that he does good work for a reasonable price or the particular contractor is well known for his expertise in specialized work that the owner contemplates.

Most work is done pursuant to competitive bidding, either public or private. The letting of public contracts is customarily regulated by statute, federal or state. Ordinarily, public contracts must be let after competitive bidding to the lowest responsible bidders.[1] Negotiated federal public contracts are permissible under certain carefully controlled circumstances,[2] and if "the public exigency will not admit of the delay incident to advertising."[3]

This discussion of errors in bids will concern bids on private and public jobs. Although the same rules should apply to negotiated contracts, the likelihood of such errors in those cases is small because of the different technique used in putting together such agreements. If a contract is negotiated, the contractor does not face the deadlines of competitive pressures of the usual bidding process. Negotiation is usually over a period of time, thus giving more opportunity to check and prevent errors from creeping into the contract price.

The usual practice in bidding is to require a contractor submitting a bid to post a bid guarantee. Such a guarantee is in the form of a bid bond or a certified check, with a provision for forfeiture in the event the bidder is low and refuses to sign the construction contract in accordance with his bid. The amount of a bid guarantee varies, depending on whether the work is federal, state, or private.

Should the low bidder refuse to sign the construction contract, his liability is usually limited in nonfederal work to the amount of his bid guarantee. Federal regulations provide that if a contractor on federal work fails to sign the contract and furnish such bond as may be required "he shall be liable for any costs of procuring the work which exceeds the amount of his bid, and the bid guarantee shall be available toward offsetting such differences."[4]

RIGHT TO WITHDRAW BID

In General

When a contractor, bidding on a public or private contract, commits an error in the preparation of his bid, he will usually seek to withdraw the bid and be relieved of his obligations thereunder. It is now recognized in every state in which the question has been presented that a contractor may withdraw his bid because of a mistake in preparation, if he can meet the following requirements:

1. The mistake is of such importance that enforcement of the bid would be unconscionable.

2. The mistake relates to a material feature of the bid.

3. The mistake did not occur through gross negligence on the part of the bidder.

4. If the bidder is allowed to withdraw his bid, the other party may be returned to the same position he was in before the bid was made.

Each of these requirements will be discussed below. Before doing this, however, it should be pointed out that bidders have been relieved of their bids

---

[1] 41 C.F.R. § 1-2.102 (1975) (Federal Procurement Regulations). State statutes contain similar requirements.

[2] *See,* for example, 41 C.F.R. §1-3.101 (b) (FPR). State statutes also permit letting of such contracts under limited conditions.

[3] 41 USC 252(c) (2). *See also* 41 C.F.R. §1-3.202(a) (FPR).

[4] 41 C.F.R. §1-10.103-3(a) (2) (FPR).

although the owners had formally accepted them. Thus, the same equitable criteria have been applied to relieve a bidder of his obligations under his bid, both before and after the owner has accepted the bid.[5]

Moreover, courts have held that the mere fact that the bid is required to be held open for a given period of time, whether by statute or agreement between the parties, does not affect the bidder's right to equitable relief under appropriate circumstances.[6]

Unconscionable Advantage

The question of whether the owner would gain an unconscionable advantage (vis-à-vis the bidder), if the bidder is not allowed to withdraw his erroneous bid, is basically a subjective decision which must be made by the court and involves a determination whether, under all circumstances, it would be unfair to hold the contractor to the bid.

In reaching this decision, it is obvious that the court is more likely to find an unconscionable advantage if the error would result in the loss to the bidder of a substantial sum of money. Indeed, it could be said that the greater the loss, the more unconscionable the contract would become. It is difficult, however, to predict the point at which an error becomes so serious as to make the advantage obtained by the owner unconscionable.

An element which has been enunciated by the courts, and which bears on the question of unconscionability, is whether the bid "patently discloses" that it is based on a mistake. This is usually determined by comparing the erroneous bid with the other bids or with an estimate of the cost of the work made by the party requesting the bids. If such a patent error exists in the bid, the owner may be charged with knowledge of the bidder's mistake, and the courts will not permit the owner to take advantage of that knowledge and bind the bidder to an unfair contract.[7]

Material Mistake

A mistake is material if it relates to an important element of the contract. In the usual case, the mistake involves the price which the bidder quotes for performing the work, specifically, an underestimation of the cost of the work. A mistake bearing on the price has consistently been held to be material.

A bid could also contain a mistake as to another aspect of the contract, for instance, the length of time within which the contractor must complete the project. All cases founded on the right of a bidder to withdraw his bid have dealt with mistakes relating to the contract price. It would seem, however, that the same principles should apply to any material mistake.

---

[5]*M. J. McGough Co. v. Jane Lamb Mem'l Hosp.*, 302 F.Supp. 482 (SD Iowa 1969); *Kenneth E. Curran, Inc. v. State,* 106 NH 558, 215 A.2d 702 (1965); *Smith & Lowe Constr. Co. v. Herrera,* 79 NM 239, 442 P.2d 197 (1968); *Board of Educ. of Floyd County v. Hooper,* 350 S.W.2d 629 (K.Ct.App. 1961); *James T. Taylor & Son v. Arlington Independent School Dist.,* 160 Tex. 617, 335 S.W.2d 371 (1960).

[6]*M. J. McGough Co., supra* note 5; *M. F. Kemper Constr. Co. v. Los Angeles,* 37 Cal.2d 696, 235 P.2d 7 (1951).

[7]*Kenneth E. Curran, Inc., supra* note 5.

Gross Negligence

The bidder must also show that his mistake did not result from gross or culpable negligence. On the other hand, failure to exercise ordinary care will not deprive him of relief.[8]

Occasionally, gross negligence will be equated to the bidder's lack of good faith, or breach of legal duty, in preparing the bid.[9] It has also been said that the bidder's mistake must have been an honest one, made without fraudulent intent or deliberation, to enable the bidder to avail himself of equitable relief.[10]

In deciding whether to relieve a bidder, some courts have distinguished clerical errors from errors of judgment. Thus, it has been held that, "[t]here is a difference between mere mechanical or clerical errors made in tabulating or transcribing figures and errors of judgment, as, for example, underestimating the cost of labor or materials."[11] Under this rule, which has been enacted into law by the legislatures of several states,[12] if the error involves a mistake of judgment, a bidder will not be permitted to withdraw his bid.

The distinction between clerical errors and errors of judgment has not been drawn in many cases. Instead, the traditional "gross-negligence" terminology is usually employed. However, in most of the cases in which the bidder has been allowed to withdraw his bid, a clerical error was involved. While it certainly is more difficult to obtain relief when an error of judgment is involved, relief will not necessarily be denied on that ground, except in those states which legislatively foreclose assistance in such circumstances. For example, a contractor misinterpreted the specifications and submitted a bid which was about 15 percent lower than the state's estimate. The court held that under the circumstances the bidder had not committed gross error and permitted him to withdraw his bid.[13]

Return of Owner to Prior Position

The final requirement is that the owner may be put in the position it occupied prior to the submission of the bid.

In determining whether this can be done, the court will consider whether the owner has expended sums in reliance on the bid submitted, whether the cost of the work has increased because of the mere passage of time, and whether the owner will have to obtain additional professional services or readvertise for bids if the bid is withdrawn.

In a fairly recent case, one of the grounds for not permitting the bidder to withdraw his bid was that the owner could not be restored to his prior position

---

[8]*M. J. McGough Co., supra* note 5; *Board of Regents of Murray State Normal School v. Cole,* 209 Ky. 761, 273 S.W. 508 (1925).

[9]*M. F. Kemper Constr. Co., supra* note 6.

[10]*Board of Regents of Murray State Normal School, supra* note 8.

[11]*M. F. Kemper Constr. Co., supra* note 6, at 11.

[12]*See,* e.g., 73 P.S. §1602 (Penna.); O.R.C. §9.31 (Ohio); and Code of Virginia, §11-20.2.

[13]*Connecticut v. F. H. McGraw & Co.,* 41 F.Supp. 369 (D Conn. 1941).

because the withdrawal notice was not made until more than forty-five days after the opening of the bids, and in the meantime the cost of materials needed for the job increased, and additional architects' and consultants' fees would be required.[14]

NOTIFICATION

As stated, a bidder may be entitled to equitable relief even if the owner accepts the bid before the bidder gives notice of the mistake and withdrawal of the bid. However, to be entitled to any relief, such notice must be given to the owner with reasonable promptness.[15] The question of whether such notice has been given, involves two factors: whether the bidder unreasonably delayed notifying the owner after the mistake was discovered and a consideration of the length of time that notification was given after the bids were opened or the bid accepted.

The sooner notice is given, the better, Thus, it appears that in all the cases in which a bidder was allowed to withdraw his bid, notice was given within one week of the submission of the bid.

An interesting question arises if the error is not discovered until after the contract for the work has been signed. No cases in point have been found. It would seem that the same principles which apply to the question: may a bidder withdraw his bid, should prevail in determining whether a contract entered into after bidding may be rescinded.

It may be that the equitable principles applicable to contract rescission generally will apply in such a situation. These principles are the same as those governing a bidder's right to withdraw his bid, except that the party seeking rescission would be held to a standard of ordinary, rather than gross, or culpable, negligence.[16]

ERRORS BY SUBCONTRACTORS

In general, the principles discussed above apply to bids made by subcontractors to prime contractors, provided the subcontractor gives notice of the error before the prime contractor's bid, which is partially based on the subcontractor's bid, is submitted to the owner. The reason for this exception is that, after the contractor has submitted his bid, he cannot be returned to his prior position. In such a case, equitable relief will be denied irrespective of whether the subcontractor's mistake involves clerical errors or an error in judgment.[17]

---

[14] *Guido and Guido, Inc. v. Culberson County*, 459 S.W.2d 674 (Tex. Civ. App. 1970).

[15] *Smith & Lowe Constr. Co., supra* note 5.

[16] *Anderson Bros. v. O'Meara*, 306 F.2d 672 (CA 5-1962).

[17] *Heifetz Metal Crafts, Inc. v. Peter Kiewit Sons'*, 264 F.2d 435 (CA 8 1959); *Cox-Hardie Co. v. Rabalais*, 162 So.2d 713 (La.App. 4 1964); *Reimann Constr. Co. v. Heinz*, 137 So. 355 (La.App.Orl. 1931); *Harris v. Lillis*, 24 So.2d 689 (La.App.Orl. 1946); *Schorr v. Nosacka*, 132 So. 524 (La.App.Orl. 1931).

RIGHT TO REFORM BID

A contract may be reformed by an appropriate court action to reflect the true intentions of the parties when the error therein is mutual.[18] In other words, when the parties have come to an agreement, but through mutual error have failed to set forth this agreement in the document executed by them, a court will enter judgment changing the contract to set forth their actual understanding. As pointed out below in the discussion of federal projects, federal regulations permit the reformation of an erroneous bid under some circumstances. But reformation is not available generally because an erroneous bid represents an error on the part of the bidder only.

Moreover, if a bidder is allowed to reform his bid after the bids are opened, the integrity of the bidding process would be destroyed, since that bidder would have the advantage of knowing the contents of his competitors' bids when resubmitting his revised bid.

FEDERAL PROJECTS

The same rules applicable to bidding on other works have been applied to bids on federal jobs. In addition, the bidder on the latter is accorded more protection under federal regulations.

Federal projects are divided into two general categories: defense contracts (i.e.: those let through a department of the Department of Defense) and nondefense contracts (those let through all other federal agencies). The regulations governing mistakes in bids are virtually the same for defense and nondefense contracts. However, as pointed out below, there is some difference, particularly when the mistake is not discovered until after the job is awarded. Unless otherwise indicated, this discussion applies to all federal projects.

Duties of Contracting Officer

After the opening of bids on a federal project, the contracting officer is required to examine the bids for mistakes.[19] Where apparent mistakes are obvious or where the contracting officer has reason to believe that a mistake exists, verification must be sought from the bidder, calling his attention to the suspected error. The request for verification should indicate to the bidder the reason for surmising error.[20] Failure on the part of the contracting officer to seek verification when he is aware or should have been aware of a possible error precludes the formation of a valid and binding contract.

---

[18]*Rolane Sportswear, Inc. v. U.S. Fid. & Guar. Co.,* 407 F.2d 1091 (CA 6 1969); *Dale Ingram, Inc. v. United States,* 475 F.2d 1177 (Ct.Cl. 1973).

[19]32 C.F.R. §2.406-1 (1974) (Armed Services Procurement Regulations) [ASPR]; 41 C.F.R. §1-2.406-1 (1975) (Federal Procurement Regulations) [FPR].

[20]*Chernick v. United States,* 372 F.2d 492 (Ct.Cl. 1967); *United States v. Metro Novelty Mfg. Co.,* 125 F.Supp. 713 (S.D.NY 1954). *See* 32 C.F.R. §2.406-3(e) (1) (ASPR); 41 C.F.R. §1-2.406-3(d) (1) (FPR).

Obvious clerical mistakes—such as the obvious misplacement of a decimal point, an obvious incorrect discount, an obvious reversal of the price f.o.b. destination and the price f.o.b. origin, or an obvious mistake in the designation of a unit—may be corrected by the contracting officer prior to award if he first obtains verification of the bid actually intended.[21] Should a contract be awarded in which a clerical error goes undetected, the bidder will be entitled to relief from the error if the contracting officer had actual or constructive notice of the error.

If upon request for verification the bidder confirms the bid as originally submitted, the contracting officer must so consider it.[22] If the bidder responds by alleging mistake, he must support the allegation by relevant evidence, such as "the bidder's file copy of the bid, his original worksheets and other data used in preparing the bid, subcontractors' and suppliers' quotations, if any, [and] published price lists," to establish the error, the manner of its occurrence and the bid intended.[23]

Should the bidder fail or refuse to furnish such evidence, the contracting officer will consider the bid as submitted, unless it is evident that acceptance of the bid would be unfair to the bidder or to the other bona fide bidders. If a contract is awarded to a bidder who fails or refuses to furnish the necessary evidence to establish the error, the bidder will nonetheless be protected against loss from the error if the contracting officer either knew or should have known of the error.[24]

Administrative Relief—Prior to Award

The federal agency (or defense department), which controls the project, may grant certain forms of administrative relief from mistakes discovered after opening of the bid but prior to award of the contract.

First, the bidder may be allowed to withdraw his bid if he so requests and there is clear and convincing evidence as to the existence of the mistake.[25] But if such evidence shows that the bid as corrected remains the lowest bid, the government may correct the bid and not allow it to be withdrawn.[26]

Second, the bidder may, upon his request, be allowed to correct his mistake if there is clear and convincing evidence of the error and the bid intended.[27] Such correction will not be allowed if it results in displacing a lower bid unless the error and the bid actually intended are substantially ascertainable from the

---

[21]32 C.F.R. §2-406-2 (ASPR); 41 C.F.R. §1-2.406-2 (FPR).

[22]32 C.F.R. §2.406-3(e) (1) (ASPR); 41 C.F.R. §1-2.406-3(d) (2) (FPR).

[23]32 C.F.R. §2.406-3(e) (1) (ASPR); 41 C.F.R. §1-2.406-3(d) (2) (FPR).

[24]*Wender Presses, Inc. v. United States,* 343 F.2d 961 (Ct.Cl. 1965).

[25]32 C.F.R. §2.406-3(a) (1) (ASPR); 41 C.F.R. §1-2.406-3(a) (1) (FPR). *See Ruggiero v. United States,* 420 F.2d 709 (Ct.Cl. 1970).

[26]32 C.F.R. §2.406-3(a) (2) (ASPR); 41 C.F.R. §1-2.406-3(a) (1) (FPR). *Chris Berg, Inc. v. United States,* 426 F.2d 314 (Ct.Cl. 1970).

[27]41 C.F.R. §1-2.406-3(a) (FPR) requires that a bid must be responsive before corrections will be allowed. *See* 38 Comp. Gen. 819 (1959).

invitation and bid,[28] In the absence of such circumstances the bidder will not be granted such relief.[29]

Doubtful cases involving pre-award relief on all federal contracts may be submitted by the agency in question to the Comptroller General for decision.[30] Even if a case is not submitted to the Comptroller General for an advance decision, the Comptroller is given the right to review any decision made by the federal agency in such matters.[31]

Administrative Relief—After Award

If a mistake in a bid is not discovered until after the award of the contract, certain other administrative relief may be granted by the agency or department in question.

First, the mistake may be corrected by an amending agreement if the amendment results in a contract more favorable to the government, and the agreement as amended does not change the essential requirements of the contract.[32] Second, the contract may be rescinded if the contract price does not exceed $1,000.[33] Third, the contract may be reformed by deleting all items involved in the error if this does not reduce the contract price by more than $1,000.[34] Fourth, the contract price may be increased—but not by more than $1,000—if the price as corrected does not exceed that of the next lowest bid.[35]

If the contract (or mistake) does not meet any of these criteria, different rules apply to a contractor's entitlement to post-award relief.

But before any post-award relief will be granted, it must be established on the basis of clear and convincing evidence that an error was made and that there was a mutual mistake or a unilateral mistake by the bidder of such a nature as to put the contracting officer on notice of the probability of the error.[36]

The test of what a contracting officer should have known is one of reasonableness, "i.e., whether under the facts and circumstances of the case there were any factors which reasonably should have raised the presumption of error in the mind of the contracting officer."[37]

In all cases involving nondefense contracts, an administrative determination made by a federal agency is subject to review by the Comptroller General,[38] and

---

[28]32 C.F.R. §2.406-3(a) (3) (ASPR); 41 C.F.R. §1-2.406-3(a) (2) (FPR).

[29]32 C.F.R. §2.406-3(a) (4) (ASPR); 41 C.F.R. §1-2.406-3(a) (3) (FPR).

[30]41 C.F.R. §1-2.406-3(e) (FPR); 32 C.F.R. §2.406-3(f) (ASPR).

[31]41 C.F.R. §1-2.406-3(e) (FPR). It is not clear whether this right of review exists for defense contracts. 32 C.F.R. §2.406-3 (ASPR).

[32]32 C.F.R. §2.406-4(a) (ASPR); 41 C.F.R. §1-2.406-4(a) (FPR).

[33]32 C.F.R. §2.406-4(b) (3) (i) (a) (ASPR); 41 C.F.R. §1-2.406-4(b) (1) (FPR).

[34]32 C.F.R. §2.406-4(b) (3) (i) (b) (ASPR); 41 C.F.R. §1-2.406-4(b) (2) (i) (FPR).

[35]32 C.F.R. §2.406-4(b) (3) (i) (b) (ASPR); 41 C.F.R. §1-2.406-4(b) (2) (ii) (FPR).

[36]32 C.F.R. §2.406-4(b) (1) and (2) (ASPR); 41 C.F.R. §1-2.406-4(c) (FPR). Additionally, 32 C.F.R. §2.406-4(b) (3) (ii) (ASPR) requires that notice of the mistake must be received prior to final payment.

[37]*Chernick, supra* note 20. *See also: Allied Contractors, Inc. v. United States,* 310 F.2d 945 (Ct.Cl. 1962).

[38]41 C.F.R. §§1-2.406-3(e) and 1-2.406-4(g) (FPR).

doubtful cases and cases in which the bidder so requests should be reviewed by the Comptroller General.[39]

Determinations as to post-award relief in defense contracts are not subject to review by the Comptroller General.[40]

Applications for post-award relief on nondefense contracts, where administrative relief is precluded because of the limitations set forth in the regulations (for instance, if the mistake involves an amount in excess of $1,000), must be submitted to the Comptroller General for decision.[41]

Such cases involving defense contracts will be referred to the contract adjustment board within the appropriate military department.[42] A contract adjustment board may amend or modify (rescission is apparently unavailable) a contract to correct or mitigate the effect of a mistake which either is so obvious that it should have been apparent to the contracting officer or involves mutual error.[43] But in order to grant such relief the board must find that "the action will facilitate the national defense"[44] and the "request therefore has been filed before all obligations under the contract (including final payment) have been discharged."[45]

If the contractor is not satisfied with the action taken by the agency to which the erroneous bid was submitted or by the Comptroller General (in appropriate cases), he may have that action reviewed either in the court of claims or by the proper United States district court.[46]

RETURN OF BID BOND

As pointed out above, a bid bond is a covenant by the bidder and his surety that he will execute a contract (and often also furnish performance and payment bonds) with the bidding authority if his bid is low. The bid bond is a type of liquidated damages—not a penalty—for the bidder's failure to enter into the contract. Such damages can be either a fixed percentage specified in the bond[47] or the difference between the low-bidder's price and the next-lowest price which the authority accepts.[48] Even where the authority's damages are in excess of the amount of the bond, it is generally held that the contractor's liability cannot exceed the amount of the bond.[49]

Where the courts have allowed the contractor to withdraw his bid because of a unilateral clerical mistake or for other equitable considerations, they require

---

[39] 41 C.F.R. §§1-2.406-3(e) and 1-2.406-4(g), (j) (FPR).

[40] 32 C.F.R. §2.406-4 (ASPR).

[41] 41 C.F.R. §1-2.406-4(i) (FPR).

[42] 32 C.F.R. §2.406-4(g) and 32 C.F.R. §17.000, *et seq.* (ASPR).

[43] 32 C.F.R. §17.204-3 (ASPR).

[44] 32 C.F.R. §17.205-1(b) (1) (ASPR).

[45] 32 C.F.R. §17.205-1(c) (1) (ASPR).

[46] *See, e.g., Henry Spen & Co. v. Laird,* 354 F.Supp. 586 (D DC 1973); *Chris Berg, Inc., supra* note 26.

[47] *A. J. Colella, Inc. v. County of Allegheny,* 391 Pa. 103, 137 A2d 265 (1958).

[48] *Brown v. United States,* 152 F 964 (CCA 2d 1907).

[49] *Bolivar Reorganized School Dist. No. 1 v. American Sur. Co.,* 307 S.W.2d 405 (Mo. 1957).

that the bid bond (or certified check) accompanying the bid be returned to the contractor and surety.[50]

It has been held that this applies in a case of a clerical error even where the official bid form provides that no plea of mistake or error is available to the prospective bidder. In one case, the court found that a provision in the bid form that bidders "will not be released on account of errors," applied only to errors of judgment, not clerical errors. To hold otherwise, said the court, would be "contrary to common sense and ordinary business understanding and would result in the loss of heretofore well-established equitable rights to relief from certain types of mistakes."[51]

Until very recently a minority view held that even where a unilateral mistake in a bid was made in good faith and the other equitable considerations discussed above were present, the contractor and surety were still liable under the bid bond. This so-called "firm-bid" rule, which started in a Pennsylvania decision,[52] was based on the ground that to hold otherwise "would seriously undermine and make the requirement or system of sealed bids a mockery; it could likewise open wide the door to fraud and collusion between contractors and/or between contractors and the Public Authority."

In 1974, the Pennsylvania legislature enacted a statute to provide for the withdrawal of a bid without forfeiture of the bid bond, where there is a clerical mistake in the bid, thereby overruling the effect of the prior jurisprudence.[53]

Similar results have occurred in Ohio and Virginia. In 1970 the Ohio Supreme Court applied the firm-bid rule.[54] Shortly thereafter the Ohio General Assembly overturned this decision by a statute providing for the return of the contractor's bid bond in those cases where it was shown that a clerical error in the bid had been made in good faith.[55] A similar decision in 1971 by the Virginia Supreme Court[56] was rendered no longer effective by similar legislation[57] adopted in 1974.

These experiences in Pennsylvania, Ohio, and Virginia indicate that the firm-bid rule is no longer viable in this country, and any further judicial adoption of the rule will be legislatively annulled.

---

[50]*M. F. Kemper Constr. Co. v. Los Angeles*, 37 Cal.2d 696, 235 P.2d 7 (1951); *Board of Educ. of Floyd County v. Hooper*, 350 S.W.2d 629 (Ky.Ct.App. 1961); *Smith & Lowe Constr. Co. v. Herrera*, 79 N.M. 239, 442 P.2d 197 (1968); *State v. State Constr. Co.*, 203 Or. 414, 280 P.2d 370 (1955); *James T. Taylor & Sons, v. Arlington Ind. School Dist.*, 160 Tex. 617, 335 S.W.2d 371 (1960); *Puget Sound Painters, Inc. v. State*, 45 Wash. 2d 819, 278 P.2d 302 (1954).

[51]*M. F. Kemper Constr. Co. v. Los Angeles*, 37 Cal.2d 696, 235 P.2d 7, 12.

[52]*Modany v. State Pub. School Bldg. Auth.*, 417 Pa. 39, 208 A.2d 276 (1965).

[53]73 P.S. §1602.

[54]*Board of Educ. of Chillicothe v. Sever-Williams Co.*, 22 Ohio St. 2d 107, 258 N.E.2d 605 (1970).

[55]O.R.C. §9.31, as amended.

[56]*City of Newport News v. Doyle and Russell*, 211 Va. 603, 179 S.E.2d 493 (1971).

[57]Code of Virginia, §11–20.2.

Chapter **23**

Changes and Extras

WILLIAM B. SOMERVILLE, ESQ.
Partner, Smith, Somerville & Case, Baltimore, Maryland

HOWARD G. GOLDBERG, ESQ.
Partner, Smith, Somerville & Case, Baltimore, Maryland

THE AUTHORITY TO ORDER CHANGES AND EXTRAS

Few projects are completed with no changes or additions to the original contract documents. Changes or additions may vary in scope from the relocation of a single window or vent to a complete redesign of the entire project. Regardless of the magnitude of the change, a contractor who wishes to ensure that he will be paid for his additional labor or material must obtain proper authorization to do the additional work either from the owner or his duly authorized representative. Disputes over payment for changes and extras frequently arise in those instances where the owner has little or nothing to do with the project during the actual construction phase. This may occur because the owner relies upon an architect or engineer to visit the site to familiarize himself with the progress and quality of the work and to determine whether the work conforms to the requirements of the contract documents. To further ensure that the contractor completes the project, the owner may also require the contractor to provide performance and payment bonds. Having taken these precautions, many owners no longer maintain a direct line of communication to the general contractor. On a day-to-day basis, the contractor will consult with an architect, project manager, or other representative of the owner. It is possible for any one of these persons to suggest a change or addition. Having received a suggestion or direction to perform additional work from an architect or project manager, the contractor must determine whether the individual in question has authority to order changes or extras.

A principal is not bound by the act of another unless that person has *authority* to act on the principal's behalf. Such authority may be *express, implied,* or *apparent. Express* authority is that authority directly granted to or bestowed upon an employee or agent in specific terms. *Implied* authority embraces acts incidental to or necessary to accomplish the acts which the employee or agent is expressly authorized to perform. For example, assume XYZ Corporation, the owner of a contruction project, appoints John Jones as vice president in charge of construction. In the corporation's bylaws, the vice president in charge of construction has certain defined functions, one of which may be to authorize changes or extras in such projects. Such a provision would be construed as providing Jones with express authority to issue changes and extras; and his approval of a change order would be binding upon his principal, in this case XYZ Corporation. On the other hand, the corporation's bylaws may provide in more general terms that the vice president in charge of construction has authority over all aspects of construction. Under those circumstances, it is fair to conclude that one of the powers incidental to Jones' express authority is the implied authority to issue change orders, and Jones' approval of a change order or extra would bind the corporation.

Problems may arise when the employee or agent has neither express nor implied authority to approve change orders or extras but proceeds to do so anyway. Suppose Bill Smith, the corporate secretary of XYZ Corporation, authorizes a change order. It is likely that he has no express or implied authority to do so. Yet, he is a corporate officer and insofar as the contractor is concerned, he is a representative of the owner. In that case the issue is whether Smith has *apparent* authority to issue change orders and extras. Apparent authority arises when a principal has held out another as his agent and has induced a third person, by virtue of that holding out, to rely upon the apparent authority of the agent. Thus, if XYZ Corporation knowingly permits an officer or employee such as Smith to deal with a contractor in matters related to construction, and if the contractor reasonably relies on Smith's apparent authority in commencing work on a change-order item, the principal, XYZ Corporation, will be bound by the agreement entered into on its behalf by Smith.[1]

The same principles apply when the owner is a partnership. Under the Uniform Partnership Act, a general partner is an agent of the partnership with respect to all acts done or obligations undertaken within the scope of the partnership business. If the contractor is authorized by a general partner to

---

[1] Restatement (Second) of Agency §27 at 103 (1958).

perform additional work, and if the contractor is aware of no restriction on the partner's authority to enter into contracts on behalf of the partnership, he may safely assume that he has been authorized to perform the work and that he will be paid either a reasonable price for the work or the agreed price, if an agreement as to price exists.

What is the result when the owner has no officer or employee at the site and the change is ordered by the owner's architect or engineer or by a government inspector? Many unfortunate contractors simply assume that an architect has the authority to authorize changes and to legally obligate the owner to pay for an increase in the contract price. Consider, however, the rather typical case where the plaintiff subcontractor sued the owner to recover $1,200 for work done and materials provided in plastering certain beams in the defendant's office building.[2] The original plans and specifications for the work contained no requirement that the beams be plastered. During the course of construction the architect decided that the beams should be plastered. The architect instructed the subcontractor to proceed with the additional work, with the assurance that he would be paid. After the work was completed, the subcontractor forwarded a bill to the architect, who marked it "approved" and sent it to the owner. The owner refused to pay the additional cost, justifying his refusal on the ground that he had not authorized any increase in the contract price. The question presented to the Court of Appeals of Maryland was whether the architect, who was the owner's agent on a project, had implied or apparent authority to bind the owner to an increase in the contract price. The court held that even though the architect was the owner's agent for certain purposes, he had neither implied nor apparent authority to authorize changes or extras or to obligate the owner to pay for an increase in the construction price.

A similar situation might arise when the owner appoints a superintendent to monitor the progress of construction. Courts generally hold that a construction superintendent who is without express authority to issue change orders has no implied or apparent authority to do so. There may be a distinction when a government inspector advises the contractor that the manner in which the work is to be done would violate a governmental code and instructs the contractor to perform additional work. In such cases courts have reached different results. Some have permitted recovery on the theory that the owner had no choice but to authorize the extra work. Others have denied recovery unless the contractor receives express authorization from the owner.

This discussion regarding the authority of an architect, engineer, or building superintendent to issue change orders is based upon the assumption that the owner has not expressly granted that person the authority to do so. In cases where the architect or engineer has been *expressly* granted authority to authorize change orders or where the construction documents *require* the contractor to follow the instructions of the architect or engineer with respect to change orders, the contractor may proceed without further instruction. In this regard,

---

[2]*McNulty v. Keyser Office Bldg. Co.*, 112 Md. 638, 76 A. 1113 (1910).

AIA Document A201 provides that an architect may authorize a change order if he "has written authority [to do so] from the Owner."[3] In those instances, the contractor is entitled to obtain a copy of the written authorization, before relying upon the architect's assertion that such a document exists.

The fact that a particular change may be an "emergency" does not necessarily alter the legal principles set forth above. Courts have been more lenient in permitting a contractor who performs additional work under an emergency situation to recover his out-of-pocket costs. In those cases, recovery is predicated upon the principle of *unjust enrichment,* an equitable doctrine which provides that one person should not receive a windfall profit at the expense of another. The contractor should be aware that it will be his burden to prove that an emergency existed and that his recoverable damages will be limited to the amount of unjust enrichment (i.e., the increase in value of the building or the amount of loss mitigated by the emergency action) and will not include his own costs, such as profit or overhead.

The only defined exception to these principles is in the area of so-called *minor changes.* Minor changes are those which have no effect upon the contract price. Many form contracts (including AIA Document A201) state that the architect has authority to order minor changes which do not involve an adjustment in the contract sum or an extension of the contract time.[4] Changes made pursuant to that provision are binding on the owner; however, out of an abundance of caution, most architects advise the owner immediately of such changes.

Although the question of the authority to issue a change order is initially a matter of concern to the contractor (who understandably wishes to be paid for his extra work), it is similarly a matter of concern to the architect, engineer, or project superintendent, who may have exceeded his authority by issuing the change order. Consider the facts of the *McNulty* case, where the architect instructed the subcontractor to proceed with the assurance that he would be paid.[5] If, as in *McNulty,* the architect did not have express authority to make such a commitment, the subcontractor (who was unsuccessful in his suit against the owner) would have a proper claim directly against the architect, on the theory that the architect had breached his implied promise that he had such authority.

THE REQUIREMENT OF A WRITTEN ORDER AND OTHER PROBLEMS

Unless otherwise specified in the construction documents, there is nothing to prevent the parties from orally contracting for changes or extras. This does not mean that the parties will be bound by oral changes in the contract documents made *before* execution of those contract documents. Once the initial contract

---

[3]American Institute of Architects *Architect's Handbook of Professional Practice,* "General Conditions of the Contract for Construction" (AIA Document A201, §12.1.2, 12th ed., 1970).

[4]A.I.A. Document A201, §12.3.

[5]*McNulty v. Keyser Office Bldg. Co., supra* note 2.

documents are executed, all previous agreements and understandings are merged into the written agreement, and any previous oral agreement which varies the terms of the written agreement is unenforceable. That rule (commonly referred to as the *parol evidence rule*) does not, however, prohibit the parties from entering into enforceable oral agreements which vary the terms of a written contract *after* execution of the original contract, as long as the construction documents do not require such changes or extras to be made in writing.

Most construction contracts have a standard provision requiring written change orders to evidence both changes and extras. Usually the construction documents require written change orders to be signed by the owner, the contractor, and by the design professional. Typical is the provision[6] in AIA Document A201, which provides as follows:

> 12.1   Change Orders
>
> 12.1.1   The Owner, without invalidating the Contract, may order Changes in the Work within the general scope of the Contract consisting of additions, deletions or other revisions, the Contract Sum and the Contract Time being adjusted accordingly. All such Changes in the Work shall be authorized by Change Order, and shall be executed under the applicable conditions of the Contract Documents.
>
> 12.1.2   A Change Order is a written order to the Contractor signed by the Owner and the Architect, issued after the execution of the Contract, authorizing a Change in the Work or an adjustment in the Contract Sum or the Contract Time. Alternatively, the Change Order may be signed by the Architect alone, provided he has written authority from the Owner for such procedure and that a copy of such written authority is furnished to the Contractor upon request. A Change Order may also be signed by the Contractor if he agrees to the adjustment in the Contract Sum or the Contract Time. The Contract Sum and the Contract Time may be changed only by Change Order.

In providing that the "Change Order may be signed by the Architect alone, provided that he has written authority from the Owner," the AIA recognized the general rule that without express authorization, an architect has no implied authority to authorize changes or extras.

It is noteworthy that the AIA form refers to "additions, deletions or other revisions." This phrase is intended to encompass changes as well as extras. In the absence of a specific reference to additions or extras, some courts have interpreted such clauses as requiring a writing only in cases of a change and not in cases of an extra. A change is defined as an alteration to an existing contract requirement concerning work which is already required to be done. An extra, on the other hand, is an addition to the contract involving work which had not been included in the original agreement. For example, if owner and builder entered into a contract to build a house and an adjoining well, a subsequent agreement to dig the well five feet deeper would involve a *change,* while an agreement to build a second well would be considered an *extra.* An agreement

---

[6]American Institute of Architects *Architect's Handbook of Professional Practice,* "General Conditions of the Contract for Construction" (AIA Document A201, 12th ed., 1970).

to relocate the dining room windows would be a change, while an agreement to include an additional window would be an extra. The person responsible for drafting the written change-order provision must thus carefully define whether extras as well as changes are included within the scope of the requirement.

There is also a second potential problem in distinguishing changes from extras. In order for any contract to be enforceable, it must be supported by legal consideration. This means that each party to the contract must receive something of value in exchange for his performance of the agreement. Courts hold that a promise to perform work which the promisor is already obligated to perform is not sufficient legal consideration. For example, if the contractor and owner agreed to relocate a window, and if there were no additional cost associated with the relocation work, an agreement to pay a sum of money over and above the contract price might well be unenforceable. Since that result is predicated on the assumption that no additional cost is associated with the change, the contractor who expects additional compensation should compile evidence of additional costs associated with the change. Since by definition an extra is not contemplated in the original contract documents, its performance is always sufficient legal consideration for a promise to pay a specified amount of money. For this reason, questions relating to the adequacy of consideration for performance of an extra rarely arise.

When the contract requires orders for both changes and extras to be in writing, the contractor must determine what type of writing will suffice. Disputes may arise as to whether a document or series of documents constitute a written change order. For example, the architect may forward information regarding his redesign of a portion of the work. If his instructions are provided by letter, there is a danger that the contractor will claim at some later date that the letter constituted a change in the construction contract. Under AIA Document A201, the contractor must provide written notice to the owner of his intention to claim an extra before considering such a letter to be a change order. Without such a provision confusion may well result unless the architect specifies that his instructions or letter does or does not constitute a change order. This question also arises when the contractor receives revised plans or specifications from the architect. There is some judicial support for the proposition that revised plans or drawings constitute a sufficient writing to satisfy the requirements of a written change order. The prudent contractor or subcontractor, however, should require a written change order in addition to revised plans.

When the contract documents require changes and extras to be in writing, courts generally hold that a contractor who fails to obtain a written change order prior to performing changes or extras will not be paid for that work. The customary change-order clause contemplates that written orders will be submitted prior to commencement of work on the new items. Some courts have refused to permit the contractor to recover in instances where he had not received the change order before commencing work.[7] In other instances,

[7]*Johnson v. Norcross Bros.*, 209 Mass. 445, 95 N.E. 833 (1911); *Hunt v. Owen Building & Investment Co.*, 219 S.W. 138 (Mo.App. 1920).

however, evidence that a written order was presented to the contractor after work was commenced, coupled with evidence that it had been the custom for changes or extras to be authorized orally and then confirmed by written change order, has been held sufficient to permit recovery.[8] This latter approach is more compatible with the obvious purpose underlying the written change-order requirement, since it is customarily inserted to provide all parties, and particularly the owner, with reliable evidence of the terms (including the cost term) of the change order or extra. The prudent contractor, however, will require the change order *before* he begins work to eliminate any possibility of confusion.

Frequently a problem arises in instances when an oral request for a change or extra is accompanied by an express oral promise to pay for the additional work but where no written change order is prepared either before or after work begins. In those cases in which the owner orally requests, directs, authorizes, or consents to the changes or extras with an express promise to pay sums over and above the contract price, courts generally hold that the contractor may recover, regardless of the existence of a clause in the contract documents requiring changes to be in writing.[9] The underlying theory is that the oral agreement is an amendment to the contract and that any contract regardless of its terms may be amended orally. While courts examine alleged oral agreements rather closely to ensure that an agreement did exist (and to prevent one party from fabricating an agreement without the other's consent), they will uphold such agreements.

Other difficulties arise where the extra work is requested, directed, or authorized by the owner with no written change order and no express agreement to pay additional monies. In some instances, courts have viewed the absence of an express promise to pay as raising an inference that the additional work was to be performed at no additional charge.[10] Other courts, however, have permitted recovery under the theory that a direction to perform work includes an implied promise to pay the additional cost of that work.[11] Such cases are stronger where the contractor can produce evidence that during the course of the work he placed the owner on notice that he expected additional monies. Such evidence may consist of periodic bills having been presented to the owner, price quotations having been forwarded to the owner, or the contractor having orally advised the owner that the item would constitute an extra. If the owner makes it clear when the work is ordered that he considers it to be included within the original contract, the contractor will normally not recover.

Finally, there is the situation in which no written change order is issued, no authorized agent of the owner directs the work to proceed, no express promise

---

[8]*Halvorson v. United States,* 126 F.Supp. 898 (D.Wash. 1954); *Crisp Co. v. S. J. Groves & Sons,* 73 F.2d 327 (5th Cir. 1934).

[9]*Sam Macri & Sons v. United States,* 313 F.2d 119 (9th Cir. 1963); *Universal Builders, Inc. v. Moon Motor Lodge, Inc.,* 430 Pa. 550 244 A.2d 10 (1968); *See also* 2 A.L.R.3d 620 §25 at 674 (1965).

[10]*Abbott v. Gatch,* 13 Md. 314 (1859); *James Reilly Repair & Supply Co. v. Smith,* 177 F. 168 (2d Cir. 1910); *Lundstrom Const. Co. v. Dygert,* 94 N.W. 2d 527 (Minn. 1959).

[11]*HiValley Constructors, Inc. v. Heyser,* 428 P.2d 354 (Colo. 1967); *C. F. Bolster Co. v. J. C. Boespflug Const. Co.,* 330 P.2d 831 (Cal.App. 1958).

to pay is made by the owner, but changes or extras are performed by the contractor with the knowledge of the owner, who makes no objection. Again the authorities are split, but many courts have permitted the contractor to recover either on the premise that the owner must have known while the work was progressing that the contractor expected payment on the theory that an owner may not equitably accept the benefits of the work and refuse to pay, especially where he stood by and failed to object.[12]

The prudent contractor will thus refuse to perform any change or extra until he receives a written order in the form specified by the construction documents. If the owner refuses to provide a written order, the contractor should consider simply refusing to perform the additional work. This holds true even if the failure to perform the additional work delays the progress of the entire job. In one reported case a tenacious contractor refused to perform any work for five full months, justifying his refusal on the owner's failure to provide a written change order for work in the critical path of the progress of the job.[13] The court there not only held that the contractor was entitled to stop work but also that he was entitled to consequential damages incurred by reason of the delay. Another alternative (remembering the architect's argument that the alleged extra is within the scope of the contract) is to perform the work under protest and seek early arbitration or adjudication.

PAYMENT FOR CHANGES AND EXTRAS

In the majority of cases the owner and contractor are able to agree on a lump-sum price for the additional work to be performed as a result of a change or extra. In other cases, the owner and contractor may prefer to have the work performed on a time and material basis, which customarily includes a fixed-percentage allowance for profit and overhead. If the owner and contractor fail to agree on a method by which the cost of a change or extra will be determined, they must look to the method prescribed in the contract documents. Normally, the contract documents not only require the contractor to perform the additional work immediately upon receipt of the change order but also set forth a formula for payment, which is similar, if not identical, to a time and materials contract. Paragraph 12.1.4 of AIA Document A201 is typical.[14]

> 12.1.4   If none of the methods set forth in Subparagraph 12.1.3 is agreed upon, the Contractor, provided he receives a Change Order, shall promptly proceed with the Work involved. The cost of such Work shall then be determined by the Architect on the basis of the Contractor's reasonable expenditures and savings, including, in the case of an increase in the Contract Sum, a reasonable allowance for overhead and profit. In such case, and also under Clause 12.1.3.3 above, the Contractor shall keep and present, in such form as the Architect may prescribe, an

---

[12]*Harrington v. McCarthy,* 420 P.2d 790 (Idaho, 1966).
[13]*Mayor & City Council of Baltimore v. Clark,* 128 Md. 291, 97 A. 911 (1916).
[14]American Institute of Architects, *Architect's Handbook of Professional Practice,* "General Conditions of the Contract for Construction" (AIA Document A201, 12th ed., 1970).

itemized accounting together with appropriate supporting data. Pending final determination of cost to the Owner, payments on account shall be made on the Architect's Certificate for Payment. The amount of credit to be allowed by the Contractor to the Owner for any deletion or change which results in a net decrease in cost will be the amount of the actual net decrease as confirmed by the Architect. When both additions and credits are involved in any one change, the allowance for overhead and profit shall be figured on the basis of net increase, if any.

As long as the quantities of material required for the change do not greatly exceed the quantities required for the base contract, unit prices will apply. AIA Document A201 provides [in ¶12.1.5] that unit prices apply where no hardship to the contractor is created. Many government contracts provide that unit prices apply as long as the quantities do not exceed a specified percentage (usually 25 percent) of the quantities specified in the base contract.

From the owner's point of view, there is one substantial problem in requiring a reluctant or hostile contractor to proceed in this manner. In *force-account* situations, the owner or his representative must use special care to ensure that he is not being charged for materials or labor which are actually being utilized on base-contract work. Many times it is difficult for even a trained inspector to separate change-order items from base-contract work and such a situation is ripe for contractor abuse. Many times contractors are able to use this concern on the part of the owner to their benefit by negotiating a favorable fixed price agreement for change-order items.

THE SURETY AND THE CHANGE ORDER[15]

Performance and payment bonds are commonplace in most construction projects. They are statutorily required on practically all state and federal public works projects. In the area of private work, payment and performance bonds are required by the prudent owner to protect against mechanics' liens and to ensure performance of the work. Unfortunately, most contractors and owners seem to think that the only communication with the surety need take place either when the bond is written or when a claim is filed. They forget that a surety bond is not an insurance policy and that although most bonds are written by insurance companies, the obligee may well owe substantially different obligations to the surety than an insured owes to an insurer under a policy of public liability insurance. Nowhere is this more true than in the area of change orders and their effect on the surety's obligation.

A surety bond creates a contractual relationship whereby one party, the surety, agrees to be answerable for the debt, default, or miscarriage of another (known as the principal). In the context of a construction project, the owner and contractor must consider that any change in the scope or nature of the debt for which the surety is answerable may release the surety in whole or in part from his contractual obligation. Before a surety agrees to guarantee the princi-

[15]For more detailed and technical treatment *see: The Forum,* vol. X, no. 1, Fall 1974, at 1 through 74.

pal's performance, it undertakes an extensive investigation into the principal's background and financial stability. It investigates its principal's (i.e., contractor's) background to determine that he is capable, financially and otherwise, of completing his contractual undertakings. More often than not, the surety will require the individuals involved to sign personal indemnity agreements, by which they personally agree to indemnify the surety in the event of a default on the part of the principal. This concern about the principal's financial capability relates directly to the effect of a change order on the surety's undertaking.

Assume that the ABC Corporation is a general contractor engaged in constructing office buildings. In January 1970 ABC contracts to construct three buildings. Each contract is in the amount of $5 million, and each requires the contractor to file a performance bond. Customarily, ABC Corporation obtains its bonds from Helpful Surety Company. Helpful has investigated ABC's business and financial capability and has decided that ABC Corporation cannot safely perform more than $20 million of work. ABC Corporation bids on a fourth job which involves construction of another $5-million building. Since a performance bond is required, ABC requests that Helpful Surety issue a bond for the additional $5 million. Because it has made an investigation into ABC's capability and has concluded that the contractor has the financial capability to perform $20-million worth of work, Helpful Surety agrees to issue the additional bond.

Once construction begins, the owner of the last project decides to expand the project from a 10-story building to a 20-story building. The architect prepares a written change order, and the owner and ABC subsequently agree on a $4-million increase in the contract price. ABC thus becomes obligated to perform a $9-million contract instead of the original $5-million contract. Neither ABC nor the owner obtains the written approval of surety. The additional work obviously extends the principal's financial obligations beyond what the surety agreed to guarantee. If ABC defaults on the last project, the owner will probably find that Helpful refuses to acknowledge any responsibility under its performance bond. In such situations, courts hold that where a creditor (i.e., principal-contractor) enters into an agreement with a principal debtor (i.e., obligee-owner) whereby the contract between the creditor and the principal debtor is materially varied or changed without the consent of the surety, the surety is discharged from his obligation.[16] The underlying theory is that the contractor and owner should not be able to unilaterally require a surety to guarantee an obligation which it never voluntarily agreed to assume. The extent to which the surety is discharged varies with the cases and the jurisdiction. On some facts, a complete discharge is possible, but clearly the trend in the cases is in the direction of a discharge *pro tanto* (i.e., only to the extent of the change) and only if the change has clearly prejudiced the surety.

Not every change involving an increase in the contract price will release the surety. The result in any particular case depends on whether the change or

---

[16]*State v. Preferred Accident Ins. Co. of New York*, 149 So. 2d 632 (1963).

extra constitutes a *material change* in the contract.[17] If a material change results, then the surety will be relieved from liability in whole or in part. On the other hand, if the change is not material or is within the limits prescribed by the bond, the surety will not escape responsibility. For example, if ABC and the owner of the first project had agreed to relocate the utility room in one building, with only a minor increase in the contract price, it is probable that a court would not hold the change to be material. On the other hand, the addition of 10 stories to the building with a $4-million increase in the contract price would be considered a material change. Extensions of time to complete the work or extensions of credit by the owner may also constitute material changes so as to release the surety.

Some sureties attempt to define those changes which will be considered material by the terms of their bond. One bond form[18] provides:

> The prior written approval of surety shall be required with regard to any changes or alterations in said contract where the cost thereof, added to prior changes or alterations, causes the aggregate cost of all changes or alterations to exceed 10% of the original contract price.

Under this form, the surety need only be advised of changes or extras when they total 10 percent of the contract price. It is good practice, however, for the owner to advise the surety of any changes in the contract which involve an increase in the contract price or an extension of time.

Perhaps the single, most important thread running through this or any other discussion of change orders and extras is the significance of careful draftsmanship of a provision relating to changes and extras in the contract documents. Neither the contractor nor the owner can afford to ignore those provisions during the course of construction, and it is important for both parties to maintain a direct line of communication throughout the construction phase.

---

[17] *State v. Preferred Accident Ins. Co. of New York, supra,* note 16.
[18] *Federal Housing Administration,* FHA Form 2452, revised January 1968, Washington, D.C.

Chapter 24

Changed Conditions

MICHAEL S. SIMON, ESQ.
New York, New York

One of the most often misconceived and misalleged construction contract claims relates to the general area categorized as *changed conditions.* In fact, the words "changed conditions" could justly be classified as words of art. More often than not, no specific contract clause is entitled Changed Conditions. This is normally true even when a contractual right to entitlement exists.

NO IMPLIED RIGHTS

It must be emphasized and reemphasized that there is no implied right to file a changed conditions claim. Too often the contractor misapplies the construction contract claim theory of changed conditions by arguing that an automatic implied right exists in every contract entitling it to compensation when conditions are encountered other than that which it unilaterally anticipated. A changed conditions claim is a creation of a contract, and *exists only when so provided in the actual contract documents.* No implied contractual right exists to collect for unforeseen conditions; collection is only pursuant to an expressed contractual right. The United States Supreme Court[1] has stated:

> The general rules of law applicable to these facts are well settled. Where one agrees to do, for a fixed sum, a thing possible to be performed, he will not be excused or become entitled to additional compensation because unforeseen difficulties are encountered. . . . Thus, one who undertakes to erect a structure upon a particular site assumes ordinarily the risk of subsidence of the soil.

Either a contract clause exists or the contractor must assume the unforeseen conditions and bear all attendant additional costs.

CONTRACT CLAUSES

Contract clauses are the basis for the changed conditions claims. Each claim is dependent upon the exact wording of the specific contract clause.

A proper changed conditions claim under one contract clause might not be proper under a differently worded clause in another contract. The extent of each claim, the procedure to be followed, and the eventual outcome depend on the contract documents.

Since the rights for changed conditions claims arise through the contract, the contract clauses must be carefully scrutinized. Two typical, but differing, changed condition clauses are commonly encountered. The first is found in the American Institute of Architects' General Conditions Form A201 (1970), Article 12.1.6.[2] Article 12.1.6 is not entitled Changed Conditions; it is part of the change orders subarticle but is the contractual basis for a changed conditions claim. It provides:

> Should concealed conditions encountered in the performance of the Work below the surface of the ground be at variance with the conditions indicated by the Contract Documents or should unknown physical conditions below the surface of the ground of an unusual nature, differing materially from those ordinarily encountered and generally recognized as inherent in work of the character provided for in this Contract, be encountered, the Contract Sum shall be equitably adjusted by Change Order upon claim by either party made within twenty days after the first observance of the conditions.

The second typical changed condition clause is found in the Armed Services Procurement Regulations which provide for a changed conditions claim under

---

[1]*United States v. Spearin,* 248 U.S. 132, 135-6 (1918). *See also: J. A. Thompson & Son, Inc. v. State of Hawaii,* 465 P.2d 148, at 155 (1970): "The State should not be placed in a position of encouraging careless bids by contractors who might anticipate that should conditions differ from optimistic expectations reflected in the bids, the State would bear the costs of the bidder's error."

[2]It is noted that AIA Document A201 has been revised and issued as the Thirteenth Edition (1976). Article 12.2 is entitled "Concealed Conditions" and changes the scope of the changed conditions coverage. However, the majority of existing contracts either incorporate the 1970 edition or are patterned after it. The reader must carefully check to see which edition is included as part of its contract or which edition its particular contract words are more similar to.

and pursuant to the contract clause entitled Differing Site Conditions. The wording of this clause, although similar in many respects to the quoted American Institute of Architect clause, provides for the filing of claims in different situations. The Differing Site Conditions contract clause,[3] 1968 edition, found in federal standard construction contract form is probably the model clause most often followed, when a clause is utilized, in contract forms. It provides:

(a) The Contractor shall promptly, and before such conditions are disturbed, notify the Contracting Officer in writing of: (1) subsurface or latent physical conditions at the site differing materially from those indicated in this contract, or (2) unknown physical conditions at the site, of an unusual nature, differing materially from those ordinarily encountered and generally recognized as inhering in work of the character provided for in this contract. The Contracting Officer shall promptly investigate the conditions, and if he finds that such conditions do materially so differ and cause an increase or decrease in the Contractor's cost of, or the time required for, performance of any part of the work under this contract, whether or not changed as a result of such conditions, an equitable adjustment shall be made and the contract modified in writing accordingly.

(b) No claim of the Contractor under this clause shall be allowed unless the Contractor has given the notice required in (a) above; *provided,* however, the time prescribed therefor may be extended by the Government.

(c) No claim by the Contractor for an equitable adjustment hereunder shall be allowed if asserted after final payment under the contract.

The importance of a careful analysis of the particular changed conditions clause in the particular contract in question is best exemplified by the drastic differences in the AIA and the federal changed conditions clauses. Although they appear to be similar to each other, in many instances entitlement might exist under the federal form but not the AIA form. The AIA form specifically covers conditions "below the surface of the ground." This is a limitation which does not exist in the federal form. The federal form talks about subsurface conditions as well as latent or unknown "physical conditions at the site." These physical conditions at the site apparently are not limited to those conditions encountered below the surface of the ground. The federal form, as well as forms similar to it, would apparently include, as part of the changed conditions claim, problems arising under contracts to existing buildings.[4] Whereas, quagmire or surface water conditions might be recognized as justifiable claims under the federal form,[5] they would face a stiffer fight under the AIA form. The argument for entitlement under the AIA form would be faced with the initial problem of proving how that surface water problem and unknown physical condition actually is the effect of a cause which could justly be deemed "concealed conditions encountered . . . below the surface of the ground."

---

[3]A.S.P.R. 7-602.4.

[4]*Pritz Associates,* VACAB No. 521, 66-1 BCA 5402 (1966); and *Transco Contracting Co.,* VACAB 921, 933, 71-2 BCA 9129 (1971).

[5]*Phillips Constr. Co. v. United States,* 394 F.2d 834 (1968).

CHANGED CONDITION CLAUSE RATIONALE

The rationale and reasoning for the insertion of such clauses in contracts has often created bitter disputes. Many owners have argued that by inserting such clauses they are only creating potential additional liability on their part. However, the insertion of a changed conditions clause is truly equitable and fair to both parties to the construction contract. By inserting such a clause, the contractor is no longer forced to put contingencies into its bid price in case unanticipated differing conditions are encountered. The contractor can bid on the information furnished to it; speculation is reduced. If drastically different conditions are encountered, the contractor will obviously lose money even when it includes some form of contingency. A bankrupt contractor is surely not to the owner's benefit. If no differing conditions are encountered, the contractor is the recipient of a windfall contingency. Obviously, in reverse, by inserting a changed condition clause, the owner eliminates the contingency factor resulting in lower bids. When a true changed condition is encountered, the owner is obligated to pay only that sum which is equitable. A properly written changed condition clause has been deemed to be for the benefit of both parties and not exculpatory.[6]

NOTICE OF CHANGED CONDITION

Although the scope and application of the changed conditions clauses vary from contract to contract, one essential ingredient seems to be similar, that is, *notice.* Most contracts specifically provide, either in the changed conditions clause itself or in a related clause, that before any claim will be recognized, the contractor must comply with the notice provisions, either actually or constructively. Specifically, the contractor is obligated to notify the owner of the changed condition prior to disturbing the conditions and/or execution of the work. Numerous cases have held that constructive and/or oral notice (less than the formal written contractual notice) was sufficient, especially where the owner has not been prejudiced.[7] However, the exceptions to the rule should not be relied upon as being sufficient notice: it is sound practice to give the formal written notice required by contract to protect one's claim. The failure to give proper notice could defeat an otherwise proper changed conditions claim.[8] The purpose for such notice is not only to permit the owner to verify the conditions,

---

[6]*James Julian, Inc. v. President & Commrs. of Town of Elkton,* 341 F.2d 205 (1965).

[7]*McCloskey & Co. and C. H. Leavell & Co.,* PSBCA No. 497, 74-1 BCA 10,479 (1974); and *M. M. Sundt Constr. Co.,* ASBCA No. 17475, 74-1 BCA 10,627 (1974).

[8]*Maverick Diversified, Inc.,* NASA BCA No. 874-19, 75-1 BCA 11,081 (1974). In a recent case the Supreme Court of Alaska went further to hold that a contractor was liable for damages since it was "required to bring his expertise into play" and, "therefore, we hold that this duty to inform the owner, regardless of his personal expertise, of potential defects in his project which come to the contractor's knowledge or should come to his knowledge is an essential element of performing any contract in a workmanlike manner according to acceptable standards." *J. R. Lewis v. Anchorage Asphalt Paving Co.,* 535 P.2d 1188 (1975).

but to also permit the owner to have the option to either have the contractor proceed with the work and pay for a changed condition, or to redesign that portion of the work so as to avoid or reduce the effect of the changed condition. The incurring of a changed condition can work to the owner's benefit by actually reducing job costs. The benefits are mutual, and its inclusion should be seriously weighed.

ACTUAL VERSUS REPRESENTED CONDITIONS (BREACH OF CONTRACT)

The changed conditions clauses as referenced above categorize two basic forms of claim. The first form of claim is when actual conditions "differ materially" or "are at variance" with the conditions indicated in the contract. In this instance, the AIA contract form seems more lenient than the federal form as there seems to be more leeway with the words "be at variance" than with "differing materially." Although the rights and results must depend upon the specific wording of the particular contract clause in question, the question of burden of proof is very important and could determine the final outcome.

Essentially what the clauses create are contractual rights to recover for what would otherwise be deemed a breach of contract. If, in fact, no changed conditions clause existed, and the actual conditions encountered did differ materially from those indicated by the contract documents, the contractor would have the basis for filing a claim for breach of contract.[9] The clause thus establishes a *contractual right* to recover in lieu of a right arising outside of the contract through a breach of contract lawsuit. However, the right of recovery is not as easy or simplistic as it appears by the face of the contract language.

The general starting point and principle of law is that an owner impliedly warrants the adequacy of its own contract documents, "if the contractor is bound to build according to plans and specifications prepared by the owner, the contractor will not be responsible for the consequences of defects in the plans and specifications."[10] The Court went on to state that "the insertion of the articles prescribing the character, dimensions, and location of the sewer imported a warranty that if the specifications were complied with, the sewer would be adequate."[11]

This leads to the next step of determining what, legally and factually, the contract says. There has been substantial litigation as to whether or not conditions are indicated or represented by the contract. The represented conditions are the basis against which the courts and arbitrators determine whether actual conditions are at variance or differ materially therewith. The parties must review the *entire* contract in order to determine what is legally represented by the contract. In other words, the question is: What does the contract state?

---

[9]*Hollerbach v. United States,* 233 U.S. 165 (1914).

[10]*United States v. Spearin, supra* note 1, at 136.

[11]*United States v. Spearin, supra* note 1, at 137. *See, Hol-Gar Mfg. Corp. v. United States,* 360 F.2d 634 (1966); *Drummond v. Hughes,* 104 Atl. 137 (1918); and 6 ALR3d 1394.

Before a claim of breach of contract for misrepresentation or claim for changed condition can be asserted under this part of the clause, the contractor must prove that positive and affirmative statements were made in the contract, that it relied on these facts, that its reliance was justified, and that the representations were not correct.[12]

> A government contract should be interpreted as are contracts between individuals, with a view to ascertaining the intention of the parties and to give it effect accordingly, if that can be done consistently with the terms of the instrument. . . . The specifications spoke with certainty as to a part of the conditions to be encountered by the claimants. . . . The specifications assured them of the character of the material,—a matter concerning which the government might be presumed to speak with knowledge and authority. We think this positive statement of the specifications must be taken as true and binding upon the government, and that upon it, rather than upon the claimants, must fall the loss resulting from such mistaken representations. We think it would be going quite too far to interpret the general language of the other paragraphs as requiring independent investigation of facts which the specifications furnished by the government as a basis of the contract left in no doubt. If the government wished to leave the matter open to the independent investigation of the claimants, it might easily have omitted the specification as to the character. . . . In its positive assertion of the nature of this much of the work it made a representation upon which the claimants had a right to rely without an investigation to prove its falsity.

However, if it is found that the contractual statements were neither "positive," "mandatory," nor "affirmative," or that they were merely "suggestive," then the Court is apt to conclude that the contractor could not justifiably rely on them. When the basis for reliance is removed, then the alleged breach is also removed, along with right for recovery.[13]

It must be noted that when one talks of "misrepresented" conditions, the contractor need not prove or even infer any evil intent or fraud on the owner's part. Fraud and misrepresentation differ. In the United States Supreme Court decision of *Christie v. United States*,[14] the Court specifically found that the evidence did not show anything other than an honest intent by the owner's engineer. However, the Court concluded that "it makes no difference to the legal aspects of the case that the omissions from the records of the results of the borings did not have sinister purpose. There were representations made which were relied upon by claimants, and properly relied upon by them, as they were positive."

When the contractor is able to prove that it justifiably relied upon certain positive representations in the contract documents, and that the actual conditions encountered were at "variance" or "materially differed," then a changed conditions claim exists.

---

[12]*Hollerbach v. United States, supra* note 8, at 171–172.

[13]*Wunderlich v. State*, 56 Cal. Rptr. 473, 423 P.2d 545 (1967); and, *Burgess Mining & Constr. Corp. v. City of Bessemer*, 312 So.2d 24 at 27 (1975).

[14]*George B. Christie v. United States*, 237 U.S. 234 (1915).

UNANTICIPATED CONDITIONS

The second form of changed conditions claim does not have an alternative remedy such as breach of contract, but is one that exists strictly by virtue of contract. The contractor need not prove that actual conditions differed from those indicated in the contract. The basis for this claim is not solely founded upon what is indicated in the contract, rather, the basis for the claim is premised on the difference between what the contractor should have reasonably anticipated to encounter on the particular contract as against what the contractor actually did encounter in the actual work and on the site. As stated by the contract changed conditions clause, a contractor must be able to prove the existence of unknown physical conditions (which by the very fact assumes that the contract does not state that such physical conditions will exist) of an *unusual* nature, which differ *materially* from those *ordinarily* encountered and generally recognized as inherent in the work in the particular contract. No breach of contract elements need be proven.

SITE INVESTIGATION AND DISCLAIMERS

Prior to the establishment of any claim or entitlement, the contractor must be able to prove that it could not have reasonably anticipated the actual conditions as encountered. In order to establish this conclusion, the contractor's obligations to inspect the site must be reviewed. The question is thus raised as to what were the contractor's legal and contractual obligations to investigate the site, conduct tests, review boring logs and samples, and in all other respects become totally conversant with all site and physical conditions. Inherent in this obligation is the fact that if a reasonable site inspection would have revealed the physical condition, it could not constitute an unknown or unusual condition, and thereby could not constitute the basis for a changed conditions claim.[15]

The obligation to inspect and investigate the site is normally one imposed by contract. The "Site Investigation" clause normally considered concurrently with the federal changed conditions clause is found in ASPR § 7-602.33, and provides:

> The Contractor acknowledges that he has investigated and satisfied himself as to the conditions affecting the work, including but not restricted to those bearing upon transportation, disposal, handling and storage of materials, availability of labor, water, electric power, roads and uncertainties of weather, river stages, tides or similar physical conditions at the site, the conformation and conditions of the ground, the character of equipment and facilities needed preliminary to and during prosecution of the work. The Contractor further acknowledges that he has satisfied himself as to the character, quality and quantity of surface and subsurface materials or obstacles to be encountered in so far as this information is reasonably ascertainable from an inspection of the site, including all exploratory work done by

---

[15]*F. H. Antrim Constr. Co.* AGBCA No. 307, 72-2 BCA 9475; and, *Utilities Contracting Co.,* ASBCA 13,261, 69-2 BCA 7932 (1969).

the Government, as well as from information presented by the drawings and specifications made a part of this contract. Any failure by the Contractor to acquaint himself with the available information will not relieve him from responsibility for estimating properly the difficulty or cost of successfully performing the work. The Government assumes no responsibility for any conclusions or interpretations made by the Contractor on the basis of the information made available by the Government.

This type of site investigation clause is similar to most clauses found in long-form contracts. The federal government clause might even be deemed reasonable and equitable in light of some of the horrendous exculpatory clauses placed into contracts by various owners.

The owner and its representatives must be forewarned that their general disclaimers and exculpatory clauses denying liability and responsibility for actual conditions which differ materially from that which they indicate in the contract, do not have the automatic force and effect as the words themselves express. This validity is enhanced when the contractual statements are not positive representations but are rather statements of possibilities or probabilities or where the contractor is not justified in relying on such representations.[16] On the other hand, disclaimer clauses have been denied force or effect when they are too strict, against public interest, or are in direct contradiction with specific representations.[17]

When a clause such as the federal site investigation clause exists, a contractor is legally bound and responsible to perform a reasonable site inspection. If such investigation would have divulged the existence of a physical condition which is not specifically referenced in the contract, then such condition would neither be unforeseen, nor unknown physical condition, nor of an unusual nature, and therefore no changed condition would exist. The real issue is: if the contractor is obligated to perform a site investigation, it is held to the responsibility of conducting a proper and reasonable inspection and discovering all facts encompassed in such reasonable inspection, whether in fact they were discovered or not.[18]

The site inspection and related clauses which attempt to totally deny any liability for the information furnished either in the contract or other annexed documents, are not looked upon favorably by the courts. In determining the applicability of such clauses the court also looks to the duration of time from the date the contractor received the bid package to the schedule bid date. Often

---

[16]*J. A. Thompson & Son v. State of Hawaii, supra* note 1; *Wunderlich v. State, supra* note 12.

[17]*United States v. Spearin, supra* note 1. It is to be noted that even where the disclaimer clauses have been given some effect, the Courts clearly indicated a lack of any wrongdoing on the owner's part. As stated in the *Thompson* case; *supra* note 1, at 154 and 155: "Here, the State correctly stated on the plans the results of the test boring. All the information in the State's possession was made available to the plaintiff. The State had no superior knowledge of the subsurface conditions, its knowledge or information having been derived from the boring of Hole No. 6. . . . We recognize that the State of Hawaii should be held liable for breach of warranty when its agency represents as a fact what in fact does not exist and the claimant acts in reliance on the representation and is damaged thereby."

[18]*J. R. Lewis v. Anchorage Asphalt Paving Co., supra* note 7.

such time is so limited as to preclude independent site investigations to the depth allegedly demanded by the bid documents, and thus many site investigation demands are nullified by the courts. Where such time has been limited in scope, courts have denied the strict enforcement of the disclaimer provisions of site investigation clauses.[19]

The rationale for these decisions is clearly established in an early New York case[20] wherein the court stated:

> It would be wholly inequitable to hold that under such circumstances where the contractor had no reasonable opportunity of discovering the truth, and where the other party had made the examination and asked for bids upon plans showing the results of such examination, the latter can be heard to say that it is not responsible, should those plans wholly misrepresent the fact.

In a recent United States Court of Appeals decision the court was faced with a factual situation which often exists. The owner let two contracts for various aspects of the work. At the time of letting the second contract, Phase II, the preliminary earth work, Phase I contract, had not been completed by the preceding contractor. The Phase II contractor assumed that the condition it would find the site in when it commenced its Phase II work would be in accord with the Phase I specifications. In upholding the district court's decision granting the contractor its claim on the basis of a changed conditions clause and breach of an implied warranty, the court[21] held:

> At the time Moorhead bid on the Phase II contract, the Phase I earth work had just commenced. Because an inspection of the site by Moorhead would not then have disclosed the difficult site conditions which it would later face due to excess moisture and lack of compaction, Moorhead in estimating its bid necessarily relied upon the City to provide a construction site prepared in accord with the specifications of Phase I. Those specifications, according to the District Court called . . . for 90% compaction of the soil embankments and cell bottoms. The Court construed the Phase I compaction specifications as implied warranties in the Phase II contract. . . . The District Court properly found liability predicated on changed conditions and breach of implied warranty as to site preparations in accordance with Phase I specifications.

Thus, the establishment of a changed condition claim under the second approach is not predicated upon representations in the contract, as it is usually assumed that the contract has not misrepresented the true facts. Rather, the claim is based on encountering unusual unanticipated conditions as set forth in the contract clause. Whether, in fact, the conditions encountered do fall within the stated basis for a changed condition must necessarily depend upon the contractor's obligations to inspect and investigate the site, and such knowledge

[19] *John Arborio, Inc. v. State of New York,* 245 N.Y.S.2d 274 (1963); *Young Fehlhaber Pile Co. v. State of New York,* 37 N.Y.S.2d 928 (App. Div. 3rd Dept., 1942); and Appeal of *Raymond International of Delaware, Inc.,* ASBCA 13121, 70-1 BCA 8341 (June 12, 1970).

[20] *Faber v. City of New York,* 222 N.Y. 255, at 260, 118 N.E. 609 (1918).

[21] *Moorhead Constr. Co. v. City of Grand Forks,* 508 F.2d 1008 (1975).

that should have been gained as a result thereof. If as a result of such site investigations the conditions are still classified as unknown latent physical conditions, fulfill the requirements of the contract clause, and are not precluded by exculpatory language, then the contractor is entitled to recover on its claim for a changed condition.

DAMAGES

Upon establishing the entitlement to a changed condition clause, the contractor is then faced with proving the damages or equitable adjustment which it is then entitled to receive. In construction claims the Courts normally require the contractor to prove with exactness each and every dollar claimed as a result from each specific alleged changed condition. The courts normally dislike granting an award on a total-cost approach, although under certain circumstances a contractor can be found entitled to all additional costs on the entire contract, above the base contract, resulting from the changed condition.[22] The equitable adjustment to which the contractor is normally entitled is "to cover increased costs which are the direct and necessary result of changed conditions, where the changed conditions led directly to disruption, extra work, or new procedures."[23]

CONCLUSION

It is of utmost importance that the contractor review—prior to bidding—the contract documents, in their entirety, to ascertain the existence of any changed conditions clause. In addition, the contractor should be fully apprised of its further obligations to perform site investigations and cannot unilaterally discount various disclaimer and exculpatory clauses inserted by the owner. If the contractor believes a changed condition does exist, immediate notice must be furnished to the owner's designated representative for such purpose, and all documents necessary to prove actual costs must be carefully and totally prepared. The changed conditions clause should prove to be a valuable asset to both the contractor and the owner when a continuing relationship exists.

[22]*Moorhead Constr. Co. v. City of Grand Forks, supra* note 20.
[23]*Appeal of Electronic and Missile Facilities, Inc.,* GSBCA 2203, 69-2 PCA 7781 (1969); *contra: G. H. Swart, Inc.,* GSBCA 2819, 71-1 BCA 8663 (1971).

Chapter **25**

Subcontractor's Entitlement to Payment Where Owner Fails to Make Payment to Prime Contractor

CHARLES YUMKAS, ESQ.

Partner, Blum, Yumkas, Mailman & Gutman, P.A., Baltimore, Maryland

An area of construction law which has been the subject of much litigation involves clauses in subcontracts which appear on the surface to condition the obligation of the prime contractor to make progress or final payments to a subcontractor only after the owner makes payment to the prime contractor. If these clauses are interpreted as making the owner's payment to the prime contractor a *condition precedent* to the prime contractor's obligation to pay his subcontractor, the subcontractor may not recover payment for work properly performed if the owner for any reason whatsoever fails, refuses, or is unable to pay the prime contractor.[1]

It is particularly important to know the legal ramifications of provisions in subcontracts which, if read literally, would appear to condition payment to the subcontractor only after payment by the owner, for many, if not most, of the subcontract forms presently in widespread use contain such provisions. An example of the language in question is found in paragraph 12.3 of the commonly used American Institute of Architects Document A-401 (January 1972

---

[1] In the context of this chapter, conditions precedent may be legally defined as acts or events which must occur or be fulfilled before a duty to perform other acts (in this case the duty to pay the subcontractor) arises. A good example of a condition precedent is the usual requirement that payment is due only after the issuance by the project architect of a certificate of final completion. Without special circumstances, where this clause appears, payment will not become due until after the certificate has been issued.

edition), *Standard Form of Agreement between Contractor and Subcontractor,* which states:

> 12.3. Unless otherwise provided in the Contract Documents, the Contractor shall pay the Subcontractor each progress payment and the final payment under this Subcontract within three (3) working days after he receives payment from the Owner. The amount of each progress payment to the Subcontractor shall be equal to the percentage of completion allowed to the Contractor for the Work of this Subcontractor applied to the Contract Sum of this Subcontract, plus the amount allowed for materials and equipment suitably stored by the Subcontractor, less the aggregate of previous payments to the Subcontractor and less the percentage retained as provided in this Subcontract.

Suppose a subcontractor signs a subcontract form with similar language to that found in the A-401 form and the project owner becomes insolvent prior to the completion of the construction, with the result that the prime contractor is not paid for work fully and properly performed by the subcontractor. Or suppose the owner merely refuses to pay the contractor for no valid reason. Would language similar to paragraph 12.3 in and of itself give the prime contractor an absolute defense to the subcontractor's claim for payment of work properly completed by him in a timely manner? The answer must depend on which state law governs the case since there is presently a divergence of views among the various state courts. The principal thrust of this chapter will be to survey and discuss those current views.

The first view, and the one finding favor in most of the recent decisions, holds that language similar to that found in paragraph 12.3 of the AIA subcontract form does not make payment to the subcontractor contingent upon the prime contractor's receiving payment from the owner. The language is construed as being an *unconditional* promise on the part of the prime contractor to pay the subcontractor, with the time of payment merely postponed until the happening of a certain event—namely, payment by the owner—or for only a reasonable period of time if it develops that payment by the owner does not take place. If for some reason the prime contractor does not receive payment from the owner within a reasonable time, the subcontractor will nevertheless be legally entitled to payment for his work. A prime example of this view is a 1968 case decided in Maryland.[2] In that case the prime contractor of a shopping center project subcontracted the paving work, the subcontract form containing the following language: "Final payment shall be made within 30 days after the completion of the work included in this Subcontract, written acceptance of same by the Architect and Owner or their authorized representatives and Full Payment therefor by the Owner."

The subcontractor completed the paving, and the contractor did the required work to complete the shopping center—all of which was approved and accepted by the project architect and the owner. However, the owner ran out of money, and the construction mortgage on the project was foreclosed. At the time of foreclosure, the owner owed the prime contractor $85,000, and the

---

[2]*Atlantic States Constr. Co. v. Drumond & Co.* 251 Md. 77, 246 A.2d 251 (1968).

contractor in turn owed the subcontractor $20,000 for the paving. Unable to successfully maintain a mechanic's lien action against the project for reasons unimportant to this discussion, the subcontractor sued the prime contractor for the balance due for the paving work. In defense of the suit, the contractor maintained that, since he had not been fully paid by the owner, he was not legally liable to pay the subcontractor because the above-quoted language constituted a contingent-payment clause making the contractor's obligation to pay the subcontractor wholly conditional on payment to the prime contractor by the owner.

The court decided that the subcontractor was entitled to recover in full, even though the prime contractor had not been paid. In the court's view, the subcontractual provisions in question did not make payment by the owner an absolute condition to payment to the subcontractor. In reaching its result, the court, adopting a rationale of a Sixth Circuit U.S. Court of Appeals decision,[3] reasoned that the parties to the subcontract never intended to transfer to the subcontractor the major credit risk which had been incurred by the prime contractor, namely the solvency of the owner. The court indicated that under normal circumstances the subcontractor looks to the solvency of the prime contractor with whom he has contracted, and it is to that prime contractor that the subcontractor looks for payment, not the owner. Therefore, the court concluded, in order to transfer the risk of owner payment from the general contractor to the subcontractor, the subcontract must contain clearly expressed provisions showing that to be the intention of the parties. In the court's view, the clause in question, while on its face appearing to make payment by the owner a condition to payment to the subcontractor, was merely "designed to postpone payment for a reasonable period of time after the work was completed during which the general contractor would be afforded the opportunity of procuring from the owner the funds necessary to pay the subcontractor." If a reasonable time elapsed without the general contractor being paid by the owner, the general contractor was liable to pay the subcontractor for work properly completed by the latter, even though the owner had failed to make payment for such work.

Other states which in recent years have similarly adopted this view that language which calls for the payment to be made to the subcontractor after payment is received from the owner does not constitute contingent-payment language are Arizona,[4] California,[5] Indiana,[6] Massachusetts,[7] North Carolina,[8] Ohio,[9] Oklahoma,[10] Oregon,[11] and Texas.[12]

---

[3] *Thomas J. Dyer Co. v. Bishop Int'l. Eng. Co.,* 303 F.2d 655 (6th Circuit, 1962).

[4] *Darrell T. Stuart Contractor v. J. A. Bridges and Rust-proofing, Inc.,* 2 Ariz. App.63, 406 P.2d 413 (1965).

[5] *Yamanishi v. Bleily & Collishaw, Inc.,* 29 Cal. App.3d 457, 105 Cal. Rpr. 580 (1972).

[6] *Midland Eng. Co. v. John A. Hall Constr. Co.,* 398 F.Supp. 981 (1975).

[7] *A. J. Wolfe Co. v. Baltimore Contractors, Inc.,* 355 Mass. 361, 244 N.E.2d 717 (1969).

[8] *Howard-Green Elec. Co. v. Chaney & James Constr. Co.* 12 N.C. App.63, 182 S.E.2d 601 (1971).

[9] *Thomas J. Dyer Co., supra* note 3.

[10] *Byler v. Great Am. Ins. Co.,* 395 F.2d 273 (10th Circuit, 1968).

[11] *Mignot v. Parkhill,* 237 Or. 450, 391 P.2d 755 (1964).

[12] *Wisznia v. Wilcox,* 438 S.W.2d 874 (1969).

A second view with a decidedly different approach to the problem was adopted by a Louisiana court in 1965 when it was called upon to decide a case which had been brought by a subcontractor against a prime contractor to recover monies claimed to be due under a fully performed subcontract containing the following language:[13]

> Progress payments will be made to Miller, based on monthly estimates approved by the Contractor, "within 10 days after receipt of payment from the Owner, . . . less 10% of each estimate to be retained until final payment which shall be made within 10 days after completion of the work included in this Contract and written acceptance by the Architect and full payment therefor by the Owner, provided evidence has been furnished by the Subcontractor, if requested, that all claims for labor and materials are settled, and provided further that all the provisions of the Contract have been complied with to the satisfaction of the Contractor."

In defense of the subcontractor's suit, the general contractor asserted that he had not obtained payment from the owner and therefore payment to the subcontractor was not due and payable. In contrast with the position taken by the Maryland court, the Louisiana court agreed with the general contractor's position, saying the following:

> An analysis of the foregoing contractual provision revealed that it imposes an obligation of making final payment on the subcontract within 10 days after (1) completion of the work, (2) acceptance by the architect and (3) *full payment for the work by the owner.* The contract is not ambiguous and its simple effect is to make payment by the owner to the prime contractor a suspensive condition to the prime contractor's obligation to make payment to its subcontractor.
>
> This provision was obviously intended to prevent the prime contractor from being compelled to assume the obligation of financing the construction of the Project in the event of default by the owner. Therefore, we must give effect to the clear intention of the parties as agreed to, and we, as usual, refrain from placing the contract upon the judicial anvil and hammering it into an unexpected shape.

It is seen that the two views are based on opposite assumptions regarding the intention of the parties to the subcontract. Those courts which have concluded that "pay-after-payment-is-received" clauses do not create a condition precedent to payment to the subcontractor have assumed that the parties intended that the financial risk of payment by the owner should remain with the prime contractor and that payment or nonpayment by the owner is irrelevant with respect to the payment obligation of the prime contractor to the subcontractor. One court even suggested that a purpose of the clause in question was to ensure the subcontractor that funds received by the prime contractor would not be diverted but would be faithfully applied on the subcontract in a timely manner.[14] However, the courts following the Louisiana reasoning hold that the clause in question shows a clear intention to shift the risk of owner payment from the prime contractor to the subcontractor. Other states which have

[13]*Miller v. Housing Auth. of New Orleans,* 175 So.2d 326 (1965).
[14]*Yamanishi, supra* note 5.

apparently adopted a similar approach to that taken by the Louisiana court are Georgia,[15] Illinois,[16] Kentucky,[17] and Connecticut.[18]

The current position of certain other state courts that have considered or at least alluded to similar clauses is difficult to accurately determine. New York presents an interesting example.

In 1933, the highest court of New York determined that a clause in a subcontract calling for "payments to be made as received from the Owner" could be construed as making payment by the owner to the general contractor a condition precedent to the contractor's obligation to pay the subcontractor.[19] In support of its decision, the court stated:

> There is, however, an express promise to pay monies "as received from the Owner," and the event upon which that promise would ripen into an absolute immediate obligation has not occurred. From the express promise to pay upon the happening of an event, an inference may be drawn that the parties did not intend or impliedly agree that payment should be made even if the event does not occur.

However, in 1975, a New York appellate court adopted an opposite view, holding that a pay-after-payment-is-received clause merely fixed the time for payment and does not establish a condition precedent.[20] Based on the divergence of the two cases, it is difficult to determine with any certainty what the law in New York currently is with respect to the problem.

Recent cases in Wisconsin[21] and Utah[22] involving clauses which on the surface appear to make payment by owner a condition precedent to the subcontractor's payment entitlement did not result in definitive rulings with respect to the issue in question. It should also be noted that a Louisiana case[23] decided after *Miller v. Housing Authority of New Orleans*[24] found that a clause requiring a developer to pay an engineer "as the developer receives its payments" was merely an outline of the method of payment and did not constitute a condition precedent.

It should be kept in mind that even those jurisdictions that have adopted the rule that pay-after-payment-is-received clauses do not create conditions prece-

---

[15]*Peacock Constr. Co. v. West,* 111 Ga. App. 604, 142 S.E.2d 332 (1965).

[16]*Standard Asbestos Mfg. Co. v. Kaiser,* 316 Ill. App. 441, 45 N.E.2d 75 (1942).

[17]*New Amsterdam Cas. Co. v. Allen Co.,* 446 S.W.2d 278 (1969) "Provided, however, that the first party may retain Ten Percent (10%) of the sums due second party until first party has received payment of the final estimate from the Department of Highways."

[18]*Star Contracting Corp. v. Manway Constr. Co., Inc.,* 32 Conn. Supp. 64, 337 A.2d 669 (1973).

[19]*Mascioni v. I. B. Miller, Inc.,* 261 N.Y. 1, 184 N.E. 473 (1933).

[20]*Schuler-Haas Elec. Corp. v. Aetna Cas. & Sur. Co.,* 371 N.Y.S.2d 207, aff'd 40 N.Y.2d 883, 389 N.Y.S.2d 348, 357 N.E.2d 1003. The subcontractor's suit was against the prime contractor's surety which contended that the language of the payment bond itself required payment by the owner to permit recovery thereunder. The court rejected the surety's interpretation of the bond. In reaching its ultimate conclusion in the case, the court did not mention the *Mascioni* case, but in support of its decision, quoted directly from the North Carolina (*Howard-Green Elec. Co., supra* note 8), Massachusetts (*A. J. Wolfe Co., supra* note 7), and Ohio (*Thomas J. Dyer Co., supra* note 3) cases.

[21]*Riley Constr. Co. v. Schillmoeller & Krofl Co.,* 236 N.W.2d 195 (1975).

[22]*Foss Lewis & Sons Constr. Co. v. General Ins. Co. of America,* 30 Utah 2d 290, 517 P.2d 539 (1973).

[23]*Subdivision Planning Engr's., Inc. v. Manner Dev. Corp.,* 290 So.2d 375 (1974).

[24]*Miller, supra* note 13.

dent might find that the presence of additional language in the subcontract would make the payment obligation conditional. After all, the ultimate determination to be made by the courts in these cases involves what the parties to the subcontract intended with respect to payment to the subcontractor. While not always clearly enunciated, the central point of the court's analysis usually is whether the parties to the subcontract intended to shift the credit risk of nonpayment by the owner to the subcontractor and used appropriate language to accomplish that intent. If the language of the subcontract clearly shows the parties' intention to condition payment to the subcontractor on payment by the owner, thereby shifting the risk of owner payment to the subcontractor, the court will have no hesitation in giving effect to that agreement. The courts have not indicated that public policy demands that the risk of payment by the owner cannot be shifted to the subcontractor. Even the aforementioned Maryland decision contained language to the effect that if the subcontract involved in the case contained express provisions unequivocally showing that payment by the owner was to be a condition to the contractor's obligation to make payment to the subcontractor, then the nonpayment by the owner would have defeated the subcontractor's right to payment.

What will constitute sufficiently clear language which will absolutely transfer the risk of owner payment to the subcontractor? Obviously the Louisiana decision and those adopting the same rationale hold that the mere pay-after-payment-is-received language is sufficient. But, as indicated earlier, most courts do not find that such language is in and of itself sufficiently unequivocal. However, if the subcontract contains a provision requiring the contractor to pay *only* after owner payment has been received, the inclusion of this additional word might make the difference.

In a 1973 Connecticut case, a court was confronted with a subcontract containing the following language:[25]

> Partial payments by the Contractor to the Subcontractor hereunder shall be made only at such time or times as payments made by the Owner to the Contractor shall include work completed by the Subcontractor, and then only in the ratio that work performed by the Subcontractor bears to all work to be done by him under this Subcontract to the extent that Contractor has received payment for such work, whichever is the lesser. In any event, payment will not be made by the Contractor to the Subcontractor until the Owner has made payment to the Contractor for the work.

The court found that the language of the subcontract did make payment by the owner a condition precedent to the subcontractor's right to receive payment from the prime contractor. Although the court's opinion did not specifically state that the inclusion of the word "only" in the subcontract language was the determining factor, there is legal precedent to the effect that a contract providing for payment only from a particular fund creates no liability to pay other

---

[25]*Star Contracting Corp., supra* note 18.

than from the fund itself.[26] An example is seen in a recent Georgia case in which the prime contractor was required to make payments to his subcontractor "from money received from the owner only."[27] There, the court decided that payment by the owner to the prime contractor was a condition which had to occur in order for the subcontractor to be entitled to payment.

This discussion has assumed that the failure or refusal of the owner to make payment to the prime contractor was not predicated on faulty work of the prime contractor. However, it is clear that a prime contractor will not be able to use the defense of nonpayment by the owner successfully if such nonpayment results from a dereliction on the part of the prime contractor himself. It is an established principle of law that one who by his conduct prevents a condition precedent from occurring will not be able to avail himself of the nonoccurrence of the condition to his benefit.[28] Thus, a general contractor whose faulty performance is the basis for nonpayment by the owner will not be able to use such nonpayment as a defense to a subcontractor's claim, even in those cases where the subcontract makes payment by the owner a condition precedent.

The principles regarding the legal effect of pay-after-payment-is-received clauses in subcontracts are equally applicable in those cases where the prime contractor's surety is being sued by the subcontractor. It is a general rule that a surety's liability is the same as that of its principal. Therefore, in the case where a prime contractor can successfully avail himself of nonpayment by the owner as a defense to the subcontractor's claim for payment, the contractor's surety under a labor-and-material bond applicable to the job can equally enjoy the same defense. And, in those cases where payment by the owner is not a condition precedent to the subcontractor's right to be paid, the surety may not successfully use lack of payment by the owner as a defense to the subcontractor's claim, unless there is language in the bond itself conditioning the surety's obligation to make payment to subcontractors and suppliers contingent upon payment by the owner. In the absence of extraordinary circumstances, the surety in these cases involving the legal effect of pay-after-payment-is-received clauses stands in the shoes of the prime contractor, and the surety's rights to assert the defense of nonpayment on the part of the owner are coextensive with those of the prime contractor.

In conclusion, the effect of clauses in subcontracts which call for a prime contractor to pay his subcontractor after payment is received from the owner

---

[26]*United States for the use of Mosely v. Mann,* 197 F.2d 39 (10th Cir., 1952); *City of Seymour v. Municipal Acceptance Corp.,* 96 S.W.2d 814 (1936); *Fidelity & Deposit Co. v. Andrews,* 244 Mich. 159, 221 N.W. 114 (1928); *Carpenter v. Sly,* 109 Cal. App. 539, 293 P. 162 (1930). The latter three cases referred to in this note do not involve construction contracts.

[27]*Sasser & Co. v. Griffin,* 133 Ga. App. 83, 210 S.E.2d 34 (1974).

[28]This general principle is recognized in 12 *Am. Jur.* (Contracts), § 329, where it states: "One who prevents or makes impossible the performance or happening of a condition precedent upon which his liability by the terms of a contract is made to depend cannot avail himself of its non-performance. In other words, he who prevents a thing from being done shall never be permitted to avail himself of the non-performance which he himself has occasioned."

varies from state to state, although there appears to be a trend of appellate courts to find that the mere language in question does not in and of itself constitute a condition precedent to the subcontractor's right to payment. Because of the uncertainty as to what the legal effect of such clauses is in numerous jurisdictions which have not made definitive rulings on the issue, parties to a subcontract should make certain that their contractual language clearly sets forth their intent with respect to payment to the subcontractor. If a prime contractor wants to be assured that he will not be required to pay his subcontractor if the owner fails to make payment for the subcontractor's work, he should insist that the subcontract include language which plainly states that payment by the owner is a condition precedent to the subcontractor's right to be paid under the subcontract. Similarly, if a subcontractor is unwilling to assume the financial risk of payment by the owner to the prime contractor, he should insist on language in the subcontract which will require payment to be made to him after his work has been completed, regardless of whether the prime contractor is paid by the owner.

Legal counsel should always be sought in order to ensure the parties that the subcontract embodies their intent on the issue of whether a subcontractor is entitled to payment if the owner fails to make payment to the prime contractor for the work completed by the subcontractor.

Chapter 26
Obtaining Time Extensions

BYRNE A. BOWMAN, ESQ.
Partner, Bowman & Pittman, Oklahoma City, Oklahoma

UNDERSTAND YOUR CONTRACT

Obtaining time extensions to avoid liquidated damages is not to be taken lightly. A contractor, whether a general contractor or a subcontractor, is in an economically hazardous business. He may encounter unexpected events and conditions that will delay his progress and cost him money. He figured his cost, and he bid or negotiated the contract price. Therefore, he should read his contract and understand the provisions for extensions of time, liquidated damages, and termination.

PRIME CONTRACT PROVISIONS
Public Contracts

Extensions of time Practically all construction contracts contain a section which establishes the completion date, a section concerning time extensions, and a section on liquidated damages. The prime contract ordinarily will fix a completion date as being a certain number of calendar days from the notice to proceed. This might be 180 days, for example. The contract may state, as in a local housing authority remodeling contract (not a federal project):

> If the work is delayed by any act or neglect by the Local Authority or its representatives, or by changes in the work, or by strikes, fire, freight embargoes, unusually severe weather, or by unforeseeable causes beyond the control and without the fault of the Contractor, then if the Contractor shall within 10 days from the beginning of such delay notify the Contracting Officer of the cause and extent thereof, the Local Authority, subject to verification of the facts and to approval by the HUD, shall extend the time for completing the work.

Thus the U.S. Department of Housing and Urban Development reserves the right to disapprove any application for a time extension.

In a federal construction contract, with the Department of the Army, Corps of Engineers, for example, the contract will state that the agency's contracting officer is the one who grants the extensions of time. Standard Form 23-A, prescribed by the General Services Administration, states in paragraph 5(d):

> The Contractor's right to proceed shall not be so terminated nor the Contractor charged with resulting damage if:
>
> (1) The delay in the completion of the work arises from unforeseeable causes beyond the control and without the fault or negligence of the Contractor, including but not restricted to, acts of God, acts of the public enemy, acts of the Government in either its sovereign or contractual capacity, acts of another contractor in the performance of a contract with the Government, fires, floods, epidemics, quarantine restrictions, strikes, freight embargoes, unusually severe weather, or delays of subcontractors or suppliers arising from unforeseeable causes beyond the control and without the fault or negligence of both the Contractor and such subcontractors or suppliers; and
>
> (2) The Contractor, within 10 days from the beginning of any such delay (unless the Contracting Officer grants a further period of time before the date of final payment under the contract), notifies the Contracting Officer in writing of the causes of delay.
>
> The Contracting Officer shall ascertain the facts and the extent of the delay and extend the time for completing the work when, in his judgment, the findings of fact justifies such an extension, and his findings of fact shall be final and conclusive on the parties, subject only to appeal as provided in Clause 6 of these General Provisions.

This section, as can be seen, is broader and more liberal than the one required by HUD, and the contractor deals directly with the contracting officer.

Liquidated damages   In the Housing Authority contract, there is a provision that if the contractor fails to complete the work within the time specified plus any extension of time granted by the local authority, he shall pay to the local authority certain liquidated damages; and in the form required by the General Services Administration, there is a similar provision.

Termination   In the HUD form, the local authority can terminate the contractor's right to proceed with the work if he "should be adjudged a bankrupt or insolvent, or if he should make a general assignment for his creditors, or fail in any substantial manner to meet any provision of the contract." Determination shall be effective upon five days' prior written notice. In the General Services Administration form, paragraph 5 of the general provisions states:

> (a) If the Contractor refuses or fails to prosecute the work, or any separable part thereof, with such diligence as will insure its completion within the time specified in this contract, or any extension thereof, or fails to complete said contract within such time, the Government may, by written notice to the Contractor, terminate his right to proceed with the work or such part of the work as to which there has been delay. . . .
>
> (b) If fixed and agreed liquidated damages are provided in the contract and if the Government so terminates the Contractor's right to proceed, the resulting damage will consist of such liquidated damages until such reasonable time as may be required for final completion of the work together with any increased costs occasioned the Government in completing the work.

The General Services form provides for a termination for default or a termination for the convenience of the government.

Contract interpretation   The invitation to bid sets forth the general conditions of the contract such as changes, extensions of time, liquidated damages, terminations, and the specifications and the plans. All the contractor can do is place a competitive bid. He has no opportunity to negotiate with another enterprise more powerful than he. For that reason, if there is a dispute as to interpretation of the contract, the boards of review and the courts will adopt the interpretation the contractor made unless it is clearly unreasonable. This is the rule of *contra proferendum*—interpretation against the offeror or drafter of the instrument. In some types of contracts, courts may call this a *contract of adhesion,* and refuse to apply harsh terms thereof when it would be inequitable to do so. Other courts may do this without calling the contract one of adhesion. Regardless of the name, this rule may help in disputes concerning defective plans and specifications.

Applications for extensions   Applications for extensions of time must be prepared with an eye to who is going to make the determination and what kind of support must be presented. In a local housing authority project the U.S. Department of Housing and Urban Development reserved the right to disapprove all applications because it finances the project. The application goes through the architect to the housing authority's contracting officer and then to someone in HUD who has plenty of forms, employees, and expense money at his disposal. All paper work must be directed toward obtaining favorable bureaucratic action from him. He may be slow, depending upon his work load, but he probably will be precise, orderly, and efficient. The applicant must be the same.

Even though at fault in several ways, the contractor nevertheless may be entitled to a time extension (or the owner not entitled to liquidated damages). In such case, he should process the application. If it is denied, and the equities are on his side, he probably will obtain relief by appealing through administrative channels or to a court. But the paper work must be done properly—which is called "exhausting the administrative remedies."

Appeals   If you have contracted with the federal government you can take an appeal to an administrative board of review on the executive side of the government. For example, you can appeal from a decision of the contracting officer for the Corps of Engineers to the Armed Services Board of Contract Appeals. This board is composed of persons who are experienced in construction contracting and have an excellent and practical knowledge of construction contract problems and construction contract law. If the contract is with a local housing authority, there is usually no way to take an administrative appeal and therefore no alternative but to prosecute a suit in court. This applies, also, to construction contracts with cities, school boards, counties, and states—practically all of which have no administrative review boards. In all these appeals, it is important to have a "track record" of documentary evidence that was made currently. A record made up after the fact will be considered but is not nearly as good.

Private Contracts

Private projects   Construction contracts on large private projects largely follow the forms of those on public projects but they may vary because the parties negotiated the terms of the contract as well as the price.

Subcontracts   A subcontract is a private contract even though it is for performance of part of a public contract. It must be read and understood. It will adopt as a part thereof many of the obligations of the public contract. The subcontractor will have some remedies afforded to him by the statutes relating to the public contract. He may have an opportunity to negotiate some of the terms of his subcontract.

SUBCONTRACT PROVISIONS

Typical subcontract paragraphs   A printed form of subcontract may contain provisions similar to these:

> 1. The Subcontractor certifies that he has examined and is fully familiar with all the terms and conditions of the prime contract, all of the component parts thereof, and its plans and specifications; the location of the job site; and the conditions under which the work is to be performed; that he enters into this contract based upon his own investigation of all such matters, including the securing of all field measurements and specification requirements and is in no way relying upon any representations or opinions made by the Contractor; and, that this contract represents the entire agreement between the parties and supersedes and voids any prior proposals or agreements relating to the work designated herein.
>
> 2. The Subcontractor agrees to be bound to the Contractor by the terms of the prime contract and any additions or changes made thereto, and to assume all the obligations and responsibilities that the Contractor assumes by that contract toward the Owner insofar as they are applicable to the work covered by this subcontract.
>
> 3. The Contractor shall have the right to order the omission or addition of the parts of the work, or materials, as omitted from or added to the prime contract by the Owner. Fair deductions or increases shall be made in the subcontract price for

such omitted or added work or materials under the terms provided for in the prime contract. No such orders, extensions of time, or any modifications of this contract shall be of any force or effect unless made in writing and duly signed by an officer of the Contractor.

4. In the event that the Subcontractor shall fail to correct, replace, and/or re-execute faulty or defective work and/or materials, fails to diligently proceed with this contract within the time provided for, enters into bankruptcy, makes a general assignment for the benefit of his creditors, or fails to make prompt payment to his materialmen and laborers, the Contractor may, at its option after 48 hours' written notice, provide any such labor and material as may be necessary, and deduct the cost thereof from any money then due or thereafter to become due to the Subcontractor under this contract, or terminate this contract and reenter and take possession of the work for the purpose of finishing it. In the event of such a breach by the Subcontractor, the Contractor shall have the right to take possession of all the tools and materials of the Subcontractor then on the job site for the purpose of completing this contract. The Subcontractor shall not be entitled to any further payments under this contract until the work is finished. At that time, if the unpaid balance is less than the expenses incurred by the Contractor in completing this work, the Contractor in addition to other remedies shall have a lien on such tools and materials to secure payment.

5. Should the Subcontractor be in default in the proper performance of his work, thereby causing delay to the Contractor or any other subcontractor working on this project, under such conditions and circumstances so as to render the other subcontractors liable to the Contractor on their subcontracts and/or the Contractor liable to the Owner on the prime contract, including the amount of any liquidated damages which may be assessed under the prime contract, the Subcontractor shall be liable for any and all loss and damages so sustained.

There may be a typed addendum to the effect that:

> In addition to and not in substitution of the Standard Subcontract Agreement, the following will in part detail the items covered by Articles II and IV thereof:
> The following sections of the Prime Contract are incorporated into this Subcontract as required for a complete installation in accordance with the Prime Contract and the applicable Plans and Specifications by this Subcontractor in part as follows:
> A. Instructions to Bidders, pages 1 through 5 of 46.
> B. General Conditions, pages 6 through 18 of 46.
> C. Supplemental General Conditions, pages 19 through 21 of 46.
> D. To complete all work under section M-1 Mechanical, pages M-1 through M-20 and Contract Drawings, Sheets M-1 through M-10, and as required or called out on other Contract Drawing Sheets as applicable to work under this Subcontract.

Applications for extensions   The subcontractor is working for the prime contractor, not the owner. He must not deal with the owner or take orders from the owner without the prime's approval. He must make all presentations, objections, and applications to the prime. The prime probably will not give him an extension or an extra unless the prime can obtain it from the owner. Therefore it is important that the subcontractor present good supporting evidence along with his application. The prime will make it a part of the prime's application.

CHANGE ORDERS

Owner delays Delays can occur due to slow action by the architect and contracting officer in negotiations for a change order and thereafter in performance of the change order. The architect and contracting officer will ordinarily grant a time extension in the change order if it is for additional work over and beyond the scope of the contract, but the contractor may consider this extension of time to be inadequate. He should therefore avoid signing the change order; or if he does sign it, he should write in a condition or exception that he is not agreeing to the number of days allowed for the time extension. He will, of course, have to proceed with that extra work even though the extension of time period is not agreed upon.

Typical contract provision This is one area where the contractor must document every step in the procedure and move as quickly as he can. In the Housing Authority contract referred to in this chapter, we find:

> *Changes in the Work; Claims:* The Local Authority, without invalidating the contract, may order extra work or make changes by altering, adding to, or deducting from the work, the contract amount and time being equitably adjusted accordingly. All such changed work shall be executed under the conditions of the contract. The value of extra or omitted work shall be negotiated in advance and stated in a change order describing the nature and extent of the change, or if the nature of extra work is such that the value thereof cannot be determined in advance, a proceed order describing the change shall be issued and this shall state the manner in which the value of the change will subsequently be determined. All change orders and proceed orders shall be based on the net cost of labor and items incidental to labor and the net cost of material delivered to the site, including local sales taxes, if any. To such items of cost there may be added, not to exceed [here follows a schedule of percentage allowances for overhead and profit]. The Contractor shall make no change in the work except in pursuance to a written order from the Local Authority, approved on its face by the HUD, except that in an emergency and without written order the Contractor may take such actions as are necessary to protect life and property. If the Contractor claims that any instructions given by the Local Authority involve extra cost or extension of time, he shall, within 10 days after receiving such instruction, and before proceeding to follow the instructions, submit his protest thereto in writing to the Contracting Officer, stating in detail the basis therefor. No such claim shall be valid unless so made.

There is bound to be a delay in these negotiations. The contractor should attempt to build a record showing that his delay was reasonable and that of the architect and contracting officer was unreasonable.

FAULTY PLANS AND SPECIFICATIONS

Ambiguities in specifications Most plans and specifications are something less than perfect. Ambiguities and uncertainties will be found. For example, the specifications may require the replacement of "missing handrails" on the back porches. The contractor, by inspection, can note where steel handrails had been imbedded in a concrete porch, and he may count 17 that are "missing." There may be 30 back porches where the handrails are intact, but there may be 10 back porches where there never were any handrails. By a stretch of the imagination, the architect and the contracting officer may contend that, where no handrails were ever installed, they are "missing" and must be replaced by the contractor. A reasonable interpretation of the specification would not indicate to the contractor that he was going to suffer the time and expense of "replacing" the additional 10 handrails. The delay incident to such a requirement by the architect and the contracting officer should be carefully documented.

Ambiguities in plans   The plans may show, either by designation or by scale, that the closet doors are to be 2 feet 6 inches wide. The contractor orders the doors and then finds that there is room for a door that is only 2 feet 4 inches wide. Or he finds that the 16 feet × 22 inches model no. 4134 medicine cabinet is too small for the space constructed for it, and he must make the space smaller in order to accommodate the cabinet. In such cases, the architect and contracting officer may deny a time extension by citing a carpentry specification that states, "All measurements and dimensions shall be verified at the job, and the Contractor shall be responsible for any work that does not fit properly."

Typical contract provision   The architect and contracting officer may deny a time extension on the basis of paragraphs like these in the general conditions:

> *Drawings and Specifications:* The intention of the documents is to include all labor and materials, equipment, power, transportation, and anything else necessary to the proper execution of the work. The plans and specifications are complementary, and what is called for by either shall be as binding as though called for in both. Discrepancies shall be called to the attention of the Local Authority, without whose decisions the matter shall not be adjusted by the Contractor, save at his own risk. In case of difference between drawings and specifications, the specifications shall govern. Large-scale details shall take precedence over drawings with smaller-scale detail. Shop drawings are required only where so called for in the specifications. The separation of the specifications into divisions is for convenience only and does not relieve the Contractor of his obligation to furnish any and all labor or material necessary to completion of the work, regardless of where specified.
>
> The drawings and specifications are intended to illustrate and describe the complete work; however, anything not expressly set forth but which is reasonably implied or necessary to the final and full completion of the work shall be executed, performed, and finished as if such items had been fully and definitely described in the drawings and specifications. Every attempt has been made in the preparation of these plans and specifications to anticipate the materials and construction of the existing buildings. It shall be the responsibility of the Contractor to check existing dimensions, details, as if such items had been fully and definitely described in the drawings and specifications.
>
> *Contractor's Responsibilities; Subcontracts; Employees:* By signing the contract, the Contractor warrants that he has visited the site and fully acquainted himself with conditions relating to construction and labor and will assert no claims against the Local Authority because of conditions regarding which he should have been on notice as a result thereof. The Local Authority may, without claim for extra cost by the Contractor, disapprove any subcontractor (1) where the proposed subcontract is for labor only or substantially for labor only; (2) for cause on the basis of its own determination; or (3) because of the fact that the proposed subcontractor is listed as ineligible to receive awards of contracts from the United States on a list or lists furnished by the HUD in effect at the time of the award of this contract.

The above sections are an attempt to place the entire burden upon the contractor for any delay or additional cost resulting from defective plans and specifications. The Housing Authority says, in effect, "We told you that you must expect to find some irregularities in the plans and specifications. Go out and look at the installation and field measure wherever you think it is necessary." This is a prime example of the importance of keeping accurate records as to the delay suffered by the contractor. Where there is a dispute, there is often a delay.

Ordinarily a contractor can rely on plans where dimensions are given. However, he should carefully examine detailed plans for notations requiring him to "field measure."

SUBMITTALS

Kinds of submittals   A construction contract ordinarily requires three kinds of submittals by the contractor to the architects and owner. Certain materials or equipment may require approval, substitutes for materials or equipment described by manufacturer's name and catalog number may be required, and submittals of shop drawings may be required.

Submittal of materials   Examples of requirements for submittals of samples of material set forth in the specifications of a contract are (in abbreviated form):

§5.02 *Samples:* Samples of all ceramic tile shall be submitted to the Architect for selection of color and finish required.

§11.03 *Contractor's Hardware Schedule:* After all samples have been approved, but prior to delivery of hardware, the Contractor shall prepare and submit to the Architect five copies of a complete schedule of all finish hardware required. Schedules shall follow requirements of specifications and shall indicate types, manufacturer's name and number, location, and finish of each item required. Approval of schedules shall not relieve Contractor of responsibility for furnishing all necessary hardware.

§11.04 *Samples:* Samples shall be furnished as requested by the Architect for approval; no hardware shall be delivered until approval is obtained.

§12.06 *Color Selection:* The Contractor for this work shall, in ample time to prevent delay in the work, secure the necessary instructions and prepare for approval a sample of every color and finish used in the work. Rejected samples shall be made over and resubmitted until approved. The Contractor shall notify the Architect who will make an inspection and approve the final shade of the color selected by the architect for the last coat. If the Contractor fails to obtain such approval, he will be required to apply another coat of finish, if necessary, to obtain the desired color without additional cost to the owner.

Submittal by catalog number   Examples of specifications by manufacturer and catalog number are:

§3.13 *Medicine Cabinets:* Existing medicine cabinets in all dwelling units shall be replaced with new cabinets with 16 × 22 inch stainless steel framed plate-glass mirror door and white enameled steel body, Model No. 4134 as manufactured by The F. H. Lawson Company, or approved equal.

§5.06 Ceramic Tile Floors: New toilet rooms in Building No. 80 shall receive adhesive-set tile floors of 2 × 2 inch unglazed "Quarryettes" as manufactured by Summitville Tiles, Inc., in Group 2 colors, grouted with waterproofed grout.

Note that "or approved equal" is not in the above section 5.06 as to "Quarryettes."

Submittal by shop drawings Examples of specification requirements for shop drawings are (abbreviated):

§3.01 Scope: The Contractor shall furnish all labor and materials to complete all miscellaneous metal as shown on the drawings or specified herein, or both as follows:
A. Steel casement windows
B. Steel handrails
C. Rolling doors
D. Garbage can racks
E. Grab bars
F. Medicine cabinets

§3.02 Shop Drawings: The Contractor shall submit complete shop drawings in accordance with the General Conditions showing dimensions, connections sizes, and all erection details. No fabrication shall be done until shop drawings have been approved.

§10.01 Scope: The Contractor shall furnish all labor and material to complete all carpentry and millwork as shown on the drawings, or specified herein, or both, as follows:
A. Millwork
B. Wood doors
C. Gypsum wallboard and steel studs
D. Wood garbage can enclosures
E. Drapery rod mounting boards

§10.03 Shop Drawings: The Contractor shall submit complete shop drawings covering all shop-built millwork, prepared by the mill, to the Architect for approval before fabrication.

Proof of delay The contractor cannot order stock items of material and equipment shipped or items fabricated and shipped until he has the required approval. Inasmuch as he is under a tight time schedule for completion, with a work progress schedule for his various subcontractors, time is of the essence to him. Any unreasonable delay of the architect and the contracting officer in approving submittals of materials, equipment, substitutes therefor, and shop drawings can be very injurious to the contractor. For that reason he should document the facts in order to support an application for extension of time when there is unreasonable delay. All submittals should be made by a formal, signed transmittal letter. Approval letters should be stamped with a date of receipt stamp. A dated, signed memorandum should be written out in longhand or dictated immediately after any telephone or personal conference concerning a submittal and placed in the file the contractor is building up on that item. If a disapproval is regarded as arbitrary and unwarranted, a memorandum should be prepared at the time. Then the same procedure should be followed on the new submittal. All efforts to locate suppliers, fabricators, and all communications with them should be documented by letters and memoranda.

Material approved schedule   The contractor should maintain a "material approved schedule," bearing in mind that the contracting officer is probably keeping one. This can be a large columnar spreadsheet which has a horizontal-line calendar across the top, with vertical columns for each day. On the horizontal lines can be the information as to the transmittal, showing the transmittal number, the item transmitted, the date of action by the architect, and the date of action by the contracting officer. A comparison of the suggested contractor's chart with that of the contracting officer's schedule is shown in Figure 26.1.

In the case of litigation an attorney's reference to the contractor's chart might be:

> Starting on line 1, at the left-hand side, and traveling along that line, we see that the ceramic tile color was transmitted as Number 1, that it was submitted on November 3, and that the architects did not act on it until 42 days later—December 14, at which time they approved it. The kitchen cabinets are listed on line 32. The cabinets for buildings 8 and 105, and the resubmittal thereof, are listed on line 33. Line 32 on the kitchen cabinets extends from November 7 to January 25, with this legend: "substitute. Uniform white birch not available. Rejected Kitcheneze cabinets. Alternate sample approved on job January 25. Kitchen cabinet architect delay 101 days, plus production program time."

On the above kitchen cabinets, the architects may have "red-lined" corrections as to various dimensions. These corrections involved the preparation and submittal of new shop drawings. In this instance there would be not only the delay in the disapproval, but the delay would be partially attributable to the subcontractor who submitted the faulty drawings.

UNOBTAINABLE MATERIALS OR EQUIPMENT

The problem   The contractor may find that he cannot obtain certain specified materials or equipment. Possibly he cannot obtain a specific type of electric transformer or white birch for fabrication of kitchen cabinets. This produces a delay, efforts to agree on a substitute, and frequently a dispute.

Contract provision   The General Services Construction Contract form states that the contractor's right to proceed shall not be terminated for default and that he shall not be charged with resulting damage, if the delay in completion of the work is due to delays of subcontractors or suppliers *arising from unforeseeable causes beyond the control and without the fault of negligence of both the contractor and such subcontractors or suppliers.* In other words, both the contractor and his supplier of transformers or white birch must be without fault and their respective delays must have been ones that they could not have reasonably expected. This provision is not present in the Housing Authority contract and in many state and municipal contracts.

FIGURE 26.1 Comparison of Contractor's Submittal Schedule with Contracting Officer's Materials-Approved Schedule

Contractor's Submittal Chart

Transaction number	Description	November	December	January
		(Vertical day columns are omitted)		
1	Ceramic tile color	11/3 ——— 42 days ———	12/14	
1A	Paint colors	11/8 ——— 50 days ———	12/27	
2	Finish hardware	11/6 ——— 71 days ———		1/16
19A	Mechanical controls		12/7 ——— 27 days ——— 1/2	

Contracting Officer's Materials-Approved Schedule

Transaction number	Description	Submitted by contractor	Received by contracting officer	Approved by architect	Approved by contracting officer	Disapproved by architect	Disapproved by contracting officer
1	Ceramic tile color	11/4	11/6	12/12	12/14		
1A	Paint colors			12/26	12/27		
2	Finish hardware	11/6	11/7	11/15	11/20		
19A	Mechanical controls	12/7	12/10	12/28	1/2		

NOTE: The submitted bar chart of the contractor graphically exhibits the delay. Note that the contracting officer's schedule does not show the date of submittal of the paint colors and that he shows approval of the finish hardware on November 20.

No contract provision   Where there is no contract provision, the contractor has no such express protection against termination or liquidated damages. Therefore it is imperative that he document the facts of the delay and particularly his efforts to locate other manufacturers or suppliers—the reason why the manufacturer of the transformers or the supplier of the white birch is unable to furnish them. (In other words, he should create a little sympathy for a problem that he did not create.)

WEATHER

Unusually severe weather   You will be entitled to an extension of time if you can reach an agreement, or prove, that you were delayed by *unusually severe* weather—which was more severe than the weather usually encountered at that time of year.

Weather summaries   Most newspapers print a daily weather summary for the day (Figure 26.2). Cut these out and put them in a notebook, and post pertinent facts to the progress chart. If the contract provides the minimum temperatures for certain interior work and certain exterior work, this should be reflected on the chart. Since the chill factor is important, it should be posted on the chart.

In order to have proof that the weather was unusually severe as compared with the average weather for the period of the delay, the "local climatological data," which is issued monthly, can be obtained by subscription (Figure 26.3).[1]

Pictures   Part of your preparation should be the taking of current pictures. If it takes one tractor to pull another tractor out of the mud, that is very convincing evidence. Pictures of flooding, deep snow, ice, and wind and storm damage are very good evidence of unusually severe weather.

Period of delay   The period of delay due to unusually severe weather will be shown on your chart, and this will be supported by the temperatures and other conditions noted thereon and the number of men shown to have been working on the project each day. (You will have obtained the number of men working on the project from the payroll reports.)

Application for extension   An application for an extension of time due to unusually severe weather can be in the form of a simple letter stating the facts. The inspector employed by the owner or the architects will be generally familiar with the facts, but the contracting officer may not. For that reason, if the application for the extension of time is denied, ask, by letter, for a reconsideration and request a conference in which you can present your evidence.

Subcontractors will have been affected by the unusually severe weather. They should file applications with the prime for extensions of time for the performance of their subcontracts.

---

[1]Available from: National Climatic Center, Federal Building, Asheville, North Carolina 28801, Att: Publications.

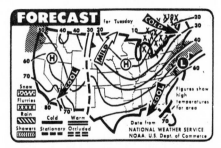

Map indicates precipitation and high temperatures forecast across the nation. (AP Map)

The Weather

CITY: Monday's skies were partly cloudy and temperatures were cooler, with the high reaching 51.

FORECAST: Fair to partly cloudy skies are expected through Wednesday, with cool temperatures Tuesday and warmer Wednesday. Winds will become light and variable Tuesday, with a high in the mid-40s.

EXTENDED OUTLOOK: Fair to partly cloudy skies with no precipitation expected through Saturday. Temperatures will be generally mild, with highs in the low to mid-60s.

State Summary

STATE: Monday's weather picture included mostly cloudy skies and gusty northerly winds. These conditions existed behind the cold front which passed through the state early Monday morning, keeping temperatures from reaching above the mid-50s. Highs ranged from 46 at Ponca City to 53 at Ardmore and Hobart.

The forecast calls for fair to partly cloudy skies through Wednesday, with highs Tuesday from the low 40s to the low 50s.

Regional Summary

Kansas will be colder and clear to partly cloudy Tuesday and Wednesday, with a slow warming trend. Highs Tuesday will be in the low 50s in the west to around 40 in the northeast.

Missouri will be sunny Tuesday with highs in the upper 20s in the northeast to the 30s in the south and west.

Arkansas will be clear and cold Tuesday, turning fair and not quite as cold Wednesday. Highs Tuesday will be near 40 in the north to near 50 in the south.

Colorado will be clear to partly cloudy over the state through Wednesday, warming in the north and east Tuesday. Highs Tuesday will be in the 40s and low 50s with 30s in the mountains.

North Texas will be cooler Tuesday and mostly fair through Wednesday, with highs Tuesday from 49 to 57.

West Texas will be partly cloudy in the north, fair in the south with a warming trend Tuesday and Wednesday. Highs Tuesday will be in the 50s.

National Summary

NATIONAL: Colder temperatures and snow have reutrned to the Midwest, with temperatures more than 20 degrees colder than Sunday. An area of rain and snow continued to move across the Midwest and by Monday afternoon was centered over the Ohio Valley. Some rain and drizzle was falling in the lower portion of the Ohio Valley, and snow showers were scattered from the Great Lakes region into Nebraska and South Dakota. There were some showers in central and southern Florida, but most other parts of the Southeast were sunny. Some minor flooding due to ice jams continues on a few rivers in West Virginia and southwestern Pennsylvania. A flash flood watch remained posted for West Virginia through Monday night. Mostly sunny skies and mild temperatures continued to dominate the western United States.

Yesterday's Temperatures

YESTERDAY'S TEMPERATURES IN OKLAHOMA CITY

1 a.m.	49	1 p.m.	... 47
2 a.m.	52	2 p.m.	...48
3 a.m.	49	3 p.m.	...49
4 a.m.	...51	4 p.m.	...50
5 a.m.	47	5 p.m.	....5:
6 a.m.	46	6 p.m.	...48
7 a.m.	44	7 p.m.	...43
8 a.m.	43	8 p.m.	...42
9 a.m.	43	9 p.m.	...51
10 a.m.	...43	10 p.m.	... 37
11 a.m.	... 43	11 p.m.	...35
Noon	45	12 Midnight	33

STATE STATIONS YESTERDAY

Stations	Pre.	High	Low
Ardmore	....	53	38
Gage	.... Tr.	51	37
Guymon	.... Tr.	47	32
Hobart	....	53	40
McAlexter	....	50	42

Okla. City Airport	 51	42
Ponca City	 46	36
Tulsa	.... .01	51	39

Highest temperature last year 71. Lowest 47. Temperatures past 87 years: Highest 81 in 1954; Lowest 1 in 1936. Sunrise and sunset data: Rises 7:17 a.m.; sets 6:12 p.m. Civil twilight: Begins 6:51 a.m.; ends 6:38 p.m. Moon data: Phase Last Quarter; rises 5:57 a.m. Feb. 16; sets 5:50 p.m. Feb. 16.

TOTAL PRECIPITATION

January 1—This date in 1973 3.63 inches
January 1—This date in 1974 . 0.10
January 1—This date in 1975 . 2.79
January 1—This date in 1976 . 0.33
January 1—This date in 1977 . 1.47
Normal January 1—This date .1.73

Figure 26.2 From *The Daily Oklahoman.* Copyright © 1977, The Oklahoma Publishing Co.

Local Climatological Data

MONTHLY SUMMARY

LATITUDE 35° 24' N   LONGITUDE   97° 36' W   ELEVATION (GROUND) 1285 FT.   STANDARD TIME USED: CENTRAL   WBAN #13967

DATE	TEMPERATURE °F MAXIMUM	MINIMUM	AVERAGE	DEPARTURE FROM NORMAL	AVERAGE DEW POINT	DEGREE DAYS BASE 65° HEATING (SEASON BEGINS WITH JULY)	COOLING (SEASON BEGINS WITH JAN.)	WEATHER TYPES ON DATES OF OCCURRENCE 1 FOG 2 HEAVY FOG 3 THUNDERSTORM 4 ICE PELLETS 5 HAIL 6 GLAZE 7 DUSTSTORM 8 SMOKE. HAZE 9 BLOWING SNOW	SNOW. ICE PELLETS OR ICE ON GROUND AT 06AM IN.	PRECIPITATION WATER EQUIVA- LENT IN.	SNOW. ICE PELLETS IN.	AVG. STATION PRES- SURE ELEV. 1304 FEET M.S.L.	WIND RESULTANT DIR.	RESULTANT SPEED M.P.H.	AVERAGE SPEED M.P.H.	FASTEST MILE SPEED M.P.H.	DIRECTION	SUNSHINE MINUTES	PERCENT OF POSSIBLE	SKY COVER TENTHS SUNRISE TO SUNSET	MIDNIGHT TO MIDNIGHT	DATE
1	2	3	4	5	6	7A	7B	8	9	10	11	12	13	14	15	16	17	18	19	20	21	22
1	49	20	35	-9	22	30	0		0	T		T	28.80	33	3.8	8.3	27	N	126	21	8	4	1
2	57	20	39	-4	22	26	0		0	0		0	28.80	28	3.6	6.0	14	NW	579	97	0	0	2
3	62	29	46	3	26	19	0		0	0		0	28.71	35	.7	9.4	17	NE	575	97	0	1	3
4	55	33	44	1	27	21	0		0	0		0	28.82	03	9.3	11.7	16	NE	534	90	0	1	4
5	50	29	40	-3	35	25	0	2	0	.13		0	28.67	14	8.2	9.5	17	SE	5	1	8	7	5
6	47	22	35	-7	30	30	0	2	0	.06		0	28.68	35	19.9	20.0	30	N	0	0	10	7	6
7	45	11	28	-14	13	37	0		0	0		0	28.74	26	4.5	9.4	17	SW	428	72	5	2	7
8	46	22	34	-8	20	31	0		0	0		0	28.84	06	4.2	9.8	17	NE	591	100	0	0	8
9	62	35	49	8	35	16	0		0	0		0	28.67	18	17.5	18.4	36	SW	519	88	4	4	9
10	56	26	41	0	36	24	0	1	6	T		T	28.76	36	3.1	17.7	29	N	0	0	10	10	10
11	34	22	28	-13	17	37	0	1	6	0		T	28.80	36	10.3	10.4	26	N	3	1	10	9	11
12	55	25	40	-1	25	25	0		0	0		0	28.82	34	2.0	5.2	15	NE	317	54	4	2	12
13	52	26	39	-1	28	26	0		0	0		0	28.97	06	2.4	4.5	15	NE	526	89	3	3	13
14	60	28	44	4	31	21	0		0	0		0	28.77	18	5.7	6.5	16	SW	521	89	1	1	14
15	60	28	44	4	30	21	0	1	0	0		0	28.73	31	3.1	5.6	15	NW	586	100	6	3	15
16	66	28	47	7	21	18	0		0	0		0	28.76	26	6.7	8.2	15	SW	587	100	0	0	16
17	71*	32	52	12	19	13	0		0	0		0	28.65	22	6.4	6.9	12	SW	587	100	0	0	17
18	65	33	49	10	32	16	0		0	0		0	28.65	18	8.3	9.1	19	SW	572	98	0	0	18
19	59	35	47	8	40	18	0		0	0		0	28.59	33	2.2	15.8	31	N	491	84	4	3	19
20	37	20	29	-10	13	36	0		0	0		0	28.98	35	16.0	16.1	29	N	586	100	0	0	20
21	40	10	25	-14	9	40	0		0	0		0	28.95	16	4.4	7.2	17	S	585	100	0	0	21
22	51	21	36	-3	16	29	0		0	T		0	28.69	17	2.1	5.5	17	S	586	100	0	1	22
23	55	25	40	2	18	25	0		0	0		0	28.81	18	2.5	6.0	12	S	586	100	0	1	23
24	60	30	45	7	28	20	0		0	0		0	28.52	18	13.0	13.2	30	SW	586	100	3	1	24
25	48	27	38	0	26	27	0		0	0		0	28.62	35	9.1	11.8	28	N	553	94	1	3	25
26	46	25	46	8	19	19	0		0	0		0	28.72	23	8.9	9.4	24	SW	576	98	1	0	26
27	65	41	53*	15	22	12	0		0	0		0	28.33	21	7.2	9.9	23	SW	514	88	8	6	27
28	40	35	42	4	22	23	0		0	0		0	28.53	34	11.9	14.5	34	N	557	95	2	2	28
29	53	23	38	1	20	27	0		0	0		0	28.49	18	1.2	7.9	19	SW	588	100	0	0	29
30	39	7	23	-14	7	42	0		0	0		0	28.49	01	13.6	17.3	41	NE	534	91	8	5	30
31	24	4*	14*	-23	-13	51	0		0	0		0	28.82	05	6.5	7.9	15	NE	562	95	3	3	31

| SUM 1635 | SUM 773 | | | | | TOTAL 805 | TOTAL 0 | | | TOTAL .19 | TOTAL 0 | FOR THE MONTH: 28.72 | 32 | 1.1 | 10.3 | 41 | NE | TOTAL 14360 | % 79 | SUM 97 | SUM 78 |
| AVG. 52.7 | AVG. 24.9 | 38.8 | -1.2 | 22 | DEP. 30 | DEP. 0 | | | DEP. -1.07 | DEP. | | | | DATE: 30 | POSSIBLE 18260 | | AVG. 3.1 | AVG. 2.5 |

NUMBER OF DAYS

| SEASON TO DATE | TOTAL 1759 | TOTAL 1702 | ≥.01 INCH 2 |
| NUMBER OF DAYS | DEP. 350 | DEP. -174 | >1.0 INCH 0 |

NUMBER OF DAYS				SNOW. ICE PELLETS
MAXIMUM TEMP. ≥ 90° 0	≤ 32° 1	MINIMUM TEMP. ≤ 32° 25	≤ 0° 0	THUNDERSTORMS 0
				HEAVY FOG 2
				CLEAR 19 PARTLY CLOUDY 5 CLOUDY 7

GREATEST IN 24 HOURS AND DATES		
PRECIPITATION .19 5-6	SNOW. ICE PELLETS 0	
GREATEST DEPTH ON GROUND OF SNOW. ICE PELLETS OR ICE AND DATE 6+		

* EXTREME FOR THE MONTH - LAST OCCURRENCE IF MORE THAN ONE.
T TRACE AMOUNT
+ ALSO ON AN EARLIER DATE. OR DATES.
HEAVY FOG: - VISIBILITY 1/4 MILE OR LESS.
FIGURES FOR WIND DIRECTIONS ARE TENS OF DE- GREES CLOCKWISE FROM TRUE NORTH. 00 = CALM.
DATA IN COLS. 6 AND 12-15 ARE BASED ON 7 OR

MORE OBSERVATIONS PER DAY AT 3-HOUR INTERVALS.
FASTEST MILE WIND SPEEDS ARE FASTEST OBSERVED
ONE-MINUTE VALUES WHEN DIRECTIONS ARE IN TENS
OF DEGREES. THE / WITH THE DIRECTION INDICATES
PEAK GUST SPEED.
ANY ERRORS DETECTED WILL BE CORRECTED AND
CHANGES IN SUMMARY DATA WILL BE ANNOTATED IN
THE ANNUAL SUMMARY

SUMMARY BY HOURS

HOUR LOCAL TIME	SKY COVER TENTHS	STATION PRESSURE IN.	TEMPERATURE AIR °F	WET BULB °F	DEW PT. °F	RELATIVE HUMIDITY %	AVERAGES RESULTANT WIND WIND SPEED M.P.H.	DIRECTION	SPEED M.P.H.
00	3	28.73	35	31	23	63	9.3	27	.3
03	3	28.72	34	30	23	66	8.6	20	.7
06	3	28.71	31	28	22	70	9.2	35	1.2
09	3	28.75	34	30	23	69	9.9	36	.6
12	3	28.74	46	37	23	43	13.5	31	2.7
15	3	28.70	49	38	21	37	14.2	30	3.7
18	2	28.71	41	34	21	48	8.7	03	1.1
21	2	28.73	37	32	23	58	8.9	16	.4

HOURLY PRECIPITATION (WATER EQUIVALENT IN INCHES)

DATE	A. M. HOUR ENDING AT 1	2	3	4	5	6	7	8	9	10	11	12	P. M. HOUR ENDING AT 1	2	3	4	5	6	7	8	9	10	11	12	DATE
1														T												1
2																										2
3																										3
4																										4
5													.03	.03	.02	T	T		T							5
6	.02	T	T	.01	.03	T									T	T			.02	.01	.02	T	T	T	6
7																										7
8																										8
9																										9
10														T						T	T					10
11	T			T	T																					11
12																										12
13																										13
14																										14
15																										15
16																										16
17																										17
18																										18
19																										19
20																										20
21																										21
22	T																									22
23																										23
24																										24
25																										25
26																										26
27																										27
28																										28
29																										29
30																										30
31																										31

noaa NATIONAL OCEANIC AND / ENVIRONMENTAL
ATMOSPHERIC ADMINISTRATION / DATA SERVICE

Daniel B. Mitchell
DIRECTOR. NATIONAL CLIMATIC CENTER

USCOMM--NOAA--ASHEVILLE   01/19/77   400

Figure 26.3

OBSERVATIONS AT 3-HOUR INTERVALS

Day	Hour	Sky cover (tenths)	Ceiling (hnds. of ft.)	Visibility: whole miles	Visibility: 16ths mile	Weather	Air °F	Wet bulb °F	Dew pt. °F	Rel. hum. %	Wind dir	Wind speed (knots)
DAY 01	00	6	UNL	20			41	32	17	38	20	12
	03	0	UNL	20			37	30	18	46	22	5
	06	8	250	20			30	27	20	66	00	0
	09	9	250	12			34	29	21	59	00	0
	12	10	16	7			47	41	34	61	36	20
	15	10	80	15			34	31	25	70	35	12
	18	0	UNL	15			32	28	21	64	36	7
	21	0	UNL	20			24	23	20	65	27	2
DAY 02	00	0	UNL	20			20	19	17	88	23	4
	03	0	UNL	20			23	22	19	85	23	6
	06	0	UNL	20			25	24	20	81	23	7
	09	0	UNL	20			33	30	24	70	25	5
	12	0	UNL	20			51	40	24	35	33	10
	15	0	UNL	20			57	43	25	29	33	8
	18	1	UNL	20			45	37	24	44	00	0
	21	0	UNL	20			38	33	26	62	11	2
DAY 03	00	0	UNL	20			33	30	25	72	17	4
	03	0	UNL	20			30	28	23	75	16	3
	06	0	UNL	20			30	28	24	78	16	7
	09	0	UNL	20			38	34	27	65	14	8
	12	0	UNL	20			59	44	25	27	23	10
	15	1	UNL	20			60	45	27	28	33	13
	18	1	UNL	20			48	40	28	46	36	8
	21	3	UNL	20			44	37	28	53	02	12
DAY 04	00	7	UNL	20			40	35	28	62	02	11
	03	5	UNL	20			39	34	27	62	04	11
	06	2	UNL	20			36	33	27	70	04	10
	09	0	UNL	15			37	33	27	67	01	9
	12	0	UNL	15			49	40	27	43	04	12
	15	0	UNL	15			55	43	26	33	03	12
	18	0	UNL	15			45	37	26	47	04	8
	21	0	UNL	15			40	34	24	53	24	8
DAY 05	00	0	UNL	15			35	31	24	64	03	6
	03	0	UNL	15			31	28	22	69	00	0
	06	6	UNL	15			30	28	25	82	16	6
	09	1	UNL	10			37	35	32	82	14	9
	12	10	11	2		RF	45	44	43	93	15	8
	15	10	28	5		RF	50	47	45	83	15	12
	18	10	14	2		RF	48	46	45	89	15	12
	21	10	5	2		RF	47	46	45	93	15	13
DAY 06	00	10	5	0	8	LF	47	46	45	93	02	5
	03	10	5	0	8	LF	47	46	46	96	35	9
	06	10	15	7			39	37	35	86	35	18
	09	10	18	6		F	36	33	29	76	35	24
	12	10	15	7			35	33	29	79	35	24
	15	10	22	8			33	30	25	72	36	21
	18	4	UNL	7			32	28	20	61	35	19
	21	0	UNL	15			26	22	09	48	35	19
DAY 07	00	0	UNL	15			22	18	06	50	35	12
	03	0	UNL	20			17	15	07	65	33	8
	06	0	UNL	20			14	12	06	70	31	3
	09	9	UNL	20			20	17	09	62	19	3
	12	9	UNL	20			36	28	11	35	19	8
	15	0	UNL	20			43	34	18	37	24	15
	18	0	UNL	20			35	30	22	59	18	7
	21	0	UNL	20			34	31	25	70	22	9
DAY 08	00	0	UNL	20			35	31	24	64	36	11
	03	0	UNL	20			31	27	19	61	36	11
	06	0	UNL	20			25	23	16	69	01	11
	09	0	UNL	15			25	22	14	63	10	4
	12	0	UNL	15			37	30	18	46	08	5
	15	0	UNL	15			45	35	19	35	14	12
	18	0	UNL	15			36	31	22	57	14	6
	21	0	UNL	15			35	31	25	67	15	8
DAY 09	00	0	UNL	15			36	33	27	70	15	8
	03	0	UNL	20			36	33	29	76	15	7
	06	0	UNL	20			38	35	31	76	16	14
	09	0	UNL	20			44	39	32	63	17	18
	12	3	UNL	20			55	46	36	49	20	25
	15	9	UNL	20			62	50	38	41	20	26
	18	10	UNL	20			55	48	40	57	17	14
	21	5	UNL	20			52	48	45	77	17	16
DAY 10	00	3	UNL	20			53	50	47	80	18	16
	03	10	13	10			54	52	50	86	18	16
	06	10	250	15			54	52	50	86	17	13
	09	10	13	7			55	53	51	86	17	5
	12	10	14	7		L	35	32	28	76	35	18
	15	10	10	5		F	28	26	22	78	35	21
	18	10	9	6		F	26	25	22	85	36	19
	21	10	12	8			27	25	21	78	02	15
DAY 11	00	10	18	10			27	24	16	63	36	16
	03	10	18	8			24	21	12	60	36	14
	06	10	18	10			23	20	11	60	36	13
	09	10	7	4		F	22	21	19	88	36	9
	12	10	13	7			27	24	16	63	35	10
	15	10	15	10			32	27	18	56	35	10
	18	10	11	8			31	28	21	66	00	0
	21	10	8	8			31	28	23	72	00	0
DAY 12	00	2	UNL	10			32	29	24	72	00	0
	03	0	UNL	15			31	28	23	72	20	4
	06	0	UNL	15			30	27	20	66	22	3
	09	0	UNL	15			31	29	24	75	21	4
	12	5	UNL	15			46	38	26	46	35	6
	15	5	UNL	15			54	42	27	35	34	8
	18	3	UNL	15			43	36	26	51	36	6
	21	0	UNL	15			41	35	27	58	05	5
DAY 13	00	0	UNL	15			39	35	29	67	04	9
	03	0	UNL	15			32	30	26	79	35	4
	06	6	UNL	15			30	29	26	85	04	7
	09	7	UNL	7			32	30	27	82	00	0
	12	1	UNL	7			45	38	29	54	13	5
	15	2	UNL	7			51	41	28	41	17	3
	18	6	UNL	10			44	38	29	56	16	3
	21	3	UNL	15			36	33	28	73	00	0
DAY 14	00	0	UNL	15			31	30	28	89	15	3
	03	0	UNL	15			30	29	27	89	15	5
	06	1	UNL	15			29	28	26	89	14	4
	09	3	UNL	8			35	34	32	89	17	6
	12	1	UNL	8			53	45	35	51	21	11
	15	0	UNL	12			59	47	34	39	21	9
	18	0	UNL	15			47	41	34	61	17	3
	21	0	UNL	15			40	37	33	76	16	4
DAY 15	00	0	UNL	15			36	35	33	89	14	4
	03	0	UNL	15			34	33	32	92	16	4
	06	0	UNL	15			33	32	31	92	00	0
	09	6	UNL	7			35	33	30	82	32	6
	12	9	UNL	8			50	42	31	48	34	9
	15	3	UNL	12			57	44	27	32	31	6
	18	6	UNL	15			46	38	27	48	32	6
	21	2	UNL	15			41	35	25	53	28	4
DAY 16	00	0	UNL	15			36	32	24	62	33	3
	03	0	UNL	20			33	29	21	61	32	7
	06	0	UNL	20			30	26	19	64	30	6
	09	0	UNL	20			33	30	24	70	23	3
	12	0	UNL	20			59	43	21	23	24	10
	15	0	UNL	20			66	46	17	15	23	14
	18	0	UNL	20			50	38	18	28	21	8
	21	0	UNL	20			46	36	20	36	22	9
DAY 17	00	0	UNL	20			43	34	20	40	22	7
	03	0	UNL	20			40	32	18	41	23	7
	06	0	UNL	20			33	28	17	52	23	6
	09	0	UNL	15			41	33	20	43	26	4
	12	0	UNL	15			61	44	19	20	20	4
	15	0	UNL	15			69	47	14	12	22	9
	18	0	UNL	20			55	41	20	25	19	7
	21	0	UNL	20			47	38	25	42	17	4
DAY 18	00	0	UNL	20			39	34	25	57	22	8
	03	1	UNL	20			40	34	24	53	16	5
	06	2	UNL	20			34	31	25	70	15	5
	09	0	UNL	15			39	35	30	70	16	6
	12	0	UNL	15			61	48	33	35	18	11
	15	0	UNL	15			65	52	39	39	20	12
	18	0	UNL	15			56	48	40	55	16	10
	21	0	UNL	15			48	45	42	80	15	6
DAY 19	00	0	UNL	15			51	50	49	93	16	10
	03	7	13	12			54	52	51	90	19	13
	06	6	UNL	10			51	49	48	90	19	12
	09	9	9	10			51	49	48	90	21	10
	12	0	UNL	12			58	50	42	55	24	10
	15	3	UNL	20			54	43	29	38	35	16
	18	0	UNL	12			50	41	29	44	36	17
	21	0	UNL	12			40	34	25	55	01	22
DAY 20	00	0	UNL	12			35	30	22	59	36	17
	03	0	UNL	15			32	28	19	59	35	16
	06	0	UNL	15			28	25	17	63	34	16
	09	0	UNL	15			26	23	15	63	35	16
	12	0	UNL	15			34	26	08	34	34	17
	15	0	UNL	20			37	28	06	27	34	16
	18	0	UNL	20			30	23	06	36	35	8
	21	0	UNL	20			22	19	09	57	36	6
DAY 21	00	0	UNL	20			22	18	05	48	02	5
	03	0	UNL	15			18	15	05	57	03	4
	06	0	UNL	15			13	12	05	70	25	3
	09	0	UNL	15			20	18	10	65	18	3
	12	0	UNL	15			32	25	09	38	15	9
	15	0	UNL	15			39	30	12	33	18	13
	18	0	UNL	20			31	25	12	45	16	5
	21	0	UNL	20			26	22	13	58	17	8
DAY 22	00	1	UNL	20			29	24	11	47	17	10
	03	7	120	15			30	25	14	51	17	6
	06	0	UNL	15			24	22	15	68	14	6
	09	0	UNL	15			29	26	18	63	17	4
	12	0	UNL	15			45	35	18	34	31	6
	15	0	UNL	20			50	37	17	27	36	6
	18	0	UNL	20			42	33	16	35	00	0
	21	0	UNL	20			36	30	17	46	00	0
DAY 23	00	0	UNL	20			31	26	17	56	22	3
	03	0	UNL	20			28	25	17	63	21	4
	06	0	UNL	20			27	24	18	69	31	5
	09	0	UNL	20			32	28	20	61	33	4
	12	0	UNL	20			48	36	16	28	11	6
	15	0	UNL	20			54	40	17	23	18	5
	18	0	UNL	20			42	33	18	38	14	6
	21	0	UNL	20			39	32	21	48	18	7
DAY 24	00	0	UNL	20			35	30	21	57	17	9
	03	0	UNL	20			37	31	20	50	18	11
	06	0	UNL	20			31	28	21	66	17	8
	09	10	UNL	20			41	35	26	55	18	14
	12	1	UNL	20			55	44	31	40	19	17
	15	0	UNL	20			59	46	32	36	19	17
	18	0	UNL	20			50	42	32	50	18	8
	21	0	UNL	15			45	42	38	77	16	8
DAY 25	00	0	UNL	15			43	41	39	86	15	6
	03	10	16	10			44	42	40	86	02	4
	06	6	16	12			37	33	26	65	36	14
	09	2	UNL	12			35	32	26	70	36	12
	12	0	UNL	20			45	37	24	44	35	19
	15	0	UNL	20			48	37	21	34	35	18
	18	0	UNL	20			39	31	17	41	34	5
	21	1	UNL	20			31	26	17	56	22	4
DAY 26	00	0	UNL	20			28	25	18	66	23	5
	03	0	UNL	20			27	25	20	75	24	7
	06	0	UNL	20			26	24	19	75	23	5
	09	0	UNL	20			34	29	21	59	23	8
	12	0	UNL	20			58	42	20	23	23	12
	15	0	UNL	20			65	45	16	15	24	16
	18	1	UNL	20			53	40	19	26	18	4
	21	0	UNL	20			46	37	22	39	20	8
DAY 27	00	1	UNL	20			44	35	21	40	19	7
	03	5	UNL	20			44	35	21	40	19	6
	06	5	UNL	20			43	35	23	45	18	9
	09	10	UNL	20			45	37	24	44	18	18
	12	10	UNL	20			56	42	23	28	23	12
	15	7	UNL	20			64	45	18	17	28	10
	18	0	UNL	20			56	41	20	25	30	2
	21	7	UNL	20			48	38	23	37	30	5
DAY 28	00	10	250	20			42	35	25	51	32	8
	03	7	UNL	20			42	36	26	53	33	11
	06	5	UNL	20			42	35	24	49	34	18
	09	0	UNL	20			36	30	20	52	36	25
	12	0	UNL	15			40	32	18	41	36	17
	15	0	UNL	20			47	37	20	34	34	8
	18	0	UNL	20			39	32	19	45	24	6
	21	0	UNL	20			40	33	21	47	25	8
DAY 29	00	0	UNL	20			42	34	22	45	27	14
	03	0	UNL	20			37	31	20	50	01	10
	06	0	UNL	20			27	24	16	63	03	5
	09	0	UNL	20			32	28	19	59	00	0
	12	0	UNL	20			45	35	17	32	14	6
	15	0	UNL	20			52	39	20	28	18	9
	18	0	UNL	20			42	34	22	45	14	5
	21	0	UNL	20			40	34	24	53	15	6
DAY 30	00	1	UNL	20			35	31	24	64	16	5
	03	3	UNL	20			35	32	27	73	18	7
	06	4	UNL	20			35	31	25	67	01	8
	09	10	UNL	7			32	27	15	49	02	24
	12	10	120	10			28	22	05	37	01	22
	15	9	100	10			19	14	-08	29	35	20
	18	0	UNL	15			14	10	-19	21	36	20
	21	0	UNL	15			09	06	-16	30	35	14
DAY 31	00	0	UNL	15			07	04	-15	35	01	12
	03	3	UNL	20			06	04	-14	39	03	8
	06	2	UNL	20			05	03	-14	40	03	6
	09	1	UNL	20			08	05	-14	35	06	6
	12	7	UNL	20			17	12	-13	25	10	4
	15	2	UNL	20			22	16	-13	20	11	6
	18	0	UNL	20			18	13	-11	26	09	6
	21	4	UNL	20			19	14	-07	31	06	7

NOTES

CEILING
UNL INDICATES UNLIMITED

WEATHER

- ■ TORNADO
- T THUNDERSTORM
- Q SQUALL
- R RAIN
- RW RAIN SHOWERS
- ZR FREEZING RAIN
- L DRIZZLE
- ZL FREEZING DRIZZLE
- S SNOW
- SP SNOW PELLETS
- IC ICE CRYSTALS
- SW SNOW SHOWERS
- SG SNOW GRAINS
- IP ICE PELLETS
- A HAIL
- F FOG
- IF ICE FOG
- GF GROUND FOG
- BD BLOWING DUST
- BN BLOWING SAND
- BS BLOWING SNOW
- BY BLOWING SPRAY
- K SMOKE
- H HAZE
- D DUST

WIND

DIRECTIONS ARE THOSE FROM WHICH THE WIND BLOWS. INDICATED IN TENS OF DEGREES FROM TRUE NORTH: I.E.. 09 FOR EAST. 18 FOR SOUTH. 27 FOR WEST. ENTRY OF 00 IN THE DIRECTION COLUMN INDICATES CALM.

SPEED IS EXPRESSED IN KNOTS: MULTIPLY BY 1.15 TO CONVERT TO MILES PER HOUR.

STATION: OKLAHOMA CITY OKLA

YEAR & MONTH: 76 12

U.S. DEPARTMENT OF COMMERCE
NATIONAL CLIMATIC CENTER
FEDERAL BUILDING
ASHEVILLE. N.C. 28801

AN EQUAL OPPORTUNITY EMPLOYER

POSTAGE AND FEES PAID
U.S. DEPARTMENT OF COMMERCE
COM-210

U.S. MAIL

FIRST CLASS

Figure 26.3

MISCELLANEOUS EXCUSES FOR DELAY

Read the contract Contracts differ in their specified excusable delays. The inclusion or omission of a particular one should be noted. If included, you can refer to it. If not included, the unusual facts may persuade a court to hold the delay to be excusable. The point is that they must be unexpected and not within your control.

Force majeure   Force majeure is a term sometimes used in private contracts. It means acts of God such as lightning, floods, storms, earthquakes, and epidemics. All these are ordinarily excuses for delays.

Strikes   Whether a delay due to a strike is an excusable delay depends upon the wording of the contract and possibly the circumstances as well.

Subcontractors   If a subcontractor causes delay to the prime, the prime contract may control. The owner may not recognize this delay. His decision may depend upon the circumstance. The subcontractor will have damaged the prime, but possibly the prime's time will be extended, and he will be fully compensated by the owner.

Suppliers   If a supplier causes delay to the prime, the prime contract may control. The owner may not recognize the delay on the basis that he had no concern as to how or when or at what price the prime would be obtaining the material or equipment. On the other hand, if a certain electric transformer is required and is no longer being manufactured, the prime has a good position. As between the prime and the supplier, there may have been a breach of a supply contract, or of a purchase order that was accepted and thereby constituted a contract. The more informal the purchase, the weaker the case.

RECORD KEEPING

Excusable delays chart   Although it is necessary for a contractor to prepare a progress chart on which he schedules the starting times for different phases of the work, and the periods different trades or subcontractors will be on the project, it is equally necessary that he have on that chart, or preferably on an excusable delays chart, current information as to what the situation really is, as distinguished from the planned progress. This second chart is what is needed as the basic record for preparation of applications for extensions of time and supportive proof that they are meritorious. This chart should have a series of vertical columns—one for each day, beginning with the notice to proceed—and a series of horizontal lines bearing appropriate legends, such as weather, the names of the subcontractors, the name of the general contractor, the number of men on the project, and the various causes for delay. The period of delay can be shown on a horizontal line—in a yellow color, for example—between the vertical column for January 15 and the vertical column for March 3. When work is in progress, a different color—for example, red—can be used on the horizontal line. A number of different lines may be required to illustrate how one cause of delay produces other delays. This is not easy, it requires time, and it will be something less than perfect, but it is better than nothing. A suggested form appears as Figure 26.4. As change orders cause delays, it can be modified and designated: Change Order and Excusable Delay Chart.

Control number sheet   There can be many problems of extra cost and delay in a large construction contract. The careful contractor, despite the time and cost, should consider giving each problem a control number and start building a file on it. On one side of the file, or as a cover page, he can maintain a control

FIGURE 26.4   Excusable Delays Chart

	November	December	January
Weather (post daily)	1, 2, 3, . . .	1, 2, 3, . . .	1, 2, 3, . . .
Temperature 8 A.M.			
Temperature 12 noon			
Temperature 5 P.M.			
Departure from normal			
Precipitation			
Wind			
Chill temperature 8 A.M.			
Weather graph (extend daily)			
Actual temperature			
Wind chill temperature			
Men on job (post daily)			
Total, subcontractor crews			
Total, prime contractor crews			
Total men on job			
Progress graph (extend daily)			
Total men on job			
Subcontractor crews			
Prime Contractor Crews			
Firms on project and days (post daily)			
Prime Contractor, Demolition			
Mechanical Sub, Demolition			
Prime, Carpentry			
Mechanical, Exterior Utilities			
Glass & Glazing Sub			
Painting Sub, Exterior			
Electrical Sub, Exterior			
Mechanical Sub, Interior			
Electrical Sub, Interior			
Tile Sub			
(Others)			

Delay Control Numbers (show a horizontal yellow bar during period of delay; red bar during period at work.)

1. Stopped up sewer lines
2. Closet door sizes
3. Exterior electrical
4. Paint material
5. Electric transformers
6. Medicine cabinets

number sheet, which will serve as a checklist and running summary. It can be cleaned up, revised, and extended from time to time. Whether typed or in longhand and whether marked up or very clean, *it should be kept current.* A list of control numbers, with their descriptions, tacked on the wall will make it easy to quickly write on the margin of any letter or informal memorandum the control number so that it will go into the right file. The file clerk, with some supervision can make initial postings to the control sheet. A suggested form for the control number sheet appears as Figure 26.5.

FIGURE 26.5 Control Number Sheet

1. *Control number:* _____
2. *Work direction:* by _____, per letter dated_____
3. *Type of work performed:*
   a. By Prime: _____
   b. By Subcontractor:_____
4. *Reference to specifications:*
   a. Section: _____; title: _____; page: _____
   b. Paragraph: _____; caption: _____
5. *No Specifications applicable:*
   a. Interpretation by prime: _____
   b. Interpretation by sub: _____
6. *Contract Drawings for Reference:* Sheets _____, _____, _____, _____
7. *No Contract Drawings Applicable:*
   a. Interpretation by prime: _____
   b. Interpretation by sub: _____
8. *Work outside scope of contract:*
   a. Additional time required: _____ to _____ (_____ days)
   b. Additional time required for delayed progress of the original contract completion date by _____ days. This can (cannot) be followed on chart.
   c. Domino effect of delay on following firms: _____
      _____
      _____
9. *Request increase in contract price:*
   a. Amount: $ _____
   b. Cost breakdown is (is not) attached in _____ pages covering reasonable cost of work interpreted not to be in original contract.
   c. Date of request: _____; date of response: _____
   d. Change order has (has not) been issued for the extra work involved and is (is not) subject to equitable adjustment in dollar value and time extensions. Number: _____ Date: _____
   e. Position of contracting officer: _____
      _____
10. *Request for time extensions for weather delay:*
    a. From _____ to _____ (_____ days) according to U.S. Weather Bureau records.
    b. Can (cannot) be followed on chart.
    c. Minimum temperature work allowed by contract: _____ degrees
    d. Following firms delayed by weather: _____
       _____
       _____
    e. Date of request: _____; date of response: _____
    f. Extension allowed (disallowed) in Change Order No. _____
11. *Disputes with contracting officer:*
    a. In dispute with contracting officer:_____
       _____
    b. Not in dispute with contracting officer:_____
       _____
12. *Disputes with subcontractor:*
    a. In dispute with _____; subcontractor: _____
       _____
    b. Not in dispute with _____; subcontractor: _____
       _____

13. *Payments for extra work:*
   a. Incurred costs for this extra work have (have not) been paid.
   b. Prime has (has not) paid the subcontractors for this extra work.
   c. Prime has (has not) paid the contract supplier for this extra material.

14. *Prime's back charges on extra work:*

Date	Number	Amount	Firm

15. *Important Correspondence:*   Letter number   Date
   a. From prime to architect: _____   _____
   b. From prime to contracting officer: _____   _____
   c. From architect to prime: _____   _____
   d. From contracting officer to prime: _____   _____
   e. Subcontract correspondence: _____   _____

16. *Comment on time delay:*
   Weather: _____
   _____
   _____

   Extra Work: _____
   _____
   _____

SUMMARY

General comment   It is most important (1) that you read your contract and (2) that you understand it. You should reproduce portions of it relative to any control number and put them in that file. This will help you because you may forget what you read. You must not depend upon friendly personal relations and warm verbal assurances to get you anywhere. Contract law is hard law. Contracts are made to fix obligations, rights, and remedies. They will be respected unless they are harsh or applied harshly. *Contracts involve dollars.* Keep records as if the contracting officer at the last minute is not going to agree. Establish a record-keeping system and work at it.

If things get really bad and you receive a "Failure to Make Progress Letter," you will be facing possible termination. Reply promptly by letter and state what you are doing to speed up progress and ask for an extension. Deliver the letter personally and inquire which trade is not progressing. Then put more men on the project, if you can.

Engaging counsel   The services of an attorney may be required. If he has to organize all the evidence and prepare charts because you failed to do so, do not complain about his fee. The best way to engage an attorney is to bring him your *organized* evidence and a written statement of your position. This may reduce his time by two-thirds, and it will enable him to analyze much quicker your position, dictate his evaluation, and then discuss with you his recommendations. You can then decide what you want to do, based on your business judgment.

If you have kept good records and adhered to notice requirements, you will have sold your application and will not need counsel.

Chapter **27**

Obtaining Adequate Compensation for Delay

JOHN B. DENNISTON, ESQ.
Partner, Covington & Burling, Washington, D.C.

There is probably no more common problem that a construction contractor has to grapple with than delay. No matter how careful and detailed the contractor's planning for the execution of a particular project, changes in the project itself, changes in the anticipated manpower, equipment, work sequence, or methods for accomplishing the project, or some other unforeseen circumstances almost invariably arise. Any of these circumstances may carry with them the potential for delaying the entire project or at least some portion of the work. The contractor's project management spend much time and effort in dealing with such eventualities in order to minimize their adverse effects.

What happens if, despite these efforts, the contractor is significantly delayed in his completion of the project? As discussed in the previous chapter, *Basis for Extension of Time,* if the delay was the responsibility of the owner or the owner's representative (such as the architect engineer or the owner's construction management firm), or if the delay arose from unforeseeable factors beyond the control and without the fault or negligence of the contractor (as from labor strikes, unusually bad weather, or acts of God), the contractor will normally be entitled to an appropriate extension of the contractually required completion date. But the benefits of such a time extension are strictly defensive; the extension prevents a default termination or the assessment of liquidated or other damages based on the contractor's excusable late performance. What about the additional expense that the contractor will almost certainly have incurred during the extended period of performance or as a result of his efforts to minimize or avoid that extended period of performance?

Under some circumstances the contractor is entitled to an increase in the contract price or to damages to compensate him for such additional delay-related expenses. This determination depends on the terms and conditions of the contract in question and on the events that gave rise to the delay.

BASIS FOR RECOVERY

Generally speaking, the contractor will not be entitled to compensation for delays that arise from unforeseeable factors over which neither the owner nor the contractor has any control—such as strikes, weather, or acts of God. The contractor, however, may well be entitled to compensation for delays which are caused by the owner or his representative or which come about because of the owner's breach of a duty or obligation—express or implied—owed to the contractor under the terms of the contract. If the contractor is delayed by the unexcused lateness of *his own* subcontractors, suppliers, or materialmen, he is also entitled to compensation from them for any reasonably foreseeable damages incurred as a result.[1]

The contractor may also be able to hold the owner liable for unforeseeable events over which neither the owner nor the contractor had any control where such delays can be traced to an earlier delay for which the owner is liable.[2]

Compensable delays are most commonly caused by changes in the work ordered by the owner or the architect engineer. The additional cost of the changed work undoubtedly will be covered by the change clause or similar clause in the contract. But implementing a significant change, or a large number of minor changes, will also frequently increase the contractor's costs of performing the *unchanged* work by causing him to delay or disrupt the latter work or to perform it in a different manner or in a different sequence than had been originally planned.

Early court and administrative tribunal decisions interpreting the change clause used in federal government construction contracts prior to 1968 held that a contractor was supposed to have anticipated such delays or disruptions of the unchanged work and therefore was not entitled to additional compensation for this type of increased expense.[3] Later decisions held that the contractor

---

[1] *General Ins. Co. of Am. v. Hercules Constr. Co.,* 385 F.2d 13 (8th Cir. 1967); *Gulf States Creosot. Co. v. Loving,* 120 F.2d 195 (4th Cir. 1941).

[2] *J. D. Hedin Constr. Co. v. United States,* 171 Ct. Cl. 70, 347 F.2d 235 (1965).

[3] *United States v. Rice,* 317 U.S. 61 (1942); *Chouteau v. United States,* 95 U.S. 61 (1877).

should be compensated for such additional costs if the impact on the unchanged work was closely subsequent in time and clearly traceable to the directed changes.[4] In any event, the federal government's construction contract change clause was modified in 1968 to overturn the earlier cases and to assure the contractor compensation for his additional costs (plus profit) incurred in performing the unchanged work. Today a contractor should be able to recover most delay-related expenses flowing from changes in the work.

Perhaps the next most common category of compensable delays in construction contracting are those caused by unanticipated subsurface conditions at the work site. Again, under current federal government construction contract clauses, where similar clauses are used in state, local, or private work, and in some jurisdictions under the modern common law, delay-related expenses resulting from differing site conditions are compensable (normally, under the special clauses, with profit) to the same extent as other expenses directly associated with the changed condition.[5]

A contractor may also incur additional expense when the owner notifies him that a change in the work is contemplated but then delays before finalizing the change or ordering the contractor to proceed with the modification. Frequently such delays occurring prior to the issuance of the final change order are held not to be compensable under the change clause of a contract.[6] Nevertheless, in many cases the contractor can recover compensation for such delays, either administratively where the contract contains a suspension-of-work clause, or in a court action for breach of the owner's implied obligation not to hinder the contractor's performance or make that performance more expensive.[7] In either type of proceeding, the contractor must show that the delay was for an *unreasonable* period of time and that the contractor thereby incurred additional costs. Normally profit on such costs cannot be recovered. In addition, the suspension-of-work clause used by the federal government prohibits the recovery of extra costs incurred more than 20 days prior to the contractor's giving notice of the act or failure to act which is causing the delay.

Another common type of compensable delay is that attributable to defective plans or specifications issued by the owner or the architect engineer governing the performance of the contractor's work. Normally the owner is held to have impliedly warranted the accuracy of such plans or specifications and hence *any* delay—whether or not unreasonable in length—and any increased costs incurred by the contractor as a result of hidden errors or conflicts in these

[4]*Paul Hardeman, Inc. v. United States*, 186 Ct. Cl. 743, 406 F.2d 1357 (1969); *Dworshak Dam Constructors*, ENG BCA 3240, 73-2 BCA ¶10039; *Power Equip. Corp.*, ASBCA 5904, 1964 BCA ¶4025.

[5]*Moorhead Constr. Co. v. City of Grand Forks*, 508 F.2d 1008 (8th Cir. 1975); *D. H. Dave, Inc. & Gerben Contr. Co.*, CASBCA 13005, 73-2 BCA ¶10191.

[6]*Cosmo Constr. Co. v. United States*, 194 Ct. Cl. 559, 439 F.2d 160 (1971); *Timmons, Butt & Head, Inc.*, ASBCA 15948, 72-1 BCA ¶9247; *Weldfab, Inc.*, IBCA 268, 61-2 BCA ¶3121.

[7]*Continental Ill. Nat'l Bank v. United States*, 121 Ct. Cl. 203, 101 F. Supp. 755, *cert. denied*, 343 U.S. 963 (1952); *Alrae Constr. Co.*, VACAB 970, 73-1 BCA ¶9872; *George A. Fuller Co.*, ASBCA 8524, 1962 BCA ¶3619.

documents (including the time to identify the errors or conflicts, to develop a solution, and to have that solution accepted by the owner or architect engineer) are compensable administratively.[8] The contractor is also normally entitled to profits on such additional expenses.

Other types of delay that are frequently encountered include: delays in the owner's issuance of a notice to proceed with the work under the contract; delays in obtaining access to all or part of the work site on which the contractor's work is to be performed; delays in the furnishing of any materials or equipment that the owner agreed to make available for the contractor's use in performing the work; and delays in inspecting, testing, or approving portions of the work as required by the contract.

In these situations the owner is generally held liable for the contractor's delay-related expenses if the contract includes an express warranty that the notice to proceed will be given, or the site will be made available, or the materials or equipment will be furnished by a specific date and the owner fails to do so for any reason.[9] If the contract does not identify a specific date by which the owner warrants that these events will take place, the owner may nevertheless be held to have impliedly agreed to give the notice to proceed, or to make the site, materials, or equipment available, or to accomplish the required inspection, testing, or approvals, within a time that is reasonable for purposes of enabling the contractor to perform his work in a timely manner. The owner can be held liable for unreasonable delays in doing so, either administratively pursuant to a suspension-of-work clause or in a breach-of-contract action in a court.[10] However, if such delays were beyond the owner's control and without his fault or negligence, the delays are not unreasonable, and there is no breach of the owner's implied obligations.[11]

[8]*W. L. Hailey & Co. v. County of Niagara,* 388 F.2d 746 (2d Cir. 1967); *Laburnum Constr. Corp. v. U.S.,* 163 Ct. Cl. 339, 325 F.2d 451 (1963).

[9]*Abbett Elec. Corp. v. United States,* 142 Ct. Cl. 609, 162 F. Supp. 772 (1958) and *T. C. Bateson Constr. Co.,* ASBCA 5985, 60-2 BCA ¶2767 ASBCA 6028, 1963 BCA ¶3692 (delayed notice to proceed); *Merritt-Chapman & Scott Corp. v. United States,* 194 Ct. Cl. 461, 439 F.2d 185 (1971) (delayed availability of a portion of the construction site); *Peter Salvucci & Sons, Inc. v. State,* 110 N.H. 136, 268 A.2d 899 (1970) and *George A. Fuller Co. v. United States,* 108 Ct. Cl. 70, 69 F. Supp. 409 (1947) (delay from failure to furnish construction models or materials).

[10]*Ross Eng. Co. v. United States,* 92 Ct. Cl. 253 (1940); *L. O. Brayton & Co.,* IBCA 641-5-67, 70-2 BCA ¶8510 and *Kraft Constr. Co.,* ASBCA 4976, 59-2 BCA ¶2347 (unreasonably delayed notice to proceed); *Paccon, Inc. v. United States,* 185 Ct. Cl. 24, 399 F.2d 162 (1968), *L. L. Hall Constr. Co. v. United States,* 177 Ct. Cl. 870, 379 F.2d 559 (1966) and *John A. Johnson & Sons v. United States,* 180 Ct. Cl. 969 (1967) (unreasonable delays caused by other contractors at the site where the owner was responsible for coordinating the work); *General Ins. Co. of Am. v. Hercules Constr. Co., supra* note 1, *Ben C. Gerwick, Inc., v. United States,* 152 Ct. Cl. 69, 285 F.2d 432 (1961) and *S. Patti Constr. Co.,* ASBCA 8423, 1964 BCA ¶4225 (unreasonably late delivery of materials or equipment); *Lea County Constr. Co.,* ASBCA 10093, 67-1 BCA ¶6243 (unexplained and hence unreasonable delays in approval of shop drawings).

[11]*Lenry, Inc. v. United States,* 156 Ct. Cl. 46, 297 F.2d 550 (1962) (contractor's access to the site delayed by a flood, an act of God over which the owner had no control); *Donald M. Drake Co. v. United States,* 194 Ct. Cl. 549, 439 F.2d 169 (1971) (interruptions to the contractor's work for the benefit of other contractors at the site not unreasonable); *Peter Kiewit Sons' Co. v. United States,* 138 Ct. Cl. 668, 151 F. Supp. 726 (1957) (owner had made diligent efforts in a vain attempt to ensure prompt delivery of concrete materials).

The contractor's rights to compensation for all these categories of delay-related expense are, of course, subject to limitation by the express agreement of the parties. Thus, if the contract provides that the owner may delay the date by which certain events will occur without liability or that he will be liable only to the extent of granting an appropriate extension of time, then the contractor will normally not be able to recover additional delay-related costs.[12]

Obviously the determination of a contractor's rights to recover delay-related expenses in any given situation is a complex question that requires careful analysis of the facts and of the provisions of the contract in question, including any pre-bid discussions or representations by the owner or his representatives. Frequently the advice of legal counsel is required. Assuming that there is a basis for the contractor to recover delay-related costs on a particular job, how does he proceed to obtain the relief to which he is entitled?

DEVELOPING A CLAIM

The first requirement is that the contractor must be in a position to ascertain promptly when events have occurred at the work site or elsewhere that have the potential to delay or disrupt the performance of the work required by his contract. In order to do this, the contractor must have developed a detailed plan and schedule for performing the work. Many construction contracts require the contractor to submit just such a plan, often in a specified format, such as one utilizing the critical path method (CPM). Careful attention and considerable effort in the preparation of this plan is important in order that it may serve as a proper foundation for any subsequent claims for delay-related expenses as well as an indispensable tool for the efficient management of the work.

Prior to the plan's submission to the owner or his representative for approval, the contractor should be satisfied that the plan represents the optimum way for him to perform the work and clearly calls out the extent to which the cooperation of, or other input from, the owner, the architect engineer, other contractors, or any other third party involved, is required. The plan or its submittal letter should contain an express statement to the effect that its achievement is dependent on the owner's cooperation or on the identified interfaces with the other parties on and off the work site.

Next, the contractor should implement a procedure for promptly identifying the extent to which the actual performance of the work deviates from the plan originally submitted to and approved by the owner. This can be accomplished by having field management personnel follow a regular format in reporting progress at the work site on a day-by-day basis, specifically including a report of whether the work planned for accomplishment that day was accomplished; and if not, why not. Based on these regular reports or any other information, the home office staff or project management personnel should be responsible for giving any required notification of a condition that potentially causes delay in the contractor's planned completion of the work. Once such notice is given, the

---

[12]*Wells Bros. v. United States,* 254 U.S. 83 (1920).

requirements of a suspension-of-work, or similar, clause are satisfied. Although such clauses also require the prompt submission of the final claim for such delays, that submission should not be made until the contractor is able accurately to estimate the effect and impact of any related delay that may be encountered.

Finally, the contractor must begin promptly to identify and, if feasible, segregate and record the additional expenses that are *actually incurred* in performing the contract *as a result* of the delay in question. Under the language of the federal government's current suspension-of-work clause, the government-caused delays must be the sole proximate cause of the delay damages for which the contractor is compensated. The existence of concurrent delays for which the government is not responsible may preclude recovery, although on occasion where both the government and the contractor are at fault, partial compensation is still granted.[13] Under the language of other versions of the clause and at common law, the test was not as strict.[14]

These expenses can vary widely depending on the particular situation involved. Typically included are the costs of idle men and equipment, losses of efficiency from the impact or ripple effect of the delay, additional overhead, escalation incident to performing the work in a later period of time, and—under certain circumstances—acceleration efforts.

Idle Men and Equipment

During a period of delay a contractor's labor force frequently cannot be used in a productive manner. If it is not practical to have idled manpower transferred to another job or to work productively on some other part of the job in question, the contractor must then decide whether to lay the men off. If good management judgment dictates that he not do so—that is, if he foresees the probable difficulty of rehiring the workers or of recruiting and training new personnel in order to be able to resume the work in a timely manner once the delay has ended—the contractor can claim their full salaries or wages and fringe benefits while idle.[15]

Similarly, a contractor must frequently keep construction equipment on standby, but idle during a period of delay. Rental payments allocable to that period, along with any storage or maintenance expenses, are recoverable.[16] Contractor-owned equipment can normally be charged for at a rate equal to 50 percent of the contractor's total actual expenses of ownership, calculated as shown by the current edition of the *Contractors' Equipment Ownership Schedule* published by the Associated General Contractors of America, Inc.[17]

---

[13]*E. H. Marhoefer, Jr., Co.,* DOT CAB 70-17, 71-1 BCA ¶8791.

[14]*Merritt-Chapman & Scott Corp.,* 208 Ct. Cl., 528 F.2d 1392 (1976); *Raymond Constructors of Africa, Ltd. v. United States,* 188 Ct. Cl. 147, 411 F.2d 1227 (1969) (trial commissioner's opinion).

[15]*Laburnum Constr. Corp. v. United States, supra* note 8, *International Builders of Fla., Inc.,* FAA CAP 67-5, 69-1 BCA ¶7706; *Hardeman-Monier-Hutcherson,* ASBCA 11785, 67-1 BCA ¶6210.

[16]*Peter Salvucci & Sons v. State, supra* note 9, *Weaver Constr. Co.,* ASBCA 12577, 69-1 BCA ¶7455.

[17]*Nolan Bros., Inc. v. United States,* 194 Ct. Cl. 1, 437 F.2d 1371 (1971); *L. L. Hall Constr. Co. v. United States,* 177 Ct. Cl. 870, 379 F.2d 559 (1966); *Grand Trunk W. R.R. v. H. W. Nelson Co.,* 116 F.2d 823 (6th Cir. 1941).

The contractor should ensure that his work site accounting records identify these unproductive expenditures on a regular and current basis.

Losses of Efficiency

Often a delay to a project will mean eventual completion of a project in a period of less favorable weather conditions than the contractor had planned on. Delays to certain portions of a project may require that other portions be done in a sequence or using methods considerably less efficient than those on which the contractor had based his bid and his work plan or CPM schedule. This situation will give rise to a category of additional delay-related direct expenses which the contractor will not be able to identify precisely and/or to reflect in his cost records, but which—properly supported—can nevertheless be recovered.

Both administrative tribunals and courts have recognized that such expenses have to be estimated in terms of a percentage loss of productivity to be applied to the actual costs of performing the impacted work under the adverse conditions involved.[18] The estimates can be made by qualified personnel employed by the contractor, or by a specially retained expert, but in either event the estimates should be made on a trade-by-trade basis for each of the qualitatively distinguishable portions of the impacted work. Whenever possible, particularly where substantial amounts are involved, the contractor should arrange for on-the-job time studies to support the level of productivity achieved in the various aspects of the impacted work under normal conditions for comparison with the lower level of productivity actually experienced under the delay-impacted conditions.

Additional Overhead

To the extent that a construction project is prolonged because of delays, work site overhead expenses for engineers, superintendents, time keepers, and insurance and bond premiums are incurred for a greater number of days. In addition, since home office overhead expenses undoubtedly remain constant, they are in effect underutilized or unabsorbed during a period of delay, especially on a relatively large project.

In order to account for these expenses a contractor should include in any delay claim an amount for work site overhead equal to the daily rate of such expense times the number of days by which the project was delayed. Similarly, administrative tribunals and courts have accepted reasonable amounts representing an allocation of the home office overhead, often calculated as follows:

$$\frac{\text{Contract billings}}{\substack{\text{Contractor's total} \\ \text{billings during the} \\ \text{period of performance}}} \times \frac{\text{Total overhead}}{\substack{\text{incurred during} \\ \text{period of per-} \\ \text{formance}}} = \frac{\text{Overhead}}{\substack{\text{allocable} \\ \text{to the con-} \\ \text{tract}}}$$

[18]*Luria Bros. & Co. v. United States,* 177 Ct. Cl. 676, 369 F.2d 701 (1966); *Freuhauf Corp.,* PSBCA 477, 74-1 BCA ¶10596; *T. C. Bateson Constr. Co.,* ASBCA 6028, 1963 BCA ¶3692; *Paccon, Inc.,* ASBCA 7890, 1963 BCA ¶3659.

$$\frac{\text{Overhead allocable to the contract}}{\text{Number of days during the period of performance}} = \text{Overhead allocable to the contract per day}$$

$$\text{Overhead allocable to the contract per day} \times \text{Number of days of delay} = \text{Unabsorbed overhead}^{19}$$

The cost data to make these calculations are usually available from the contractor's normal accounting records.

Escalation Effects

When a project is significantly delayed, the contractor must perform a portion of it during a later period of time than he based his bid on. In an inflationary economy this may mean that his costs of completing the job rise. Any such cost increase arising during a period of compensable delay should be included in the delay claim.[20] Wages, material costs, and equipment rentals are most frequently affected, but other elements of expense, including overhead expense, may also be involved. Special attention must be paid to ensure that the amount of such increases are identified (or reasonably estimated) and recorded.

Acceleration Efforts

Another category of expenses that may arise from delays to a project and be compensable to the contractor under certain circumstances are expenses related to acceleration efforts.

Suppose the contractor has encountered excusable delay on a project, has given notice of the delay to the owner, and has requested an appropriate extension of time to complete the job. If the owner denies the request and clearly indicates that the contractor must meet the original schedule, the contractor should then give a further notice that he will proceed to accelerate his performance and complete the job by the original date. Any additional costs reasonably incurred in that attempt will then also be compensable, either administratively under the change clause of the contract or in a court action for breach of contract.[21]

These costs may include wage overtime or shift premiums, higher prices paid to subcontractors or materialmen for expedited performance or deliveries, and losses of efficiency resulting from the use of overtime, extra shifts, untrained or less skilled laborers or from work during adverse weather conditions. Except for costs associated with efficiency losses, data concerning these

[19]*Luria Bros. & Co. v. United States, supra* note 18, *J. D. Hedin Constr. Co. v. United States, supra* note 2, *Grand Trunk W. R.R. v. H. W. Nelson Co., supra* note 17, *Southern New England Contr. Co. v. State,* 165 Conn. 644, 345 A.2d 550 (1974); *Shore-Calnevor, Inc.,* ASBCA 15715, 73-1 BCA ¶9837; *Eichleay Corp.,* ASBCA 5183, 60-2 BCA ¶2688. *Cf. Kansas City Bridge Co. v. Kansas City Struc. Steel Co.,* 317 S.W.2d 370 (Mo. 1958).

[20]*Keco Ind., Inc.,* ASBCA 15184, 72-2 BCA ¶9576; *International Builders of Fla., Inc., supra* note 15.

[21]*Nat Harrison Assoc. Inc. v. Gulf States Util. Co.,* 491 F.2d 578 (5th Cir. 1974); *Canon Constr. Corp.,* ASBCA 16142, 72-1 BCA ¶9404; *Day & Zimmerman-Madway,* ASBCA 13367, 71-1 BCA ¶8622; *L. O. Brayton & Co., supra* note 10.

costs are usually available from accounting records kept in the normal course of business. The costs of efficiency losses have to be established by properly supported estimates and expert opinion, as discussed above.

PRESENTING THE CLAIM

A claim for compensation for delay-related expenses, perhaps more than any other type of construction contract claim, should be carefully prepared and reduced to writing prior to presentation to the owner or his representative.

So many such claims have been presented and even litigated on the basis of poorly defined theories of entitlement and on the basis of exaggerated or inadequately supported costs that there is a tendency for owners automatically to discount the amounts claimed by a substantial factor. Unless the contractor has carefully laid out the basis of his claim and marshalled probative supporting evidence in his initial presentation, the claim is very likely to be substantially rejected regardless of its true merits. The contractor is then left with an unhappy choice: forgo a meritorious claim or endure lengthy and expensive administrative disputes or court proceedings to obtain the compensation to which he is entitled.

Obviously a contractor should not enter any negotiation, certainly not one seeking compensation for delay, without being prepared to negotiate and compromise where appropriate. Entitlement to compensation for delay may involve debatable legal issues, such as the extent of the owner's implied obligations to have prevented a particular type of delay encountered, or whether float time on the contractor's CPM schedule for performing the work was for the owner's or the contractor's benefit. The amount of any appropriate compensation may turn on such judgmental factors as what portion of a delay actually incurred was unreasonable and therefore compensable, what portion of any delay costs was contractor-caused rather than owner-caused, or what would labor and equipment productivity have been in the absence of the adverse delay-caused conditions.

Although these are all legitimate areas for negotiation and compromise, a claim that is well organized and supported as fully as it is practical to do so, depending on the magnitude of claim, will maximize chances for a reasonable and expeditious settlement and will also afford a realistic basis on which the contractor can decide whether to press for more compensation by litigation.

CONCLUSION

The keys to success in a contractor's obtaining adequate compensation for delay are (1) the *early* recognition of owner-caused deviations from the contractor's optimum plans and schedule for accomplishing the project and (2) the prompt gathering of *on-the-job data* to *document* the impact of those delays on the remainder of the job. Even modest amounts of hard corroborating data can produce a substantial negotiated recovery that the contractor might otherwise never obtain or obtain only after protracted litigation.

Chapter **28**

Exceptions to No-Damage-for-Delay Claims

ROY S. MITCHELL, ESQ.
Partner, Lewis, Mitchell & Moore, Washington, D.C.

THE NO-DAMAGE-FOR-DELAY CLAUSE

Uses

No-damage-for-delay clauses are found in both private construction contracts and in contracts awarded by many state, local, and municipal governments. No such clause is presently utilized by the federal government in its standard form construction contracts. In legal terminology a no-damage-for-delay provision is an exculpatory clause; that is, it is a clause which excuses one of the parties to a contract from liabilities which he would otherwise incur. Such clauses are ordinarily upheld as valid by courts, but they are strictly interpreted and limited to their literal terms in order to avoid forfeitures.

The liability sought to be avoided by the use of a no-damage-for-delay clause is the obligation to pay financial compensation for delay, disruption, or interference suffered by a contractor during performance of a construction contract.

Normal rules of contract law will ordinarily impose liability for owner-caused (or, in the case of subcontracts, prime-contractor–caused) delays in a variety of circumstances absent such a clause. Use of no-damage-for-delay clauses, therefore, represents an attempt by owners and prime contractors to avoid these and related liabilities. The extent to which this attempted denial of liability has been upheld, or limited by judicially recognized exceptions, is the subject of this chapter.

Typical Clauses and Their Scope

Two typical no-damage-for-delay clauses found in prime contracts read as follows:

> No payment or compensation of any kind shall be made to the Contractor for damages because of hindrance or delay from any cause in the progress of the work, whether such hindrances or delays be avoidable or unavoidable. . . .
>
> No charges or claim for damages shall be made by the Contractor for any ordinary delays or hindrances, from any cause whatsoever, during the progress of any portion of the work embraced in this contract. Such delays or hindrances shall be compensated for by an extension of time as above provided.

Similarly, a representative clause from a subcontract states:

> When extension of time for strikes, fire, casualties, or for any other reason beyond its control has been granted to the Contractor by the Owner or its representative as set forth in the General Contract, the same extension, to the extent applicable, shall be granted said Subcontractor; it being expressly agreed, however, that the Contractor shall not be liable to the Subcontractor for any such delays or for any other reason whether caused by the Contractor or its other Subcontractors, the Owner or other independent Contractors of the Owner except to the extent and amount that the Contractor is actually paid therefor by the Owner, Subcontractor, or others for the specific use and payment of Subcontractor's claim.

As is apparent from the above examples, no-damage-for-delay clauses vary significantly in their specific terms, and such variations will have a considerable effect on the extent to which a given clause will protect an owner or prime contractor from liability. For example, the second prime contract clause, above, refers to "ordinary delays or hindrances." In general, therefore, only those ordinary sources of delay contemplated by the parties at the time the contract was entered into would be within the protection of this particular clause. Conversely, any delay of a type not ordinarily encountered during a construction project would be beyond the protection of the clause, and the owner would remain liable.

An important distinction is made in case law between delay and interference. Often, courts hold that *delay* refers only to situations in which the contract completion date is extended, whereas *interference* indicates performance problems or inefficiencies which result in increased cost whether or not the final completion date has been changed. Thus, a no-damage-for-delay clause may not exclude recovery for interference.

Effect of Clause

As previously noted, the no-damage-for-delay clause is, in general, held to be a valid exculpatory provision enforceable in court. Such clauses are given a strict construction, however, since they involve a forfeiture by one party of recognized contract rights. Among the rights potentially forfeited by such clauses are:

1. Compensation for delays caused by the other party to a contract
2. Compensation for delays caused by third parties to a contract
3. Compensation under a clause granting time extensions for delays but which is silent as to money

The waiver of the above potential rights through use of a no-damage-for-delay clause carries harsh pecuniary results for a contractor. Accordingly, courts closely scrutinize the language of such clauses, refusing them application beyond their precise terms, and resolving any ambiguities in favor of the contractor. The time-worn axiom that "the law does not favor forfeitures" has been invoked on numerous occasions to avoid unjust or inequitable application of such clauses. As a result, several well-defined exceptions to no-damage-for-delay clauses have been developed by the courts, as follows.

EXCEPTIONS

Preliminary Factors in Assessing Applicability

Whenever a delay situation is encountered during performance of a contract containing a no-damage-for-delay clause, three basic inquiries must be made in order to determine the applicability of the clause to the type of damage suffered. The first and most important area to be examined is the scope of the clause as evidenced by its express language. The clause may reference not only delay but hindrance, interference, and disruption of work as well. Recovery may also be limited by language including avoidable as well as unavoidable delays, and the clause may purport to cover both reasonable and unreasonable delays.

Second, one must examine the specific type of damage which has occurred. Some distinction has been made by the courts between simple delays which merely postpone the completion date of a contract, and increased costs incurred as a result of piecemeal performance or other disruptions which do not necessarily extend the performance date.

Finally, the type and source of the delay must be reviewed. Delays of a type generally encountered during performance of a construction contract will, in general, be covered by the clause, while unusual delays not contemplated by the parties will not be. Similarly, delays caused by willful misconduct or fraud by one of the parties will usually be beyond the protection of the clause as will delay caused by active interference.

The following sections discussing the recognized exceptions to the no-damage-for-delay clause should be read with these specific factors in mind.

Although court precedent is helpful, reference in any particular dispute must always be to the precise contract language, type of delay, and damages alleged.

Delays Not Contemplated by the Parties

Once the previously enumerated preliminary inquiries have been made, the primary question to be addressed in ascertaining whether a particular claim is precluded by the no-damage-for-delay clause is whether, at the time the contract was entered into, the parties intended that the specific type of delay was to be covered by the clause. Generally, types of delay not contemplated by the parties at the time of the contract will not be exempt from liability, and a contractor will retain his right to recover for damages caused by such a delay.

The most common situation in which delay is held to be beyond the contemplation of the parties involves denial of job-site access. In general, and in the absence of express contract language to the contrary, the delays contemplated by a no-damage-for-delay clause are considered to be delays in the progress of the work, not failure to allow work to begin. Site-availability delays, unless specifically provided for, are usually held to be beyond the scope of the clause. Several cases have made the important distinction between delays in the performance of a contract and delays in allowing performance to begin.

One such case involved a contract with the state of Idaho to widen and improve a segment of state highway.[1] In order to allow the work to begin it was necessary to remove privately owned utility poles. The contract obligated the state to schedule pole removal with the utility company, but a no-damage-for-delay clause specifically limited the contractor's right to damages.

When the poles were not removed within the time specified by the contract, the contractor sued for his delay costs. The court analyzed the dispute by examining the types of delay contemplated by the parties at the time of contract execution. In doing so, a distinction was made between delays resulting from the failure of the state to *schedule* pole removal and delays resulting from the utility company's late removal of the poles once the schedule had been prepared. The phrase "within the time specified" in the no-damage-for-delay clause presumed, in the opinion of the court, that the state would formulate a pole removal schedule. Hence, failure to schedule removal was a source of delay not contemplated by the parties at the time they entered into the contract, and the no-damage-for-delay clause did not bar recovery for additional costs caused by this type of delay.

Numerous disputes have also centered about the liability of a party, often a state agency or local municipality, for delay costs resulting from its failure to procure timely rights-of-way needed to begin performance of a construction project. Again, the distinction is usually made in such situations between delays encountered by a contractor in the progress of the work and those encountered in seeking to begin the work. In general, unless the contract expressly states otherwise, delays in allowing the work to begin will *not* be held to have been within the contemplation of the parties. Recovery for delay costs incurred as a

[1]*Grant Constr. Co. v. Burns*, 92 Idaho 408, 443 P.2d 1005 (1968).

result of a party's failure to perform contract obligations necessary to commence work, such as obtaining rights-of-way, or granting site access, may thus be had even where a no-damage-for-delay clause is contained in the contract.

In determining whether a particular type of delay is within the contemplation of the parties, the precise language and scope of the no-damage-for-delay clause in the contract will be the controlling consideration, and a key word or phrase within the clause can be determinative of the validity of a contractor's claim. One such dispute involved a contract to improve and extend a city water supply system.[2] The contract required the city to deliver all pipe necessary for the job to the contractor, but exonerated the city from liability for damages caused by delay. When the city delayed in ordering pipe, the contractor suffered increased labor and equipment costs. In a subsequent lawsuit he was allowed recovery of these costs on the grounds that the no-damage-for-delay clause involved did not contemplate delays in furnishing *material*. The clause did, however, preclude recovery for various other sources of delay to which express reference was made.

In accordance with the rule that the intent of the parties controls the scope of a no-damage-for-delay clause, specific contract terms may negate the general assumption that site access delays, as opposed to performance delays, are not within the purview of such a clause. Thus, in a case involving the construction of parking ramps for a city agency, a contractor was delayed by a job site accident which killed two of his workmen and forced some work to be redone.[3] The contractor sought damages, despite the presence of a no-damage-for-delay clause in the contract, on the grounds that the accident caused delays in site access. The court rejected this contention, however, stating that the contractor had been prevented from working at part of the site only and that the parties had contemplated *some* delay in site availability.

Depending upon the particular clause in question, certain delays encountered during contract performance may also be beyond the contemplation of the parties. During performance of a contract to clean, paint, and waterproof the state capitol building in Albany, New York, a contractor was forced to suspend his sandblasting operation because the resultant noise interfered with state legislature sessions.[4] The resultant delay caused the contractor to incur increased labor costs since he was forced to schedule overtime work. He was allowed to recover these costs despite the no-damage-for-delay clause in the contract since, in the opinion of the court, it was beyond the contemplation of the parties. A similar holding involving overall scheduling of a construction project in Texas was reached in an extensive and well-written opinion in *Housing Authority of the City of Dallas v. Hubbell*.[5]

As with most exceptions to any general rule, it must be remembered that the exceptions to the coverage of the no-damage-for-delay clause are themselves

[2]*Sandel & Lastrapes v. City of Shreveport*, 129 So.2d 620 (La. App. 1961).
[3]*Cunningham Bros. v. City of Waterloo*, 254 Iowa 659, 117 N.W.2d 46 (1962).
[4]*W. L. Waples Co. v. State*, 178 App. Div. 357, 164 N.Y.S. 797 (1917).
[5]325 S.W.2d 880 (Tex. Civ. App. 1959).

quite narrow. The question of what delay was contemplated by the parties at the time the contract was executed is one of fact and contract interpretation. The vast majority of delays—those which are most commonly encountered—will, by their very nature, be within the contemplation of the parties at the time of contract. These include the bulk of performance delays and those caused by foreseeable site conditions. Unusual performance delays or delays in allowing the work to begin must be very carefully analyzed and characterized in order to bring them within this exception to the clause.

Active Interference

The no-damage-for-delay clause is often used to attempt to insulate a party to a contract from liability for delay caused by his own negligence or his failure to act in fulfillment of a legally recognized duty. Consistent with the reluctance of courts to enforce contractual provisions which involve forfeitures of legal rights, such a clause ordinarily will not relieve a party from the consequences of his negligence *unless* the word "negligence" expressly appears in the terms of the clause. Typically, this is true regardless of the apparent intent of the parties.

Even when a no-damage-for-delay clause successfully avoids liability of a party for his own negligence, however, acts or omissions of that party which actively interfere with the progress of the work will often be beyond the protection of the clause. This active interference may take many forms. One good example involved delays encountered in the construction of a portion of the Pennsylvania Turnpike.[6] Before the work could begin, a second contractor was required to perform fill work. The turnpike commission ordered road construction to begin even though the fill had not been completed, and commencement of the construction was thus impossible. Pursuant to the contract, the contractor was granted a time extension for the period of the delay, but the turnpike commission relied upon a no-damage-for-delay clause in denying the contractor any recovery for his delay costs.

The contractor subsequently brought suit on the theory that the no-damage-for-delay clause was inapplicable because the commission itself had caused the delay by ordering work to proceed with the knowledge that the job site was unavailable. The court agreed, holding that, because the commission ordered the contractor to begin work when it knew that this was impossible and positively interfered with the contractor's performance by its *failure* to act in an essential matter necessary to the prosecution of the contract, the clause could not provide any protection from liability. The commission's failure to ensure that fill work was completed on time was therefore a source of delay not covered by the no-damage-for-delay clause, and the contractor was held to be entitled to recover his delay costs.

The active interference exception to no-damage-for-delay claims is closely related to the earlier exception involving delays beyond the contemplation of the parties. Since every contract carries an implied obligation that neither party

---

[6]*Gasparini Excav. Co. v. Pennsylvania Tpke. Comm.*, 409 Pa. 465, 187 A.2d 157 (1963).

will hinder or interfere with the performance of the other, it is natural to presume that the parties similarly would not contemplate that such a source of delay would be within the scope of a no-damage-for-delay provision. As a result, these two theories have been merged on several occasions in cases in which a no-damage-for-delay clause has been held not to apply to a dispute involving active interference.

In a case concerning a state bridge construction project, the contractor who was to supply steel was delayed when a caisson collapsed due to the faulty work of another contractor.[7] The state nevertheless required that the steel contractor continue to make steel available on the job site. The steel had to be stored during the delay period and later had to be repainted. The court allowed recovery despite the no-damage-for-delay clause in the contract, stating that the delay constituted active interference on the part of the state and that such delay was beyond the contemplation of the parties.

Many other acts (or failures to act) have been found to constitute active interference so as to avoid the effects of a no-damage-for-delay clause. The failure of a state to provide heat for a construction site, as required by the contract, was held to have resulted in active interference, and the contractor was allowed to recover his costs for resultant delays even though a no-damage-for-delay clause was present in the contract.[8] Other acts which have been found to constitute active interference include the opening to other contractors of a roadway on which the contractor claiming delay was working, delay in awarding a contract for other work necessary to the completion of the claimant's work, and issuance of notice to proceed when necessary materials were two years late in delivery.

Perhaps the best example of a case in which active interference was held to override a no-damage-for-delay clause, however, is *Housing Authority of the City of Dallas v. Hubbell.*[9] The clause in this case purported to relieve the city from liability for delay damages for any hindrance or delay in the progress of the work, whether the delays were avoidable or unavoidable. The city maintained that the provision completely protected it from liability for any delays unless the delays were caused by fraud, bad faith, or a willful intent to injure the contractor. The delays for which the contractor sought recovery in the ensuing trial were found to have been caused by the failure of the city to furnish master construction schedules, plan development and construction of the project, coordinate the various prime contractors on the project, and otherwise permit the work to proceed in an orderly fashion. The court rejected the city's contentions and held that the clause did not preclude the imposition of damages for the above-mentioned delays since they were caused by the active interference of the city. The court stated the general rule that no-damage clauses may protect a party from delays caused by forces beyond his control or by his negligence or mistakes in judgment. The court went on to say, however,

---

[7]*American Bridge Co. v. State,* 245 App. Div. 535, 283 N.Y.S. 577 (1935).
[8]*De Riso Bros. v. State,* 161 Misc. 934, 293 N.Y.S. 436 (1937).
[9]*Housing Auth., supra* note 5.

that such a clause does *not* give a party "a license to cause delays wilfully, by unreasoning action, without due consideration and in disregard of the rights of other parties."[10]

Although the active interference doctrine is a well-established exception to no-damage-for-delay clauses, a contractor should be aware that this exception is, again, a narrow one. If properly drafted, such clauses can insulate a party from the consequences of his own negligence or mistaken judgment, both of which are common sources of delay. In order to invoke the active interference exception, therefore, more than mere negligence must ordinarily be shown. A party must have failed to use due diligence in attempting to proceed properly under the contract or taken an action which has, in fact, interfered with the progress of the work. In the absence of such active interference, the protection of the no-damage-for-delay clause will be available.

Unreasonable Delays

A third exception to the no-damage-for-delay clause has been established in those cases dealing with delays of unreasonable duration. Generally, a delay will be unreasonable if it is of such length as to justify the party delayed in treating the contract as ended. There is no firm rule as to what length of time must be involved, and it is thus impossible to state a blanket rule defining delays which will be considered unreasonable. All the facts and circumstances involved in a particular delay situation will be examined by a court in determining when a delay is so unreasonably long that it precludes application of a no-damage-for-delay clause.

Although a contractor would often be justified in terminating his performance and abandoning the contract in cases involving unreasonable delays, he ordinarily need not do so in order to be entitled to delay damages. He may usually continue his performance and also collect damages. It is also worth remembering that the unreasonable delay exception, like that recognized for active interference, is closely related to the exception established for delays beyond the contemplation of the parties. The parties clearly cannot be held to have contemplated the occurrence of delays so serious in nature as to strike at the heart of a contract.

Illustrative of the cases in this area is one involving a contract with the New York City Board of Education to remove certain structures from a proposed school site.[11] The relevant clause provided that the contractor was only to receive a time extension if his work was delayed by any act or omission of the city. The contractor was subsequently delayed for nearly a year because the city failed to demolish an existing building on the site. The court found the clause to be inapplicable, since the delay was so unreasonable that the contractor was entitled to treat it as an abandonment of the contract. The delay went to the heart of the contract, according to the court, and did not involve a merely peripheral matter.

[10]*Housing Auth., supra* note 5, at 891.
[11]*John T. Brady & Co. v. Board of Educ.,* 222 App. Div. 504, 226 N.Y.S. 707 (1928).

Factors other than the length of the delay must also be considered in order to determine whether a particular delay is of unreasonable duration. Foremost among these will be the question of the foreseeability of the delay, since foreseeable delays will ordinarily fall within the scope of a no-damage-for-delay clause. Also important will be the nature of the delay. In the above case, the one-year delay in the simple demolition of a building was considered unreasonable, but a different result might have been reached had the delayed work been extremely complicated or involved a novel, untried process.

Whether a delay of the length involved might naturally be expected to result in undue damage is also of importance. Thus, in a suit for breach of contract for unreasonable delay in furnishing plans, specifications, and notice to proceed under a sewer construction contract, a contractor was allowed recovery despite the presence of a no-damage-for-delay clause which expressly included delays in furnishing plans or rights-of-way.[12] Of importance in the court's decision was the fact that the damage for which compensation was sought, the cave-in of open sewer lines, was the natural result of the unreasonable delay.

Fraud or Bad Faith

A final major exception to the no-damage-for-delay clause is found in situations where delays result from fraud or bad faith by one of the parties. The courts will not allow a party to escape from liability under a no-damage-for-delay clause when the delay is caused by his own intentionally false statements or acts. If the clause were allowed to serve such a purpose, the basic requirement of fair dealing which underlies all contracts would be seriously eroded. Stipulations against liability for fraudulent acts are uniformly unenforceable as being against public policy.

Cases in which fraud will be held to override a no-damage-for-delay clause most often involve intentionally false statements in order to induce the other party to enter into a contract. It is a general rule of law that a party induced by fraud to enter into a contract may, upon discovery of the fraud, elect either to rescind the contract or continue his performance and seek recovery in court for any damages he may have suffered as a result of the fraud. The no-damage-for-delay clause does not alter this general rule, and a contractor's right to delay damages is ordinarily preserved even though he continues to perform a fraudulently induced contract containing such a clause.

The way in which fraud may neutralize a no-damage clause is illustrated by a case involving the construction of a county housing project.[13] The middle portion of the project was to be located on a county-owned strip of land. During bidding, litigation arose concerning annexation of the strip, and the low bidder was requested by the county to keep his bid open for an additional period of time to allow resolution of the title problems. Several months later the housing authority informed the contractor that all obstacles in connection with annexation of the strip had been overcome, and the contract was executed. Notice to

---

[12]*Hawley v. Orange County Flood Cont. Dist.*, 211 Cal. App. 2d 708, 27 Cal. Rptr. 478 (1963).

[13]*Maurice L. Bein, Inc. v. Housing Auth.*, 321 P.2d 753 (Cal. App. 1958).

proceed was issued immediately, but a few days later the contractor was given a second notice ordering him to suspend performance until further annexation problems could be solved. The county assured the contractor that annexation would be completed within 10 days, but the contractor was denied access to the overall job site for over two months, and was not allowed to work on the county-owned strip until a year later.

The contractor suffered considerable damages as a result of these delays in that his work was carried on in a piecemeal and inefficient manner, and coordination of the project was severely hindered. Increased overhead, loss of labor efficiency, and loss of use of equipment were the major sources of increased costs. In addition, the contractor had prepared a progress schedule, approved by the housing authority, which would have been met had the county not delayed in acquiring the strip.

When the contractor subsequently sued to recover his delay costs, the county based its defense upon a no-damage-for-delay clause in the contract which denied liability "for damages because of delay or hindrance or delay from any cause in the progress of the work, whether such hindrance or delay be avoidable or unavoidable." The court overruled this defense, however, since the county (1) informed the contractor that all obstacles relating to the county-owned strip had been overcome, (2) *knew* at the time this information was given that there was still to be a lengthy delay, (3) made these statements for the purpose of inducing the contractor to enter into the contract, and (4) knew that the contractor was ignorant of the true facts.

Thus, the knowledge and actions of the parties will be the key factor in determining whether fraudulent inducements may avoid a no-damage-for-delay clause. Statements of fact known to be false or concealment of facts which induce a party to enter into a contract can constitute fraud. Liability for any delays resulting from such false statements or concealments will fall upon the party guilty of the fraud, regardless of the presence of a no-damage-for-delay clause in the contract.

To summarize, then, no-damage-for-delay clauses are valid and will be enforced by the courts according to their terms. However, they will be narrowly construed in order to avoid the harshness of forfeiture, and the four major exceptions outlined above may provide an avenue of relief for contractors under appropriate factual circumstances.

Chapter **29**

Liability for Liquidated Damages

W. ROBERT WARD, ESQ.
Partner, Weller, Friedrich, Hickisch & Hazlett, Denver, Colorado

DONALD LAWRENCE, JR., ESQ.
Associate, Weller, Friedrich, Hickisch & Hazlett, Denver, Colorado

INTRODUCTION

Most contracts for construction of public works and large private projects contain what is typically termed a *liquidated* or *stipulated* damage provision.

Liquidated damage provisions are creatures of contract. They are products of agreement and, theoretically at least, of negotiation. Such a clause represents the attempt of the parties to agree in advance on the financial consequences which will result from default. The most common type of provision is one embodying a specified dollar amount to be assessed for each day of delay in completion of the construction. There is no legal requirement that such clauses specify dollar amounts. They may be tied to any readily ascertainable standard.[1] The damages agreed upon may be less than or greater than the damages which in fact result from default.[2] If the provision is an enforceable liquidated-

---

[1]*Broderick Wood Prod. Co. v. United States,* 195 F.2d 433 (10th Cir. 1952), *Lee v. Bergesen,* 58 Wash. 2d 462, 364 P.2d 18 (1961).

[2]*Southwest Eng. Co. v. United States,* 341 F.2d 998 (8th Cir. 1965), *cert. denied,* 382 U.S. 819.

damage clause, both parties are bound by its terms. Thus, in some cases, the defaulting party will be liable for a lesser amount in liquidated damages than could be recovered in the absence of the agreement.[3]

For one reason or another, not all contracts are completed in conformity with the terms and the question becomes whether, under the circumstances, the parties are bound by a purported liquidated damage clause.

LIQUIDATED DAMAGES OR PENALTY?

If the provision is truly one for liquidated damages, it is enforceable, and both parties are bound by it. If it provides instead for a penalty, neither party is bound, and the party in default is liable for the actual damages suffered by the other.[4]

The conceptual distinction between a genuine liquidated damage and a penalty provision is somewhat fuzzy. This lack of clear distinction sometimes makes it difficult to determine into which of these pigeonholes a particular provision fits better and contributes to uncertainty in contract drafting. For these reasons, the balance of this chapter will focus on the apparent reasons for courts labeling such clauses as either "genuine liquidated damage" clauses or "unenforceable penalty" clauses; and will furnish some suggestions and guidelines to consider in drafting a liquidated damages clause.

Historical background From the early judicial decisions on the validity of purported liquidated-damage provisions, even the casual reader will discern a marked hostility to them. One phrase recurring in these cases is that courts "look with disfavor" upon such clauses. The result was that in cases of doubt, the courts opted in favor of construction as providing for penalties, and so refused enforcement. There is now a clear judicial trend away from this hostility.[5] Increasingly, and perhaps as an acknowledgment of chagrin at some of the early decisions, courts are "looking with candor"—if not with favor— upon such provisions, at least in contracts between parties of relatively equal bargaining power and economic clout.[6] Some courts are now declaring that they will look with favor upon such clauses.[7] Presumably, what these courts mean is that in borderline cases they will opt for construction as enforceable liquidated-damage provisions rather than as penalty clauses.

Which contracts may include a liquidated damage provision Damages for breach of virtually every contract associated with construction may be liquidated in advance by agreement. A liquidated damage clause may be inserted into the prime contract, the prime contractor's contracts with subcontractors

---

[3]*Georgia Ports Auth. v. Norair Eng. Corp.*, 127 Ga. App. 864, 195 S.E.2d 199 (1973); *Gruschus v. C. R. Davis Contr. Co.*, 75 N.M. 649, 409 P.2d 500 (1965); *Brower Co. v. Garrison*, 2 Wash. App. 424, 468 P.2d 469 (1970) (*as amended and modified*).

[4]*Russ Mitchell, Inc. v. Houston Pipe Line Co.*, 219 S.W.2d 109 (Tex. Civ. App. 1949).

[5]*Wise v. United States*, 249 U.S. 361 (1919); *Gustav Hirsch Organization v. East Ky. Rural Elec. Coop. Corp.*, 201 F.Supp. 809 (E.D. Ky. 1962).

[6]*Wise v. United States*, 249 U.S. 361 (1919); *Southwest Eng. Co. v. United States*, 341 F.2d 998 (8th Cir. 1965), *cert. denied*, 382 U.S. 819.

[7]*S. L. Rowland Constr. Co. v. Beall Pipe & Tank Corp.*, 14 Wash. App. 297, 540 P.2d 912 (1975).

and materialmen, and the subcontractors' contracts with their subcontractors and material suppliers.

The principal use of such a clause is liquidation of damages for delay in delivery of materials or completion of the contract, although damages for delay in completion of certain critical phases of the contract may also be liquidated by agreement.[8] Obviously, if the contractor is subject to liquidated damages for delay, it is advisable to include comparable provisions in subcontracts and supplier orders to protect the contractor.

Expected damages to be "uncertain"   It is often stated and universally agreed that the parties may contract for liquidated damages only in those instances in which, at the time of entering into the contract, damages might reasonably be expected to result from the breach and also appear to be uncertain, not readily ascertainable, or difficult of proof.[9] The theoretical justification underlying a liquidated damage clause is that it is an attempt to quantify in advance these uncertain damages.[10]

There is no real reason to deny parties to a contract the freedom to predetermine just compensation for such damages, or to force them to the additional expense, delay, and uncertainty inherent in litigation after the fact.[11]

Liquidated damages must be a reasonable forecast of damages which might be expected   Paradoxically, it is only those provisions which appear to courts to represent a reasonable forecast of this admittedly uncertain and perhaps unascertainable amount which qualify as enforceable provisions.[12] Many courts have indicated that it is the "intent" of the parties to the contract that is determinative on this question.[13] If it appears that the provision was intended as a reasonable method of providing for compensation in the event of default, it will be upheld.[14] If it appears that the parties intended the clause only as a scare tactic to secure conforming performance or to impose punishment for default regardless of actual damage, it will be invalidated.[15]

This focus on intent is not the subjective inquiry one might expect. Instead it is only a legal conclusion reached on the basis of the reasonableness of the provision in light of all the circumstances. Since intent is an element the courts consider in evaluating the enforceability of the provision, a recital of that intent and the items contemplated by the parties in the provision is of some value.

---

[8]*Hillsborough County Av. Auth. v. Cone Bros. Contracting*, 285 So.2d 619 (Fla. App. 1973); *Georgia Ports Auth. v. Norair Eng. Corp.*, 127 Ga. App. 864, 195 S.E.2d 199 (1973).

[9]*Gustav Hirsch Organization v. East Ky. Rural Elec. Coop. Corp.*, 201 F.Supp. 809 (E.D. Ky. 1962); *Otinger v. Water Works & Sanitary Sewer Bd.*, 278 Ala. 213, 177 So.2d 320 (1965); *Parsons Constr. Co. v. Metropolitan Util. Dist.*, 107 Neb. 709, 104 N.W. 2d 272 (1960).

[10]*Gustav Hirsch Organization v. East Ky. Rural Elec. Coop. Corp.*, 201 F.Supp. 809 (E.D. Ky. 1962); *Dineen v. United States*, 71 F.Supp. 742 (Ct. Cl. 1947), *cert. denied*, 333 U.S. 842, *rehearing denied*, 334 U.S. 816; *Otinger v. Water Works & Sanitary Sewer Bd.*, 278 Ala. 213, 177 So.2d 320 (1965).

[11]*Wise v. United States*, 249 U.S. 361 (1919).

[12]*Southwest Eng. Co. v. United States*, 341 F.2d 988 (8th Cir. 1965), *cert. denied*, 382 U.S. 819; *Gruschus v. C. R. Davis Contr. Co.*, 75 N.M. 649, 409 P.2d 500 (1975).

[13]*Wise v. United States, supra* note 13.

[14]*Gruschus v. C. R. Davis Contr. Co.*, 75 N.M. 649, 409 P.2d 500 (1975).

[15]*S. L. Rowland Constr. Co. v. Beall Pipe & Tank Corp.*, 14 Wash. App. 297, 540 P.2d 912 (1975).

Time at which reasonableness determined   It is to be remembered that enforceability of such a provision is almost always litigated after the fact. Typically, the contractor has defaulted and is either suing the owner for release of funds which the owner claims as liquidated damages or is being sued by the owner for such damages. This has led to no little confusion regarding the point in time on which the court should focus to determine whether the amount stipulated was reasonable, in light of what appeared to the contracting parties.

Consequently, there are two lines of decisions, one conceptually consistent with intent at the time of contracting as the key to enforceability and one line wholly inconsistent. The first line of decision focuses on the time at which the parties entered into the contract and asks whether the agreed amount is reasonable in light of what they contemplated (or might have contemplated had they thought about it at all) at the time concerning future damages.[16] The second line asks whether, in light of the absence of actual damages or the amount of damage actually sustained as a result of the breach, the agreed amount is reasonable, not grossly disproportionate or extravagant. The latter is the view voiced by a minority of courts. However, one suspects that it is an unarticulated basis for other decisions appearing to follow the first line of cases. Some courts appear to make both inquiries.[17]

The clear weight of authority is with the first line of cases. Accordingly, no actual damages need be proven.[18] All that need be proven is the agreement, that it was a reasonable forecast of actual damages to be expected upon breach, and the breach itself.[19]

Increasingly, one finds courts making a third and distinct comparison, especially in cases of liquidated damages specified per each day of delay. The per-day-delay damage amount is compared with the total contract price.[20] There is no real rationale offered to justify such a comparison. It would appear to have little relationship to the reasonableness of the amount of damage one might expect upon delay, other than interest or carrying charges on progress payments previously made. Significant damage might be expected to result from delay in completion of some contracts of relatively small dollar amounts, and relatively insignificant damage—other than interest—might be expected to follow delay in completion of some contracts for large sums. None of the decisions which mention this factor appear to have turned on it, but it is a factor which should be considered by one drafting a liquidated-damage clause.

Types of uncertainty in expected damage against which liquidated damage clause may insure   Damages to be reasonably expected to result from breach may also be expected to be uncertain, not readily ascertainable, or difficult of

---

[16]*Bethlehem Steel Co. v. Chicago,* 234 F.Supp. 726 (N.D. Ill. 1964); *Gustav Hirsch Organization v. East Ky. Rural Elec. Coop. Corp.,* 201 F.Supp. 809 (E.D. Ky. 1962); *Anne Arundel County v. Norair Eng. Corp.,* 275 Md. 480, 341 A.2d 287 (Md. App. 1975).

[17]*Parsons Constr. Co. v. Metropolitan Util. Dist.,* 107 Neb. 709, 104 N.W.2d 272 (1960).

[18]*Southwest Eng. Co. v. United States,* 341 F.2d 998 (8th Cir. 1965), *cert. denied,* 382 U.S. 819.

[19]*Dineen v. United States,* 71 F.Supp. 742 (Ct. Cl. 1947), *cert. denied,* 333 U.S. 842, *rehearing denied,* 334 U.S. 816.

[20]*Otinger v. Water Works & Sanitary Sewer Bd.,* 278 Ala. 213, 177 So.2d 320 (1965); *Anne Arundel County v. Norair Eng. Corp.,* 275 Md. 480, 341 A.2d 287 (Md. App. 1975).

proof for a number of reasons. It may be that whether any damage at all would result from default is uncertain at the time of agreement. Although damage of some sort might be expected, uncertainty might be the result of inability to forecast whether the items of damage expected would be allowed by a court in the event of default and litigation. Anticipated damages might not be readily ascertainable because of the difficulty of documenting the precise amounts. Finally, one always takes the risk in pursuing judicial remedies that for one reason or another the court will rule against him. In short, the uncertainty prerequisite to validity of a liquidated damage provision may be the product of any one of a myriad of factors.

Effect of contract language It should be emphasized that the label placed upon the provision is not determinative. Provisions labeled liquidated damages have frequently been held to actually provide for a penalty and therefore have been declared invalid. Somewhat less frequently, provisions labeled penalty clause or containing the words "forfeit," "penalty," or terms of similar import have been held actually to provide for liquidated damages.[21] In short, the language employed by the parties is given some weight by courts ruling on the validity of such clauses but certainly is not the decisive, nor even the most important, factor. However, it is submitted that provisions couched solely in terms of penalty or punishment are more likely to be held invalid than those using language more readily associated with compensation.

DRAFTING THE LIQUIDATED DAMAGE CLAUSE

The threshold question in drafting a liquidated damage provision is whether the contract is one which qualifies for an enforceable liquidation of damages, that is, whether the damage upon breach is expected to be of an uncertain character, not readily ascertainable, or difficult of proof.

Contracts for public works construction are typically of this character. Delay in completion of a water treatment facility designed to meet projected needs, for example, could be expected to result in some damage to the governmental unit contracting for it. If the projected growth in demand in fact occurred, delay could be expected to result in the necessity of buying and importing water, rationing it, and banning noncritical uses. To measure such damages after the fact would be most difficult. Perhaps more significant, but less tangible, damage might also be expected, such as adverse effects on land development and industrial relocation decisions. Surely, these damages might be expected and are real even though essentially intangible. The contract is undoubtedly a candidate for an agreement as to reasonable compensation for such damages.

The second step, of course, is to arrive at a figure which will provide that reasonable compensation upon default.

This is at best a difficult task, and the more uncertain the expected damages, the more difficult it is to determine a reasonable figure for liquidated damages. Nevertheless, some effort must be made. The agreed damage upon default

---

[21]*Ross v. Loescher,* 152 Mich. 386, 119 N.W. 193 (1908).

need not be accurate, it need only be a reasonable estimate. This gives the parties some necessary margin for error, and allows for relatively rough estimates of the more intangible expected damages. It is suggested that the provision include a recitation of the uncertainty of the damages to be expected upon default, the reasons they appear to the parties to be uncertain and that the parties agree that the liquidated damages specified are intended to provide reasonable compensation for these damages in the event of default.

The method for collection of liquidated damages assessed should be spelled out. One of the principal appeals of such a provision is the fact that one need not resort to litigation for collection of the damages upon default. If the contract so provides, the nondefaulting party may set off the amount of damages claimed against any earned progress payments due under the contract or against the retainage or other monies due under the contract.

Avoid language with a penal connotation. Terms such as "penalty" and "forfeit" should be avoided. Terms with connotations of negotiation, agreement, and reasonableness ought to be employed. It should be clear from the provision that the parties are aware of the difficulties resulting from delay and are attempting to spell out the solution in advance.

Finally, in the event of default, it should be remembered that there is the possibility of litigation of the validity of the liquidated damage clause. A determination of invalidity does not void the entire contract, but only prevents enforcement of the agreed damages, and allows recovery of such actual damages as are proven. Actual damages must be documented and causally related to the default. Of course, some courts require a reasonable relationship between these actual damages and the amount stipulated as liquidated damages as a condition of validity of the liquidated damage provision. Care should be exercised in documenting actual damages.

CONCLUSION

In the construction industry, the liquidated damages clause is used primarily regarding damages for delayed performance to avoid the problems of proof of actual damages from such breach. When the contract provision for liquidated damages is reasonable under the particular circumstances, the provision is enforceable upon such breach. A carefully drafted liquidated damage provision can simplify and expedite determination of damages due to such a breach. It is suggested the drafter make a careful review of the principles and authorities previously referred to and the court decisions in his own jurisdiction to assist in drafting an effective and enforceable liquidated damage clause.

Chapter **30**

Liability of the Architect-Engineer to the Contractor and Subcontractor

THEODORE W. GEISER, ESQ.
Partner, McElroy, Connell, Foley & Geiser, Newark, New Jersey

SCOPE OF THE WORK

Liability means the exposure of the professional to civil suits for money damages at the instance of contractors and subcontractors performing work upon the project designed and/or supervised by the professional. Not treated in this section are the rights of the professional vis-à-vis the owner, nor the rights of third persons, such as adjoining landowners, workmen, and others who may be affected by the performance of the professional.

Also excluded from the scope are the relationships among professionals engaged in the same project, whether independently employed or retained by the owner or jointly engaged with each other, as in the case of an architect-engineer joint venture, or where one is a subcontractor to the other.

GENERAL CONDITIONS

Architect-Engineer Defined

The disciplines of architecture and engineering are interrelated and to a large extent interdependent. It is safe to say at this writing that there is no practical distinction made by the law in spelling out the duties and responsibilities of each to other. Cases dealing with architects may be applied to engineers and vice versa. It is also fair to say that the law does not impose upon either the responsibility of an absolute guarantee of work performed. The key word here is "absolute," since the law may, under certain circumstances, find a "warranty" of accuracy—similar to that imposed upon a manufacturer of goods—that plans, for example, are *reasonably* fit to serve their intended purpose.

Relationship of the Architect-Engineer to Others

Here is the touchstone of the law. The living-room lawyer will be very well equipped to discuss and understand the law—even with lawyers—if he understands that the critical point of all disputes is the *relationship* between the disputants. Law seeks to regulate society by prescribing a set of rules establishing rights and correlative duties among the members of that society, to the end that optimum harmony may be achieved and maintained, and by providing the machinery necessary to compensate one for the breach of a duty owed to him by another.

Putting to one side the duties owed by each individual to society as a whole, for the breach of which criminal sanctions may be applied, most rights and duties with which the law is concerned may be classified generally as arising out of contract or tort. Now, contract rights and duties are voluntarily assumed by agreement of the parties and may be thought of as being special, or custom-made, so to speak, for the particular situation. Assuming that the terms of the contract are not violative of public policy, each party is entitled to performance by the other, and if there be a breach by one of the parties, causing damage to the other, the law provides a remedy.

As for torts, these may be defined as civil wrongs committed by one to the damage of another, arising not from any contract between them but rather by reason of their relationship, one to the other, in the society. Thus, I have a duty to exercise reasonable care in the operation of my automobile so as not to interfere unreasonably with your right to operate your car or to walk across the street. The important consideration is always the relationship, because rights and duties spring only from the relationship.

In recent years, the courts have mirrored broadening social concepts, responsive to increasing demands in our society favoring an expansion of the obligations we owe to each other. In part, this may be due to what is called *risk distribution*. As a consequence, it is the obligation of a manufacturer to see to it that a product placed by him in the stream of commerce is reasonably fit for its intended purpose, and today he may be held liable for breach of that duty to the ultimate consumer or, indeed, to *anyone* who might foreseeably be injured by the product. Not so very long ago the same manufacturer would have been insulated against such liability where there was no *privity*, that is, no contract between the manufacturer and the injured person; no relationship, no duty. However, upon the hypothesis that the damage which may be caused by the product ought to be an incident of cost, borne (and presumably passed on in price) by the manufacturer, the law now is that a sufficient relationship exists between the manufacturer and the "foreseeable" injured person to justify liability on a tort basis.

All this may seem a roundabout way to arrive at the destination, but it is necessary background, for in the construction industry the relationships among the many people involved in a project are complex and varied. At the apex of the contract triangle we usually find the owner, who has contracted with the architect-engineer and separately with the prime contractors. Vertically, the primes have contracted with several tiers of subcontractors and vendors. Ordinarily there is no lateral integration between the professionals and the contractors, although there may be, if the owner has provided for such integration. For example, all the owner's contracts may contain an arbitration provision cross-referenced so as to require the professional and the prime to arbitrate any differences they may have between themselves. Since the architect-engineer often prepares all contract documents, he enjoys an enviable position in terms of self-protection as draftsman of the construction contracts.

One of the most important relationships which must be analyzed and defined is the relationship between the owner and the professional, because the relationship of the contractor and subcontractor to the professional is seriously affected by this determination. It may be that the professional is part of the owner's staff, a salaried employee. In such a situation he is merely the agent of the owner and, as such, acts as the alter ego of the owner. As in any other case of simple agency, the contractor is entitled to look to the owner for damages occasioned by any wrongful conduct of the agent.

Frequently, however, the owner engages the professional on a consulting basis under a contract for his services. This presents a much more complicated problem, especially where the construction contract provides for the resolution of disputes in the first instance by the professional. Where the professional acts as an arbiter of disputes, it is said that he is functioning in a quasi-judicial role and that he is not liable to the contractor except for arbitrariness, bad faith, or fraud. Put another way, this means that even if his decision is erroneous (and perhaps even negligently made), he is invulnerable to suit for damage at the instance of *either* the owner or the contractor.

But even in situations where the professional is an "independent consultant," it may be that he acts as the owner's *agent* in some situations. Reference to the general conditions of the construction contract will determine in what areas the owner has implicitly designated the professional as his representative. In typical cases this will be found to be so in such areas as approval of shop drawings, construction schedules, material samples, and the like.

Indeed, as a practical matter the concept of the architect-engineer acting as an independent "arbitrator" between the owner and the contractor is more fanciful than real. The owner is commonly unsophisticated in construction matters and in practice the professional makes or controls all important decisions. This can often be proven in court by a careful review of all the documents underlying the administration of the contract. Further, the construction contract itself, probably prepared by the professional, is so onerous by its terms that the literal application of its provisions by the professional leaves very little room for him to decide a dispute upon an equitable basis. Finally, the plain fact is that he is paid by the owner.

Yet, a good deal of construction contract litigation against the professional by contractors and subcontractors grows out of the misapprehension on his part that the foregoing circumstances require, or at least permit, him to side with the owner against the contractor. The law is not ingenuous. A responsible and growing body of judicial authority exists for the proposition that the architect-engineer may be personally liable to the contractor or subcontractor where he fails to perform his duties in keeping with the usual and accepted standards of his profession at the time and place in question (professional standards, like the law, vary according to geography and chronology and the state of the art), and such failure can be shown to have caused damage to the contractor.

It is true that there is ordinarily no contract relationship between the professional and the construction contractor, but the law recognizes that where a person undertakes to do an act which, if negligently performed, involves a foreseeable risk of harm to another who justifiably acts in reliance upon the other, there may be tort liability.

This leads us to another dimension of this matter of relationships, to which we now turn.

Plans and Specifications

As we have said, the professional is usually a controlling presence in the entire construction process. When the independent consultant undertakes the preparation of plans and specifications, he moves into an area of heavy exposure not only to his client but to the contractors and subcontractors who will one day bid in reliance upon these documents. Certainly his potential for liability in design is far greater than in inspection, which will be dealt with later.

In the design phase the architect-engineer is caught in an economic vise. He must endeavor to perform his professional work within the dollar limits of his contract with the owner, and it is a rare case indeed when the owner gives the professional carte blanche. Ideally, he would like to secure comprehensive subsurface information, but borings cost money. He would prefer to take several weeks to search out and examine local records concerning water tables and other geologic information, but time and money do not always permit such thoroughness. A definitive soils study might be indicated, but who will pay for it?

On the other hand, the contractor who bids upon the project has little choice; he *must* rely upon the plans and specifications. The risk involved in competitive bidding coupled with the very limited time available to bidders to estimate cost will not permit any substantial investment in making thorough independent studies, notwithstanding the boilerplate warnings and disclaimers in the bidding documents. So there is something to be said on both sides.

As to liability of the professional to contractors and subcontractors for design shortcomings, it may be well to quote from the *Restatement of Torts*,[1] which provides that:

---

[1] *Restatement of Torts*, § 552 (1938).

One who in the course of his business or profession supplies information for the guidance of others in their business transactions is subject to liability for harm caused to them by their reliance upon the information if

(a) he fails to exercise that care and competence in obtaining and communicating the information which its recipient is justified in expecting, and

(b) the harm is suffered

(i) by the person or one of the class of persons for whose guidance the information was supplied, and

(ii) because of his justifiable reliance upon it in a transaction substantially identical therewith.

The above quotation is *not necessarily* representative of the law in any given state, but it appears to be the general direction in which the law is moving in this field. Against the argument on behalf of professionals that the risk burden is unfairly cast upon them, the response is offered that the risk must fall somewhere, and they are in the best position to avoid the damage. How?

If the owner is unable or unwilling to pay for the desirable subsurface exploration, he may make the absence of such information clearly known to prospective bidders—not by the boiler-plate method, but by a definitive statement applicable to the particular project. If the professional has not prepared the plans and specifications "in keeping with the usual and accepted standards in the profession," the owner may say so and set forth the respects in which they are deficient. If he is aware (or should be) of a subsurface condition which may affect the cost of the work, he may say so and set forth the reasons for concern.

The professional who performs on a scissors-and-paste basis in the preparation of contract documents is in for trouble, and it will not do to say that the consulting contract was not sufficiently funded to allow a proper job to be done. If this is the case, he should not have taken the job in the first place.

As to latent defects in the plans themselves, the professional may be liable upon the same basis to the contractor or subcontractor who justifiably relied on them. In unit-price contracts the professional may be somewhat less exposed than in lump-sum work, since payment will be made according to actual quantities; but even here he may be subject to suit by the contractor where there is, for example, a serious underrun and where the contractor is able to prove that the professional knew or should have known that his estimated quantity was grossly overstated.

The best counsel that can be given the professional in minimizing his exposure to liability in design is a simple one: full and fair disclosure of everything known and candid warnings addressed to the unknowns. Only by thorough and strict adherence to this proposition can the bulk of the risk be effectively transferred to the contractors.

Inspection of the Work

The well-advised owner will contract with the same consultant for both design and inspection services. Some years ago, the function of the professional during the construction phase was described as "supervision," but the implications of this word raised the spectre of liability of the professional because it suggests control, to some degree, of the method and manner of doing the work by the professional. The term "inspection" is a euphemism for the same function, and although there may be some ambiguity in the AIA standard form of construction contract, there is no doubt that a measure of control over the performance of the work is, and properly should be, reserved to the professional.

Lawyers and judges have come to recognize the need to cut through some of the broad contract language dealing with the role of the professional, and reliance upon insulating language in the construction contract which seeks on the one hand to reserve power to the professional while avoiding responsibility is a doubtful defense. In a real-life context, the orderly construction of any project depends upon the sensible administration of the project by the contractor and the professional. Except in isolated instances, the owner is not in the building business and is likely to be guided almost entirely by the professional. It is safe to say that every responsible contractor is anxious to have a responsible architect or engineer on the project, and the professional earnestly hopes that the contract will be awarded to an equally responsible contractor. Their common goal ought to be to build and complete the project and to avoid friction and controversy which will, in the end, prove trying and expensive to both.

The exposure of the professional to liability to the prime contractor and to subcontractors is relatively more narrow in the inspection phase than in design. Nevertheless, the professional holds the power of economic life or death over the contractor in the administration of the contract. Progress payments to the contractor commonly depend upon certificates to the owner by the professional on a periodic basis, and the contractor has anticipated this cash flow. Change orders are issued and priced out upon the recommendation of the professional, job progress is directly affected by the timeliness of professional action upon shop drawings, extensions of time often must be determined by the project, and so on. Where the professional acts or fails to act in a manner consistent with the usual and accepted standards of his profession as they exist at a given time in an area, he may well wind up as a central defendant in a suit by the contractor and subcontractors for damages. This standard, to which we have earlier referred, is commonly known as *negligence,* and this concept does not depend upon privity of contract.

An interesting corollary is the proposition that the professional may even be liable to the contractor's bonding company where he has negligently caused an acceleration of payments to the contractor. This is because the surety company which has guaranteed performance of the contract by its principal (contractor) is entitled to rely upon retainage as well as all contract balances for work not performed. Obviously, if the contractor is paid at a rate more rapid than that prescribed in the contract, should he default, the bonding company would find less money left against completion cost than it was entitled to expect.

In summary, the only safe position for the professional is one which coincides perfectly with the highest ethical precepts: make certain that the contractor is paid fully and prudently in accordance with the contract documents, but not more or earlier than he is entitled to expect.

Approval of shop drawings, samples, and the like is a perfectly simple matter. The contractor should carefully document the chronology of submissions, and the professional should act responsibly with respect to such admissions.

As to change orders, this generic term includes both extra work and reduction orders. These are the safety valves of construction contracts, through which the necessary adjustments may be made during the course of the work to ensure the orderly completion of the project. Once again, the professional is the key to the resolution of unforeseen problems which arise during the course of the performance of the contract work. Serious liability problems may arise because, as a practical matter, the adjustment of the contract work must take place in the field when the problem becomes manifest, even though the contract usually provides that the contractor will not be paid for extra work in the absence of a written and regularly approved change order. The paperwork takes time, and no one really expects (or wants) the contractor to await the processing of the papers before he goes to work. In practice, the contractor does the work on the basis of verbal instructions from the professional. If a quarrel develops over the terms of the written change order, the professional may well be in the soup. There is no absolute means of avoiding this problem short of accelerating the bureaucratic process.

COURT PROCEDURES

Although legal procedures vary somewhat from state to state, a basic understanding of the procedural aspect of civil litigation is of critical importance. When we speak of the liability of one person to another and of how rights and duties spring out of relationships, such concepts are not entirely meaningful without an understanding of how they are implemented. Subject to local variations, the fundamentals of civil litigation are fairly standard throughout the United States and in the federal courts. Suit is commenced with the filing, by the *plaintiff*, of a *complaint*, stating in very general terms the nature of his grievance against the defendant or defendants. Each defendant files his *answer* to the complaint together with any *counterclaim* he may have against the plaintiff and also any *crossclaim* he may have against any other defendant.

When all the affirmative and defensive pleadings have been filed, issue will have been joined, and all parties are now entitled to have *discovery* of each of the other parties. Some states allow discovery prior to the joining of the issue. There are a number of tools available to the lawyer in the discovery process, the most common of which are *interrogatories*, which are written questions addressed to the subject matter of the dispute to which the other party is required to respond in writing, and *depositions*, which consist of the oral examination of parties and witnesses, under oath, with testimony transcribed by a court reporter. If you have been exposed to these procedures, you know what a drain it is upon your staff, not to mention the very considerable legal costs. The very nature of construction cases is such that vast amounts of time are needed in order to properly prepare the case for trial, and the cost is commensurate with the time required.

Another procedural aspect must be taken into account. In most jurisdictions there is a liberal *third-party practice*. This means that where A sues B, and B believes that C is or may be liable to B for all or part of the damages claimed by A, B may be permitted to drag C into the proceedings as a *third-party defendant*.

Thereupon, A will automatically amend his complaint so as to sue C directly. Because of the tripartite nature of construction regulations, the tactical decisions assume major importance. At first glance, the contractor may think it obvious that he ought to sue both the owner and the professional in the same action, but this may not be necessary or prudent. In his suit against the owner, the architect-engineer will often be the most important witness, since in the eyes of judge or jury his elite status carries with it the implication of our knowledge. The aura of credibility surrounding the professional will be an important factor at the trial, and the contractor may not wish to alienate the professional by suing him in the first instance. Frequently the owner's attorney may bring in the professional by way of third-party complaint, and the contractor may thereby profit from a greater degree of objectivity on the part of the professional. If the owner does not react by suing the professional, the contractor may amend his complaint and add the professional as a defendant, if circumstances suggest that this is desirable.

Alternate options are available to contractors. It is sometimes useful, when representing the contractor, to bring independent actions separately against the owner and the professional. Of course, one cannot collect the same money from two people, but it is completely possible to maintain independent suits at the same time, thereby offering the possibility of two bites at the apple. In addition, the contractor's attorney is able to examine all the files and records of the professional and to take his deposition in a proceeding in which the owner is not entitled to participate, in this phase arming himself for trial against the owner. By pursuing this course, the owner's attorney, who may have been reluctant to sue the professional, may opt to do so in order to lay the foundation for consolidation of the two cases, and this is perfectly agreeable to the contractor's attorney since it will now be apparent to the court or jury that *both* the contractor and the owner are suing the professional.

Frankly, it is open season on the professional, and the trend in this direction continues, as witness the mountainous increases in the cost of errors and omissions insurance coverage. The important lesson to be learned from this takes us back to the earlier observations as to the conduct of the professional in design and inspection phases. His most effective shield against liability is the strict adherence to the highest principals of his profession. At this juncture it is appropriate to quote two excerpts from a decision of the New Jersey Supreme Court a few years ago.[2] The facts of the case are not important to this discussion, but the quotations will serve to demonstrate the sensitivity of the judicial branch of government to the problems of construction contracts:

> The work to be performed is grounded in the principles of free enterprise and competition. The scope of such an undertaking requires those who accept the invitations to bid to be well versed, or advised, in contract law and forms together with comparable efficiency in accounting and engineering departments. Otherwise their financial doom is spelled. It is common knowledge that the owner, or sponsor,

---

[2]*Terminal Constr. Corp. v. Bergen County Hackensack R. San. Sewer Dist. Auth.*, 18 N.J. 294, 113 A.2d 787 (1955).

"writes its own ticket" and the competing market of contractors is obliged to bid and perform in conformity thereto, or to avoid that field of endeavor.

However, this does not mean that a contractor is not entitled to enjoy just treatment within the terms of the contract. If it were otherwise the construction of vital public and municipal projects would suffer by the failure of qualified bidders to enter the field for fear of risks beyond those which are foreseeable. It is grave enough to meet calculated risks in good business practice. The public authority which chooses the contract terms is not exempt from the operation of the basic principle of construction of contracts, that where ambiguities exist they are to be taken most strongly against the draftsman. . . .

We are of the opinion that acts or inaction of the engineer in exercise of authority vested in him or it by the owner under the contract is denominated fraudulent in the legal sense where the engineer's act or inaction was arbitrary and without reason, and that this rule applies even where the owner was not a direct participant in the engineer's fraud.[3] In this we are in accord with the expression of law made by the Superior Court, Appellate Division, in the present matter that: "Fraud in this connection has a broader connotation than is ordinarily implied. In addition to its ordinary significance, in construction contracts it includes arbitrary action and gross mistake."[4]

The philosophy of the law in this respect has been stated to be: "If the engineer has acted in good faith after fair investigation of the facts, the courts give conclusive effect to his decision as the parties agreed."[5] It has been said that the decided cases are generally in accord, and that if the architect or engineer has acted fraudulently or has committed a gross mistake the contractor is entitled to payment.[6,7]

The underlying rationale of this philosophy of constructive fraud is that in determinations under this type of contract the "high point in the Architect's (or engineer's) practice of his profession" lies in those instances "when in order to do justice to the Contractor he has to oppose the desire of his employer, the Owner."[8] It has been said that the architect or engineer occupies a position of trust and confidence, and that "he should act in absolute and entire good faith throughout," and that when he acts under a contract as "the official interpreter of its conditions and the judge of its performance" he should "side neither with the Owner nor with the Contractor" but exercise impartial judgment.[9]

LAWYERS

For centuries, lawyers have been regarded with something less than fondness in every society, but the discipline exists and will continue to exist because it is necessary to resolve disputes by some means less sanguine than combat. The real function of the lawyer, however, is not the trial of cases but the giving of

[3]*Rizzolo v. Poysher,* 89 N.J.L. 618,625, 99A. 390 (E.&A. 1916).
[4]AM. JUR. BLDG. and CONSTR. CONTS., § 34, Restatement of the Law, Contracts § 303.
[5]3 Corbin, *Contracts* § 652, at 600 (1951).
[6]Grismore, *Contracts* § 164, at 252–253 (1947).
[7]*Massman Const. Co. v. Lake Lotawana Ass'n.,* 240 Mo.App. 469, 210 A.W.2d 398, 402 (Ct.App. 1948).
[8]Parker and Adams, *The A.I.A. Standard Contract Forms and The Law,* 1954, p. 54.
[9]American Institute of Architects, *The Handbook of Architectural Practice,* 1943, Chap. 8, pp. 19, 20; Chap. 48, p. 81.

advice so as to avoid foreseeable controversy and to minimize risks. It is virtually impossible to conduct business in today's complex society without the advice of a competent attorney.

Relatively few lawyers are involved in construction contract law, and this is probably because it requires the assimilation of a considerable volume of knowledge in a very complicated field. Lawyers commonly charge fees on the basis of time, and the client is understandably unhappy about having to pay the attorney for the time necessary to educate him in the construction business. Consequently, construction law problems are dealt with by a relatively small number of lawyers who have been through the mill so many times that they can quickly grasp the nature of the particular case and come rapidly to grips with the problem.

This article will have served its purpose if it has afforded the reader enough of an overview of the patterns of responsibility growing out of the relationships of all of those engaged in construction work, while at the same time encouraging all concerned to discuss particular problems with competent counsel at the earliest possible time—ideally before the problem amounts to more than a cloud on the horizon. This is not always possible, but it is always to be desired, because after a dispute has congealed, the parties tend to polarize and the reasoning process is inhibited.

Finally, the proper business of society is progress, and the friction of dispute is wasteful. The investment made in securing experienced and sage advice will yield manifold returns.

Part Seven

Contract Rights

Chapter **31**

Contractor's Rights and Remedies When the Owner Breaches

WILLIAM F. HAUG, ESQ.
Partner, Jennings, Strouss & Salmon, Phoenix, Arizona

INTRODUCTION

On February 16, 1903, George and John entered into a contract[1] under which John agreed to dig a trench and lay pipes for a boiler which George was building on his land. George agreed to pay John $3,450 for the work, to be paid in monthly cash payments as the work progressed.

When John began to excavate the trench, he quickly learned that the subsoil conditions were not what George had told him to expect. The earth, among

Acknowledgment: The author's deep appreciation is extended to his two associates, Charles Santaguida and Grady Gammage, Jr., without whose help he could not have accomplished this chapter.

[1]This example is based loosely on *Philadelphia v. Tripple*, 79 A 703 (1911).

other difficulties, was extremely rocky, and there was major water seepage. To make matters worse, on several occasions George changed his mind on what course the trench should follow. In one instance, John had to backfill part of the trench due to one of these changes.

On October 15, 1903, John had completed one-half of the work. By this time he had spent about $2,500 on materials and labor. He had received payment of $900. At this point it was clear that John was going to lose a considerable amount of money by the time he finished the project.

John, however, never did finish the project because on October 16, 1903, George wrote to John telling him that he was not satisfied with the speed with which the project was being completed; that he was to stop work on the project; and that he and his men, tools, machinery, and materials had to be removed from the work site within five days.

John replied to George's letter advising him that he would comply with his request, adding, however, that he intended to charge George for the expenditures he had made on the project.

Since they were unable to settle their differences, George and John went to court. John said he should be paid $2,500 since he had spent that much on the work. George said that John should be paid only one-half of the agreed-on price of $3,450 because only one-half of the work was done. The court determined that John should be paid $2,500.

The next year, George's neighbor, Hubert, also needed pipes laid to connect to a boiler he had built. He had seen John's work on George's property and asked him to do the job. John and Hubert agreed that the price would be $4,000 and that monthly progress payments would be made.

This time the work went along smoothly. By June, John had completed one-half of the work at a cost of only $800. He had received progress payments totaling $1,800. On June 3, 1904, however, Hubert wrote John that he was not satisfied with the speed of the work and that he should discontinue work on the project. John replied that he intended to stand by their agreement and was willing to do the work he had promised.

When Hubert refused to pay John for any other work done, John stopped work and the parties went to court. Hubert, who had talked to George, said that John should be paid $800, the amount of money that he had spent on the work. John said that he was entitled to be paid the agreed price of $4,000, minus the $1,600 it would have cost him to complete the project, a total of $2,400.

The court again agreed with John and awarded him $2,400, the amount of profit he would have earned if the contract had been performed.

Not every contractor is as successful as John. Many contractors, when faced with a losing contract, such as the one with George, would find the court unwilling to give them the amount of money actually spent on the project. On the other hand, there have been cases where a contractor, who has a money-making contract, will not be paid the contract price, but only his expenses. The purpose of this chapter is to describe what a contractor should do in order to maximize the amount of money he can recover from the owner when he is faced with a situation where the acts of the owner entitle him to stop work on a project.

THE RIGHT TO STOP WORK

Frequently, because of the actions of the owner, a contractor has the right to stop work on a project. The contractor's right to stop work can be derived under different theories of law. First, the contract itself might give the contractor the power to *terminate* the contract on the occurrence of certain events. Second, the contractor and the owner might agree to *rescind* the contract; that is, they might agree to end their contract. Third, the contractor might be *excused* from performing under the contract because of a material breach by the owner. The rights of the contractor to secure compensation for the work he has performed and the amount of money he will recover vary according to which theory the contractor has elected to use to justify the stopping of work. In addition, certain acts of the owner may justify the contractor's cessation of work under one theory but not under the others.

Termination

Rights and remedies created in the contract   A contract may expressly give either or both parties the power to terminate the contract on the occurrence of certain events. When a contractor elects to exercise the power of termination, he is relieved of his obligation to perform further on the contract; that is, he is not required to do any of the things he originally obligated himself to do. The contract may also specify obligations which the owner must fulfill if the contractor elects to terminate the contract.

Events triggering the right to terminate in the AIA contract   In order to determine when a contractor has the power to terminate a contract, one must read the contract. This is because the contract creates the power to terminate and controls the situations when the power can be exercised. Using the AIA standard contract[2] as an example, we find that the contractor's power to terminate the contract is created in Article 14, which provides:

> **Termination of the Contract**
> 14.1 TERMINATION BY THE CONTRACTOR
> 14.1.1 If the Work is stopped for a period of thirty days under an order of any court or other public authority having jurisdiction, or as a result of an act of government, such as a declaration of a national emergency making materials unavailable, through no act or fault of the Contractor or a Subcontractor or their agents, or employees, or any other persons performing any of the Work under a contract with the Contractor, or if the Work should be stopped for a period of thirty days by the Contractor for the Architect's failure to issue a Certificate for Payment as provided in Paragraph 9.7, or for the Owner's failure to make payment thereon as provided in Paragraph 9.7, then the Contractor may, upon seven days' written notice to the Owner and the Architect, terminate the Contract and recover from the Owner payment for all Work executed and for any proven loss sustained upon any materials, equipment, tools, construction equipment and machinery, including reasonable profit and damages.

---

[2]AIA Document A201, *General Conditions of the Contract for Construction* (August 1976 ed.)

Article 14 tells us that the owner and contractor agreed to two things regarding termination by the contractor: first, the events which must occur before the contractor has the power to terminate the contract and, second, the rights and duties of the parties once the contract is terminated.

Article 14 lists four events which can trigger the contractor's power to terminate the contract. The contractor may give the architect and the owner seven days' written notice of his intent to terminate the contract if work is stopped for 30 days:

1. By an order of a court or other public authority
2. By an act of government
3. By the contractor because the architect has failed to issue a certificate for payment
4. By the contractor because the owner has failed to make payments which are due

Let us examine how each of the four events might occur.

Court Order.   Work could stop as the result of a court order under a number of circumstances. For example, an owner might contract to have a glue factory built on land next to a residential area. The adjacent landowners, upon learning of the plans of the owner, go to court and claim that a glue factory would be a nuisance in the neighborhood. The court, before determining whether the building should ultimately be constructed, issues an order temporarily stopping work on the factory until the case is fully argued by both sides. Although the owner might eventually win the lawsuit brought by the homeowners, the contractor, after work has been stopped for 30 days, has the power to terminate the contract after giving 7 days' written notice to the architect and owner.

Governmental Act.   The second event stated is that work is stopped for 30 days as the result of an act of government. Suppose, for example, that the owner and the contractor agreed to build a one-story warehouse and loading dock. The parties' agreement provided that work on the project was to commence on August 1. The zoning of the lot on which the structure is to be built permits such a use. The city building code requires, however, that a building permit be secured prior to the start of construction on any new structure. Due to administrative backlog, a building permit was not issued until September 15, although the owner had filed all necessary plans and forms for the permit to have been received by August 1. On August 31, after work had been stopped for 30 days, the contractor had the right to terminate the contract.

Architect's Failure to Issue a Certificate for Payment.   The third possible event is that work is stopped for 30 days because the architect fails to issue a certificate for payment. The explanation of how this event can occur is somewhat complex because a number of subsidiary events must occur before the contractor is allowed, initially, to stop work because of the failure of the architect to issue a certificate for payment.

Basically, if the architect fails to issue a certificate for payment within seven days after receipt of the contractor's application for payment, the contractor may, upon seven days' written notice to the owner and the architect, stop the work until the amount owing has been received.[3] The application for payment, which is based on a schedule of values of the various portions of the work, must be submitted at least the day before each payment becomes due. The contractor must substantiate that the work and materials covered in the application have been performed or delivered, and he must deliver title to the work and materials clear of all liens.[4]

If the architect declines to issue a certificate for payment due to the fault of the contractor, the contractor cannot stop the work. Failure to issue the certificate will be deemed the fault of the contractor if the work has not progressed to the point indicated or if the work is not of the quality called for in the specifications. Other justifications for refusing to issue a certificate for payment, which are deemed the fault of the contractor, include the failure of the contractor to remedy defective work, the filing or probable filing of third-party liens, the failure of the contractor to make payments properly to subcontractors, reasonable doubt that the work can be completed for the unpaid balance of the agreed-upon price, damage to another contractor, reasonable indication that the work will not be completed on time, or unsatisfactory prosecution of the work by the contractor.[5] Essentially, if the contractor fails to perform as promised, the architect will be justified in refusing to issue a certificate for payment. If the architect is justified in refusing to issue the certificate, the contractor is not justified in stopping the work. On the other hand, if the contractor has performed in accordance with his promise and he has properly filed an application for payment, then he is justified in stopping work if the architect fails to issue a certificate for payment.

An example may clarify how these provisions operate. A contractor and an owner agree to build and pay for a private residential structure. The contract provides that progress payments will be made at three intermediate points and a final payment made when the structure is completed. The contractor submits a schedule of values which indicates that 25 percent of the work will be completed with the pouring of the basement, 50 percent with the erection of the exterior walls and roof, and 75 percent with the completion of the interior walls. The contractor proceeds with the work, completes the foundation, and receives the first progress payment. He then submits an application for payment to the architect for the second progress payment. He also submits documentation which indicates that the exterior walls and roof have been completed and that there are no liens on the work or materials. The architect refuses to issue a certificate of payment because workmen for one of the subcontractors have not been paid, although the contractor has, in fact, paid the subcontractor. The architect tells the contractor he will not issue the certificate until the contractor has pressured the subcontractor into paying his workmen. Seven days after the application for payment has been submitted, the contractor writes to the architect and owner warning that he will stop work on the

---

[3] AIA Document A201 (1976 ed.), ¶ 9.7.1.
[4] AIA Document A201 (1976), ¶ 9.2 and 9.3.
[5] AIA Document A201 (1976 ed.), ¶ 9.6.

project. Seven days after giving this written notice to the architect and owner, the contractor stops work. After the work has been stopped for 30 days, which is 44 days after the application for payment has been submitted (7 days for architect to issue certificate and 7 days written notice of intent to stop work plus the 30-day work stoppage), the contractor has the power to terminate the contract. It should be noted that if the contractor had not paid the subcontractor, the architect would have been justified in refusing to issue the certificate. The stopping of the work by the contractor would not be authorized under the contract and the contractor could be liable for damages.

Owner's Failure to Make Payment.   The fourth event which can occur is that the work is stopped for 30 days because of the failure of the owner to make payments when due. The circumstances and procedures under which this event can occur are similar to when work is stopped due to the architect's failure to issue a certificate. The owner is required to pay only after the architect has issued a certificate, and he is justified in refusing to pay, despite the issuance of a certificate, for any of the reasons that would justify the refusal to issue a certificate. Thus, if the contractor does not properly perform his obligations, the owner may be justified in refusing to make payments. On the other hand, if, seven days after a certificate has been issued, an owner unjustifiably refuses to pay, the contractor can give written notice of his intent to stop work. After seven days, the contractor can stop work. After the work has been stopped 30 days, the contractor can terminate the contract if he has given the architect and owner seven days' notice of his intent to do so.[6]

Remedies under the AIA Standard Contract.   In addition to stating the events which trigger the contractor's power to terminate, Article 14 of the AIA contract determines the amount of money he can recover after he invokes his power. Article 14 provides that the contractor can recover: (1) for the work he has performed, (2) losses he has sustained on the materials and equipment, and (3) reasonable profits and damages.

The contractor's recovery for the work he has performed will be measured by the contract price. In other words, if he has performed one-half of the agreed-upon work before he terminates the contract, he can recover one-half of the contract price. In addition, he can recover for any loss which he can prove he sustained on any materials or equipment which he purchased in order to perform. If the value of the materials which he purchased to enable him to perform dropped in value, he can recover the difference in price from the owner. Finally, the contractor can recover a reasonable profit and damages. If the contractor would have made a profit on the remaining work, he can recover that amount even though the work is not performed. The contractor can also recover damages which he suffers.

A simple example will illustrate how the contractor's recovery is measured. The contractor and owner agree to build a house for $35,000. In computing his bid, the contractor determined that his costs for building the house would be

---

[6] AIA Document A201 (1976 ed.), ¶ 9.7.

$30,000 and that he would realize a profit of $5,000. After half the project has been completed, the contractor terminates because the owner has failed to make payments as agreed. At this point, the contractor has spent $15,000 on the work actually completed. In addition, he has purchased materials which were to be used in completing the remainder of the house at a cost of $9,000. He has also rented equipment to be used for the remainder of the project for $4,000. He is able to sell the materials he had purchased for $8,000, and the owner of the equipment is willing to take it back for a cost of $500. During the 30 days the work was stopped due to the failure of the owner to make payments, the contractor lost $750 due to the rental cost of the equipment and other overhead expenses. The contractor's recovery would be measured as shown in Table 31.1.

TABLE 31.1

Payment for work performed: One-half the contract price since one-half the work was performed	$17,250
Loss on materials and equipment:	
Materials	1,000
Equipment	500
Lost profit and damages: Lost profit (one-half of the reasonable profit is paid in the amount recovered for payment of work performed)	2,500
Damages	750
Total Recovery	$22,000

As will be explained later, the amount the contractor may recover when he elects to terminate the contract may vary from the amount he could recover if he were to elect to rescind the contract or to sue for breach.

Rescission

By agreement   Like the original contract between the parties, the rescission of a contract is an agreement made by the owner and the contractor. In the original contract the parties agreed to do something. In rescinding the contract, the parties agree that they will not do what they had originally agreed to do. The rescission of a contract is similar to a termination of a contract in that it is based on the agreement of the parties. Unlike an agreement to terminate a contract, which is part of the original contract, an agreement to rescind the contract is a separate agreement, apart from the original contract, and entered into after the original contract was created.[7] For example, in the original contract, the contractor agreed that he would build a two-story house in

[7]Calamari and Perillo, *Contracts*, § 339 (1970).

Chicago in accordance with plans furnished by the owner, and the owner agreed to pay the contractor $35,000 when the house was completed. After the contract was signed, both parties had second thoughts about the advisability of actually performing on the contract. The contractor, after the contract was signed, was offered the opportunity of constructing a larger building but would be unable to do so because his men and equipment would be tied up building the two-story house. The owner was transferred to another city, and the two-story house in Chicago would do him no good. The owner and contractor can agree to release each other from their obligations under the contract. Their agreement is a rescission of the contract.

It is not necessary that both parties actively desire the rescission of the contract. It is possible that, although the contractor is still willing to build the house, the owner, because he has been transferred, no longer wants to pay for it. The owner may tell the contractor that, if the contractor builds the house, he will not pay for it unless he can find a buyer for it. If the contractor agrees to treat the contract as put to an end, the contract is rescinded even though the contractor may feel that he has lost money as a result. It should be noted that the contractor is not compelled to agree to or accept the owner's offer of rescission. As will be discussed later, the contractor can treat the owner's acts as a breach of the contract and, although he does not build the house, hold the owner liable on the contract. The important distinction is that, if the contractor agrees to treat the contract as put to an end, the contract is rescinded, and both parties are relieved of the obligation to perform.

The parties' agreement to rescind the contract can provide that one party will be obligated to pay for services already rendered or for losses which the other party suffers as a result of the rescission. For example, if the parties agreed to rescind the agreement to build the house because the owner had been transferred, they could agree that the owner pay for work already done on the house, or that the owner would pay the contractor his expenses in preparing to build the house, or that the owner would pay the contractor the amount of profit he would have made under the contract. Although such an agreement to pay these sums may be implied by a court, it is preferable that the parties specify in writing any payments which are to be made or any obligations which are not discharged.[8]

By court implied agreement   At times the law will operate as though the owner and the contractor had agreed to rescind the contract although, in fact, the parties never did enter into such an agreement. This can occur when the owner commits an act which constitutes a material breach of the contract. Just what material breach means and what conduct on the part of the owner would constitute a material breach of a contract will be discussed later. At present, it is enough to know that a material breach of a contract excuses the contractor from performing further on the contract. When an owner materially breaches a contract, the law states that such conduct is like an offer to rescind the contract. The law reasons that, if the owner does not fulfill his obligations under the

[8] *cf. Johnston v. Gilbert,* 382 P.2d 87 (Ore. 1963); *Anderson v. Copeland,* 378 P.2d 1006 (Okla. 1963).

contract, he must be willing to see the contract between the parties put to an end. It will, therefore, treat a material breach of a contract as an offer to rescind which the contractor can accept.[9]

Once a contract has been rescinded in this manner, the law acts as though the contract had never existed. Neither the contractor nor the owner can claim any rights or benefits which he would have had under the contract. As we will discuss later, this determination of the law to treat the contract as though it never existed will affect the amount of money which the contractor can recover for any work he has performed or for any materials he has sold to the owner.

Excused Performance

Material breach: a critical but elusive concept   Actions taken by one party to a contract may have consequences to the other party beyond operating as an offer to rescind. Often a breach of contract by one party will *excuse* the counterperformance due from the other party. All contracts are based on an exchange of consideration. *Consideration* can be money, work, a promise not to do something, or another sort of promise. Without consideration on both sides of a contract, it will usually not be binding on the parties.

Breach of a contract occurs when one of the parties fails to live up to his side of the bargain. His consideration may have failed (e.g., his check bounces, or he fails to fulfill his promise), he may have delayed too long in performing his obligations, or he may have gone bankrupt. In any such event, a breach has occurred.

As explained in the last section, some of these breaches can be seen as an offer to rescind the contract—an offer made by the breaching party to the other party. Such a breach will only constitute an offer to rescind when it is material. This concept of materiality is equally critical in the area of excuse of performance, for when a breach of contract is material, it *excuses* the counter-performance of the other party. The fact that material breach may either excuse counterperformance or be seen as an offer to rescind the contract is not as mysterious as it may seem. It means that in many cases the contractor is given a choice: he may accept the offer to rescind, thereby voiding the contract, or he may simply cease his own performance and treat the contract as still in existence. This choice is called an *election of remedies*. The way in which this election is made, the factors which go into an intelligent choice, and the consequences of such a choice are dealt with below.

It is very difficult to briefly explain the concept of material breach. Essentially, a breach is *material* if it "goes to the essence of the contract."[10] Material breaches are those which destroy or, at least, severely impair the purpose for which the contract was made. For example, suppose an owner and a builder signed a contract agreeing that the owner would pay the contractor $50,000 for

[9]Calamari and Perillo, *Contracts,* § 239 (1970).
[10]*See, e.g. United States v. Western Cas. and Sur. Co.,* 498 F.2d 335 (9th Cir. 1974); 5 Corbin, *Contracts* § 1104 at 562 (1964); *Restatement, Contracts* § 274; *Crofoot Lumber, Inc. v. Thompson,* 329 P.2d 302 (Cal. App. 1958).

a four-bedroom, two-bath house. If the contractor built a three-bedroom, one-bath house, he would, undoubtedly, be held to have materially breached the contract, and the owner would be excused from paying. Failure to install a single electrical plug, however, would almost certainly not be material. The owner would still have to pay although he could recover damages for the missing plug.

This chapter deals with owner breach, however, and particular examples are developed below. Although failure by the owner to supply the vacant land on which to construct the house would almost certainly be a material breach, a three-hour delay in a single progress payment is almost as certainly not material. Obviously, such extreme examples are simple. The problems arise more frequently in more ambiguous situations. Generally, the analysis must consider the importance of this particular bit of performance to the other party at the time the contract was made. One relevant question is: Would the other party have made his bargain if he knew this breach would occur? If not, it is likely that the breach is material.

Nature of breaches *Failure of Performance by the Owner.* Both the contractor and owner promise to perform certain acts when they enter into a contract. Generally speaking, the owner's primary obligation is to pay for the work done by the contractor. At times, however, the owner will also undertake obligations which are directly related to the work itself. An owner, for example, can promise to make certain materials or plans available to the contractor, or he may undertake the responsibility of seeing that the necessary building permits are secured. If the owner fails to perform one of these obligations and, as a result, the contractor is unable to proceed with the work as planned, the owner has committed a material breach, and the contractor is excused from performing further.

One way that an owner can materially breach is illustrated by an agreement between an owner and a contractor to construct a storage dam. The owner agreed to deliver at the dam site all cement, gravel, sand, steel, and other metal work which was to be a permanent part of the dam. In addition, the owner agreed to supply compressed air in sufficient quantities to operate the contractor's power shovels. Finally, the owner agreed to excavate the cutoff trench early enough that the contractor would not be delayed. The owner failed to deliver the materials on time. Instead, deliveries were frequently late and in insufficient quantities. As a result, the contractor was seriously delayed and finally had to stop work when winter set in. The delay was aggravated by the fact that the owner failed to provide sufficient compressed air. Finally, progress on the cutoff trench was slower than promised with the result that the contractor was still further delayed. These failures of the owner to perform as promised were of such a nature that they prevented the contractor from performing his obligation as planned. As a result, the owner had materially breached, and the contractor was excused from further performance.

Another obligation which owners frequently undertake is to secure the issuance of a building permit. For example, the parties may agree to build a low-cost apartment building with construction to commence immediately after the issuance of building permits. Suppose the owner never secures the necessary permits because he abandoned the project when his financier disapproved of his proposed specifications. The failure of the owner to secure the building permits is a material breach, and the contractor is excused from performance.

Delay in Performance by Owner. The matter of whether or not a contractor may cease work because some owner caused delay is somewhat unclear. Cases are split, and their reasoning emphasizes various points in regard to this problem. The materiality of the delay and the quality of the contract as "entire" or "severable" may both be important factors.

Owner-caused delay may take several forms, including the failure of the owner to properly coordinate work with the contractor, demands by the owner for major unexpected changes in work, and failure by the owner to make timely progress payments. Often courts dealing with this question speak in the language of rescission. In fact, as explained above, rescission is a distinct legal theory differing from excuse. In any delay-of-performance situation either rescission or excuse might be used as a theory to seek relief. In both cases the test on whether or not the contractor may stop work in response to the delay caused by the owner revolves around the seriousness (materiality) of the owner-caused delay. Rescission is proper only where the owner has manifested some intent to end the contract. Delay alone might not always manifest such intent unless coupled with a repudiation of the rest of the contract. In any event, the seriousness-of-delay test is also quite properly applied to a determination of whether the owner's actions are sufficient to *excuse* the contractor's further performance. If the owner's delay is material, then the contractor should have the right to suspend all further performance.

Failure to make progress payments. The situations in which failure to make progress payments will excuse counterperformance by the contractor are not entirely clear. One legal authority expresses the opinion that the contractor, on nonpayment of an installment of the contract, might refuse to perform further until such payment is made and if delayed for a long and unreasonable period of time, might refuse to go on with the work altogether, although a day's delay in payment would not justify permanent cessation of the work.[11] Some cases suggest a stricter standard and have held that any delay by the owner in making payments does not operate to excuse the contractor's performance unless such failure prevents further work by the contractor.[12] Some of these cases even suggest that if the contractor does not immediately stop work after the owner's actions, he can be considered to have elected to continue with the contract.[13]

In each case, whether or not failure to make a progress payment is material would be decided based upon the amount of the payments, the number of payments to be made, the work to be done, and so on. The cases noted above would suggest that the material breach standard is met only where nonpayment of the installment actually prevents further work by the contractor. This is an extremely difficult test to meet.

---

[11] 2 Williston, *Contracts* 626; 2 Williston, *Sales* (2d ed. § 467-E).

[12] *See, e.g., Knutson v. Metallic Slab Form Co.,* 128 F.2d 408 (5th Cir. 1942); *Greenlee County v. Cotey,* 155 P. 302 (Ariz. 1916).

[13] *Knutson, supra.*

More recent cases and the modern trend generally hold that in building and construction contracts calling for performance of labor and supplying of materials, a stipulation for payments from time to time during work is so material that a substantial failure to pay excuses further performance by the contractor.[14] Most cases using this standard would excuse the contractor's performance not only when the owner's delay prevented further work but would also allow such an excuse in many other situations. However, "materiality" retains some meaning; a brief delay in making a payment would certainly not totally excuse the contractor.[15]

Many cases on this question speak not only in terms of the materiality of the owner's breach but also of the quality of the contract as "entire" or "severable."[16] *Severable,* here, means that the contract in question can be treated as a series of separate bargains, each with its own work to be done and with its own consideration or payment. If the contract is found to be severable, the court will separate each of these bargains into smaller contracts and enforce them individually.

Severability is a legal conclusion reached by the court in each case. If, for example, each progress payment is tied to a specific task, the contract is more likely to be seen as severable. So, if the owner were to pay $5,000 on completion of a foundation, $5,000 on completion of wall framing, $5,000 on finishing the roof, and $5,000 on final completion of the building, the court might sever the contract into as many as four component bargains.

If the court were to decide the contract was severable in such a case, then when the owner failed to make the third $5,000 payment, the contractor could stop work and claim that his further performance is excused. The reasoning behind this analysis also really involves a question of material breach. If the contract is indivisible (entire), the failure to make one single payment is not seen as sufficient to excuse counterperformance by the contractor. But, if each task is tied to each payment in a series of severable mini-contracts, then any failure to pay is a total, and, therefore, *material* breach as to that section of the total agreement.

Many cases treat only the question of severability and do not mention the materiality of the breach. Others analyze the problem in exactly the opposite way, while some cases examine both questions. In practice, the test and the result are the same. If the breach is material, or if the contract is severable, the contractor's performance is excused on the owner's breach. The only important distinction is that the severability of a contract depends upon the original intent of the parties. When arguing for severability, the fact that payments are apportioned to actual work done is treated as evidence of an intent to make the

---

[14]*See* cases cited at 17A C.J.S. 672 n. 34–35; *see also Gabriel v. Corkum,* 196 P.2d 437 (Ore. 1948).

[15]The effect of delay in making a progress payment has been much litigated in California. The law there generally appears to be that a "substantial" failure to pay will justify *rescission,* but only in the most extraordinary circumstances will such a breach provide an excuse of performance allowing the contractor to sue for contract damages. *See Integrated, Inc. v. Alec Ferguson Elec. Contr.,* 250 Cal. App. 287, 58 Cal. Rptr. 503 (1967). Many of the California cases fail to properly distinguish between rescission and excuse. *See* cases cited *id,* at 58 Cal. Rptr. 509–510.

[16]*See, e.g., Baker Sand & Gravel Co. v. Rogers Plumb. & Heat. Co.,* 154 SO 591 (Ala. 1934).

contract severable. The question of the materiality of owner's breach does not depend on the intent of the parties.

The context in which the right of the contractor to stop work upon the owner's failure to make progress payments has usually been litigation over whether the contractor may suspend performance and recover damages for the idleness of his workers during the delay. Some cases have allowed such recovery while others have refused to allow any recovery for delay beyond interest on the payments.[17] In each case the test has either been based on materiality of breach or severability of the contract.[18]

It should be noted that in many cases provisions in the contract will deal with this problem. Frequently, building and construction contracts contain express provisions against the recovery of damages resulting from delay caused by the owner. These provisions have been held to be valid and, when applicable, effectively preclude the contractor from recovering damages for delay. This means that, while the contractor has the right to stop work, he will not be able to recover for the idleness of his employees during the suspension period. Provisions in the contract authorizing the owner to suspend work, under certain conditions, without compensation to the contractor have also been held valid but have been held, in some particular circumstances, not to preclude the contractor from recovering all damages resulting from the delay caused by the default of the owner.[19]

The final conclusion on failure to make progress payments as an excuse to performance, then, is that such failure may, or may not, be a material breach acting to excuse counterperformance. If the failure to pay prevents further performance by the contractor, it is clearly material. Probably any prolonged delay of a significant payment would also constitute material breach.

Failure to coordinate work. The failure to make progress payments is not the only context in which owner-caused delay could operate to excuse further work by the contractor. Such a situation could arise when the owner had delayed in preparing the work site so that the contractor could not proceed or when the owner was so uncooperative in delivering materials that the contractor could not perform at the required time. For example, suppose a homeowner made a contract with one contractor to build several houses and a contract with a roofing company to roof each of the houses. However, the owner failed to have the house builder begin performance early enough for the houses to be completed when anticipated. As a result, the roofer was unable to roof the houses. By the time they were finished, he was obligated to perform another job.[20]

If the roofer had agreed to complete the work by a specific date, the failure of the owner or of some person for whom the owner is responsible to make a

---

[17]13 Am. Jur. 2d, "Building and Construction Contracts," §§ 48–50. *cf. Underground Constr. Co. v. Sanitary Dist.,* 11 N.E.2d 361 (1937); with *O'Rourke Eng. Const. Co. v. New York,* 241 NYS 613 (1930).

[18]*See Cases* cited at *Anno.,* 115 A.L.R. 65 at 75–76 (1938).

[19]13 Am. Jur. 2d, "Building and Construction Contracts," §§ 48–50; *Anno.,* 10 A.L.R.2d 803 (1950); 115 A.L.R. 80 (1938).

[20]*Stark v. Shaw,* 155 Cal. App.2d 171, 317 P.2d 182 (1957); *cert. denied,* 356 U.S. 937 (1958).

payment or perform a task to ensure the completion of the houses in time would act as an excuse to the contractor's performance. The contractor can, of course, recover damages caused by the owner's delay.

Should the owner's delay involve failure to cooperate, the contractor must establish that the owner obligated himself to have it done on a certain date and have materials and property ready for such work and that the contractor was delayed by the owner's failure to do so. In analyzing whether the owner's uncooperative actions justify the contractor's stopping work, the contractor should again ask: Is the owner's action a material breach?

Anticipatory Breach by the Owner.   At times an owner will have second thoughts about a project after he has entered into a valid contract with a contractor. The owner may try to talk the contractor into agreeing to rescind the contract. If he is unsuccessful, the owner may simply announce that he is not going to go through with the deal. Under some circumstances, such a repudiation of the contract by the owner will entitle the contractor to stop work on the project and immediately sue for damages.

Broadly speaking, an owner can act to repudiate a contract in three ways: First, he can make a positive statement that he will not, or cannot, go through with his part of the bargain. For example, an owner had entered into a contract to have a private residence built in Chicago. After signing the contract, the owner was transferred by his employer to work in the company's Cleveland office. The owner then notified the contractor that he no longer needed the house and that he would not pay for it if it were built. The acts of the owner constituted a repudiation of the contract.[21]

A second way an owner could repudiate a contract is by selling his interest in the land, or some other item he needed in order to perform on the contract.[22] Suppose, for example, that the owner, upon learning that he had been transferred to Cleveland, sold the property on which he had planned to build the house. One of the obligations the owner had undertaken in his contract with the builder was to provide the builder with access to the work site. Since he had sold the land, the owner could no longer do this. The selling of the land, therefore, constituted a repudiation of the contract.

A third way the owner could repudiate the contract is by doing some act which would make his performance under the contract impossible or *apparently* impossible.[23] For example, the contract between the owner and the builder may provide that the owner will furnish plans drawn by a particular architect. When the owner learns that he has been transferred, he fires the architect before the plans have been completed. The owner has made it impossible for him to furnish the plans and has, therefore, repudiated the contract.

When an owner repudiates his contract with the builder, the builder generally must stop work on the project. The builder can do this under several theories. As discussed above, the builder can treat the owner's acts as an offer to rescind the contract. By accepting this offer, the builder can agree to put the

---

[21]*Restatement, Contracts* § 318(a) (1932).

[22]*Restatement, Contracts* § 318(b) (1932).

[23]*Restatement, Contracts* § 318(c) (1932).

contract to an end and, thereby, *rescind* the contract. The repudiation of the contract also acts as a *breach of the contract* which *excuses* the builder from his obligation to perform. The builder can choose to sue immediately on the contract or he can sue when the time for the owner's payments become due. Under most circumstances the builder cannot ignore the owner's repudiation and continue work on the project. Generally speaking, the builder must act in a manner which keeps the damages resulting from the owner's act to a minimum.

An owner can retract his repudiation if the builder has not acted in reliance on it.[24] If this occurs, the contract continues as though nothing has happened except that the builder may be given an extension of time for the delay caused. Suppose the owner, after telling the builder he is not going to pay for the house because he has been transferred to Cleveland, writes the builder a few days later and tells him he has changed his mind because he now realizes that it would be unfair to try to avoid his responsibilities. He tells the builder to finish the house and that he will pay for it and sell it to someone else. If the builder has not relied in some way on the owner's earlier repudiation, he is obligated to finish the construction of the house. On the other hand, if the builder has changed his position because of the repudiation, the builder is not now obligated to build the house.[25] For example, if the builder had undertaken a new commitment, based on the assumption that he would not be working on the owner's house, the builder would not have to build the house. Similarly, if the builder had started a lawsuit against the owner, he would not have to build the house.

Inability of the Owner to Perform.   In any given project the contractor may also be presented with the right to stop work as a result of the owner's inability to perform his part of the contract. Possible examples of owner inability include failure of the owner to own the work site, bankruptcy of the owner, or insolvency of the owner. All three of these actions by the owner might be treated as rescission as well as an action which excuses performance by the contractor. As we previously noted, this overlap is a problem throughout this area but it is especially acute here where any of these particular actions by the owner may be seen as an offer on his part to rescind the contract. For example, a voluntary petition in bankruptcy by the owner may act, not only as a breach of contract, excusing the contractor from performance, but also as an offer by the owner to the contractor to rescind the contract. These actions can also be analyzed as repudiations, as developed above.

Generally, here, in regard to the actions by the owner excusing performance by the contractor, the same analysis as developed above in regard to delay by the owner is applicable: Is the owner's action a material breach? However, in this instance, the materiality inquiry may also go to testing whether or not the owner's actions constitute an offer to rescind. It will often be up to the contractor to choose the theory most advantageous to him.

Failure to own work site. Suppose an owner contracts for a builder to erect a hamburger stand for him at "the lot located at the southeast corner of Mill and Broadway, designated as 2451 East Broadway and as Lot 67 in Tract 412 in the

---

[24]*Restatement, Contracts* § 319 (1932).
[25]*Restatement, Contracts* § 323 (1932).

City of Bisbee." When the contractor first visits the site with his crew he finds that it is not a vacant lot, as the owner represented, but has a fast-food market built on it. He then discovers that the owner does not even own such a lot. Is the contractor excused from performing? Probably so, for the owner's action may be a material breach. However, if the only problem were that the contract should have read "southwest" corner and that lot is as represented, material breach would probably not have occurred.

The more frequent problem arises where the owner has not fully perfected his title before the contract calls for the builder to commence construction. In such a case, if the builder has not begun work, he will probably refuse to do so until title is perfected. The owner's failure to clear title in time can be analyzed as an owner-caused delay as explored above. If the delay time is material, the contractor is probably excused. What if partway through the work, the contractor discovers that the owner has failed to gain clear title? The answer now may depend on how defective the title is, on how much the owner must do, and how long it will take him to clearly own the land. In each case the question remains: Is the owner's failure a material breach?

Bankruptcy or insolvency of the owner. The authorities are not in universal agreement as to the right of the contractor or other party to any contract to be excused from performing on bankruptcy or insolvency of the other party. Some authorities speak in terms of the right of the solvent party to rescind.[26] Others simply state that the prospective inability to perform the contract arising on insolvency is not a sufficient condition to excuse the other party from his obligation.[27] However, the trend may be that prospective inability to perform, including present insolvency or bankruptcy, does discharge the obligation of the other party to perform.[28]

Classically, it was said that in order to excuse the other party's counterperformance, the present disability of a party must be so complete as to place it beyond the power of that party to perform his obligations in every respect.[29] Insolvency would not necessarily meet this test. Today, more courts would probably hold that the contractor would not have to perform on discovery of the owner's insolvency.[30] These cases would treat insolvency as a material breach. A voluntary petition in bankruptcy by the owner would be treated similarly.

Election of Remedies

As previously discussed, many times a contractor can choose to stop work either because he treats the contract as rescinded or because his performance is excused because of a material breach by the owner. A contractor is required to

---

[26]*Brady v. Oliver,* 147 S.W. 1135 (Tenn. 1911).

[27]*Arizona Title Ins. & Trust Co. v. O'Malley Lumber Co.,* 484 P.2d 639, 647 (Ariz. App. 1971).

[28]*Restatement, Contracts* § 287 (1932).

[29]*Brady v. Oliver,* 147 S.W. 1135 (Tenn. 1911).

[30]Many cases view present insolvency or bankruptcy as anticipatory repudiation and cite *Central Trust Co. v. Chicago Auditorium Ass'n.,* 240 U.S. 581 (1916).

do one or the other; he cannot treat the contract as rescinded for some purposes and breached for other purposes. Requiring the contractor to choose between these remedies is what is known as *the election of remedies.*

Once an owner has elected to rescind a contract, he cannot later make a claim for damages for any breach of the contract.[31] On the other hand, after a contractor indicates that he intends to treat a contract as valid and continuing after a breach by the owner, he cannot later claim that the contract was rescinded by the same conduct.[32] In view of the fact that the contractor's amount of recovery may vary depending on whether he treats the contract as rescinded or breached, it is important that the contractor understand what he must do to rescind the contract and what he must do to keep the contract alive.

Conduct by the contractor which indicates that he considers the contract as put to an end will indicate that the contract has been rescinded. The contractor's words may indicate that he considers the contract as put to an end. For example, after the owner has failed to pay the contractor over a long period, the contractor may write the owner telling him: "The whole deal is off because you have not paid me as we agreed. As far as I am concerned, it was a big mistake for me to get involved in this project in the first place." This letter would be a strong indication that the contractor was treating the failure of the owner to make the required payments as an offer to rescind the contract, which he accepted. The contractor would not be allowed to change his mind later and decide that he would rather keep the contract alive and sue the owner for damages.

The acts of the contractor can also indicate an intention to rescind the contract. If the acts of the contractor are inconsistent with the continuing existence of the contract, they will be treated as indicating his intent to rescind. If the owner failed to make payments, the contractor could reclaim materials which he had sold and delivered to the owner. The act of reclaiming the materials would be viewed as indicating that the contractor intended to treat the contract as rescinded. In addition, if the contractor accepted a return of money which had been deposited with the owner to ensure his completion of the work, or if he released his surety, this would indicate a rescission of the contract. Similarly, an offer to return payments made by the owner would indicate rescission.

On the other hand, any conduct by the contractor which indicated that he intended to treat the contract as valid and subsisting would indicate that he had elected to treat the owner's conduct as a breach of the contract for which he could recover damages.[33] For example, the contractor could indicate a willingness to continue to perform on the contract despite the fact that the owner had breached it. Another way a contractor could indicate that he considered the parties' contract to be valid would be to demand that the owner perform under the contract. Finally, the contractor could sue the owner for breach of contract.

---

[31]*Larsen v. Johannes,* 86 Cal. Rptr. 744 (1970).
[32]*Ely v. Bottini,* 3 Cal. Rptr. 756 (Cal. App. 1960).
[33]*Dover Shopping Center v. Cushman's Sons,* 164 A.2d 785 (N.J. Super., 1960).

The essential fact to establish an election to treat the contract as breached, rather than rescinded, is conduct on the part of the contractor which indicates that he does not consider the contractual relationship between himself and the owner as put to an end. This issue is generally considered to be one of fact. In other words, a jury could be asked to decide whether, based on the acts and conduct of the contractor and the owner, the contract had been put to an end or whether the contractor had indicated that he intended to hold the owner liable for a breach of the contract.

The contractor should consider certain factors in deciding between these remedies beyond merely the differences in recovery which are available. One such consideration is that, if a rescission action is pursued, the contractor may lose any lien rights against the owner.[34] Another consideration is how much of the work on the job has already been done by the contractor. The exact impact of this factor on the contractor's ability to rescind the contract is unclear. It is possible, however, that if the contractor has done too much work on the project, he may be barred from electing to rescind the contract.

Up to this point we have treated the difference between rescission and excuse of performance (electing to keep the contract alive) as a choice left entirely up to the contractor when the owner materially breaches. There may be some limits on that choice based on the way the owner's breach is manifested to the builder, but, for the most part, material breach may be treated either as an excuse of performance or as an offer to rescind. The only major limitation on this election grows out of a common-law doctrine on the remedy of *restitution*.[35]

Restitution, as explained below, is the remedy which follows after rescission. It seeks to return the parties to the status quo before they made their bargain. At common law, a party who had fully performed his part of the contract, or any major divisible part of his performance, could sue for the amount due on the contract. While this may not seem substantially different from the *quantum meruit* or "quasi-contract" recovery explained below, such an action was considered to be one for enforcement of the contract rather than rescission of it. Because this remedy was possible, recission was often held not be available in such a situation.

The result of this was that at some point the nonbreaching party would have performed enough of his part of the bargain that he could no longer rescind. He had to sue on the contract. The point at which this occurred was unclear but was often expressed as being when the debt became *fully liquidated*.

In construction contracts this doctrine fits together with the doctrine of *substantial performance*.[36] This doctrine allows the contractor to recover from the owner on the contract when he has done very nearly what the contract called

---

[34]*See, e.g., Davidson v. Clearman,* 391 S.W.2d 48 (Tex. 1965); but *cf., Foster v. Terry Contr.,* 310 N.Y.S. 2d 76 (App. Div. N.Y., 1970).

[35]In regard to the substantial performance limitation, *see,* 5 Corbin, *Contracts,* § 1110, at 585 *et seq.* (1963).

[36]A classic case here is *Jacob & Young v. Kent,* 129 N.E. 889 (N.Y. 1921); *See also, Anno.,* 76 A.L.R.2d 815, *et seq.,* § 5.

for. This is a relaxation of the old common-law rule that a party could recover on a contract only if he performed exactly. Substantial performance means, for example, that the contractor could recover even though he painted one room of a house the wrong color or failed to install exactly the desired sort of light switches. The owner could still collect damages for the difference (if he could prove such damage), but the contractor would be able to sue on the contract.

There is no set formula for determining what constitutes substantial performance. Generally, it may be thought of as not doing the exact thing promised but doing something else that is just as good, or at least good enough to satisfy the owner. The contractor must have made a good faith attempt to perform.

Because the contractor is usually allowed to sue on the contract debt when he has substantially performed, some courts have held that, after substantially performing, he may no longer seek to rescind the contract.[37] This would mean that at some point in his work, the point at which his actions become substantial performance, the contractor's election of remedies on the owner's breach is constrained. He may treat his further performance as excused and sue on the contract itself, but he may not seek to rescind the agreement.

Other cases and legal commentators have criticized and rejected this result.[38] Especially where the owner's breach is total, such as where he refuses to pay at all, the contractor should be allowed to rescind without regard to the extent of his own performance. Nonetheless, some courts favor the older approach and, in making an election of remedies, the contractor should consider the possibility that he may be denied the right to rescind if he has substantially performed.

THE CONTRACTOR'S REMEDIES: DAMAGES AND RESTITUTION

Throughout this chapter we have attempted to deal with situations of default by the owner where the contractor is suing on the various theories explained above. The major difference in these theories lies in the amount of damages the contractor can recover. Although on many occasions the actions of the owner will only allow the contractor to sue on one theory, in at least an equal number of instances, a suit can be brought on various theories, each of which may result in a different measure of damages. It is the purpose of this section to explain how damages are measured under these various theories.

This section is concerned not only with what the contractor may recover by way of money damages, but also with his remedies in terms of recovering materials which he has in some way delivered to the owner. In some cases he can get these goods back while in other instances he must settle for getting the price of the goods from the owner.

In regard to damages, it is important to note that what we are considering here are general contract damages. In each instance examined below special

[37] *cf., United States for Use and Benefit of Harkol, Inc. v. Americo Constr. Co.,* 168 F.Supp. 760 (D.C. Mass. 1958).
[38] 5 Corbin, *Contracts* § 1110, at 589–590 (1963).

and consequential damages may also be recoverable. Examples of special and consequential damages might include damages for delay, for loss of another contract by reason of relying on this one and so on. The contractor is entitled to recover whatever damages should have been reasonably within the parties' contemplation when the contract was made.

Contractual Clauses on Damages

First, it is important to point out that many contracts, especially construction contracts, often include special clauses dealing with the damage amounts recoverable. These clauses, if carefully written, are usually upheld by courts considering the contracts.

Liquidated damages   Liquidated-damage clauses fix damages which will be recoverable in the event of a breach. Such a clause is often used in a construction contract to fix the amount of recovery of damages recoverable by the owner in the event of breach by the contractor. An example is the $250-a-day or $1,000-a-day clause which assesses amounts against the contractor for each day he is working beyond the due date. Such clauses are allowed and enforceable only if the amount fixed is a reasonable forecast of the proper compensation for the harm that is suffered and if the harm is impossible or very difficult to estimate accurately. Such daily assessments against the contractor are usually upheld. This chapter deals, of course, only with the rights of the contractor against the owner. The use of liquidated-damage provisions against the owner is fairly rare in the construction contract, but such a clause could be inserted in the contract and would be upheld if it met the two-pronged test above. If the clause is not a reasonable forecast of damages, it will be considered a penalty clause and will not be enforced.

No-damage-for-delay clauses   A more frequently used clause which deals with the recovery by the contractor against the owner is the so-called no-damage-for-delay clause. Such a clause is often inserted in a construction contract to preclude the claims on the part of the contractor for damages due to delay caused by the owner. The validity of such provisions has generally been assumed.[39] When such a clause is found in the contract, the arguments will generally center around whether or not a particular delay falls within the terms of the particular provision. We have dealt with the various kinds of delay by the owner which may amount to breach of the contract or an offer to rescind. Each of these types of delay may or may not be covered by a particular no-damage clause inserted in the contract. Cases have construed no-damage clauses in situations involving delay by the owner in procuring right-of-way, delay by the owner in readying the site, failure of the owner to furnish materials to the contractor, changes in the plans made by the owner, suspension of work on order of the owner, and other situations.[40]

---

[39]*See, Lichter v. Mellon-Stewart Co.,* 196 F. Supp. 149 (D.C. Pa. 1961); *Cunningham Bros. v. Waterloo,* 117 N.W.2d 46 (Iowa, 1962); *Humphreys v. J. B. Michael & Co.,* 341 S.W.2d 229 (Ky., 1960); *American Pipe & Constr. Co. v. Harbor Constr. Co.,* 317 P.2d 521 (Wash. 1957). See Liability for Liquidated Damages, this *Handbook.*

[40]On no-damage clauses in particular situations, *see, Anno.,* 10 A.L.R.2d 801; See also, Exceptions to No Damage for Delay article, this *Handbook.*

Restitution

Restitution is the remedy that goes hand in hand with rescission of the contract. Rescission has been explained above. Briefly, the entire basis of rescission of the contract is the notion that the parties have agreed to end the contract. Therefore, the contract no longer exists for the purposes of determining remedies and assessing damages. In rescission, any contractual clauses on damages are irrelevant.

Restitution is a remedy which is based, then, on the absence of any contract. While rescission is the most frequent situation in which this will arise, restitution may also be applicable where no contract was ever formed. If there is some defect in the contract itself, or in the negotiations which took place, or in the way in which the intent of the parties was translated onto paper, it may be possible to claim that a contract was never formed and to seek restitution.

Restitution seeks to return the parties to the status quo before they ever entered their now aborted agreement. To do this, two things must be done. First, the contractor must be able to recover any materials he has delivered, and, second, the contractor must be paid for the reasonable value of any work he has performed.

The right to reclaim goods delivered to the work site   During the course of working on the project it is necessary, of course, that the contractor assemble materials and equipment at the work site. If the contractor determines to stop work by rescinding the contract, he would, naturally, like to reclaim both his materials and equipment. In addition, the contractor would like, if possible, to take back materials which he has sold to the owner but which the owner has not paid for, or which the contractor believes he will not pay for. We will examine three broad categories of circumstances when a contractor may seek to reclaim materials he has delivered to the work site: (1) when the contractor seeks to recover materials and equipment which belong to him and to which the owner does not have title, (2) when the contractor seeks to recover goods he has sold to the owner but he then learns that the owner is insolvent, and (3) when the contractor seeks to reclaim materials sold to the owner for which the owner fails to make payments.

Recovery by the Contractor of His Own Materials and Equipment.   A great many of the materials and equipment at the work site will not be owned by the owner of the land. The contractor will assemble materials which are to be incorporated into the project but which, at a particular moment in time, are still owned by the contractor. When work on the project comes to a halt, the contractor has the right to remove these items. If the owner refuses or in some way impedes the contractor in reclaiming the goods, the contractor can enlist the help of the sheriff or some other official to recover his property. This is usually done by securing a *writ of replevin* from a court. Essentially, this is a request to the court by the contractor which says, in effect, "Give me back my property."

This process can be explained by an example. Suppose work on a college dormitory was stopped by the contractor because the college had failed to make progress payments on time. Prior to the time that the contractor stopped work on the dormitory, he assembled a large quantity of bricks and tiles which were to be used in the construction of the dormitory. The bricks and tiles were delivered to the work site in trucks which belonged to the contractor. Some of the bricks had been unloaded from the trucks, but the remainder of the material was still in the trucks. Also, in the trucks were some wood beams which were to be delivered to another, unrelated project. When the contractor notified the college that he intended to stop work on the project, the college caused mounds of sand to be dumped all around the contractor's trucks and materials to prevent the contractor from removing them. If the college refused to let the contractor take his trucks and bricks, the contractor should seek a writ of replevin. Armed with this writ, the sheriff would help the contractor in securing his property from the college.

In addition, the contractor could collect damages from the college for interfering with the contractor's removal of his property. If the truck or materials were seriously damaged or stolen while they remained on the work site because the college prevented their removal, the college would be compelled to pay for them. Even if nothing was damaged, the college would be required to pay the contractor to compensate him for his lost use of the truck and materials.[41]

Reclaiming Materials Sold on Credit When the Owner is Insolvent.   During the course of construction, the contractor will frequently sell some materials not incorporated into the structure to the owner on credit. Article 9 of the standard AIA contract requires that such sales be made if the contractor is making an application for payment based in part on materials not yet incorporated into the structure. Title to materials and equipment must pass to the owner free of all liens and claims by either the contractor or third parties. The result of compliance with the provision of the AIA contract is that the contractor sells the materials to the owner without any security for their payment. Our concern is what happens if, after transferring title to the owner, the contractor learns that the owner is insolvent and will be unable to pay for the materials.

First, since the contractor sold the materials to the owner without retaining a security interest in the goods, the contractor cannot assert the remedies which a secured lender would normally use. Generally speaking, his right to reclaim the materials will be governed by §2-702 of the Uniform Commercial Code (UCC). Essentially, the UCC provides that when the contractor learns that the owner has received goods on credit while he is insolvent, the contractor can reclaim the goods if he makes demand for their return within 10 days of the time that the owner received them. The 10-day period does not apply if the owner made a misrepresentation of his solvency, *in writing,* to the contractor within three months of the delivery of the materials, on which the contractor relied. Although the contractor can reclaim the goods under these circumstances from the owner, his right to reclaim the goods is subject to the rights of third parties who also have an interest in the goods. These third parties will generally be construction lenders or a trustee in bankruptcy. The law is unsettled at this

[41]Prosser, *Torts,* §§ 14,15 (4th ed. 1971).

point whether the construction lender or the trustee in bankruptcy would be able to claim the goods ahead of the contractor.[42]

The manner in which §2-702 operates can be illustrated as follows: The contractor is engaged in constructing a private residence. He submits an application for payment for work done to the point where interior walls have been completed. Part of the work which is to be done at this point is the installation of insulating material, but the insulation has not been installed although the material has been delivered to the work site. Since the insulating material is work which is covered by the application for payment, the contractor submits a bill of sale for these materials, along with other documents, in the application for payment. Seven days later, the architect issues a certificate for payment, but he also tells the contractor that he probably will not be paid because the owner is now insolvent. The contractor immediately delivers to the owner a written demand that the insulation materials be returned to him. At this point, the contractor is entitled to recover the insulating materials. Two days later the owner files for bankruptcy. That same day the contractor is notified by both the construction lender and the trustee in bankruptcy that they each claim to be entitled to the materials ahead of the contractor. At this point, if not earlier, the contractor needs to consult an attorney to determine his rights to the materials. In some states the contractor may still have the right to recover the materials, in others, the construction lender or the trustee in bankruptcy will get the materials.

Reclaiming Goods When the Owner Fails to Pay.   After the contractor has submitted an application for payment and the architect has issued a certificate for payment, payment becomes due seven days later. If the owner fails to make the payment when due and demanded, the contractor can reclaim—as against the owner—materials which have been sold to the owner but which have not been paid for. The UCC provides that the contractor may cancel the contract if the owner fails to make a payment when due.[43] The cancellation of a contract is a peculiar remedy which exists only in the UCC. It has characteristics of both rescission and excuse due to material breach. If the contractor cancels the contract, the owner has no right to retain the materials as against the contractor. If the owner has sold the materials to a third party, however, the contractor could not reclaim the materials from the third party. It may also be that, if one of the owner's creditors secured a lien against the materials while the materials were in the owner's possession, the contractor could not reclaim the goods. The contractor should move quickly when he wants to recover materials because of failure of payment, to cut down the risk that a third party will intervene and cut off his right to reclaim.[44]

Quantum meruit and damages in restitution   The second part of restitution's quest to return the parties to status quo is to award to the contractor the value of

[41]Prosser, *Torts,* §§ 14,15 (4th ed. 1971).

[42]Frank R. Kennedy, *The Interest of the Reclaiming Seller,* under Article 2 of the *Code,* 30 *The Business Lawyer 833 (1975).*

[43]Uniform Commercial Code, § 2-507, 2-703(f).

[44]3A Bender's U.C.C. Service, Duesenberg & King, Sales and Bulk Transfers § 13.02 (1966).

any work he has done. This is done on a legal theory called *quantum meruit* or quasi-contract. To determine the amount the contractor should be awarded in *quantum meruit,* the contract price is completely *irrelevant.*[45] The contract no longer exists because it has been rescinded. The *quantum meruit* measure of damages is only applicable when the contractor has performed to some degree. If the contractor rescinds the contract before he has done any work, he will recover nothing. The contract does not exist; therefore the contractor cannot recover his anticipated profits.

If the contractor has performed to some extent, he will be able to recover in *quantum meruit* for the reasonable value of the work he has performed. Since the contractor did work with the expectation of being paid and the work he performed was of benefit to the owner, to allow the owner to receive such a benefit without paying for it would be unjust enrichment. Since there is no contract, the only way to determine the amount the contractor should receive is to admit testimony on the reasonable value of the work he has done.

At the same time, *quantum meruit* recovery is also not available if the contractor has done too much work. As explained above, rescission is not available where the contractor has substantially performed. In such a situation he has no alternative to a suit on the contract itself.

In the range between where the contractor has done some work but has not substantially performed, *quantum meruit* recovery is available as an alternative to recovery on the contract. If the contractor chooses to treat the contract as rescinded, he may have restitution and *quantum meruit.*

An example will aid in explaining how *quantum meruit* damages are measured.[46] Contractor and owner entered into a contract to build a home. The contract price was $50,000. Suppose, first, it would actually cost the contractor $30,000 to build the house. When he has spent $10,000, the owner commits a material breach. If the contractor is able to elect to treat the contract as rescinded and he does so, he will recover $10,000, the amount he has expended. In fact, he is allowed to recover this $10,000 only if such expenditure was reasonable. This is a limit on *quantum meruit* recovery, which is not simply for the amount expended by the parties suing but, rather, for *reasonable value* of the work the party has done. Problems often arise as to how this value is measured. The general rule is that the measure is the reasonable value of the benefit to the owner, not the burden to the contractor.[47] The reasonable value of the goods and services is generally considered to be the amount for which they could be obtained under like circumstances.[48] Generally, this measure is considered to include some amount for profits and overhead. Depending on

---

[45]That is, it *should* be irrelevant. Many courts fail to understand this distinction. *See, United States v. Western Cas. & Sur. Co.,* 498 F.2d 335 (9th Cir. 1974) where the appellate court had to remedy such an error made by the lower court.

[46]Throughout this section, the *Restatement, Contracts,* §§ 329, 333–335, 346–351 (1932) are useful sources.

[47]Williston, *Contracts* (3d ed.) §1482 (1970).

[48]*Wunderlich v. United States,* 240 F.2d 201 (10th Cir. 1957).

how broadly "profits" and "overhead" are defined, courts have allowed contractors to recover for both items so long as no double recovery is evident.[49]

In the examples below we will assume that the amount spent by the contractor was, in fact, reasonable. Under *quantum meruit,* therefore, he would be able to recover $10,000. Notice, again, that for figuring the contractor's recovery here, the $50,000 contract price is totally irrelevant.

If the contractor, here, had substantially performed, as, for example, if he had spent $28,000 of the $30,000 cost and done everything except paint the interior of the house, he might not be able to sue in *quantum meruit* for the value of his services but would have to sue on the contract, as explained below.

Suit on the Contract

The alternative to rescission, discussed above, was called *excuse of performance.* There, we discussed situations in which the owner's material breach operated to excuse further performance by the contractor. The contractor's corollary right in such a case is a suit on the contract. Just as rescission affords the remedy of restitution, excuse affords the remedy of suit on the contract. The differences in the measure of damages between restitution and suit on the contract are quite pronounced and will often determine which theory the contractor chooses in seeking redress.

Delivered goods and materials   If the contractor brings suit on the contract, claiming his performance is excused due to some breach by the owner, he has no right whatsoever to seek the return of materials he has delivered. This is the first obvious difference to a suit in restitution. The reason is that, by suing, the contractor has affirmed the contract. The remedy here does not seek to return the parties to the status quo but, rather, to give them the "benefit of the bargain."

General contractual measure of damages   In accord with the policy of giving the parties the benefit of their bargain, the general rule here is that the contractor, as the party not in default, is entitled to be made whole, to be put in the position he would have been in had the contract been performed.

How Damages Are Figured.[50]   Let us again consider our example where the contractor is to build a house for the owner at a contract price of $50,000. Whenever the owner breaches, the contractor is entitled to the benefit of his bargain, that is, the profits he anticipated in contracting to build the house. This can be expressed in two ways: (1) Expected Profits + Amount Expended or (2) Contract Price − Cost of Completion. The two formulas yield exactly the same result.

Let us again assume that the contractor's cost of construction is $30,000.

---

[49]*Continental Cas. Co. v. Schaefer,* 173 F.2d 5 (9th Cir. 1949); *Central Steel Erec. Co. v. Will,* 304 F.2d 548 (9th Cir. 1962).

[50]This section draws heavily on two excellent articles by Judge Clarence Guittard: "Building Contracts: Damages and Restitution," 32 TEXAS BAR J. 91 (1969); "Judge's View of Construction Litigation," Construction Contracts Program from an ABA National Institute, October 1967.

Suppose the owner breaches before any work is performed by the contractor. The contractor is entitled to recover $20,000. This is figured as:

$50,000 contract price or $20,000 anticipated profit
−30,000 cost to complete +00,000 amount expended
$20,000 $20,000

Even if the contractor has performed in part, the damages are measured in exactly the same way. For example, in the same situation as above, suppose the contractor has spent $10,000 at the time the owner breached. His damages would now be $30,000. This is figured as:

$50,000 contract price or $20,000 anticipated profit
−20,000 cost to complete +10,000 amount expended
     ($30,000 cost
     −10,000 spent)
$30,000 $30,000

In each situation, the contractor is entitled to reimbursement for what he has spent plus the entire profit he anticipated. In most of these examples the owner would have made progress payments to the contractor. In such a situation, the payments actually made would be subtracted from the damages which the contractor could recover.

In the above examples we have assumed a contract which was favorable to the contractor. This is not always the case and, in many cases, the owner may try to show that the contract did not include such a large quantity of anticipated profit as the contractor will claim. Suppose that our contract, again, was for a $50,000 house but the owner can show that it would have cost the contractor $55,000 to build the house. Obviously, it is unlikely in such a situation that the owner would breach at all but, if he does, he would attempt to show in court that the contractor had no anticipated profits. In such a situation, if the contractor had not performed at all, the contractor would not be able to recover using our formula. The contract price of $50,000 minus the estimated cost of $55,000 leaves a loss of $5,000 to the contractor. In the second example above, where the contract is partly performed, let us also assume that, in fact, the contract would have cost the contractor $55,000 to perform. In such a situation, where the contract cost more to complete than the contractor anticipated, we would still start with his expenditures, which in the example were $10,000; but in such a case instead of adding his anticipated profit, we would subtract his anticipated loss of $5,000. In this case, damages would be figured as:

$50,000 contract price or −$ 5,000 anticipated loss
−45,000 cost to complete +10,000 amount spent
     ($55,000 cost
     −10,000 spent)
$ 5,000 $ 5,000

The general measure of contract damages thus works very well when the contractor can show that he had a profitable contract, for he will be able to recover the entire amount of his anticipated profit. However, when it is clear that the contractor had a losing contract, the measure is extremely unfavorable because it forces the contractor to bear the cost of the entire losing contract. Of course, if the contract had gone through to completion, the contractor would have been forced to bear the entire loss on the contract. The reason for this result in both cases is that the general measure of damages is based on the contract price itself in connection with the anticipated cost to the contractor. Any time the contractor can be said to be suing on the contract, damages will be figured in the manner explained above.

The General Measure and Quantum Meruit Compared. Let us continue with our two examples in order to compare the damage recoveries under restitution and a suit on the contract.

In both cases, the contract price is $50,000. In case A, the contractor's actual cost is $30,000. In case B, the contractor's actual cost is $55,000. Case A is, thus, from the contractor's standpoint, a profitable contract, and case B is a losing one.

First, in Table 31.2, let us consider both cases in a situation where the owner breaches before any work is done by the contractor.

TABLE 31.2

Case A: Profitable Contract

Quantum meruit	Contract damages
Recovery = $0	Recovery = $20,000
(No work = no recovery)	(Recover all anticipated profits)

Case B: Losing Contract

Quantum meruit	Contract damages
Recovery = $0	Recovery = $0
(No work = no recovery)	(No anticipated profits— only a $5,000 anticipated loss)

Now, in Table 31.3, suppose the owner breaches after the contractor has expended $10,000 in labor and materials.

TABLE 31.3

Case A: Profitable Contract

Quantum meruit	Contract damages
Recovery = $10,000	Recovery = $30,000
(Recover reasonable value of work done)	(Anticipated profit of $20,000 + value of work done)

Case B: Losing Contract

Quantum meruit	Contract damages
Recovery = $10,000	Recovery = $5,000
(Recover reasonable value of work done)	(Value of work done—$5,000 loss bargained for)

Obviously, the lesson of these examples is that *quantum meruit* is a preferable measure of damages in those circumstances where the contractor has performed some work on a losing contract. Under the restitution–*quantum meruit* approach, he can recover the value of those services without bearing any amount of his anticipated loss. This difference should influence contractors in choosing between rescission and excuse of performance. It must also be noted that while *quantum meruit* seems to be a vastly preferable remedy where the contractor has partly performed on a losing contract, a problem may arise because in rescinding the contract, or treating it as rescinded, the contractor would lose lien rights against the owner where the lien is created by the contract.

CONCLUSION

After reading this chapter, one should understand how John, the contractor described in the introduction, was able to maximize the amount of money he recovered from the owner when work on the project was halted. In his contract with George he realized that he was losing money. When George told him to stop work on the project, he recognized that this was an anticipatory breach, or repudiation of the contract, which entitled him to either rescind the contract or sue for breach. John was careful to elect to rescind the contract by telling George that he would agree to put their contract to an end. He did not call on George to fulfill his obligations on the contract or in any other way act as though they still had a viable contract. When he came into court, the judge awarded him the amount of money he had spent as a measure of the reasonable value of the work he performed.

With Hubert, of course, the situation was different. When Hubert repudiated the contract by telling John to stop work, John called on Hubert to live up to his part of the contract. John also offered to do his part under the contract. John's behavior made it clear that he intended to preserve his rights under the contract. As a result, the judge awarded John damages measured by the contract price.

John's success, in short, was based on three important determinations: First, he determined if he had the right to stop work. He read his contract to see if it gave him the power to terminate. Then, he checked to see if the owner had done some act or said something that the law would treat as an offer to rescind the contract. He also checked to see if the owner had committed a material breach which would excuse him from performing.

The second determination John made was how much money he would recover under each theory. If he had a losing contract, he might recover more money by rescinding the contract.

Third, after determining which theory offered him the greater recovery, John was careful to elect the right one. He did not act as though the contract were at an end when he wanted to recover contractual damages, and he did not act as though the contract was still viable when he wanted to rescind. Because he understood the distinction between termination, rescission, and breach, John was not the victim of events. Instead, he consciously controlled events to ensure that he would recover the maximum amount of money when work was halted due to the acts of the owner.

Chapter **32**

Recovery of Interest
and Attorneys' Fees

HUGH E. REYNOLDS, JR., ESQ.
Partner, Locke, Reynolds, Boyd & Weisell,
Indianapolis, Indiana

INTRODUCTION

Under certain circumstances either party to a construction contract or contracts to furnish construction materials may be entitled to interest or attorneys' fees. These circumstances may arise out of the nature of the dispute, the contract language, applicable statutes, applicable case law, or any combination of these factors. The reader is cautioned not to assume if a case citation supports a position, that this is the current law in that state at that reading. The law changes from time to time. Statutes may be passed by legislatures, and case law may be changed by court decisions. The reader should discuss specific facts with his attorney before reaching a definitive conclusion on any such point.

The purpose of this article is to point out the various circumstances which may give rise to the existence or nonexistence of such obligations. In general, the law currently tends to favor the recovery of interest in most contract obligations that do not involve an attempt to recover consequential damages. Conversely, the law still tends to look with disfavor on permitting recovery of attorneys' fees.

If a party is entitled to recover funds due under a contract, the delay in the payment caused by a dispute or litigation has deprived the successful party of the use of the money due him for that time. The normal compensation for being thus deprived of the use of money (whether voluntarily or involuntarily) is interest. Such interest, if awarded, is usually termed *prejudgment interest.*

Conversely, the imposition of attorneys' fees tends to penalize or discourage a party from asserting what he believes to be his rights under the law. Consequently, most statutes providing for recovery of attorneys' fees occur in a situation where there is a strong public policy to be served by forcing one side of a potential controversy to discharge its obligation or refuse to do so at its peril. In the normal circumstances, however, the law prefers that each party have equal right to make claim under an instrument or with respect to a dispute. Imposing on a litigant the obligation to pay the opponent's attorneys' fees, if the former is proved wrong, would seriously impair that right. In general a statute or contract provision which provides attorneys' fees to either party if it prevails rather than to only one party is more likely to be enforced wholeheartedly by a court.

RECOVERY OF INTEREST

Circumstances under which interest may be recoverable vary from state to state. However there is some uniformity on many points. Interest may be recoverable in any of the following situations:

1. The contract expressly provides for the recovery of interest under certain circumstances.

2. There is a statute providing for recovery of interest under the circumstances pertaining to the litigation or dispute.

3. The circumstances of the delay in payment or the nature of the case place it within a class where, under the case law of the given state, interest is recoverable if the person claiming money is successful.

4. Custom, usage, or prior practice between the parties could give rise to an obligation to pay interest. (This would be considered an implied-in-fact contract and will be discussed as such.)

Recovery of Interest Pursuant to Contract

The provisions of the construction contract may provide expressly for the recovery of interest. For example, AIA form 201A contains a recommended provision which provides for recovery of interest at the legal rate in the place where the work is being performed on money not paid when it is due to either party.

Other forms may be drafted to provide interest only to the contractor, or only to the owner, in the event of a dispute which results in an award of damages to one or the other. This could include recovery of an unpaid contract balance or an award for extras or even on damages for delays if that is specified. The courts will be much more likely to enforce provisions precisely as written if they apply equally to both parties to the contract and not only to one party.

For example, in *Ansco Constr. Co. v. Ocean View Estates,*[1] suit was brought against the general contractor for recovery for labor and materials in construction of streets, curbs, and gutters. The subcontract provision required payment within 10 days after completion of a portion, and if the account was not paid when due, interest was added at the rate of 10 percent per annum. This provision was enforced. In that case, the contract also provided for recovery of attorneys' fees, and that provision was also enforced.

In many instances the purchase order for materials used in construction contains language stating interest is charged at a certain percent in the event payment is not made pursuant to the invoice within a stated period of time. This period of time is often either 30, 60, or 90 days (most often the first). It is not certain, however, in what manner these provisions may be enforced in the event a dispute arises and a determination is made that less than all the money claimed under the invoice is due and owing. For example, where the quantity delivered is incomplete or portions of the goods delivered do not meet contract specifications, the full invoice amount is not due. In such a case the enforcement of the contract provision relating to interest may stand or fall on more general principles of case law. An attempt to predict the result in such a case is difficult. If the implication of the provision in the invoice is that interest is sought on the entire amount due and, particularly, if the claim asserted is for the entire amount shown in the invoice and it is later determined that less than the entire amount is due, there is a chance that the provision will not be enforced. However, the more probable result is that interest would be awarded even if recovery were for less than the amount claimed if, in fact, the greater portion of the amount claimed was in fact determined to be due and owing.

Interest may also be recoverable under the theory that custom or usage allows recovery of interest for delayed payment. This is what the law calls an *implied-in-fact contract.* Such a recovery pursuant to custom would arise where in the applicable industry within the local area (or nationwide if the facts showed this to be so) interest were allowable for delay in payment. The creation of a custom depends upon two facts. First that a given practice is followed for a considerable period of time and secondly that, when the practice has been followed, the circumstances show that the parties consider it obligatory. This obligation may arise initially with the concept that it is a moral or business obligation rather than one that is formally binding in law. However with the passage of time continued following of the custom can ripen into one that is legally binding. Such an obligation by the way of custom would not depend upon the usage between the two parties to the contract themselves, but rather on the industry-wide usage. However, contrary usage by the parties could negate the custom.

Recovery of interest pursuant to usage or practice would arise where the two

[1]337 P.2d 146 (Cal. App. 1959).

parties to this specific contract in their prior conduct had customarily charged and paid interest for delayed payment of claimed amounts under similar circumstances as those that exist in the present dispute. For example, a contractor had purchased goods for a number of years from a given supplier. In instances in which an obligation became more than 90 days past due, the supplier charged interest for such past-due obligation, and the interest was paid by the supplier. If a dispute arose, and such a delay in payment occurred, by reason of the prior usage and practice between these two parties a court would be quite likely to find that interest at the same rate and under the same circumstances would also be allowable.

It should be pointed out that such a custom or practice would not be absolutely binding on the court. The court would undoubtedly look to the circumstances of the original transactions and also to whether there were unusual circumstances related to the dispute which might make the custom or prior usage and practice irrelevant or not enforceable.

Recovery of Interest Pursuant to Statute

There are a number of statutory provisions that may apply in various states which provide for the recovery of interest that could be pertinent to construction contracts.

Statute allowing recovery of interest upon any debt arising by virtue of contract Some states have statutes which provide arbitrarily for recovery of interest on any amount found due under a contract.

The State of New York has the following statute (in part):

> 46. §501. Interest to verdict, report or decision.
> (a) Actions in which revocable. Interest shall be recovered upon a sum awarded because of a breach of performance of a contract.

Numerous cases construing that or predecessor statutes have allowed recovery of interest in construction contracts. See for example, *High Quality Homes, Inc. v. Palmer.*[2]

Such a statute would apply not only if the court determined that a contractor was entitled to a sum as the unpaid balance of a construction contract, but also would apply if it was determined that the owner was entitled to recover monies because the cost of completing work required under the contract exceeded any unpaid contract balance. Normally such statutes apply whether or not the prevailing party has recovered the entire amount claimed. For example, if the contractor were to claim a balance due of $50,000, but the case ultimately resulted in a $40,000 verdict because of the allowance of $10,000 for uncompleted or improperly completed work, prejudgment interest would still be recoverable on the amount awarded. The date from which interest is payable is normally also set forth in the statute. Sometimes it is the date upon which the obligation matures. That, in turn, must be determined by the underlying construction contract. If the construction contract is silent on that point, it is the

[2]283 App. Div. 954, 130 N.Y.S.2d 360, reh den 283 App. Div. 1079, 131 N.Y.S.2d 902 (1954).

time when one would normally expect such an obligation to be paid. In other cases courts may look to the date of an invoice or demand for payment or the date upon which the suit was filed (often termed *the date of judicial demand*).

Such a statute may not apply to certain consequential damages such as lost profits due to breach of contract if they were not capable of ascertainment until final determination in court. On the other hand, it might apply to *consequential damages* arising by virtue of breach of an indemnity agreement. For example, where the contractor had agreed to indemnify the owner for damages sustained by the owner through the contractor's negligence, if the owner were required to pay a judgment in litigation and had a right of indemnity over against the contractor, this could well be considered a circumstance where (although such recovery is technically classified as consequential damages) it is of such a nature that the court would enforce recovery of interest under such a statute.

Recovery of interest on an account stated   An *account stated* generally involves the presentation of accounts for payment in a written statement on a regular basis showing the balance due without prompt objection or where the account is admitted. Some states have statutes that allow interest for the failure to pay such an account.

The state of Indiana has the following statute:[3]

> Date from which interest allowed.—Interest at the rate of eight per cent [8%] per annum shall be allowed. . . .
> (b) And from the date an itemized bill shall have been rendered and payment demanded on an account stated, account closed or for money had and received for the use of another and retained without his consent.

This assumes that later litigation establishes that the account stated was stated accurately and was recoverable. While this situation would more normally occur in connection with the purchase of materials it may be applied to a construction contract assuming the contractor follows an appropriate invoicing procedure in sequence with the billing provisions of the contract whether for partial payment or for final payment, particularly if the request for payment has an architect's approval.

Statutes may contain provisions allowing interest where damages are "liquidated" or are "certain" or have similar criteria   Normally these statutes are simply declaratory of much of the case law. See for example, the Colorado statute discussed in *Jim Arnott, Inc. v. L & E, Inc.* in which the court said:[4]

> In a claim for payment pursuant to a contract, the fact that the amount due thereunder is disputed does not render the claim *unliquidated* [emphasis added] for the purpose of awarding interest pursuant to § 5-12-102 C.R.S. (1971 PermSupp., C.R.S. 1963, 73-12-102).

The criteria for a "liquidated" claim will be discussed under the section on case law.

[3]Burns' Indiana Statutes § 24-4.6-1-103.
[4]539 P.2d 1333 (Col. App. 1975).

A District of Columbia statute which allows postjudgment interest says that nothing in the statute should prevent the jury or court from including prejudgment interest as an element of damages if necessary to fully compensate the plaintiff. It has been construed to give discretion to allow or disallow prejudgment interest in construction cases.[5]

Other circumstances   Some statutes provide for recovery of interest for past-due indebtedness or delayed payment under certain limited circumstances. Many states provide for recovery of interest by virtue of mechanic's lien statutes. For example, the Illinois statute discussed in *William Aupperle & Sons v. American Nat'l Bank & Trust Co.* states that the recovery shall include interest on the amount due.[6]

No extensive discussion of the mechanic's lien law is necessary. Most jurisdictions do allow interest either by statute or by case law, particularly if the amount of the debt is clearly ascertainable.

Other statutes may provide for recovery of interest in the case where a bill is presented and a purported payment is made upon a check that is thereafter returned for insufficient funds. There are also other possible circumstances peculiar to a transaction that call for recovery of statutory interest.

A few statutes provide for recovery of interest prospectively. Some states, for example, require that under certain circumstances retainage either may or must be escrowed and the escrow is interest-bearing. Such interest accrues to the benefit of the payee on a debt that has not yet matured.

Recovery of Interest Pursuant to Case Law

Case law generally provides for recovery of interest under one of three basic philosophies. In a given state, several of the three may be applied as law. In other peculiar circumstances state case law provides for such recovery in selective circumstances. However, these circumstances do not normally arise in the construction field. One basis for recovery of interest occurs where the debt is liquidated or otherwise ascertainable with certainty. This determination is normally made as a matter of law (that is, by the judge) rather than as a matter of fact (that is, by the trier of the facts whether judge or jury). The second class of cases are cases in which the court looks not to the nature of the debt, but to the nature of the wrong. Thus, interest is awarded more in the nature of a penalty for unreasonably withholding the funds due. This determination is normally made by the trier of the facts. The third circumstance is where by case law, rather than statute, courts have held that interest is recoverable as a matter of right. A review of these cases would tend to show, however, that they usually apply in cases where the amount recovered was, if not ascertainable, at least based on mathematical calculation and not on an assessment of intangibles.

Criteria to determine whether prejudgment interest may be awarded for debts which are "liquidated" or "ascertainable with certainty"   The following cases illustrate circumstances where courts have determined whether interest was recoverable on claims arising in the construction field. A contractor was denied

---

[5]*Dyker Bldg. Co. v. United States,* 86 App. D.C. 297, 182 F.2d 85 (1950).
[6]329 N.E.2d 458 (Ill. App. 1975).

recovery of interest in *United States v. Zelonky* where it amended its complaint to allow credit for mistaken installation of improper paneling in a post office cafeteria.[7] The court found the claim could not be liquidated in view of the amendment made at the last moment. The same test was used in *Stevens Construction Corp. v. Carolina Corp.,* which was an action for recovery of an unpaid balance on a construction contract.[8] The court found that the plaintiff's claim had to be considered unliquidated in view of the multiplicity of issues that were difficult to resolve except with the aid of 13 days of trial and a genuine dispute as to the degree of substantial payment.

In *Chas. T. Main, Inc. v. Massachusetts Turnpike Authority,* however, interest was awarded on fees for an engineering firm.[9] The defendant had asserted that the amount could not be ascertained until litigation between it and a different plaintiff had been determined. The court held that this was not sufficient grounds to withhold payment to the engineer, and hence the amount due was an unpaid liquidated account and bore prejudgment interest.

In *Mitchell v. Flandro,* the court granted an award of prejudgment interest for breach of contract in the erection of an automobile sales and service building. It was held that the amount owed was capable of ascertainment by mere mathematical processes. This result was reached in part by the interpretation of an existing statute.[10]

Alley Construction Co. v. Minnesota involved a highway construction contract.[11] The court disallowed prejudgment interest except on a small undisputed amount since the damages required decision and computation upon multiple theories and the result was based upon the evaluation of the evidence. Hence, it was not readily ascertainable prior to the verdict.

The mere fact that the party against whom the claim is made has put forward a *setoff* or counterclaim does not make the claim of the plaintiff unliquidated and does not necessarily preclude the award of prejudgment interest. In *Herbert & Brooner Construction Co. v. Golden,* a builder brought an action against the owner to enforce a mechanic's lien.[12] The owner counterclaimed for damages for delay and defective workmanship. The court considered the builder's claim to be liquidated despite the assertion of the counterclaim.

The cases tend to hold the amount ascertainable where the contract itself contains language or terms which permit such ascertainment such as a fixed-price contract in which the amount of the payments previously made can be ascertained. Another example is a unit-price contract. A court might award interest based upon whether it was a legal dispute over contract interpretation or one over measurement. For example, in *Aetna Casualty & Surety Co. v. United States,* prejudgment interest had been allowed upon the subcontractor's recovery for excavation work. The amount owing was considered ascertainable since

[7]209 F.Supp. 305 (D. Wis. 1962).
[8]217 N.W.2d 291 (Wis. 1974).
[9]196 N.E.2d 821 (Mass. 1964).
[10]506 P.2d 455 (Ida. 1972).
[11]219 N.W.2d 922 (Minn. 1974).
[12]499 S.W.2d 541 (Mo. App. 1973).

the amount of yardage that had been removed was not disputed but rather which of two unit prices per yard specified in the subcontract was applicable.[13]

Where the issues are complicated by claims for increased compensation because of increased costs resulting from delay or other owner breach, such enhancement of damages may also serve to make the claim unliquidated and foreclose the recovery of prejudgment interest.

In some instances, the court will look to the disparity or lack of disparity between the amount demanded and the amount eventually awarded as a test as to whether the claim was ascertainable. For example, in *Portage, Indiana School Construction Corp. v. A. V. Stackhouse Co.,* prejudgment interest was disallowed where the original invoice was for approximately $30,000, the complaint prayed for approximately $67,000 and the judgment was entered for the plaintiff for approximately $47,000.[14]

Courts may also consider the number and complexity of issues between the litigants. In *United Pacific Insurance Co. v. Martin & Luther General Contractors, Inc.,* the number of claims and counterclaims by and between the prime contractor, subcontractors, lien claimants, the owner, and the surety caused the court to deny recovery of prejudgment interest on the grounds the claim was far from being readily computable.[15]

Discretionary allowance of prejudgment interest   The reasoning for the discretionary viewpoint is that the prevailing party has been deprived of the use of its money during the period of the dispute. Interest compensates him for this loss of use. Whether the amount of money could or could not have been readily ascertained at the time the dispute arose does not change the loss of use of the money. One cannot possibly be fully compensated without the award of interest.

For example, in *E. I. DuPont DeNemours & Co. v. Lyles & Lang Construction Co.,* the court[16] sustained an award of prejudgment interest even though it did not think the claim was either liquidated or determinable with sufficient certainty. The court felt that compensation was a fundamental principle of damages and that one who uses another's money should pay for such use. In the exercise of its discretion the court stated it was permitted to allow recovery of interest.

Fanning & Doorley Construction Co. v. Geigy Chemical Corp. indicates that courts may be influenced by what they believe are equities in reaching an interest award. In that case the prejudgment interest was allowed only from the period of *judicial demand.*[17] *Black Lake Pipe Line Co. v. Union Construction Co.* awarded prejudgment interest on a recovery in *quantum meruit,* which was based on opinions of the value of the work rather than a fixed price.[18]

In applying this theory, courts consider the case as a whole; determine the

[13]365 F.2d 997 (8th Cir. 1966).
[14]287 N.E.2d 564 (Ind., 1972).
[15]455 P.2d 664 (Wyo. 1969).
[16]219 F.2d 328 (4th Cir.S.C. 1955) *cert. den.* 349 U.S. 956, 75 S.Ct. 882.
[17]305 F.Supp. 650 (D. R.I. 1969).
[18]520 S.W.2d 486 (Tex. Civ. App. 1975).

basic merits of the underlying dispute, the complexity, the unreasonableness of the delay in payment, and the impact on the prevailing party from the withholding of funds; and then reach a determination that interest should or should not be allowed.

Allowance of interest as a matter of right   Although the number is still small, an increasing number of courts ignore all the other criteria and assert as an absolute matter of right that, if recovery is allowed, in suits on contract (or in some instances in any suit dealing with damages that are not tangible—such as pain and suffering) prejudgment interest must be allowed on the entire amount of the verdict. These cases follow the assumption that loss of use of the money is an inevitable element of damage and must be compensated to its logical conclusion. An example of these cases is *Beck v. Lawler.*[19]

Mechanics of Recovery of Interest

In case of litigation or disputes in which one party recognizes some money as owing to the other, it may make a tender of the amount admittedly due and owing. At a minimum, the making of such a tender and keeping it good by deposit of funds with the clerk (in the event litigation is commenced) would prevent recovery of interest where the amount eventually awarded the prevailing party is only equal to or less than that amount. A tender reasonably covering the known indebtedness may even foreclose any recovery of prejudgment interest by the prevailing party even if awarded a sum greater than that tendered.

The time when the interest may commence to run may be established by statute, by contract, or by common law. For example, if the payment provisions of a construction contract required payment within 30 days of approval by the architect, interest would run from the end of that 30-day period. The rate of interest may be either specified by contract or statute.

ATTORNEYS' FEES

In general, attorneys' fees incurred by a successful party are not recoverable for the reasons stated earlier. Numerous cases support this view. Attorneys' fees may be considered and allowed in certain cases involving intentional torts (such as malicious prosecution) or otherwise calling for punitive damages or where a fund is created or preserved by a party's actions. However, these cases are not usually pertinent to the construction field. In construction cases, attorneys' fees may be recovered pursuant to a contract providing for such fees, pursuant to statute, or (in Alaska) pursuant to court rule.

Recovery of Attorneys' Fees Pursuant to Statute

In a few states attorneys' fees are awarded by statute to the prevailing party. These usually operate only where the losing party has shown bad faith or has

---

[19]422 S.W.2d 816 (Tex. Civ. App. 1967).

been unreasonable in its handling of the litigation. Such statutes are found in Georgia and Puerto Rico.[20]

There may be specific statutes that award attorneys' fees in limited cases, such as mechanic's lien statutes, statutes awarding attorneys' fees for improper refusal to honor certain insurance contracts, statutes relating to dishonor of certain negotiable instruments, and the like. The first instance is especially pertinent to the construction field. Other statutes are quite varied and not capable of definitive discussion in the space available.

In the first half of this century some mechanic's lien statutes providing for recovery of attorneys' fees were declared unconstitutional, particularly where the attorneys' fees were awarded only if the alleged lien holder prevailed. As recently as 1972, such a statute was held unconstitutional in *Gaster v. Coldiron.*[21] However, in general, such statutes have been upheld, particularly where attorneys' fees are provided for the "prevailing party." In some states where attorneys' fees are provided by statute on mechanic's lien cases, the court may limit this to prosecution of the action in the trial court and exclude attorneys' fees for services performed on appeal. Furthermore, such statutes generally are enforced only if the lien is held to be valid. In an action in which the lien holder prevails in enforcement of the debt but not enforcement of the lien, attorneys' fees normally would not be authorized against the losing party. An analysis of the present statutes discloses that a clear majority of the states do provide for attorneys' fees in mechanic's lien cases.

Award of Attorneys' Fees Pursuant to Contract

A contract provision providing for attorneys' fees would normally be enforced. However, it may be subject to the usual rules of contract construction, including the rule that it is construed most strongly against the party drafting the instrument. This would be particularly true where it provides attorneys' fees only to one side and not to both sides. Many cases hold that, without a contract or statutory provision, attorneys' fees are not recoverable in actions on construction contracts. Often these provisions will be narrowly enforced. For example, in *Woods v. Langenbeck,* even though the contract provided for attorneys' fees, it was limited to those incurred in order to take possession or complete the residence upon default.[22] In this instance, the damages awarded the owner were for correction of deficiencies and no attorneys' fees were awarded.

[20]Ga. Code § 20-1404, Rules of Civil Procedure of the Commonwealth of Puerto Rico 44.4(a).
[21]297 A.2d 384 (Del. 1972).
[22]318 So.2d 134 (La. App. 1975).

Chapter **33**

Problems of Breach of Contract in a Shortage Economy

MORGAN P. AMES, ESQ.
Partner, Cummings and Lockwood, Stamford, Connecticut

PAUL E. KNAG, ESQ.
Associate, Cummings and Lockwood, Stamford, Connecticut

THE SHORTAGE PROBLEM

Since the so-called Arab oil embargo of 1973–1974, awareness of the significance of shortages has increased markedly, and even though the short-term crunch of that embargo is now history, shortages continue to pose a critical threat to the economy in general and to the construction industry in particular.

Shortages can and do result from a wide variety of factors, and almost any product or material may at some point be in short supply.

Potential shortages of petroleum products are particularly significant because shortages of these products can so easily result in shortages of a wide variety of other commodities, and because the potential for future shortages of petroleum products is great. As an official United States government study has stated, "it is extremely difficult to envision circumstances which would make the United States ever again economically self-sufficient in oil and gas."[1]

There are also a sizable number of other commodities for which the United States depends on limited foreign sources,[2] and this means a substantially increased chance of disruption in the market for these commodities.

In addition to shortages caused by lack of adequate raw materials, a wide variety of other problems can and do create shortage difficulties.

Shortages can be caused by strikes, by transportation disruptions, by natural disasters, by business failures, and by governmental regulations or business practices discouraging investment in a particular industry or threatening profitability.

Whatever the cause, a shortage means problems.

Shortages threaten profit margins of the supplier since materials may be available to the supplier, if at all, only at a price which exceeds the contract price to the buyer. Shortages threaten profit margins of the contractor since the contractor may have to curtail productive activities because of unavailability of needed materials and also because the contractor may end up paying more than the anticipated price for the materials in question.

Because of this, a shortage will usually lead affected persons to consider whether existing contractual commitments can or should be met. In turn, the promisee will have to consider what steps, if any, are appropriate to counter such a threat.

In order to determine the proper course of action in this context, a variety of practical and legal questions must be reviewed.

Is the supplier excused from performance under the contract? If not, what can be done about its failure to comply with its contractual obligations? If so, is performance excused completely or is the supplier obligated to make shipment at a later date, or in a lesser quantity, or both? To what extent, if any, is substituted performance required? Should the contract be renegotiated? How can supplies be protected after existing contractual commitments end?

These questions must not be answered in an ivory tower framework since a practical approach to problems of a shortage economy is the approach which is most likely to yield favorable results. Nevertheless, being practical necessarily involves making some attempt to answer the legal questions which arise in this context.

---

[1]Brobst and Pratt, Eds., *United States Mineral Resources,* U.S. Government Printing Office, 1973, p. 493.

[2]"Mineral Needs and the Environment Today and Tomorrow," *Final Report of the National Commission on Minerals Policy,* June 1973, Tables 2.2 and 4.B.1.

PROBLEMS OF BREACH OF CONTRACT BY THE SELLER OR PROVIDER

The Legal Basis for a Claim of Excuse for Breach of Contract to Deliver Goods in Short Supply

The law has long recognized that holding a party to the literal terms of its contractual undertakings may in certain circumstances become inequitable. Accordingly, in limited circumstances, the law makes provision for excusing a party from obligations which have become extraordinarily difficult or impossible to fulfill because of circumstances not foreseen or which were not taken into account when the contract was made. This rule of law, sometimes known as the law of *force majeure* or *impossibility* of performance, in some cases may permit a seller in a shortage context to be excused in whole or in part from its contractual obligations.

The *Restatement of Contracts*—a generally accepted statement of principles of contract law—describes the basic legal rule of force majeure as follows:

> . . . where, after the formation of contract facts that a promisor had no reason to anticipate, and for the occurrence of which he is not in contributing fault, render performance of the promise impossible [and as is explained in § 454 "impossible" also includes "impracticable"], the duty of the promisor is discharged.[3]

With respect to a contract for the sale of goods, this principle is set forth in the Uniform Commercial Code[4] which has been enacted as law in most states, and which provides that—except insofar as a seller has assumed a greater obligation and subject to certain conditions, including a requirement for seasonable notice—delay in delivery or nondelivery does not constitute a breach of a contract if:

> . . . performance as agreed has been made impracticable by the occurrence of a contingency the non-occurrence of which was a basic assumption on which the contract was made or by compliance in good faith with any applicable foreign or domestic governmental regulation or order whether or not it later proves to be invalid.

Although the Code, unlike the *Restatement of Contracts,* is applicable only to a contract for the sale of goods, this section of the Code is another good statement of the generally applicable law of force majeure.[5] Hence, while a construction contract per se (as opposed to a builder's contract with its supplier) is probably not a "contract for the sale of goods" covered by the Code, similar principles are applied in determining whether a contractual obligation is excused.

Thus, the general rule is that a contractual obligation will be excused by a shortage (or other event which is claimed to excuse performance) if such shortage or other event:

---

[3] *Restatement of Contracts* § 457.

[4] Uniform Commercial Code (hereafter sometimes referred to as the "Code"), § 2-615.

[5] *Restatement of Contracts* § 454, 457, 469; Corbin, *Contracts,* § 1320 *et seq.*

- Makes performance as agreed "impracticable"
- Is an event whose nonoccurrence was assumed at the time the contract was made (or as the *Restatement* puts it, results from facts which the promisor had no reason to anticipate and for the occurrence of which he is not in contributory fault)

Although it is simple enough to state the rule, it is anything but simple to determine when and how it applies.

Performance must be impracticable One important feature of the Code's statement of the rule of force majeure is that it uses the term "impracticable" rather than "impossible." The use of the word *impracticable* emphasizes the commercial context of the rule, and makes clear, as has long been recognized, that *impossibility* includes circumstances where performance—although possible in the strictest sense of that word—is rendered highly impracticable.

What this means is that mere unexpected difficulties will not be a basis for an excuse even though performance is rendered unprofitable, but that where extreme and unreasonable effort would be necessary to fulfill the contract, performance will be deemed impracticable or impossible.

For example, in one case in Washington, D.C., an oil company was held excused from its contract to deliver oil at a particular time because of the existence of 6-foot snow drifts.[6] Performance if possible at all would have been possible only through very extreme and unreasonable efforts.

Similarly, a contract for the excavation of soil that was partially under water was impossible insofar as it related to such soil under water even though it was not literally impossible to excavate the soil.[7]

On the other hand, a steel fabrication contract was not impossible even though the columns as designed may have been extremely difficult to make and even though the contractor claimed that "the tight construction schedule set out in the contract made production of two hundred faultless columns impossible." The court held that performance may have been extremely difficult and unprofitable, but it was not impossible.[8]

Similarly, no extreme and unreasonable difficulty was found where a contract for the transportation of goods became 33⅓ percent more expensive after the closing of the Suez Canal in 1967 forced a ship to travel around the Cape of Good Hope to reach its destination.[9]

Unprofitability is not enough. In order to be impracticable, performance under the contract must be possible, if at all, only at "excessive or unreasonable cost,"[10] and even though cost may exceed the contract price by 100 percent or more, such cost may still not be regarded as excessive or unreasonable.[11]

Nevertheless, Comment 4 to § 2-615 of Uniform Commercial Code makes clear that "a severe shortage of raw materials or of supplies due to a contin-

---

[6]*Whelan v. Griffith Consumers Co.,* 170 A.2d 229 (D.C. Mun. 1961).

[7]*Mineral Park Land Co. v. Howard,* 172 Cal. 289, 156 P. 458 (1916).

[8]*Ballou v. Basic Constr. Co.,* 407 F.2d 1137, 1140–41 (4th Cir. 1969).

[9]*American Trading & Pro. Corp. v. Shell* Int'l. Mar. Ltd., 453 F.2d 939 (2nd Cir. 1972).

[10]*Moss v. Smith,* 9 C.B. 94 (1850).

[11]*Publicker Indus., Inc. v. Union Carbide Corp.,* 17 U.C.C. Rep. 989, 992 (E.D.Pa. 1975).

gency such as war, embargo, local crop failure, unforeseen shutdown of major sources of supply or the like" *can* be a basis for excuse when it causes a "*marked increase in cost*" as well as when it "altogether prevents the seller from securing supplies necessary to his performance." (emphasis added).

Hence, there is *some* point at which "mere unprofitability" becomes "extreme and unreasonable cost" which constitutes "impracticability." Unfortunately, though, there is no well-defined guide as to where that threshold is.

The impracticability must be caused by an event the parties assumed would not occur Under § 2-615 of the Code, even if performance has become impracticable, such performance is not excused unless the impracticability was caused by "the occurrence of a contingency the non-occurrence of which was a basic assumption on which the contract was made."

Under the *Restatement of Contracts,* this requirement is stated in terms of "facts that a promisor had no reason to anticipate and for the occurrence of which he is not in contributing fault."

While the Code does not expressly mention this problem of the seller's own fault, it is clear that under the Code, as well as under the *Restatement* and other authorities, there is no basis for an excuse where the seller is fully or partially responsible for the inability to perform.[12]

Since a seller cannot claim to be excused by his own fault, a contract is not normally excused by an event which occurred after the time for performance has passed.[13] Also a seller will be responsible for any impairment of its particular source of supply or other factors which are personal to it.[14]

However, if performance from a particular source of supply or by a particular person or entity is shown to have been contemplated by the parties at the time the contract was made, failure of such a source of supply may justify an excuse,[15] provided the supplier does everything in his power to ensure the continued availability of such supply through the use of long-term contracts or other appropriate devices.[16]

On the other hand, merely because an event is beyond the seller's control does not necessarily mean that the nonoccurrence of the event was "a basic assumption of the contract" or that the event was unforeseen.

Although it is a difficult task indeed for any court to determine the parties' unexpressed assumption in making a contract, if a particular event was foreshadowed at the time the contract was made, the absence of an express excuse is a substantial indication that the parties did not intend the occurrence to excuse performance.

This is particularly true in relation to problems involving increase in price.

[12]Uniform Commercial Code § 2-615, Comment 5.

[13]*M. W. Fruit Co. v. Sissell,* 371 S.W.2d 896 (Texas App. 1963).

[14]*Deardorff-Jackson Co. v. National Produce Distrib., Inc.,* 447 F.2d 676 (7th Cir. 1971).

[15]*International Paper Co. v. Rockefeller,* 161 App. Div. 180, 146 N.Y.S. 371 (3d. Dept. 1914); *Low's Ezy-Fry Potato Co. v. J. A. Wood Co.,* 4 U.C.C. Rep. 483 (U.S. Dept. of Agric. 1967).

[16]Uniform Commercial Code § 2-615, Comment 5, citing *Canadian Ind. Alcohol Co. v. Dunbar Molasses Co.,* 258 N.Y. 194, 179 N.E. 383, 80 A.L.R. 1173 (1932) and *Washington Mfg. Co. v. Midland Lumber Co.,* 113 Wash. 593, 194 P. 777 (1921).

Unless there is some *unforeseen cause* of the price increase, there will be no excuse since parties normally *do* foresee that prices are likely to rise.[17] In fact, as the Uniform Commercial Code commentary recognizes, the risk of market fluctuation is "exactly the type of business risk which business contracts made at fixed prices are intended to cover."[18]

The sale of goods made in the context of a shortage or possible shortage would therefore normally *not* be subject to avoidance because of such shortage since the contract price and other terms presumably took such shortage into account.[19]

Even where a shortage prompts the government to step in and impose an allocation formula, companies which have entered into contracts in the context of a developing shortage without proper regard for their ability to deliver may be liable to the purchaser for damages for breach of contract.[20]

But foreseeability does not always control. Courts may find a particular circumstance that the parties did not intend to require compliance with the contract terms upon the happening of an unusual event, even though such event was foreseen or foreshadowed at the time the contract was made.[21]

The court will also be expected to look to the commercial context and custom in making the determination of when the seller should properly be excused. If, for example, the seller promotes his product as a "revolutionary break-through," it cannot later claim to be excused when it experiences engineering difficulties.[22]

Similarly, if a contract can fairly be said to have been made for the purpose of hedging possible market fluctuations or shortages, courts will be most unlikely to permit the seller to make any claim of excuse.

Given all the factors which a court must consider, whether an excuse is available in any particular set of circumstances may well be uncertain. Courts are therefore urged to "pray for the wisdom of Solomon"[23] in their efforts to apply the rule fairly!

However, in lieu of dependence on the wisdom of Solomon, which in practice the courts sometimes fail to exhibit, parties may wish to clarify the basis of their relationships by appropriate contractual provisions.

The Role of Appropriate Contractual Provisions

Under the Code and other authorities, it is established that the rules just discussed may be affected, supplemented or modified by appropriate contrac-

---

[17]*Maple Farms, Inc. v. City School Dist.*, 76 Misc. 2d 1080, 352 N.Y.S. 2d 784 (Sup. Ct. 1974).

[18]Uniform Commercial Code § 2-615, Comment 4; *Neal-Cooper Grain Co. v. Texas Gulf Sulphur Co.*, 508 F.2d 283 (7th Cir. 1974).

[19]*See e.g. Madeirense do Brasil, S/A v. Stulman Emrick Lumber Co.*, 147 F.2d 399 (2nd Cir. 1945).

[20]*International Paper Co. v. Federal Power Comm.*, 476 F.2d 121, 126 (5th Cir. 1973); *Monsanto Co. v. Federal Power Comm.*, 463 F.2d 799, 808 (D.C. Cir., 1972).

[21]*Transatlantic Fin. Corp. v. United States*, 363 F.2d 312 (D.C. Cir. 1966); *Fratelli Pantanella, S.A. v. International Com'l Corp.*, 89 N.Y.S. 2d 736 (S.Ct. 1949).

[22]*United States v. Wegematic Corp.*, 360 F.2d 674, 677 (2nd Cir. 1966).

[23]*American Trading & Pro. Corp. v. Shell Int'l. Mar. Ltd.*, 453 F.2d 939 (2nd Cir. 1972), citing 6 A Corbin, *Contracts* § 1333, at 372 (1962).

tual provisions.[24] Because of this, many contracts do provide some sort of excuse in the event of an occurrence of specified risks such as shortages, weather risks, fires, transportation accidents, strikes, and governmental actions. Sometimes such clauses merely reiterate the general rules which are recognized as a matter of law, relating to an excuse for impossibility due to the occurrence of an unforeseen contingency.

More frequently, however, such clauses have as their intent a desire to alleviate some of the uncertainties which might otherwise apply under the application of these rules of excuse due to impossibility. Most importantly, a clause providing an excuse from performance may include a provision for excuse upon the happening of specified events which in fact are foreshadowed at the time the contract is made.

The contractual language may also vary the degree of impracticability needed for an excuse. For example, it may be provided that a contract is excused to the extent that specified events make performance "more difficult," or performance may be excused where "prevented" by specified events. "More difficult" suggests a more liberal standard than "impracticability" while the word "prevented" is at least as strict as "impracticability."

Where the intent of a contract clause is to depart from the general rule of excuse which would otherwise be applicable, it is important that the provision be explicit and specific. Otherwise, the courts may be inclined to interpret contractual provisions strictly and may tend to prefer to interpret them to be in accordance with the general principles of law outlined above which would be applicable in the absence of such provisions.

For example, in one case, a contract was entered into providing broadly for excuse upon any change in conditions "presently existing in the home building industry" which rendered the seller "unable to procure promptly, as and when needed, labor and material."[25] Despite the apparent effort to create a broad ground for excuse, the court refused to permit an excuse because of increased costs since the seller was still able to perform.

Similarly, where a clause provided that "sellers are not responsible for strikes, fires, accidents, or anything beyond their control," the term "anything beyond their control" was held to include only those events that are similar to those specifically named.[26]

For this reason, it is normally desirable from the point of view of the supplier to insert a clause into sales contracts dealing specifically with possible shortage problems and providing that the supplier will be excused in the event a shortage makes performance more difficult.

Another thing that a contract may provide for is an excuse from performance based upon the actions or nonactions by a third party. For example, a

[24]Uniform Commercial Code § 2-615.

[25]*Hudson v. D & V Mason Contr., Inc.*, 252 A.2d 166, 168 (Del. Sup. Ct. 1969).

[26]*Krulewitch v. National Import. & Trad. Co.*, 196 App. Div. 544, 186 N.Y.S. 838 (1st Dept. 1921). *See also Monolith Portland Cement Co. v. Douglas Oil Co.*, 303 F.2d 176, 180 (9th Cir. 1962), where the contract provided an excuse for specific causes and "any other cause whatsoever beyond the control of such party, whether similar or dissimilar to the causes herein enumerated."

contractor may condition performance of a construction contract on the continued availability of his existing sources of supply or labor, or the contract may provide specifically what sources of supply the contractor is looking to or intends to look to for specific goods.

On the other hand, if the parties agree, the contract may rule out in advance any possible claim for an excuse due to shortages or, alternatively, may require payment of a stipulated sum in liquidated damages or for some other alternative performance in the event of an inability to deliver as promised.

Another approach would be to give the buyer the right to purchase from alternative sources upon nonperformance by the seller, with an unqualified right to compensation from the seller for the difference between the contract price and the purchase price.[27]

It may also be desirable to spell out in the contract the effect of any claim of excuse. When should the event permit delay but not excuse performance completely? When should performance be excused completely? When should delayed or partial performance be required? Should substituted performance be permitted or required? What notice of a claim of excuse should be given?

A different approach, which is particularly reasonable where a buyer is in a position to pass on his own costs, is for the contract to contain appropriate *price-escalation* or *cost-plus* provisions.

These can be most effective in assuring supply, since in the absence of emergency government restraints, it is usually possible to obtain needed supplies if the price is right—even in the context of an extreme shortage. However, from a business point of view, cost-plus or price-escalation clauses will not by any means be the best solution in all or even most instances, nor are they a panacea even when they are used.

Hence, at times when a claim of excuse is made, and when this occurs, it will be necessary to determine precisely the effect of such a claim on the contractual relationship between the parties.

The Extent of the Excuse

Just because performance as agreed is excused does not mean that the seller is completely excused from its contractual obligations, since the seller may still be required to render or at least offer substituted, delayed, or partial performance under the contract.

Substituted performance   The circumstances under which substituted performance is required are quite limited. Unless authorized by the contract, substituted performance is not required unless it involves only an *unsubstantial variation* of the contract terms.

One example of this given in the *Restatement of Contracts*[28] is as follows:

> A, a contractor enters into a contract with B to build a house and to use for the plumbing and drainage a certain make of pipe. Before the time for performance

---

[27] *Swift Textiles, Inc. v. Lawson*, 135 Ga. App. 799, 219 S.E.2d 167 (1975).
[28] *Restatement of Contracts* § 463, Ill.4.

that type of pipe is no longer manufactured and cannot be obtained. Other pipe adequate in quality can be obtained at no greater cost. A is under a duty to erect the building with the substituted pipe.

Section 2–614 of the Code specifically requires substitute performance where there is a commercially reasonable substitute with respect to the type of carrier, the agreed manner of delivery, the agreed berthing, loading, or unloading facilities, or the agreed manner of payment (where such manner of payment is prevented by governmental regulation).

Delayed or partial performance   The right to delayed or partial performance does not depend upon whether such delayed or partial performance constitutes an unsubstantial variation from performance as agreed. Partial or delayed performance must always be offered unless the event which rendered full timely performance impracticable also renders partial or delayed performance impracticable.

Allocation   In accordance with this rule, both the Code and the *Restatement of Contracts* require that a supplier allocate production and deliveries among its customers where there are insufficient quantities to fill all outstanding contractual commitments.[29]

However, the question of how the allocation is to be made may become a topic of bitter dispute.

Under the Code, the seller may "allocate in any manner which is fair and reasonable" and "may at his option include regular customers not then under contract as well as his own requirements for further manufacture."

Yet, for a seller to be put in the position of being "fair and reasonable" inevitably means that the seller will allocate in the ostensibly fair and reasonable way that best suits its financial interest.

In this context, it may be asked:

- Is it fair and reasonable for a seller to agree to give a bigger allocation to those customers who agree or have agreed to renegotiate the contract price upward?
- Is it fair and reasonable for a seller to prefer customers who make available to the seller other goods which are also in short supply?
- Is it fair and reasonable to meet one's own needs first and then meet those of others on a pro-rata basis?
- Is the customer's need revelant?
- Should supplies on hand by customers be considered in determining need?
- Is it fair and reasonable to prefer certain classes of customers to others?
- Who are the regular customers and what should their allocation be?
- To what extent can existing contracts be affected by additional contractual commitments assumed by the supplier in a shortage context?

Without providing firm answers to these questions, the Code[30] does indicate

---

[29]Uniform Commercial Code § 2-615(b), *Restatement of Contracts* § 464.

[30]Uniform Commercial Code § 2-615, Comment 11.

that the normal rule of allocation should be pro rata apportionment: "in case of doubt [the seller's] contract customers should be favored and supplies prorated evenly among them regardless of price."

Similarly, the *Restatement of Contracts* provides that *ratable apportionment* is the proper means of apportionment.[31]

In any event, it is clear that some fair means of apportionment is required and that a supplier may not arbitrarily cut off one customer despite existing contractual commitments while continuing to supply others.

Right to notice of excuse   Under the Code, the buyer has the right to "seasonable" notice of any claim of excuse pursuant to § 2-615.

The notice must indicate whether delayed performance is being offered, whether there will be an allocation, and the estimated quota.

Under § 2-616(2) of the Code, the buyer then has a reasonable time, not exceeding 30 days, to notify the seller that it agrees to accept the allocation or delay. If it does nothing or refuses the offer, the contract will be terminated, and—provided the seller's claim for excuse is valid—any unexecuted portion of the contract will be discharged.[32]

In the case of the construction contract itself, as has already been pointed out, the Code probably does not apply, and hence this seasonable notice provision of the Code does not apply. Nevertheless, it appears clearly desirable for any person claiming an excuse from a contract to notify the other party; and if practicable, to offer partial performance, substituted performance, or late performance; and await acquiescence from the other party before proceeding to actually render the delayed, partial, or substituted performance.

Practical Considerations Concerning Shortage Problems

In a shortage situation, the buyer normally has as a paramount goal a desire to assure itself an adequate supply of the affected commodity, without the same regard for cost which might normally be exhibited by such buyer. In this context, the seller is tempted to do everything possible to avoid its preshortage contractual obligations in order that it may make as many sales as possible at market rather than the lower contract price. Accordingly, whether or not an excuse is properly available, the seller may demand a price higher than that specified in the contract as a condition of its agreeing to fulfill the terms of its contract. Alternatively, a compromise might involve an appropriate arrangement ensuring continued supplies for the buyer in connection with an agreement for higher prices to be paid to the seller.

Given a threat by the seller to cut off supplies, the buyer may conclude that the commercially reasonable manner in which to proceed is to agree to the higher price in order to get the needed supplies. In that case, even if the seller is willing to give nothing in return for the higher price except for the originally

---

[31] *Restatement of Contracts* § 464.

[32] Under § 2-616(3) of the Code the right of a *buyer* to *terminate* a contract upon a claim of excuse by the seller under § 2-615 is not affected by any contractual provision made in advance of trouble which requires the buyer to stand ready to take delivery whenever the product becomes available. However, the seller cannot contractually avoid his duties in the event of an excuse under § 2-615.

agreed-upon performance, the buyer will probably still be bound by any agreement by it to pay a higher price.

As a general principle of law, in order for a contract to be binding on the parties, there must be valid *consideration*. In other words each of the parties must agree to do something for the other. However, in the case of a modification of an existing contract, no consideration is necessary under the Code provided the modification is made in good faith,[33] and even where no excuse is available it is not a sign of bad faith in a commercial context for a seller to ask a buyer for a higher price where the contract has come to involve a loss to the seller due to a market shift.[34]

A renegotiation of a contract in the context of a shortage will, of course, be made with full contemplation of the problems associated with the shortage. Therefore, where a contract is renegotiated after the shortage has arisen, any claim for excuse due to the shortage would be obviated in the absence of contractual provisions to the contrary.

Legal Remedies for Breach of Contract in the Shortage Context

Although renegotiation may prove to be the most practical solution to problems of breach of contract, there are times when despite the attendant costs, acrimony, and delay, a lawsuit may be the most appropriate course of action.

However, in order to make the decision as to whether to accept the risks and burden of litigation, an evaluation must be made not only as to the question of whether the buyer's legal position is valid but also as to what remedies may be available in a lawsuit and as to how these will serve the business needs of the potential plaintiff.

If a buyer is seeking possible money damages only, and if it is willing to have its lawsuit pending for several years awaiting a trial on the merits, there will be no problem as to remedies.

However, if the buyer is hoping to get the court to order the seller to actually deliver goods to it, problems of the timing and availability of remedies become significant.

In such an event, the buyer will wish to consider specific performance, injunctive relief, replevin, and possibly attachment as remedies which can supplement or be obtained in lieu of a possible damage remedy.

Specific performance is the most obvious remedy for someone interested in obtaining deliveries of goods in accordance with a contract. Where the court orders specific performance, the seller is under court order to deliver the goods as required by the contract, and the seller can then be punished by contempt proceedings if no deliveries are made.

However, under the Code, specific performance is only available "where the goods are unique or in other proper circumstances."[35]

Where suitable quantities of the materials are available, even though the price

---

[33]Uniform Commercial Code § 2-209.
[34]Uniform Commercial Code § 2-209, Comment 2.
[35]Uniform Commercial Code § 2-716(1).

thereof considerably exceeds the contract price, a court will not order specific performance.

On the other hand, one "other proper circumstance" for permitting specific performance is that the goods are in short supply and cannot be obtained from other sources.[36] Hence, when the shortage of supply is so severe that the material is wholly unavailable at any price, specific performance may be available.

However, even assuming that specific performance is available, it is normally quite unlikely that the court will award this remedy in time to alleviate the immediate problem of supply cutoff, since specific performance, like damages, is normally awarded only as a final disposition of a lawsuit and is subject to the normal problems of docket congestion and trial delays.

The efficacy of this specific performance remedy may therefore be dependent upon the concurrent availability of a preliminary injunction to force continuation of supply pending disposition of the case.

Such a preliminary injunction would probably be available only where there had been a past history of shipments from the buyer to the seller, where a continuation of shipments constituted a maintenance of the status quo, and where the scarce supply would cause the plaintiff to suffer irreparable injury if no injunction were awarded.[37]

However, where there is a substantial possibility that the seller is excused by contract or under § 2-615 of the Code, where the threat of substantial injury is less than clear, where the preliminary injunction is not really preserving the status quo but rather is changing it, or where other equities mitigate in favor of the seller, preliminary relief may not be available.

Hence, only in limited circumstances is specific performance available, and the circumstances under which a preliminary injunction will be available are even more limited.

Also of limited availability is the remedy known as *replevin*.

Replevin is proper only where the goods are not available elsewhere *and* where specific goods have been *identified with* the buyer's contract with the seller. (Goods identified with the contract are goods which have been designated in the contract, or shipped, marked, or otherwise designated by the seller as goods to which the contract refers.)[38] However, where replevin is available, it can be a swift, effective remedy since a writ of replevin authorizes an officer of the court to physically seize goods and turn them over to the buyer, and normally the court will act promptly upon a request for such relief.

It may also be possible to get the goods in short supply away from the seller by *attaching* the goods, although the purpose of this remedy would normally be

---

[36]Uniform Commercial Code § 2-713, Comment 3; § 2-716, Comment 2.

[37]*Kaiser Trading Co. v. Associated Metals & Min. Corp.,* 321 F. Supp. 923 (N.D.Cal. 1970).

[38]Uniform Commercial Code § 2-716(3); *see also* § 2-501 for definition of goods identified to the contract. Replevin is available without showing that goods are unavailable elsewhere where the goods have been shipped but "under reservation" and the seller has offered and tendered satisfaction of the security interest giving rise to the "reservation." Uniform Commercial Code § 2-716(3); *see also* § 2-505.

to secure possible money damages. However, the availability of attachment varies widely from state to state, and an attachment would normally be subject to dissolution upon the posting by the defendant of an appropriate bond. Hence, this remedy may ensure payment of damages but is not designed to ensure availability of supply.

Thus, there are several possibilities for quick, effective relief. However, in a shortage context, there is also a substantial possibility that a lawsuit will give no basis for quick court-ordered relief.

Before a buyer decides to go to court, it should be well prepared to deal with the likely delays involved and the limitations on the remedies which may be awarded as a result of a lawsuit.

ANTITRUST VIOLATIONS, FRAUD, INDUCING BREACH OF CONTRACT, AND UNFAIR COMPETITION

Although this chapter deals with the problem of breach of contract in the shortage context, persons confronted with shortage problems may also wish to consider whether any of their noncontractual rights have been violated. In this context, it may be appropriate to investigate the possibility of antitrust violations, fraud, interference with contractual relations by third parties, and unfair competition.

When goods are in short supply, the opportunities to restrain competition in possible violation of the Sherman Antitrust Act are multiplied. Sellers who compete with their own customers are tempted to cut off the customers in order to eliminate competition. Buyers are tempted to try to induce suppliers to cut their competitors off in violation of their contractual promise or to indirectly do so in connection with efforts to assure their own supply. Also, sellers are tempted to tie a sale of the goods in short supply to some other product which is not in short supply, and this may also create antitrust problems.

Possible violations of the Robinson-Patman Act, which prohibits price discrimination between purchasers under certain circumstances, become more likely as every sale becomes the subject of *ad hoc* negotiation.

Furthermore, a shortage may actually be the result of an antitrust violation as, for example, where a monopolist keeps the price of a commodity artificially low in order to make entry by competitors into the market unprofitable or where competitors conspire with each other to restrict supply.

Fraud, sharp dealing, and numerous forms of unfair competition also may be experienced where there is a shortage. In particular, the temptation to request suppliers to breach their contracts with others is great, and this may constitute inducing breach of contract. Where proof of such conduct exists, there may be an appropriate basis for civil and sometimes even criminal relief.

Hence, whenever a buyer is trying to evaluate possible modes for relief in a shortage context, an evaluation should be made by competent legal advisors as to whether the problems being experienced result in part from antitrust violations, inducements of breach of contract by third parties, fraud, or unfair competition.

PROBLEMS OF BREACH OF CONTRACT BY THE BUYER

The Buyer as a Middleman

In a sense, the contractor is a middleman; it buys materials from its suppliers and then turns around and uses that material in connection with the construction project.

The buyer-contractor will normally try to claim as an excuse from its own construction contract any excuse claimed by its supplier, although this may not always be possible. However, in this sense the buyer is not acting as a buyer but rather is asserting an excuse similar to that being asserted by its own seller, and therefore the legal efficacy of such an excuse will be based on the principles which have already been discussed.

Frustration of Purpose

Another type of breach of contract by a buyer in the shortage context is the breach which results from the fact that a buyer will not wish to take delivery of goods or services which cannot be utilized because of the shortage problems.

For example, if a sudden shortage of natural gas prevented any new hookups of residential properties to natural gas lines, a contract to put in piping necessary for such a connection would be frustrated in its essential purpose, and the buyer might be justified in terminating such a contract provided the natural gas shortage was unanticipated.

However, insofar as a contract for the sale of goods is concerned, the buyer's intended end use is not normally considered the purpose of the contract where the goods can be used for other purposes or resold.[39]

In fact, § 2-615 of the Code does not even mention the possibility of an excuse for the buyer because of the occurrence of an event whose nonoccurrence was a basic assumption of the contract. Nevertheless, where there is a frustration of the purpose of a contract because of an event the parties assumed would not occur, the buyer is excused. Again, possibilities for renegotiation should be explored in this area as an alternative to the necessity for a lawsuit.

After the Shortage Ends

The third and perhaps most significant type of breach of contract by a buyer occurs after the shortage has passed. In this context, prices will normally fall almost as rapidly as they rose when the shortage situation began. As such, buyers will be anxious to find a way to avoid their contracts with their suppliers in order to try to take advantage of the falling market and avoid the obligations assumed at exorbitant rates at the height of the shortage.

Suddenly, those who pressed hardest to assure themselves of a supply at all cost end up with the biggest problems. Contracts which once were an assurance

---

[39]*See Amtorg Trading Corp. v. Miehle Printing Press & Mfg. Co.*, 206 F.2d 103 (2d Cir. 1953) [where the purchaser of machinery intended to export it to the USSR but was prevented from doing so by governmental regulation; the court held that the contract was not excused as there was no frustration of purpose].

of supply threaten to put the buyer at a competitive disadvantage. Generally, there will be no unanticipated event and no impracticability to justify an excuse by the buyer in this context.

Also, the buyer's principal promise is to pay money, and that is a promise which is unlikely to become impracticable.

Therefore, what buyers can and will do is to insist upon all their rights under the Code to refuse acceptance or revoke acceptance of the goods as shipped. The most important right in this connection is the right of the buyer to reject delivery in the event the goods fail to conform to the contract requirements.[40]

Since substandard or irregular materials become common when there is a shortage, it is quite possible that contractual commitments may be avoided by careful insistence by the buyer upon conformity with the purchase order requirements.

When the shortage is over, a buyer may suddenly discover such deficiencies or alleged deficiencies in shipments already received as well as in shipments received thereafter. A buyer who makes such a discovery may attempt to revoke acceptance or to claim nonacceptance of nonconforming goods which might have been shipped during the shortage crisis.

With the tables turned, the sharp dealing supplier suddenly finds that his customers are anxious to return the treatment they experienced when the shortage was on. It is at this point that most of the litigation generated by shortages actually starts. The seller has less to lose by bringing suit than the buyer did when the tables were turned and is less concerned about immediate relief. Thus, the protracted battle for the ultimate apportionment of the gains and losses is left for disposition by the courts in the normal course.

CONCLUSION

Shortages inevitably prompt widespread efforts to avoid contractual commitments made under different market conditions.

In general, the legal rules concerning whether performance is excused are vague, and it may be difficult to predict whether a legal excuse will be available in the absence of clear contractual provisions relating to the problem.

Furthermore, even if no excuse is available, a seller may still choose to breach his contract unless the buyer will renegotiate. Hence, renegotiation is often the most practical way to ensure continued supplies.

In any event, before litigation is commenced, in addition to careful consideration of the question whether a proper claim for excuse is available to the seller, consideration should be given to the remedies which may be available for breach of contract and also to whether any noncontractual violations have been committed, as for example possible antitrust, inducement of breach of contract, fraud, and unfair competition.

The buyer is most likely to attempt to avoid contracts immediately after the shortage when prices start to drop, and ironically that is when most shortage-prompted lawsuits actually begin.

[40]Uniform Commercial Code § 2-601.

Part Eight

Special Collection Remedies Provided by Law

Chapter **34**

Mechanic's Liens on Private Projects

ROBERT LEE AGER, ESQ.
Seattle, Washington

DEFINITIONS AND PURPOSE

Webster, who for years has been trying to help us make sense out of the English language, defines[1] *liens* as follows:

> . . . a charge upon real or personal property for the satisfaction of some debt or duty ordinarily arising by operation of law.

"Mechanic's" is a word used before the word "lien" in most of the statutes. However, *mechanic* can mean a general contractor or a subcontractor, a laborer or a supplier of material to either contractor, or anyone else who is a laborer or a supplier of material to either, or anyone else whose labor or materials have been incorporated in some construction for the owner.

---

[1]*Webster's Seventh New Collegiate Dictionary,* 1967, G. C. Merriam Co., 1970.

A lien is a time-and-action gate. Two things are required:

1. To go through the right gate at the right time
2. To take the correct action while going through the gate

A precautionary note: Liens are created by legislatures and take the form of statutes. Lien statutes of each state differ from those in other states. Legislatures constantly change lien laws in an effort to balance the equities between the many competing claimants. In addition, the requirements are sometimes overly technical. Consequently, the advice of a local attorney is essential. The material contained here is not legal advice, nor a substitute for a local lawyer but is intended, instead, to inform.

Contracting is a high-risk business. According to one national authority,[2] 39 percent of the contractors go broke in the first two years, and 67 percent are through within seven years. These are chilling statistics, not only for the general contractor, but for his labor and material suppliers, his subcontractors and their labor and material suppliers, and lower-tier contractors.

Legislators have created liens in favor of those who furnish labor or materials in a private construction contract. Properly *perfected,* a lien is a claim on the land of the owner which can be enforced by foreclosure and sale of the owner's land. This is the most effective method by which the construction contract claimant can secure payment. A lien on the owner's property effectively prevents him from selling the property without paying the lien or from using the land as security for borrowing.

Liens are created by statutes and statutes do not lend themselves to a summary. Each of the words in the statute is intended to be meaningful, and each word is intended to mean what it says. Similarly, the many statutes of the 50 states do not lend themselves to a summary. Furthermore, there is risk in discussing statutes in generalities. The Table of Statutory Requirements (see the appendix) is merely a guide, and the particular state statute must be consulted. With this in mind, however, it is possible to look at the broad patterns of legislative intention. Common to almost all statutes are instructions on:

- Who may claim a lien
- How the claim is made
- When the claim is made
- Where the claim is made
- Duration of the claim
- Priority of the claim
- Owner's defenses
- Foreclosure procedures

These subjects will each be discussed below and without reference to any specific statute.

WHO MAY CLAIM A LIEN

The following persons, whether they are individuals or corporations, usually may claim a lien against real property of the private owner, provided that they

[2]Overton Currie.

meet the other requirements. These persons will almost always have the right to claim a lien:

General contractor
Laborer of general contractor
Supplier of general contractor
Subcontractor of general contractor

In addition, certain others may also have a right to claim a lien under certain additional circumstances:

Laborer of subcontractor
Supplier of subcontractor
Sub-subcontractor

[Certain support services such as architects, engineers, and other government lien claimants such as taxing agencies are omitted for this discussion.]

The language varies. West's Annotated Civil Code[3] includes all

> ... Mechanics, materialmen, contractors, subcontractors, lessors of equipment, artisans, architects, registered engineers, licensed land surveyors, machinists, builders, teamsters, and draymen, and all persons and laborers of every class performing labor upon or bestowing skill or other necessary services on, or furnishing materials or leasing equipment to be used or consumed in or furnishing appliances, teams, or power contributing to a work of improvements.

Illinois, on the other hand, has a different way of saying it; Illinois includes

> ... Any person who shall ... furnish materials, fixtures, apparatus or machinery, forms or form work or fill, sod or excavate ... or do landscape ... or raise or lower any house ... or remove any house ... or perform any services as an architect, structural engineer, professional engineer or land surveyor ... or drill any water well thereon ... or furnish or perform labor or services in superintendent time-keeping, mechanic, labor or otherwise ... or furnish material, fixtures, apparatus, machinery, labor or services.[4]

These statutes are quoted in part to illustrate differences in wording and to emphasize the need for looking at the particular statute involved.

Despite these differences, the statutory pattern is clear: The closer the claimant is to the owner, the better the possibility that he is one of the persons who has the right to claim a lien.

In certain instances, however, more remote claimants may qualify—namely those who may have a charge for the use of tools or appliances for preparatory or fabricating work done on materials intended for use on the job,[5,6] or cases in which labor is used in examination, repair or servicing of fixtures, machinery or other attachments.[7] The answer depends upon the statute, and courts differ widely on the subject.

A subcontractor who has agreed with a general contractor to undertake a portion of the construction for a predetermined price is clearly one who

---

[3]*West's Annotated Civil Code,* § 3110.
[4]Ill. Ann. Stat., Ch. 82, § 1.
[5]3 ALR3d 573.
[6]25 ALR2d 1370.
[7]51 ALR3d 1087.

furnishes labor and materials within the meaning of the various statutes. Similarly, the materialman who furnishes the lumber, the concrete, the nails, the paint, the plasterboard or other obvious building materials is equally, obviously, furnishing something covered by the statute. The carpenter, the mason, the iron worker, fork-lift operator, hired directly by the general contractor, and the other obvious building trades who furnish labor are also furnishing something covered by the statute.

Supposing the contractor rents a power saw and a planer from the local supply store. Are these materials within the meaning of the statute? Some states categorically provide that rental of tools is covered, and others do not. If the contractor burns out an engine bearing in one of his trucks, a spherical roller bearing in his power shovel, or a ball bearing in a rented power saw, is the supplier of these replacement parts entitled to a lien because he furnished material? The answer again is in the statutes.

Do the materials have to be incorporated in the work, or delivered to the job site, or simply ordered? The cases are at wide variance. Actual use, for example, would appear to be a possible prerequisite in Arkansas, California, Hawaii, Illinois, Indiana, Kentucky, Maine, Michigan, New York, Ohio, and Oklahoma. The issue appears to be doubtful in Missouri, Nebraska, Pennsylvania, and Tennessee. In the balance of the states, either furnishing or delivering the materials will sustain the lien.[8]

The conclusion as to who may file the claim cannot be answered categorically. The statutes and decisions are at wide variance. However, an examination of the statutes of all 50 states and some of the decisions leads to the observation, first that the more directly connected the labor and material are to the general construction contract, the more apt they are to be covered by the lien statute; second, if the claimant can show that what he furnished was of direct economic benefit to the owner in the construction of the facility, the more the courts are apt to be sympathetic with the claim.

HOW THE CLAIM IS MADE

Preliminary notice   Prior to the discussion of formal requisites of filing a claim, the subject of preliminary notice must be discussed because in many statutes some form of preliminary notice to the owner may be required in order to enable the claimant, if unpaid at the end of the job, to claim a lien successfully. Generalities on this subject are dangerous, as the requirements vary from state to state. However, it is safe to state the general rule that the general contractor usually need not give preliminary notice to the owner. The purpose of notice, after all, is to give the owner information that he otherwise would not have—namely, that someone unknown to him is working on his property and may claim a lien. If the owner has actual notice, the giving of formal notice would seem, therefore, unnecessary.

Some form of preliminary notice before the work has been completed

[8] 39 ALR2d 394.

appears to be required in Alabama, Florida, Louisiana, Massachusetts, Michigan, Nevada, New Hampshire, North Carolina, Ohio, Oregon, Rhode Island, Texas, Vermont, Virginia, Washington, and Wisconsin for subcontractors. Direct labor is seldom, if ever, required to file a preliminary notice, but subcontractors, materialmen, and lower-tier contractors are required to file such a notice. The notice varies by state. In Florida,[9] for example, it must be served before the commencement of construction or not later than 45 days from the commencement:

> This notice must be served before commencing or not later than 45 days from commencing to furnish his services or materials but in any event before the date of furnishing the affidavit under subsection (3) (d)1., of this section, or abandonment, whichever shall occur first.

Michigan appears to require a 90-day preliminary notice for those who do not have a direct contractual relationship with the owner.[10]

Preliminary notice requirements are serious, and the failure to file a notice when required will defeat the claim even though all other requirements are met.

NOTICE OF LIEN

All lien claimants are required to file some form of written notice if they remain unpaid after having completed their portion of the construction contract. The form of notice is almost invariably described in the statute, and therefore it, too, varies from state to state. The form must always be signed by the claimant and usually verified, that is, given under oath. Other usual requirements are a description of:

- The claimant
- The work or materials performed or delivered
- The owner
- The real property against which the lien is claimed

Oklahoma[11] requires

> . . . a statement setting forth the amount claimed and the items thereof as nearly as practicable, the names of the owner, the contractor, the claimant, and the description of the property subject to the lien, verified by affidavit.

New York[12] requires

> 1. The name and residence of the lienor; and if the lienor is a partnership or a corporation, the business address of such firm, or corporation, the names of partners and principal place of business, and if a foreign corporation, its principal place of business within the state.
>
> 1-a. The name and address of the lienor's attorney, if any.

[9]Fla. Stat. Ann. § 713.06.
[10]Mich. Stat. Ann., § 26.281, Mich. Comp. Laws Ann., § 570.1.
[11]42 Okla. Stat. Anno., § 141.
[12]N.Y. Lien Law § 9 (McKinney 1954).

2. The name of the owner of the real property against whose interest therein a lien is claimed, and the interest of the owner as far as known to the lienor.

3. The name of the person by whom the lienor was employed, or to whom he furnished or is to furnish materials; or, if the lienor is a contractor or subcontractor, the person with whom the contract was made.

4. The labor performed or materials furnished and the agreed price or value thereof, or materials actually manufactured for but not delivered to the real property and the agreed price or value thereof.

5. The amount unpaid to the lienor for such labor or materials.

6. The time when the first and last items of work were performed and materials were furnished.

7. The property subject to the lien, with a description thereof sufficient for identification; and if in a city or village, its location by street and number, if known. A failure to state the name of the true owner or contractor, or a misdescription of the true owner, shall not affect the validity of the lien. The notice must be verified by the lienor or his agent, to the effect that the statements therein contained are true to his knowledge except as to the matters therein stated to be alleged on information and belief, and that as to those matters he believes it to be true.

Although the form of notice appears to be simple, substantial questions arise concerning the sufficiency of the description of the owner,[13] or of the property,[14] or of the work.[15] These must be made clear because the successful lien claimant gains priority over nonlien claimants and courts are inclined to the view that to gain priority, the claimant must comply strictly with the statute. Care must be exercised that the correct name of the real owner is given, and this should not be too hard to obtain.

The question arises as to whether it is necessary to give a legal rather than a common description of the real property.[16] There seems to be a general tendency among courts to relieve the lien claimant from the requirement of a strict legal description given by the lien claimant, if it is sufficient to identify the property. Reference should be made to the statute.

The type of work must be described with some particularity, a number of courts feeling that, where the specific nature of the work was not indicated, the lien notice was defective and the lien disallowed.[17]

WHEN THE CLAIM IS MADE

By all odds, the most difficult question is the time frame within which the final claim must be made and filed. Once again, the subject is entirely statutory, and the time limits vary widely. Therefore, exteme care must be taken to consult the particular statutes involved. The time may be as short as 30 days in Massachusetts,[18] 45 days in Hawaii,[19] or as long as six months in Alabama[20] and four

---

[13]48 ALR3d 153.
[14]52 ALR2d 12.
[15]27 ALR2d 1169.
[16]52 ALR2d 12.
[17]27 ALR2d 1169.
[18]Mass. Gen. Laws Ann., Ch. 254 § 8.
[19]Hawaii Rev. Laws, Ch. 507.

months in North Carolina.[21] Obviously, it is impossible to generalize about these vital requirements. They are covered in the appendix, Table of Statutory Requirements. Reference should be made to that table, and the statute should be read in order to ascertain the correct filing time.

WHEN THE TIME STARTS TO RUN

In most jurisdictions, the most common provisions are that time shall be calculated from the completion of the construction. The question always exists as to *what is completion,* and once again, the answer to this question is purely statutory. Generally speaking, however, substantial completion is sufficient.

Occasionally, trouble can arise where the lien claimant had a contract with the general contractor and later entered into an independent contract with the owner. If the time periods for filing are different, the issue exists as to which time period should be used; and in this regard there is a division of authority, and the individual case law of the particular state must be consulted.[22]

WHERE THE CLAIM IS MADE

This subject consists of two parts, the first one having been covered in the sense that a copy of the notice must always be given to the owner.

The second part of the question is whether the claim must be filed in a particular place. The answer is yes. The actual location depends again upon the particular statute, and it would be unfortunate if one were covered, having complied with all the necessary requirements, but either filed the claim in the wrong place or failed to file it at all. Places vary widely. It could be the judge of probate of the county,[23] the county recorder,[24] the office of the clerk of the circuit court of the county,[25] the town clerk of the town in which the building is situated,[26] or the office of the Prothonotary of the county where the property is situated.[27] As a general rule, the lien is filed with that office where records of real estate transactions would be available. The obvious reason is that the lien is an actual recorded charge on the land. A filing or recording fee is almost always charged.

DURATION OF CLAIM

The duration of the claim is spelled out by statute, and this term means that length of time which the lien will remain a charge upon the land. All the statutes provide that the lien must be reduced to judgment or some other form

---

[20]Code of Alabama, Title 33, § 42.
[21]General Laws of N.C., § 44A-12.
[22]78 ALR2d 1165.
[23]Code of Alabama, Title 33, § 41.
[24]Ariz. Rev. Stat., § 33–993.
[25]Ark. Stat., § 51–613.
[26]Conn. Gen. Stat. Ann., § 49-34.
[27]Del. Code Ann., 25-2712.

of judicial undertaking or suit must be commenced in order to foreclose the lien.

As with the other statutory requirements, these vary from state to state. For example, in Michigan[28] the duration is one year, as is the case in Minnesota[29] and Mississippi.[30] In Nebraska[31] it is two years, but in New Hampshire[32] it is 90 days. In North Carolina it is 180 days,[33] whereas in North Dakota[34] it is three years unless the owner files a written demand, in which event suit to enforce the lien must be commenced within 30 days.

These samplings will indicate the need for specific reference to the particular statute involved.

OWNER'S DEFENSES

Owners do not like liens. They have nothing to gain by them and everything to lose. Therefore, it is not surprising to find that they assert defenses of many different kinds. The first, and most obvious, defense to the owner is the failure of the claimant to comply with the statute in every respect, and this has been covered previously.

The second defense of the owner is actually one arranged for in the drafting of the construction contract. He may insist upon the insertion of a provision of a construction contract waiving the lien, or otherwise get the contractor to agree not to file a lien. In addition, he may insist upon such a clause being inserted in subcontracts. Clear and unambiguous clauses in construction contracts to that effect have been enforced, and contractors have been precluded by reason of their no-lien agreement from asserting a mechanic's lien in Colorado, Illinois, Indiana, Iowa, Maryland, New Jersey, New York, Texas, and Utah.[35] In addition, Illinois, Indiana, and Pennsylvania have statutes which provide, in essence, that if a no-lien contract is properly filed or recorded in the designated office, it has the effect of barring a subcontractor's or materialman's lien.

In addition, the contract between the general contractor and the subcontractor or materialmen in which the latter waives its right to a mechanic's lien or agrees not to file it is also held generally valid and effective and will preclude the enforcement of a lien. This has been seen in the decisions of California, Indiana, New York, and Pennsylvania.

The third defense is statutory, as the statutes of a number of states provide, in substance, that the owner may, within a certain number of days of the start of construction, give notice that he will not be responsible for, nor will his land be subject to, any lien. He usually posts a notice in writing to that effect in some

[28]Mich. Stat. Ann., § 26.289 Mich. Com. Laws Ann., § 570.9.
[29]Minn. Stat. Ann., § 514.12.
[30]Miss. Code Ann., § 360.
[31]Rev. Stat. of Neb., Ch. 52.
[32]N.H. Rev. Stat. Ann., Ch. 447:9.
[33]Gen. Stat. of N.C., § 44A-13.
[34]N.D. Cent. Code, Ch. 35-27-25.
[35]76 ALR2d 1087.

conspicuous place or otherwise brings it to the attention by other notice provisions. The question has arisen in Alaska, Arizona, California, Indiana, Massachusetts, Minnesota, Nevada, New Mexico, Oregon, and South Dakota;[36] and reference should be made to the specific case and statutory law in those states for further explanation.

The fourth defense the owner asserts is probably not a defense but is derived from those portions of the lien statutes which give him the right to shorten the time in which a lien may be filed or enforced by filing some form of notice to that effect.

In the statutes of some of the states are provisions which give the owner the ability to file or record a notice of completion and thus shorten the time in which a lien may be claimed. Typical of such statutes are those in Washington[37] and California.[38]

Finally, the need for accuracy in preparing and filing the lien goes beyond the possibility of losing the lien. In the event the amount of the lien is specified incorrectly, it may lead to recovery of damages from the person whose property was improperly liened.[39]

CONCLUSION

The conclusion is obvious: Mechanic's liens are highly technical, and the statute must be read, understood, and followed if a construction contract creditor is to have a charge upon the owner's land. The advice of a local attorney is invaluable.

APPENDIX: Table of Statutory Requirements

State	Preliminary notice requirement	Notice of claim, recordation requirement	Duration of lien
Alabama			
Code of Ala. Tit. 33, § 37		*P,* 6 months[a]	6 months[d]
		S, 4 months[a]	
		L, 30 days[a]	
Alaska			
A.S. 34.35.050	None required	90 days[a]	6 months[b]
Arizona			
A.R.S. § 33-981	None required	*P,* 90 days[c]	6 months[b]
		S, 60 days[c]	
Arkansas			
A.S.A. § 51-601	None required	120 days[a]	15 months[b]
California			
West's Annotated Civil Code § 3110		90 days[al]	90 days[c]

[36] 85 ALR2d 949.
[37] Rev. Code Wash. Ann., Ch. 60.04.
[38] *West's Annotated Civil Code,* § 3117.
[39] *Puget Sound Plywood v. Mester,* 86 Wash. 2d 135.

APPENDIX: Table of Statutory Requirements (*Continued*)

State	Preliminary notice requirement	Notice of claim, recordation requirement	Duration of lien
Colorado			
C.R.S. § 38-22-101		3 months[a]	6 months[a]
Connecticut			
C.G.S.A. § 49-33		60 days[a]	1 year[b]
Delaware			
25 Del C. § 2702	None required	P, 30 days[e]	Refer to 25 § 2711
		S, 90 days[a]	
Florida			
F.S.A. § 713.01 and 713.05		90 days[a]	1 year[b]
Georgia			
G.A. Code Ann. § 67-2001	None required	3 months[a]	12 months[d]
Hawaii			
H.R.S. § 507-41	None required	45 days[c]	3 months[b]
Idaho			
I.C. § 45-501	None required	P, 90 days[f]	6 months[b]
		S, 60 days[f]	
Illinois			
S.H.A. ch. 82		4 months[c]	2 years[c]
Indiana			
I.S.A. § 32-8-3-1		60 days[a]	1 year[b]
Iowa			
I.C.A. § 572.2	None required	P, 90 days[a]	2 years[g]
		S, 60 days[a]	
Kansas			
K.S.A. § 60-1101	None required	P, 4 months[a]	1 year[b]
		S, 3 months[a]	
Kentucky			
K.R.S. § 76.010		6 months[a]	12 months[b]
Louisiana			
L.S.A. 9:4801		60 days[a]	1 year[b]
Maine			
10 M.R.S.A. § 3251	None required	90 days[a]	120 days[a]
Maryland			
Ann. Code of Maryland, 1974 § 9-101		180 days[a]	1 year[b]
Massachusetts			
M.G.L.A. c. 254 §§ 1, 3 and 4		P, 30 days[h]	60 days[b]
		S, 30 days[i]	
		L, 40 days[a]	
Michigan			
M.C.L.A. § 570.1		90 days[a]	1 year[b]
Minnesota			
M.S.A. § 514.01	None required	90 days[a]	1 year[a]
Mississippi			
Miss. Code Ann. § 356	None required	None required	12 months[d]
Missouri			
V.A.M.S. § 429.0l0		P, 6 months[d]	6 months[b]
		S, 4 months[d]	
		L, 60 days[d]	

APPENDIX: Table of Statutory Requirements (*Continued*)

State	Preliminary notice requirement	Notice of claim, recordation requirement	Duration of lien
Montana			
R.C.M. § 45-501	None required	90 days[al]	2 years[b]
Nebraska			
R.R.S. 1943 § 52-101	None required	P, 4 months[a] S, 3 months[a] M, 4 months[a]	2 years[b]
Nevada			
NRS 108.222		90 days[al]	6 months[b]
New Hampshire			
RSA 447:2		30 days[a]	90 days[a]
New Jersey			
N.J.S.A. 2A:44.66		4 months[a]	4 months[a]
New Mexico			
N.M.S.A. § 61-2-2		P, 120 days[c] S, 90 days[j]	1 year[b]
New York			
32 McKinney's Statutes § 3	None required	4 months[a]	1 year[b]
North Carolina			
G.S. 44A-8		120 days[a]	180 days[a]
North Dakota			
N.D.C.C. § 35-27-02		90 days[al]	3 years[d]
Ohio			
O.R.C. § 311.12		60 days[a]	6 years[b]
Oklahoma			
42 O.S. 1971 § 141	None required	P, 4 months[a] S, 90 days[a] M, 4 months[a] L, 4 months	1 year[b]
Oregon			
O.R.S. § 87.010		P, 60 days[c] S, 45 days[a]	6 months[b]
Pennsylvania			
49 P.S. § 1301		4 months[a]	2 years[b]
Rhode Island			
G.L. § 34-28-1		P, None required S, 40 days[a] M, 4 months[a]	1 year[b]
South Carolina			
C.L.S.C. § 45-251		90 days[al]	6 months[a]
South Dakota			
S.D.C.L. § 44-9-1		120 days[al]	6 years[a]
Tennessee			
T.C.A. § 64-1102	None required	P, None required S, 90 days[d] L, 90 days[d] M, 90 days[d]	1 year[a]
Texas			
Vernon's Ann. Civ. St. Art. 16-5452		P, 120 days[d] S, 90 days[d]	4 years[d]

APPENDIX: Table of Statutory Requirements (*Continued*)

State	Preliminary notice requirement	Notice of claim, recordation requirement	Duration of lien
Utah			
U.C.A. § 38-1-3	None required	P, 80 days[e] S, 60 days[e]	12 months[e]
Vermont			
9 V.S.A. § 1921	None required	60 days[d]	3 months[d]
Virginia			
Va. Code Ann. § 43-1		90 days[c]	6 months[k]
Washington			
R.C.W. § 60.04.040		90 days[a]	8 months[b]
West Virginia			
W.Va.C. § 38-2-1		P, 90 days[c] S, 60 days[j] M, 90 days[a] L, 90 days[a]	6 months[b]
Wisconsin			
W.S.H. § 289.01		6 months[a]	2 years[b]
Wyoming			
W.S. § 29.4		P, 4 months[d] S, 90 days[d]	180 days[b]

[a]Commences with the date of claimant's last performing or furnishing materials.

[b]Commences with the date the lien is filed of record.

[c]Commences with the date of completion of the principal contract.

[d]Commences with the date the indebtedness accrues or becomes due and owing.

[e]Commences with the expiration of 90 days after the date of claimant's last performing or furnishing materials.

[f]Commences with the date of completion of project or the date of claimant's last performing or furnishing materials, whichever is later.

[g]Commences with the expiration of 90 days for the original contractor and commences with the expiration of 60 days for all others.

[h]Commences with the date the original contract is to be performed.

[i]Commences with the date the subcontract is to be performed.

[j]Commences with the date of completion of the subcontract.

[k]Commences with the time when the memorandum of lien is recorded or after 60 days from the time the structure was completed or work terminated, whichever is the last to occur.

[l]Owner can change the duration of the notice of claim requirement.

NOTE: P = The principal or original contractor. S = The subcontractor, unless otherwise specified, includes all parties except the original contractor. L = Laborer. M = Material furnisher.

Chapter **35**

Mechanic's Liens on
Public Projects

LOUIS AUERBACHER, JR., ESQ.
Newark, New Jersey

Mechanic's liens on public projects (sometimes called Municipal Mechanic's Liens) are available as a remedy to those furnishing labor or material by subcontract or otherwise on public works projects in certain states.[1] The lien which applies to public improvements is created by statute which, of course, varies. Reference is required to the particular statute in each of the respective states in order to determine the precise requirements of that state.

This right of lien is usually intended to permit one supplying material, labor, or acting as a subcontractor supplying such, to have a right to assert a claim against public contract funds. It is intended to create a right of claim or lien against funds (to the extent of the contractor's liability) due or to become due to the contractor from the public agency. It should be noted that there is no right against the public agency as such. The remedy applies only to funds due or to become due to the contractor on the public contract to whom such labor or material was supplied. The remedy as stated is applicable only to the funds themselves.

Other states permit the remedy as to most public agencies in their state such as a county, city, town, public commission, or public board which is authorized by law to make contracts. This right of lien is limited to the public bodies described in the pertinent statute. For example, in the State of New Jersey it does not apply to a contract involving the state government itself.

---

[1]California, Colorado, Illinois, Indiana, Iowa, Kentucky, Louisiana, Maine (but only to public buildings), Massachusetts, New Hampshire, New Jersey, New York, Ohio, South Dakota, Texas (on contracts under $15,000), Washington (State of), Wisconsin. An old decision in the State of Kansas seems to indicate that there is some such right. The case is *Fidelity & Deposit Co. v. Stafford* 165 P, 837. Similarly as to the State of Utah, the case of *Mellen v. Vondor-Horst Bros.* 140 P, 130.

Laws in the various states creating this type of lien are to be construed in accordance with the precise language of the particular law involved. In most of these with statutes granting lien claim rights there are also provisions for surety bonds to be provided. These bonds give a right to the claimant against the surety on the bond but do not affect the right of a claimant to proceed directly against contract monies of the contractor in the possession of the public body as a municipal mechanic's liens.

It is a prerequisite that there be a contract balance due or to become due to the contractor under the contract with the public body in order for such lien claim to be effective.

The pertinent statutes usually require the filing of a notice of the lien claim with the public body or an official thereof. There is also usually a provision giving a time limitation for such filing. This is generally before the work is completed or accepted or within a short period thereafter.

The usual form of statute requires that the public body serve notice upon the contractor to show cause why the claim should not be paid. If the contractor does not indicate a dispute in the form required by the statute, the public body without an order of the court can make payment to the claimant and may deduct that amount from any amount which might be due the contractor.

Unpaid labor and materialmen who file such liens and are not paid are required to institute proceedings and file an appropriate pleading setting forth their claims. The statutes usually prescribe that an action must be brought within a limited time; if not, the lien claim is ineffective. Usually the claimant first bringing the action is required to join all others who may have filed claims. The court then determines the validity and priorities, if any, of the liens as well as the amount due from the public agency to the contractor which would be available. In some states the costs of completion are deducted from the contract balances. The amount due or to become due to the contractor determines the amount available for the lien claims.

There are usually also provided methods whereby the lien claim may be discharged, usually a statement that the claim has been paid (a satisfaction) filed by the claimant. The termination of the proceedings would also be a means of discharge of the lien claim.

Many public bodies permit the filing of a surety bond by the contractor to take the place of the lien claim so that monies held for the lien claim by the public body may be released to the contractor. This, in many cases, may be important to the contractor so that his funds, which are needed for the performance of the contract, are not unduly retained. The surety bond then replaces the lien and the claimant may, if entitled to a recovery, proceed against the bond.

The laws providing for such liens are usually liberally construed by the courts in favor of the claimants and are very often based on equitable principals rather than upon strict legal rules, since such rights and procedures are held to be highly remedial.

On the question of priority of the claim as against claims of the contractor's general creditors or assigns, it has been held that unpaid furnishers of labor or materials in the performance of a public contract have an equitable right in the funds due and owing the contractor but still in the possession of the public body, and this right is prior and superior to the claims of the contractor's general creditors or assigns.[2] This applies whether or not there is a statutory bond in effect protecting such labor and material suppliers.

The chief points to bear in mind respecting municipal mechanic's liens claims where applicable by statute are that:

1. The claimant be one who has furnished labor and material to a public project by subcontract or otherwise

2. There are contract funds due the contractor or which will become due from the public body

3. There exists no right against the public body itself

4. Service of appropriate notice is necessary in accordance with the statute

5. Institution of proceedings is required in accordance with the statute

Below is a typical form of notice to be used where it is in accord with the pertinent statute.

APPENDIX: Municipal Mechanic's Lien

To Whom It May Concern:

Notice is hereby given by M_____ N_____, a municipal mechanic's lien claimant who resides at No._____ Street in the City of __ _____, County of _____, *(State of)* _____, that he has performed labor and has furnished materials which have actually been performed and used in the execution and completion of a certain contract for the erection and completion of a public school house made by and between the Board of Education of the City of _____ and the C_____ Building and Construction Co., a building contractor on the _____ day of _____, 19_____, and duly filed with the Clerk of the County of _____.

1. The aforesaid public school is located at No._____ Street in the City of _____.

2. The aforesaid labor and materials have been performed for and furnished to the C_____ Building and Construction Co. by the claimant in pursuance of a contract made by and between the claimant and the Company and dated _____, 19_____.

3. The following is a statement of the labor and materials furnished by the Company to _____ Company.

(Insert Statement)

4. The amount of the claimant's demand, after the deduction of all just credits and offsets, is the sum of $_____, which is the amount claimed as justly due and owing to the claimant by the _____ Company which is the building contractor.

5. A lien is hereby claimed for the sum of $_____, being the full value

---

[2]*Stroud Oil Reclaim. Co. v. Community State Bank* 475 P2d 819 (1970).

of the labor and materials furnished by the claimant, on the monies in the control and possession of the Board of Education of the City of _____, which are due or to become due on the aforesaid contract between the Board of Education of _____ and the _____ Company.

Dated: _____ 19_____

_____
(Signature)

State of _____:

              : SS

County of _____:

    M_____ N_____, of full age, being duly sworn upon his oath according to law, deposes and says:

    1. I am the claimant who is filing the foregoing notice of a claim for a mechanic's municipal lien.

    2. I have read the foregoing notice and the facts, matters and things set forth therein are true.

_____
(Signature)

(Jurat)

Chapter **36**

Surety Bonds

KENNETH E. LEWIS, ESQ.
Partner, Anderson, McPharlin & Conners, Los Angeles, California

ROBERT F. CUSHMAN, ESQ.
Partner, Pepper, Hamilton & Scheetz, Philadelphia, Pennsylvania

FEDERAL BOND LAWS

The Miller Act

History A mechanic's lien is not enforceable on publicly owned property. It is and has been the policy in the United States that public property not be subjected to any kind of encumbrances. However, in recognition of the equitable obligation to secure payment for labor and material supplied to publicly owned property, and in lieu of the mechanic's lien, the concept of the labor-and-material bond developed. The idea was that this bond would serve as an alternate source of security for the payment of labor and material claims, thus protecting laborers and materialmen, while keeping the public property free of liens.

In addition to the labor-and-material bond, there is a second type of bond, generally known as a performance bond. When the government began utilizing private persons for construction of public buildings, the need to protect itself from contractors' default soon became apparent. The performance bond protects the government by guaranteeing the performance of the contractor.

The desire to protect the government from insolvent contractors, as well as the desire to secure the payment of laborers and materialmen on public projects, led to the enactment of the Heard Act in 1894. The Heard Act required that

> . . . any person or persons entering into a formal contract with the United States for the construction of any public building . . . shall be required before commencing such work to execute the usual penal bond, with good and sufficient sureties, with the additional obligations that such contractor or contractors shall promptly make payments to all persons supplying him or them labor and materials in the prosecution of the work provided for in such contract.

The Heard Act contemplated a single bond providing both the protection of a performance bond and a labor-and-material bond.

The Heard Act soon ran into procedural and technical difficulties most of which were eliminated in 1935 when Congressman John Miller, later a distinguished U.S. District Judge, authored and brought about the passage of the statute that bears his name. The Miller Act[1] became effective October 23, 1935; the Heard Act was repealed effective that date.

The Statute

The Miller Act provides that before any contract exceeding $2,000 in amount for the construction, alteration, or repair of any public building or public work of the United States is awarded to any person, such person shall furnish to the United States: (1) a performance surety bond in such amount as the officer awarding the contract shall deem adequate for the protection of the United States and (2) a separate payment surety bond for the protection of certain suppliers of labor and material in a sum equal to one-half of the contract price, when the total amount payable by the terms of the contract is not more than $1 million, and in a sum equal to a smaller fraction of the contract price where the total amount payable, by the terms of the contract, is more than $1 million.

The statute and subsequent amendments provide that:

1. Persons dealing directly with the general contractor are entitled to bring suit on the payment bond if not paid within 90 days after the day on which the last of their labor or material was provided.

2. Persons having no direct contractual relation with the general contractor, but contracting with a subcontractor of a general contactor, have a similar right of action *provided that* they give written notice to the general contractor within 90 days from the date they last provided labor or material for which they are making claim. This notice must state "with substantial accuracy the amount

---

[1]The Miller Act, 40 U.S.C.A. § 270a–270f.

claimed and the name of the party to whom the material was furnished." It should be sent by registered mail, postage prepaid, to the general contractor.

3. Any person desiring to bring suit on a Miller Act payment bond must do so within one year after the day upon which he last performed labor or supplied material.

4. The Comptroller General is required to provide certified copies of the Miller Act payment bond and the general contract to which it pertains upon the written application of any person stating by affidavit that he has supplied labor or materials on the bonded project.

A 1966 amendment to the Miller Act makes the payment bond surety liable for certain federal income withholding taxes (subject to proper notice from the government) which the general contractor fails to set aside and pay to the government with respect to the general contract.

Which Public Contracts Are Covered

Under the Miller Act, any contract "exceeding $2,000 in amount for the construction, alteration, or repair of any public building or public work of the United States" must be bonded. This requirement would apply to any agency of the United States government entering into a contract of this type with a private person or company. There are, however, exceptions. First of all, the government contracting officer involved can waive the Miller Act bond requirements where the contract is to be performed in a foreign country, and it would be impracticable for the contractor to obtain bonds there. Also, due to the size of the contracts involving national defense, the Secretaries of the Army, the Navy, and the Air Force may waive the requirement that Miller Act bonds be obtained in certain cost type contracts. The Secretary of the Treasury, as contracting officer for the Coast Guard, has the same right. Recently, the Miller Act was amended to provide that the Secretary of Commerce can also waive the bond requirement with respect to contracts under the purview of the Merchant Marine Act or the Merchant Ship Sales Act.

Who Is Protected by the Miller Act

In spite of the broad wording of the statute providing protection to "every person who has furnished labor or material in the prosecution of the work," there are limitations as to who is entitled to recover on the Miller Act payment bond. The courts have held that subcontractors (S) and materialmen (M) who have a direct contractual relationship with the prime contractor (PC) may bring suit on the bond. These are "first-tier claimants." The courts have held that subcontractors and materialmen having a contractual relationship with a subcontractor of the prime contractor may also bring suit on the payment bond. These are "second-tier claimants." These relationships are demonstrated in Figure 36.1. Anyone more remote than a second-tier claimant has no right of action on the bond.

One of the early disputes concerning interpretation of the Miller Act related to the statutory definition of subcontractor. The United States Supreme Court in *Clifford F. MacEvoy v. United States for Use and Benefit of Calvin Tomkins Co.*

```
        (PC)
       /    \
     /        \
   (M)        (S)   First-tier claimants
            /    \
          /        \
        (M)        (S)   Second-tier claimants
```

Fig. 36.1 PC = Prime Contractor. M = Materialman. S = Subcontractor.

addressed this issue.[2] In that case, MacEvoy, the general contractor, had purchased building material from Miller. Miller had purchased these materials from Tomkins and, although Miller was paid by MacEvoy, Miller failed to pay Tomkins. Tomkins gave MacEvoy the notice required by the statute and filed suit on MacEvoy's Miller Act bond. In effect, Tomkins claimed status as a second-tier claimant. The court denied the claim of Tomkins on the ground that Miller was not, under the statute, a subcontractor. The court defined the term subcontractor, in the context of the Miller Act bond, as "one who performs for and takes from the prime contractor a specific part of the labor or material requirements of the original contract, thus excluding ordinary laborers and materialmen."

It appears that the MacEvoy decision would have been different had Miller contracted with MacEvoy for "a specific part of the material requirements of the original contract." This distinction between one who simply provides materials to a prime contractor and one who provides to a prime contractor specific materials for the material requirements on the prime contract, has been subject to much criticism. The distinction is better drawn in two subsequent Circuit Court of Appeals cases. The first, *Brown and Root, Inc. v. Gifford-Hill Co.,* was a suit in which it was held that the plaintiff materialman could not recover.[3] Pearl had agreed with the prime contractor to furnish all the sand and gravel needs of the prime contract. Pearl then purchased some of its sand and gravel from the plaintiff. The court held that Pearl was not, under these circumstances, a subcontractor and that Pearl's supplier could not recover on the payment bond. An agreement that a subcontractor will supply all materials for the prime contract, thus does not satisfy the "specificity" requirement of *MacEvoy*.

A similar holding was reached in *United States for Use of Bryant v. Lembke Construction Co.*[4] Adams agreed with the prime contractor to supply all concrete required in the job. Adams then contracted with Bryant for sand and gravel to be used in mixing the concrete, but Bryant was not paid. The court noted that Adams did not take from the prime a specific part of the material requirements of the prime contract. Adams' supplier, Bryant, was not dealing with a subcontractor and was therefore not allowed to recover on the bond.

A case where a materials supplier was held to a subcontractor is *United States for Use of Wellman Engineering Co. v. MSI Corp.* in which the prime contractor entered into an agreement with Seneca to manufacture and supply, but not install, hydraulic lift mechanisms for missile silos.[5] Seneca contracted with the

---

[2]MacEvoy, 322 U.S. 102 (1944).
[3]319 F.2d 65 (5th Cir. 1963).
[4]370 F.2d 293 (10th Cir. 1966).
[5]350 F.2d 285 (2nd Cir. 1965).

plaintiff, Wellman, for certain of the hydraulic parts. In Wellman's suit, Seneca was held to be a subcontractor, thus entitling Wellman to recover, for the reason that Seneca provided items not readily available on the open market.

It would therefore appear that a person supplying materials to a prime contractor is more likely to be accorded the status of subcontractor for purposes of second-tier claimants where the materials supplied are custom made. General types of construction material, such as sand, gravel, or paint, are not likely to give rise to a subcontractor status to the party supplying them. On the other hand, materials which are manufactured or customized to the unique specifications of the prime contract will support a finding of subcontractor status and thus protect second-tier materialmen.

One other exception is worthy of note: In a situation where a first or second tier party is other than a bona fide entity, the court might allow recovery on a Miller Act bond for a party otherwise too remote. For example, in *Fine v. Travelers Indemnity Co.*, plaintiff supplied labor and materials to a second-tier subcontractor.[6] The Court "telescoped" and found that this second-tier subcontractor was a sham company, created solely to spread profit, but not to perform work on the project. The holding was that the plaintiff had in fact contracted with the first-tier subcontractor and was thereby entitled to recover on the bond.

Miller Act Notice Requirements

Persons providing labor or material directly to the prime contractor (PC) are not subjected to any notice requirement by the Miller Act. The contractor knows or should know whether he is indebted to the subcontractors (S) and material suppliers (M) with whom he deals. These persons (first-tier claimants) need merely wait 90 days from the day on which the last of their labor was performed or material supplied and, if not paid by that time, may file suit.

For persons other than those dealing directly with the prime contractor, however, notice *is* required in order to have a right of action on the bond. The statute provides that a second-tier claimant (that is, any person having a contractual relationship with a subcontractor of the prime contractor but with no express or implied contractual relationship with the prime), must give written notice to the prime. See Figure 36.2.

The notice must be given within 90 days from the date on which the labor or material for which the claim is made was last furnished. The notice must state "with substantial accuracy" the amount claimed and the identity of the subcontractor with whom the claimant dealt. The statute indicates that the notice

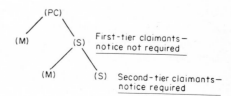

Fig. 36.2 PC = Prime Contractor. M = Materialman. S = Subcontractor.

[6]233 F. Supp. 672 (W.D. Mo. 1964).

should be sent by registered mail, postage prepaid, addressed to the prime contractor at the place where he maintains his office or conducts his business, or where he resides, and that service of the notice may also be made by the United States Marshal in the same fashion in which he would normally serve a court summons.

The notice requirements of the Miller Act have, understandably, led to a substantial amount of litigation. The courts have been extremely liberal in dealing with the problems related to form and content of the notice. For example, in *Fleisher Engineering & Construction Co. v. United States for Use of Hallenbeck,* it was held that the statutory requirement of notice "by registered mail" was not mandatory so long as it is demonstrated that written notice was actually received by the prime contractor.[7]

The liberality of the courts in construing the content required in the notice is reflected in *United States for Use of Kelly-Mohrhusen & Co. v. Patnode Co.*[8] In that suit, plaintiff's attorney telephoned the prime contractor to advise that the subcontractor involved was in bankruptcy and that the plaintiff looked to the prime contractor for payment of the goods supplied to the bankrupt subcontractor. He was advised by the prime contractor that funds would be available for this purpose. The attorney then confirmed the telephone conversation with a letter in which he neglected, however, to identify the subcontractor. Even though the statute requires the notice to state the name of the party to whom the material or labor was furnished, the court held that the letter, considered together with the telephone conversation, satisfied the statute. Plaintiff was allowed to recover.

The Ninth Circuit Court of Appeals has recently held in *United States for Use of Bailey v. Freethy* that two letters written to the prime contractor were sufficient to constitute notice under the statute.[9] The court held that the critical factor as to the content of the notice is that it "must inform the prime contractor, expressly or by implication, that the supplier (of material or labor) is looking to the [prime] contractor for payment of the subcontractor's bill."

The provision of the act that notice be served by mailing it to the contractor at any place where he maintains an office or conducts his business or to his residence is generally followed and consequently has not given rise to much controversy.

The timeliness of notice, however, is a controversial subject. The courts have viewed notice as a legitimate and reasonable requirement of the statute. Notice, of course, is for the protection of the prime contractor. The prime, upon being notified, can withhold from funds otherwise due his subcontractors, sums sufficient to satisfy the labor and material suppliers who had put him on notice. There is a split of authority on the issue of whether notice must be *sent* within 90 days or *received* within 90 days. In one suit, it was held that as long as the notice was sent within 90 days, there was compliance with the statute. There is

---

[7]311 U.S. 15 (1940).
[8]457 F.2d 116 (7th Cir. 1972).
[9]469 F.2d 1348 (9th Cir. 1972).

legal opinion to the contrary, however, and it is therefore preferable that the second-tier claimant be sure that his notice is actually received by the prime contractor within 90 days.[10]

The general rule is that for a single or *entire* contract, the 90-day-notice measuring period begins to run from the date the last material or labor for which the claim is made was furnished. Where there were two series of deliveries of materials to a subcontractor, and more than 90 days expired between the completion of the first series and the beginning of the second series, notice made within 90 days after the completion of the second series has been held not to be effective as to the first series.[11] The reasoning is that a later shipment should not be permitted to revive a Miller Act liability that has extinguished and thereby place in jeopardy payments properly made by the prime to his subcontractor in the interval. A second-tier materialman should therefore protect himself and give notice to the prime if a delivery of materials on a project is interrupted for a period approaching 90 days.[12]

The courts have, on occasion, bent over backward to find that notice was timely given. For example, in *United States ex rel. General Electric Co. v. Gunnar I. Johnson & Sons,* it was held that the electrical system involved was not completed until two defective parts, without which the system was not operational, were delivered.[13] The bulk of the system had been previously installed, but notice was given more than ninety days after all work had terminated, other than the installation of these two replacement parts. A contrary decision was reached in *United States ex rel. General Electric Co. v. H. E. Lewis Construction Co.,* in which plaintiff delivered two fixtures to replace those broken by the subcontractor.[14] Notice was given more than 90 days from the completion of the fixture deliveries, but within 90 days from the date of the delivery of the replacements. The court held that the delivery of the replacements was not the determinative date and that the plaintiff failed to notify the prime contractor in time. The theory of the later case is that if the period of notice were extended by the replacement of these minor defective parts, shrewd suppliers would leave a few defects in their work to give them an edge.

A unique case is *United States for Use of Dukane Corp. v. U.S.F. & G. Co.* where materials were delivered on a credit basis, and subsequently other materials were delivered on a c.o.d. basis.[15] The court held that the delivery of the c.o.d. materials did not extend the 90-day notice period. The court's reasoning was that notice is required within 90 days of last providing labor or materials *for which the claim is made.* Plaintiff was not making a claim for the materials delivered c.o.d. so notice was necessary within 90 days of the last credit delivery.

---

[10]*United States for Use of Crowe v. Continental Cas. Co.,* 245 F. Supp. 871 (E.D. La. 1965).

[11]*United States for Use of Westinghouse Elec. Supply Co. v. Endebrock-White Co.,* 275 F.2d 57 (4th Cir. 1960); *see also United States for Use of J. A. Edwards & Co. v. Peter Reiss Constr. Co.,* 273 F.2d 880 (2nd Cir. 1959), *cert. denied,* 362 U.S. 951 (1960).

[12]*United States for Use of I. Burack, Inc. v. Sovereign Constr. Co.,* 338 F. Supp. 657 (D.C. N.Y. 1972).

[13]310 F.2d 899 (8th Cir. 1962).

[14]375 F.2d 194 (2nd Cir. 1967).

[15]422 F.2d 597 (4th Cir. 1970).

With regard to labor, the general rule is that the 90-day period begins to run from the last date work called for in the contract was supplied. Work done for the purpose of correcting defects or for the purpose of making repairs does not usually extend the 90-day period.[16]

In order to ensure that there be no 90-day problem on a Miller Act claim, it is important that notice be given promptly after the conclusion of any contract or agreement and promptly after the completion of each series of deliveries of materials.

When and Where Suit Must Be Brought

The statute, as amended in 1959, specifically provides that suit must be filed within one year after the day on which the last labor or material was furnished. This is not the same standard used in determining whether the 90-day notice was given in time. The notice provision requires the notice within 90 days of furnishing the labor or materials "for which the claim is made." In calculating the one year for filing suit, however, the court looks only to the last day upon which labor or materials were furnished. The suit can seek recovery for labor and materials furnished more than one year *prior to* suit so long as timely notice for that labor or material was given.[17]

As in the case of notice, supplying labor or materials to correct defects does not, as a general rule, extend the time for filing suit—nor does the making of final inspections.[18]

There have been situations in which the surety was barred from asserting the one-year statute. They arise only when the surety acted in such a fashion as to encourage the claimant to delay the institution of suit.[19] Generally the courts are strict in enforcing the one-year provision.

Miller Act suits are to be brought "in the name of the United States for the use of the person suing, in the United States District Court in which the contract was to be performed and executed and not elsewhere." This rule is subject to qualification only where the written agreement pursuant to which the plaintiff has filed suit provides for mandatory arbitration. Where the arbitration clause is enforceable by local law, the federal court, on a timely motion, will stay the outcome of the litigation pending arbitration.[20] Initiation of arbitration does not, however, eliminate the requirement that the Miller Act suit be commenced within one year.[21]

[16]*Johnson Service Co. v. Transamerica Ins. Co.,* 349 F. Supp. 1220, *aff'd* 485 F.2d (5th Cir. 1973).

[17]*General Elec. Co. v. Southern Constr. Co.* 383 F.2d 135 (5th Cir. 1967) rev. 229 F. Supp. 873 (1964 and 236 F. Supp. 742 (1964. *See United States for Use of Harris Paint Co. v. Seaboard Sur. Co.* 437 F. 2d 37 (5th Cir. 1971) *aff.* 312 F. Supp. 751.

[18]*General Ins. Co. of America v. United States for Use of Audley Moor & Son,* 406 F.2d 442 (5th Cir. 1969), *cert. denied,* 396 U.S. 902 (1969).

[19]*United States for Use of Atlas Erection Co. v. Continental Cas. Co.,* 357 F. Supp. 795 (E.D. La. 1973); see also *Sam Finley, Inc. v. Pilcher, Livingston & Wallace, Inc.,* 314 F. Supp. 654 (D.C. Ga. 1970).

[20]*United States for Use of Capolino Sons, v. Electronic & Missile Facilities, Inc.,* 364 F.2d 705 (9th Cir. 1966), *cert. denied,* 385 U.S. 924.

[21]*United States for Use of Wrecking Corp. of Am. v. Edward R. Marden Corp.,* 289 F. Supp. 141, *aff'd* 406 F.2d 525 (D. Mass. 1968).

Types of Claims Recoverable

Labor furnished for the construction, alteration, or repair of a public building or public work is covered by the Miller Act payment bond. This would include manhours spent on the project, at the then prevailing hourly rate or the amount specified in the claimant's agreement. A subcontractor whose sole function was to provide labor of some sort, without regard to materials, could surely recover on the payment bond. The problems which arise invariably involve the question of what is included within the concept of materials.

The courts have moved away from the nineteenth-century notion that a claimant can recover only if the materials supplied were incorporated into the constructed unit. Today, it would be safe to state that recovery can be made under a Miller Act payment bond for the following:

1. Items incorporated into and made a part of the building structure.
2. Items used or consumed in erecting the structure.
3. The cost of repairs on equipment made necessary by its use on the construction.
4. Rental costs for equipment used on the construction.
5. Other materials furnished in the prosecution of the contract.

An early case concluded that anything indispensable to the completion of the work contracted for fell within the meaning of materials under the Miller Act.[22] Another early case decided that the value of room and board, including groceries, was recoverable under a Miller Act payment bond where the location of the work was so remote that such provisions had to be made.[23] Fuel consumed, such as gasoline or coal, is also covered so long as it is actually consumed in the construction process. On the other hand, insurance premiums charged a contractor, in the nature of workmen's compensation or otherwise, have been held not to be covered under a Miller Act bond.[24]

Equipment rental is a subject which has been repeatedly litigated. The general rule is that the Miller Act provides protection for the rental of equipment the use of which is necessary in the work of construction.[25] The courts are careful to analyze rental claims to confirm that the amount claimed is the true and fair rental value of the equipment involved and not a payment toward the purchase price on the sale of equipment which is not covered under the bond.

The replacement of parts and equipment is covered by the bond where they are damaged, destroyed, or consumed in the prosecution of the project. However, should the replacement substantially increase the value of the machinery, rendering it available for other projects, then there is no bond coverage. In this latter case, the replacement is deemed a capital expenditure: the Miller Act is not intended to provide a source of investment capital.

---

[22]*United States for Use of Watsabaugh & Co. v. Seaboard Sur. Co.,* 26 F. Supp. 681 (D.C. Mont. 1938), *sustained* 106 F.2d 355 (1939).

[23]*John P. Brogan v. National Sur. Co.,* 246 U.S. 257 (1918).

[24]*United States for Use of General Accident Fire & Life Assur. Corp. v. Maguire Homes, Inc.,* 186 F. Supp. 659 (D. Mass. 1959).

[25]*Riebel & Hartman, Inc. v. United States for Use of Codell Constr. Co.,* 238 F.2d 394 (6th Cir. 1956).

The act covers a reasonable value of equipment specifically purchased for a Miller Act job, and which would not be valuable or available for other jobs.[26] The limitation on this rule is demonstrated in one suit where the cost of a laborer's tools was held not recoverable in a suit on the bond.[27]

In some cases, the courts have made the distinction that replacement of permanent equipment is not covered by a Miller Act bond. On the other hand, repairs which were made necessary as a consequence of ordinary wear and tear on a Miller Act job are covered by the bond.

In *United States for Use of J. P. Bryne & Co. v. Fire Assoc. of Philadelphia* plaintiff sold to the prime contractor heavy duty tires for earth-moving equipment.[28] It was contemplated and agreed that the tires would be substantially used up by the prime on the project. However, there was an unexpected stoppage of work, and the tires were not actually consumed. The court held that the claimant did not have to show that the tires were in fact substantially consumed in the project, but rather only that he reasonably contemplated that they would be. The court here held the surety liable to the seller of the tires for their reasonable value.

Transportation-related costs are under most circumstances protected by a Miller Act payment bond. For example, a railroad which had transported construction materials for use in the construction of a United States post office furnished labor within the purview of the bond.[29]

In *Bill Curphy Co. v. Elliot* plaintiff brought suit for the repayment of money it had loaned to a Miller Act subcontractor for the purpose of meeting its payroll.[30] The court held that even if the borrowed money had been wholly applied to the payment of the cost of labor or material, there was no coverage. Money was not "labor and material furnished."

A unique line of cases has developed concerning substituted materials. In *Commercial Standard Insurance Co. v. United States ex rel. Crane Co.* the plaintiff furnished steel pipe to a contractor for use in a Miller Act project.[31] The contractor, however, used his own pipe on the project and stockpiled the material provided by the plaintiff. The court held that the plaintiff had furnished the pipe in the prosecution of the work and that the claim was therefore valid.

Liability for Attorneys' Fees, Costs, and Interest

There is no provision in the Miller Act for the award of attorneys' fees in a Miller Act suit. This led to a number of lawsuits and conflicting rules. Prior to 1974, the general rule was that the successful Miller Act plaintiff's entitlement

---

[26]*Continental Cas. Co. v. Clarence L. Boyd Co.*, 140 F.2d 115 (10th Cir. 1944); see also *United States for Use of Wyatt & Kipper Eng., Inc. v. Ramstad Constr. Co.*, 194 F. Supp. 379 (D. Alaska 1961).

[27]Burack, Inc., *supra* note 14.

[28]260 F.2d 541 (2nd Cir. 1958).

[29]*Standard Accident Ins. Co. v. United States for Use of Powell*, 302 U.S. 442 (1938).

[30]207 F.2d 103 (5th Cir. 1955).

[31]213 F.2d 106 (10th Cir. 1954).

to attorneys' fees was determined by reference to the prevailing policy of the state in which the suit was heard.[32] The United States Supreme Court has recently changed this rule. In *F. D. Rich Co. v. United States for Use of Industrial Lumber Co.* the court reaffirmed the "American Rule" governing the award of attorneys' fees in federal court litigation.[33] The American Rule is that attorneys' fees are not recoverable unless there is a statute or enforceable contract specifically providing for them. Although the lower court had followed the former general rule and applied the "public policy of the State where the suit was heard," the Supreme Court held that the Miller Act was an exclusively federal remedy. The Court deemed it wise "to extricate the Federal Courts from the morass of trying to define State policy." Consequently, without bad faith or vexatious delay on the surety's part, attorneys' fees cannot be collected by a Miller Act claimant.

Unlike the recent ruling of the United States Supreme Court with respect to attorneys' fees, a plaintiff's right to interest is still determined by the law of the state in which the contract and bond were performed.[34] The majority rule would appear to be that interest should be allowed to a successful Miller Act plaintiff from the date upon which the amount of the claim became admittedly due. However, if there is a legitimate dispute as to the entitlement or the amount of the claim, interest may be awarded only from the date of entry of judgment.[35]

The Federal Rules of Civil Procedure providing for the award of costs to the prevailing party in a civil suit have been held applicable to Miller Act claims. The prevailing party, whether claimant or defendant, can recover his costs, although the purview of this term is limited. Only items such as filing fees, costs of service of process, and costs of deposition transcripts are normally awarded. Attempts to include attorneys' fees as a cost have, at times, succeeded in the past. However, in light of the recent ruling in *F. D. Rich Co.,* this will not happen in the future.[36]

Conclusion

The Miller Act provides a safe and relatively clear-cut procedure for the protection of the United States government and for the protection of persons providing labor and material on a bonded federal construction contract. Although areas of the statute are unclear and have led to litigation, suppliers of labor and/or materials on a Miller Act job can protect themselves by first ascertaining that they fall within a recoverable tier before entering into their contracts, and second, by complying with the notice and time for suit requirements after they do.

---

[32] *United States for Use of Pritchard Prod. Corp. v. Fullerton Constr. Co.,* 407 F.2d 1002 (4th Cir. 1969).
[33] 417 U.S. 116 (1974).
[34] *Illinois Sur. Co. v. John Davis Co.,* 244 U.S. 376 (1917).
[35] *United States for Use of Carter-Schneider-Nelson, Inc. v. Campbell,* 293 F.2d 816 (9th Cir. 1961), *cert. denied,* 368 U.S. 987.
[36] *Rich, supra* note 35.

Other Projects

The Atomic Energy Commission requires bid, payment, and performance bonds of its prime contractors on fixed-price construction contracts. On a cost type of contract, however, Miller Act bonds are not required, but prime contractors are required to secure Miller Act type of bonds for subcontractors.

The Small Business Administration requires 100 percent performance and payment bonds.

The United States Department of Housing and Urban Development (HUD), Federal Housing Administration, requires a performance bond and a payment bond for its larger construction and rehabilitation projects.

STATE PUBLIC WORK BONDS

Introduction and History

There are primarily two reasons why each of our states now requires its public works contractors to furnish surety bonds for the protection of suppliers of labor and material. The first is moral: a recognition of its obligation as an owner to see that those supplying its construction projects are paid in full. The second is practical: the acceptance of the reality that subcontractors of higher quality will bid to their contractors, and probably at lower prices, when payment is guaranteed by a corporate surety.

State statutes also require bonds guaranteeing performance of their construction contracts. Most, but not all, require two separate contract bonds which avoids the possibility of the owner exhausting the penal sum (the face value) of the bond in completing the work of its breaching contractor, leaving suppliers and subcontractors with little or no protection.

State bond statutes often apply to contracts of their political subdivisions, their counties, cities, water, sewer and school districts, as well as their junior taxing authorities.

In spite of the complexity of statutory bond requirements and the lack of uniformity of court decisions, it is apparent that both the purpose of the statutes and the trend of the court decisions are designed for and lead to (1) the protection of the creditor, to see that he is paid for the work that he performs on the public project and (2) the protection of the public, to see that it has its project properly completed.

Summary of Notice and Time for Suit Provisions

A detailed analysis of public works bond legislation in each state, as well as reference to the principal court decisions interpreting these statutes, is beyond the scope of this chapter.

The amount of bond coverage; what projects are covered; the smaller construction contract exclusions; the nature of labor and material covered under these statutes; requirements pertaining to place of suit; waiting periods necessary before filing suits; notice provisions to the surety, the municipality, the principal contractor (both as to time for notice and contents thereof); procedures to obtain copies of payment bonds; time periods for commencing suit; and, most important, the special provisions applicable to each state public works bond statute, must be explored or bond rights can be lost.

Generally in determining what constitutes labor and material under state statutes, state courts follow decisions of federal courts. For example, where there is no specific reference to equipment in a state statute, most courts have followed the federal decisions and hold that coverage for rental of equipment is included. For the most part, recovery is not limited to material actually incorporated in the work, but covers labor and material fabricated for or supplied in the prosecution of work whether used or not. As a general rule, unless there is an express provision covering insurance premiums and taxes, they are not given bond protection.

Whether overalls for workmen or veterinary services for mules of a road contractor are "materials used in the prosecution of the work" and therefore covered under the bond, and whether rental of tools or freight charges or unemployment compensation, workmen's compensation, or other state and local taxes are within the coverage of the bond, are often matters of court interpretation. As statutes vary, so do court decisions within the different jurisdictions. None of these questions can be answered categorically.

Of primary concern to a labor and material supplier seeking protection under the state bond statutes are the two *time* requirement categories under the payment bond. These requirements are, first, the time within which notice must be given to preserve bond rights, and second, the time within which suit must be brought against the bonding company. A failure to meet these requirements will result in absolute forfeiture of bond rights. These time requirements are set forth on a statewide basis, but because they are subject to legislative change and court interpretation, they should be considered as guidelines and not legal advice or legal opinion on specific facts.

ALABAMA

Notice Required: To surety—45 days prior to the institution of suit.

Time for Suit on Bond: Must be commenced not later than one year from the date of final settlement of the contract.

ALASKA

Notice Required: To principal contractor—Within 90 days of performance of work or furnishing of material for which claim is made if claimant has no contractual relationship with principal contractor.

Time for Suit on Bond: Must be commenced not later than one year from the date of final settlement of the contract.

ARIZONA

Notice Required: To principal contractor—Within 90 days of performance of work or furnishing of material for which claim is made if claimant has no contractual relationship with principal contractor.

Time for Suit on Bond: Must be commenced not later than one year from the date on which the last of the labor was done or performed or materials were furnished or supplied for which claim is made.

ARKANSAS

Notice Required: No special statutory provisions.

Time for Suit on Bond: Within six months from the date that final payment is made on the contract.

CALIFORNIA

Notice Required: No special notice is required from a claimant having a direct contractual relation with the original (general) contractor. However, a claimant having no such direct contractual relation must give written preliminary bond notice to the original contractor within 90 days from the date of having furnished the last labor, services, equipment, or materials for which claim is made.

Time for Suit on Bond: An action on a public works bond must be brought within six months from the time within which the claimant may file a stop notice. Claimant may file a stop notice only if done within 30 days of the recordation of the notice of completion or notice of cessation or, if no such notice is recorded, within 90 days after completion of the project or cessation of labor thereon.

COLORADO

Notice Required: Person furnishing labor or material to contractor or subcontractor, at any time up to and including the time of final settlement for the work contracted to be done, which final settlement shall be duly advertised at least 10 days prior thereto in the county or counties where the work was contracted for and wherein such work was performed, may file with the official awarding the contract, a verified statement of the amount due and unpaid, whereupon such official shall withhold payments from contractor sufficient to ensure the payment of such claim, until the same has been paid or the claim has been properly withdrawn. However, such funds shall not be withheld longer than 90 days following the date fixed for final settlement, unless an action is commenced within that time to enforce such unpaid claim and notice thereof is filed with the public body by whom the contract was awarded.

Time for Suit on Bond: Within six months after the completion of the public work.

CONNECTICUT

Notice Required: To principal contractor—Within 90 days of performance of work or furnishing of materials for which claim is made if claimant has no contractual relationship with principal contractor.

Time for Suit on Bond: Within one year after the day on which the last of the labor was performed or materials were supplied by the claimant.

DELAWARE

Notice Required: No special statutory provision.

Time for Suit on Bond: If the bond so provides, no suit shall be commenced after the expiration of one year following the date on which the successful bidder ceases work on the contract, otherwise suits may be commenced at any time within three years following the date the last work was done on the contract.

DISTRICT OF COLUMBIA

Notice Required: To principal contractor—Within 90 days of performance of work or furnishing of material for which claim is made if claimant has no contractual relationship with principal contractor.

Time for Suit on Bond: Within one year after the date on which the claimant supplied the last of his labor or material.

FLORIDA

Notice Required: (a) To surety—A claimant who is not in privity with the contractor and who has not received payment for his labor, materials or supplies, shall within 90 days after performance of the labor or complete delivery of materials and supplies, deliver to the surety written notice of the performance of the labor or delivery of the materials or supplies and of the nonpayment.

(b) To principal contractor—A claimant, except a laborer, who is not in privity with the contractor and who has not received payment for his labor, materials or supplies shall, within 45 days after beginning to furnish labor, material or supplies for the prosecution of such work, furnish the contractor with a notice that he intends to look to the bond for protection. A claimant who is not in privity with the contractor and who has not received payment for his labor, material or supplies, shall within 90 days after performance of the labor or after complete delivery of all the material or supplies, deliver to the contractor written notice of the non-payment.

(c) To municipality—Application to governmental entity having charge of the work.

Time for Suit on Bond: Within one year from the performance of the labor or completion of delivery of the materials and supplies.

GEORGIA

Notice Required: To principal contractor—Within 90 days of performance of work or furnishing of material for which claim is made if claimant has no contractual relationship with principal contractor.

Time for Suit on Bond: Within one year after the completion of the contract and the acceptance of the public building or public work by the proper public authority.

HAWAII

Notice Required: A creditor instituting a first suit must give personal notice of the pendency of the suit to all known creditors. In addition thereto, notice by publication for at least three successive weeks is required to be given in some newspaper of general circulation in the state (county) at least once in each of three successive weeks, the last publication to be at least one month before the expiration of the five-month period hereafter referred to.

Time for Suit on Bond: If the state starts suit the claimant must intervene therein. If no action is brought by the state within two months from the completion and final settlement of any contract, the claimant upon applying therefor and furnishing an affidavit to the superintendent of public works or other officer representing the state in the matter of such contract that labor or materials for the prosecution of such work have been furnished by him, and that payment therefor has not been made, will be furnished with a certified copy of the contract and bond upon which he is authorized to bring an action in the name of the state in the Circuit Court of the circuit in which the contract was to be performed and not elsewhere, for his use and benefit. This separate action by the claimant shall not be commenced until after complete performance of the contract and final settlement thereof, but must be commenced within four months after the performance and final settlement and not later.

IDAHO

Notice Required: To principal contractor—Within 90 days of performance of work or furnishing of material for which claim is made if claimant has no contractual relationship with principal contractor.

Time for Suit on Bond: No such suit shall be commenced after the expiration of one year from the date on which claimant performed the last of the labor or furnished or supplied the last of the material for which such suit is brought, except that if the claimant is a subcontractor of the contractor, no such suit shall be commenced after the expiration of one year from the date on which final payment under the subcontract became due.

ILLINOIS

Notice Required: Every person furnishing material or performing labor, either as an individual or as a subcontractor for any contractor with the state or any political subdivision thereof, has a right to sue on the bond provided, however, that any person having a claim for labor or material as aforesaid shall have no such right of action unless he shall have filed verified notice of claim with the officer, board, bureau or department awarding the contract within 180 days after the date of the last item of work or the furnishing of the last item of materials.

Time for Suit on Bond: The statute provides that no action shall be brought on the bond until the expiration of 120 days after the date of the last item of work or the furnishing of the last item of materials, except in cases where the final settlement between the public body and the contractor shall have been made prior to the expiration of the 120-day period, "in which case action may be taken immediately following such final settlement, nor shall any action of any kind be brought later than six months after the acceptance by the State or political subdivision thereof, or the building project or work."

INDIANA

Notice Required: To surety—On state highway, road, and bridge contracts, a claimant is required, within one year after the acceptance of the improvement by the State Highway Commission, to furnish to the surety a statement of the amount due.

Time for Suit on Bond: Except in the case of state highway, road, and bridge contracts, no suit shall be brought against the surety until the expiration of 30 days after the filing of the verified duplicate statement, but action must be commenced within 60 days from the date of the final completion and acceptance of the public building or public work. In the case of state highway, road, and bridge contracts, suit may not be brought on the bond until the expiration of 60 days after the furnishing of the statement of the amount due to the surety. Suit on such bond may be instituted at the expiration of such period of 60 days, but the suit must be commenced within 18 months from the date of the final acceptance of such highway or improvement.

IOWA

Notice Required: No part of the unpaid fund due the contractor shall be retained on claims for material furnished other than material ordered by the general contractor or the authorized agent thereof unless such claims are supported by a certified statement that the general contractor has been notified within 30 days after the materials are furnished, or by itemized invoices rendered to the contractor during the progress of the work, of the amount, kind, and value of the material furnished for use upon said public improvement. Claimant may file with the officer charged by law to issue warrants in payment of the public improvement an itemized, written statement of his claim. In case of highway improvements for the county, claims shall be filed with the county auditor of the county letting the contract.

Time for Suit on Bond: Claims may be filed with the proper officer at any time before the expiration of 30 days immediately following the completion and final acceptance of the improvement, and at any time after said 30-day period if the public corporation has not paid the full contract price and no action is pending to adjudicate rights in and to the unpaid portion of the contract price. The court may allow claims to be filed during the pendency of any action, at any time after the expiration of 30 days and not later than 60 days following the completion and final acceptance of the public improvement.

KANSAS

Notice Required: A claimant for labor, materials, or supplies furnished in the construction, improvement, reconstruction, and maintenance of a state highway system may not sue on the bond unless, within six months after the completion date of the contract, according to the records of the State Highway Commission, there be filed with the State Highway Commission an itemized statement of the amount of the indebtedness.

Time for Suit on Bond: On bonds other than state highway bonds, no action shall be brought on the bond after six months from the completion of the public improvement. On bonds given in connection with the construction, improvement, reconstruction, and maintenance of the state highway system, no action may be brought after one year from the completion of the contract.

KENTUCKY

There is no general statute in Kentucky requiring general contractors to produce a bond for the protection of labor and materialmen. However, subcontractors may recover on a bond conditioned for payment of labor and material bills. The statutory limitation of the time for commencing a civil action upon a bond or obligation for the payment of money or property is fifteen years after the cause of action has accrued. (However, a reasonable limitation of the time for suit, if set forth in a bond, such as one year, etc., may be upheld by a Court.)

LOUISIANA

Notice Required: Before any person having a direct contractual relationship with a subcontractor, but no contractual relationship with a contractor, shall have a right of action against the contractor or the surety on the bond furnished by the contractor, he shall record his claim or give written notice to said contractor within 45 days from the recordation of the notice of acceptance by the owner of the work or notice by the owner of default.

Time for Suit on Bond: Within one year from the registry of acceptance of the work or notice of default of the contractor.

MAINE

Notice Required: To principal contractor—Within 90 days of performance of work or furnishing of material for which claim is made if claimant has no contractual relationship with principal contractor.

Time for Suit on Bond: Within one year from the date on which the last of the labor was performed or material was supplied for the payment of which such action is brought.

MARYLAND

Notice Required: To principal contractor—Within 90 days of performance of work or furnishing of material for which claim is made if claimant has no contractual relationship with principal contractor.

Time for Suit on Bond: Must be commenced not later than one year from the date of final acceptance of the work performed under the contract.

MASSACHUSETTS

Notice Required: To principal contractor—Within 65 days of performance of work or furnishing of material for which claim is made if claimant has no contractual relationship with principal contractor. Special provisions are set forth for specially fabricated material.

Time for Suit on Bond: Within one year after the date of last performance.

MICHIGAN

Notice Required: To principal contractor—No notice is required by a claimant having a contractual relationship with the principal contractor. A claimant not having a direct contractual relationship with the principal contractor does not have a right of action upon the payment bond unless:

(1) Claimant has within 30 days after furnishing the first of such material or performing the first of such labor served on the principal contractor a written notice which shall inform the principal of the nature of the materials being furnished or to be furnished or labor being performed or to be performed and identifying the party contracting for such labor or material and the site for the performance of such work or the delivery of such materials.

(2) Claimant has given written notice to the contractor and the governmental unit involved within 90 days from the date on which the claimant performed the last of the labor or furnished or supplied the last of the material for which the claim was made, stating with substantial accuracy the amount claimed and the name of the

party to whom the material was furnished or supplied or for whom the labor was done or performed.

Time for Suit on Bond: One year from the date on which final payment was made to the principal contractor.

MINNESOTA

Notice Required: To municipality—No action shall be maintained on the bond unless, within 90 days after the completion of the contract and the acceptance thereof by the proper public authority, the claimant shall file a written notice specifying the nature and amount of his claim and the date of furnishing the last item thereof in the office of the commissioner of insurance, in case the contract is for the performance of work for the state or any department thereof, or in the office of the county auditor, in case the contract is let by any county, municipal corporation, or other public board or body, of the county in which such municipal corporation, public board or body is situate, and if situate in two or more counties then such notice shall be filed in the office of the county auditor of each of the counties. The official with whom the claimant files written notice shall mail one copy to each of the sureties on the bond and to the principal contractor.

Time for Suit on Bond: One year after the service of the notice.

MISSISSIPPI

Notice Required: To creditors—Notice of the pendency of suit shall be made by publication in some newspaper of general circulation published in the county or town where the contract is being performed if there be such paper; otherwise, in a paper having a general circulation therein, for at least three weeks, the last publication to be at least one week before the trial of the suit.

Time for Suit on Bond: If the municipal corporation starts suit, subcontractors and materialmen intervene therein. If no suit is brought by the municipality within six months from the completion and final settlement of the contract, claimant may start suit.

Suit by subcontractors and materialmen may not be instituted until after (1) complete performance of the contract, (2) final settlement thereof, (3) the public body has published notice thereof in some newspaper published in the county or, if there be none, then in some newspaper having a general circulation therein. Suit must be commenced within one year after performance and final settlement of the contract and not later, provided that, if the contractor quits or abandons the contract before its completion, suit may be instituted by any such claimant on said bond and shall be commenced within one year after such abandonment and not later. An amendment of May 15, 1962, sanctions intervention by other claimants where suit has been instituted under the contract bond. However, such intervention must occur within the time limited for such persons to bring an original action. It also permits the surety to require all known claimants under the bond to be joined as parties in any action thereunder.

MISSOURI

Notice Required: None

Time for Suit on Bond: The Revised Code of General Ordinances for St. Louis contains a section providing that no suit shall be instituted on the bond after the expiration of 90 days from the completion of the public contract.

MONTANA

Notice Required: To principal contractor—Not later than 30 days after the date of the first delivery of the provender, material, supplies, or provisions to any subcontractor or agent of any person, firm, or corporation having a subcontract with respect to the prosecution of said public work. Notice is required to be given to the municipality within 90 days from and after the completion of the contract.

Time for Suit on Bond: None

NEBRASKA

Notice Required: To principal contractor—Within four months of performance of the work or furnishing of material for which claim is made if claimant has no contractual relationship with principal contractor.

Time for Suit on Bond: Not later than one year after final settlement of the principal contract.

NEVADA

Notice Required: No notice is required by a claimant having a contractual relationship, expressed or implied, with the principal contractor. Any claimant who has a direct contractual relationship with any subcontractor of the contractor who gave such payment bond, but no contractual relationship, expressed or implied, with such contractor, may bring an action on the payment bond, only:
1. If he has, within 30 days after furnishing the first of such materials or performing the first of such labor, served on the contractor a written notice which shall inform the latter of the nature of the materials being furnished or to be furnished, or the labor performed or to be performed, and identifying the person contracting for such labor or materials and the site for the performance of such labor or materials.
2. After giving written notice to such contractor within 90 days from the date on which the claimant performed the last of the labor or furnished the last of the materials for which he claims payment.

Time for Suit on Bond: Must be commenced not later than one year from the date claimant performed the last of the labor or furnished the last of the material for which claim is made.

NEW HAMPSHIRE

Notice Required: In order to obtain the benefit of such bond any person, firm, or corporation having any claim for labor performed, materials, machinery, tools, or equipment furnished as aforesaid, shall within 90 days after the completion and acceptance of the project by the contracting party, file in the office of the secretary of state, if the state is a contracting party, or with the Department of Public Works and Highways, if the state is a party to said contract by or through said department, or in the office of the clerk of the superior court for the county within which the contract shall be principally performed, if any political subdivision of the state is a contracting party, a statement of the claim; a copy of which shall forthwith be sent by mail by the office where it is filed to the principal and surety.

Time for Suit on Bond: One year after filing of claim as above.

NEW JERSEY

Notice Required: Must give notice to surety prior to acceptance of the public improvement or within 80 days thereafter.

Time for Suit on Bond: Must be commenced within one year from the date of acceptance of the building, work, or improvement.

NEW MEXICO

Notice Required: To principal contractor—Within 90 days of performance of work or furnishing of material for which claim is made if claimant has no contractual relationship with principal contractor. Claimant must also notify public body of commencement of suit.

Time for Suit on Bond: Within one year after date of final settlement of the contract.

NEW YORK

Notice Required: To principal contractor—Within 90 days of performance of work or furnishing of material for which claim is made if claimant has no contractual relationship with principal contractor.

Time for Suit on Bond: No action on a payment bond shall be commenced after the expiration of one year from the date on which the claimant performed the last of the labor or furnished the last of the material for which such action is brought, except that if the claimant is a subcontractor of the contractor no such action shall be commenced after the expiration of one year from the date on which final payment under the subcontract became due.

NORTH CAROLINA

Notice Required: To principal contractor—Within 90 days of performance of work or furnishing of material for which claim is made if claimant has no contractual relationship with principal contractor.

Time for Suit on Bond: At any time after the expiration of 90 days after claimant performed the last of the labor or furnished the last of the material for which he claims payment, but no such suit may be commenced after the expiration of the "longer period of one year from the day on which the last of the labor was performed or material was furnished by the claimant, or one year from the day on which final settlement was made with the contractor."

NORTH DAKOTA

Notice Required: To principal contractor—Within 90 days of performance of work or furnishing of material for which claim is made if claimant has no contractual relationship with principal contractor.

Time for Suit on Bond: Suit must be commenced within one year after completion of the claimant's contribution of labor, material, or supplies. Prior to 1973, suit had to be brought within six months after the first publication of notice to file claims was given by the contractor or surety.

OHIO

Notice Required: At any time after furnishing labor or material, but not later than 90 days after the acceptance of the public improvement by the duly authorized board or officer, claimant shall furnish surety a statement of the amount due.

Time for Suit on Bond: Suit must be commenced not later than one year from date of acceptance of the public improvement.

OKLAHOMA

Notice Required: To principal contractor—Within 90 days of performance of work or furnishing of material for which claim is made if claimant has no contractual relationship with principal contractor. Claimant must give notice to the surety as well within 90 days.

Time for Suit on Bond: No action shall be brought on said payment bond after one year from the date on which the last of the labor was performed or materials or parts furnished for which such claim is made.

OREGON

Notice Required: To principal contractor—Within 90 days of performance of work or furnishing of material for which claim is made if claimant has no contractual relationship with principal contractor. A notice of claim in writing substantially as set forth in the statute must be presented to and filed with the secretary of state, or clerk or auditor of the public body which let the contract, prior to the expiration of six months immediately following the acceptance of the work. This notice must be signed by the person making the claim and becomes a public record.

Time for Suit on Bond: A claimant who has filed notice of claim with the municipality as above required, or his assignee, may institute an action on the contractor's bond in the circuit court of the state or the federal district court of said district not later than two years after the acceptance of the work.

PENNSYLVANIA

Notice Required: To principal contractor—Within 90 days of performance of work or furnishing of material for which claim is made if claimant has no contractual relationship with principal contractor. .

Time for Suit on Bond: No suit shall be commenced prior to 90 days from the date on which claimant furnished the last of the labor and material for which said claim is made, but such suit must be commenced not later than one year from the date on which the last of the labor was performed or material was supplied for the payment of which such action is brought.

PUERTO RICO

Notice Required: To principal contractor—Within 90 days of performance of work or furnishing of material for which claim is made if claimant has no contractual relationship with principal contractor. (Registered Mail.)

Time for Suit on Bond: Suppliers or sellers of materials, equipment and tools to the subcontractor are required to wait 30 days from the date of mailing of notice to the contractor before instituting suit on the contractor's public work bonds. Suit must be instituted by all claimants within six months after final acceptance of the work by the Commonwealth of Puerto Rico.

RHODE ISLAND

Notice Required: To principal contractor—Within 90 days of performance of work or furnishing of material for which claim is made if claimant has no contractual relationship with principal contractor.

Time for Suit on Bond: Under the May 20, 1975, amendment no suit shall be commenced after the expiration of two years, or under the maximum time limit as contained within the labor or material payment bond, whichever period is longer, after the day on which the last of the labor was furnished or material or equipment supplied by claimant.

SOUTH CAROLINA

Notice Required: To principal contractor—Within 90 days of performance of work or furnishing of material for which claim is made if claimant has no contractual relationship with principal contractor.

Time for Suit on Bond: Must bring suit within one year for the date of the final settlement of the contract.

SOUTH DAKOTA

Notice Required: To principal contractor—No special statutory provisions except in the case of highway construction contracts. A person having a direct contractual relationship with a subcontractor but not with a highway contractor has a right of action on the contractor's bond upon his giving written notice to said contractor within six months from the date on which such person did or performed the last of the labor or furnished or supplied the last of the material for which his claim is made, stating with substantial accuracy the amount claimed and the name of the party to whom said material was supplied or furnished or for whom said labor was done or performed. Such notice shall be served by registered mail, postage prepaid, addressed to the contractor at the place he maintains his principal office or conducts his business or his residence, or in any manner authorized by the laws of South Dakota for the service of process. Personal notice of the pendency of such suit must be given to all known creditors and, in addition thereto, notice shall be given by publication in some newspaper of general circulation published in the county where the contract is being performed for at least three successive weeks, the last publication to be at least three months before the time limited for suit.

Time for Suit on Bond: Claimant may start suit at the expiration of six months from the completion and final settlement of the public contract, but suit must be commenced within one year thereafter.

TENNESSEE

Notice Required: (1) To principal contractor—Within 90 days after the completion of the public work; (2) To municipality—Within 90 days after completion of the public work to support a suit on the highway contractor's bond; to share in retained percentage within 30 days after the last advertisement of proposed final settlement between highway department and contractor.

Time for Suit on Bond: Several persons entitled may join in one suit on the bond or one may file a bill in equity on behalf of all such who may, upon execution of a bond for costs, by petition assert their rights in the proceedings, provided that action shall be brought or claims so filed within six months following the completion of such public work or the furnishing of such labor or materials. All actions on bonds furnished under the highway code shall be commenced before the expiration of one year following the date of the first publication of the notice required to be published in some newspaper in the county where the work was done, etc.; that settlement is about to be made, notifying all claimants to file notice of their claims with the department.

TEXAS

Notice Required: In 1959 Texas enacted a new public works bond statute known as the MacGregor Act. The detailed statutory provisions for notice involve:
(1) All claimants having a direct contractual relationship with the prime contractor.
(2) Claimants who do not have a direct contractual relationship with the prime contractor.
(3) Notices with respect to unpaid retainages.
(4) Notices required for unpaid bills other than notices solely for retainages.
An analysis of the time requirements under these detailed categories is beyond the scope of this article.

Time for Suit on Bond: Suit may not be filed prior to the expiration of 60 days after the filing of the claim. No suit may be brought on the payment bond after the expiration of one year after the date on which suit may be first brought thereon under this statute.

UTAH

Notice Required: To principal contractor—Within 90 days of performance of work or furnishing of material for which claim is made if claimant has no contractual relationship with principal contractor.

Time for Suit on Bond: A period commencing 90 days after the date on which the claimant performed the last of the labor or furnished the last of the material for which he claims payment but such action must be commenced as follows: "provided, however, that no such suit shall be commenced after the expiration of one year from the date on which the claimant performed the last of the labor or furnished or supplied the last of the material for which such suit is brought, except that if the claimant is a subcontractor of the contractor, no such suit shall be commenced after the expiration of one year from the date on which final payment under the subcontract became due."

VERMONT

Notice Required: The amendment approved May 31, 1961, reads that in order to obtain the benefit of such bond the claimant must file with the highway commissioner a sworn statement of his claim within 90 days after the final acceptance of the project by the State of Vermont or within 90 days from the time such taxes or contributions to the Vermont Employment Security Board are due and payable.

Time for Suit on Bond: Within one year after filing his claim with the commissioner of highways, claimant must institute suit on the bond, with notice and summons to the contractor, the surety and the commissioner of highways, to enforce such claim, or must intervene in a suit theretofore instituted. Such suit must be brought in the county where the creditor resides or, if he is a nonresident, in the county of Washington, petitions to intervene shall be brought in any county where their prior suit is pending.

VIRGINIA

Notice Required: No statutory requirement.

Time for Suit on Bond: Within one year after the day on which the person bringing such action last performed labor or last furnished or supplied materials. Every such action shall be brought in a Virginia court of competent jurisdiction in and for the county or other political subdivision of the Commonwealth of Virginia in which the project, or any part thereof, is situated, or in the United States district court for the district in which the project, or any part thereof, is situated, and not elsewhere.

WASHINGTON

Notice Required: (1) To principal contractor—Every person, firm, or corporation furnishing materials, supplies or provisions shall, not later than 10 days after the date of the first delivery of such materials, supplies, or provisions to any subcontractor or agent of any person, firm, or corporation having a subcontract for the construction, performance, carrying on, prosecution or doing of such work, deliver or mail to the contractor a notice in writing, stating, in substance and effect that such person, firm, or corporation has commenced to deliver materials, supplies, or provisions for use thereon, with the name of the subcontractor or agent ordering or to whom the same is furnished, and that such contractor and his bond will be held for the payment of the same. No suit may be maintained in any court against the contractor or his bond to recover for such material, supplies, or provisions or any part thereof unless this notice has been given. (2) To municipality—Creditor shall not have any right of action on the bond unless, within 30 days from and after the completion of the contract with an acceptance of the work by the executive action of the municipal officers, the creditor shall present to and file with such public official a notice in writing in substance of claim. This notice must be signed by the person or corporation making the claim or giving the notice, and after being presented and filed, the notice becomes a public record.

Time for Suit on Bond: No statutory provision.

WEST VIRGINIA

Notice Required: No special statutory provision.

Time for Suit on Bond: No special statutory provision.

WISCONSIN

Notice Required: No statutory provision.

Time for Suit on Bond: Not later than one year after the completion of the work under the contract.

WYOMING

Notice Required: To municipality—Claimant must notify the municipality of the beginning of his suit, giving the name of the parties, describing the bond sued upon, and stating the amount and nature of his claim.

Time for Suit on Bond: Suit must be brought within one year after the date of the first publication of notice of final payment of the contract.

BONDS ON PRIVATE CONSTRUCTION PROJECTS

Most private construction is not bonded, particularly where contracts are negotiated or result from invitational bids. However, California, Florida, Louisiana, Mississippi, Utah, West Virginia, and Wisconsin have statutes extending bond protection to private work. These statutes have been held to be constitutional. Generally speaking, the protection of the claimant's payment bond rights are achieved by perfection of his statutory mechanic's lien rights. For example, California law provides that, where the surety has recorded its payment bond within the county where the work is to be performed, the claimant must perfect his mechanic's lien or, in the alternative, give written notice to the surety in order to recover on the payment bond. California further provides that the claimant must bring suit against the private works surety within six months after completion of the work of improvement.

The most commonly used bond forms on private projects are those recommended by the American Institute of Architects (AIA form 311). This form does not require notice by a claimant who had a direct contract with the principal contractor but requires notice by registered or certified mail within 90 days after furnishing the last work or material by claimants who did not deal directly with the principal contractor. Moreover, this notice must be served upon any two of the following: the principal (the general contractor), the owner, or the surety.

The authors recommend that owners and architects choosing to require bonds of their general contractors, require that their contractors furnish AIA-approved bonds (forms follow Chapter 40, Claims against Bonding Companies—How and When to File). The chief beneficiary of forms used by architects who elect to modify or devise their own forms are usually not the owners or unpaid suppliers of labor and material, but the attorneys who are engaged to litigate their meaning.

BID BONDS

The purpose of the bid bond is to provide the owner with security if the lowest bidder fails to execute the contract. In some situations where contracts have called for the issuance of payment bonds and they were not furnished, unpaid laborers and material suppliers have been permitted to recover against the bid bond surety.

Chapter **37**

Construction Trust-Fund Statutes

CHARLES A. GILMARTIN, ESQ.
Partner, Gilmartin, Wisner & Hallenbeck, Ltd., Chicago, Illinois

INTRODUCTION

There are three primary types of special protection afforded by the law to those engaged in the construction industry, to ensure payment for labor and material furnished. The two remedies which usually come to mind are the mechanic's lien (against either property or funds) and the right to recover under a payment bond. The third area can be roughly characterized as *construction trust-fund statutes.*

A construction trust-fund statute, in its simplest form, is a statute which declares that the funds paid to a contractor are trust funds held by the contractor as a trustee, for the benefit of subcontractors and material suppliers. A trust is a relationship recognized by the law in which one party, the trustee, holds money or property for the benefit of another party, the beneficiary. Although these basic observations are valid, the intricacies that have arisen in each state which has enacted a construction trust-fund statute require a more detailed examination.

Fourteen states have enacted some form of construction trust-fund statute.[1] In three of these states, the statute has either been declared invalid by case decision, repealed or both.[2] Thus, there are presently eleven states with subsisting construction trust-fund statutes.

These eleven jurisdictions may be divided into three categories: those which impose criminal penalties only;[3] those which impose civil liability only;[4] and those having either separate criminal and civil statutes, or having criminal statutes which have, by case decision, been held to create civil liabilities.[5] The criminal penalties imposed are fairly serious, most states providing not only for fines, but also for several years of imprisonment. Excluding those states which appear to have firmly concluded that their statutes are criminal in nature only, and excluding those states which have either declared their statutes invalid or repealed them, the real area of interest is limited to ten states.[6]

In six of these ten states,[7] the statute is a fairly simple criminal statute, so that available civil remedies and the rules governing them can be determined only by examining the case law in those states. In the remaining four states,[8] the civil liability is created by the statute itself, rather than by case decision, and is thus governed by both statutory and case law. The case law in these four jurisdictions is fairly extensive. Particularly in New York, the statute itself is quite lengthy and complex.

From the foregoing, it is obvious that in order to accurately determine the applicable rules in each state, one must carefully examine the statutory and case law in that particular jurisdiction. Nevertheless, bearing this caution in mind, certain general observations may be made with respect to civil liability.

First, one must distinguish the applicability of the statutes as between public and private projects. Second, it is often important to determine when the trust duty arises and whether it is enforceable against anyone other than the contractor. Third, does the failure of a trust beneficiary to file and pursue a lien claim or a bond claim prejudice his right to enforce trust liability? Fourth, what problems arise with respect to sales on general account? Finally, can rights

[1]Arkansas (Ark. Stat. Ann., § 51-601); California (*West's Ann. Penal Code*, § 506); Delaware (6 Del.C. § 3501-3505); Georgia (Ga. Code Ann. 26-1802 and 26-1808 [formerly 26-2812]); Michigan (M.C.L.A. § 570.151, 570.152); Minnesota (M.S.A. § 514.02); Nebraska (R.R.S. 1943 § 52-123, 51;124); New Jersey (N.J.S.A. 2A:44-147 [148] and 2A:102-10); New York (McKinney's Consolidated Laws of New York Annotated, Lien Law, § 70 et seq); Oklahoma (42 O.S. 152, 153); South Carolina (Code of Laws of South Carolina, § 45-301 and § 45-302); South Dakota (SDCL 1967 22-38-8); Washington (RCW 9.54.080 and 9.54.010[3]); Wisconsin (W.S.A. 289.02[5], 289.16, 706.11, 943.20).

[2]California, Georgia, and South Dakota.

[3]Arkansas.

[4]Oklahoma.

[5]Delaware, Michigan, New Jersey, New York, Washington, and Wisconsin. It is unclear whether civil liability exists in Minnesota, Nebraska, and South Carolina.

[6]Delaware, Michigan, Minnesota, Nebraska, New Jersey, New York, Oklahoma, South Carolina, Washington, and Wisconsin.

[7]Delaware, Michigan, Minnesota, Nebraska, South Carolina, and Washington.

[8]New Jersey, New York, Oklahoma, and Wisconsin.

under construction trust-fund statutes be enforced by persons other than the trust beneficiaries themselves?

PUBLIC VERSUS PRIVATE PROJECTS

In New York and Wisconsin, there are separate construction trust-fund statutes for public and private projects. In Michigan, only private work is covered by the construction trust fund statute. One of New Jersey's statutes clearly covers public work, but the existence of any trust duty as to private work would have to arise from the applicable criminal statute, and the most recent case on New Jersey law indicates that the existence of a civil duty on a private project is questionable.[9]

In Delaware, there are cases involving both public and private projects, so that the construction trust-fund statute presumably applies to both. In Oklahoma, the construction trust-fund statute speaks of "lienable" claims. However, liens are not permitted on public property. Nonetheless, a recent case has held that the statute is applicable to public work, apparently on the theory that the claims were of such a nature that they would have been lienable, had they been on a private project.[10] In Washington, the situation is similar to that in Oklahoma, in that the construction trust-fund statute refers to labor or material "where any lien might lawfully be filed," and liens on public property are prohibited. How this provision will be construed remains to be seen. It is unclear if there is any civil liability at all in Minnesota, Nebraska, and South Carolina. If such a liability were held to exist, it appears that in Minnesota it would apply only to private work.[11] Nebraska is in much the same position as Washington. In South Carolina, the statute is worded in such a manner that it could arguably apply to public work, but all the decided cases thus far seem to involve private projects only.

TRUST DUTIES

Several statutes and interpretive decisions hold that the trust comes into existence only once the funds are actually paid to the contractor. Consequently, if the funds are still held by the owner (or public body), there may be no trust. This distinction often becomes unimportant since, if the money has never been paid to the contractor, he has never had an opportunity to apply it improperly. The funds, therefore, ultimately will be used to pay subcontractors and material suppliers anyway. But the distinction should not be ignored. For example, in one case the court reached what appears to be an erroneous conclusion, holding that an assignee of the contractor's accounts receivable prevailed over a

[9]*First Natl. State Bank v. Carlyle House, Inc.*, 102 N.J. Super. 300, 246 A.2d 22 (1968).

[10]*U.S. Fid. & Guar. Co. v. Sidwell*, 525 F.2d 472 (10th Cir., 1975).

[11]Minn. Stat. Ann., § 514.02, refers to § 514.01, and the cases under the latter section indicate that a lien cannot be filed against public property.

supplier, on the theory that the trust never arose until the funds were paid to the contractor. Since the funds involved went directly from the owner to the assignee, the court held that no trust ever arose.[12] This ruling seems to ignore the basic legal principle and that an assignee takes by assignment only those rights which the assignor has. If the contractor would have been subject to trust duties, it seems illogical to allow an evasion of those duties by a mere assignment of accounts receivable.

A second aspect of trust duties, and as a practical matter probably the most important area, is whether a beneficiary of a construction trust-fund statute can trace the funds into the hands of a person wrongfully paid by the contractor. While the applicable law of the particular state involved must again be consulted, the general rule is that for any person who gets the funds from the contractor to be liable to pay them over to a trust beneficiary, that person must have had actual knowledge not only of the trust character of the funds, but also that the contractor was violating his trust duty by paying them to the person involved. In other words, merely knowing that money came from a job covered by a construction trust-fund statute is not enough. The person receiving the money must also know he is receiving it at a time when the contractor has failed to pay his subcontractors and suppliers on that job. Some cases also hold that if the facts known to the person receiving the funds are sufficient to show *bad faith,* the subcontractor or material supplier can recover the money. Thus, the person receiving the money might not have specific knowledge that the subcontractors and material suppliers of a contractor on the particular job involved are unpaid, but if at the time of receiving the funds he knew that the contractor was about to file bankruptcy, this could be bad faith.

FAILURE TO PERFECT LIEN OR BOND CLAIM

Most cases appear to hold that the failure of the subcontractor or supplier to perfect an available bond claim or lien claim will not prejudice his right to enforce the trust liability. Further, in some states the coverage afforded by the construction trust-fund statute is broader than that allowed by the mechanic's lien statute. For example, in Wisconsin, the applicable statute for private projects was amended in 1955 to allow recovery not only for lienable claims, but for all "labor and material used for such improvements."[13]

EFFECT OF SALES ON GENERAL ACCOUNT

In several of the states, in the case of a material supplier, the issue of sales on general account arises. Most of the courts hold that a trust exists only for the benefit of those material suppliers whose materials actually went into the job. Therefore, if the material suppliers sold on general account, without specific

---

[12]*National Bank v. Eames & Brown, Inc.,* 50 Mich. App. 447, 213 N.W.2d 573 (1974). For an opposing view, *see Selby v. Ford Motor Co.,* 405 F.Supp. 164 (E.D., Mich., 1975).

[13]*Weather-Tite Co. v. Lepper,* 25 Wis. 2d 70, 130 N.W.2d 198 (1964).

allocation to particular jobs (or documentation to show delivery to particular jobs), the material supplier faces much the same problem he would with a mechanic's lien claim. He cannot prove which materials were supplied to what jobs. Consequently, he cannot qualify as a trust beneficiary on any of the projects.

ENFORCEMENT OF TRUST RIGHTS

There are several cases involving a third party (usually a surety company) who has paid a qualified subcontractor or material supplier. Those cases hold that such a third party does acquire the rights of the trust beneficiary to enforce the trust, or in legal terminology, the third party becomes *subrogated* to the rights of the trust beneficiary.

One generally becomes concerned about these special protections only when a contractor fails to pay, which in turn very often occurs when the contractor is in serious financial difficulty. Consequently, one can expect that in most such cases, any money coming into the contractor's possession will not remain there for long. The result is that, as a practical matter, subcontractors and material suppliers will often try to tie up the funds before they are ever paid to the contractor, or attempt alternatively to trace those funds into the hands of the person that the contractor paid. Therefore, once it is determined that a subcontractor or material supplier is a trust beneficiary, one must examine the statutes and decisions of the particular jurisdiction involved to determine the rights of the beneficiary to proceed against an owner who has not yet paid the contractor, or against persons already wrongfully paid by the contractor.

In those jurisdictions with the construction trust-fund statutes, the law is far from fully developed. Though it may at first appear that a given construction trust-fund statute is inapplicable, further attention is usually required. For example, one might not have easily guessed several years ago that many of the jurisdictions with what appeared to be purely criminal statutes would decide that those statutes gave rise to a civil liability, yet they often have. A right to recover under a construction trust-fund statute may exist in favor of one who has no lien or bond rights. In short, careful attention to the statutes and cases involved may be well warranted.

Construction trust fund statutes are useful tools. To the extent they impose civil liability, they may allow subcontractors and material suppliers either an additional source of recovery—or perhaps the *only* source of recovery—for labor and material furnished. To the extent they impose criminal liability, they serve to deter unauthorized applications of contract funds. Like any tool, the utility of a construction trust-fund statute is limited only by the skill of the craftsman employing it.[14]

---

[14]See 78 A.L.R. 3d—validity and construction of statute providing criminal penalties for failure of contractor who has received payment from owner to pay laborers or materialmen.

Part Nine

Collection Procedures

Chapter **38**

Collection Procedures in the Construction Industry

MARK R. KOENIG, ESQ.
Manager, Credit and Accounts Receivable, Commercial Division,
Honeywell Inc., Minneapolis, Minnesota

OVERVIEW

General comments This section is limited to an outline of procedures used in collecting money for material supplied and labor performed on a construction project. Although it is recognized that there are many different debtor-creditor relationships on a project, there is a great deal of similarity in successful collection procedures and methods used. Thus, although the writer's comments in this article may be addressed primarily to material suppliers and subcontractors selling to a subcontractor, these same comments are quite universally applicable. Wherever a relationship *more* remote from the prime contract (e.g., where your contract is with a material supplier to a subcontractor) exists, and where that relationship may cause problems, the writer will try to point out those problems.

There are basic collection principles and procedures common to all good collection departments in all industries. These will not be considered in this piece, since there are a number of good publications and periodicals available covering that field. Rather, this section will be devoted to those collection procedures peculiar to the construction industry and to the relationships and motivations of various parties within this industry, since these motivations will dictate the shape and form of effective collection procedures.

As in any collection system, emphasis must be placed on regular and effective collection procedures. No matter what the contractor customer's financial picture seems to be on his last financial statement, the creditor cannot afford to lower his guard. This industry is much more volatile than most others, and the financial position of the established contractor tends to change much more rapidly than that of an established manufacturer. The very large sales-to-net-worth position of the average contractor should give the credit executive fair warning that a very small loss as a percent of sales can wipe out the contractor's net worth in a hurry. Thus, your collection personnel must be in tune to the extreme danger of listening to the contractor's request for extended payment terms due to a "temporary" working capital shortage.

When you start work   As soon as you become aware that labor has been performed or material has been shipped to a job, you must make a determination as to whether legal protection will be maintained under lien and/or bond laws as covered elsewhere in this handbook, or whether you intend to look solely to your customer for payment. Your answer will depend upon a number of factors. If your product is not readily identifiable to a specific job, it is entirely possible that you will not be able to maintain protection for reasons mentioned in other sections relating to lien and bond laws. Another factor will be the location of the job since the statute of the state where the job is located determines the lien and bond requirements, except where the job site is federally owned, and the job is bonded under federal statute. If the statute of that state requires a pre-lien or pre-bond notice within a certain period of time after first delivery of materials or performances of labor, that notice requirement must be complied with at this time.

We have already seen in other sections of this handbook that maintaining lien or bond protection runs the gamut from a relatively easy requirement in some states to a most arduous requirement in others. In several states, no real protection is available. Thus your determination at this point is basically a cost-versus-benefits analysis wherein you weigh the odds of collecting directly from the customer against the cost of maintaining lien or bond protection on the project. This cost analysis should consider additional time spent by the collector to maintain such protection. Each contract should be treated as a separate entity unless the owner of the project is treating two or more of your orders as a single contract with the general contractor, in which case it is normally advisable to lump your contract in the same manner.[1]

Once the billing on a project begins, your own follow-up will of course be dictated by your terms and position on the project as a general contractor, subcontractor, or material supplier.

---

[1]Note that we are here talking about maintaining protection as a *precautionary* measure. We assume that the determination has already been made to extend open-account credit to the customer. Elsewhere in this manual another author has spoken to the subject of extending credit and with the various security devices available at the time the credit is extended.

If you had determined that the customer was not worthy of open-account terms, and that a letter of credit or some other bank plan was necessary, you will already have set up the arrangement and must be sure that the proper billing formats are used and that all documentation as required by the agreement is meticulously provided.

If some other security device was agreed upon, you must now follow up for payment on the contract billings based upon the protective device you have employed. Whether or not you have decided to maintain your lien or bond protection on a project, your primary emphasis will no doubt be in attempting to collect first from your customer himself. Relying upon collecting from parties other than your customer, and based upon lien or bond protection available, will result in extremely slow-turning receivables. Every credit manager worth his salt knows that cash is much more valuable than a receivable in the construction industry, no matter how gilt-edged that receivable might be. Thus, he must first consider collecting from the customer directly.

If lien rights are to be maintained   If your customer is not of sufficient quality that lien and bond protection can be ignored, a further analysis now must be made relative to the laws involved. Be sure to note the different strategy if you intend to rely upon a lien on property as opposed to the lien on funds. In the latter case, of course, your lien goes only to the funds unpaid on a project. It is therefore necessary to provide required statutory notices relatively early to ensure that sufficient funds are being withheld to cover you and other people who resort to liens on that project. Additionally, it should be noted that priorities are different in each state as to who has first call between lienors. In some states, whoever files the lien first has priority over claimants who file liens later.

Reliance upon bond rights   If you are relying upon a bond, you must determine the terms of that bond unless it is a statutory bond, since private bonds can require anything (including the filing of a lien) in order to maintain protection. In a very few states only, private bonds can be statutory in that the law might state that the owner will avoid liability for liens if he takes out a bond in the format prescribed by statute. Without this statutory requirement, there is normally no way for the furnisher of labor or equipment to determine what requirements exist other than by reviewing the bond itself. In many cases, of course, the bond supplied is only for the protection of the owner. If one hears that a private job is bonded, he cannot even be certain that the bond is a *payment* bond unless he reviews it. The owner might very well have required only a performance bond. Further, care must be exercised so that federal government turnkey jobs are not confused with the normal government jobs where the federal government is the owner of the property involved. On turnkey jobs, the job is billed and completed by private interests with an agreement to sell to the government at the completion of the job. In such cases, and although the federal government might require bonds, the job can be treated as a private job with lien rights prevailing, assuming that the property on which the job is constructed is owned by private interests at the time of construction.

If the job is a federal project requiring a Miller Act bond, we caution you to be certain that you are not too far removed in the contracting tier to obtain protection. The same situation may well prevail under state statutory lien or bond protection where you can be cut off at a certain tier level on protection afforded. For example, bond protection may be extended to one who contracts with a subcontractor, but possibly not to one who contracts with a sub-subcontractor. In view of this situation, you must be on guard for two or more companies with similar names increasing the number of tiers above you. Although relatively uncommon, cases have arisen where a general contractor will create one or more separate corporations with similar names and toss those corporations into the contracting tier, thereby attempting to insulate themselves from liability by placing normally a third-tier subcontractor into the position of fourth-tier subcontractor or lower. Although a subcontractor placed in that position may well be able to prevail ultimately in court based upon the claim that creation of the second corporation was a sham or subterfuge, legal action of this nature is often not worthwhile pursuing in view of the cost involved. Thus, from a practical standpoint, the unscrupulous party may succeed.

A further task you must perform is to analyze bonding companies providing the statutory or private bond. An approved list of bonding companies is published by the federal government each year and is obtainable from them. This may give you some idea as to how the United States Government views the various surety companies providing performance and payment bonds on their projects. However, inclusion upon that list is by no means an assurance that the bonding company involved is solvent, and will be around next year to pay valid claims lodged against them. It seems that every year or two a bonding company providing a substantial amount of bonding capacity is forced to close its doors as a result of losses incurred in their surety business. Do not forget that a claim against a surety company is only as good as the surety company itself. And note also that a bonding company which requires you to sue them to collect on a valid claim must also have its value discounted, and that this factor should weigh in determination as to whether to maintain your bond right intact on a private job, as opposed to filing a lien, which may well turn out to be the cheaper and quicker method available to secure payment.

COLLECTION PROCEDURES

Collecting from Your Customer

General comments and payment terms   If you are a material supplier with discount terms, your most effective follow-up will necessarily be different from that of a material supplier without discount terms. Similarly, both of these suppliers' collection procedures will differ from those of a subcontractor with terms calling for payment at such time as the customer is paid by his customer. In the case of material suppliers, there is normally no question of when the money is due—whether your terms be "net/30," "2%/10, net/30," or whatever. On the other hand, if you accept terms of payment calling for payment to you when your customer is paid, the situation is completely different. In this latter situation, payment for monthly progress billings can be expected by about the tenth of each month if your contract is directly with the owner, the twentieth of the month if you have contracted with the prime contractor, and the thirtieth if your contract is with one who has contracted with the prime contractor. Again, this will partly be dependent upon terms of the contract itself and on how much time it allows for your customer to process your payment after he receives his.

If your contract calls for your customer to retain a certain part of the monthly progress payment, you should have negotiated terms calling for no more retainage than is being withheld from him at any point in time on that job. The amount of retainage withheld varies considerably from one job to the next. Normally, retainage on private and state work calls for retaining 10 percent of each billing until final completion, with subsequent reductions in that retainage depending upon the amount of work left to be done. Federal government contracts for construction normally require payment for 90 percent of progress billings (with 10 percent retained) until 50 percent completion, with 100 percent payment for all billings thereafter if the inspector is satisfied that the work has progressed satisfactorily and that billings are proper. More recently, many federal contracts have been let with no retention required, particularly by the General Services Administration. Retainage required on state and munici-pal (including school board) contracts is normally 10 percent, although there are exceptions such as Massachusetts which holds only 5 percent. Recent legislation trends toward a reduction in required retainage.[2]

If your terms call for payment when your customer receives his payment, it may be necessary for you to check with some other source to determine whether or not your customer has been paid. In such cases, the architect will normally provide you with information as to whether payment has been made to the prime contractor. If your customer is a subcontractor, note that payment to the prime contractor does not necessarily mean that payment has been made to your customer. In such cases, you may wish to check with the prime contractor to determine whether he has yet paid your customer. When you call and find that your customer has not been paid for your past-due billings, this contact may put pressure on the prime contractor to pay your customer so that he can in turn pay you. And if your customer has been paid, the architect or prime contractor will frequently put pressure upon your customer to pay, thus eliminating the need for you to take lien or other action on your part detrimen-tal to work progress.

Note also that certain recent decisions may require your customer to make final payment to you in a reasonable time after you have completed your work (unless there is a dispute where your work is involved), despite a contract provision which would seem to allow your customer to delay payment to you until he receives his final payment on a project.[3]

---

[2]Payment terms should also include *favorable* aspects of your customer's terms with his customer. In some states, retainage is deposited in an account bearing interest, with that interest payable to the contractors. In this situation, you should insist that your share of the interest be passed along to you. It is your job to collect this interest, and your collection policy should say so. Every dollar of interest collected is a dollar of profit, after deducting the nominal collection costs.

[3]*See* Chapter 25, "Subcontractor's Entitlement to Payment Where Owner Fails to Make Payment to Prime Contractor," by Charles Yumkas.

In your collection policy, outside parameters should be set as deadlines for holding further orders, stopping work, notifying other parties, and filing lien or bond actions. Each of these four will put pressure on the customer to pay—a pressure over and above that which you can generate through collection letters or telephone follow-ups. These parameters should be written into your policies, with any deviation subject to management approval. The purpose for the approval requirement is not so much to check on the work of the collector as it is to obtain unbiased and fresh input into the decision. Further, this will provide an impetus to change the policy when necessary due to frequent exceptions. As is true in dealing with customers in any industry, however, collection activities must be tailored to your particular customers on an individual basis as much as possible.

Holding approval on a new order   Holding a future order can be an effective collection tool in construction as it is in all other credit areas. If this tool is being used, it is necessary that the customer be notified in writing as to why the action is being taken and amount of past-due indebtedness which you will require to be paid before shipment of the new order. Not reducing your position to writing may result in severe consequences later if the customer attempts to backcharge you for damages due to your nondelivery of equipment on that order. And backcharges for delay of completion are frequent in the construction industry.

Stopping work on the job with past-due billings   When you are not being paid for the work you have done on a job, there should be no need to continue to deliver material, or to do any further work on the job until such time as you have been paid for work already done in accordance with the terms of your contract. If your customer is in breach of the contract terms by not paying you as agreed in that contract, if that breach is a *material* breach, and if you have not previously breached the contract yourself, you should be entitled to hold guarantee or other work pending his remedy of that breach. In many states, you are required to serve notice before stopping work. Whether or not such legal requirements exist, it should always be your practice to give your customer sufficient notice to allow him time to make payment and thereby assure your continued performance.

It can readily be seen that there are numerous potential legal problems involved with stopping work. In reviewing your remedies for breach of contract, if there is any question regarding your right to stop work, your attorney should be consulted as the best source of information regarding legal remedies and rights you have available to you. In this area, as in any area of construction law, the applicability of the Uniform Commercial Code must be carefully determined, primarily because the Uniform Commercial Code deals in many places with contracts between merchants. Most contractors do not fit that definition. Again, it is imperative that the customer be notified in writing when this action is taken. The first reason: If you have only one or two men performing labor on the job spasmodically, or if your material shipments are intermittent, the customer might not even know that you have stopped work, and no pressure is generated if he is not aware of your action. Secondly, you must substantiate your position in writing to avoid any potential backcharges. Whenever you stop work due to lack of payment, all parties should be told that any extra costs you incur as a result of your being forced to stop work will be charged back to the customer and that you will expect an additional sum to be paid by your customer to cover those costs.

Notifying other parties   We earlier alluded to the procedure of checking with an architect or general contractor regarding the status of payment on jobs. This is also a method of putting pressure on your customer to effect payment. All the parties above your customer in the contracting-tier relationship are normally anxious that a job be completed on time and without any liens being filed. Actually filing a lien or bond action is a fourth method and, again, particular to the construction industry.

Extreme care must be taken to notify only those who have a proper interest in knowing that you are not being paid on a project. Generally speaking, those outside the direct contracting tier with the exception of the bonding company, architect, and possibly the lending agency, have no particular need for that information.

Treat each job separately   (The following paragraph applies to the situation where the customer is to pay you on each contract as he receives his payment. If your terms are otherwise, this paragraph is not applicable.) At this point, it should be noted that there will normally be no problems if you treat each job with a customer as a separate entity. This statement presumes common sense and reasonable application of good credit principles with no arbitrary application of cash between jobs. As a general rule, you should never apply cash to a specific job without obtaining your customer's approval to do so. If obtained verbally, this approval should be confirmed in writing. Whenever this rule is ignored, there is an excellent chance that your customer, a bankruptcy trustee, or a general contractor will disagree with your cash application two or three years later, and you will end up writing off some money. When you have a customer paying promptly on three jobs and slow on one, there need be no hesitation about stopping work on that one job, filing a lien on that job, and taking any other such action as may be necessary to effect reasonably prompt collection on the receivable due. Some of your customers will favor your intervention actively on the job where you are not being paid, since his prompt payment on three out of four jobs probably indicates that he is not being paid on the fourth job either. In fact, your customer may be hesitant to proceed in that aggressive manner against his customer and will probably welcome your intervention as a party over whom he theoretically has no control. When you get your money, he will also get his. Thus, your activities in treating each job separately (where terms call for payment to you as your customer is paid) should be limited only by your relationships with your own customer and not by any concern for a potential legal problem which normally does not exist.

Trust doctrine   Several states have adopted a trust-doctrine statute relating to construction work. The basic legal theory involved is that money received by owners or contractors for use in constructing a certain building, or for payment of obligations incurred in constructing that building, are trust funds which must first be used for payment of all obligations relating to that project in particular. Diversion of these funds for any other purpose makes the person criminally liable for that diversion. In some states, there are civil remedies as well. Although it is certainly unethical and most likely illegal to threaten anyone with *criminal* action under these statutes, everyone should be aware of their existence in certain states and of civil remedies available in certain instances.

This trust doctrine can be valuable as a tool where a customer takes bankruptcy and the trustee lays claim to funds owed to your customer on a job where you are also unpaid. Where the trust doctrine exists, it can often be argued convincingly that the trustee, if he were to receive those funds, would simply hold them in trust for you and other unpaid suppliers on *that specific* job. At least in states where there is a civil remedy, the trustee will often agree to your being paid those funds directly.

Collection of retainage   Your contract may call for the reduction of retainage as work proceeds on a project. In such cases, it is often necessary to ask for this reduction when it is due. Seldom will a contractor volunteer the information. In fact, you can often perform a service for your customer by pointing out to him that a reduction is in order, since he will often be unaware that he too is entitled to more money.

When speaking of retainage collection, two factors are of prime importance. First, you must have a system established to get the work done properly, with minor problems cleared up in a hurry. Secondly, you should have a procedure established to enable you to check periodically on all customers, good and bad, to make sure they have passed along any retainage deductions to which you are entitled.

Some customers want a separate invoice to process for retainage payment. At times, a procedure as simple as issuing a bill will quickly bring payment of a sizeable retainage. Also, this is the time to look at the contract again to determine whether you are entitled to interest on that money. If so, ask for it.

Other collection devices   The threat of placing his account for collection often does not cause particular concern to the contractor, since he can usually invent some excuse for not paying—an excuse which will at least get him past the courthouse steps. This lack of concern is even greater in view of the recent court decisions which limit as unconstitutional many laws which creditors relied upon to quickly tie up funds due contractors on other jobs for payment due on a different job. Again, your attorney is the best source of information in this area.

At times, your customer will admit he cannot pay you due to a shortage of cash and will ask you to go along with a deferred-payment plan of some type. That may include notes, postdated checks, or simply an agreement that you will wait for a given period of time for your money. If you intend to maintain lien or bond protection in cases of this nature, it is absolutely essential that you obtain the approval of the surety company involved and/or any other parties who might also be liable under a lien or bond claim. If you do not obtain that approval, you may well lose your right to proceed against any other third parties if your customer does not pay you directly. In all cases where you have been unable to collect directly from your customer, be certain that no guarantee work is done on any of your equipment and that no guarantee labor is performed on the job.

If the owner on a project, or any other party, is anxious to have you honor a guarantee, they should be willing to pay for that service. If a major problem should surface, they may well be willing to pay your entire open balance. Do not forget that your guarantee is an item of value which should not be given away if you will be unable to collect for it from your customer.

If all other pressure fails, and you are about ready to place the customer's account for collection, you may wish to present his bank with a sight draft and request that his bank have the customer honor that draft. This rather subtle pressure at times prods the customer into paying.

Filing lien or bond action   Actually filing a lien or bond action is usually a last resort. Note carefully that lien and bond laws are normally very strictly construed, which simply means that the courts will make certain that all t's are crossed and all i's are dotted before they grant the relief sought by a claimant or lienor. If the law states that you must notify the general contractor within thirty days from the date you last deliver material to the job, notice to the general contractor on the thirty-first day will generally cause you to lose your security interest in its entirety. Courts are simply not anxious to make an individual pay twice for the same material, as the general contractor must often do if he has already paid the contractor when a lien has been filed or a proper bond claim asserted. Note especially that this date of last work can relate to the date the project was abandoned, or the date you last performed even if you never finished.

Collecting from Third Parties

This subject is of sufficient importance to the collection process in the construction industry that we shall treat rather extensively with each of these parties, their interest, and their normal reaction to an approach. It is most important to realize that nearly all these parties have no contract with you. Thus, they have no *contractual* obligations to fulfill when you are not being paid. According to the law, there is no *"privity of contract."* Thus, they must be very cautious in all dealings with you to protect the party with whom they *do* have a contract.

Collecting from general contractors   General contractors are normally interested in delivering a completed and satisfactorily constructed project to their customer (the owner) on time, free and clear of all liens. Most contracts between owners and general contractors require that the building be delivered free and clear of liens. Thus, at least in those states where lien rights are substantial, most general contractors are concerned when one of their subcontractors does not pay his material suppliers or subcontractors as soon as he gets the money to do so from the general contractor. Similarly, most general contractors have in their contracts with the subcontractor a clause which allows them to take some affirmative action if a lien is filed on a project, the subcontractor becomes bankrupt, or even if they become aware of unpaid claims against that subcontractor. Without this clause in their contract with the subcontractor, general contractors do not have complete legal authority to pay off such obligations directly. At the same time, they normally have sufficient legal clout from one term or another of their subcontract to enable them to take appropriate action on behalf of the unpaid material supplier or subcontractor. Several points are worthy of further note.

Depending upon his own contractual rights at this point, the general contractor may agree to enter into a separate contract with you to get you to return to work on a contract and finish up the project. He may simply issue a purchase order for the balance due you on a project. Such an order legally executed by the general contractor at that point is normally binding, and is one of the best methods available to an unpaid supplier or subcontractor to ensure reasonably prompt payment from that point forward and ultimate payment on past-due billings as well. However, the terms of the order must be reviewed specifically to be certain that they meet with approval.

A joint-check agreement by the general contractor may also be effective in preventing further payment delays. However, care should be taken to require a guarantee of the general in addition to his agreement to pay by joint check. Further, a careful analysis of the legal problems involved in guarantees is necessary for you to understand the potential pitfalls of this method of operating. It should be pointed out that a joint-check agreement alone is simply that, namely, an agreement to issue a check payable jointly to you and your customer. There is some question as to whether that agreement is legally enforceable. Even if it is, the third-party obligation is fulfilled when he issues that check, even though the check is not a negotiable instrument without the endorsement of both payees. If your customer is bankrupt, you may indeed have a difficult time in convincing the trustee in bankruptcy to sign the check on behalf of the bankrupt debtor and turn that check over to you. More likely, he will try to negotiate with you for your endorsement of the check so that he can put it into funds for disbursement to general creditors and may even petition the court to require your endorsement. Thus, if there is any danger of insolvency by your customer, you should always insist upon the joint check being accompanied by a guarantee signed by an officer (preferably the president and chairman of the board) of the general contractor.

It should be noted that in certain states the contractor has the right to rely upon an affidavit of his subcontractor that all his material suppliers and sub-subcontractors have been paid.[4] Upon receipt of such an affidavit, the general contractor may pay the subcontractor without fear of further liability for the amount of that payment. Any liens filed for work included in that payment are worthless as against the property. Where this situation exists, or may exist, you should again make every effort to notify the general contractor early if you are not being paid promptly for your billings. Even where such laws exist, the general contractor normally has no right to rely upon an affidavit of his sub-subcontractor when he has prior notice from a material supplier or subcontrac-

---

[4] *See* Fla. Stat. § 713.06; Ill. L. 193 at 230, § 21; Mich. Stat. § 570.4; Ohio Stat. § 1311.04.

tor to his sub-subcontractor that payment has not been made promptly by that particular subcontractor.

In certain cases, general contractors have been known to pull the wool over the eyes of ill-informed subcontractors or material suppliers to sub-subcontractors they have paid already by acting as though their liability under the lien or bond law is limited to the money they are holding, even when they have full liability in fact. These contractors are definitely in the minority, since most general contractors are helpful, and many will even pay you directly the amount they are withholding from one of their subcontractors despite the fact that they are aware that you do not have lien or bond rights on a particular project.

If this situation does exist, and the general contractor is wary of paying you the money which is really payable to his subcontractor, it is possible that an indemnification agreement signed by your company will give him sufficient legal protection to obtain his agreement to a direct payment of those funds to you. Any such agreement would be signed by your firm, and would simply agree to indemnify and hold the general contractor harmless from any action brought by any party against them for money allegedly due and owing to your customer from the general contractor, if that action was brought relative to those specific funds paid to you directly. This agreement should include the stipulation that you be notified of any action brought by any third party within 5 or 10 days after service of papers in the action. Other requirements should be dictated by your own legal counsel.

Any agreement with a general contractor designed to ensure payment is a new contract. Thus, it should specifically recite the full agreement, must be in writing, and signed at least by the general contractor, and must recite the *consideration*. A letter signed by someone in the general contractor's organization who is authorized to bind the general contractor is sufficient. It should recite both how much and when you are to be paid. It should read basically as follows:

> In return for returning to work and completing the obligation under the contract entered into with (*your customer's name*) we (*general contractor*) will guarantee payment for your invoices on this project. The total sum of _____, plus additions and minus deductions to the contract, will be paid to you promptly by (*general contractor*) within 30 days after your invoices are rendered monthly on this project.

It should be signed by the president or another officer authorized to sign the document and should have an affidavit at the bottom properly attested, affirming his right to sign the guarantee. Again, your attorney should approve the format. If the general contractor is to pay your billings by joint check, it should be clearly spelled out that this alone will not end his obligation to you. Rather, you are looking to him to guarantee full payment, with the choice of joint check being his decision, thus making it his responsibility to make sure that the money reaches you one way or the other and on time.

Collecting through the architect The primary concern of the architect as representative for the owner is to make sure that the owner receives the building that he has contracted for, on time, and without liens or other encumbrances. Further, some architects feel a moral obligation to see that material suppliers and subcontractors are paid in full to the greatest extent possible. On the other hand, some architects exhibit no particular interest in payment problems of a subcontractor or material supplier. If the architect is concerned, he can be a valuable source of pressure on all parties, to make sure that you are paid, and promptly. In return, he will normally ask only that you deliver as you are required to by your contract. His main pressure point is that he could stop the flow of all funds to the general contractor on a job. This would bring to a halt all payment by those further down in the contracting tier, and everyone can become quite upset in a hurry. And even those architects who are not concerned enough to stop payment or make any calls are often willing to provide you with copies of any bonds which might be required, or at least with information as to who has and has not been paid.

Collecting from owners If there is an architect who is sympathetic and willing to assist, there is no need normally to go to an owner. At times, however, the owner interjects himself into the picture in view of the threat of a lien filing or work stoppage. Aside from those few cases where you are dealing with a combined owner/general contractor, owners will generally not involve themselves except to the extent of attempting to put pressure on you through your sales force to resume work or not file a lien. Your own marketing policy will dictate your response to this type of owner activity. Where he does become interested in assisting you, however, the owner, like the architect, can and may tie up all funds on a job pending assurance that you will be paid. Again, the effect can be most beneficial.

In a few states, a statute gives the owner the right to pay directly those who have given notice of their unpaid status.[5] Even without such legislation, at times the owners have funds and are agreeable to paying but may *require* that you first file a lien in order to give them the clear right to pay you directly. When owners are reluctant to make payment to you, you may wish to *volunteer* a lien filing despite the additional expense, and particularly where your customer is or may be insolvent. Despite an intervening bankruptcy, your filing the lien will normally provide you with a prior right to the funds and eliminate any challenge by

---

[5]Statutes allow owners to pay claimants directly, with varying requirements short of judgment, in the following states (designation of "public work" refers only to state and municipally owned projects, and *not* to federally owned projects): (a) Colorado (private work), (b) Florida (private work), (c) Indiana (public work), (d) Kentucky (public work), (e) Michigan (public work), (f) Minnesota (private work), (g) Nebraska (private work), (h) New Jersey (private work), (i) North Dakota (private work, but only after work is completed), (j) Oklahoma (private work), (k) Pennsylvania (private work), (l) Rhode Island (private work), (m) South Dakota (private work—statute allows direct payment on public work with a court order), (n) Texas (private work), (o) Wisconsin (public work—statute allows direct payment on private work when a bond is furnished in lieu of lien rights), (p) Wyoming (public work, but only after completion, payable from final payment money).

a trustee in bankruptcy regarding a payment made to you directly rather than your customer. This procedure is highly recommended whenever doubt exists as to the solvency of your customer.

Collecting on municipal mechanic's liens In some states, a statute enables you to collect directly from funds which the owner is holding on a public project. This remedy is particularly valuable in a state like New Jersey, where you cannot even commence suit on the bond until many months after acceptance of the project. To expedite collection in these states and where the owner has sufficient funds to pay your claim, it is often advisable to rely upon this collection method as the more favorable compared with filing a bond claim. Wherever you have alternative remedies, however, you should weigh the costs. If your customer is broke, you will probably have a clear claim against a bonding company. Normally, that claim can be collected from a reputable bonding company without incurring any attorney's fees. Filing a municipal mechanic's lien, on the other hand, may well cost you some attorney's fees. Thus, the size of your claim may dictate which way to turn.

Collecting from bonding companies A bonding company's position on a contract is normally that of guaranteeing that their principal will perform in accordance with the contract and will pay all obligations under his contract. This often includes payment of obligations not only of those with whom he has contracted directly but also of those with whom his subcontractors have contracted. Since the bonding company guarantees only that its principal will meet these obligations, the bonding company has no liability under its bond as long as its principal is solvent. It is most important to recognize this fact. If your customer has already been paid and goes bankrupt, it is not the general contractor's bonding company, but rather the solvent general contractor who must pay twice by paying you even though he has already paid your customer for your materials. Where the bonding company's principal is bankrupt, however, liability is clear and the obligation is immediate.

Most bonding companies will honor their just obligations with reasonable promptness. There are some exceptions, where a bonding company has been known to make continued assurances to claimants verbally that they will check into the status of the claim for month after month, with the result that the claimant never does take the action required by statute to perfect his claim, normally in the area of suing within a certain statutory period. Thus, by the time claimant wakes up, it is too late for him to perfect his rights, and the bonding company simply walks away. Do not get caught in this trap.

In most cases, bonding company claim agents are considerably overworked. Very frequently, claims handled by one agent may be cleared expeditiously, where another claims agent for the same company in another office may well cause you to file suit in order to collect on a legitimate claim. In such cases, it is recommended that this be called to the attention of sufficiently high management authority within that bonding company. If that does not suffice, a letter to the state insurance commissioner of the state where a legitimate claim is not being handled properly will often succeed in obtaining much faster resolution of the problems. Many state insurance commissioners are ineffective, but there are likewise many who do an extremely efficient and effective job of policing surety companies writing bonds within their jurisdictions.

There is one further bond claim which should be mentioned in passing. Certain states require a contractor to be licensed, and to post a bond for a nominal amount to guarantee his performance. When a contractor simply disappears, this bond may be available to pay your claim. Though this is a rather long shot, it occasionally romps home a winner.

Collecting through interim lending institutions   On most major private projects, funding is provided by two separate sources. The short-term financing to provide money during the course of the job is provided by a bank or other source of short-term funds. These funds are then disbursed during the course of a job either by the institution itself or some third party, often a title company with a local office. Normally it is this local disbursing agency which is responsible for insuring that disbursement is made only after proper lien waivers, affidavits of payment, or other such papers are provided by the general contractor. At times, this disbursing agency may be a title company which guarantees clear title to the property after construction has been completed. In those cases, the role of the title company becomes very close to that of a surety. In addition to the potential legal ramifications this poses due to licensing requirements in certain jurisdictions, there is also an increasing reluctance on the part of third parties such as title companies to make any such guarantees. This is especially true in jurisdictions where mechanic's liens take priority over recorded mortgages. In those jurisdictions, very few third parties will assume the obligations we are referring to. When this does occur, however, it is clear that the disbursing agency has a direct interest in avoiding any liens or other such encumbrances on the property.

Even where there is no such guarantee, most such disbursing agencies feel it is their duty to do everything in their power to avoid any lien filings. Although their manpower restrictions normally prevent their requiring lien waivers from parties lower than subcontractors to the general contractor, and though they do not actively solicit input from parties below that tier, they are usually very responsive to notification by any lower subcontractor or material suppliers who are not being paid for progress billings. Even where there is no legal obligation to provide protection to the owner, these agencies normally feel that it is a moral obligation to protect such material suppliers or subcontractors, or at least to protect the owner from the problems of clearing liens wherever possible. And although they will often refuse to issue joint-payment checks at the credit-approval stage where you are looking for third-party security, they may issue such joint checks later on when you are not being paid properly for your monthly billings. More often, their approach to the situation is simply to hold payment for any further billings of the general contractor on the job, which action immediately calls the attention of all parties to your plight, and frequently results in one of the parties above you in the contracting tier accepting liability for your presently outstanding and future billings as well.

Collecting through lien filing and foreclosure   Although filing a lien is often an effective method for securing an outstanding receivable, it should be considered only as a last resort since it is a legal device and therefore is subject to all the delays encountered whenever legal measures are resorted to. In the case of a dispute, it is especially ineffective, since the result is often to cement each party in the position they presently find themselves, with the result that no compromise is thereafter possible. Even when this does not occur, there is often a sufficient number of disputes that the customer feels he should fight all the way. In most jurisdictions, he can do so very effectively by simply posting a bond in the amount of the lien, thereby leaving only foreclosure procedures which can be very protracted and time-consuming. Thus, filing a lien may well be a costly alternative (in terms of money and time) to reaching an agreement with some party above the customer in the tier as to how you will be paid the remainder due on a project. But there are also positive results to be gained. Even lienors second to the mortgage often gain a reasonably good bargaining position when the time comes to close the permanent financing on a building. Although the organization providing the interim financing may simply assign its rights as a prior recorded mortgage holder (usually a position prior to the lienors), normally the permanent financiers have their own forms and are not satisfied with relying as assignee on the forms required by the interim lendor. In these cases, the owners are often forced to deal with lienors whose rights are normally superior to any mortgage filed later, as the new mortgage would be.

Despite potential problems, there should be no hesitancy to use the remedy when it appears that doing so will hasten collection or secure a questionable receivable. For the reasons mentioned earlier, prompt lien filing is necessary when a lien-on-funds situation is available, and where priorities depend on order of lien filing.

As is true in most areas, it can readily be seen that lien filings should be chosen carefully to fit the situation. Another section of this *Handbook* is devoted to this area much more extensively, and a local attorney's advice is often sought by the experienced credit manager, particularly where there may be a question as to the constitutionality of the existing lien statutes within that state.

MISCELLANEOUS ITEMS FOR CONSIDERATION

Backcharges   One of the major abuses in the construction industry is that of improper backcharges. A backcharge is simply a bill sent to you by your customer for any of a number of reasons. Perhaps the most frequent backcharge, and one which is most often justified, is that for hoisting wherein the general contractor provides a lift in a building for the use of all tradesmen, and charges you by the hour for the use of that lift in hauling your men or materials up and down in the building involved. There are many other causes for backcharges, including costs which your customer says he incurred because you did not do your job properly or on time or costs he maintains he incurred when he does some work he claims *you* should have done by the terms of your contract. It is well known in the industry that certain unscrupulous contractors make it a practice of attempting to increase their profit level on a job—and sometimes even to produce *all* their profit on a job—as a result of improper backcharges to their subcontractors. These backcharges are then deducted from payments made against progress billings, with the result that your customer is holding the amount of the backcharge in cash, and you must sue him in order to obtain payment, or file a lien or bring suit against a bond to accomplish the same result. In any event, the burden is upon you to take action since he has your money. Since subcontractors are often in need of cash at the close of the job and are anxious to clear the job from their books, many settle short of the full balance due them simply to meet those needs.

There is no way to avoid backcharges entirely. Similarly, there is no way to be in the driver's seat, since your customer is normally holding the money and therefore cares little if the backcharge is ever resolved. When the backcharge is proper, your object in the collection department is to get the backcharge reduced to a proper figure and then have the proper party within your organization issue credit to reduce the balance outstanding to the proper amount. When the backcharge is *not* justified, your object is to try to put the shoe on the other foot by making it at least mutually beneficial between the customer and yourself to resolve the backcharge at the earliest possible time. Perhaps the best method for doing this is to file a lien, bring suit against a payment bond, or take any such other action which will not only secure the balance outstanding, but will also give your customer some incentive to resolve the matter at the earliest possible time. If your customer desires to continue to do business with you, it is clear that pressure can be put upon him by holding future orders or requiring cash in advance until that improper backcharge is cleared.

In large organizations, it is often a long way from the sales department to the collection department. Since crediting a backcharge will often adversely affect the sales organization's profit-and-loss statement, there is sometimes a reluctance by the sales department to credit promptly those backcharges which are legitimate. Normally, your sales representatives are the ones who can most properly determine the legitimacy of any such backcharges. In order to provide them with the proper incentive to credit those backcharges which are legitimate, resolve those which are partly legitimate and bring suit on those which are not, outstanding backcharges can be charged back directly against the responsible unit's profit-and-loss statement until resolution. If favorably resolved, that same charge would be credited to the proper profit column.

Until such time as the backcharge is finally resolved, your continued input as an experienced collector will often prove most beneficial to whoever in your organization is charged with the responsibility to resolve the matter. Although it is true that some backcharges are unavoidable, it would prove most beneficial for your organization to consider maintaining a log on all jobs to include particularly any verbal agreements when a dispute arises, how the dispute was resolved, and specifically what was said by each of the parties. Any written notes of this nature can be used by a witness to refresh his memory on the witness stand as to what was said by whom, and are often very effective if the matter comes to trial. Far better than this, however, is the practice of reducing everything agreed upon to writing. Making it a practice of doing so on each and every job will reduce the number of disputes considerably and will eliminate much hard feeling between you and your customer if you conscientiously provide your customer with a copy of these notes at the time they are taken.

Extra work orders   Whenever you are requested to do work over and above the work required by your contract, you should receive a signed order requesting that work, and agreeing to the amount to be paid for that work. It should be signed by someone who has authority to sign such documents. Without contractual requirement to the contrary, this work order in writing should always be demanded before the work proceeds. At times, you may be faced with what is termed in government contracting a *PDL clause*. This is facetiously referred to as a "proceed-and-decide-later" clause. Actually it is a *price-determined-later* clause. Even in such cases you normally have the right to require a written work order requiring that you proceed, even though you may not have the right to require that the price be negotiated in advance. Even in such cases, it is wise to immediately begin price negotiations rather than wait until the end of the job to resolve them all, since only a minimum amount—if anything—will be paid to you until the price is finally determined.

Lien waivers   In order to ensure that liens will not be filed on a job, architects, owners, payment disbursing agencies, or other parties may require lien waivers from you or from your subcontractors or material suppliers on a job. A lien waiver is simply a legal instrument signed by someone in authority and stating that the signing party releases any rights to file a lien on a project up to a certain dollar amount, or for labor and/or materials provided up to a certain date, or possibly waiving entirely and forever the right to file a lien on a specific project. Third parties have a right to rely upon such lien waivers, and any payment which they make to your customer as a result of a lien waiver signed by you will effectively preclude you from filing a lien to the extent of the waiver given. At the same time, it is generally true that those third parties must actually *rely* upon that lien waiver in making the payment if the waiver is to have any force and effect. Thus, if a payment was made to your customer before you issued the lien waiver, or if it could be shown that no reliance was placed on the lien waiver at the time the payment was made to your customer, that lien waiver will often have no force and effect and will not bar you from later filing a lien for the amount involved.

You are often forced into a difficult position by your customer when he maintains he cannot pay you until he receives his money on a project, and at the same time the party who is to pay your customer is requiring a lien waiver from you before he makes that payment. Assuming you do not wish to go to that third party and request a payment directly to you for the amount of your waiver, a reasonably effective method to help ensure that you will receive your fair share of the payment to your customer is to require a trust receipt from your customer. This is simply a legal document signed by your customer wherein he agrees to hold your portion of the money he receives in trust for you until he has the opportunity to disburse the money to you. Any violation of the trust position your customer is placing himself in would normally be considered a criminal act subject to whatever penalty might be applied to such act by the laws of the state involved. Since most people are anxious to avoid criminal liability for violation of trust, there is usually sufficient incentive for your customer to make sure that you are paid reasonably promptly after he receives his money.

Qualifications for the effective collector   Collecting in the construction industry is a vocation in which the faint-hearted will not long survive. Contractors in all tiers are generally honest—but tough. They ask no quarter and give none. To be effective, the collector must enjoy dealing with people in person and on the phone. He must be a salesperson, selling the customer on paying. And since the contractor is nearly always short of cash, this means selling the customer on paying you *instead of* thirty others who are owed money by this same customer. In sales, there are generally five or so major competitors. In collecting, everyone who is trying to get money from the customer is your competitor, including Uncle Sam and other taxing authorities. Thus, an outgoing individual who loves to negotiate and has excellent communication skills, with a flair for public relations, is your best candidate for collection work, assuming his feelings are not easily hurt.

Danger signals   Each experienced credit employee in the construction industry has his pet signals of future trouble for a contractor. In the short run, those signals are clear. But what can indicate trouble one, two, or three years from now?

There are three primary leading indicators. (Obviously, these are not always true and must be applied judiciously.) First is the death or retirement of an active father who established the business, leaving the son or sons to run the business. Lacking the father's instinct for the business and his contacts, there is often trouble two years later.

The second results from the effort of a local contractor to become the biggest in the area. In order to accomplish this, he begins taking more marginal work. His financial resources, probably already stretched at the lower volume, are usually seriously below what is needed at the higher volume level.

Lastly, the move out of his normal working area is a precarious one for most contractors. This is why the normal approach is to joint venture in the new area. Otherwise, a contractor's control methods and top personnel are stretched too thin. Further, a union contractor faces the problem of going to the bench for all his laborers. What is on the bench is not usually the cream of the crop.

In my experience, these three have contributed most frequently to the demise of the established contractor. All three can be observed far ahead of the severe financial difficulty which often follows.

CLOSING COMMENTS

Collecting in the construction industry requires one to keep an eye on the strict requirements of local lien and bond laws, while giving primary emphasis to employing good collection practices. This includes early notification to third parties who can not only help you collect your money, but also can often protect themselves from paying twice for the same materials. But most important, it requires frequent contact and communication with the customer and careful attention to his problems.

Even though bad debt losses are relatively low (as a result of the protection afforded by lien or bond rights against third parties), cash flow tends to be very slow for subcontractors and often for material suppliers as well. Legal problems are frequent, although most are resolved by good-faith compromise rather than court action. New problems occur daily. Misunderstandings, delays, and frustrations are commonplace. Yet this is understandable, for though it is the largest, the construction industry is the least structured in the country.

Collecting money in this industry is indeed a challenging assignment—but never dull.

Chapter **39**

Applicability of the Uniform Commercial Code to Construction

H. G. WHITTON
Collection Manager, Bethlehem Steel Corporation, Bethlehem, Pennsylvania

RICHARD S. CRONE, ESQ.
Partner, Crone and Zittrain, Pittsburgh, Pennsylvania

INTRODUCTION

The Uniform Commercial Code is the largest undertaking ever attempted in the area of uniform statutory law and has, with some variance, been adopted in substantially identical form in 49 states, the District of Columbia, and the Virgin Islands. Louisiana has adopted portions of the code relating to commercial paper, bank deposits, and letters of credit but has not adopted the sales or secured transactions articles of the code so that most of what follows hereafter is not applicable to the State of Louisiana.

The code itself purports to be a unified treatment of all commercial law, dealing with all phases which may ordinarily arise in the handling of a commercial transaction from start to finish. It is intended to be not only uniformly adopted by all states but also uniformly interpreted by all courts. It is divided into nine articles covering such topics as sales, commercial paper, bank deposits and collections, letters of credit, bulk transfers, warehouse receipts, bills of lading, investment securities, chattel paper, and secured transactions. The sales article of the Uniform Commercial Code is of primary importance to contractors and material suppliers.

EFFECTS ON CONTRACTORS AND MATERIAL SUPPLIERS

The sales article of the code is not, by its terms, restricted to a "sale" (defined as a transaction involving transfer of title for a price) but instead uses the terms "contract or transaction" to define its general applicability.[1] Obviously a material supplier whose function in a construction project is simply to furnish raw or finished materials to a construction site is covered by the sales article of the code. It is equally obvious that a contractor whose sole function is to furnish labor to the project is not covered by the sales article. The difficult problems arise where a contractor or supplier furnishes both labor and materials. A typical situation creating a problem of the applicability of the code would involve the delivery and installation of a swimming pool or a furnace or a generator. Where faced with such an issue, the courts have generally looked at the predominant character of the transaction. If it really is a sale of goods, then it is subject to the sales article of the Uniform Commercial Code even though a substantial amount of service is to be rendered in installing the goods. On the other hand, if it is predominantly a construction agreement, it is not covered by the sales article of the code even though the furnishing of material and apparatus is an incident to the performance of the contract. The deciding factor, therefore, is whether the contract involved the sale of a machine or similar apparatus with the setting up or installation only incidental to the sale or whether the contract is really a building or construction agreement and the furnishing of material and apparatus is merely an incident thereto. Whether a particular contract is covered by the code can be of extreme importance where issues involving the statute of limitations, unconscionability, or warranty are concerned.

CONTRACT RIGHTS

Where a contract or transaction comes within the purview of the code, the code imposes an obligation of good faith or honesty in fact in both the performance and the enforcement of the contract.[2] It permits consideration of the past course of dealing between the parties and of trade usages provided they do not specifically conflict with the express terms of the agreement.[3] Indeed, the

---

[1] Article 2 of the Uniform Commercial Code (Hereafter UCC) is the sales article. Section references under this article appear as § 2-101, etc. This specific reference is to § 2-102.
[2] § 1-203.
[3] § 1-205.

course of performance of a contract subject to the sales article is relevant to determining the meaning of the agreement unless it violates the express terms of the contract. Where a course of performance is accepted or acquiesced in without objection, it is relevant to show a waiver or modification of any term inconsistent with it. A very important portion of the code relates to unconscionable contracts or clauses and provides that, if a contract or a clause is unconscionable at the time it is made, a court may refuse to enforce the contract or enforce the remainder of the contract without the unconscionable clause or so limit the application of the unconscionable clause as to avoid any unconscionable result.[4] In essence, the court is given the power to consider whether, in the light of the general commercial background and the commercial needs of the particular trade or case, the clauses involved are so one-sided as to be unconscionable. A clause in a contract limiting the time for complaints where latent defects may be involved or a blanket clause prohibiting rejection of shipments by the buyer has been held unconscionable. A combination of the "good-faith" and "unconscionability" provisions of the code may serve, in proper cases, to extricate a contractor or supplier from a bad contract.

Ordinarily, a contract for the sale of goods for a price of $500 or more is not enforceable unless in writing signed by the party against whom enforcement is sought.[5] Subject to that qualification, a contract for the sale of goods may be made in any manner sufficient to show an agreement even though one or more of the terms are left open provided that the parties have intended to make a contract and that there is a reasonably certain basis for giving an appropriate remedy for breach. The code differs from standard contract law with respect to acceptance or written confirmation of an offer in that the code permits an acceptance or written confirmation to create a contract even though it states terms additional to or different from those offered or agreed upon unless the acceptance is expressly made conditional on assent to the additional or different terms.[6] In other words, between a contractor and a material supplier, these additional terms would become part of the contract unless the offer expressly limits acceptance to the terms of the offer, or they materially alter the offer, or notification of objection to them is given within a reasonable time.

The terms of a written contract intended by the parties as a final expression of their agreement may not be contradicted by evidence of any prior agreement or of a contemporaneous oral agreement but may be explained or supplemented by a course of dealing or usage of trade or by course of performance.[7] A signed agreement excluding modification except by signed writing cannot be otherwise modified but may be waived.[8]

An interesting provision of the sales article of special importance to construction projects provides that, unless otherwise agreed, all goods called for by a contract for sale must be tendered in a single delivery, and payment in full is

[4]§ 2-302.
[5]§ 2-201.
[6]§ 2-207.
[7]§ 2-202.
[8]§ 2-209.

due at the time and place at which the buyer is to receive the goods.[9] In other words, the code contains a presumption against extension of credit. Payment and delivery are presumed to be concurrent.

Unless the contract provides otherwise, delay in delivery or nondelivery in whole or in part is not a breach of contract if performance as agreed has been made impracticable by the occurrence of a contingency the nonoccurrence of which was a basic assumption on which the contract was made or by the compliance in good faith with any applicable foreign or domestic governmental regulation or order.[10] In such cases, the seller must allocate production and deliveries among his customers and must notify the buyer that there will be a delay or nondelivery. In essence, the code supplies statutory relief in cases of impracticability or frustration of performance. However, an increase in cost alone or even a collapse in the market are generally insufficient to come within the definition of excuse under the code unless brought about by some unforeseen contingency which alters the essential nature of the performance.[11] The code provides an excuse in cases of war, embargo, or unforeseen shutdown of major sources of supply causing a marked increase in cost or altogether preventing the seller from securing supplies necessary to his performance. In the event notice of a material or indefinite delay is received by a buyer, the buyer may terminate the contract or agree to take his available quota. If he does nothing within 30 days, the contract lapses.[12] These provisions are of special importance in these days of energy crises and gasoline shortages.

WARRANTIES[13]

The code imposes in every contract for sale a warranty by the seller that he is conveying good title to the goods and that their transfer is rightful and that the goods are free from any security interest or other lien or encumbrance. Express warranties are created where any statement or promise is made by the seller to the buyer which relates to the goods and becomes a basis of the bargain. In such event, the goods must conform to the statement of fact or promise involved. Further, any description of the goods or any sample or model which is made a basis of the bargain creates an express warranty that the goods will conform to the description or the sample or model. It is not necessary that the seller have a specific intention to make a warranty. Thus, specification data sheets of manufacturers have been held to bind the manufacturer to the statements and descriptions contained therein.

In addition to those warranties expressly made by a seller, there is implied in every contract for sale a warranty of merchantability, that is, that the goods are at least such as will pass without objection in the trade under the contract

---

[9]§ 2-307.
[10]§ 2-615.
[11]UCC comment 4 to § 2-615.
[12]§ 2-616.
[13]*See generally* §§ 2-312 to 2-318 inclusive.

description and are of fair or average quality and are fit for the ordinary purposes for which such goods are used. In addition, every contract of sale, where the seller at the time of contracting has reason to know any particular purpose for which the goods are required and that the buyer is relying on his skill or judgment to select or furnish suitable goods, includes an implied warranty that the goods shall be fit for such purpose.

Words disclaiming an express warranty are inoperative. The implied warranties of merchantability or fitness for a particular purpose may be excluded or modified by specific language in the agreement or by course of dealing or course of performance or usage of trade and remedies for breach of warranty can be limited by contract.

The implied warranties imposed by the code are, of course, in addition to any promises made by the seller in the contract itself. The exclusion or modification of warranties and the limitation of remedies for breach of warranty are matters which are subject to the general good-faith and unconscionability provisions of the code and, therefore, require great care. It is suggested that material suppliers who desire to exclude or modify warranties or to limit remedies for breach of warranty contact counsel for the preparation of language sufficient to accomplish these purposes under the law of the state involved.

RIGHT OF REJECTION OR REVOCATION

The code imposes a general obligation upon the seller to tender goods which conform to the contract, that is, which are in accordance with the obligations assumed under the contract. Where goods fail in any respect to conform to the contract, the buyer may reject the whole, accept the whole, or accept any commercial unit or units and reject the rest.[14] Rejection must be within a reasonable time after delivery or tender and the buyer is obligated to promptly notify the seller that he has rejected the goods. If the goods have already been delivered, the buyer must hold them with reasonable care at the seller's disposition for a time sufficient to permit the seller to remove them. It is important in connection with the rejection of nonconforming goods that the buyer state specifically the defect which has caused him to make the rejection.[15]

Once a buyer has accepted goods, he cannot thereafter revoke his acceptance, if he had knowledge that the goods failed to conform with the contract, unless he reasonably assumed that the nonconformity would be seasonably cured or remedied. A buyer may revoke acceptance within a reasonable time after he discovers or should have discovered the ground for it and before any substantial change occurs in the condition of the goods, provided he notifies the seller of his revocation and provided that he had not discovered the nonconformity either by reason of difficulty of discovery before acceptance or by reason of the seller's assurances.[16]

[14] § 2-601.
[15] § 2-605.
[16] § 2-608.

In transactions covered by the Uniform Commercial Code there are some rights afforded the parties which go beyond normal contractual rights and obligations with respect to assurance of performance. The code provides that when reasonable grounds for insecurity arise with respect to the performance of either party, the other may in writing demand adequate assurance of due performance and until he receives such assurance may, if commercially reasonable, suspend any performance for which he has not already received the agreed return.[17] For example, if a material supplier is concerned about the ability of his customer to pay, and reasonable grounds for this concern exist, he may withhold delivery and demand in writing adequate assurance of payment. If the purchaser fails to provide such assurance of due performance within 30 days, it is considered a repudiation of the contract and the seller may consider the contract breached.

REMEDIES[18]

Under the code, where a seller discovers the buyer to be insolvent, he may refuse delivery except for cash, including payment for all goods theretofore delivered under the same contract, and stop delivery of goods in the possession of a carrier and, in addition, subject to the rights of a buyer in ordinary course or other good-faith purchaser or lien creditor, may reclaim, within 10 days after receipt, any goods received by the buyer on credit. Unfortunately, bankruptcy courts in some areas of the country, regard the code as in direct conflict with the Bankruptcy Act and deny the right of reclamation.[19]

Where the buyer wrongfully rejects or revokes acceptance of goods or fails to make a payment due on or before delivery or repudiates the contract in whole or in part, the seller may withhold delivery, stop delivery by a carrier, and resell the goods, recovering from the buyer the difference between the resale price and the contract price together with incidental damages. Specific notice requirements and the method of resale are provided by the code.

Where a seller fails to make delivery or repudiates the contract or delivers nonconforming goods justifying rejection or revocation of acceptance, the buyer may cancel the contract, recover so much of the price as has been paid, and *cover* or purchase goods in substitution for those due from the seller, recovering from the seller as damages the difference between the cost of cover and the contract price together with any incidental or consequential damages. Where the goods are unique, the buyer may secure specific performance of the contract to deliver. The right to consequential damages is particularly important in cases of breach of warranty inasmuch as consequential damages include reimbursement for any loss resulting from the general or particular requirements and needs of the seller as well as damages for injury to property resulting

---

[17]§ 2-609.

[18]UCC-Sales, Part 7, §§ 2-701 to 2-725 inclusive.

[19]*In re Federal's, Inc.*, 17 UCC Rep. 407 (E.D. Mich., 1975) and *In re Telemart Enterprises, Inc.*, 17 UCC Rep. 881 (1975), 524 F.2d 761 (1975).

from the breach. If, for example, a manufacturer sells a waterproof membrane which, in fact, leaks, the purchaser may recover, as consequential damages, reimbursement of all costs in remedying the defect including not only the cost of cover but also damages from delay and from any other result of the breach.

The Uniform Commercial Code provides that an action for breach of any contract for sale must be commenced within four years after the cause of action has accrued. This may, by original agreement between the parties, be reduced to a period not less than one year and may not be extended to more than four years. Thus, a contractor or supplier subject to the provisions of the Uniform Commercial Code may find that his responsibility may exceed the normal one-year guaranty period which is so often provided in the general conditions of a construction contract.

SECURED TRANSACTIONS

The secured transactions article of the code is intended to provide a simple and unified structure within which the immense variety of secured financing transactions can go forward with greater certainty. This particular portion of the code is relevant where a material supplier who furnishes an item such as a furnace, boiler, or air conditioning unit for installation in an existing structure wishes to protect himself by perfecting a security interest in his product prior to incorporating it into the building. Ordinarily, goods incorporated into a structure in the manner of lumber, bricks, tile, cement, glass, metal work, and the like cannot be protected by a security interest unless, under the applicable law of the state, the structure remains personal property. The code provides that a security interest which attaches to goods before they become fixtures takes priority as to the goods over the claims of all persons who have an interest in real estate except subsequent purchasers for value, subsequent lien creditors, or creditors with a prior encumbrance of record to the extent that they make subsequent advances, provided that the subsequent purchase is made, the lien obtained, or the subsequent advance under the prior encumbrance is made or contracted for without knowledge of the security interest and before it is perfected. Once the security interest is perfected, it takes priority over not only the owner but the subsequent purchaser or creditor as well. A material supplier who secures and perfects a security interest in goods prior to their attachment to the property may, on default (that is, the failure of his purchaser to pay when due), remove the goods from the real estate, but he must reimburse any encumbrancer or owner of the real estate who is not the debtor for the cost of repair of any physical injury caused by the removal. It must be remembered that this provision of the code does *not* apply to structural materals. Where it does apply, however, and a security interest in the goods as chattels has attached before the goods are affixed to the property, the secured party gets priority over all prior claims, and if he perfects his interest by filing, over subsequent claims to the real state as well. Before attempting to exercise this right of removal, it is recommended that the contractor or supplier confer with counsel to assure himself of the legality of his actions.

Chapter **40**

Claims against Bonding Companies: How and When to File

PENROSE WOLF, ESQ.
Hartford Accident & Indemnity Co., Hartford, Connecticut

How and when to file a claim on a construction surety bond may be a topic of no present interest for you or your company. Hopefully, you will not have occasion in the future to file such a claim but, especially in today's volatile climate, the knowledge of how and when will be important. Therefore, some preliminary facts concerning bonds will be useful.

Performance bonds and labor-and-material payment bonds have come into widespread use since about the turn of the century and approximately coincident with the imposition of bonding requirements by the federal government on public projects. In fact, however, suretyship has been in use since ancient times. The first example of bonds on the federal level was the Heard Act (1894), followed by the Miller Act (1935). Presently, every state, as well, requires that contractors on certain public work furnish a bond to protect labor and materialmen. While the statutory requirements vary somewhat from state to state, the intent generally is to require contractors to furnish performance bond to ensure completion of the work pursuant to the construction contract and to furnish labor-and-material payment bond to ensure payment to subcontractors and other creditors for work, labor, and materials actually furnished or intended to be furnished to the project.

The purpose of this article is not to summarize the statutory requirements of the federal Miller Act or of each state, but rather to discuss the essential elements of how and when to file a claim, with some brief preliminary comment on the types of bonds.

This discussion will not include reference to claims by the obligee on the performance bond as this area has been treated by other articles of this *Handbook* with considerable precision and depth.

DEFINITION OF BOND

A contract bond, essentially, is a guarantee of performance by the contractor and assures the owner-obligee that the contractor to whom the construction contract has been awarded will perform the contract in accordance with plans and specifications and that the labor and material bills incurred in performance of the contract will be paid, but with certain limitations. The bond is not a contract of insurance and, unless specially conditioned and certainly in its standard forms most frequently encountered, will not cover all the contingencies which can occur on a construction project.

PARTIES TO THE BOND

Briefly, the terms encountered when reading a bond include *principal, obligee,* and *surety.* The principal is the contractor or subcontractor who has the obligation to perform the underlying construction contract or subcontract. The obligee, sometimes called the owner and who may also be the general contractor, is the other party to the construction contract and the party to whom the obligation on the performance bond runs, that is, the party to whom the duty of performance is owed in the event of default by the principal. The surety, the third party to the bond, is in effect the guarantor, whose assurance the obligee holds that, if the principal fails in the obligation of performance, the surety will assume that obligation.

TYPES OF BONDS

Performance Bonds

The performance bond (Figure 40.1) is a contract indemnifying the obligee against loss resulting from the failure of the contractor-principal to perform the construction contract in accordance with the plans and specifications. This bond, with some few exceptions depending upon the language of the bond and

BOND NO............................

HARTFORD ACCIDENT AND INDEMNITY COMPANY
Hartford Plaza
Hartford, Connecticut 06115

PERFORMANCE BOND
(NOTE: THIS BOND IS ISSUED SIMULTANEOUSLY WITH PAYMENT BOND ON PAGE 2, IN FAVOR
OF THE OWNER CONDITIONED FOR THE PAYMENT OF LABOR AND MATERIAL.)

KNOW ALL MEN BY THESE PRESENTS:

That..
(Here insert the name and address, or legal title, of the Contractor)

as Principal, hereinafter called Contractor, and the HARTFORD ACCIDENT AND INDEMNITY COMPANY, a
corporation organized and existing under the laws of the State of Connecticut, with its principal office in the City of
Hartford, Connecticut, as Surety, hereinafter called Surety, are held and firmly bound unto...............................
....
(Here insert the name and address, or legal title, of the Owner)

as Obligee, hereinafter called Owner, in the amount of...
....Dollars ($..),
for the payment whereof Contractor and Surety bind themselves, their heirs, executors, administrators, successors, and
assigns, jointly and severally, firmly by these presents.

Whereas, Contractor has by written agreement dated..
entered into a contract with Owner for..

in accordance with drawings and specifications prepared by..
(Here insert full name, title and address)

....
which contract is by reference made a part hereof, and is hereinafter referred to as the CONTRACT.

Now, Therefore, the condition of this obligation is such that, if Contractor shall promptly and faithfully
perform said CONTRACT, then this obligation shall be null and void; otherwise it shall remain in full force and effect.

The Surety hereby waives notice of any alteration or extension of time made by the Owner.
Whenever Contractor shall be, and declared by Owner to be in default under the CONTRACT, the Owner having
performed Owner's obligations thereunder, the Surety may promptly remedy the default, or shall promptly

   (1) Complete the CONTRACT in accordance with its terms and conditions, or

   (2) Obtain a bid or bids for completing the Contract in accordance with its terms and conditions, and upon
determination by Surety of the lowest responsible bidder, or, if the Owner elects, upon determination by the Owner
and the Surety jointly of the lowest responsible bidder, arrange for a contract between such bidder and Owner, and
make available as Work progresses (even though there should be a default or a succession of defaults under the contract or contracts of completion arranged under this paragraph) sufficient funds to pay the cost of completion less
the balance of the contract price; but not exceeding, including other costs and damages for which the Surety may
be liable hereunder, the amount set forth in the first paragraph hereof. The term "balance of the contract price,"
as used in this paragraph, shall mean the total amount payable by Owner to Contractor under the Contract and any
amendments thereto, less the amount properly paid by Owner to Contractor.

Any suit under this bond must be instituted before the expiration of two (2) years from the date on which final payment under the CONTRACT falls due.

No right of action shall accrue on this bond to or for the use of any person or corporation other than the Owner
named herein or the heirs, executors, administrators or successors of the Owner.

Signed and sealed this   day of   A. D. 19

Witness...   ....(Seal)
    (If Individual)   (Principal)

Attest...   ....(Seal)
    (If Corporation)   (Title)

                                   ....(Seal)

HARTFORD ACCIDENT AND INDEMNITY COMPANY

Attest...   By..(Seal)
                                               (Title)

Form S-3213-4 Page 1. Printed in U. S. A. 12-'70
(A. I. A. Form—Document No. A-311, February. 1970 Edition
Approved by The American Institute of Architects)

Fig. 40.1 This document has been reproduced with the permission of Hartford
Accident and Indemnity Company. Further reproduction, in part or in whole, is not
authorized.

BOND NO. ....

HARTFORD ACCIDENT AND INDEMNITY COMPANY

Hartford Plaza
Hartford, Connecticut 06115

LABOR AND MATERIAL PAYMENT BOND

(NOTE: THIS BOND IS ISSUED SIMULTANEOUSLY WITH PERFORMANCE BOND ON PAGE 1, IN FAVOR OF
THE OWNER CONDITIONED FOR THE FULL AND FAITHFUL PERFORMANCE OF THE CONTRACT.)

KNOW ALL MEN BY THESE PRESENTS:

That........ .... ,
(Here insert the name and address, or legal title, of the Contractor)

as Principal, hereinafter called Principal, and the HARTFORD ACCIDENT AND INDEMNITY COMPANY, a
corporation organized and existing under the laws of the State of Connecticut, with its principal office in the City of
Hartford, Connecticut, as Surety, hereinafter called Surety, are held and firmly bound unto ....

.... ,
(Here insert the name and address, or legal title, of the Owner)

as Obligee, hereinafter called Owner, for the use and benefit of claimants as hereinbelow defined, in the amount of

....
(Here insert a sum equal to at least one-half of the contract price)

....Dollars ($......................................),
for the payment whereof Principal and Surety bind themselves, their heirs, executors, administrators, successors, and
assigns, jointly and severally, firmly by these presents.

Whereas, Principal has by written agreement dated...
entered into a contract with Owner for...

in accordance with drawings and specifications prepared by...

.... ,
(Here insert full name, title and address)

which contract is by reference made a part hereof, and is hereinafter referred to as the CONTRACT.

Now, therefore, the condition of this obligation is such that, if the Principal shall promptly make payment
to all claimants as hereinafter defined, for all labor and material used or reasonably required for use in the performance
of the CONTRACT, then this obligation shall be void; otherwise it shall remain in full force and effect, subject, however,
to the following conditions:

 1. A claimant is defined as one having a direct contract with the Principal or with a sub-contractor of the Principal for labor, material, or both, used or reasonably required for use in the performance of the contract, labor and
material being construed to include that part of water, gas, power, light, heat, oil, gasoline, telephone service or rental
of equipment directly applicable to the CONTRACT.

 2. The above named Principal and Surety hereby jointly and severally agree with the Owner that every claimant
as herein defined, who has not been paid in full before the expiration of a period of ninety (90) days after the date on
which the last of such claimant's work or labor was done or performed, or materials were furnished by such claimant,
may sue on this bond for the use of such claimant, prosecute the suit to final judgment for such sum or sums as may
be justly due claimant, and have execution thereon. The Owner shall not be liable for the payment of any costs or
expenses of any such suit.

 3. No suit or action shall be commenced hereunder by any claimant,

  (a) Unless claimant, other than one having a direct contract with the Principal, shall have given written notice
to any two of the following: The Principal, the Owner, or the Surety above named, within ninety (90) days after
such claimant did or performed the last of the work or labor, or furnished the last of the materials for which said
claim is made, stating with substantial accuracy the amount claimed and the name of the party to whom the materials
were furnished, or for whom the work or labor was done or performed. Such notice shall be served by mailing the
same by registered mail or certified mail, postage prepaid, in an envelope addressed to the Principal, Owner or Surety,
at any place where an office is regularly maintained for the transaction of business, or served in any manner in which
legal process may be served in the state in which the aforesaid project is located, save that such service need not
be made by a public officer.

  (b) After the expiration of one (1) year following the date on which Principal ceased work on said CONTRACT,
it being understood, however, that if any limitation embodied in this bond is prohibited by any law controlling the
construction hereof, such limitation shall be deemed to be amended so as to be equal to the minimum period of limitation permitted by such law.

  (c) Other than in a state court of competent jurisdiction in and for the county or other political subdivision of
the state in which the project, or any part thereof, is situated, or in the United States District Court for the district in
which the project, or any part thereof, is situated, and not elsewhere.

 4. The amount of this bond shall be reduced by and to the extent of any payment or payments made in good
faith hereunder, inclusive of the payment by Surety of mechanics' liens which may be filed of record against said
improvement, whether or not claim for the amount of such lien be presented under and against this bond.

Signed and sealed this   day of   A. D. 19

Witness...   ....(Seal)
(If Individual)   (Principal)

Attest...   ....(Seal)
(If Corporation)   (Title)

                   ....(Seal)

           HARTFORD ACCIDENT AND INDEMNITY COMPANY

Attest...   By...(Seal)
                          (Title)

Form S-3213-4 Page 2. Printed in U. S. A. 12-'70
(A. I. A. Form—Document No. A-311, February, 1970 Edition
Approved by The American Institute of Architects)

Fig. 40.2 This document has been reproduced with the permission of Hartford
Accident and Indemnity Company. Further reproduction, in part or in whole, is not
authorized.

the facts of the situation, is solely for the use of the named obligee, and subcontractors and other creditors have no basis for claim upon it. Language frequently found in the performance bond is:

> Now, Therefore, the condition of this obligation is such that, if Contractor shall promptly and faithfully perform said Contract, then this obligation shall be null and void; otherwise it shall remain in full force and effect.

Labor-and-Material Payment Bonds

The labor-and-material payment bond (Figure 40.2) is the one with which we are primarily concerned in this article. The bond is required in order that the persons for whose benefit the bond is exacted shall be paid in full without regard to the status of what may be due to the contractor or to his subcontractors under his contract, or what may be due to the public authority from the surety under the construction performance bond.[1] An example of the operative language of this kind of bond is:

> Now, Therefore, the condition of this obligation is such that, if Principal shall promptly make payment to all claimants as hereinafter defined, for all labor and material used or reasonably required for use in the performance of the Contract, then this obligation shall be void; otherwise it shall remain in full force and effect, subject, however, to the following conditions.

Federal and State Bonds

Both the federal government and all of the states require bonds on public works projects. The statutory requirements of these bonds may differ somewhat between federal and state, and the requirements among the several states are not uniform and vary somewhat in language and intent. However, the basic obligation in both the performance and labor-and-material payment bonds used in any jurisdiction does not differ substantially from the examples used in this article. Of course, one must always refer to the controlling statutes in the particular jurisdiction to be certain of the requirements imposed upon creditors, and an excellent summary of the requirements of both the Miller Act and the statutes of each state is to be found in the *Credit Manual of Commercial Laws*.[2]

Private Bonds

Most private contracts also require performance and labor-and-material payment bonds to be furnished by the contractor. (See Figures 40.3 and 40.4.) Examples of language from bond forms used in private contracts are:

> *Performance:* Now, Therefore, the condition of this obligation is such that, if Contractor shall promptly and faithfully perform said Contract, then this obligation shall be null and void; otherwise it shall remain in full force and effect.

---

[1]*Extruded Louver Corp. v. McNulty,* 1962, 34 Misc. 2d 566, 226 N.Y.S.2d 220, *reversed on other grounds,* 18 A.D. 2d 661, 234 N.Y.S.2d 902.

[2]"Bonds on Public Works," *Credit Manual of Commercial Laws,* published each year by the National Association of Credit Management.

THE AMERICAN INSTITUTE OF ARCHITECTS

AIA Document A311

Performance Bond

KNOW ALL MEN BY THESE PRESENTS: that

(Here insert full name and address or legal title of Contractor)

as Principal, hereinafter called Contractor, and,

(Here insert full name and address or legal title of Surety)

as Surety, hereinafter called Surety, are held and firmly bound unto

(Here insert full name and address or legal title of Owner)

as Obligee, hereinafter called Owner, in the amount of

Dollars ($

for the payment whereof Contractor and Surety bind themselves, their heirs, executors, administrators, successors and assigns, jointly and severally, firmly by these presents.

WHEREAS,

Contractor has by written agreement dated   19   , entered into a contract with Owner for

(Here insert full name, address and description of project)

in accordance with Drawings and Specifications prepared by

(Here insert full name and address or legal title of Architect)

which contract is by reference made a part hereof, and is hereinafter referred to as the Contract.

AIA DOCUMENT A311 • PERFORMANCE BOND AND LABOR AND MATERIAL PAYMENT BOND • AIA ®
FEBRUARY 1970 ED. • THE AMERICAN INSTITUTE OF ARCHITECTS, 1735 N.Y. AVE., N.W., WASHINGTON, D. C. 20006

1

PERFORMANCE BOND

NOW, THEREFORE, THE CONDITION OF THIS OBLIGATION is such that, if Contractor shall promptly and faithfully perform said Contract, then this obligation shall be null and void; otherwise it shall remain in full force and effect.

The Surety hereby waives notice of any alteration or extension of time made by the Owner.

Whenever Contractor shall be, and declared by Owner to be in default under the Contract, the Owner having performed Owner's obligations thereunder, the Surety may promptly remedy the default, or shall promptly

1) Complete the Contract in accordance with its terms and conditions, or

2) Obtain a bid or bids for completing the Contract in accordance with its terms and conditions, and upon determination by Surety of the lowest responsible bidder, or, if the Owner elects, upon determination by the Owner and the Surety jointly of the lowest responsible bidder, arrange for a contract between such bidder and Owner, and make available as Work progresses (even though there should be a default or a succession of defaults under the contract or contracts of completion arranged under this paragraph) sufficient funds to pay the cost of completion less the balance of the contract price; but not exceeding, including other costs and damages for which the Surety may be liable hereunder, the amount set forth in the first paragraph hereof. The term "balance of the contract price," as used in this paragraph, shall mean the total amount payable by Owner to Contractor under the Contract and any amendments thereto, less the amount properly paid by Owner to Contractor.

Any suit under this bond must be instituted before the expiration of two (2) years from the date on which final payment under the Contract falls due.

No right of action shall accrue on this bond to or for the use of any person or corporation other than the Owner named herein or the heirs, executors, administrators or successors of the Owner.

Signed and sealed this   day of   19

_____   { _____
        (Witness)   (Principal)   (Seal)
                                           {
                                           { _____
                                                                    (Title)

_____   { _____
        (Witness)   (Surety)   (Seal)
                                           {
                                           { _____
                                                                    (Title)

AIA DOCUMENT A311 · PERFORMANCE BOND AND LABOR AND MATERIAL PAYMENT BOND · AIA ®
FEBRUARY 1970 ED. · THE AMERICAN INSTITUTE OF ARCHITECTS, 1735 N.Y. AVE., N.W., WASHINGTON, D. C. 20006

2

40-7

THE AMERICAN INSTITUTE OF ARCHITECTS

AIA Document A311

Labor and Material Payment Bond

THIS BOND IS ISSUED SIMULTANEOUSLY WITH PERFORMANCE BOND IN FAVOR OF THE
OWNER CONDITIONED ON THE FULL AND FAITHFUL PERFORMANCE OF THE CONTRACT

KNOW ALL MEN BY THESE PRESENTS: that

(Here insert full name and address or legal title of Contractor)

as Principal, hereinafter called Principal, and,

(Here insert full name and address or legal title of Surety)

as Surety, hereinafter called Surety, are held and firmly bound unto

(Here insert full name and address or legal title of Owner)

as Obligee, hereinafter called Owner, for the use and benefit of claimants as hereinbelow defined, in the

amount of

(Here insert a sum equal to at least one-half of the contract price)   Dollars ($

for the payment whereof Principal and Surety bind themselves, their heirs, executors, administrators,
successors and assigns, jointly and severally, firmly by these presents.

WHEREAS,

Principal has by written agreement dated   19   , entered into a contract with Owner for

(Here insert full name, address and description of project)

in accordance with Drawings and Specifications prepared by

(Here insert full name and address or legal title of Architect)

which contract is by reference made a part hereof, and is hereinafter referred to as the Contract.

AIA DOCUMENT A311 • PERFORMANCE BOND AND LABOR AND MATERIAL PAYMENT BOND • AIA ®
FEBRUARY 1970 ED. • THE AMERICAN INSTITUTE OF ARCHITECTS, 1735 N.Y. AVE., N.W., WASHINGTON, D. C. 20006   **3**

Fig. 40.4   This document has been reproduced with the permission of The American Institute of
Architects (AIA). Further reproduction, in part or in whole, is not authorized. Because AIA
documents are revised periodically, users should ascertain from AIA the current edition of the
document reproduced above.

LABOR AND MATERIAL PAYMENT BOND

NOW, THEREFORE, THE CONDITION OF THIS OBLIGATION is such that, if Principal shall promptly make payment to all claimants as hereinafter defined, for all labor and material used or reasonably required for use in the performance of the Contract, then this obligation shall be void; otherwise it shall remain in full force and effect, subject, however, to the following conditions:

1. A claimant is defined as one having a direct contract with the Principal or with a Subcontractor of the Principal for labor, material, or both, used or reasonably required for use in the performance of the Contract, labor and material being construed to include that part of water, gas, power, light, heat, oil, gasoline, telephone service or rental of equipment directly applicable to the Contract.

2. The above named Principal and Surety hereby jointly and severally agree with the Owner that every claimant as herein defined, who has not been paid in full before the expiration of a period of ninety (90) days after the date on which the last of such claimant's work or labor was done or performed, or materials were furnished by such claimant, may sue on this bond for the use of such claimant, prosecute the suit to final judgment for such sum or sums as may be justly due claimant, and have execution thereon. The Owner shall not be liable for the payment of any costs or expenses of any such suit.

3. No suit or action shall be commenced hereunder by any claimant:

a) Unless claimant, other than one having a direct contract with the Principal, shall have given written notice to any two of the following: the Principal, the Owner, or the Surety above named, within ninety (90) days after such claimant did or performed the last of the work or labor, or furnished the last of the materials for which said claim is made, stating with substantial accuracy the amount claimed and the name of the party to whom the materials were furnished, or for whom the work or labor was done or performed. Such notice shall be served by mailing the same by registered mail or certified mail, postage prepaid, in an envelope addressed to the Principal, Owner or Surety, at any place where an office is regularly maintained for the transaction of business, or served in any manner in which legal process may be served in the state in which the aforesaid project is located, save that such service need not be made by a public officer.

b) After the expiration of one (1) year following the date on which Principal ceased Work on said Contract, it being understood, however, that if any limitation embodied in this bond is prohibited by any law controlling the construction hereof such limitation shall be deemed to be amended so as to be equal to the minimum period of limitation permitted by such law.

c) Other than in a state court of competent jurisdiction in and for the county or other political subdivision of the state in which the Project, or any part thereof, is situated, or in the United States District Court for the district in which the Project, or any part thereof, is situated, and not elsewhere.

4. The amount of this bond shall be reduced by and to the extent of any payment or payments made in good faith hereunder, inclusive of the payment by Surety of mechanics' liens which may be filed of record against said improvement, whether or not claim for the amount of such lien be presented under and against this bond.

Signed and sealed this   day of   19

_____
(Witness)

                (Principal)   (Seal)

                (Title)

_____
(Witness)

                (Surety)   (Seal)

                (Title)

AIA DOCUMENT A311 • PERFORMANCE BOND AND LABOR AND MATERIAL PAYMENT BOND • AIA ®
FEBRUARY 1970 ED. • THE AMERICAN INSTITUTE OF ARCHITECTS, 1735 N.Y. AVE., N.W., WASHINGTON, D. C. 20006   **4**

40-9

Labor-and-Material Payment: Now, Therefore, the condition of this obligation is such that if the Principal shall promptly make payment to all claimants as hereinafter defined, for all labor and material used or reasonably required for use in the performance of the Contract, then this obligation shall be void; otherwise it shall remain in full force and effect, subject, however, to the following conditions.

HOW TO MAKE CLAIM

A basic rule on this point is: Follow *carefully* the terms of the bond and be sure to obtain a copy. If a Miller Act contract is involved, the Comptroller General of the United States is required to furnish a certified copy of the bond and contract upon receipt of an affidavit (Figure 40.5) from a supplier of labor and materials that he is unpaid.[3] The various state laws have similar provisions which require the contracting party to furnish a copy of the bond upon receipt of an appropriate affidavit and perhaps a nominal fee. Of course, the claimant can write to the surety and request a copy, which ordinarily is furnished promptly. The architect on the project is another alternative source.

Carefully review the bond requirements as to whom notice of claim must be given, as generally, notice, if required, must be given to more than one party. Note also that, under most forms of labor-and-material payment bonds, a claimant who is in a contractual relationship with the principal on the bond is not required to give notice as a prerequisite to filing a lawsuit, but a claimant who has no contractual relationship with the principal on the bond must give the notice. For example, under the Miller Act, one in privity of contract with the general contractor has no notice requirement, but a remote furnisher, that is, one who is at least one tier removed from the subcontractor level, must give notice to the contractor within 90 days from the date on which such person did or performed the last of the labor or furnished or supplied the last of the material for which such claim is made.[4] In the various states, the notice requirement will vary somewhat and must be examined carefully, although a number of states have adopted public work statutes similar to the Miller Act and which carry the same provisions.[5] Under the private forms of bonds, the AIA documents require no notice of one who is in privity of contract with the general contractor but notice to any two of the principal, the owner (obligee) or the surety if no contractual relationship with principal exists. (Figure 40.4).

Other forms of private bonds, often used on private contracts where the AIA form is not used, carry similar reporting requirements.

Having given the requisite notice within the prescribed time, the claimant must also carefully observe the time limitation within which to file suit at the other end of the time interval. Again, this is generally to be found either stated in the form of bond or in the statutes if federal or state projects are involved. An in-depth discussion of these points, abundantly cited, is found in Chapter 36, "Surety Bonds," by Lewis and Cushman, in this *Handbook.*

[3]40 U.S.C. 270(c).
[4]40 U.S.C. 270b(a).
[5]*See* Credit Manual of Commercial Laws, *supra* note 2.

FIGURE 40.5   Affidavit to Comptroller General for Certified Copy of Contract and Bond

STATE OF   : : ss.
COUNTY OF

_____, being duly sworn according to law, deposes and says that he is an attorney for   , a corporation (hereinafter called "claimant"), and that he is authorized to make this application and affidavit on its behalf:

1. Heretofore, The United States of America, acting by and through the   entered into an agreement dated _____, 19___, being Contract No.   , with   , a corporation (hereinafter called "contractor"), of   , for the construction of (insert here contract designation and location of project), in accordance with drawings and contract documents prepared by   , architects.

2. Pursuant to the provisions of said contract and the Act of Congress in such case made and provided, said (name of contractor), as principal, and (name of surety), as surety (hereinafter called "surety"), furnished to The United States of America their certain joint and several payment bond dated _____, 19___, in the penal sum of $, conditioned for the payment to all persons supplying labor and material in the prosecution of the public work described herein.

3. On _____, 19___, claimant entered into a written agreement with contractor to furnish and to provide   required in the construction and completion of the said project.

4. Thereafter, claimant furnished all of the material required of it by the aforesaid agreement, and was paid from time to time by contractor the aggregate sum of $, leaving due, owing and payable a balance of $, with interest; which balance contractor, without legal justification or excuse, has failed and neglected to pay to claimant.

5. The material upon which the aforesaid indebtedness is based was furnished by claimant and supplied upon the faith and credit of the payment bond referred to in Paragraph 2 hereof.

6. Wherefore, claimant applies to the Comptroller General of the United States for a certified copy of the contract and the payment bond referred to in Paragraphs 1 and 2 hereof, for the purpose of maintaining legal proceedings for the recovery of the aforesaid indebtedness against contractor and/or surety on the said payment bond.

7. Claimant hereby offers to pay for such certified copy such fee as the Comptroller General has fixed or may fix to cover the cost of the preparation thereof.

Sworn to and Subscribed   (Insert claimant's name)
before me this _____   By _____
day of _____, 19___   Attorney

_____
      Notary Public
My Commission expires _____.

WHEN TO MAKE CLAIM

Each of the forms of bonds discussed contains a time limitation for giving notice of claim and filing suit thereon. Each bond form must be examined in detail on these crucial points. While this time limitation is a matter for the claimant's lawyer, it must be considered by the claimant to the extent that the case is given to the lawyer with adequate time remaining to prepare the lawsuit.

The discussion thus far presumes a situation in which the claimant is unlikely to receive payment without substantial effort and perhaps litigation on his part. But, what of the very common situation in which a claimant is unpaid by his contracting party, the account is now overdue, and the claimant is uncertain or uneasy as to the debtor's ability to pay? What then should be done with the account? Should notice, if required, be given to the parties? Even if not required, should it be given? Generally, the answer is yes, assuming of course that the debt in fact is due and owing under the terms of the contract or, expressed differently, has matured into an obligation to pay. If so, notice probably should be given if the account is substantially overdue or due and payable longer than that period which is reasonable, as well as normal, to the particular business, trade, or industry. This format, if followed consistently, should avoid the trap which closes on so many creditors whose credit policy is a bit too lax. This procedure may raise protest from major suppliers, but economic realities should override other considerations.

A collateral benefit to the surety from this notice of overdue account is in uncovering potential loss situations at an earlier date than might otherwise occur.

On the other hand, the claimant must be cautious not to give notice if, in fact, the account is not then due and owing, on the terms of the contract.

In short, claimants will be within an acceptable time frame if (1) they carefully follow the time requirements imposed by the bond *and* (2) follow reasonable credit principles applicable to the trade or business. Always note that, if notice is required, the time requirement can be crucial to preservation of the right to file suit on the bond.

SUBSTANCE OF NOTICE REQUIREMENT

The notice requires no particular form or formality. It must be in writing and should identify the project and the parties to the contract or subcontract under which the account is claimed and should otherwise be sufficiently descriptive to permit the general contractor, obligee, or surety to identify the contract and project involved. It is wise to send the notice registered or certified mail, although this is not absolutely necessary.[6] The notice should be as precise, accurate, and detailed as the facts permit, stating the amount presently claimed and showing derivation of the amount by reference to the total contract amount, prior amounts paid, and retainage withheld. The notice should state with substantial accuracy the amount claimed and the name of the party to whom the material was furnished or for whom the labor was performed.[7] The notice does not require the precise formality, however, of a mechanic's lien claim and notice of intent usually required of a mechanic's lienor or for a statutory claim on the fund, where permitted. A form of notice and demand for payment appears as Figure 40.6.

[6]*United States ex rel. Hallenbeck v. Fleisher,* 311 U.S. 15 (1940).
[7]*Liles Constr. Co. v. United States,* 415 F.2d 889 (5th Cir. 1969).

FIGURE 40.6   Notice and Demand for Payment

_____, 19____

ABC Construction Company   (Name and address of contractor)

_____ Casualty Company (Name and address of surety)

Gentlemen:

By writing dated _____, 19____, The United States of America, acting by and through the   entered into an agreement (Contract No.   ) with ABC Construction Company for the construction of (description of project and location).

ABC Construction Company, as principal, and _____ Casualty Company, as surety, furnished to The United States of America a joint and several payment bond dated _____, 19____, in the penal sum of $, conditioned upon the payment to all persons supplying labor and material in the prosecution of the project described herein.

On _____, 19____, XYZ Company entered into a written agreement with ABC Construction Company to furnish and to provide (description of material, equipment, etc. furnished) required in the construction and completion of the project described above. A true and correct copy of this agreement is attached hereto.

Thereafter, XYZ Company supplied all of the material required by its agreement, whereupon there became due, owing and payable to XYZ Company the sum of $, made up as is more particularly set forth in the summary attached. ABC Construction Company has paid XYZ Company the aggregate sum of $, leaving due, owing and payable a balance of $, with lawful interest.

ABC Construction Company, without legal justification or excuse, has failed, neglected and refused to make payment to XYZ Company of this indebtedness in the sum of $, with interest, or any part thereof.

XYZ Company states that the (materials, supplies, equipment, etc.) were supplied to, for, toward, in and about the construction of the project referred to herein upon the faith and credit of the bond furnished by _____ Casualty Company, inuring to the use of laborers and materialmen, including XYZ Company.

Demand is hereby made upon you and each of you, the contractor and surety for the payment of this indebtedness in the amount of $, with lawful interest. You and each of you are hereby further notified that, unless the amount due and owing is forthwith paid, suit will be instituted upon the bond.

XYZ COMPANY

By _____

Title:

1. Duplicate originals to be sent by certified mail.
2. Copy to be sent to your attorney.

CLAIMS COVERED BY THE BONDS

The answer to this point is long, detailed, and has been the subject of much litigation. The topic is much too expansive and detailed to be reviewed here except in the most general terms. For those who want to examine the subject in more detail, the _Credit Manual of Commercial Laws_ is an excellent summary of the case law, both on the federal and state level, and the subject is also discussed in depth in Chapter 36 "Surety Bonds," by Lewis and Cushman.

Generally, however, all labor, material, equipment, and supplies necessary to and required for completion of the contract or subcontract are included. For a precise determination on this point, there is no alternative to careful examination of the terms of the bond, the relevant federal or state statutes and adjudicated cases—all of which, in most instances, is a matter for counsel.

As an example, the Miller Act provides[8] that the contractor shall furnish

> . . . a payment bond with a surety or sureties satisfactory to such officer for the protection of all persons supplying labor and material in the prosecution of the work provided for in said contract for the use of each such person.

The American Institute of Architects' labor-and-material payment bond (Figure 40.4) provides coverage for

> . . . all labor and material used or reasonably required for use in the performance of the Contract . . . labor and material being construed to include that part of water, gas, power, light, heat, oil, gasoline, telephone service or rental of equipment directly applicable to the Contract.

Private forms of bonds generally use the same or similar language.

Therefore, as is readily apparent, the language of the labor-and-material payment bonds most frequently encountered is not really as precise or descriptive as one might wish, and the consequence is a very large number of adjudicated cases, which at least will provide the background for an informed decision.

SUMMARY

If your company is a claimant or potential claimant on a construction project: (1) Obtain a copy of the labor-and-material payment bond or bonds (depending upon your status in the respective tiers of contractors) and become thoroughly familiar with the requirements; (2) send the requisite notice to all necessary parties; (3) be certain that your notice is as specific and detailed as the facts permit; (4) be certain to observe the time limitations imposed by the bond and/ or the statutes, and (5) be aware of the limitation in the bond or statutes within which suit may be filed and refer the matter to counsel well ahead of this deadline.

Chapter 41

When to File a Federal Contract Claim

McNEILL STOKES, ESQ.
Stokes & Shapiro, Atlanta, Georgia

INTRODUCTION

During the performance of a construction contract, changes are frequently made in the contract requirements. As construction technology develops and becomes more advanced and complex, the cost of making changes in projects becomes greater. Ideally, many changes can be prevented if enough time is taken in developing, reviewing, and checking the original drawings and specifications. Unfortunately, this ideal cannot always be attained, and even on a well-thought-out construction project, the government, the architects, the engineers, the general contractor, or the subcontractors may find it necessary to change the original plans.

There are many reasons for issuing a change order. It may be necessitated by the further development of the government's requirements, incorporation of construction improvements, deletion of unneeded features, equipment changes, unavailability or slow delivery of specified items, correction of contract document errors, resolution of coordination problems, and changes to include applicable code requirements or technological improvements. The contractor, in many cases, is entitled to extra compensation, called an "equitable adjustment" of the contract price, or to an extension of the completion date, or to both. The government will not volunteer these remedies; the contractor must affirmatively claim them. Because the contractor must first recognize these situations before he can make the claim and seek legal assistance in obtaining the appropriate remedy, the focus of this chapter is identification of the claim. The following chapter discusses the steps necessary to protect one's legal rights, and how to file a federal contract claim.

Certain generalizations, however, have been made for the sake of brevity, and the legal doctrines discussed may vary according to the particular facts of each case, the applicable law, and the specific wording of the contract clauses. Although frequent reference is made to Standard Form 23-A, which is the standard set of general provisions used in government construction contracts, the particular agency may vary the wording of the clauses and may exclude some standard clauses and include others not in Standard Form 23-A. The contractor should be aware of these limitations on the materials in these two chapters, and in no case should he substitute these materials for competent legal advice in a specific fact situation.

The construction contract is between the government and the prime contractor; the government usually has no contract whatsoever with the subcontractors or suppliers. Therefore, all references to contractor in this chapter are to prime contractor, although in most instances the same or similar principles apply to subcontractors. When certain provisions of the contract between the prime contractor and the government are required to be incorporated into the subcontract or where government actions have caused an increase in the cost or length of performance of the subcontract, the subcontractor may be entitled to relief indirectly from the government. The peculiar problems of this procedure will be discussed in Chapter 42.

A preliminary issue in identifying a potential claim is the distinction between breach of the contract and a change in the contract requirements by the government. The first arises when the government takes some action prohibited by the contract or fails to take some action required by the contract. In order to obtain a remedy for a breach of contract, the contractor must file suit in a court of law. Upon proof of a breach, the contractor may be entitled to damages for the government's breach and to a termination of his obligation to complete the construction project. By contrast, a claim arises from some act or omission by the government which is explicitly permitted by the contract but for which the contractor is nevertheless entitled to an equitable adjustment and/or a time extension.[1] The types of claims and their remedies are set forth in the

[1]*United States v. Utah Constr. & Min. Co.*, 384 U.S. 394 (1966).

general conditions of the contract in the sections labelled changes, differing site conditions, termination for default—damages for delay—time extension, suspension of work, and termination for convenience of the government.

Even if the changes clause describes the situation the contractor faces, the contractor must determine that the extra work falls within the scope of the contract. This is the test to distinguish between a change and a breach. This determination depends upon the facts of each case, so there is no easy rule to follow. In general, the changed work must be regarded as fairly and reasonably within the contemplation of the parties when the contract was entered into.[2] Factors to be considered are whether the magnitude, quality, and original purpose of the contract are changed.[3] As an example, the elimination or addition of an entire building would not normally be held to be within the scope of the contract,[4] whereas minor structural variations would usually be considered to be within the general scope of the contract.[5]

Another example of a change fundamentally affecting the magnitude of the performance required is a case in which the contractor built an airplane hangar which collapsed because of defective specifications. Although the hangar was reconstructed according to the change and the rebuilt hangar was essentially identical to the original, the undertaking was so great as to be a cardinal change in the contract and, therefore, outside the scope of the contract.[6] A third example of an order constituting a breach occurred where the required earth-moving work was increased from 7,950 to 13,000 yards, necessitating bringing equipment 100 miles back to the job site.[7] The function of the end product, the cost of the change, the time and manpower necessary to complete the change, and the ability of the present contractor to perform the change are all important factors in determining whether the change is within the general scope of the contract. If the contractor determines that the change is not within the scope of the contract, the change order is a breach of contract upon which the contractor may file suit in court.

The requirement of the disputes clause, that the contractor must proceed with any work under dispute pending final resolution of the disagreement, does not apply if a change does not, in fact, fall within the scope of the contract. Under these circumstances the contractor is not obligated to perform and cannot be held in breach of contract.[8] Conversely, where the change does fall within the general scope, if he refuses to perform, he is liable for breach of the

---

[2]*Freund v. United States,* 260 U.S. 60 (1922).

[3]*Wunderlich Contr. Co. v. United States,* 351 F.2d 956 (Ct. Cl. 1965).

[4]*General Contr. & Constr. Co. v. United States,* 84 Ct. Cl. 570 (1937) (one out of seventeen buildings deleted).

[5]Comptroller General's Decision No. B-178662, 20 CCF ¶83,060 (May 9, 1974).

[6]*Edward R. Marden Corp. v. United States,* 442 F.2d 364 (Ct. Cl. 1971).

[7]*Saddler v. United States,* 287 F.2d 411 (Ct. Cl. 1961).

[8]*United States v. Spearin,* 248 U.S. 132 (1918). *See* Appeal of Yukon Service, Inc., 69-2 BCA ¶7843 (1969).

contract.[9] However, where the work falls within the scope, but the government treats it as a new procurement and awards the work to another contractor, the contractor working under the main contract cannot compel the government to issue a change order and let him perform the change.[10]

Whereas a breach of contract is always prosecuted in court unless the parties reach a settlement, the procedure for making a claim differs and is set out in the contract and in the regulations issued by the government agency administering the contract. There are three phases of making a claim: (1) claim recognition and documentation;[11] (2) claim presentation; and (3) appeal. The first phase begins even before the claim has arisen.

CHANGE ORDERS

Too often general contractors and subcontractors fail to recognize the legal implications of problems that arise during the performance of construction contracts which may increase the cost of performing the contract. Extra work or changes in contract requirements may arise in many forms, not always apparent to the contractor performing the work. Until the contractor recognizes and identifies the situations in which he is entitled to extra compensation, he cannot obtain relief. The contractor must, therefore, educate not only himself, but also the key members of his staff and field personnel who are likely to encounter these situations, to recognize the elements of changes which may give rise to a compensable claim.

The changes clause in Standard Form 23-A (April 1975 Edition) provides, in part:

> 3. CHANGES
> (a) The Contracting Officer may, at any time, without notice to the sureties, by written order designated or indicated to be a change order, make any change in the work within the general scope of the contract, including but not limited to changes:
> (1) In the specifications (including drawings and designs);
> (2) In the method or manner of performance of the work;
> (3) In the Government-furnished facilities, equipment, materials, services, or site; or
> (4) Directing acceleration in the performance of the work.
> (b) Any other written order or an oral order (which terms as used in this paragraph (b) shall include direction, instruction, interpretation, or determination) from the Contracting Officer, which causes any such change, shall be treated as a change order under this clause, provided that the Contractor gives the Contracting Officer written notice stating the date, circumstances, and source of order and that the Contractor regards the order as a change order.

---

[9]*Stoeckert v. United States*, 183 Ct. Cl. 152 (1968); Appeal of Dave & Gerben Contracting Co., 1962 BCA ¶ 3493 (1962); Appeal of James Stewart Co., 1963 BCA ¶ 3669 (1963).

[10]*Hunkin Conkey Constr. Co. v. United States*, 461 F.2d 1270 (Ct. Cl. 1972).

[11]Because documenting the existence of a claim is at least as important in proving the claim and its amount as it is in initially identifying the claim, it is discussed in the following chapter on claims procedures.

(c) Except as herein provided, no order, statement, or conduct of the Contracting Officer shall be treated as a change under this clause or entitle the Contractor to an equitable adjustment hereunder.

(d) If any change under this clause causes an increase or decrease in the Contractor's cost of, or the time required for, the performance of any part of the work under this contract, whether or not changed by any order, an equitable adjustment shall be made and the contract modified in writing accordingly.

The changes clause provides for two categories of change orders. The first is the formal change order, which is always in writing and identifies itself as a change order. This is the more often encountered type of change order, and it constitutes a clear admission by the government that a change has been made and that the contractor is entitled to an equitable adjustment in the contract price and to an increase in the time in which he has to perform the contract.

The second type of change order is a constructive change order, so-called because its existence must be "constructed" by inference from the surrounding circumstances. Any written or oral order or any act or admission of the government may be the basis for a constructive change order as long as its effect is to require the contractor to perform the work in addition to or in a different manner from that specified in the original contract documents. A constructive change order has the same effect under the changes clause as a formal change order.

In order for a formal or constructive change order to bind the government, the person issuing the change order must have the authority to do so. Unless the order is authorized by the proper person, the government may not be required to pay for it. The changes clause allows the contracting officer or his authorized representative to issue change orders. In order for a representative to have the power to obligate the government to pay for a change, this power must actually have been delegated to him. It is not enough that his title or his duties would lead the contractor to believe that he has the necessary authority.[12] The burden is placed on the contractor to determine whether the official he is dealing with has the authority to issue the change.[13] Ideally, the contractor should deal only with the designated contracting officer, but this is often impractical. If the contractor is not absolutely certain that the person he is dealing with has the authority to issue a change order, he should obtain from the contracting officer a written statement of that official's authority.

An alternative method of protecting against performing unauthorized work is to send the contracting officer a written report of the instructions received by the representative and state that these instructions require extra work for which the contractor, if required to perform, will make a claim. The contracting officer may tell the contractor not to proceed with the work, in which case the contractor is relieved of any duty to perform; or the contracting officer may acquiesce in the instructions by affirmatively issuing a change order or by

[12] *Federal Crop Ins. Co. v. Merrill*, 332 U.S. 380 (1947); *Richards & Assoc. v. United States*, 177 Ct. Cl. 1037 (1966).

[13] Appeal of Edward Hines Lumber Co., 76-1 BCA ¶ 11,854 (1976).

silence or failure to repudiate the instructions.[14] In the latter case, if the contractor later performs the work and the contracting officer accepts it, the contractor may be entitled to claim an equitable adjustment in spite of the fact that the contracting officer never expressly authorized the change.

CONSTRUCTIVE CHANGES

As a general rule, if an unwritten change would be enforceable when formalized in writing and signed by the person instigating the change, it is an enforceable constructive change order. In practice, constructive change orders may not be easy to identify because the identity and authority of the person responsible for the change order is not always ascertainable, and it is often difficult to determine whether the change falls within the scope of the contract.

A constructive change order need not be a direct order. It may be a mere suggestion which nevertheless indicates to the contractor that he has no practical alternative but to follow a certain course of conduct. It may be implied from a threat to terminate for default. A course of government conduct which requires the contractor to perform extra work qualifies as a constructive change order, even if the contracting officer refuses to issue a formal change order.[15] However, being held to perform a task agreed to in the contract is *not* a constructive change order,[16] nor is voluntary acceptance of a suggestion which the contractor is free to refuse.[17] In each case, the contractor must prove that the work was *not* included in the contract, that he had no practical alternative but to perform the work, and that he suffered delay or added expense as a result. Several distinct categories of constructive changes have been consistently recognized by the courts, and all contractors should be familiar with them.

Geographic Changes

Geographic changes are often made pursuant to an oral order by the contracting officer or his authorized representative and are "constructive" only because they are not issued in written form. They are, therefore, easy to identify. Examples include orders changing the location of the field office[18] or the material storage area,[19] errors in government staking of the site,[20] and failure to provide access to the site.[21]

---

[14]Imputed knowledge plus inaction on the part of the contracting officer have been held to constitute an implied ratification of the change order. *Williams v. United States,* 127 F. Supp. 617 (Ct. Cl. 1955).

[15]*Turnbull, Inc. v. United States,* 389 F.2d 1007 (Ct. Cl. 1967). An exception to this rule is a request by the contracting officer for a price quotation on a contemplated change. The contractor was denied an equitable adjustment for costs incurred in preparing a proposal in Appeal of B.W. Horn Co., 67-2 BCA ¶ 6583 (1967).

[16]Appeal of Paul E. McCollum, Sr., 76-1 BCA ¶ 11,746 (1976).

[17]Appeal of Mountain Builders, Inc., 76-1 BCA ¶ 11,861 (1976).

[18]Appeal of Melrose Waterproofing Co., 1964 BCA ¶ 4119 (1964).

[19]Appeal of John McShain, Inc., 73-1 BCA ¶ 9981 (1974).

[20]Appeal of Discount Co., 74-1 BCA ¶10,511 (1974).

[21]*Id.*

Defective Plans and Specifications

A contractor who enters into an agreement to perform work under detailed plans or design specifications has no right to depart from those specifications.[22] To protect the contractor, the government is held to impliedly warrant that, if the specifications furnished by the government are followed, the resulting work will meet the contract requirements and the contractor will not be put to undue expense.[23] The contractor has the right to rely on the accuracy of plans and specifications without making an independent investigation.[24] This warranty is breached when specifications prove to be erroneous[25] or incomplete[26] or when the completed work violates an ordinance or statute and when the contractor incurs additional costs in attempting to perform. Not only is this breach of warranty a defense to any government claim of contractor default, but also the contractor can recover an equitable adjustment in the contract price and the time and expense for any delay caused by attempting to comply with the defective specifications.[27]

The more detailed the specifications, the better chance the contractor has of successfully asserting his claim. The extent of the detail is an indicator of the extent to which the government has assumed the risk of overcoming any difficulties. In addition, greater detail makes the task of determining the cause of the difficulty substantially easier. A distinction between design specifications and performance specifications can be drawn on the basis of the detail as an indicator of the government's assumption of the risk. Because performance specifications do not set out in detail the method of performing the contract, the government does not warrant the sufficiency of the method of performance. Difficulty in meeting performance specifications is better understood in terms of impossibility of performance.[28]

A limitation of the warranty doctrine is that, when the error in the plans or specifications is obvious, the contractor has the duty to inquire about the discrepancy and to seek instructions.[29] The theory is that, where the contractor is put on notice that an error exists, the government must be given the opportunity to correct the error and avoid the unnecessary costs of attempted compliance with the erroneous specifications. A corollary to this principle is that, when a contractor discovers a hidden defect in the specifications, he should stop work immediately and report the difficulty to the contracting

---

[22]*Laburnum Constr. Corp. v. United States,* 325 F.2d 451 (Ct. Cl. 1963).

[23]*Quiller Constr. Co. v. United States,* unreported (Ct. Cl. 1975); Appeal of Arthur Painting Co., 76-1 BCA ¶ 11,894 (1976).

[24]*Blount Bros. Constr. v. United States,* 346 F.2d 962 (Ct. Cl. 1965); *Wunderlich Contracting Co. v. United States,* 240 F.2d 201, *cert. denied,* 353 U.S. 950 (1957); Appeal of Massey-Judge Constructors, Inc., 76-1 BCA ¶ 11,737 (1976).

[25]*J.D. Hedin Constr. Co. v. United States,* 347 F.2d 235 (Ct. Cl. 1965).

[26]Appeal of Markowitz Bros., 1964 BCA ¶ 4167 (1964).

[27]*Jonal Corp. v. District of Columbia* (DDC, No. 656-73, November 27, 1973) (unreported), *aff'd.* 533 F.2d 1192 (D.C. Cir. 1976).

[28]*See* the subsection Impossibility in this chapter.

[29]Appeal of S & S Constr., 76-1 BCA ¶ 11,759 (1976).

officer at once. The responsibility for added expenses and delays from that point on is placed with the contractor if he decides to proceed with the work or to try to correct the problem. However, any wasted time and expense incurred *before* the contractor should reasonably be aware of the error or *after* the contractor gives the government notice of the defect is chargeable to the government.[30]

Where a defect is discovered[31] or is obvious and should be discovered[32] before the contract award is made, the contractor must notify the government, even if the contract documents do not specifically require that he do so. If the government ignores the contractor's request for clarification, the government has assumed the risk that the contractor may incur added expense not covered by the bid. If, however, the contractor assures the government that he can meet the specifications despite any defects which are reasonably discoverable, the risk of added costs is on the contractor and he may not be allowed an equitable adjustment for later remedying the defect. In no case, however, is the contractor required to conduct an independent pre-bid evaluation of the specifications to discover any hidden defects.

Misinterpretation of the Specifications

Where specifications are not defective, there may nevertheless be disagreement as to their meaning. If the contracting officer or his authorized representative misinterprets the specifications and requires performance not called for by the contract, the contractor is entitled to an equitable adjustment in the contract price for the contractor's increased cost of performance, plus a reasonable profit thereon for a constructive change.

Typically, the contracting officer or the architect misinterprets the specifications. The problem is often that the architect designed a cow barn and the contracting officer expects a cathedral. The contracting officer under the guise of interpreting the specifications may state that he had intended the work to be included. The answer to this assertion is that the contractors are specifications readers and not mind readers. Contractors base their estimate of the cost on the work shown in the plans and specifications and not on the architect's or the contracting officer's intention to include an additional floor in the building.

As long as the contractor's interpretation is reasonable, his interpretation will usually be favored over even an equally reasonable interpretation by the government.[33] If the contractor's interpretation is unreasonable and the government's is reasonable, the contractor is not entitled to a constructive change. To determine whose interpretation is more reasonable, the courts follow cer-

---

[30]*Molony & Rubien Constr. Co. v. United States,* unreported (Ct. Cl. 1976).

[31]*Blount Bros. Constr. Co. v. United States,* 346 F.2d 962 (Ct. Cl. 1965).

[32]*John McShain, Inc. v. United States,* 462 F.2d 489 (Ct. Cl. 1972); *Mountain Home Contractors v. United States,* 425 F.2d 1260 (Ct. Cl. 1970).

[33]Appeal of Brezina Constr. Co., 65-1 BCA ¶ 4638 (1965). In *United Pacific Ins. Co. v. United States,* 497 F.2d 1402 (Ct. Cl. 1974), the court went one step further to hold that the contractor's *reasonable* interpretation would be followed even in the face of a *more* reasonable government interpretation.

tain rules of interpretation. Words in the specifications are given the meaning which would be understood by a reasonably intelligent person acquainted with all the operative usages and customs of the trade and knowing all the facts and circumstances prior to and at the time of entering into the contract.[34] Sometimes the application of this rule alone will be sufficient to decide the case.

If the problem cannot be resolved using this general rule, more technical rules must be applied.[35] There are four primary rules of interpretation. First, technical words are given their technical meaning unless the circumstances or an applicable usage of the trade indicates a different meaning. Custom and usage of the particular trade are commonly applied either to supplement the terms of the contract or to clarify an ambiguous provision of the contract. Where the custom or usage of the trade is clear and regularly observed and was known or should have been known to both parties to the contract, it will be considered a part of the original contract and not a constructive change.[36] However, even a well-established custom or usage may be overridden by an express contradictory term or provision in the contract.[37] A custom or usage may be proved by referring to an industry code, such as the National Electrical Code,[38] or by having other contractors in the same trade testify as to the common trade understanding of the term in question. One of the most convincing ways a contractor can support his own interpretation is to check with the other bidders who bid on the contract or subcontract to determine how they interpreted the specifications in question.[39] The contractor should then get a letter or appropriate statement from the bidders who agree with the contractor's position. Of course, any evidence or documentation that the government initially interpreted the specifications in question similarly to the contractor should be presented.[40]

The second general rule of interpretation is that a writing is interpreted as a whole, and all writings forming part of the same contract are interpreted together.[41] No single word, phrase, or sentence should be interpreted out of the context of the rest of the contract.[42] This means that all the provisions of the contract should be read in such a way as to be meaningful, reasonable, and consistent with the rest of the contract.[43] An interpretation which gives a

[34]*Kenneth Reed Constr. Corp. v. United States,* 475 F.2d 583 (Ct. Cl. 1973); *J.B. Williams Co. v. United States,* 450 F.2d 1379 (Ct. Cl. 1971).

[35]*See* Appeal of Randolph Engineering Co., 58-2 BCA ¶ 2053 (1958).

[36]*Bromion v. United States,* 411 F.2d 1020 (Ct. Cl. 1969); Appeal of DeMatteo Constr. Co., 76-1 BCA ¶ 11,845 (1976).

[37]*Merando, Inc. v. United States,* 475 F.2d 603 (Ct. Cl. 1973).

[38]Appeal of Blinderman Constr. Co., 76-1 BCA ¶ 11,807 (1976); Appeal of Santander Constr., Inc., 76-1 BCA ¶ 11,798 (1976).

[39]Appeal of L.B. Samford, Inc., 76-1 BCA ¶ 11,684 (1976).

[40]*Norcoast Constructors, Inc. v. United States,* 448 F.2d 1400 (Ct. Cl. 1971).

[41]Appeal of Hoel Steffen Constr. Co., 76-1 BCA ¶ 11,853 (1976); Appeal of Knutson Constr. Co., 76-1 BCA ¶ 11,677 (1976).

[42]Appeal of Neste, Brudin & Stone, Inc., 76-1 BCA ¶ 11,829 (1976).

[43]Appeal of Massey-Judge Constructors, Inc., 76-1 BCA ¶ 11,737 (1976).

reasonable and effective meaning to all the contract language is preferred to one that leaves part of the language unreasonable or meaningless.[44] If the general provisions of the contract are inconsistent with the specific requirements, the specific provisions ordinarily prevail over the general.[45] Similarly, provisions which have been typed onto the contract generally control over the printed boiler-plate terms and general conditions of the contract.

The third principle of interpretation is that all circumstances accompanying transactions between the contractor and the government related to the contract may be taken into consideration, with the exception of oral statements by the parties as to what they intended a writing to mean.[46] Discussions prior to the signing of the contract may be used to interpret or explain the meaning of a word, symbol, or drawing, but not to contradict or add to the terms of the contract. In addition, the contractor's past experience with the government may be relevant to interpreting an ambiguity.[47]

Finally, when a court is unable to choose between more than one reasonable meaning, the ambiguity is construed against the one who drafted the document. Because the government uses a standard general contract form drafted by the government and usually drafts the specific contract requirements as well, the contractor's interpretation will be followed in most cases. The reason for this principle is that the government chose the words in the contract and had the opportunity to phrase its provisions in the clearest manner possible. The contractor is not penalized for placing a reasonable interpretation on ambiguous provisions.[48]

The contractor has the duty to seek clarification of any major patent discrepancies, obvious omissions, or drastic conflicts in the provisions of the contract.[49] There is no duty to seek clarification, though, where the contractor innocently construes a subtle ambiguity in his favor,[50] but a contractor who deliberately seeks to profit from an ambiguity in the contract which he knows to be an error by the drafter may not recover from a constructive change if he has not sought clarification from the contracting officer.[51] Therefore, if a contractor intends to rely on his own interpretation of an ambiguity, he should inform the contracting officer of the ambiguity and seek clarification.[52] If the contracting officer fails to clear up the questionable provision, the government will be held to have

---

[44]*United Pacific Ins. Co. v. United States*, 497 F.2d 1402 (Ct. Cl. 1974); Appeal of Modern Constr., Inc., 74-1 BCA ¶ 10,510 (1974).

[45]*Southwest Eng. Co. v. United States*, unreported (Ct. Cl. 1975); *Klingensmith v. United States*, 505 F.2d 1257 (Ct. Cl. 1974); Appeal of Randall H. Sharpe, 1964 BCA ¶ 4124 (1964).

[46]Appeal of Robert McMullan & Son, 76-1 BCA ¶ 11,758 (1976).

[47]*Singer-General Precision, Inc. v. United States*, 427 F.2d 1187 (Ct. Cl. 1970).

[48]*Gholson, Byars, & Holmes Constr. Co. v. United States*, 351 F.2d 987 (Ct. Cl 1965).

[49]*Woodcrest Constr. Co. v. United States*, 408 F.2d 406 (Ct. Cl. 1969), *cert. denied*, 398 U.S. 958 (1970).

[50]*John McShain, Inc. v. United States*, 462 F.2d 489 (Ct. Cl. 1972); Appeal of Robert L. Guyler Co., 76-1 BCA ¶ 11,690 (1976).

[51]*Ring Constr. Corp. v. United States*, 162 F. Supp. 190 (Ct. Cl. 1958).

[52]*Merando, Inc. v. United States*, 475 F.2d 603 (Ct. Cl. 1973).

waived the right to complain of the interpretation placed on the contract by the contractor.[53]

The contractor may not be able to claim a compensable constructive change when he performs the work according to an interpretation of the contract which is more costly to him without first protesting and receiving a direction by the contracting officer to perform the work according to that interpretation. In the absence of a protest, the contractor's voluntary performance may be taken to show that both parties intended the contract to be interpreted to require the more costly performance.[54] If, however, there has been a direction from the contracting officer to perform the work according to an interpretation of the contract that the contractor believes is unreasonable or contrary to what the parties intended, the contractor must follow the contracting officer's directions and perform the work in that manner. The contractor's recourse is to seek an equitable adjustment in the contract price.[55]

Method of Performance

When performance standards are set for the end result but the method of performance is not specified, the contractor is entitled to choose a method for meeting performance specifications which is less expensive than other possible methods. The contractor can follow any industry practice unless prohibited and may choose any reasonable and feasible method[56] as long as the performance specifications are met. If the contractor is directed by the government to use any method more expensive than his reasonable choice, then a constructive change arises and he is entitled to recover the difference in cost between the two methods as well as the cost of modifying any work in progress.[57]

Similarly, where two or more optional methods are specified, the contractor may choose the least expensive option.[58] Even if it is discovered that the least expensive option is not feasible, the contractor can recover the cost difference, because the specifications gave the contractor the choice of using that method.[59] However, if the government reserves the option of choosing one particular method of performance over another, a subsequent order to follow a certain method is not a constructive change.

A compensable constructive change may also occur from a direction by the contracting officer to change the sequence of the work which increases the cost of performance.[60] In any case, however, the contractor must prove that the

---

[53]*Beacon Constr. Co. v. United States,* 314 F.2d 501 (Ct. Cl. 1963).

[54]Appeal of Marinell & Campbell, Inc., 1963 BCA ¶ 3948 (1963).

[55]The contractor's obligation to proceed is discussed more fully in Chapter 42, "How to File a Federal Contract Claim," in the section entitled Disputes.

[56]Appeal of Main Cornice Works, Inc., 65-2 BCA ¶5019 (1965).

[57]Appeal of R.C. Hedreen Co., 76-1 BCA ¶ 11,816 (1976); Appeal of Beacon Constr. Co., 68-2 BCA ¶ 7197 (1968).

[58]Appeal of Dawson Eng. Co., 1963 BCA ¶ 3759 (1963).

[59]*United Pacific Ins. Co. v. United States,* 497 F.2d 1402 (Ct. Cl. 1974).

[60]Appeal of Mech-Con Corp., 65-1 BCA ¶4574 (1964); Appeal of Hill & Moore Constr. Co., 1963 BCA ¶ 3709 (1963).

ordered change was the cause of the increased cost of performance. If some other condition for which the contractor is responsible caused the increased cost, the contractor cannot recover.[61]

In order to recover for a constructive change because of alternate methods of performance, there must be a direction from the contracting officer or his authorized representative designating the more expensive method. If the contractor merely voluntarily selects the more expensive method, he cannot recover. For example, if the contractor specifies the more expensive method in his bid, even if no method is required by the specifications, he will be bound by his voluntary choice of that method and may not claim a constructive change. This is an exception to the rule for constructive changes applied by some courts that no actual direction is necessary if the extra work is done with the contracting officer's knowledge and approval.[62] In addition, mere acceptance by the contractor of a suggestion by the government may not constitute a constructive change.[63]

Rejection of "Or-Equal" Substitutions

The contract specifications may allow the contractor to choose the materials or equipment he uses under an "or-equal" provision. These clauses, which are common in government construction contracts, provide for the use of a particular brand-name product or its "equal" or provide that the brand names are used merely as a "standard of quality." Under these clauses the contractor is entitled to substitute materials or equipment which are equivalent to the materials or equipment specified in the contract. Furthermore, the contractor is entitled to the benefit of an honest judgment by the contracting officer of the quality of a proposed substitute. If the contracting officer rejects the substitution of materials or equipment which are less expensive but *equal* in performance, then a constructive change has occurred.

The word "equal" as used in or-equal clauses does not mean that the substitute is required to be identical in every respect to the brand name specified in the contract as a standard of quality. The substitute may be equal and at the same time have a somewhat different design. Equality is to be defined by the quality and performance of the substitution as compared to that of the brand-name product. If the substitute functions as well as the specified equipment or material, it should be accepted by the contracting officer as satisfying the or-equal clause.[64] Even if the name brand itself is inadequate the government is liable for an equitable adjustment, although the defective-specifications rationale is more appropriate in this instance. However, if the contractor chooses what he believes to be the equivalent of a satisfactory brand name and it does not meet the specifications, the contractor is not entitled to an equitable adjustment.

---

[61]Appeal of Baize Int'l, Inc., 1963 BCA ¶ 3963 (1963).
[62]*Chris Berg, Inc. v. United States*, 455 F.2d 1037 (Ct. Cl. 1972).
[63]Appeal of Orndorff Constr. Co., 67-2 BCA ¶ 6665 (1967).
[64]*Sherwin v. United States*, 436 F.2d 992 (Ct. Cl. 1971).

Impossibility

When it is impossible to meet the requirements of the plans and specifications, a contractor has the right to some relief in attempting to perform the contract. The impossibility may be the result of overambitious performance specifications, of an action by the contractor himself, or of some external force beyond the control of both parties to the contract. Before impossibility is recognized as a constructive change, certain prerequisites must be met.

First, the contractor must prove that performance was actually or practically impossible. Mere economic hardship is not sufficient to prove impossibility.[65] Actual impossibility occurs when erroneous design specifications describe an impossible task, when defective performance specifications establish a standard which cannot be met, or when the performance called for by the contract is beyond the capabilities of present technology, although in the future a means of accomplishing the task may be developed. The test for actual impossibility is an objective one; the contractor must prove that the contract could not be performed by any contractor. Subjective factors, such as inadequate financial resources or insufficient skill on the part of the contractor, are not normally considered.[66]

Practical impossibility occurs when the contractor is physically capable of completing performance, but to require him to do so would be unreasonable or commercially impracticable. Examples are when an unreasonable work schedule is established, when performance becomes illegal, and when—through no fault of the contractor or any subcontractor—a sole-source supplier becomes unavailable.[67] The commercial circumstances must require such extreme and unreasonable difficulty and expense that performance is not practical within existing commercial circumstances and the basic terms of the contract. Again, mere hardship or excessive costs are not sufficient to prove practical impossibility.

In addition to proving actual or practical impossibility, the contractor must show that he did not assume the risk that performance would be impossible. The theory is that the government impliedly warrants that its specifications, designs, drawings, and other data are suitable for their intended use and that it is possible to comply with them. The risk of impossibility is thus placed on the government, and the contractor need not make an independent check to determine whether the specifications and plans are in fact feasible. However, the risk may be shifted to the contractor where he knew or should have known of the difficulty or impossibility, where he offers his own specifications or design, where the government is relying on the contractor's special technical expertise, or where he expressly assumes the risk.

A distinction is drawn between design specifications and performance specifi-

---

[65]*Stock & Grove, Inc. v. United States,* 493 F.2d 629 (Ct. Cl. 1974); *Transatlantic Financing Corp. v. United States,* 259 F. Supp. 725 (D.D.C. 1965); Appeal of Huber, Hunt & Nichols, Inc., 76-1 BCA ¶ 11,788 (1976).

[66]Appeal of Blount Bros. Constr. Co., 1963 BCA ¶ 3760 (1963).

[67]Appeal of Norit Constr. Corp., 76-1 BCA ¶ 11,890 (1976).

cations. The contractor assumes the risk that design specifications are impossible to comply with only where he writes them or where the risk is obvious.[68] Where only performance specifications are set out and the contractor is given a free hand at choosing the method of performance, then the contractor is held to have assumed the risk that the standard set out for the final product cannot be obtained. The government is not deemed to have warranted that the performance goal can be met unless it also sets out optional methods of meeting that goal.

Before signing a contract, a contractor should carefully weigh the risk of offering his own design, realizing that he will be responsible for any errors or impossibility. He should also check the statement of the work for obvious errors and to make sure that he can meet the performance goals. The contractor should not take a follow-on contract if the previous contractor encountered impossibility if the specifications have not been modified to make the performance possible. Knowledge of the previous unremedied defects may preclude recovery.

If a contractor is successful in proving impossibility, he is accorded two separate remedies. In general, the contractor is entitled to the cost of attempting to comply with the impossible requirements plus a profit. In addition, if the government has already terminated the contract for default and is seeking to hold the contractor liable for liquidated damages, impossibility is a defense to this action. Where performance is only temporarily impossible, the contractor is entitled to a time extension without penalty.

Nondisclosure of Technical Information

When the government fails to disclose information to the contractor which is crucial to evaluating the costs and to bidding on the job or to determining the method of performance, the performance may be delayed or made impossible or more expensive. Even if the contractor later obtains the information and can proceed with the performance of the contract as modified by the information, he is entitled to an equitable adjustment for any extra costs occasioned by nondisclosure of the pertinent information and to an extension of time if performance was delayed or set back.[69] If the contractor has been terminated for default, the termination is modified into one for the convenience of the government, thus entitling the contractor to his costs and profit.

The doctrine of nondisclosure is relatively new, and its supporting theories and requisite elements are often difficult to predict. For example, some courts consider nondisclosure to be a breach of contract rather than a change.[70] In general, however, the contractor must prove four elements in order to recover under the changes clause: first, that the information was crucial to a proper estimation of costs or method of performance; second, that the contractor was unable to obtain the information through normal investigation; third, that the government had access to the information; and fourth, that the government

---

[68]*Quiller Constr. Co. v. United States,* unreported (Ct. Cl. 1975).
[69]Appeal of J.W. Bateson Co., 76-1 BCA ¶ 11,814 (1976).
[70]*The American Ship Building Co. v. United States,* unreported (Ct. Cl. 1975).

had actual or constructive knowledge of the fact that the contractor was lacking this information. Practically speaking, in order to prove that the information was crucial and to calculate the expenses incurred for nondisclosure, the contractor must be able to identify a specific problem which access to the information would have solved. Examples of undisclosed information which may qualify for treatment under the constructive change theory are subsurface conditions, technical information, the financial ability of the sole source supplier, the status of a predecessor contractor, and the government's plans to award other contracts. The contractor should check the specifications to make sure that they do not place on him the risk of discovering certain crucial information.

Government-furnished Property

Additional work required of the contractor because of defective property, equipment, and materials furnished by the government to the contractor also gives rise to a compensable constructive change. Three categories of such changes are recognized: failure to furnish, delay in delivery, and unsuitability for intended use. The government impliedly warrants that the property that it agrees to furnish is suitable for the use intended under the contract. Examples include defective models, erroneous data or information, and erroneously marked parts.[71]

The contractor is entitled to an increase in the contract price for his increased cost of performance in procuring suitable property or for expenditures required to make the unsuitable property suitable for his performance. Such costs include costs for inventorying and replacing defective government-furnished property, for abnormal but necessary handling, for repair, and for obtaining replacement parts. In addition, the contractor can recover the costs of and receive a time extension for any resulting disruption and delay. However, relief may not be allowed a contractor for any unreasonable vain attempts to make defective government-furnished property meet the contract specifications. When the contractor considers the material furnished by the government to be unsuitable, he should notify the contracting officer at once of the unsuitability and of his claim for a constructive change.

Overinspection

Inspection by the contracting officer or his authorized representative which requires more than the contract requires may be the basis of a constructive change order. Overinspection may take the form of administering tests not required, applying an overly high standard of compliance,[73] making excessive or repetitive tests, and changing the time or manner of the inspection.[74] According to the general rule, the inspector must be specifically authorized by

---

[71]Appeal of Sutton Constr. Co., 1963 BCA ¶ 3762 (1963).

[72]Appeal of Power City Constr. & Eqpt., Inc., 68-2 BCA ¶ 7126 (1968).

[73]Appeal of Warren Painting Co., 61-2 BCA ¶ 3199 (1961).

[74]Appeal of Gordon H. Ball, Inc., 1963 BCA ¶ 3925 (1963); Appeal of Pacific Car & Foundry Co., 60-1 BCA ¶ 2505 (1960).

the contracting officer to issue change orders or his action must be ratified or acquiesced in by the contracting officer or his authorized representative.[75] An infrequent exception to this rule occurs when, due to emergency circumstances, failure to comply with directions would result in materials becoming unusable. In that case, the contractor is obligated to follow the orders of the unauthorized inspector and will be given an equitable adjustment for the change.[76]

Rejection of Conforming Work

Rejection of conforming work occurs when an inspector unjustifiably rejects the work without performing the required tests[77] or when the tests are properly conducted but the inspector is erroneous in his judgment that the work does not conform to the established standards.[78] The contractor is entitled to an equitable adjustment for his cost in redoing the conforming work, but the contractor will not be compensated if the work does not actually meet the contract requirements and was justifiably rejected.

The standard of performance required of a contractor is governed by the specifications[79] and is supplemented by the applicable customs and practice of the trade.[80] Often the contract itself will provide that a particular trade standard or code, such as the National Electric Code, will govern performance.[81] Insistence on a higher standard is a constructive change. A common contract term requires the use of "first-class workmanship." This phrase has been interpreted to mean that skillful, average work conforming to industry standards is sufficient. If no standard of workmanship is expressly stated in the contract, a promise by the contractor to use good workmanship is implied.

The inspection and acceptance clause of Form 23-A specifies that work not conforming to specifications must be corrected unless it is in the public interest to accept the work and adjust the contract price downward. Public interest would demand a downward adjustment where, for example, the contractor had in good faith substantially complied with the contract but made slight and insignificant deviations, or where the reconstruction or repair would involve unreasonably high expenditures which would amount to "economic waste."

DIFFERING SITE CONDITIONS

Differing site conditions are covered by a clause separate from the changes clause, but are nevertheless treated as changes in that the contractor may claim an equitable adjustment and a time extension for them. The purpose of the differing-site-conditions clause is to eliminate from the contractor's bid any contingency for increased costs resulting from discovery during performance

[75]*L.B. Samford, Inc. v. United States,* 410 F.2d 782 (Ct. Cl. 1969).
[76]Appeal of Barden & Sons, 65-2 BCA ¶ 4874 (1965).
[77]Appeal of D.R. Kincaid, Ltd., 65-1 BCA ¶ 4810 (1965).
[78]Appeal of Day & Zimmermann-Madway, 71-1 BCA ¶ 8622 (1970).
[79]Appeal of E.W. Sorrells, Inc., 70-2 BCA ¶ 8515 (1970).
[80]Appeal of Healy Tibbits Constr. Co., 73-1 BCA ¶ 9912 (1973).
[81]Appeal of Mishara Constr. Co., 66-1 BCA ¶ 5308 (1966).

of unexpected site conditions. The contractor is assured by the clause of full payment of costs and profit if unforeseen conditions are discovered, and the government is required to compensate for the costs of such conditions only when they occur.

The differing-site-conditions clause provides as follows:

4. DIFFERING SITE CONDITIONS

(a) The Contractor shall promptly, and before such conditions are disturbed, notify the Contracting Officer in writing of: (1) Subsurface or latent physical conditions at the site differing materially from those indicated in this contract, or (2) unknown physical conditions at the site of an unusual nature, differing materially from those ordinarily encountered and generally recognized as inhering in work of the character provided for in this contract. The Contracting Officer shall promptly investigate the conditions, and if he finds that such conditions do materially so differ and cause an increase or decrease in the Contractor's cost of, or time required for, performance of any part of the work under this contract, whether or not changed as a result of such conditions, an equitable adjustment shall be made and the contract modified in writing accordingly.

There are two types of changed conditions for which relief may be granted to the contractor. Type I conditions are subsurface or latent physical conditions at the site which differ materially from those indicated in the contract. To recover for Type I changed conditions, the contractor must show that the conditions expressly or impliedly stated in the contract were incorrect. For example, if the method specified for performing the work necessarily requires certain site conditions, the contract is said to imply the existence of those conditions.[82] The contractor does not have to show that the government was at fault in misrepresenting the conditions; the contractor need show only that a material difference exists.[83]

The second type of conditions are those which are unknown to both parties and are of an unusual nature so as to be reasonably unanticipated. No reference, therefore, is made to Type II conditions in the contract. The conditions need not be freak conditions as long as they would not be anticipated by the reasonable contractor. To be reasonable, a contractor's expectations must be based on information gathered from a thorough examination of the contract documents, a reasonable site inspection,[84] and sound construction experience. Other relevant factors include customs of the trade, common knowledge of the industry, manufacturer's instructions and recommendations for materials and equipment, and traditional assumptions made in bidding on a construction job.[85] Reasonableness is measured from the time of bidding and not from the time of beginning performance or of encountering the conditions.

Differing site conditions may be above the ground or below the ground. However, it is more difficult to show that above-ground conditions were

---

[82]*Foster Constr. C.A. v. United States,* 435 F.2d 873 (Ct. Cl. 1970).

[83]*Id.; Jefferson Constr. Co. v. United States,* 392 F.2d 1006 (Ct. Cl.), *cert. denied,* 393 U.S. 842 (1968).

[84]Appeal of George E. Jensen Contractor, Inc., 76-1 BCA ¶ 11,741 (1976); Appeal of Bromley Contracting Co., 76-1 BCA ¶ 11,734 (1976).

[85]Appeal of Redman Service, Inc., 1963 BCA ¶ 3897 (1963).

reasonably unanticipated. The contractor is required by clause 13 of Standard Form 23-A to conduct a general site inspection and is held to notice of conditions which could be reasonably discovered thereby. If the contract indicates that certain conditions are present, but a reasonable pre-bid site inspection would have revealed the true conditions, the contractor may not be able to recover for a constructive change. A reasonable site inspection, however, does *not* include such steps as reengineering the site or verifying test borings. Although contracts other than Form 23-A may include a clause requiring bidders to verify *all* site conditions, disclaiming any guarantee of specifications, or containing other broad exculpatory language, courts are reluctant to enforce such broad and unfair language.[86]

The contractor should be alert to identify differing site conditions so that he can claim a constructive change for them. The different types of differing site conditions include, but are not limited to, subsurface rock,[87] subsurface water or permafrost,[88] erroneous contour lines,[89] and unknown utilities.[90] The differing-site-conditions clause does not include nonphysical conditions such as political, economic, or labor changes, nor does it include abnormal weather conditions, such as hurricanes or flooding, or extensions of work into winter weather.[91] The general rule is that the physical condition must have existed at the time the contract was executed,[92] but recovery has been allowed when an unanticipatible man-made condition has occurred after the contract was made if the government could have controlled the situation.[93] Where the narrow test for differing site conditions is not met, the contractor should consider whether he can sue for breach of contract for nondisclosure of material information.[94]

ACCELERATION

Acceleration of the time for performance occurs when the contractor is proceeding on schedule and the government orders him to speed up, or when the contractor is entitled to an excusable delay and the government does not allow him the full time extension to which he is entitled. In order for a compensable acceleration to occur when the contractor is not behind schedule, the contractor must actually be threatened with default. A mere insistence that it is urgent for

---

[86]*Woodcrest Constr. Co. v. United States,* 408 F.2d 406 (Ct. Cl. 1969); *United Contractors v. United States,* 368 F.2d 585 (Ct. Cl. 1966).

[87]*See, e.g., Tobin Quarries, Inc. v. United States,* 84 F. Supp. 1021 (Ct. Cl. 1949); Appeal of American Structures, Inc. 76-1 BCA ¶ 11,683 (1976).

[88]*Virginia Eng. Co. v. United States,* 101 Ct. Cl. 516 (1944).

[89]Appeal of Poblete Constr. Co., 68-1 BCA ¶ 6860 (1968).

[90]*Nelse Mortensen & Co. v. United States,* 301 F. Supp. 635 (E.D. Wash. 1969); *Henry v. United States,* 250 F. Supp. 526 (N.D. Miss. 1965).

[91]Appeal of B & W Constr. Corp., 76-1 BCA ¶ 11,693 (1976). *But see* discussion of excusable delays in the section entitled Acceleration.

[92]*Arundel Corp. v. United States,* 96 Ct. Cl. 77 (1942).

[93]*Hoffman v. United States,* 340 F.2d 645 (Ct. Cl. 1964).

[94]*See Potashnik v. United States,* 105 F. Supp. 837 (Ct. Cl. 1952).

the contractor to speed up work not accompanied by threats will usually be insufficient to constitute a constructive change.[95]

The courts have required a minimal showing of certain key elements before allowing relief on an acceleration constructive change following an excusable delay. There must be an excusable delay for which the contractor is entitled to an extension of time. The contractor must have requested an extension of time, and the owner must have failed or refused to grant the extension to which the contractor is entitled. The contractor must have been required, either expressly or impliedly by the conduct of the owner's representatives, to complete the contract without an extension, and the contractor must have completed the contract on time and actually incurred the extra cost. Of course, if the contractor himself has caused the delay, it is not an excusable delay and the contractor cannot claim a constructive change for being required to perform on schedule.[96] It is therefore important to be aware of which delays are excusable and which are not.

The excusable delay provision of Standard Form 23-A can be found in section d(1) of the clause entitled Termination for Default—Damages for Delay—Time Extensions (the default clause) and provides as follows:

> (d) The Contractor's right to proceed shall not be so terminated nor the Contractor charged with resulting damage if:
> (1) The delay in the completion of the work arises from unforeseeable causes beyond the control and without the fault or negligence of the Contractor, including but not restricted to, acts of God, acts of the public enemy, acts of the Government in either its sovereign or contractual capacity, acts of another contractor in the performance of a contract with the Government, fires, floods, epidemics, quarantine restrictions, strikes, freight embargoes, unusually severe weather, or delays of subcontractors or suppliers arising from unforeseeable causes beyond the control and without the fault or negligence of both the Contractor and such subcontractors or suppliers.

This section requires, first, that the cause of the delay be unforeseeable and, second, that the contractor not be at fault and not have control over the causes of the delay. In general, excusable delays can be classified as acts of God or nature, acts of the government, and acts of third persons. In all cases the contractor has the duty to mitigate the delay. For example, where a strike causes a transportation delay, the contractor should find an alternative means of transportation.[97]

The excusable delay for unusually severe weather is often the source of confusion. Only when the weather is *unusually* severe for the place and time of year will it result in an excusable delay.[98] Blizzards in Minnesota in the winter, for example, are normal, not unusually severe, and a contractor cannot claim a

[95]Appeal of Mountain Builders, Inc., 76-1 BCA ¶ 11,861 (1976).
[96]Appeal of Square Constr. Co., 76-1 BCA ¶ 11,747 (1976).
[97]*Nelson Constr. Co. v. United States*, 87 Ct. Cl. 375 (1938); Appeal of Arizona Plumbing & Heating Co., 60-2 BCA ¶ 2702 (1960).
[98]Appeal of Tidewater Tennis Courts, 76-1 BCA ¶ 11,810 (1976).

time extension for the resulting delay. The contractor should anticipate normal variations in the weather in pricing the job and in setting up his work schedule. It is not necessary that the unusually severe weather occur on consecutive days or for a major percentage of the total contract time, so long as the severity of the weather actually causes the delay in performance. For example, if a contractor in Florida encounters an ice storm which he could have avoided by completing the contract on time, the delay attributable to the ice storm may nevertheless be excusable. However, if the late start forces the contractor to work into the winter months, the weather-caused delay is not excusable because the weather was not unusually severe.

Delays caused by a subcontractor or a supplier, which may not be the fault of the general contractor or the government, also cause problems. Such a delay will be excusable only if the subcontractor experiencing the delay as well as any intervening contractor is without fault or negligence in causing the delay, and no contractor along the line has assumed the risk of delay.[99] Where the delay is attributable to a sole-source subcontractor, the problem of proving that the contractor did not assume the risk of delay by selecting him is particularly difficult. However, if the contractor had no choice but to use that subcontractor or supplier, he can argue that the government assumed the risk by expressly or constructively limiting his choice to that subcontractor by the nature of the contractual obligation.

SUSPENSION OF WORK AND TERMINATION FOR CONVENIENCE

When the government itself causes an excusable delay but does not order an acceleration, no constructive change has been ordered because the changes clause requires an acceleration order and the delay clause recognizes only the right to a time extension. In order to obtain an equitable adjustment, therefore, the contractor must look to the suspension-of-work clause, which provides as follows:

> 17. SUSPENSION OF WORK
> (a) The Contracting Officer may order the Contractor in writing to suspend, delay, or interrupt all or any part of the work for such period of time as he may determine to be appropriate for the convenience of the Government.
> (b) If the performance of all or any part of the work is, for an unreasonable period of time, suspended, delayed, or interrupted by an act of the Contracting Officer in the administration of this contract, or by his failure to act within the time specified in this contract (or if no time is specified, within a reasonable time), an adjustment shall be made for any increase in the cost of performance of this contract (excluding profit) necessarily caused by such unreasonable suspension, delay, or interruption and the contract modified in writing accordingly. However, no adjustment shall be made under this clause for any suspension, delay, or interruption to the extent (1) that performance would have been so suspended, delayed, or interrupted by any other cause, including the fault or negligence of the

---

[99]Appeal of David M. Cox, Inc., 76-1 BCA ¶ 11,821 (1976). *See* Clause 5(d) (1), Standard Form 23-A (April 1975 edition).

Contractor or (2) for which an equitable adjustment is provided for or excluded under any other provision of this contract.

Under the suspension-of-work clause the contractor can recover only for that portion of the delay which is unreasonable and cannot receive a profit on the cost.[100] Reasonability of the delay may be determined by the urgency of the job, the extent to which additional costs are incurred, and the extent to which the delay interferes with other portions of the work. One situation to which the suspension-of-work clause applies is when the government indicates that a change order is contemplated but fails to issue one. The contractor is faced with the problem of whether to proceed with the original work, which could result in wasted effort and a useless end product, or to suspend work pending issuance of the order, which would result in unnecessary costs should the order never be issued. Because of this dilemma, the contractor can recover under the suspension-of-work clause if he stops work, regardless of whether a change order is ever issued.

In addition to suspending the work, the government can at any time terminate the contract for its own convenience under the termination clause.[101] The contractor is entitled to costs reasonably incurred prior to termination, plus a profit on the portion of the job completed before termination. The government termination order will direct the contractor to refrain from incurring further costs. The contractor must cease all work at once, because he cannot recover for additional work in process without a written authorization from the contracting officer.

However, certain inevitable costs will continue even after the termination order is issued. These include direct costs, unabsorbed overhead costs, and settlement expenses. Direct costs are those for labor, materials, and services which cannot be immediately discontinued, and they are fully recoverable. They include such items as severance pay for terminated employees, costs of holding employees on the payroll pending reassignment to another job, payment of invoices and unexpired equipment leases, and removal of equipment from the job site.

To the direct costs, an amount representing overhead is added. Only where the contractor can prove certain overhead expenses were incurred as a result of the termination and were not otherwise absorbed can the contractor recover for overhead. Although the actual computation of overhead should be done by an accountant, the procedures outlined in the next chapter for tracing costs of changes are relevant.

Finally, settlement expenses, such as termination or settlement of subcontracts, costs of disposing of property acquired for or produced under the contract, and the expenses of preparing and presenting settlement claims and data, are recoverable as long as they are necessary and the amount is reasonable. However, the professional services of attorneys and accountants related to a board or court appearance are not recoverable.[102]

---

[100]*Ross Eng. Co. v. United States,* 92 Ct. Cl. 253 (1942).
[101]Appeal of James E. McFadden, Inc., 76-1 BCA ¶ 11,772 (1976).
[102]See note 24, *supra.*

Chapter 42

How to File a Federal Contract Claim

McNEILL STOKES, ESQ.
Stokes & Shapiro, Atlanta, Georgia

INTRODUCTION

What procedure a contractor will follow to recover the costs of his extra work will depend upon whether he characterizes the order to perform that work as a change order or as a breach of contract. The proper characterization depends upon whether the change is within the scope of the contract.[1] The line between a change and a breach is often very thin, and the contractor may have difficulty in predicting whether the board or court will agree with his choice. Whether a breach by the government will later be treated by the boards and courts as a breach may depend upon the contractor's response to the breach. Acceptance and performance of the order, treating it as a change rather than a breach, may be taken as an indication that the parties contemplated that such changes would

---

[1]*See* Introduction, Chapter 41.

be within the scope of the contract. The contractor may later be "estopped" from or denied the right to claim that a breach occurred.[2]

The contractor must make the initial decision whether to follow the procedures required for filing a claim, authorized in general by the Wunderlich Act,[3] or to file suit in the Court of Claims under the Tucker Act[4] for breach of contract. If the contractor files suit under the Tucker Act, by the time the court determines that the facts present a claim and not a breach, the 30-day time limit for filing a claim[5] will have expired. The contractor may be left without any avenue of recovery. By contrast, if the contractor files a claim, and the board of contract appeals or the court ultimately determines that the facts support a breach, he may still be able to file suit in the court of claims for the breach because the statute of limitations for suits in the court of claims is six years.[6]

As a practical matter the contractor should always comply with the procedure for filing a claim whenever there is the slightest question of whether the change is a breach or gives rise to a claim. Even if the board of contract appeals reaches a decision adverse to the contractor, the contractor can still present his suit for breach to the court. The court can then disregard the board's decision and make its own determination of whether the case is one of breach and what the merits of the contractor's case are.

GIVING NOTICE OF THE CLAIM

If a contractor does not follow the prescribed procedure for asserting his claim, the government may assert that it has been damaged by the lack of notice or by the late notice. For example, if the contractor delays in notifying the contracting officer that he has encountered unanticipated rock in the course of the excavation, the government may claim that it was not given the opportunity to verify the quality and quantity of rock before it was removed. If the contractor discovers that the specifications contain an error and he persists in trying to overcome or circumvent that error, the government may claim that the government was not given the opportunity to minimize the costs of the change. Where the claim is for "impossibility of performance," the government may wish to alter the job or avoid it. The contractor should therefore be very careful to follow the required procedures for giving notice.

Where extensions of time for giving notice are allowed, the contractor should not count on being given an extension, but should give notice within the normal time period. However, where the contractor has neglected or has been unable to give notice within the required time, he should give notice as soon as he possibly can, because the deadline may be waived or the government may be

---

[2]*See Silberblatt & Lasker, Inc. v. United States,* 101 Ct. Cl. 54 (1944); Appeal of Harwell Constr. Co., 66-1 BCA ¶ 5329 (1966).

[3]41 U.S.C. §§ 321, 322 (1965).

[4]28 U.S.C. § 1491 (1973).

[5]*See* Filing and Negotiating the Claim, *infra.*

[6]28 U.S.C. § 2501 (1965).

unable to show that it has been harmed by not receiving notice within the time period required.[7]

The first step in the claims procedure is giving the contracting officer notice of the change. If the change order is a formal one, the government already has notice because it issued the written order; the contractor needs only to acknowledge the order by signing it. However, if the order contains a price or a maximum price for the change with which the contractor is not satisfied, he should make a note on the notice that his signature acknowledges receipt only and that he does not agree to the stated price.

If the change order is a constructive one, the work may already be in progress and the contracting officer may be totally unaware that the contractor considers his statement or action to be a constructive change order. The contractor is therefore required to inform the contracting officer of the constructive change order, including the date it occurred, the source of the order, the circumstances surrounding the order, and specific notice that the contractor regards the order as a constructive change order.[8] No set form is required for this notice, but it must be in writing.[9]

It is extremely important to submit this notice as soon as possible after discovering the change, because the contracting officer may take the position that the contractor is not permitted to recover change-related costs incurred more than 20 days before the notice is issued.[10] There are two exceptions to this limitation: The first is for differing site conditions, of which the contracting officer must be notified immediately and before the site conditions are disturbed;[11] the second is for defective specifications for which a contractor may recover any costs reasonably incurred in attempting to comply with the specifications even if the costs are incurred more than 20 days prior to notice.[12]

If, in addition to or because of a formal or constructive change order, the contractor encounters an excusable delay in the work, he must give the contracting officer written notice of the delay and its cause within 10 days of the beginning of the delay.[13] The contractor should at the same time request an extension of time for performance. Two specific notices, then, are required: one of the constructive change and a second of the resulting delay. If the government contests the excusability of the delay and threatens to terminate for default, the contractor should give notice that he considers this threat to be an acceleration and a constructive change order. If the contracting officer indicates to the contractor that he is going to issue a change order on a particular

---

[7]By contrast, where the government has not been prejudiced by the late notice, the Board may be willing to waive the time limit. *See* Appeal of Mil-Pak Co., 76-1 BCA ¶ 11,836 (1976); Appeal of R.C. Hedreen Co., 76-1 BCA ¶ 11,816 (1976); Appeal of Flex-Y-Plan Industries, Inc., 76-1 BCA ¶ 11,713 (1976).

[8]*See* Standard Form 23-A, clause 3(b).

[9]*Id.*

[10]*See* Standard Form 23-A, clauses 3(d) and 17(c).

[11]*See* Standard Form 23-A, clause 4(a).

[12]*See* Standard Form 23-A, clause 3(d).

[13]*See* Standard Form 23-A, clause 5(d)(2).

matter but delays in actually issuing it, causing the contractor a delay pending issuance of the order, the contractor should give notice to the contracting officer that he is stopping work under the constructive suspension of work order unless ordered to proceed.[14]

Although the requirements for timely notice of a claim may be waived by the government,[15] the contractor should make every attempt to comply with the time limit because he cannot be certain that it will be waived. However, the contractor must be certain to give all notices of delay, change, or work suspension before he accepts final payment for the contract, because claims asserted after final payment may not be considered.[16]

However, a contractor or subcontractor who performs extra work and is otherwise entitled to be paid for it will not automatically lose his money just because he has failed to follow procedural technicalities in the contract. Experience has shown that the courts hesitate to deny a just claim because of such technicalities. Instead, they have recognized several areas which will allow a general contractor or subcontractor to recover for extra work, changed work, or delays even though no written notice was ever given.

The courts have recognized that these notice requirements serve two functions: (1) they give the government or architect an opportunity to correct any problem which is going to result in extra cost and (2) they protect the government from "surprise" claims after the job is over. Since the notice provisions are placed in the contract for the protection of one of the parties, the courts have found that these notice provisions can be waived by that party in situations where the failure to give the required notice does not have an adverse effect on the party who was to receive the notice. For example, the courts have found that the government may waive written notice of extra work, changed work, or delays where the owner had actual knowledge of the circumstances and the contractor considered them to amount to a compensable change in the work.

If the government had knowledge of the circumstances that formed the basis of the claim, then the courts and the Board of Contract Appeals have held that formal notice is not required.[17] Only in a very unusual and compelling case, however, will the courts permit a claim to be considered after final payment.[18]

The contractor need not postpone giving notice because he cannot fully explain the cause of the constructive change or because he cannot yet calculate the length of the time extension or the amount of the equitable adjustment to which he is entitled. This notice need not contain any such information; its sole purpose is to give the contracting officer notice of the fact of delay or change so that he can take the appropriate measures to avoid further expenses or delay.

---

[14]*See* Standard Form 23-A, clause 17(b).

[15]*See, e.g., Ardelt-Horn Constr. Co. v. United States,* 21 CCF ¶ 84,096 (1975); *Southwest Eng. Co. v. United States,* 21 CCF ¶ 83,909 (1975).

[16]*Pearson Dickerson, Inc. v. United States,* 115 Ct. Cl. 236 (1950). *See* Standard Form 23-A, clauses 3(f), 4(c), 5(d)(2), 7(e), 17(c).

[17]Appeal of Beacon Constr. Co., 68-2 BCA ¶ 7197 (1968).

[18]*See, e.g.,* Appeal of Jackson & Church Co., 68-1 BCA ¶ 6815 (1968).

FILING AND NEGOTIATING THE CLAIM

After the notice of change and the notice of delay, if applicable, have been submitted, the next step in the claims procedure is the filing of the claim itself with the contracting officer. The claim may be submitted along with initial notice, but it is not necessary to do so. Where the claim is for damages due to suspension of work or to delay, it must be filed as soon as possible after the delay or suspension ceases.[19] Where the claim is for a formal change, the contractor has 30 days from receipt of the change order to file the claim with the contracting officer.[20] For a constructive change order, the contractor has 30 days from when he filed notice of the constructive change with the contracting officer.[21] The claim, like the notice, must be filed before final payment.[22]

There is no required form for a claim, but it must be in writing and it must contain a statement of the "general nature and monetary extent" of the claim.[23] This requirement is general and does not give a contractor much guidance in deciding how to phrase his claim. He should keep in mind that the primary object of the claim is to convince the contracting officer of the merit of his claim, both as to its existence and its amount. In addition, if negotiation attempts are unsuccessful and the contracting officer denies the claim, the claim documents will be the basis for an appeal of that decision to the appropriate board of contract appeals. A well-prepared claim is a valuable tool for appeal. The contractor will avoid having to make extensive preparations for the appeal, and the well-prepared claim document itself will impress upon the administrative and judicial judges the contractor's sincerity and seriousness in making the claim.

Because of the time and expense involved in appealing the contracting officer's decision, a contractor should make every effort to negotiate a settlement of the claim with the contracting officer. Even if he must settle for less than he feels he is entitled to, he may be saving money in the long run because attorney's fees, accountant's fees, expert witness fees, travel expenses, and all other expenses of prosecuting a claim are usually not recoverable.[24] The contractor must deduct these anticipated expenses from what he reasonably believes the appeals board or court should award him in order to determine the net amount he stands to gain. He should further consider the fact that, unless the contract expressly provides, he cannot recover interest on the overdue adjustment even if he wins the suit.[25] This figure should be compared with the

---

[19]*See* Standard Form 23-A, clause 17(c)(2).

[20]*See* Standard Form 23-A, clause 3(e).

[21]*Id.*

[22]*See* Standard Form 23-A, clause 3(f).

[23]Standard Form 23-A, clause 3(e).

[24]*Brezina Constr. Co. v. United States,* unreported (Ct. Cl. 1974); *United States ex rel. E. & R. Constr. Co. v. Guy H. James Constr. Co.,* 390 F. Supp. 1193 (M.D. Tenn. 1972); Appeal of H. & J. Constr. Co. 76-1 BCA ¶ 11,903 (1976); Appeal of Granite Constr. Co., 76-1 BCA ¶ 11,748 (1976).

[25]28 U.S.C. § 2516 (1965). Standard Form 23-A, clause 19, provides for interest on the amount determined owed to the contractor from the date of the written appeal or the date payment was due, whichever is later, to the date of final decision by the board or judgment by the court.

contracting officer's offer to determine which alternative—settle or appeal—is the more advantageous.

Due to the potential expense of an adverse decision by the contracting officer, the contractor should not cut corners in preparing a claim for the contracting officer's decision. Even if the contracting officer appears to favor the contractor's claim, the mere fact that the contracting officer has not yet made the equitable adjustment or extended the time for performance belies this attitude. The contractor should assume that he has a full burden of persuasion and should prepare his claim with the same degree of care and thoroughness that he would prepare it for presentation to the board or the court. A detailed claim with accurate and complete supporting data and legal authority should serve not only to convince the contracting officer of the merits of the claim but also to demonstrate the contractor's conviction that he is entitled to the adjustment and is willing to pursue an appeal if necessary. By contrast, a claim which is not fully documented serves neither purpose; in fact, it could encourage the contracting officer to disallow the claim on the assumption either that the contractor is not prepared or willing to appeal if necessary or that any appeal would be decided in the contracting officer's favor. Thus, the claim should be prepared with sufficient detail and persuasiveness to convince a neutral party unfamiliar with the facts that the contractor merits the relief he is seeking.

Specifically, the claim document should first contain a statement of the facts. All details relevant to the claim should be included. The facts may be illustrated or supplemented with photographs taken before and after the change, expert reports submitted on the cause and effect of the change, and graphs and drawings relevant to the change. These documents carry much more weight than an unsupported narrative of the relevant events. They present an independent and unbiased view from the perspective of a third party, which enhances the credibility of the claim. In addition, the photographs and drawings can often communicate what the written word cannot. Even if the narrative portion is sufficiently clear and explicit, these visual stimuli serve to emphasize and reinforce the factual statement.

The contractor must show not only that his statement of the facts is what actually occurred, but he must also establish that those facts entitle him to relief because they constitute a change. The basis for asserting a claim for relief is always a specific contract clause.[26] It is, therefore, imperative that the clauses under which the claim is made be cited and, preferably, quoted. The contractor may also need to refer to the portions of the plans and specifications which support the claim. He must show: (1) what the contract required him to do, (2) what he was actually required to do in the course of performance, and (3) that the contract recognizes this difference as a change for which the contractor is entitled to be compensated.

Because the facts together with the contract documents seldom present a clear-cut and irrefutable claim, it is helpful and sometimes absolutely necessary

---

[26]*See* note 1 and Chapter 41, When to File a Federal Contract Claim.

to support the claim with legal authority. Previous cases decided by the boards and courts may have already disposed of the question involved in the claim. Where cases on point are not available, cases having similar facts or applicable reasoning may be persuasive. In some instances a particular law and cases decided under it may be relevant or controlling. Discussing the legal authority for the claim serves as objective support of the claim and may convince the contracting officer that an adverse decision on the claim would be overturned on appeal. In addition, it supplies the contracting officer, who is acting in the government's interest, with an objective rationale for acting in favor of the contractor by making the equitable adjustment or excusing the delay. Of course, the assistance of an attorney is demanded here, as it may also be in other aspects of the claims procedure.

In addition to presenting a convincing claim, a contractor can boost a claim's persuasive power by never filing any claim of which the contractor himself is not convinced of the merits. Such frivolous claims may serve only to decrease the impact and convincing quality of valid claims. They are also a waste of effort, because they are almost certain to be disallowed. It is hardly worth preparing 10 empty claims in the hope that the contracting officer may allow one of them.

By contrast, a contractor should not hesitate to file a claim for an adjustment to which he is entitled. Failure to demand what he has earned does not improve the working relationship with the contracting officer; it only encourages the contracting officer to issue more changes under the guise of suggestions or to insist on extra work, confident that the contractor will not seek an equitable adjustment or a time extension for the change.

The contractor can recover only what he asks for, both in terms of deciding initially to file the claim and then in computing the sum to request. The contractor, therefore, in addition to prosecuting all valid claims, should claim all costs to which he is entitled. In other words, the contractor should give himself the benefit of every doubt, although he certainly should not demand what he is not entitled to. The government will, no doubt, operate on the same principle, and a fair value can be agreed on between the two parties' figures. To facilitate the bargaining procedure, the contractor should beforehand assess which elements of the cost or time extension are fixed and nonnegotiable and which elements and to what extent he is willing to compromise in response to complementary government concessions.

Until the contracting officer issues a final written decision, the negotiations are still open and the contractor has not lost. When the contracting officer indicates to the contractor what his objections to the claim are, the contractor should be prepared to defend his position with both facts and law.

DISPUTES

The contracting officer and the contractor may encounter a difference of opinion as to a factual issue in the contract. For example, the contractor may contend that he is not required by the contract to perform certain work, while the contracting officer asserts that the work is required by the contract and refuses to issue a change order for it. The contractor, however, does not have the right to stop work pending settlement of the dispute. The disputes clause of Form 23-A provides as follows:

> 6. DISPUTES
>
> (a) Except as otherwise provided in this contract, any dispute concerning a question of fact arising under this contract which is not disposed of by agreement shall be decided by the Contracting Officer, who shall reduce his decision to writing and mail or otherwise furnish a copy thereof to the Contractor. The decision of the Contracting Officer shall be final and conclusive unless, within thirty days from the date of receipt of such copy, the Contractor mails or otherwise furnishes to the Contracting Officer a written appeal. . . . *Pending final decision of a dispute hereunder, the Contractor shall proceed diligently with the performance of the contract and in accordance with the Contracting Officer's decision* [Emphasis added].

Until a final resolution of the issue is reached, the contractor must perform the work in accordance with the contracting officer's instructions.[27] His remedy is to claim a constructive change for the added work and to appeal a claim rejection if necessary, but not to stop work altogether, even if the duty to proceed with the work causes him to become insolvent.[28] However, when a contractor is faced with bankruptcy if he performs the disputed work, the alternative prospect, a default termination and liquidated damages for not complying with the disputes clause, may not be very threatening.

There are two exceptions to the disputes-clause provision. The first occurs when the dispute centers on whether a change falls within the scope of the contract.[29] Where the change falls outside of the scope of the contract, the contractor is under no obligation to perform the work and may refuse to proceed with the work pending resolution of the dispute.[30] However, if the contractor is wrong in his estimation that the work is outside the scope, he will not be protected from default if he stops work.

The second exception to the disputes clause requirement occurs when the contractor is unable to proceed with the contract requirements or a change because he has not been given sufficient instructions as to how to proceed. If the contractor has made a good faith effort to resolve the problem and he has informed the government of the difficulty, he is not obligated to proceed until the contracting officer clarifies the instructions, and he cannot be terminated for default.[31] Furthermore, the contracting officer's inaction may lead to costs which are compensable under the suspension-of-work clause.

The full impact of the disputes clause can be appreciated when it is realized that any difference of opinion as to whether a change or an excusable delay has

---

[27]*American Dredg. Co. v. United States,* 21 CCF ¶ 84,078 (1975).

[28]*See, e.g., Preuss v. United States,* 412 F.2d 1293 (Ct. Cl. 1969). In that case defective specifications cost the contractor $275,000 and placed him in such a weak financial position that he was forced to stop work; nevertheless, the court held that the government had not caused the financial problems and resulting work stoppage, so a default termination and liquidated damages were upheld.

[29]*See* note 8 and Chapter 41, When to File a Federal Contract Claim.

[30]*United States v. Spearin,* 248 U.S. 132 (1918).

[31]Appeal of Lutz Co., 68-1 BCA ¶ 6767 (1967).

occurred or as to the amount of equitable adjustment or time extension warranted is considered to be a dispute covered by the disputes clause. Thus, where a contractor is trying to negotiate a claim with the contracting officer, he must continue to perform according to the contracting officer's instructions despite the fact that the contracting officer is unwilling to compensate the contractor for the extra work. Although this dilemma seriously weakens the contractor's bargaining position, his only recourse is to appeal the contracting officer's decision to the appropriate board of contract appeals.

PRICING THE CLAIM

It cannot be overemphasized that identifying the specific extra and documenting it for later proof is the single most important step in the government contract claims procedure. The specific extra may be caused by a change order, a constructive change order, a delay, a suspension-of-work order, or a termination for the convenience of the government. As mentioned above, there are several types of remedies to which the contractor may be entitled, singly or in combination, depending upon the nature of the injury: added costs, profit, a time extension, and a modification of a default termination into a termination for convenience. Both the nature of the remedy and the extent to which it will be granted are determined by the specificity of proof of injury. The need for complete supporting details is shown more clearly when the appropriate relief is an equitable adjustment of the contract price and the contractor must prove how much he is entitled to.

Timing of pricing   Change orders may be unilateral or bilateral. In a bilateral change order, the price is agreed upon in advance by negotiations between the parties. Bilateral change orders are more favorable to the government because contractors often estimate their prospective costs to be less than the costs actually incurred. If the contractor decides to enter into a bilateral agreement, however, he should add a contingency to cover against unforeseen costs or he should retain an option to modify the price after performance under certain conditions.

Under the unilateral-change-order method the contracting officer issues the order directing performance of the change, and the price is determined after performance by computing the contractor's actual provable costs and adding a profit. The contractor is entitled to receive his actual costs because the equitable adjustment is based on actual reasonable costs incurred, and not on the value of the extra work to the government. However, the contractor may be placed in an uncomfortable negotiating position in that the government has received the benefits of the work and is in no hurry to reach a price agreement, whereas the contractor has already paid those expenses out of his pocket and is eager to be reimbursed. For this reason some contractors are hesitant to enter into a unilateral change agreement.

A unilateral change order may contain a notation that the price may not exceed a certain dollar limit. The contractor should refuse to sign such an order, or if he does sign it, he should make a clear notation on the order that his signature acknowledges receipt of the order only and that the price is still to be fully negotiated under the changes clause without regard to the limitation. The contractor should, however, be aware that this maximum price, although not enforceable if not agreed to, may reflect the amount which the agency has budgeted for this contract, and it may be difficult, if not impossible, to recover more.

Elements of the price   Where the contractor negotiates a price after performance, the price is, in general, the difference between the cost of the work as originally required and the cost of the performance of the work as changed, making adjustments for any cost savings to the contractor and taking into account overhead and profit. There is no required formula for computing overhead. Instead, any reasonable accounting method may be used to determine the amount of overhead which is attributable to the change. The parties, of course, can stipulate in the contract itself what amount will be added as overhead for any changes ordered during execution of the contract.

The rate of profit is generally the same rate as allowed on the original contract.[32] However, where the work is extremely complex, where the risk assumed by the contractor is great, or where the contractor has invested a large amount of capital into the change, a greater profit allowance might be appropriate.

Methods of pricing   There are three acceptable methods of proving costs, one of which is preferred. This is the procedure of specifically proving the amount and reasonableness of each item claimed as well as the causal connection between the change order and the cost increase. The recoverable items include: the direct costs of additional labor and material; the added labor costs due to inefficiency, such as congestion of the work site and fatigue; the costs of additional time spent by supervisory personnel; general administration and overhead costs; the expense of storage beyond the time contemplated; premium prices for accelerated delivery of materials; loss of rental value of fixed assets; the cost of idle construction equipment; and any other costs which in fact were caused by the change and which are reasonable and provable.[33]

When a contractor cannot prove his costs item by item, he may be able to use the "total-cost" method. This method is permitted only when the contractor's bid was realistic, his actual costs were reasonable, he was not responsible for any portion of the added costs, and it is impossible to determine his actual costs.[34] The computation is made by adding the total expenditures on the contract and subtracting the bid. To the difference is added a sum for profit.

When the facts do not fit within the narrow requirements for using the total-cost method, the contractor may qualify for the "jury-verdict" method. This method is not favored by the courts and government contract boards of appeal, and they require that the contractor present clear proof of his injury and that

---

[32] Profit is not recoverable, however, on added expenses attributable to a work suspension for the government's convenience. *See* Standard Form 23-A, clause 17(b).

[33] *Bruce Constr. Corp. v. United States*, 324 F.2d 516 (Ct. Cl. 1963).

[34] *Meva Corp. v. United States*, 511 F.2d 548 (Ct. Cl. 1975); *Continental Consol. Corp. v. United States*, 20 CCF ¶ 83,761 (1972); *Turnbull, Inc. v. United States*, 389 F.2d 1007 (Ct. Cl. 1967).

he show that no more reliable method for computing the amount is available.[35] There must be sufficient evidence of the costs to enable a court or jury to make a fair and reasonable approximation of the cost of the change.

DOCUMENTING THE CLAIM

Because the jury-verdict and total-cost methods may be used only in certain limited circumstances, the contractor should protect himself by keeping accurate and complete records of all expenses related to the contract and should segregate all items relating to a particular change. In addition, all other details of the contractual relationship should be preserved so that the contractor can later prove that his version of the facts is accurate in all respects. Such details are needed to prove the existence of the claim as well as to show the nature and amount of the appropriate remedy.

All invoices for materials and services should be filed, and records or memoranda should be retained of all the telephone calls, trips, conferences, and letters relating to specific matters which the contractor might later recognize as changes. When any difficulties in performance are encountered, the contractor should obtain expert reports, samples, and photographs concerning the condition.

Notes or memoranda should be kept of telephone or oral conversations. The content of each contact with representatives of the owner or other contractors should be noted. Then, as soon as possible, these notes should be translated into a written memorandum for the file or a confirming letter to the other party to the conversation. These notes, memoranda, or letters have the dual purpose of implying agreement by the other party if he remains silent after the receipt of a confirming letter, and also of preserving a written record.

In addition to these reports, photographs showing the nature and location of the changed work should also be made a part of the file. Photographs can be the ultimate help in documenting the exact factual situation and may even furnish details previously unnoticed or not noted elsewhere.

These procedures are helpful when done as a routine, even in the absence of unusual circumstances, because they document the progress of the work and may help in spotting changes not noticed at the time. In addition, the contractor may find that it is useful or necessary to compare a situation as it existed before the claim arose with the status after the facts constituting the claim occurred. The only way to be able to make this comparison is to make documentation a routine.

Depending on the magnitude and complexity of the claim for extra work, experts may be needed to present expert opinions, analyses, and reports on the subject matter of the claim. An expert can serve the dual purpose of supporting the claim and advising the contractor on the specifics of the claim. The contractor should not formulate his claim and then hire an expert at the last

[35]*Meva Corp. v. United States,* Id.

moment before presenting a claim. Rather, calling in an expert should be among the first steps when it becomes clear that a substantial claim for extras may exist.

Also relevant in presenting a claim is evidence of the customs and practices of the trade of the particular contracting field. These customs or trade practices amplify plans and specifications and are implicitly incorporated into a contract provided they are not contrary to express provisions of the contract. In addition to "fleshing out" the terms of the plans and specifications, proof of customs and trade practices may be an absolute necessity when questions arise about the standards of workmanship.

It is important that the contractor be specific in establishing that the cause of the added expense was a particular change. For example, if the contractor is claiming a delay due to an unusually large rainfall, it is not enough that he state that the average rainfall for that month is x inches, while the rainfall actually experienced was an average of y inches. He should state that it rained a particular amount on each day, compare it to the average rainfall for that season, detail the effect of the rain on performance that day, and total the number of days lost due to rain.[36] The availability of detailed cost data makes the proof procedure easier and more convincing and also puts the contractor in a better position to negotiate the claim with the contracting officer and avoid the expense and delay of adversary proceedings. Inability to substantiate the amount of a claim will likely lead to its disallowance.

In addition to documenting the time and money expended on a contract change, a contractor should preserve a record of the scope of the change and the authority of the person ordering the change. These facts are needed to prove that the government is obligated to pay for the contractor's efforts.[37] All written communications concerning the claim should be preserved because they may be useful in showing that the change was within the scope of the contract or that the government agent had the proper authority. All oral communications should be put in writing. The contractor should insist upon receiving from the contracting officer a written confirmation of all oral orders and suggestions and a written statement of authority for all persons dealing with the contractor as the contracting officer's authorized representatives. If the contracting officer fails to provide such written documents, the contractor should take it upon himself to send to the contracting officer a letter restating the orders or authority. If the contracting officer fails to object to the contractor's written statement, his silence operates as a confirmation.[38] If the orders being confirmed originated from an agent of whose authority the contractor is unsure, the contracting officer's silence is a ratification of those orders and is as effective as if the contracting officer himself had issued them. Even if the oral communication does not involve an order or a question of authority, it is a good idea to make a memorandum of it or, even better, to write a letter to the other

---

[36]*See* Appeal of B.D. Click Co., 76-1 BCA ¶ 11,739 (1976).

[37]*See* Chapter 41, When to File a Federal Contract Claim.

[38]*See, e.g., Gresham & Co. v. United States,* 470 F.2d 542 (Ct. Cl. 1972); *William v. United States,* 127 F. Supp. 617 (1955); *Appeal of Allied Contractors,* 1964 BCA ¶ 4379 (1964).

party summarizing the communication. Such records are very helpful in later reconstructing the facts which support the claim.

APPEAL

Board proceedings[39]

If the contracting officer agrees to the price stated by the contractor in his claim, the contract will be amended to reflect the equitable adjustment, and the claim process is terminated. If the contracting officer does not agree to the contractor's price, he will issue an order denying the claim or stating the price he will pay for the change. This order, to be appealable, should state that it is final and that the contractor has a right of appeal and should also advise the contractor how to obtain an appeal.[40] However, if the contracting officer fails or refuses to issue a final decision within a reasonable time, the inaction itself becomes an appealable order.[41]

If the contractor does not wish to accept the claim denial or the price offered by the contracting officer, he must follow the contract procedures for appeal.[42] This procedure is set up in the disputes clause and requires that the contractor submit to the appropriate appeals board written notice of appeal within 30 days of receipt of the contracting officer's final decision.[43] Subcontractors should note that the 30-day period for them begins to run on the day the *prime* contractor receives the contracting officer's final decision. This is because the government's contract is with the prime contractor, not the subcontractor. Failure of the prime or subcontractor to appeal a final decision within the time limit is excusable in three instances:[44] if the contracting officer fails to inform the contractor that his order is final and must be appealed,[45] if the contracting officer agrees to reconsider the claim within the 30-day period,[46] or if the final decision is that the contract is being terminated for default, and the contractor

---

[39]It should be noted that the specific procedures followed by the different boards of contract appeal vary. The following is a generalized discussion intended to give the contractor an outline approach to board proceedings in general. For a specific guide as to the steps required for an appeal, the contractor should consult the regulations set out by the agency administering the particular contract.

[40]Failure to include such language prevents the decision from becoming final and relieves the contractor of the necessity of appealing where the contract is subject to the Armed Services Procurement Regulations. *Bostwick-Batterson Co. v. United States,* 283 F.2d 956 (Ct. Cl. 1960).

[41]Appeal of Dubois & Son, Inc., 57-1 BCA ¶ 1306 (1957). However, failure to issue a final decision may also be treated as a breach of contract, permitting the contractor to bypass the appeals procedure and sue directly in court. *United States v. Peter Kiewit Sons,* 345 F.2d 879 (8th Cir. 1965); *Johnson v. United States,* 173 Ct. Cl. 561 (1965); *Langenfelder & Son v. United States,* 169 Ct. Cl. 465 (1965).

[42]*Schlesinger v. United States,* 383 F.2d 1004 (Ct. Cl. 1967).

[43]*See* Standard Form 23A, clause 6(a).

[44]The General Services Administration Board of Contract Appeals allows *no* exceptions to the 30-day time limit. *See* appeal of Grunley-Walsh Constr. Co., 72-2 BCA ¶ 9687 (1972); appeal of Ginley-Soper Constr. Co., 67-2 BCA ¶ 6535 (1967).

[45]*See* note 40, *supra* and accompanying text.

[46]*See e.g.,* Appeal of Herman Adams, 59-2 BCA ¶ 2454 (1959).

later appeals from the contracting officer's assessment of liquidated damages.[47] Failures to appeal within the time limit may be excusable in other instances,[48] but under no circumstances should the contractor *expect* his delay in filing to be excused.

No particular form is required for notice of appeal, although the particular agency may make standard forms available for the contractor's convenience. The notice of appeal, usually in triplicate, should include the contract number, the name of the agency administering the contract, a brief statement of the contracting officer's decision, and a clear and express statement that the letter is notice of appeal of that decision. The notice should be signed by the contractor, his authorized representative, or his attorney, and should be addressed to the agency head but sent to the contracting officer. It is a good idea to send the notice by certified mail in order to have proof that the contractor mailed the notice within the prescribed time limit.

Where the contracting officer has failed or refused to issue a final decision, the contractor may wish to state in the letter a particular reason that the delay in issuing a final order is unreasonable or that the contractor is in particular need of an immediate appeal. Although an appeal letter following refusal to make a decision may be sent directly to the board of contract appeals instead of through the contracting officer, sending it through the contracting officer may prompt him to issue the final decision. Although the board may decide not to grant the requested appeal, it will probably at least inform the contracting officer that unless he issues a final decision, the board will hear a later appeal on the issue.

When the contracting officer receives a notice of appeal, he is required to forward it to the board within a set time limit. When the board receives the notice, it sends the contractor a copy of the board's rules. The contracting officer is also required to submit to the board any papers he has pertaining to the claim. Copies of these are sent by the board to the contractor. The contractor is then required to send to the board any additional papers in his possession which are not already in the file. The board, in turn, forwards copies of these to the government attorney.

The contractor has the option of representing himself or being represented by an attorney. The contractor is aided by the fact that the rules of evidence used in court may be relaxed or ignored in board hearings. In addition, the board may have a simplified procedure for dealing with small claims.[49] If the contractor's claim is small, he may decide that it is not worth the expense of obtaining an attorney, particularly since his legal fees are not recoverable even if he wins.[50]

However, the contractor should realize that the government will be represented by an attorney. If he chooses to appeal without the assistance of counsel, the judge presiding over the board appeal may take a more active role in

---

[47]Appeal of Atlas Fabrics Corp., 1962 BCA ¶ 3264 (1962).
[48]*J.R. Youngdale Constr. Co. v. United States,* 504 F.2d 1124 (Ct. Cl. 1974).
[49]*See, e.g.,* Rule 12 of the General Services Administration Board of Contract Appeals.
[50]*See* note 24, *supra.*

examining witnesses and eliciting the contractor's side of the story. However, the contractor should realize that it may be difficult for the judge to be an impartial decision maker and at the same time to protect the contractor's interests. Furthermore, the contractor is responsible, at a minimum, for knowing and abiding by the board rules. The decision to represent oneself should be made by carefully weighing all these factors and considering the difference between the contractor's claim and the contracting officer's decision, which is the amount the contractor stands to lose.

In order to be able to make an informed and intelligent decision whether to proceed with or without an attorney, the contractor should be acquainted with the general nature and procedure of a board hearing. Board hearings closely resemble court hearings. The parties file pleadings, make motions, and submit evidence. When the appeal is docketed, or put in line to be heard, it is assigned a docket number, and notice of docketing is sent to the contractor along with a copy of the board rules. The contractor has a set time limit from receipt of this notice to file a complaint in triplicate. The complaint simply sets forth the essential facts, the theory upon which the claim is based (*e.g.*, differing site conditions) and the relief sought (*e.g.*, an equitable adjustment of *x* dollars plus a time extension of *y* days). Although no specific form is required, the complaint should identify the contract number and the docket number, and the facts should be divided into numbered paragraphs. The complaint normally follows the form for a complaint in a court suit.

The government has a certain time after receipt of the contractor's complaint in which it must file its answer. The answer denies or admits each paragraph of the complaint, sets out the defenses the government has, and may assert a counterclaim. The board may extend the time limits for filing the complaint and the answer without penalty.

Because the complaint and answer are very general and give only the barest outline of the facts, each party may supplement them with, for example, motions for a more definite statement (of the answer or complaint), interrogatories (lists of questions which the other party must answer), inspection of designated documents, and a prehearing conference (at which the parties decide on what they agree or disagree about, discuss their view of the case, and limit the number of witnesses, among other things). At any time during this procedure the government may move that the appeal be dismissed for lack of jurisdiction. Upon such a motion, the appeals board may dismiss any claims that are based on breach of contract and other theories that are not covered by the contract itself.

After the government files its answer, the contractor may have the option of demanding a hearing or allowing the board to decide the claim on the basis of the written record established. Even if the contractor does not demand a hearing, the government may. If the parties agree to dispense with the hearing phase, the board may allow them to submit any additional documentary evidence they wish. Each party is allowed to object to the evidence submitted by the other on the grounds that it violates the rules of evidence followed by the board, and each party is allowed to refute the evidence of the other with additional evidence of its own. When the board notifies the parties that the record is closed, each may present its argument either orally or in the form of a written brief. However, neither side may present additional evidence. The board decides the case on the basis of the record and the arguments.

Because a case decided without a hearing does not provide ample opportunity for presentation of evidence, it is not suitable for complicated claims nor is it desirable for a claim in which a large sum of money is at stake. The value of this procedure is in expediting claims in which the parties are in substantial agreement as to the facts, but disagree as to the law, and in cases where the cost of the hearing would consume any possible recovery.

If one of the parties requests a hearing, both are permitted—after both of their optional opening statements—to present witnesses, either personally or through a deposition (a formal question-and-answer session subject to cross-examination and written down by a court reporter), and to offer documents and physical evidence. The formal rules of evidence used in courts of law are not uniformly followed in board hearings. Some boards have dispensed with them, while others allow the Administrative Law Judge to relax them. The primary limitation on the admissibility of evidence applied by the boards is that it must be presented in an orderly manner, and it must be useful in proving a relevant point. All documents and physical evidence must be "authenticated" (someone must testify as to their identity and accuracy) and experts must be "qualified" (their credentials stated). At the close of the evidence each party is entitled to make a closing statement or an oral argument, although any argument is better presented in a written brief.

After a transcript of the hearing is made available, the parties will ordinarily exchange briefs, which are written summaries and arguments of their side of the case. Although no special form is required for the brief, it is generally prefaced by a statement of the facts, quoting key testimony or documents which were entered into evidence. Then each issue is separately discussed, citing the law applicable to the issue. The law relied upon may include board decisions, court decisions, statutes, regulations, and other legal materials.

When the briefs have been exchanged, the parties may present their oral arguments. The claim is then ready for decision by the board. The board's decision normally contains two portions: (1) findings of facts and (2) conclusions of law. In other words, what the board decides really happened is made the basis for applying the law.

After receipt of the board's decision either party can move for a reconsideration. The motion can request either that the record be reopened or that the board reconsider its decision based on the present record. The motion should state what relief is sought and why the claim should be reconsidered.

Court proceedings

A timely appeal of a final board decision is the only way a contractor can obtain a court hearing of a contract claim.[51] However, the board's findings of *fact* are

---

[51]*James McConnen & Sons v. United States,* 21 CCF ¶ 84,150 (1976); *McGarvie v. United States,* 20 CCF ¶ 83,103 (1974). By contrast, a suit for breach of contract cannot be heard by any board but must be brought initially before a court. *Bethlehem Steel Corp. v. Grace Line, Inc.,* 416 F.2d 1096 (D.C. Cir. 1969).

generally final.[52] The exception is where they are so divergent from the evidence that they are an abuse of the board's power to resolve factual conflict. Under the Wunderlich Act this test is whether the board's findings are "fraudulent or capricious or arbitrary or so grossly erroneous as necessarily to imply bad faith, or [are] not supported by substantial evidence."[53] Thus, if the contractor or the government appeals the board decision to the Court of Claims or to the United States District Court (the contractor may appeal to the District Court only if the claim is under $10,000),[54] the court will accept as the truth the board's findings of fact if they meet this test and will consider only the issues which relate to erroneous conclusions of law.

An erroneous legal conclusion is always reviewable by the court.[55] Because the facts are final, no additional evidence may be submitted. Instead, the parties present briefs and oral arguments that interpret the board's fact findings to their advantage, applying the law favorable to their case. The court may either reach its own decision as to the applicable law and enter judgment or it may "remand" the case (refer it back) to the board for further consideration of certain issues (usually the computation of the equitable adjustment in light of the court's decisions as to the law governing the case).

This summary of the procedure for appealing a decision by the contracting officer mentions only the major steps involved. It does not fully reveal the complexity of the process, both in terms of what must be done in order to follow the required procedure and with respect to possible timing and tactics of that procedure. It is a difficult undertaking for an attorney who does not routinely appeal claims decisions, and it is far more complex to a layman who is not even familiar with legal procedures and concepts. Unless the contractor has little to lose, he is best advised to secure legal representation.

SPECIAL PROBLEMS OF SUBCONTRACTOR CLAIMS

Because a subcontractor has no contract with the government, the subcontractor cannot sue the government, even if the government directly causes a change which affects the subcontractor.[56] The only exception to this rule occurs when the prime contractor has assigned the entire contract to the subcontractor with the government's knowledge and consent, so that the subcontractor is substituted in the place of the general contractor. The assignment must be formally executed; the fact that the subcontractor performed all the work under the contract is, by itself, insufficient.[57] A requirement that the government approve the terms of any subcontract[58] or the incorporation of the terms of the general

[52]*See* Standard Form 23-A, clause 6(a).
[53]41 U.S.C. § 321 (1965).
[54]28 U.S.C. §§ 1346, 1491 (1976, 1973).
[55]41 U.S.C. § 322 (1965). *See also* Standard Form 23-A, clause 6(b).
[56]*Beacon Constr. Co. v. Prepakt Concrete Co.,* 375 F.2d 977 (1st Cir. 1967).
[57]*Hunt v. United States,* 257 U.S. 125 (1921).
[58]*Sullivan & Sons v. United States,* 129 Ct. Cl. 63 (1954).

contract into the subcontract[59] will not suffice to create the necessary government-subcontractor relationship.

In almost all cases, therefore, the subcontractor must either prosecute a claim in the name of the prime contractor or have the prime contractor prosecute the claim for the subcontractor.[60] There are several problems with this procedure, the most apparent of which is that it requires the cooperation of the prime contractor. Any procedure in the name of the prime contractor requires the prime contractor's permission, even if he has no active role in presenting the case. Where the prime contractor prosecutes the claim for the subcontractor, taking an active role, the outcome of the case may, in addition, depend upon the extent to which the prime contractor is convinced that the subcontractor has a valid claim. In either situation, the subcontractor may need the prime contractor's records or the testimony of his employees in order to present a convincing argument. In addition, the subcontractor may not submit his claim after the prime contractor has released the government from all liability on the contract by giving a final release, agreeing to modification, or accepting final payment. Once the government has been released under the prime contract, all claims against it are foreclosed.[61]

The prime contractor's willingness to cooperate may depend upon several factors. First, he may erroneously believe that he cannot be liable to the subcontractor for the amount of the equitable adjustment to which the subcontractor is entitled; or he may believe that if the claim is successful, he will have to pay part of it. Second, he may fear that the subcontractor could use any statements or documents of the prime contractor in a subsequent suit between the subcontractor and the prime contractor if the government claim is unsuccessful. Third, he may be using his right to refuse to sue as leverage to compel the subcontractor to grant certain concessions or as an enticement to elicit favors from the government.

By contrast, the prime contractor may sincerely believe that the subcontractor has a valid claim and may feel that he has a legal and moral obligation not to interfere with that claim. In addition, the prime contractor may, under the terms of his contract, receive an upward equitable adjustment of his own contract price in the form of a markup or a profit on the subcontractor's price adjustment. As a last resort, the prime contractor could be threatened with suit under the Miller Act or for a breach of contract.[62]

There are two clauses which a prime contractor might include in the subcontract which could aggravate the subcontractor's difficulties in recovering against the government. The first is an exculpatory clause which states that the prime contractor has no liability whatsoever to the subcontractor for damages resulting from government action. Under a clause like this, the government may take

---

[59]*Continental Ill. Nat'l Bank v. United States,* 112 Ct. Cl. 563 (1949).

[60]*Warren Bros. Roads v. United States,* 123 Ct. Cl. 48 (1952); *Stout, Hall & Bangs v. United States,* 27 Ct. Cl. 385 (1892); Appeal of American Structures, Inc., 76-1 BCA ¶ 11,683 (1976).

[61]Appeal of Martin Constr. Co., 66-2 BCA ¶ 5894 (1966).

[62]*See* note 66, *infra* and accompanying text.

the position that the prime contractor cannot recover from the government on behalf of the subcontractor, because the government's liability to the prime contractor is limited to the damages the prime contractor actually suffers. This rule is referred to as the *Severin* doctrine after the case that established the rule.[63] Because of this rule, the subcontractor should refuse to sign any contract containing a clause such as this. Instead, the subcontractor should insist that the contract contain a clause which indicates that the prime contractor is clearly obligated to pay over to the subcontractor the recovery in a suit on a government liability to the subcontractor.

It should be noted, however, that subsequent cases have so modified the *Severin* doctrine as it applies to claims under the general contract, that it now has virtually no applicability to government contract claims.[64] Thus, even where the subcontract contains an exculpatory clause, the subcontractor may recover from the government through the general contractor.

The second dangerous clause is one that states that the prime contractor is liable to the subcontractor only to the extent of any recovery from the government. If the subcontractor does not impose on the prime contractor the duty to faithfully prosecute any subcontract claim against the government, he may not be liable to the subcontractor if he never even attempts to recover from the government. The difference between the two clauses is that, in the first, the prime contractor cannot recover from the government and is never liable to the subcontractor, whereas, in the second, the prime contractor may be insulated from liability if he does nothing and is liable only for the amount paid to him by the government if he recovers on the claim. There should be some means for insuring that the prime contractor will prosecute the subcontractor's claim in good faith. To solve this dilemma, the subcontract should also include a clause obligating the prime contractor to diligently prosecute any subcontractor claims arising from government action.[65]

If the prime contractor violates the clause obligating him to pursue the subcontractor's government claims, the subcontractor can either sue the prime contractor for breach of the contractual obligation to pursue the subcontractor's claim or file a suit under the Miller Act. In a suit for breach of contract, the subcontractor can not only recover the claim, if proven, but may also be able to obtain damages for his inability to recover against the government within a reasonable time.

The subcontractor may also file suit under the Miller Act.[66] Because the subcontractor is not permitted by law to obtain a mechanic's lien on government property, the Miller Act was enacted to protect the subcontractor's right to payment for his services.[67] It requires the prime contractor to furnish a

---

[63]*See Severin v. United States,* 99 Ct. Cl. 435 (1943), *cert. denied,* 322 U.S. 733 (1944).

[64]*See Southern Constr. Co. v. United States,* 364 F.2d 439 (Ct.Cl. 1966); *Blount Bros. v. United States,* 346 F.2d 962 (Ct. Cl. 1965); Appeal of Horner Constr. Co., 59-2 BCA ¶ 2321 (1959).

[65]*See* Appeal of Burn Constr. Co., 76-1 BCA ¶ 11,778 (1976).

[66]40 U.S.C. § 270a–270e (1969).

[67]*St. Paul Fire & Marine Ins. Co. v. United States ex rel. Dakota Elec. Supply Corp.,* 309 F.2d 22 (8th Cir. 1962).

surety bond which guarantees payment to the subcontractor for all work performed under the contract. If the subcontractor is not paid within 90 days after finishing the portion of the work on which the claim is made, he can file suit against either the prime contractor or his surety.

The subcontractor, to ensure recovery on government claims, should first be certain that the subcontract clearly obligates the prime contractor to prosecute such claims for the subcontractor or to allow him to prosecute them himself in the name of the prime contractor. The clause which prevents the subcontractor from recovering from the prime contractor more than the amount of the judgment against the government is permissible under these circumstances. If the prime contractor violates his duty to prosecute, the subcontractor can then sue him for breach or sue him under the Miller Act.

Part Ten

Arbitration

Chapter **43**

Arbitration of Construction Disputes

GERALD AKSEN, ESQ.
General Counsel, American Arbitration Association, New York, New York

INTRODUCTION

Arbitration in the construction industry has become the accepted mode of claims and dispute settlement. Since 1966 all major segments of the building community have provided for arbitration between owners, architects, engineers, general subcontractors, and lower-tiered subcontractors. Thus, for example, the standard form contracts of the American Institute of Architects, the Associated General Contractors, and the National Society of Professional Consulting Engineers provide that:

> All claims, disputes and other matters in question between the Contractor and the Owner arising out of, or relating to, the Contract Documents or the breach thereof . . . shall be decided by arbitration in accordance with The Construction Industry Arbitration Rules of the American Arbitration Association then obtaining unless the parties mutually agree otherwise (AIA Doc. 201-1976 §7.9).

Nine major industry and professional construction associations (American Consulting Engineers Council, American Institute of Architects, American Society of Civil Engineers, American Society of Landscape Architects, American Sub-Contractors Association, Associated General Contractors, Associated Specialty Contractors, Inc., Construction Specifications Institute, and National Society of Professional Engineers) have participated with the American Arbitration Association (AAA) in creating the Construction Industry Arbitration Rules. The AAA has established a National Construction Industry Arbitration Committee and regional advisory committees to improve the available panel of knowledgeable arbitrators, to serve as a conduit for information, and to advise the AAA on administrative problems. In 1975, the AAA administered 1,793 construction arbitrations involving over $100 million in claims. Thus, it is timely to review the procedures before and during the arbitration process.

The construction industry has shown a recent marked preference for arbitration instead of litigation for five principal reasons: speed, cost, expertise, privacy, and practicality.

Speed.   Arbitration is generally *faster* than litigation in resolving claims. Although some construction cases may require several years in arbitration, according to a 1974 survey the vast majority of AAA cases are resolved within nine months.

Cost.   There are costs attached to arbitration. However, the expense is usually reasonable or moderate when compared to the cost of a lawsuit.

Expertise.   Arbitrators in construction cases are usually selected because of their knowledge of the building trade. A typical panel might consist of an architect, a contractor, and an attorney familiar with construction contracts and claims. The arbitrator's ability to use what the courts call *judicial notice* helps reduce the cost considerably. By contrast, since judges cannot be familiar with the intricacies of every business that comes before them in lawsuits, a great deal more time is required to put on expert and general witnesses to testify to mundane facts.

Privacy.   The arbitration hearing normally takes place in private. Lawsuits are subject to being heard in open court with attendant press and publicity that may unduly damage a business reputation while the trial is in progress.

Practicality.   Arbitration produces a more practical forum in several ways. It is simpler as a process. Whereas court procedures and rules are spelled out in detailed and lengthy volumes of civil procedure, arbitration procedures are based more upon a commonsense businessman's approach to hearing the material and relevant evidence. The arbitrator usually schedules the hearings at the parties' convenience. A judge has many cases to schedule, whereas the construction arbitrator has only the one case to hear at a time. The entire arbitration process gives the parties and their counsel greater flexibility in time, place of hearings, and accommodation to local needs.

PROCEDURES BEFORE ARBITRATION

Many procedures should be followed before commencing a construction arbitration. Being well prepared may prove the difference between lengthy and quick proceedings at a later stage. Often, assumptions by counsel have resulted in unnecessary motion practice over such questions as applicable law, arbitrability, jurisdiction, locale, and appropriate arbitrators. If, however, the following checklist of items is reviewed, the chances are better that the arbitration will proceed more smoothly.

1. Check Contract Arbitration Clause.

Arbitration clauses in the standard form documents are voluntary and subject to change. It is always appropriate to determine whether the parties during contract negotiations either deleted the arbitration clause or made changes in it. For example, parties may have amended the clause language to provide that the hearings take place in a particular locale. More important is the fact that standard form contracts are frequently changed, and one should not assume the appropriate contents of a particular contract. In construction agreements this is particularly true. Many building contracts give rise to years of construction. The agreement may have been negotiated in 1970, the job may have begun in 1971, and the project may not have been completed until 1975. Claims or disputes may not arise until 1976. The 1976 industry documents may be quite different from the contracts signed in 1970. Thus, determining the applicable contract language is essential. Several court decisions have already demonstrated that changes in form documents can cause litigation.

An interesting question may arise where parties choose to avoid the contract provisions in favor of still another agreed-upon arbitration mechanism. It is most likely that courts will permit the parties to resort to the Construction Industry Arbitration Rules even where a contract has prescribed a certain procedure. In Minnesota, for example, the State Department of Administration included an arbitration clause in its form construction contracts designating the Governor as its arbitrator. The clause contained the following language:

> In case any dispute or controversy arises between consultant and state out of any provision herein contained, such dispute or controversy shall be referred to the Governor of the State of Minnesota for arbitration and his decision shall be final and binding on both parties.

A dispute arose between the architect-planner and the state owner over the design and construction of a parking ramp. The particular issue concerned a time extension requested by the contractor for completing construction of the ramp. The Governor declined to act as arbitrator and instead designated the AAA to arbitrate the dispute. The court[1] upheld the award rendered by the AAA-appointed arbitrator, stating:

> Indeed, it appears that the governor routinely refers these arbitration matters to the American Arbitration Association. Thus, there appears to be no reason why the

---

[1] *State of Minnesota v. McGuire Architects-Planners, Inc.* 245 N.W.2d 218 (Minn. S. Ct. 1976).

state and parties with which it contracts could not simply and directly name the AAA, or some other disinterested person or entity, to act as arbitrator in contract disputes.

2. Determine Applicable Law.

At one time arbitration law was primarily governed by state arbitration statutes. Recently, however, the Federal Arbitration Act[2] has been playing a more prominent role, particularly in construction agreements. The Federal Arbitration Act enacted on February 12, 1925, was intended to override the long-standing judicial hostility to arbitration on public policy grounds, and to make arbitration agreements "valid, irrevocable, and enforceable." It was not until 1967, however, that the United States Supreme Court held that the Federal Arbitration Act created national substantive law for interstate commerce and maritime transactions.[3] Since most construction work involves interstate elements such as labor or materials crossing state lines, it clearly involves commerce and will be covered by the federal rather than a state arbitration statute.

The significant question is whether the parties in carrying out the terms of their construction agreement *contemplated* substantial interstate activity. It does not matter whether the parties actually crossed state lines. The test[4] as articulated by the then chief judge of the second circuit was:

> The significant question, therefore, is not whether, in carrying out the terms of the contract the parties *did* cross state lines, but whether, at the time they entered into it and accepted the arbitration clause, they *contemplated* substantial interstate activity. Cogent evidence regarding their state of mind at the time would be the terms of the contract, and if it, on its face, evidences interstate traffic, . . . the contract should come within § 2. In addition, evidence as to how the parties expected the contract to be performed and how it was performed is relevant to whether substantial interstate activity was contemplated.

The importance of the applicability of the Federal Arbitration Act cannot be overstated. It brings to the construction contract a single national uniform law; coupled with the American Arbitration Association's Construction Industry Arbitration Rules, it helps move the building industry toward a more cohesive nationwide standard of procedures and laws in settling claims and disputes. In the long run this should benefit the entire construction field—from owners to builders to design professionals. Where parties were forced to rely upon hostile or uncertain state arbitration laws, the arbitration mechanism could not function in a prompt fashion, thus depriving the parties of their intended bargain.

As of this writing, 14 states still do not enforce contractual agreements to arbitrate future claims that may arise under a building or design contract. One state even goes so far as to refuse to apply its modern arbitration law to construction contracts. By having recourse to the Federal Arbitration Act, these few remaining outmoded statutes are properly avoided.

[2]9 U.S.C. 1 *et seq.*
[3]*Prima Paint Corp. v. Flood & Conklin Mfg. Co.*, 388 U.S. 395 (1967).
[4]*Metro Indus. Painting v. Terminal Constr. Co.*, 287 F.2d 382, 387 (2d Cir.) *cert. den.* 368 U.S. 817 (1961).

Federal law has gone far toward encouraging the full use of the arbitral process. The federal judiciary has fashioned a liberal policy of promoting arbitration both to accord with the original intention of the parties and to help ease the current congestion of court calendars. The U.S. Supreme Court put a stamp of approval upon the liberal policy doctrine even to the point of holding that an arbitration clause is "separable" from the agreement embodying it.[5] Under this doctrine even claims of fraudulent inducement of the contract are proper matters for the arbitrator's determination. Only if the allegation is fraudulent inducement of the arbitration clause will the issue be determined by the federal court.

Under section 4 of the federal act a district court judge may specifically enforce an arbitration provision once he is satisfied that the making of the arbitration agreement and the failure to comply with it are not at issue. The Supreme Court has stated that "a federal court may consider only issues relating to the making and the performance of the agreement to arbitrate."

What has literally happened under the federal law is that there has emerged a "presumption of arbitrability" applied to the majority of issues arising from construction contracts containing arbitration clauses. However, in those instances where the construction job clearly contemplates only *intra*state elements, then parties must be familiar with the applicable state arbitration law. As already indicated, some states will not enforce a future arbitration clause;[6] some states have no arbitration statute[7] and depend entirely on common-law doctrine and at least one state has refused to permit construction contract arbitration clauses to be covered by its arbitration statute.[8]

A recent encouraging decision emerged from West Virginia. Although the state arbitration law does not empower the courts to compel arbitration of future claims, a party may nonetheless be required to honor its agreement to arbitrate before the AAA as a condition precedent to litigation.[9]

3. Avoid Waiver of Legal Rights.

Since arbitration is purely a contractual right agreed upon voluntarily between parties to resolve their disputes privately rather than through litigation, it is relatively easy to waive that contractual right. A claimant seeking relief in court by serving a summons and complaint may waive his right to later file arbitration. In state courts, the waiver usually becomes fixed when the defendant files an answer to the suit. Recent federal cases, however, have found waiver only where the demand for arbitration comes long after the suit commenced and when both parties had engaged in extensive discovery.[10] In one federal court[11] it was stated:

---

[5]*Prima Paint Corp., supra* note 3.
[6]Alabama, Georgia, Iowa, Kentucky, Mississippi, Missouri, Montana, Nebraska, North Carolina, South Carolina, Tennessee, and West Virginia.
[7]*E.g.,* Oklahoma and Vermont.
[8]Texas Civ. Stat. Ann. Title 10, Art. 224.
[9]*Board of Educ. v. Harley Miller, Inc.,* 221 S.E.2d 882 (W. Va. 1975).
[10]*Gavlik Constr. v. H. F. Campbell,* 526 F.2d 777 (3rd Cir. 1975).
[11]*Carcich v. Rederi A/B Nordie,* 389 F.2d 692, 696 (2d Cir. 1968).

We believe it is not the inconsistency of a party's actions, but the presence or absence of prejudice which is determinative of the issue of waiver.

Particular care should also be exercised when parties are seeking judicial relief along with arbitration. The most common situation in construction is where a claimant contractor files a lien on the premises for work and labor performed. Actions to foreclose mechanic's liens are commonplace in the industry. The question always arises, however, as to whether the arbitration clause is waived under such circumstances. Some states such as New York have enacted special legislation making clear that the filing of a lien does not constitute a waiver of arbitration.[12] In other jurisdictions the case law has found waiver. Accordingly, steps should be taken in these latter jurisdictions to protect the right to arbitration by filing the demand for arbitration together with the lien proceeding to clearly indicate the filing party's intent not to forgo its right to arbitrate.

Similar waiver problems can also arise where a contractor files a notice of claim against a public owner. It is common for local governments to have 90-day time limits within which to file notices of claim. In New York, for example, CPLR 9802 was held not to mean that a contractor waived his right to arbitrate when it filed a notice of claim against a local village on Long Island.

However, failure to give timely notice of claim against a city school district under a state's education law will amount to a permanent denial of the right to seek arbitration.

All applicable contract and statutory time limits must be met or a party may indeed have waived its right to arbitration. The standard form AIA "cost-of-work" language provides that all work has to be performed within one year and that all claims for extensions of time must be made in writing. These provisions must be honored unless it can be shown that they have been waived.

4. Understand Overlapping Statutes.

There are times when parties will be faced by other federal or state laws that may have impact upon arbitration. Already discussed were lien laws. Another very recent statutory development has been the introduction of compulsory arbitration of some construction contract claims. North Dakota, for example, has a compulsory arbitration statute covering highway construction disputes.[13] Where the arbitration is required rather than voluntary, there may be significant differences in the applicable law. In such a jurisdiction one could not waive arbitration, nor argue arbitrability. Nor is it clear whether a party could challenge awards under the standards promulgated by voluntary arbitration statutes. Where compulsion rather than free choice is the law, appropriate adherence to local statutory and judicial guidelines becomes essential.

---

[12]*See e.g. A. Burgart, Inc. v. Foster-Lipkins Corp.,* 30 N.Y.2d 901, 335 N.Y.S.2d 562 (1972).

[13]N.D.C.C. § 24-02-26 was held constitutional. *See e.g. Nelson Paving Co. v. Hjelle,* 207 N.W.2d 225 (1973); *Hjelle v. Sornsin Constr.,* 173 N.W.2d 431 (1969).

Statutes dealing with bonding rights may also be called into question in arbitration. Thus, where a subcontractor brought suit on a general contractor's payment bond, the latter moved to stay the litigation pending arbitration. The federal court held that the state statute granting a subcontractor the right to sue on a bond required for public works projects did not create an exception to the arbitration act and the general contractor was entitled to a stay of the action. Applying state law, the court reasoned that there was no intention under the state bonding act to render meaningless a contractual agreement to arbitrate.[14]

Potentially, some confusion exists between the Miller Act and the Federal Arbitration Act. The Miller Act, designed to protect both suppliers of labor and material and the government itself by requiring that bidders in federal projects furnish both performance bonds and labor-and-material "payment bonds," provides: "Every suit instituted under this section shall be brought in the name of the United States for the use of the person suing, in the United States district court for any district in which the contract was to be performed and executed and not elsewhere, irrespective of the amount in controversy in such suit." This provision appears in conflict, in part, with the Federal Arbitration Act, which provides that arbitration agreements will be enforced in the federal courts. A number of cases, however, have sustained arbitration under the federal act on the ground that the Miller Act does not prescribe an exclusive remedy. Stated in simple terms, most courts hold that the Miller Act provisions were venue provisions designed to benefit defendants in some cases and not designed to prohibit materialmen from voluntarily substituting arbitration.

5. Determine Contracting Parties.

Construction disputes often involve more than two parties. They are not similar to the usual buy-sell contracts where, typically, there are controversies between two parties: a buyer and a seller. Multiple-party disputes are more often than not found in construction. A subcontractor seeks payment for its work from the general contractor, the contractor in turn argues that the dispute is really with the owner, and the owner says he retained an architect to make these construction decisions and to deal with the contractors. Where all the parties are signatories to arbitration clauses, it may be possible to resolve all these questions in arbitration. But where some of the parties to the construction job did not agree to arbitrate claims they cannot be compelled to do so. Thus, in a recent case decided by the Minnesota Supreme Court involving multiparty actions, where some of the parties were bound to arbitration agreements and some were not, the court balanced the policies favoring arbitration with the interests of the other parties and the policies supporting joinder of parties and claims and permitted a litigation to proceed.[15] The court noted that of the five parties involved, three could not be compelled to arbitrate since they were not bound to contracts containing arbitration clauses.

[14]*Warren Bros. v. Cardi Corp.*, 471 F.2d 1304 (1st Cir. 1973).
[15]*Prestressed Concrete v. Adolfson & Peterson*, 240 N.W.2d 551 (Minn. 1976).

CONSOLIDATION

Knowing the contracting parties is also important for determining not only who is subject to arbitration, but also whether the contracting parties can be subjected to a consolidated arbitration. The American Arbitration Association's construction rules do not contain any specific provision regarding consolidation of construction cases.

The present AAA administrative policy with regard to multiparty cases is to initiate the arbitration and/or counterclaim(s) as filed by the moving party—even though separate contracts may be involved, thereby providing the parties with an opportunity to proceed jointly if they so desire. However, should one or more parties object to such a procedure, the cases will be separated and processed individually, unless a court orders otherwise. In separately instituted arbitrations, cases may be consolidated whenever all the parties mutually agree or if consolidation is ordered by the court. Without such agreement or court order the cases will be administered as separate cases in accordance with the existing contractual relationships of the respective parties.

The federal and state courts have tended to arrive at differing conclusions on whether they will judicially order consolidation of multiparty clauses. Research discloses that New York, Pennsylvania, and Minnesota have permitted consolidation whereas Michigan, New Jersey, and Massachusetts have not. Some federal courts have also granted consolidation of construction arbitrations.

Recently, however, parties have by contract regulated the use of consolidation and joinder. The new 1976 AIA documents, for example, now state:

> No arbitration arising out of or relating to the Contract Documents shall include, by consolidation, joinder or in any other manner, the Architect, his employees or consultants except by written consent containing a specific reference to the Owner-Contractor Agreement and signed by the Architect, the Owner, the Contractor and any other person sought to be joined. No arbitration shall include by consolidation, joinder or in any other manner, parties other than the Owner, the Contractor and any other persons, substantially involved in a common question of fact or law, whose presence is required if complete relief is to be accorded in the arbitration. No person other than the Owner or Contractor shall be included as an original third party or additional third party to an arbitration whose interest or responsibility is insubstantial. Any consent to arbitration involving an additional person or persons shall not constitute consent to arbitration of any dispute not described therein or with any person not named or described therein.

GOVERNMENT AS A PARTY

Another primary reason for determining the contracting parties is because a governmental entity is very often an owner in construction. In addition to having to comply with all the special laws and regulations that apply to cities, towns, villages, counties, states and federal agencies, government's role in arbitration must also be researched for special applications.

A primary method of obtaining federal court jurisdiction exists when there is diversity of citizenship between the two contracting parties. However, where a contractor sought to compel arbitration with a state building authority, a federal court found it lacked jurisdiction because a state is not a "citizen" for diversity purposes. The court reasoned that the building authority was really an arm or alter ego of the state. Since a state is not considered a "citizen" for purposes of creating diversity and since the Federal Arbitration Act requires an independent basis of jurisdiction, the action was dismissed.[16]

Governmental bodies are also subject to arbitration and attempts to renege on signed arbitral agreements have been thwarted by the courts. A leading case involved the Dormitory Authority of the State of New York.[17] After a public bidding, it awarded an electrical contract for a new structure on the campus of the State University. The contract was concluded prior to the creation of the Construction Industry Arbitration Rules. However, the contract, as drafted by the Dormitory Authority, stated that in

> all disputes between parties, as to the interpretation of this contract, or in performance of same, except cases where the decision of the Architect is final . . . either party may demand that the matter in dispute be submitted to arbitration in accordance with provisions of the Standard Arbitration Procedure of the American Arbitration Association.

The electrical work was to be completed within 540 days. Because of delays allegedly caused by the Authority, the work took an extra 183 days after the scheduled completion date. The Authority rejected any settlement of the dispute, and the electrical contractor demanded arbitration. The Authority sought to defeat arbitration because, "in carrying out a governmental function . . . (education), sovereign immunity protects it from the operation of the arbitration clause which it had inserted into the contract." New York's highest court first determined that the State Dormitory Authority was not entitled to sovereign immunity in any event because the enabling legislation creating it envisioned a "separate existence" and was therefore not identical with the state.

More important, however, was the strong language of the court when it said, "Assuming the validity of the Authority's argument that it is identified with the State, we hold that the State itself is not insulated against the operation of an arbitration clause in a contract because the power to contract implies the power to assent to the settlement of disputes by means of arbitration."

PROCEDURES DURING ARBITRATION

The Construction Industry Arbitration Rules were first promulgated by the AAA on March 8, 1966. Since that time, all construction cases have been administered pursuant to these special rules unless for some reason the parties' contracts call for other rules or procedures.

There are several differences between the construction rules and the AAA's commercial arbitration rules. First, they have been prepared exclusively for

---

[16]*McDevitt & Street Co. v. Georgia Bldg. Auth.*, 343 F. Supp. 1238 (N.D. Ga. 1972).
[17]*Dormitory Auth. of the State of N.Y. v. Span Elec. Corp.*, 18 N.Y. 2d 114, 271 N.Y.S.2d 983 (1966).

construction industry claims and disputes. Second, the rules are under the guidance of the National Construction Industry Arbitration Committee and the representative of the nine associations and professional societies that comprise the committee. Third, the arbitrators used on construction cases are all persons nominated by and experienced in the building business. Other differences include: a standard $100 filing fee due when the case is filed; service by the arbitrators without compensation for the first two days of hearing, unless the parties otherwise agree; and a presumption that three arbitrators will comprise the arbitral tribunal as opposed to one in an ordinary commercial case.

1. Commencing Arbitration

The arbitration is initiated by either party to the contract. For instance, if there is a dispute between an owner and an architect, either one may initiate proceedings by serving notice on the other of a demand for arbitration. The association has specially prepared forms available for such purposes. Copies may be obtained at any AAA regional office. Information on the demand for arbitration should include the nature of the claim, the type of relief that is being sought, and the applicable arbitration provision of the contract. One copy should be sent to the other party to the arbitration and two copies forwarded to the nearest AAA regional office, together with the appropriate fee called for in the fee schedule of the construction rules. Once a copy of the demand has been received by the association, all further administrative duties will be handled by a tribunal administrator assigned by the AAA to the case.

2. Answering Statement

The party upon whom the demand is served is permitted seven days within which to make an answering statement. Should no answering statement be received by the association, it is assumed that all claims are denied.

3. Locale

The next step involves determining the locale of the hearings. Normally the parties will agree on the locale of the hearing. Most often it takes place at the construction site or nearby. However, from time to time there is a dispute between the parties as to where the arbitration should be heard. For example, there may be an owner from one state, a contractor from a second state, an architect from a third state and the building site in a fourth state. In this situation, it is not unusual for the parties to disagree as to where the arbitration should be scheduled. Where the contract does not specify a particular locale for the hearing, the parties are requested to advise the AAA in writing as to why they desire the hearing at a particular place. The AAA then makes a final and binding determination as to where the hearings shall be scheduled. In reviewing the locale applications, the association considers eight factors in arriving at its decision: (1) location and convenience of the parties, (2) location and convenience of witnesses and documents, (3) location of the construction site, (4) relative cost to the parties, (5) where the contract was signed, (6) the law applicable to the contract, (7) place of any previous court actions, and (8) location of the most appropriate panel of arbitrators.

4. Selecting Arbitrators

After determining locale comes selection of the arbitrators. The association maintains a nationwide panel of arbitrators who are experts in the field of construction disputes, consisting of architects, engineers, contractors, subcontractors, material suppliers, and attorneys familiar with construction contracts and claims. Despite the fact that the AAA has the authority to appoint arbitrators, it is the normal policy to submit lists of names of the prospective arbitrators to the parties to enable them to participate in the selection process. To give parties in the construction industry the most acceptable arbitrators, the association maintains a full-time panels department with the sole task of thoroughly reviewing each panel member before he or she may be used as an arbitrator. No one may serve on a case who has any interest in the outcome of the proceedings, either financial or personal. Even after the appointment has been made by the association, either party may offer a factual objection which, after consideration by the administrators, may result in the removal of the arbitrator from the case.

The rules provide a standard procedure under which impartial arbitrators are selected with or without the cooperation of the disputing parties. Under the construction industry rules, a party may name an arbitrator or specify a method by which the arbitrator is to be appointed. If the parties' contract has neither named an arbitrator nor specified a method of appointing him, the arbitrator is appointed pursuant to a procedure whereby each party to the dispute receives an identical list of names and is requested to delete the name of any proposed arbitrator that the party finds unacceptable. The lists are returned to the association and from among those persons who have been approved on both lists, in accordance with the order of preference of the parties, the AAA invites the acceptance of the arbitrators to serve.

5. Scheduling Hearings

Once the hearing site has been selected, and the parties have returned their list of arbitrators, the arbitrators sign an oath of office and schedule the hearings. It is usual, however, for the tribunal administrator to discuss with the parties when they would like the hearings to be scheduled. The parties are given at least five days written notice of the scheduled hearing. Parties generally welcome the AAA procedures, which allow them to indicate their preferences for the date of the hearing on a calendar which they receive when the case is initiated. This convenient device is quite different from appearing in court because the parties and their attorneys are able to participate in choosing a hearing date that is convenient for both. It is possible to obtain adjournments or continuations from the tribunal administrator and the arbitrators whenever necessary and appropriate.

6. Conduct of Hearings

The hearing itself is conducted in very much the same manner as a hearing before a court referee, except that it is even more relaxed and flexible. However, strict rules of evidence do not apply and a stenographic record is not kept unless the parties agree otherwise.

The arbitrators, not being bound by strict rules of evidence or procedure, are usually quite liberal in receiving evidence. This is especially true in light of the fact that a refusal to hear relevant or material testimony may constitute grounds for vacating an award. It is important to remember that an arbitrator's action in receiving evidence offers no assurance that it will be given the weight or bearing that the offering party intends. Attorneys representing architects, engineers, and contractors will do well to bear this in mind, for it may relieve anxiety and obviate needless argument one way or the other. Visual aids and working drawings of a particular building or fixture therein, which may be the basis of the dispute, are always welcome, and arbitrators seem to prefer working with such aids.

The order of proceedings is not unusual. The complaining party or his counsel presents the claim and proofs and the witnesses who are then subject to questions and other cross-examination. Thereafter, the responding party or his counsel presents the defense and proofs, and witnesses who also submit to questions and examinations. The arbitrator may vary this procedure at his discretion, but he must afford full opportunity to all parties and their counsel for the presentation of material and relevant proofs. The making of opening and closing statements is usually helpful. The submission of briefs and memoranda is also helpful, but both opening statements and submission of briefs are within the discretion of the arbitrators.

Unless the parties have agreed otherwise, the arbitrators may not conduct an independent investigation of the construction site. This is important to remember, because in many controversies and claims arising out of construction contracts, parties and their attorneys want the arbitrator to view the site for a better understanding of the issues at hand. In order for the arbitrator to make this inspection, however, he must do it either in the presence of the parties or must have their express permission to visit the area independently. In the event that the parties or any of them are not present at the inspection or investigation, the arbitrator should make a verbal or written report to them and afford an opportunity for the receipt of comment and/or testimony in relation thereto.

During the course of the arbitration, there should be no communication between the parties or their counsel and an arbitrator other than at the hearings. Any time parties wish to contact the arbitrator, such communication should be directed to the tribunal administrator for transmittal to the arbitrator. In this manner, all the parties are assured that the proceedings will be fair and impartial, and no one has the opportunity to present evidence to the arbitrator that the other side is not aware of.

7. The Award

After the hearings are closed, it is usual for the arbitrators to reserve decision. Under the construction industry rules, however, the award must be made promptly, in any event not later than 30 days from the date the hearings were closed, and must be rendered in writing. The arbitrator has the authority to grant any remedy or relief which he deems just and equitable so long as it is within the terms of the agreement of the parties. Thus, for example, if an arbitrator feels that specific performance of a particular part of the construction job would be inappropriate, he has the authority to award monetary damages.

Oftentimes, it is possible for the parties to settle their dispute during the course of the arbitration. When this is done, it is possible for the arbitrator to enter into a consent award. Such a consent award may, at a later time, help the parties avoid unnecessary disputes as to the appropriate terms of their settlement.

8. Prehearing Conference

There has been one interesting new development in the processing of construction industry claims. Over the years, parties have suggested that there should be a way of speeding up processing of large claims. In an attempt to meet this need, the AAA instituted the use of a prehearing conference as a means of expediting certain large, complicated construction cases. Under this procedure, which is still relatively new to the association, a regional director convenes an informal meeting of the parties or their attorneys prior to the hearing to arrange for exchanges of information and stipulation of uncontested facts and—where possible and appropriate—to resolve certain collateral issues by discussion and mediation. From time to time, an arbitrator rather than an association executive may be used to convene the prehearing conference. As the AAA has gained experience with this procedure, it has developed an internal checklist of 24 items that are discussed with the parties. The parties are made to understand that should they wish to discuss the substance of their claims and any counterclaims, any such discussions would be in the strictest confidence insofar as the arbitration was concerned. The important thing to remember is that the objective of the prearbitration conference is to expedite rather than delay the ultimate disposition of the dispute. Whenever a given conference either lags or becomes counterproductive, it is immediately terminated.

Many of the prehearing conferences have resulted in the parties' discontinuing arbitration and settling the claims directly. In others, there has been success in weeding out a large number of claims that the parties did not wish to discuss until they were in the hands of a neutral. Under the AAA's auspices, they were willing to dispose of major portions of some of the claims, thereby making it easier for the arbitrator to ultimately rule on those that could not be settled. It is too early to tell whether the prehearing conference is an unqualified success. The association, however, is pleased with the cooperation it has received from the parties and their counsel because much depends on the spirit of cooperation in a prehearing conference. It is hoped that the continued availability under AAA auspices of this prearbitration procedure will provide an additional method by which large construction industry claims may be more promptly administered.

Chapter **44**

Arbitration May Help You Collect Faster

GIRARD R. VISCONTI, ESQ.
Partner, Abedon & Visconti Ltd., Providence, Rhode Island

INTRODUCTION

Arbitration has become an effective tool for the resolution of contract, labor,[1] and safety[2] disputes in the construction industry. Although arbitration is not always the answer, its virtues are many in comparison to those of the sometimes costly and time-consuming legal process. The following is an analysis of these various attributes, which should give the reader sufficient information as to the positive aspects of arbitration so that he can determine whether or not and when arbitration is right for him.

It is important to note that in the construction industry the right or duty to arbitrate a dispute is generally self-imposed. That is, the parties to a construc-

---

[1]*United Steel Workers v. Warrior & Gulf Navig. Co.*, 363 U.S. 574 (1960).
[2]*Gateway Coal Co. v. United Mine Workers*, 414 U.S. 368 (1974).

tion contract, to be bound to arbitrate, must at the time they contract mutually consent to the arbitration of all or some disputes which might arise under the contract. Thus, it is essential that the various parties to such a contract (contractors, suppliers, owner, and architect) understand how arbitration will affect them should such a dispute develop, since arbitration, if agreed upon, will be compulsory.

The following is a basic arbitration clause which is often recommended for use in construction contracts:

> All claims, disputes, and other matters in question, arising out of or relating to the interpretation or performance of this contract or the breach thereof, shall be promptly referred to the American Arbitration Association to be resolved in accordance with the then existing construction industry rules. Any award shall be final and binding upon the parties.

PRACTICAL ADVANTAGES OF ARBITRATION

Essentially, six factors make arbitration an effective tool for the settlement of disputes in the construction industry: time, cost, expertise, convenience, informality, and privacy. Any of these factors may be individually significant to a party who is contemplating arbitration.

Time

For one who is attempting to collect money owed or settle a controversy arising under the terms of a construction contract, the passing of time can significantly diminish the chances of a successful recovery or resolution. Problems can arise both while construction is in progress and after it has been completed. Consider for example the situation where a subcontractor and the general contractor during construction are in dispute over whether or not certain work as set forth in the specifications or drawings is within the subcontractor's scope of work. Such a dispute could delay the progress of the project for months and increase the costs to all substantially if the matter was litigated. Arbitration, however, which usually takes a few months to complete, could settle the dispute with little or no interruption to the progression of work. Furthermore, many arbitration clauses contain language which requires a contractor to "carry on the work and maintain the progress schedule during any arbitration proceedings unless otherwise agreed by him and the owner in writing."[3] These factors lean heavily in favor of arbitration for the resolution of disputes which occur while work is in progress. After a construction project is substantially or finally completed, arbitration may be utilized to determine such factors as balances due, punch list disputes, or warranty coverage.

Due to the instability of the construction industry, the passage of time can often determine whether or not collection can be made on a past-due account. Statistics show that 63 percent of all construction contractors will survive in the

---

[3]AIA Document A201, General Conditions of the Contract for Construction, 1976 ed., article 7.9.3.

industry for no longer than five and one-half years.[4] Add to this the fact that it can literally take years for a case to reach trial in the overburdened state judicial systems. Thus, as every year passes from the date of completion the chances of total or even partial recovery are reduced. Inflation, which is rampant in the industry, will also eat away at any recovery. Construction dollars recovered at a later date will have decreased in real value at a rate of approximately 10 percent per year.

The procedures which govern arbitration are oriented toward the speedy resolution of disputes. Any form of arbitration must be authorized by statute. Most states have adopted what is known as the Uniform Arbitration Act, which governs the arbitration of private matters.[5] Some states also have statutes which specifically provide for arbitration in regard to public works projects.[6] The specific details of how and when arbitration is to be conducted in any given situation will be governed by the terms of the construction contract which can include general and supplemental conditions, specifications, addenda, and modifications, any one of which may contain arbitration procedures. Therefore, all contract documents should be considered in determining arbitration procedures, including prearbitration conditions.

It should not be forgotten that the parties to a construction contract can voluntarily submit a dispute to arbitration even though there is no arbitration clause in their contract.[7] In doing so, the parties will agree as to what procedure they will follow in conducting the arbitration.

The timetable for arbitration begins when one party makes a demand for arbitration. The time period in which demand must be made can be limited by the terms of the parties' contract or by applicable arbitration statutes. Thus, arbitration often is commenced before litigation normally would be initiated.

Once demand is made, arbitration usually moves very quickly to its conclusion. For example, under the construction industry arbitration rules, the American Arbitration Association must submit a list of prospective arbitrators immediately to each party.[8] The parties have seven days to object to the names on that list. The arbitrators are then appointed and ordinarily hearings will be scheduled within two months. The arbitrators then, in most cases, must make the award within a specified number of days. The Construction Industry Arbitration Rules require that the award be made "not later than 30 days from the date of closing the hearings."[9]

---

[4]O. Currie and A. Coleman, *Construction Default: The Contractor's Bond,* "Litigation with a Surety," PLI, New York, 1976, p. 67.

[5]The following states have enacted arbitration statutes: Alaska, Arizona, Arkansas, California, Connecticut, Delaware, Florida, Hawaii, Illinois, Indiana, Kansas, Louisiana, Maine, Maryland, Massachusetts, Michigan, Minnesota, Nevada, New Hampshire, New Jersey, New Mexico, New York, North Carolina, Ohio, Oregon, Pennsylvania, Rhode Island, South Dakota, Texas, Virginia, Washington, Wisconsin, and Wyoming. There is also a Federal Arbitration Act. 9 USC 1 et seq.

[6]Maine, Nevada, and Rhode Island.

[7]The American Arbitration Association will provide forms for this purpose.

[8]Construction Industry Arbitration Rules, § 13.

[9]Construction Industry Arbitration Rules, § 41.

The abbreviated procedure of the arbitration proceeding facilitates the speedy resolution of disputes which if litigated could take years to reach finality. Gone are the prehearing motions and extensive discovery which often delay trial in the state and federal judicial systems for months. Also avoided is the large backlog of cases which have the effect in some states of detaining trial for three years after a case has been assigned for trial.

The finality of an arbitration award must be considered when the factor of time becomes important. Under most state arbitration statutes, the award of the arbitrators cannot be overturned or vacated except under very limited circumstances, such as fraud, partiality of arbitrators, or where the arbitrator has exceeded his power.[10] The state and federal judicial systems, on the other hand, with their overburdened appellate courts, offer further opportunity for delay.

It is also significant to note that arbitration, like litigation, encourages the settlement of disputes by the parties prior to the time that hearings are held. According to the American Arbitration Association, approximately 60 percent of all construction cases settle after demand for arbitration is made.[11]

Arbitration then, in most cases, will mean that disputes will be settled faster and money will be collected sooner than they would have been had the parties resorted to litigation.

Cost

Arbitration, like litigation, is expensive. In fact, at first glance arbitration appears to involve greater expense than litigation. The following are typical costs incurred in an arbitration proceeding:

American Arbitration Association fees   There is an initial filing fee of $100 when arbitration is commenced. The balance of the administrative fee of the AAA is based on the amount of the claim as shown in Table 44.1.

Arbitrator's fee   Under the AAA rules the first two days are served without compensation, but on occasion an honorarium of $100 or more may be given by the parties. After the first two days, the arbitrators are paid on a per diem basis at a rate determined by the parties, usually $150 to $250.

---

[10]A typical statute (General Laws of Rhode Island, 1956, as amended, § 10-3-12) reads as follows: Grounds For Vacating Award: In either of the following cases said court must make an order vacating the award upon the application of any party to the arbitration.

(a) Where the award was procured by corruption, fraud or undue means.

(b) Where there was evident partiality or corruption on the part of the arbitrators, or either of them.

(c) Where the arbitrators were guilty of misconduct in refusing to postpone the hearing, upon sufficient cause shown, or in hearing legally immaterial evidence, or refusing to hear evidence pertinent and material to the controversy, or of any other misbehavior by which the rights of any party have been substantially prejudiced.

(d) Where the arbitrators exceeded their powers, or so imperfectly executed them that a mutual, final, and definite award upon the subject matter submitted was not made.

[11]G. Aksen, *Construction Contracts,* "Role of Arbitration in Construction Contracts," PLI, New York, 1976, p. 304.

TABLE 44.1

Amount of claim	Fee
Up to $10,000	3 percent (minimum $100)
$10,000 to $25,000	$300, plus 2 percent of excess over $10,000
$25,000 to $100,000	$600, plus 1 percent of excess over $25,000
$100,000 to $200,000	$1350, plus ½ percent of excess over $100,000

Attorney's fee The attorney's fee is determined by the party and its attorney.

In the long run the arbitration of construction disputes will save money.[12] Arbitration encourages the early settlement or determination of a dispute. Thus, if one is owed money, the chances of recovery will be greater when the other party is still in existence and is a viable enterprise. Furthermore, the inflation factor will be reduced to a minimum.

Arbitration is also less costly because the procedure is uniform. If the dispute takes place out of state, vagaries of unfamiliar laws and costs will not exist. An attorney, who is familiar with a particular firm and the problems associated with it, will be able to represent it in any arbitration proceedings anywhere in the country. All these factors lead to predictability, which will in the long run allow better assessment of any given dispute and resolve the dispute at less expense.

Also important in regard to the cost factor is the flexibility of arbitration. As one authority has stated, arbitration is a "mobile and informal tribunal which is not tied to a fixed location and can meet and hold hearings at almost any time or place agreed upon by the parties."[13] Thus, the parties involved can schedule the hearings at a time which is not disruptive to their daily business or work schedules. The trial calendars of our state and federal courts are not so accommodating.

Since arbitrators, under the Construction Industry Arbitration Rules, are experts in the construction field, an arbitration proceeding very likely will be shorter in duration than a court trial. Expensive and time-consuming explanation of the details of the construction business, which may be required with a judge or a jury, is unnecessary. Furthermore, the hearing will not be governed by all the rules of evidence which can disrupt the presentation of testimony.

As was noted previously, the ability to appeal an arbitration award is very limited. The potential for savings here is tremendous since appellate review of trial court decisions is a very costly process. Attorneys must spend many hours researching, writing briefs, and preparing for arguments. The chances that an arbitration award will be subject to appellate review are far less likely than those of a trial court decision in regard to the same dispute.

[12]Comisky & Comisky, "Commercial Arbitration—Panacea or Nightmare," 47 TEMP. L. Q. 457 (1974); Mentshikoff, "Commercial Arbitration," 61 COLUM. L. REV. 846 (1961).

[13]Lippman, "Arbitration As An Alternative to Judicial Settlement," 24 MAINE L. REV. 215, 218 (1972).

Convenience

The convenience of an arbitration proceeding is one of its outstanding features.[14] While the judicial process very methodically moves along and demands attendance when it is ready, the flexibility of arbitration ensures that all parties meet when and where they desire. Other business concerns can be given proper attention when required, and the case can be properly prepared because the parties know precisely when it is going to take place.

The consolidation of all disputes which arise in regard to a construction project is another recognized attribute of arbitration. Although usually not mandatory, consolidation may be voluntarily agreed upon. For example, the owner of a project may have a claim against the general contractor, who may assert it against a subcontractor, who in turn may assert it against his supplier. The end result may be three separate arbitration hearings with contradictory awards. The consolidation of the hearings into one eliminates this problem.

Informality

The atmosphere surrounding arbitration is less hostile than that of a trial. The formality of the trial court with its detailed rules of evidence and set procedures can create animosity between the parties which may never dissipate. The more relaxed atmosphere of the arbitration hearing will tend to reduce this hostility. In a business where it is very likely that two disputing parties will want to be put, or will be put, in a position where they will have to work together again, the importance of keeping conflict to a minimum cannot be overemphasized. Arbitration provides an excellent forum for this purpose.

Expertise

One of the great assets of construction arbitration is the fact that the arbitrators are familiar with the construction industry and its rather unique methods and terminology. This can be significant because it will take less time to get to the heart of the dispute. The chances of one side confusing and deceiving the decision makers will be diminished. There will be fewer surprise decisions.

Under the Construction Industry Arbitration Rules, the arbitrators are selected from what is known as the Construction Industry Panel, which is made up of persons "qualified to serve by virtue of their experience in the construction field." Furthermore, each of the parties may object to the appointment of an arbitrator if they doubt his ability or objectivity. Thus, in arbitration, a party has a certain degree of control over who will determine the outcome of a dispute in which he is involved.

Privacy

Arbitration is essentially a private means of dispute resolution. The public does not have a right to view the hearings, and there is no public record of what takes place or what is said in the hearings. This can be important where a party wants

---

[14]Aksen, "Resolving Construction Contract Disputes Through Arbitration," 23 Arb. J. 141 (1968).

to avoid publicity or prevent the disclosure of confidential information such as a trade secret.[15] Also, the embarrassment of a public hearing, which often contributes to hostility between the parties, is avoided.

PRACTICAL POINTS

It is essential that arbitration be commenced properly. One should always obtain legal advice.

In filing a demand for arbitration, carefully follow the procedure set forth in the contract documents. At the very least a demand for arbitration should contain the following information: the name and address of the parties, the name of the project, the architect/engineer, the issue or issues to be arbitrated and the relief requested.

It is important that the issues presented and the relief requested in the demand be properly phrased. For example, the issue may be "whether or not a masonry subcontractor is required under his contract to *tooth* exterior brick work in the alteration of an existing building," and the proper relief may be a "change order and an extra."

A subcontractor in a dispute over how a particular item of work is to be done, with the architect insisting that it be done a certain way, should demand arbitration of the dispute, proceed to do the work in accordance with the architect's instructions, and notify the other parties that the work is being performed "under protest and without prejudice." If the arbitration award is in his favor, he will be awarded costs plus overhead and profit for the work not required but performed under protest. If the award is not in his favor, he will have performed the work at a lower cost as compared to the general contractor performing the work or subcontracting it out and later backcharging his firm. He may be required to proceed with the disputed work anyway as many contracts contain clauses which state that the contractor must "carry on the work and maintain the progress schedule during any arbitration proceedings."

On occasion it may be appropriate for the parties to submit an "agreed statement of facts" to the arbitrators. Such a statement could include all relevant facts, the issues presented, the relief sought by each party and all related documents. The parties then submit written or oral arguments with little or no testimony.

In some cases the parties, usually a subcontractor and a general contractor, may want to agree prior to the hearing on the payment of a lump sum for the disputed work. The agreement should be in writing and presented to the arbitrator. Such a lump-sum payment is helpful because, win or lose, both parties know exactly what they may recover or have to pay.

In the alternative, the parties may agree that the disputed work be performed, pending arbitration, on a time-and-material basis plus a certain per-

---

[15]Notes, "An Analysis of a Technique of Dispute Settlement: The Expanding Role of Arbitration." 7 SUFFOLK U. L. REV. 618 (1973).

centage for overhead and profit. A daily time sheet recording labor and material performed should be acknowledged in writing by both parties, to prevent future controversy over the amount and value of labor and material provided.

If no method of compensation is agreed upon, the claimant must present to the arbitrator evidence of the amount and value of such items as labor or material provided in relation to the disputed work. The contract documents will usually provide the percentage for overhead and profit. If no such percentage is included in the contract, the claimant can present evidence of the traditional or prevailing percentages in the construction industry.

ARBITRATION OF LABOR DISPUTES

An arbitration clause in collective bargaining agreements may prove to be a very useful tool. The Supreme Court has held that a union may not resort to such measures as the strike, slowdown, or picket line when the collective bargaining agreement between the parties contains an arbitration clause which applies to the disputed matter. Furthermore, if the union refuses to arbitrate and strikes, an employer may seek injunctive relief to enjoin the strike and compel the union to arbitrate.[16]

CONCLUSION

Arbitration is an excellent device to resolve construction disputes—especially money and contract interpretation disputes. Of the various factors noted above perhaps the most important is the time element. Arbitration's greatest advantage is the speed with which it can resolve a dispute. Without arbitration, the parties may have to wait several years for the courthouse to call.

---

[16]*The Boys Markets, Inc. v. Local 770, Retail Clerks Union,* 398 U.S. 235 (1970).

Chapter **45**

The Disadvantages of Arbitration

MAX E. GREENBERG, ESQ.

**Senior Partner, Max E. Greenberg, Trayman, Cantor, Reiss & Blasky,
New York, New York**

Theoretically, arbitration is a most desirable means of determining a controversy. The parties agree on an objective arbitrator or panel of arbitrators who are knowledgeable as to trade practices, conditions, and costs and who can quickly and understandably arrive at a just result. Unfortunately, practice and theory do not always coincide. In determining whether you should or should not arbitrate, consideration should be given to many problems that can arise in connection with an arbitration.

THE APPOINTMENT OF ARBITRATORS

Generally, arbitration agreements provide for two methods of designating arbitrators. If the matter is not one to be arbitrated in accordance with the rules of the American Arbitration Association, usually it is provided that each side will designate one arbitrator and the two shall, in turn, designate an umpire. In the event the two cannot agree on the umpire within a reasonable period of time, it is usually provided that the third arbitrator or umpire shall be designated by a justice of a designated court or some other designated person. More often than not, there is difficulty in obtaining the umpire. Each side is suspicious of the persons proffered by the other. If the matter is then referred to a justice of a court, the probabilities are that he will not designate a person who is familiar with the trade and its practices but some party member or other person known to the justice. Although normally the judges designated are fair in an attempt to designate an umpire, it has occurred that a judge has been approached as to whom he should designate. A fair arbitration, or certainly one complying with the theoretical objectives of an arbitration, is not obtained under these circumstances.

Where the arbitration is in accordance with the rules of the American Arbitration Association, the practice is for the association to send out a duplicate list of proposed arbitrators. Each side marks off those whom they do not desire. If there are common names left on the two lists, then appointment is made from those not marked off. This is at least a reasonably prompt method of obtaining arbitrators. Customarily, if there are no common names left on the first list, a second list is sent out. If after the second list is promulgated there are still no common names, then the Arbitration Association will itself designate the arbitrators. Whether they are as objective and competent as one might hope is not ensured. The lists are customarily made up by clerical forces employed by the Arbitration Association. Sometimes they are unbalanced in that representatives of particular trades outweigh those of another trade or the representative of one of the trades involved is not designated at all. Frequently, lawyers are designated with a statement that they are familiar with construction contract matters. They may *not* be familiar with such matters. They may have had some smattering of experience in connection with one or more matters, but they may be far from knowledgeable in the field. Other arbitrators, assuming that a lawyer would know what the law is and how a matter should be handled, may be much influenced by this lawyer who in fact may be all but incompetent. Unless we know that a lawyer actually is experienced in the field, it is our practice to strike their names from the list.

Where there are a number of parties involved in the arbitration, such as a general contractor, a subcontractor, an owner, an architect or engineer, even under the practices of the American Arbitration Association, it is extremely difficult to arrive at names satisfactory to all. We are aware of instances where it actually took years simply to arrive at the designation of arbitrators even under the rules of the American Arbitration Association.

WHEN ARBITRATION IS DESIRABLE

If the matter to be arbitrated is comparatively simple in that it will not involve hearings of more than a few days and the parties can agree on a single arbitrator in whom they have confidence, we believe that under these circumstances the designation of such an arbitrator would be highly satisfactory and desirable.

UNDISCLOSED FAVORITISM OF ARBITRATOR

Another consideration, in arriving at a determination whether to arbitrate, is the approachability or possible favoritism of the arbitrator or arbitrators. There is more likelihood of such occurrences in arbitration than in a matter in a court particularly where the parties have a right to a jury trial. It is true that sometimes judges are approached, but that occurs less frequently than might be the public understanding. However, among arbitrators it may be far more frequent. We have had experience with matters where the third arbitrator actually had been doing business with the other side but did not disclose that fact at the time of his appointment and not until after an award in favor of the other side. We then were able to discover that he had in fact been employed as an engineer by the other side. In order to upset that award, it was necessary for us to go all the way to the United States Supreme Court, which did upset the award under the circumstances.

In another instance, after an unfavorable award, we ascertained that the third arbitrator had been in constant telephone communication with the other side during the arbitration. That award was upset. It is not always easy to find out these facts, however.

On another occasion, during the course of the hearings it developed that one of the arbitrators had been engaged in business with the parent company of one of the parties. Millions of dollars were in controversy, but the American Arbitration Association refused to remove him. It was necessary to go through court proceedings to have him removed.

In another instance, we were approached by a third person with a statement that two of the arbitrators were in disagreement and that the decision would be made by the third arbitrator. It was suggested that an arrangement could be made with the third arbitrator. It was refused, of course. We nevertheless obtained a favorable award. Whether the suggestion by the third person had been made with the knowledge or consent of the third arbitrator we do not know. These examples are cited only to demonstrate what can happen in an arbitration, not to suggest that they occur regularly.

PROTECTIVE PROVISIONS DISREGARDED

When building and construction contracts are made, many clauses are inserted which will protect against claims. They are inserted for that very purpose. Yet, if there is an arbitration, these clauses will not bind the arbitrators. The arbitrators are not bound by rules of law. They can make their own law. Under the circumstances, all these protective clauses can be utterly disregarded. In agreeing upon an arbitration, this problem also should be kept in view. It may be well to understand what a party is waiving if he agrees to an arbitration. Unless he had the protective clauses he might not even have made the contract originally.

PROTRACTED HEARINGS

Our greatest objection to arbitration, however, relates to controversies which will involve a long period of hearings. A delay claim, a claim for interferences, claims involving large numbers of controverted items which would take possibly a number of weeks or several months on a trial become very costly, long-lived matters in an arbitration. Claims which could be disposed of on a continuous trial of several weeks or months may literally take many years to determine in an arbitration. The problem is that the arbitrators will not sit continuously when hearings are commenced. They will sit one day a week or at most, several days a week. They may not sit again for another week or another month. The dates have to be agreed upon between the arbitrators and the parties and it is frequently difficult to arrive at a date satisfactory to all parties. When hearings are resumed, it is necessary to refresh one's self as to all of the testimony previously given and to study the matter all over again. The time of the arbitrators on these hearings is customarily paid for. In addition, it is advisable and usual to have minutes taken, which is costly. We are familiar with arbitrations which actually extended over a period of five years or more. We are also advised concerning a present arbitration pending for seven years which has not yet been determined or even concluded.

In addition, on these long-lived arbitrations, it is not easy to get the type of arbitrator that one would like to have. The experienced, well-qualified person is usually too busy to spend all the time necessary on the arbitrations even though he or she is paid. The result is that the arbitrators are more likely to be persons who are not so well-known or qualified and therefore are not so preoccupied with their own business as to make it difficult for them to act as arbitrators on a long-lived matter. There is no quick determination which is expected in connection with an arbitration; it is far more costly than appearing in court because of the necessity of paying the arbitrators over a period of years, obtaining minutes of hearings, spending time to renew familiarity with matters that had gone before and in connection with continued preparation and re-preparation after long periods between hearings, etc. Under these circumstances it is far more efficient and economical to dispose of the matter in accordance with normal court procedures.

THE FUTURE OF ARBITRATION

If a means could be found whereby practice and theory could be made to conform, then arbitration would indeed be far more desirable than a court proceeding before a court or jury unfamiliar with the particular trade. It has been suggested by this writer that the industry itself provide for a corps of permanent, highly paid, well-qualified arbitrators who will act as professionals in this particular field of endeavor. They would be in a position to sit continuously when arbitration proceedings are instituted to come to a prompt and understandable conclusion. It is suggested that a very small addition to the cost of each contract price would provide a huge fund available for the purpose suggested. As a matter of fact, the tunneling industry is presently attempting to work out the adoption of a procedure along these lines in cooperation with the American Arbitration Association. They are not providing, however, that the arbitrators would be paid by the industry. They would provide for payment by the parties to the arbitration, which may be expensive. It still could be more desirable than other forms of litigation where large sums are involved and complicated long-lived matters are required to be determined. It is the intermittent hearings, sometimes far apart from one another, which make arbitration under these circumstances so expensive, undesirable, and protracted. It is also these circumstances which preclude the highly qualified personnel one would like to have engaged as arbitrators from being engaged due to the necessity of giving attention to their own affairs.

Chapter **46**

Enforceability of Arbitration Provisions

KENNETH M. CUSHMAN, ESQ.
Partner, Pepper, Hamilton & Scheetz, Philadelphia, Pennsylvania

INTRODUCTION

Whether one party to an agreement to arbitrate disputes must judicially compel the other party to that agreement to arbitrate will be determined by how the parties regard the relative strength of their position and how they perceive the forum of arbitration, as opposed to a formal trial, as affecting the ultimate outcome of the case. A prospective owner will rarely consider the relative merits of arbitration when he prepares the contract for construction, and usually it is the architect who suggests the form of contract to be used. Since the American Institute of Architects favors arbitration, the standard American Institute of Architects' contract contains an arbitration clause, and often this clause or a variation of it is incorporated into the owner–general contractor agreement.[1] As a result, it is when a dispute arises that the parties for the first time focus on the full effect of the arbitration clause.

---

[1]The provisions of the current AIA General Conditions which pertain to arbitration are set forth in the appendix to this chapter.

Typical of the type of dispute giving rise to arbitration litigation is when the contractor seeks to recover a substantial delay claim against a local public body, or the reverse position, that is, when the public body attempts to assess liquidated damages against a contractor whose contention it is that any delays were the result of inadequate plans and specifications furnished by the architect, unforeseen project conditions, and the failure of the owner to coordinate the work of multiple prime contractors. Usually, at this point, the owner wants to avoid arbitration so that a local jury or judge can teach this nonlocal contractor with a corporate surety that when a party signs a contract, he is required to strictly adhere to its terms or bear the consequences of not doing so. At the same time, the contractor will realize that local juries will probably be reticent to award large delay damage verdicts to contractors—especially if this will result in an increase in local taxes—and that the best way to get a fair hearing is to proceed before independent arbitrators.[2]

It is not the purpose of this chapter to weigh the relative merits of arbitration but rather to analyze the process of how and why agreements to arbitrate and awards pursuant thereto will or will not be enforced. The primary focus will be on the United States Arbitration Act[3] and the arbitration law of the Commonwealth of Pennsylvania, which like many other states in the United States has, in addition to retaining common-law rights of arbitration, adopted a form of the Uniform Arbitration Act.[4]

The typical arbitration statute[5] provides that:

> A provision in any written contract . . . to settle by arbitration a controversy thereafter arising out of such contract, or out of the refusal to perform the whole or any part thereof, or an agreement in writing between two or more persons to submit to arbitration any controversy existing between them, at the time of the agreement to submit, shall be valid, irrevocable and enforceable, save upon such grounds as exist at law or in equity for the revocation of any contract.

Generally, these acts contain other essential provisions, such as: (1) power of a party to obtain a court order directing the other party to proceed to arbitration; (2) authority for the court to stay any action filed in violation of an agreement to

---

[2]This is not to imply that owners will always seek to avoid arbitration and that contractors will always find it to their advantage to pursue same. Many a contractor's lawyer feels more comfortable arguing before a jury that this big public utility or that this gigantic corporate owner did not deal "fair and square" with this little contractor with the result that the contractor will be put out of business unless he receives a substantial verdict. If this is the case, it is likely that the owner will prefer arbitration to avoid the prejudices of a jury.

[3]9 U.S.C. § 1-14 (1970).

[4]Uniform Arbitration Act of 1927. *See also* K. M. Cushman, "Arbitration and State Law," 23 ARB. J. 162 (1968). At common law, arbitration agreements were revocable at any time before award, *Vynior's Case.* 77 K B 595 (1609) as they ousted the jurisdiction of the court. *Kill v. Hollester,* 1 Wils, 129 (1746). Even today, a large number of states retain this common-law revocability doctrine or hold that only agreements to arbitrate existing controversies are valid. Askin, "Resolving Construction Contract Disputes Through Arbitration," 23 ARB. J. 141 (1968).

[5]5 P.S. § 161 (Penna.) (1963).

arbitrate; (3) proceedings which permit courts to appoint arbitrators if the parties have not designated a selection method; (4) procedures to compel attendance of witnesses at arbitration hearings; (5) procedures for the modification, vacation, or appeal from arbitration awards; and (6) methods for turning the award of the arbitrators into an enforceable judgment.

When drafting an arbitration clause, particular attention should be directed to any "magic words" required by the arbitration act under which the contract is likely to be scrutinized. For example, in order for the Michigan Arbitration Act to be applicable, the arbitration clause must contain language that the parties "agree that a judgment of any Circuit Court shall be rendered upon the award made pursuant to such submission."[6]

It is universally acknowledged that since arbitration is contractual, a party cannot be required to submit to arbitration any dispute which he has not agreed to arbitrate.[7] Moreover, since the arbitrators derive their power and authority from the agreement under which they are appointed, an award outside the scope of that agreement is not binding unless the parties additionally agree to this submission prior to the time of the award.[8] Consequently, if one party to an agreement which contains an arbitration clause prefers to litigate instead of arbitrating, it is not unlikely that such party will contend one or more of the following: (1) the dispute in issue is outside the scope of the arbitration clause; (2) there is no valid or enforceable agreement to arbitrate; (3) there has been a waiver, revocation, or breach of the agreement to arbitrate. Such a position may require the party seeking arbitration to move the court having jurisdiction to compel arbitration. Procedurally, the issue is usually raised in the following manner: (1) the party seeking to avoid arbitration institutes suit and the party desiring arbitration files a Petition to Stay Legal Proceedings and Compel Arbitration; (2) the party who desires arbitration files a Demand for Arbitration and the party seeking to avoid arbitration files a Complaint in Equity to Enjoin Arbitration Proceedings; (3) one party refuses to proceed with arbitration, and the party seeking same files a Petition to Compel Arbitration.

COMPELLING ARBITRATION UNDER THE FEDERAL ARBITRATION ACT

In *Prima Paint Corp. v. Flood & Conklin Mfg. Co.,*[9] a party to an agreement which contained an arbitration clause sought to avoid submitting to arbitration by alleging that he was fraudulently induced to enter into the contract which resulted in the entire agreement being void.

The Supreme Court of the United States referred to § 2 of the Federal Arbitration Act[10] which provides:

---

[6]*E. E. Tripp Excav. Contractor, Inc. v. County of Jackson,* 60 Mich. App. 221. 230 N.W.2d 556 (1975).
[7]*Atkinson v. Sinclair Refining Co.,* 370 U.S. 238 (1962).
[8]*J. P. Greathouse Steel Erectors, Inc. v. Blount Bros. Const.,* 374 F.2d 324 (D.C. Cir. 1967).
[9]388 U.S. 395 (1967).
[10]9 U.S.C. § 2 (1970).

A written provision in any maritime transaction or a contract evidencing a transaction involving commerce to settle by arbitration a controversy thereafter arising out of such contract or transaction, or the refusal to perform the whole or any part thereof, or an agreement in writing to submit to arbitration an existing controversy arising out of such a contract, transaction or refusal, shall be valid, irrevocable and enforceable, save upon such grounds as exist at law or in equity for the revocation for any contract.

The Court noted:

[T]he Federal Arbitration statute is based upon and confined to the uncontestable federal foundations of control over interstate commerce and admiralty.

Consistent with this announced principle, the Court held that under federal law, a general attack on a contract for fraud is to be decided by the arbitrators and that only where the claim of fraud in the inducement goes specifically to the arbitration provision itself should it be decided by the court rather than the arbitrator.

Prima Paint leaves no doubt that if the requirements for invoking the Federal Arbitration Act are met,[11] then under the preemption doctrine, the federal policy toward arbitration will prevail over any conflicting state policy as to enforcing agreements to arbitrate.

The criteria for sufficient interstate commerce to bring into play the Federal Arbitration Act's provisions for enforcing agreements to arbitrate was explained in *Metro Industrial Painting Corp. v. Terminal Construction Co.*[12] At issue was a subcontract which called for certain painting work to be performed at a Florida construction project. Although the court acknowledged that all the painting was to take place within the State of Florida, it nevertheless held that since 20 percent of the work force including supervisory personnel were transported from New York, and since much of the painting materials were purchased from states outside of Florida, the transaction involved commerce so as to require the application of federal law.

The significance of the foregoing is that federal substantive law requires that an agreement to arbitrate be liberally construed in favor of arbitration.[13] As stated by the United States Supreme Court in *United Steel Workers v. Warrior & Gulf Navigation Co.*[14]:

An order to arbitrate the particular grievance should not be denied unless it may be said with positive assurance that the arbitration clause is not susceptible of an

---

[11]The precursor to the federal preemption doctrine as ultimately established in *Prima Paint* was the Supreme Court's decision in *Bernhardt v. Polygraphic Co. of America*, 350 U.S. 198 (1956), which held that in order for the Federal Arbitration Act to apply, there must be interstate commerce, but that the existence of interstate commerce alone without diversity of citizenship would not confer federal jurisdiction.

[12]287 F.2d 382, 384 (2nd Cir. 1961), *cert. denied* 368 U.S. 817 (1961).

[13]*Lundgren v. Freeman*, 307 F.2d 104 (9th Cir. 1962); *Metro Ind. Paint. Corp. v. Terminal Constr. Co.*, *supra*.

[14]363 U.S. 574, 582–583 (1960).

interpretation that covers the asserted dispute. Doubts should be resolved in favor of coverage.

So too, state courts must enforce this federal policy of liberality in favor of arbitration if the requisite interstate commerce is found to exist, notwithstanding the fact that their state law as to revocation of agreements to arbitrate may be inconsistent. As was stated in *Aerojet-General Corp. v. Non Ferrous Metal Refining, Ltd.*[15]:

> [S]tate rules allocating functions between court and arbitration do not control and in actions involving arbitration provisions in interstate transactions, the Federal Act overrides the inconsistent provisions of arbitration acts of the several states, regardless of the forum in which they are brought.

The consequence of the foregoing is that if state courts must follow the federal liberality toward arbitration in construing contracts which involve interstate commerce and which contain an arbitration clause, such as the standard AIA contract, virtually all disputes—including but not limited to claims for delay damages[16] and claims for breach of contract and/or wrongful termination of contract[17]—will no longer be considered as arising outside of the contract, but rather will be subject to arbitration.

COMPELLING ARBITRATION UNDER STATE LAW

The Pennsylvania judicial evolution toward arbitration is instructive as to what other state courts will do when faced with similar issues.

Pennsylvania, like many other states, still retains common-law arbitration notwithstanding the passage of an arbitration act. The present state of the law is that if the agreement to arbitrate does not refer to the Arbitration Act, or if neither of the parties attempts to follow the act, the arbitration will be considered one at common law.[18]

Since Pennsylvania has abolished the common-law doctrine which permitted one party to an arbitration agreement to unilaterally revoke his consent,[19] the major distinction between common-law arbitration and statutory arbitration is in the standard of review for an arbitration award which will be discussed later in this chapter. At common law, it was a requirement that a decision by a panel

[15] 37 A.D.2d 531, 322 N.Y.S. 2d 33, 34 (1971); *see also REA Express v. Missouri Pacific R.R. Co.,* 447 S.W.2d 721 (Ct. Civ. App. Texas 1969); *Network Cinema Corp. v. Glassburn,* 357 F. Supp 169 (S.D.N.Y. 1973); *Litton RCS, Inc. v. Penna. Turnpike Comm.,* 376 F. Supp 579 (E.D. Pa. 1974) *aff'd.* 511 F.2d 1394 (1975).

[16] *Aberthaw Constr. Co. v. Centre County Hosp.,* 366 F. Supp. 513 (M.D. Pa. 1973) *aff'd.* 503 F.2d 1398 (1974).

[17] *Formigli Corp. v. Alcar Builders, Inc.,* 215 F. Supp. 166 (E.D. Pa. 1963) *aff'd.* 329 F.2d 79 (1963).

[18] *John A. Robbins Co. v. Airportels, Inc.,* 418 Pa. 257, 210 A.2d 896 (1965); *Capecci v. Joseph Capecci, Inc.,* 11 Pa. D.&C.2d 459 *aff'd.* 392 Pa. 32, 139 A.2d 563 (1958).

[19] *Mendelson v. Shrager,* 432 Pa. 383, 248 A.2d 234 (1968).

of arbitrators had to be unanimous in order to be binding except if otherwise specified in the agreement.[20]

Like the Federal Arbitration Act, the Pennsylvania Arbitration Act provides a method by which a party can compel a recalcitrant party to arbitrate disputes properly referable to arbitration under the terms of their agreement.[21]

The evolution of the present day rules as to timeliness of demand and what issues are referable to arbitration in the construction industry should begin with the case of *Emmaus Municipal Authority v. Eltz.*[22] In *Eltz*, the Pennsylvania Supreme Court had a factual situation before it where the owner had terminated the contractor's right to proceed for allegedly failing to perform under the terms of the contract. The contractor took the position that all claims for damages were to be arbitrated, and the owner contended that only technical matters which arose during the life of the contract were subject to arbitration. The Pennsylvania Supreme Court first set forth the parameters in construing arbitration agreements and stated: "(1) that arbitration agreements are to be strictly construed and that such agreements should not be extended by implication . . . , and (2) that when the parties agree to arbitration in a clear and unmistakable manner, then every reasonable effort will be made to favor such agreements."

The court then noted that the contract did not clearly state what was to be arbitrated and therefore, based on the clause in the contract which required a demand for arbitration "be filed in no case later than the time for final payment," along with the clause wherein the contractor agreed that it would not cause delay of the construction during any arbitration proceeding, concluded that the parties intended that the arbitration procedure be utilized only during the life of the contract and not after its termination.[23]

Similarly, in *Westmoreland Hospital Ass'n. v. Westmoreland Constr. Co.,*[24] the Pennsylvania Supreme Court refused to enforce the arbitration provisions of a construction contract which contained a "no-work-stoppage" and a "no-demand-after-time-of-final-payment" clause, where the contractor had accepted final payment and had not demanded arbitration until seven months after the contract was completed.[25]

In 1975 the attitude of the Pennsylvania Supreme Court toward arbitration appeared to change. In *Flightways Corp. v. Keystone Helicopter Corp.,*[26] Pennsylvania adopted the federal *Prima Paint* rule that a general attack on a contract for fraud is to be decided by arbitration and only where the claim is fraud in the inducement of the arbitration clause itself should the issue be decided by the

---

[20]*Scholler Bros. v. Otto A. C. Hagen Corp.,* 158 Pa. Super. 170, 44 A.2d 321 (1945) lists the requirements which at common law were prerequisites for a valid award.

[21]5 P.S. § 163 (1963).

[22]416 Pa. 123, 204 A.2d 926 (1964).

[23]*See also Hussey Metal Div., Copper Range Co. v. Lectromelt Furnace Div., McGraw-Edison Co.* 471 F.2d 556 (3rd Cir. 1973) which applied Pennsylvania law and followed *Eltz.*

[24]423 Pa. 255, 223 A.2d 681 (1966).

[25]*See also Bange v. Harrisburg West Motor Inn, Inc.,* 429 Pa. 654, 240 A.2d 370 (1968).

[26]331 A.2d 184 (1975).

court rather than the arbitrator. The court concluded that, "when one party to an agreement to arbitrate seeks to enjoin the other from proceeding to arbitrate, judicial inquiry is limited to the questions of whether an agreement to arbitrate was entered into and whether the dispute involved falls within the scope of the arbitration provision."

In *Muhlenberg Township School District v. Pennsylvania Fortunato Construction Co.,*[27] the School Authority attempted to avoid its agreement to arbitrate and contended among other things that the contractor's demand for arbitration came too late under the terms of the contract, notwithstanding the fact that a demand for arbitration was filed prior to final payment. Without even referring to its decision in *Eltz,* the Pennsylvania Supreme Court held:

> The question whether the contractor's demand for arbitration was timely is one of interpretation of the agreement and not one of the existence or scope of the arbitration provision; it is thus outside the bounds of our review and its resolution must be left to arbitration.

Finally, in *Chester City School Authority v. Aberthaw Construction Co.,*[28] the School Authority terminated the general contractor's agreement after it refused to repair flood water damage to an uninsured school building after it was substantially completed. (The day before the flood damage occurred, the architect inspected the building and concluded it was substantially complete.) The arbitration clause was that contained in the American Institute of Architects' Document A201, September 1967, and provided that "all claims, disputes and other matters in question arising out of or relating to this contract or the breach thereof . . . shall be decided by arbitration."

The court refused to follow *Eltz,* and held that the arbitration clause was broad in scope and therefore applied to the dispute of responsibility to pay for the damages caused by the flood and for delay damages and that under the language of the contract, a unilateral repudiation or a termination of the contract would not foreclose the right to resort to arbitration.

It must therefore be concluded that Pennsylvania courts will restrict their inquiry to determining whether or not the dispute reasonably falls within the parameters of the arbitration clause, and if so, they will probably order arbitration unless the demand is so blatantly untimely that it results in the dispute being considered as outside the scope of the agreement to arbitrate.

SCOPE OF THE ARBITRATION

Since arbitration is a function of contract, a party will only be required to arbitrate disputes which he agreed to submit to that forum. The question then posed is who determines whether or not a particular dispute falls within the arbitration clause: The arbitrators or the court?

In *Bel Pre Medical Center, Inc. v. Frederic Contractors, Inc.,*[29] the contractor

[27]333 A.2d 184 (1975).
[28]333 A.2d 758 (1975).
[29]21 Md. App. 307, 320 A.2d 558 (1974).

sought to enjoin arbitration after the owner filed his demand more than 30 days after the architect certified to substantial completion of the building and directed final payment to the contractor except for a small amount retained for a punch list. The arbitration clause in question was the standard AIA contract form which called for arbitration of all claims, disputes, and other matters in question arising out of or relating to the contract, and further required that the demand for arbitration be made within a reasonable time after the claim, or within the relevant statute of limitations. Another portion of the contract, however, required that demand for arbitration be made within 30 days of the architect's decision.

After an exhaustive review of arbitration history in Maryland, the Maryland Court of Appeals held that if it is apparent that the issue which is sought to be arbitrated lies beyond the scope of the arbitration clause, the opposing party should not be compelled to submit to arbitration; but that in a situation where it is not clear as to whether the subject matter of the dispute falls within the scope of the agreement to arbitrate, the legislative policy in favor of the enforcement of agreements to arbitrate dictates that the question be decided by the arbitrators as opposed to the court and that a court should not deprive the party seeking arbitration of the arbitrators' skilled judgment by attempting to resolve this type of ambiguity.

Although the issue of the scope of the agreement to arbitrate is normally raised prior to the arbitration proceedings by means of a complaint in equity to enjoin the arbitration, this issue is also properly raised after the arbitration proceedings are concluded as a ground for vacating or modifying the arbitration award if the arbitrators exceeded their power by considering claims outside of the submission and if the complaining party did not waive this defense by attendance and participation at the hearing without objection. In *E. E. Tripp Excavating Contractor, Inc. v. County of Jackson,* the dispute revolved around the necessity of the owner rerouting portions of a sanitary sewer line because of unsatisfactory soil conditions. The owner stopped the contractor from proceeding in the area where the unsatisfactory soil condition was discovered. Thereafter, attempts to negotiate a price and completion-date change order proved futile and when the contractor refused to proceed with the reroute work until there was an agreed-upon method of payment for same, the owner defaulted the contractor and terminated his right to proceed, notwithstanding the fact that the contractor was performing work on the nondisputed portions of the project.

Prior to the termination, the contractor filed a demand for arbitration with the American Arbitration Association to have arbitrators decide the controversy which had arisen between the parties. Both the owner and contractor filed their claims with the American Arbitration Association and thereafter proceeded to select arbitrators. After it terminated the contract, the owner-County took the position that it revoked its agreement to arbitrate and accordingly did not participate in the arbitration proceedings, which continued on in an ex-parte manner pursuant to rule 29 of the American Arbitration Association's construction industry rules. (After the contract was terminated, the contractor amended its Demand for Arbitration to include damages resulting from wrongful termination.) The arbitrators granted a lump-sum award to the contractor of $870,565, and the owner resisted confirmation of the award by contending among other things that the clause in the contract which provided that "all decisions of the engineer shall be final except in cases where time and/or financial considerations are involved, in which case the decision will be subject to arbitration" did not give the arbitrators power to award damages for termination of the contract.

In a landmark decision, the Michigan Court of Appeals held that (1) Michigan Municipal Authorities have the power to enter into agreements to arbitrate, (2) that the county waived its right to assert the defense that Tripp failed to pursue the statutory method for filing claims against public authorities,[30] (3) that for there to be statutory arbitration, specific language must be in the arbitration clause that a judgment can be entered on the award which language was not present in this contract, and (4) that the owner had not specifically revoked its agreement to arbitrate. The court then concluded that, although the arbitration clause conferred power on the arbitrators to award compensation because of the rerouting, the arbitrators exceeded the scope of their authority in awarding damages for the breach of contract in terminating the contract. The matter was sent back to the arbitrators who were to differentiate damages awarded for the breach of contract from damages found causally connected to the reroute change order, thereby allowing the arbitrators to make a decision within the scope of the arbitration agreement. (On remand the arbitrators awarded the contractor $570,565, and this award was confirmed and the Authority was mandamused to pay the award.

Waiver

Since the right to arbitrate is contractual, it can be waived like any other contract right. The modern case law trend is that while a delay in demanding arbitration will not constitute a waiver, the taking of an inconsistent act, such as the filing of a complaint in court, results in the party filing the complaint losing his right to compel arbitration.

Since the filing of a demand for arbitration does not toll the statute of limitations, a subcontractor must file his complaint in the appropriate court in a timely manner in order to preserve his right against the prime contractor's labor and material surety bond.[31] To avoid this dilemma, it is suggested that the subcontractor institute suit against the surety and in the complaint specifically allege that "the purpose of filing the Complaint is to toll the statute of limitations, and by so filing, subcontractor does not intend to relinquish his right to arbitration."[32]

---

[30] *See also Pa. Turnpike Comm. v. Sanders & Thomas, Inc.,* 12 Pa. Com. Ct. 145, 316 A.2d 127 *aff'd.* 336 A.2d 609 (1975).

[31] *United States ex rel. Wrecking Corp. of America v. Edward R. Marden Corp.,* 406 F.2d 525 (1st Cir. 1969).

[32] *McElwee-Courbis Constr. Co. v. Rife,* 133 F. Supp. 790 (1955). *See also* E. H. Cushman, *Arbitration and The Miller Act,* Proceedings of the ABA Section of Ins., Negligence and Compensation Law, 149 (1967).

Confirmation of Arbitration Awards and Standards of Review

An arbitration award is not self-executing. Accordingly, the prevailing party must move the appropriate court to have the award confirmed as a judgment. Once this is accomplished, the judgment has the same effect as any other judgment.

In order to avoid an arbitration award being entered as a judgment under the Federal Arbitration Act, the losing party must file within three months after the award is filed or delivered either a motion to vacate or a motion to modify the award. Section 10 of the Federal Arbitration Act[33] permits an award to be vacated when:

> (a) the award was procured by corruption, fraud or undue means . . .
>
> (b) where there was evident partiality or corruption in the arbitrators, or either of them.
>
> (c) where the arbitrators were guilty of misconduct in refusing to postpone the hearing upon sufficient cause shown, or in refusing to hear evidence pertinent and material to the controversy; or of any other misbehavior by which rights of any party have been prejudiced.
>
> (d) where the arbitrators exceeded their power, or so imperfectly executed them that a mutual, final, and definite award upon the subject matter was not made.

Section 11 of the Federal Arbitration Act permits modification of an award where there was an evident miscalculation of figures; where the arbitrators based their award upon matters not submitted at the hearing; where the award was imperfect in form; or where modification is necessary to effect the intent of the award and promote justice between the parties.[34]

Under either section of the Federal Arbitration Act, it is extremely difficult to convince a court to overturn the award of arbitrators, the philosophy being that having agreed to arbitration, the parties should be bound by the result. In rejecting assaults on arbitration awards, courts have noted that arbitrators may make lump-sum awards and need not write opinions explaining their reasons,[35] that arbitrators are the sole judge of the facts and the law,[36] that rules of evidence need not be followed,[37] and that arbitrators could consider, in addition to the evidence presented to them, facts known through their own personal knowledge.[38]

However, in *Commonwealth Coatings Corp. v. Continental Casualty Co.*,[39] the United States Supreme Court vacated an arbitration award when one of the arbitrators did not reveal he had past business dealings with one of the parties. Normally, only when an award is in "manifest disregard" of the law or the rights of the parties, will it be overturned by a federal court.[40]

---

[33] 9 U.S.C. § 10 (1970).

[34] 9 U.S.C. § 11 (1970).

[35] *Hale v. Friedman*, 281 F.2d 635 (D.C. Cir. 1960).

[36] *Marcy Lee Mfg. Co. v. Cortley Fabrics Co.*, 354 F.2d 42 (2nd Cir. 1965).

[37] *Local 18, Newark Stereotypers' Union v. Newark Morning Ledger Co.*, 397 F.2d 594 (3rd Cir. 1968).

[38] *American Almond Prod. Co. v. Consolidated Pecan Sales Co.*, 144 F.2d 448 (2nd Cir. 1944).

[39] 393 U.S. 145 (1968).

[40] *Sobel v. Hertz Warner & Co.*, 469 F.2d 1211 (2nd Cir. 1972); *Trafalgar Shipping Co. v. International Milling Co.*, 401 F.2d 568 (2nd Cir. 1968).

If the award of arbitrators is at common law, the review standards for overturning the arbitrators' award are equally, if not more, rigid. The rule and the rationale for same was set forth in *Allstate Insurance Co. v. Fioravanti:*[41]

> If the appeal is from a common law award appellant, to succeed, must show by clear, precise and indubitable evidence that he was denied a hearing, or that there was fraud, misconduct, corruption or some other irregularity of this nature on the part of the arbitrator which caused him to render an unjust, inequitable or unconscionable award, the arbitrator being the final judge of both law and fact, his award not being subject to disturbance for a mistake of either.

The Pennsylvania Arbitration Act provides broader grounds for modifying an arbitration award, and permits a court to modify or correct an award "where the award is against the law, and is such that had it been a verdict of the jury, the court would have entered a different or other judgment notwithstanding the verdict."[42]

The above-quoted clause has been the vehicle by which courts have overturned substantial arbitration awards in favor of contractors on the grounds that the arbitrators failed to follow the requirements of the contract[43] and in another instance was the instrument by which the court permitted a contractor to recover substantial delay damages despite a no-damage-for-delay clause in the contract.[44]

CONCLUSION

Although views differ as to the ultimate advantages and disadvantages of arbitration, it must be recognized that the resolution of disputes by arbitration is a process which calls for technical skills and deliberate analysis if an arbitration award is to be entered as a final judgment.

APPENDIX: Provisions in General Conditions of the Contract for Construction AIA Document A201 (1976 Edition) Which Pertain to Arbitration

2.2.9   Claims, disputes and other matters in question between the Owner relating to the execution or progress of the Work or the interpretation of the Contract Documents shall be referred initially to the Architect for decision which he will render in writing within a reasonable time.

2.2.10   All interpretations and decisions of the Architect shall be consistent with the intent of and reasonably inferable from the Contract Documents. In his capacity as interpreter and judge, he will endeavor to secure faithful performance by both the Owner and the Contractor, will not show partiality to either, and will

---

[41]451 Pa. 108, 299 A.2d 585 (1973).
[42]5 P.S. § 171 (1963).
[43]*Scott Township School Distr. Auth. v. Branna Constr. Corp.*, 409 Pa. 136, 185 A.2d 320 (1962).
[44]*Gasparini Excav. Co. v. Pennsylvania Turnpike Comm.*, 409 Pa. 465, 187 A.2d 157 (1963).

not be liable for the result of any interpretation or decision rendered in good faith in such capacity.

2.2.11   The Architect's decisions in matters relating to artistic effect will be final if consistent with the intent of the Contract Documents.

2.2.12   Any claim, dispute or other matter in question between the Contractor and the Owner referred to the Architect, except those relating to artistic effect as provided in Subparagraph 2.2.11 and except those which have been waived by the making or acceptance of final payment as provided in Subparagraphs 9.9.4 and 9.9.5, shall be subject to arbitration upon the written demand of either party. However, no demand for arbitration of any such claim, dispute or other matter may be made until the earlier of (1) the date on which the Architect has rendered a written decision, or (2) the tenth day after the parties have presented their evidence to the Architect or have been given a reasonable opportunity to do so, if the Architect has not rendered his written decision by that date. When such a written decision of the Architect states (1) that the decision is final but subject to appeal, and (2) that any demand for arbitration of a claim, dispute or other matter covered by such decision must be made within thirty days after the date on which the party making the demand receives the written decision, failure to demand arbitration within said thirty days' period will result in the Architect's decision becoming final and binding upon the Owner and the Contractor. If the Architect renders a decision after arbitration proceedings have been initiated, such decision may be entered as evidence but will not supersede any arbitration proceedings unless the decision is acceptable to all parties concerned.

7.9   ARBITRATION

7.9.1   All claims, disputes and other matters in question between the Contractor and the Owner arising out of, or relating to, the Contract Documents or the breach thereof, except as provided in Subparagraph 2.2.11 with respect to the Architect's decisions on matters relating to artistic effect, and except for claims which have been waived by the making or acceptance of final payment as provided by Subparagraphs 9.9.4 and 9.9.5, shall be decided by arbitration in accordance with the Construction Industry Arbitration Rules of the American Arbitration Association then obtaining unless the parties mutually agree otherwise. No arbitration arising out of or relating to the Contract Documents shall include, by consolidation, joinder or in any other manner, the Architect, his employees or consultants except by written consent containing a specific reference to the Owner-Contractor Agreement and signed by the Architect, the Owner, the Contractor and any other person sought to be joined. No arbitration shall include by consolidation, joinder or in any other manner, parties other than the Owner, the Contractor and any other persons substantially involved in a common question of fact or law, whose presence is required if complete relief is to be accorded in the arbitration. No person other than the Owner or Contractor shall be included as an original third party or additional third party to an arbitration whose interest or responsibility is insubstantial. Any consent to arbitration involving an additional person or persons shall not constitute consent to arbitration of any dispute not described therein or with any person not named or described therein. The foregoing agreement to arbitrate and any other agreement to arbitrate with an additional person or persons duly consented to by the parties to the Owner-Contractor Agreement shall be specifically enforceable under the prevailing arbitration law. The award rendered by the arbitrators shall be final, and judgment may be entered upon it in accordance with applicable law in any court having jurisdiction thereof.

7.9.2   Notice of the demand for arbitration shall be filed in writing with the other party to the Owner-Contractor Agreement and with the American Arbitration Association, and a copy shall be filed with the Architect. The demand for arbitration shall be made within the time limits specified in Subparagraph 2.2.12 where applicable, and in all other cases within a reasonable time after the claim, dispute or other matter in question has arisen, and in no event shall it be made after the date when institution of legal or equitable proceedings based on such claim, dispute or other matter in question would be barred by the applicable statute of limitations.

7.9.3   Unless otherwise agreed in writing, the Contractor shall carry on the Work and maintain the progress during any arbitration proceedings, and the Owner shall continue to make payments to the Contractor in accordance with the Contract Documents.

Part Eleven

Financial Difficulties and Bankruptcy

Chapter **47**

Obtaining Financial Aid
from Your Surety

J. PAUL McNAMARA, ESQ.
Partner, McNamara and McNamara, Columbus, Ohio

WILLIAM McCABE, ESQ.
**Surety Claim Counsel, American International Group, New York,
New York**

The contractor faced with the problem of trying to obtain financial aid from his surety can prepare himself for this task by studying the list of items of information the surety will want to consider. No two problems are identical, but certain basic concerns are similar in every situation of financial distress. The authors of this chapter have experience working with and for sureties so that our approach bears the imprint of the surety. Nonetheless, a contractor and his attorney, his accountant, his engineer and his superintendent will present the contractor's case for financial aid with more likelihood of success if the contractor and his associates are prepared to furnish promptly to the surety the items of information outlined.

When the contractor is in default in the performance of his contract or faced with a declaration of default, the surety has these alternatives:

1. Do nothing and deal with a claim of the owner at some future date.

2. Obtain a new contractor and enter into a contract between the surety and the contractor for completion.

3. Obtain a new contractor and present that new contractor to the owner to contract with the owner to complete the contract.

4. Arrange for financial assistance to the contractor who is principal in the bond executed by the surety.

In our case the contractor wants the surety to choose alternative 4, so the contractor must be able to convince the surety that this choice is economically wise and feasible.

The surety will, in most cases, have the benefit of the assistance and advice of an attorney, an accountant, an engineer, and in some cases a surety consultant. The surety consultant is one who has developed an expertise in analyzing construction contract problems, including defaults, and in managing the completion of the contract on behalf of the surety.

When the contractor asks the surety for financial aid, the surety will seek the answers to these questions:

1. What is the condition of the financial affairs of the contractor?
2. What is the ability of the contractor, his subcontractors, and suppliers or materialmen to complete the construction project?
3. What is the financial status of each contract or construction project, and what is the estimated cost to complete each?
4. What is the physical status of each contract or construction project?

There is no way to allocate a relative value to each of these areas of concern of the surety. Surety A may attribute greater weight to one factor, and surety B may attribute greater weight to another factor. In every case the contractor will be ahead who can answer the questions outlined in each of the four areas listed above.

With respect to the condition of the financial affairs of the contractor, the surety will want the answers to these questions:

1. Does the contractor have a current statement of assets and liabilities? Is it prepared by an independent certified public accountant? Are similar statements for prior years available for comparison and study?
2. Does the contractor have a current operating statement showing income and expense? Who prepared this statement and are earlier statements available?
3. Are there bank loans, and what is the status of each? Are such loans secured?
4. Are there any unpaid subcontractors, suppliers, and materialmen? If there are several contracts, are the claims of such creditors allocated to each contract?
5. Are there unbonded contracts, and are the claims of creditors allocated to each such contract?
6. What is the status of federal, state, and local tax liabilities?
7. Does the contractor have assets which can be liquidated to provide cash?
8. Is the contractor involved in litigation? Are his attorneys prepared to give a brief written analysis and summary of each pending case?
9. Is the contractor prepared to show (on the statement in 2 above or otherwise) the indirect and administrative cost in his operation?
10. Can the contractor show what he has done with the contract proceeds on each contract? Has he diverted funds from the contract presently in trouble to pay debts on a completed contract or to pay debts on an unbonded contract?
11. What is the status of each unbonded contract?

With respect to the ability of the contractor, subcontractors, and suppliers or materialmen to complete the construction project, the surety will want the answers to these questions:

1. Is the contractor experienced in the kind of work involved?

2. Is the contractor experienced in the area where the work is being performed?

3. What is the working relationship between the contractor and the owner? What is the working relationship between the contractor and the architect and engineer? What is the working relationship between the contractor and the other prime contractors on the project?

4. Does the contractor have competent job supervision?

5. Does the contractor have competent office and financial management?

6. Does the contractor have a capable labor force available?

7. Does the contractor have sufficient tools and equipment to perform the work?

8. Does the contractor have experienced and competent subcontractors? Are the subcontractors bonded? Are the subcontracts fixed-price contracts?

9. Have purchase orders been placed for all the important materials? Are the purchase orders for materials at fixed prices? Are the materialmen and suppliers experienced and competent?

With respect to the financial status of each contract or construction project and the estimated cost to complete each such contract, the surety will want the answers to these questions:

1. What is the percentage of work completed?

2. What is the contractor's estimate of the cost to complete?

3. What is the estimated cost to complete prepared by the surety's engineer or the surety's consultant?

4. What is the estimated cost to complete or bid to complete obtained from one or more potential completing contractors?

5. Does the contractor have claims for extra work?

6. Have change orders been issued either increasing or decreasing the work to be performed?

7. Has the contractor been overpaid or improperly paid?

8. Are there claims against the project or the contract funds such as judgment executions, tax levies, liens, and attested accounts?

With respect to the physical status of each contract or construction project, the surety will want the answers to these questions:

1. Is there some special difficulty in the work to be performed?

2. What time will be required to complete the work? How does this time compare with the completion date fixed in the contract?

3. Is provision made for liquidated damages in the contract?

4. Will there probably be delay damage claims or other kinds of claims against the contractor? Does the contractor have delay damage claims or other kinds of claims?

5. Is the work in place properly performed and substantially in accordance with the plans and specifications? Does the owner claim that there is substantial corrective or remedial work to be performed?

6. Are the standards provided in the contract to test the acceptability of the work reasonably clear?

7. Is there substantial punch-list work to be performed?

If the contractor goes to his surety for financial aid and is prepared to answer the foregoing questions and supply with reasonable accuracy the information required by those questions, the surety will be able to make a decision. Granting the contractor financial aid is a decision made by the surety only after a careful consideration of all the facts developed by the foregoing questions. In granting financial aid to the contractor, the surety enters the contracting business and for all practical purposes, the surety undertakes a risk not limited by the penal sum of the performance bond. No surety undertakes this risk without the conviction that to grant financial aid to the contractor is economically wise and economically feasible. Again, the alternatives from which the surety may choose are these:

1. Do nothing and face a claim of the owner.
2. Obtain a new contractor to contract with the surety to complete.
3. Obtain a new contractor to contract with the owner to complete.
4. Provide financial aid to the contractor bonded by the surety.

If the contractor has convinced the surety to select alternative 4, there are two methods of financing that are most commonly used, and the contractor should be familiar with these two methods. The first method is a direct loan from the surety to the contractor. The second method is for the surety to guarantee a bank loan to the contractor. Depending upon the circumstances, the surety will probably require that the contractor agree to the following:

1. The pledge or mortgage of the contractor's assets to secure the surety for the loans (this will sometimes include personal assets)
2. Joint control of all funds, including contract proceeds and loan proceeds
3. The right of the surety to participate in the office management
4. The right of the surety to terminate the advancement of funds by the surety or the advancement of funds by the lending institution
5. A definite date and plan for repayment by the contractor which may include liquidation of the contractor's assets

An understanding of the kinds of transactions a surety may make is best illustrated by setting forth an actual agreement in which the surety loaned the contractor funds to complete and an actual agreement by which the surety guaranteed a bank loan to the contractor. Although the terms of each agreement are actual, the names, places, amounts, and identities are fictional.

First, an agreement by which the surety loaned the contractor funds:

AGREEMENT

THIS AGREEMENT made and entered into, this 1st day of May, 1976, by and between Lakeside Construction Co. of Columbus, Ohio, hereinafter called Contractor, and The Atlas Surety Company, hereinafter called Surety,

WITNESSETH:

WHEREAS, the parties as Contractor-Principal and Surety executed a performance bond in the sum of $2,200,000 and payment bond in the sum of $2,200,000 to Mack Company in connection with a subcontract between Contractor and Mack

Company for work in the construction of a building for National Rubber Company, Columbus, Ohio; and

WHEREAS, the Contractor represents to Surety that Contractor lacks sufficient working capital and is requesting financial assistance from Surety to complete the subcontract work;

NOW, THEREFORE, it is agreed between the parties as follows:

1. Surety agrees to provide to Contractor such financial assistance, as, in Surety's uncontrolled and unlimited discretion and judgment, Surety deems advisable to carry out the purposes of this agreement in accordance with and subject to the conditions of this agreement. Contractor and Surety agree that Surety has the right, in Surety's uncontrolled and unlimited discretion and judgment, to terminate the advancement of funds hereunder at any time and for any reason that Surety deems sufficient, without liability of Surety for so doing; provided, however, that if Surety ceases to advance funds, Surety nevertheless agrees to see to the payment of payroll earned during the week of such termination and all payroll taxes due for payroll earned through that period. The Contractor will execute and deliver to the Surety all instruments necessary to perfect a security interest in the equipment of Contractor on the job and Contractor will execute and deliver to Surety mortgages on real estate owned by Contractor in Ohio and Indiana.

2. Surety reserves to Surety the right of Surety to pay obligations of Contractor for which Surety may be liable with regular claim drafts of Surety.

3. All funds advanced by Surety (except as hereinafter provided in paragraph 3) and all contract earnings will be placed in one or more bank accounts jointly controlled by the parties.

4. All advances made by Surety before the execution of this agreement and all advances by Surety hereunder shall bear interest at six percent (6%) per annum on the outstanding principal balance from the date of advance to the date of repayment. On July 1, 1976, and every three months thereafter the Contractor shall sign a promissory note in terms acceptable to Surety and Contractor for all money advanced by Surety to the joint control accounts herein provided in the preceding three-month period together with said interest at 6% per annum on each advance in that three-month period from the date of advance to the date of such promissory note with interest thereafter to run from the date of each promissory note. None of the principal or interest on the promissory notes shall be payable prior to January 1, 1977, and if prior to that date the Contractor pays the accrued interest on the promissory notes to January 1, 1977, then, at Contractor's option, all such promissory notes shall be extended for an additional period of one year and will become due and payable on January 1, 1978, provided, however, that if by January 1, 1978, the Contractor has diligently presented and prosecuted the claims of contractor for additional compensation and damages or both against Mack Company and other parties liable for such claims, and the claims have not been finally determined, then Surety, upon payment to it of all accrued interest and one-half of all sums due on such promissory notes, will extend said notes for the remaining one-half due thereon for one additional year or until said claims are so determined, whichever first occurs.

5. During the time this agreement is in force and effect, Contractor agrees that the Contractor will not voluntarily contract for any additional or new construction work, either bonded or unbonded, without express written consent of Surety.

6. The execution of this agreement shall not change the relationship of principal and Surety which now exists between the Contractor and the Surety. The

rights and remedies provided to the Surety and the Contractor in this agreement shall be and are in addition to and not in substitution of the rights and remedies presently vested in the parties by law and by the terms of agreements of indemnity. No delay, omission, or failure by Surety to exercise any rights and remedies accruing to Surety under this agreement or otherwise shall constitute a waiver or release by Surety of any of such rights and remedies.

7. This agreement is solely for the benefit of the parties hereto and no right shall accrue hereunder to any third party.

Executed by the parties hereto on the date and at the place shown below.

Signed in the presence of: LAKESIDE CONSTRUCTION CO.

_____   _____
                                                                                            President

_____   _____
                                                                                            Secretary
                                                                            Date: _____
                                                                            Place: _____

Signed in the presence of: THE ATLAS SURETY COMPANY

_____   *By* _____
_____   *Its* _____
                                                                            Date: _____
                                                                            Place: _____

In some direct loans from the surety to the contractor, the surety deposits to the bank account of the contractor only that amount of money required to pay the checks being issued by the contractor and certified by the bank on that day. In this way there is no time at which the contractor has funds of the surety in the contractor's possession. This is sometimes called an *overdraft system* and sometimes called a *zero balance system.*

Second, an agreement by which the Surety agreed to guarantee a bank loan to the Contractor and an agreement for trust account for the deposit and disbursement of the proceeds of the bank loan:

AGREEMENT

THIS AGREEMENT, entered into by and between Atlas Surety Company (hereinafter referred to as Surety), Lakeside Construction Company, Columbus, Ohio, (hereinafter referred to as Contractor); The Columbus Trust Company, Columbus, Ohio; The Commercial Bank, Dayton, Ohio; and Clark National Bank, Springfield, Ohio (hereinafter referred to as Banks).

WHEREAS, Surety executed performance and payment bonds for Contractor on numerous projects which are at various stages of completion; and

WHEREAS, Banks have heretofore extended credit to Contractor; and

WHEREAS, Contractor lacks sufficient working capital to continue operations inasmuch as additional working capital cannot be obtained through usual lending sources; and

WHEREAS, Contractor has requested Surety to assist in arranging necessary working capital for Contractor to continue operations and complete existing contracts, to provide adequate time to liquidate certain equipment to pay indebtedness to Banks, part of which indebtedness is secured by construction equipment; and

WHEREAS, Surety has analyzed the contracts in various stages of completion, the financial position of Contractor, and developed pertinent information as to disputed accounts receivable; and

WHEREAS, Surety will assist Contractor in obtaining financing for continued operations, performance of contracts, and liquidation of equipment conditioned upon the agreement by the Banks to accept payment of interest and take no steps for the collection of the principal indebtedness so long as Surety continues in its arrangement with Contractor for financing which Surety can discontinue at its sole discretion with immediate advice to Banks and Contractor,

NOW, THEREFORE, in consideration of the mutual promises and agreements contained herein, it is mutually understood and agreed as follows:

1. Surety will procure financing for Contractor by means of a guaranteed bank loan, the proceeds of said loan to be deposited in bank of Surety's choice and Surety will jointly control proceeds of said loan;

2. Surety at its sole discretion may discontinue the procurement of additional funds for Contractor and Surety agrees it will immediately notify Contractor and Banks in the event of a decision to discontinue financing arrangements;

3. Contractor by letter attached hereto and made a part hereof, agrees to liquidate specific equipment at the earliest reasonable date that it is not needed for existing projects, the proceeds from the sale of said equipment to be applied to Contractor's indebtedness to Banks;

4. Banks agree, upon receipt of interest of loans presently outstanding, to make no demand on Contractor for payment of principal as long as Surety continues to arrange for working capital for Contractor;

5. Contractor will pay to Clark National Bank a maximum of $100,000 of the contract balance upon receipt thereof from the Portsmouth Sewer contract covered by Surety's Bond No. 12345, which contract is presently in litigation. The payment of $100,000 is to be made to the Bank after payment of amounts currently due materialmen, subcontractors, and for other obligations which constitute an obligation under Surety's bond. Likewise, any payment made by the Surety prior to the collection of the contract funds on that contract shall be repaid to the Surety before payment to the Bank.

6. All funds collected by Contractor on contracts with State of Ohio, Department of Transportation as covered by bonds of Surety as set out on the attached schedule, shall be first applied to obligations due materialmen, subcontractors and suppliers, which claims constitute a claim under Surety's bonds aforesaid, and the cost to collect said contract balance, the remaining balances to be paid 75% in reduction of Contractor's indebtedness to Banks and 25% to be utilized at Surety's discretion to reduce obligations under guaranteed loan arrangements or payment of materialmen, subcontractors, or suppliers claims for which the Surety may be liable.

IN WITNESS WHEREOF we set our hands and seals this___ day of___, 19___.

Signed in the presence of: ATLAS SURETY COMPANY

_____   By _____

_____   Date _____

                                                            Place _____

                                                            LAKESIDE CONSTRUCTION COMPANY

_____   By _____

_____   Date _____

                                                            Place _____

COLUMBUS TRUST COMPANY

	By _____
	Date _____
	Place _____

Signed in the presence of:

THE COMMERCIAL BANK

	By _____
	Date _____
	Place _____

CLARK NATIONAL BANK

	By _____
	Date _____
	Place _____

AGREEMENT FOR TRUST ACCOUNT

THIS AGREEMENT, made and executed by and between Lakeside Construction Company, Columbus, Ohio (hereinafter referred to as Lakeside), Atlas Surety Company (hereinafter referred to as Atlas), and The National Bank of Columbus, Columbus, Ohio (hereinafter referred to as Bank),

WITNESSETH:

WHEREAS, Atlas, as surety, has executed on behalf of Lakeside, as principal, bonds as set forth in schedule attached hereto and marked Exhibit A, and

WHEREAS, Lakeside has appealed to Atlas for financial assistance and Atlas has heretofore given financial assistance to the extent of guaranteeing payment of a loan or loans obtained by Lakeside from the Bank in the sum of $200,000 and hereafter Atlas will guarantee payment of additional loans to Lakeside in an amount to be determined solely and exclusively by Atlas, and

WHEREAS, the parties hereto desire to set forth in this Agreement for Trust Account the terms and conditions upon which proceeds of the loans and the proceeds of the contracts bonded by Atlas shall be received, deposited, managed and disbursed,

NOW, THEREFORE, in consideration of the premises and the execution by Atlas of guarantee or guarantees of payment of loans to be obtained by Lakeside, it is mutually understood and agreed as follows:

1. All funds received by Lakeside as proceeds of contracts for which bonds are listed in Schedule A attached hereto, and funds received by Lakeside as proceeds of loans, payment of which is guaranteed by Atlas, and all funds received by Lakeside from any other source whatsoever (except as such other funds are committed by prior agreement approved by Atlas) shall be deposited in an account in the Bank entitled "The Atlas Account in Trust for Lakeside." The funds deposited and to be deposited in that trust account shall be trust funds for the sole purpose of (1) paying for labor and materials supplied, subcontractors and other job costs in the prosecution of the work provided for in the contracts for which bonds are listed on the schedule attached hereto marked Exhibit A, (2) payment for the loan or loans to Lakeside, payment of which is guaranteed by Atlas, (3) indemnifying and saving harmless Atlas in accordance with agreements of indemnity heretofore executed by Lakeside. When all of the aforesaid purposes have been fully performed to the satisfaction of Atlas and Atlas has issued a certificate in writing to the Bank so stating, the balance in the account, if any, shall be paid to Lakeside. No check shall be drawn upon that trust account and no withdrawal shall be made therefrom except for the purposes hereinabove stated. Checks shall be drawn upon the trust

account and such withdrawals shall be made only by check bearing two signatures: One of the following representing Atlas _____, and one of the following representing Lakeside _____ or _____. In the event of the death, resignation, or incapacity of any of the persons authorized to sign such checks, Atlas or Lakeside shall designate in writing a substitute to sign such checks.

2. Atlas, in its sole discretion, may at any time terminate the aforesaid trust account and direct that all funds in that trust account, or so much thereof as is necessary, be applied by the Bank in payment of the loans to Lakeside, payment of which is guaranteed by Atlas. At the time of such termination by Atlas the balance, if any, in the trust account after payment of loans by the Bank shall be applied, to the extent necessary, to indemnify and save harmless Atlas in accordance with the agreements heretofore executed by Lakeside. Any balance thereafter remaining shall be paid to Lakeside.

3. The Bank shall be Trustee of the funds deposited in the above entitled trust account provided, however, that Lakeside assumes full responsibility for the acts of the Bank as Trustee. Lakeside shall by appropriate power of attorney and any such additional instrument required by the Bank authorize and empower the Bank to endorse any and all checks received by the Bank on any of the contracts for which bonds are listed in Exhibit A attached hereto or from other sources and the Bank shall deposit the proceeds of such checks in the aforesaid trust account. Lakeside and Atlas agree to execute any instruments required by the Bank to protect and indemnify the Bank from any liability arising out of this Agreement and the performance thereof by the Bank. The Bank shall furnish Atlas the customary account of receipts and disbursements in connection with the trust account and all checks paid from that account, and Atlas shall furnish Lakeside duplicate photocopies of such accounts and checks.

4. The rights afforded Atlas by the terms of this Agreement are in addition to and not in lieu of any other rights which Atlas may have as against Lakeside by law or under the terms of any other agreement and shall inure to the benefit of Atlas, its co-sureties and its and their reinsurers.

5. An executed copy of this Agreement shall be delivered to the Bank, Lakeside and two copies to Atlas. The Bank is hereby authorized and directed to honor each and every check drawn against the trust account when signed as herein designated, if such check be presented to the Bank prior to receipt by the Bank of certificate of termination of the trust account. It is expressly understood and agreed that the Bank shall have no duty to make inquiry as to the purpose of any check.

The parties hereto have hereunto set their signatures and seals on the date and at the place hereinafter set forth.

Signed in the presence of: LAKESIDE CONSTRUCTION COMPANY

_____   *By* _____

_____   *Date* _____

Place _____

ATLAS SURETY COMPANY

_____   *By* _____

_____   *Date* _____

Place _____

THE NATIONAL BANK OF COLUMBUS, OHIO

_____   *By* _____

_____   *Date* _____

Place _____

(EXHIBIT A OMITTED)

Some sureties require contractors to execute a power of attorney to the surety in connection with the agreement to give financial aid to the contractor. The following is a form of power of attorney:

POWER OF ATTORNEY

KNOW ALL MEN BY THESE PRESENTS, That Lakeside Construction Company, Columbus, Ohio (hereinafter referred to as Grantor) does hereby make, constitute and appoint Atlas Surety Company, Columbus, Ohio (hereinafter referred to as Atlas), the true and lawful attorney in fact for Grantor and in Grantor's name, place, and stead to do and perform any and all acts, deeds, and things which in the exclusive judgment of Atlas may be necessary and proper including, but not limited to, any and all acts and deeds necessary or requisite, in the exclusive judgment of Atlas (a) to carry out and perform the contracts entered into by Grantor and (b) to carry out and perform the indemnity agreements executed and delivered by Grantor to Atlas in connection with the bonds executed by Atlas, as surety for Lakeside Construction Company, as principal, including, but not limited to the following:

1. To establish bank account or accounts and to sign checks on and withdraw funds from any bank account maintained by Grantor and Atlas, or either of them, which in the exclusive judgment of Atlas may be necessary or expedient.

2. To receive and collect any and all sums due or owing Grantor and to receipt therefor and to endorse any checks made payable to Grantor and to receive the proceeds of such checks.

3. To discharge any employee of Grantor when in the exclusive judgment of Atlas, such discharge is justified.

4. To terminate the authority and employment of any officer of Grantor when in the exclusive judgment of Atlas such termination is justified.

5. To employ in the name of Grantor, agents, attorneys, employees, contractors, and any person, firm, or corporation deemed necessary in the exclusive judgment of Atlas to assist in the performance of the contracts of Grantor and also to discharge any agent, attorney, employee, contractor, or other person, firm, or corporation employed by Grantor in connection with the performance of any or all of the aforesaid contracts.

6. To do in the name of Grantor any and all things necessary to complete the construction contracts of Grantor.

7. To contract for, in the name of Grantor, any and all labor, material, supplies, services, equipment, equipment rental, and any and all other things necessary and requisite, in the exclusive judgment of Atlas, to complete the contracts of Grantor.

8. To execute and deliver all requests, requisitions, estimates, receipts, releases, and any and all other instruments, documents, and writings necessary, in the exclusive judgment of Atlas, in performing and completing the contracts of Grantor.

9. To bargain, sell, and convey in fee simple by deed with or without covenants of general warranty, or other covenants usual or customary in a warranty deed, or by land contract, for such price and upon such terms of credit, and to such person, firm, or corporation, as Atlas shall think fit, the whole or any part of any lands, tenements, or hereditaments owned by Grantor or any interest therein.

10. To sell and convey by bill of sale or other proper instrument of conveyance

with customary warranties, terms, and provisions, for such price or prices, and upon such terms of credit or otherwise, and to such persons, firms, and corporations as Atlas shall deem best, all or any part of the personal property of Grantor.

In consideration of the obligations assumed or to be assumed by Atlas, this power of attorney is irrevocable by Grantor, and Grantor shall observe and recognize the same until this power of attorney is terminated by Atlas.

Grantor hereby authorizes and empowers Atlas to substitute from time to time any attorney in fact under Atlas with the same powers and authority, with full power of substitution and removal of any such attorney in fact.

Giving and granting unto Atlas full power and authority to do and perform all and every act and thing whatsoever requisite and necessary, or which Atlas shall deem requisite and necessary to be done in and about the premises as fully to all intents and purposes as the said Grantor might or could do and with full power of substitution and revocation, hereby ratifying and confirming all that Atlas or its substitute shall do or cause to be done by authority hereof.

IN WITNESS WHEREOF, Grantor, by its duly authorized president and secretary, has executed this instrument this _____ day of _____, 1976.

Signed in the presence of: LAKESIDE CONSTRUCTION COMPANY

_____   By _____

Its President

_____   And _____

Its Secretary

(ACKNOWLEDGMENT)

The foregoing agreements are typical. The variations of these agreements will be as numerous as the variations in the circumstances that surround the problems of the contractor and the surety and the bank, if one is involved.

While the probability of the success of the contractor in obtaining financial aid from his surety is not predictable in terms of percentages, the reading on the other side of the coin is much clearer. Failure in 100 percent of the cases can be predicted where the contractor fails to provide the information needed by the surety.

Chapter **48**

Rights of the Surety under Contract Bond Indemnity Agreements

RICHARD MARLINK, ESQ.
President, Richard Marlink & Associates, Cherry Hill, New Jersey

INTRODUCTION

The requirement by surety companies that contractors execute agreements of indemnity in connection with the delivery of construction contract bonds is a time-honored practice. This chapter deals with some of the most important rights and remedies the execution of these agreements gives to the surety. In general, these rights materially improve the position of the surety by enabling it to better protect itself from loss and to make financial recovery from the contractor and its guarantors. The rights created by these indemnity agreements have been a favorite subject for discussion and study.[1] In this chapter,

[1]*See* Clare M. Vrooman, "Various Aspects of the Surety's Right of Indemnity," *ABA Proceedings,* Section of Insurance Law, 1940, and *e.g.* Indemnity and Surety's Rights in the Fidelity and Surety Law Bibliography, 1946–1971, Section of Insurance, Negligence and Compensation Law, ABA, 1972.

attention is focused on these rights and we will examine how they relate to each other and how they affect the construction contractor and his co-indemnitors.

The traditional indemnity agreement required by the surety industry as part of the consideration for delivery of construction bonds can take the form of a specific agreement relating to one bonded construction project or it can be a continuing type of agreement relating to all bonds subsequently issued in behalf of the contractor.

Under common law a surety is entitled to reimbursement of its loss from its principal.[2] In most cases this is a right without a remedy, as generally the loss incurred by the surety was triggered by the financial inability of its principal to meet its obligations. Consequently, the surety will frequently require indemnity of other parties, such as the spouse of a contractor operating as an individual, or the chief officers and owners (and perhaps their spouses) of a closely held corporation or related corporations.

THE RIGHT TO INDEMNITY FROM LIABILITY

The indemnification agreement formalizes the common-law obligation of the contractor to reimburse the surety for loss arising out of the principal-surety relationship and extends it to third-party indemnitors.

First, and most important, it creates a right in the surety to be indemnified from liability. This gives the surety the right to demand action by the contractor and third-party indemnitors before it has made a single loss payment and at a time when it only anticipates that it may have a loss. The right to indemnity against liability can be triggered not only by a default in the performance of the contract work but also by the failure to pay a bill when due.[3]

The right to indemnity against liability (as opposed to loss) becomes particularly important when the unpaid suppliers of labor and material have a delayed right of action against the surety. Under the Miller Act, which requires performance and payment bonds on federal projects, the supplier of labor and material must wait until 90 days after supplying the last of the labor and material for which claim is made before it can bring suit on the payment bond.[4] In New Jersey, there is no right of action on the payment bond until 80 days after acceptance of the work[5] and many other states have similar provisions in their public work statutes. The practical effect of the right to indemnity against liability coupled with the delay in the right to sue on the payment bond gives the surety time to negotiate with the indemnitors and, if negotiation fails, time to bring suit before it becomes necessary to make a loss payment.

Next, the indemnity provision broadens the right to indemnity to include expense as well as loss. The surety can recover such expense as attorneys' and accountants' fees, and engineers' and surety consultants' fees.

---

[2] 74 Am. Jur. 2d, *Suretyship*, § 171. *See also Pearlman v. Reliance Ins. Co.*, 371 U.S. 132 (1962).
[3] *Martin v. Nation Sur. Co.*, 300 U.S. 588 (1937).
[4] 40 U.S.C. 270b.
[5] N.J.S.A. 2A: 44–145.

THE RIGHT TO DEMAND THE DEPOSIT OF COLLATERAL

This provision, sometimes called reserve-deposit, provides quite simply that, if the surety finds it necessary to establish a reserve to cover a possible liability, the indemnitor, on demand, will deposit a sum of money with the surety equal to the reserve, as collateral security.

Courts will enforce the right of a surety to recover from an indemnitor prior to payment of a loss. Frequently, however, courts require that the liability be legally imposed before recognizing that right.[6] In some jurisdictions, suit against the indemnitor can be brought after judgment but before payment of the judgment.[7] Generally, the courts will require that the surety has incurred a loss rather than only a threat of loss to have the right to indemnity. The effect of these decisions largely is to nullify the advantage to the surety of the right to indemnity against liability. A great many, if not most, of the contractor problem cases follow this script: They start with an increasing flow of notices of unpaid bills and disputes with subcontractors. The contractor gives the surety an explanation which on its face may be logical, that is, that the bill is not due because an item is missing, something supplied is not correct, or the work or material has not been accepted by the owner. The contractor then agrees at his own expense to defend both himself and the surety when the supplier or subcontractor files suit. Sometimes the surety arranges its own defense, asks for a judgment over against the principal and brings a third-party action against indemnitors. With court calendar congestion, resolution may be five years after commencement of the action and the right to indemnity against liability is a hollow one.

In short, the legal right to indemnify against liability will not usually save the surety from payment of a loss. By the time the surety has incurred a legal liability, it usually will be required to pay the loss and will not have time to prosecute a suit against an indemnitor to judgment.

The right to demand the deposit of collateral creates for the surety a more efficient procedure. Under the reserve-deposit provision generally used, the indemnitor agrees that, if for any reason the surety shall deem it necessary to set up a reserve, the indemnitor will deposit with the surety a sum equal to that reserve as collateral security. All insurance companies are required to set up reserves against potential liability. These reflect the best estimate of the liability of the company, which can be penalized for inadequate reserves.

The reserve-deposit provision is set in motion when the surety establishes a reserve and follows it with a demand for collateral equal to the amount of the reserve. The agreement generally requires the deposit to be made with the surety "on demand." If the deposit is not forthcoming, the surety files suit.[8]

---

[6] 41 Am. Jur. 2d, *Indemnity,* § 31.

[7] *McArthur Bros. v. Kerr,* 213 N.Y. 360, 107 N.E. 572 (1915).

[8] *See e.g.* Louis Auerbacher, Jr., "Quia Timet: Relief by Summary Judgment on Indemnity Agreement," *Insurance Counsel Journal,* October 1972.

The reserve-deposit remedy is equitable in nature and consequently requires that the surety must exercise good faith and reasonable judgment.

THE RIGHT TO INFORMATION

Indemnity agreements have always had some sort of provision requiring the contractor to furnish information and give the surety access to its books and records. Some agreements authorize banks, supply houses, credit reporting agencies and others to furnish information about the contractor.

The courts have upheld the right of an insurance company to examine the books and records of an insured for premium audit purposes, and it is reasonable to suppose that a surety would be given the same right of examination to establish the facts. Getting the facts at that time, however, may not help the surety demonstrate that it acted reasonably in establishing a reserve, as the facts are needed before the reserve is set up or suit is started. When a contractor agrees to access under the provisions of an indemnity agreement, to refuse information is difficult.

Usually, a brief examination will disclose the principal subcontractors and suppliers.

The amount demanded by the surety seldom covers every potential liability and often is later amended.

The indemnitor who resists the demand for collateral on the ground that it is unreasonable usually finds it difficult to sustain his position when, in the face of his written agreement to furnish information, he refuses to do so.

THE AGREEMENT THAT CONTRACT FUNDS ARE TRUST FUNDS

Under this provision, the contractor agrees that the proceeds of all bonded contracts are trust funds for the payment of all persons to whom the contractor incurs obligations in the performance of the contract. The contractor also agrees that, on demand by the surety, it will set up a separate trust account for these funds and that withdrawals will be by checks signed by the contractor and countersigned by the surety.

This declaration of trust adds little to the legal and equitable rights the surety already has to funds in the hands of the owner. However, the provision, from an operating point of view, creates for the surety an agreement by the contractor to place contract funds in a trust account and to give the surety countersignature control over disbursements. The concern of a surety dealing with a contractor under financial pressure is that contract funds will be diverted to payment of noncontract obligations. With the funds in an account over which the surety has signature control, such diversions can be prevented.

THE ASSIGNMENTS BY THE CONTRACTOR

To obtain for the surety an interest in the contractor's assets as collateral security against loss, the indemnity agreement will have an assignment clause covering contract funds, equipment, subcontracts, and claims against subcontractors, and which becomes effective on the happening of certain acts of default.

The assignment is undoubtedly good as between the contractor and the surety but, when the contractor is in financial difficulty, there are third parties who assert rights to these same assets. The assignment generally is not effective against these third parties because the interests conveyed generally have not been perfected under the Uniform Commercial Code. Ordinarily, the assignment gives the surety the right to engage in a race for assets, but little more.

The Model General Agreement of Indemnity used by many sureties provides that the agreement is a security agreement and financing statement in accordance with U.C.C. provisions. Business considerations, however, make impractical the filing of these agreements as is required to perfect the interest under the code. These are filed by the surety after the contractor's troubles are apparent and generally too late to be of substantial help. When problems occur and the surety determines that a U.C.C. filing is necessary, the practice is for the contractor to sign financing statements tailored to eliminate controversy over the adequacy of the description of the property covered and to permit duplicate filing, where required.

THE SURETY AS ATTORNEY-IN-FACT FOR THE INDEMNITOR

Most Agreements contain a clause which authorizes the surety, as attorney-in-fact, to execute documents necessary to convey title to the property assigned and to provide the surety with the protection contemplated by the indemnity agreement.

If the contractor refuses to sign, the surety will do so as attorney-in-fact and, in this capacity, may endorse checks or vouchers as well as documents relating to completion of the contract.

AGREEMENTS RELATING TO CLAIMS AGAINST THE SURETY

The surety is liable only when its principal is liable. If a surety pays a loss for which its principal is not liable, it is a volunteer and, therefore, cannot recover. Faced only with an obligation to indemnify against loss, a recalcitrant indemnitor can require the surety to litigate each claim as a condition precedent to reimbursement. Three clauses in most indemnity agreements affect this situation.

First, a clause whereby the surety can pay or compromise any claim or demand on the bond and the payment shall be binding on the indemnitor as long as it was made by the surety in the reasonable belief that it was liable. Of course, the surety must act in good faith, which includes giving the indemnitor notice of its intention to make the payment. Notice by the surety to the indemnitor is necessary because of a second clause whereby the indemnitor agrees to deposit collateral with the surety equal to the amount of the claim.

The third is the clause whereby a sworn statement or voucher or other evidence of payment by the surety shall be either conclusive or prima facie evidence of the fact of legal liability therefor and the amount of the payment.

The practical effect of these three clauses is to assist the surety in cutting through frivolous or sham defenses by an indemnitor. The clauses do not give a surety a free hand, and it must always act reasonably. Nevertheless, their combined weight would seem to shift the burden of proof to the indemnitor to demonstrate that the surety acted unreasonably or in bad faith.

THE RIGHT TO TAKE POSSESSION OF THE WORK

Most indemnity agreements recite that, in the event of default, the surety has the right to take over the work and complete it or cause it to be completed. The exercise of this right is at the sole option and discretion of the surety and, perhaps more than any other, must be exercised in good faith and with care.

In the event of problems short of default by obligee, the surety may attempt to obtain a voluntary letter of default from the contractor. Absent either of these, the surety's takeover of the work under this clause must be carried out reasonably, in good faith, and in a manner not prejudicial to the interest of its principal if its position is to be sustained in subsequent litigation.[9]

Frequent observations have been made over the necessity for the surety to act in good faith in the exercise of the rights obtained under the indemnity agreement. The surety must be careful to document the reasons for the takeover and its activities thereafter for there are at least two areas of possible attack on the surety. First, the indemnitor may raise the defense that the actions of the surety precluded the indemnitor from completing the contract and he was thereby relieved of liability. Second, although infrequently raised, the surety may be accused of having dominated the contractor's business, to the prejudice of the contractor.

MISCELLANEOUS PROVISIONS

Most indemnity agreements contain other clauses permitting the surety to refuse to write the final bond on a project on which it wrote the bid bond, providing that each indemnitor shall be jointly and severally liable, that a release of one indemnitor is not a release of any other indemnitor, and providing for an indemnitor the power to terminate liability thereunder with respect to bonds thereafter issued.

---

[9]*Seaboard Sur. Co. v. Dale Constr. Co.*, 230 F.2d 625 (1st Cir. 1956), *Resolute Ins. Co. v. Norbo Trading Corp.*, 165 S.E.2d 441 (1968), *New Amsterdam Cas. Co. v. Lundquist*, 198 N.W.2d 543 (1972).

Chapter 49
Legal and Illegal Transfers

ROBERT R. HUME, ESQ.
Hart & Hume, New York, New York

We deal here with situations where a debtor has treated title to his property, whether by sale, gift, or other method of transfer, so as to attempt to place that property beyond the reach of his creditors. The affected creditor must try to realize on such property, the title to which is now in person or entity other than the original debtor, in a manner which preserves its nature as collateral for specific indebtedness, without unduly prejudicing the debtor's rights of alienation.

The history of legislative and judicial efforts to cope with this paradoxical objective of the creditor formally commences in sixteenth century England with the first statutory recognition of the problem: the Statute of Fraudulent Conveyances (13 Eliz. c: 519n).

The statute was directed against any transfer of property by a debtor when made with the intent to hinder, delay, or defraud creditors. Eventually supplemented by a second act particularly concerned with fraudulent conveyances of land,[1] this law and its successors recognized the need to afford some remedy against debtors' fraudulent conveyances not only to those creditors as of the date of the challenged transfer but to the category of creditors whose relationship with the debtor formally commenced subsequent to the suspect conveyance. Criminal sanctions were imposed by these laws against the transferring debtor.

As a result of these criminal sanctions, the standards for proof of debtor's intent became the critical focus of judicial efforts to apply the statute. Direct proof of intent is usually difficult to obtain, and the courts soon developed what were called *badges of fraud,* that is, factual circumstances surrounding the disposition of property which raised at least an inference if not a presumption of fraud. The development of a law of constructive fraud was fundamentally a tailoring of the broad statutory remedies to a fashion more compatible with the sophisticated and flexible response to these transfers which is provided by today's civil remedies. *Constructive fraud* encompasses those acts, contracts, and transactions which, though not originating in any actual evil design or contrivance, are deemed by law and public policy as equally reprehensible with actual fraud because of their tendency to deceive other persons and violate the private confidences and agreements which underlie our substantially free enterprise commercial system.[2]

Concomitant with the growth of the case law of constructive fraud, and the increasing tendency to examine debtor's conveyances from the perspective of the creditor's civil remedies, a widespread recognition has developed of the social and commercial need for a systematic approach to both a debtor's rights in his property and a creditor's conditional rights in the same property as collateral. Out of this recognition, accelerated as it was by the increasing utilization of third-party credit instruments and other negotiable evidences of debt among transacting commercial classes, arose the enactment of recording statutes affecting chattel mortgages and conditional sales. These recording statutes formalized bona fide credit transactions without impinging on the case law of constructive fraud and the remedies available to creditors as to transfers deemed suspect thereby.

THE UNIFORM FRAUDULENT CONVEYANCE ACT

As recording acts implementing security interests became more widespread, the desirability of similar codification of the rights and remedies of creditors against fraudulent conveyances became apparent.

In 1915 the National Conference of Commissioners on Uniform Laws decided to draft a uniform act, and in 1918 the conference approved the final form of The Uniform Fraudulent Conveyance Act which was adopted by the following states:

---

[1] *See* 27 Eliz. c4, 1584-5.

[2] The most celebrated case under the Statute of Fraudulent Conveyances was Twyne's Case, Star Chamber, 1601 3 Coke, 80b, 76 Eng. Rep. 809 which held that a sale or gift of chattels without transfer of possession is constructively fraudulent.

Arizona (1919)   New York (1925)
California (1939)   North Dakota (1943)
Delaware (1919)   Ohio (1961)
Idaho (1969)   Oklahoma (1965)
Maryland (1920)   Pennsylvania (1921)
Massachusetts (1924)   South Dakota (1919)
Michigan (1919)   Tennessee (1919)
Minnesota (1921)   Utah (1925)
Montana (1945)   Virgin Islands (1957)
Nevada (1931)   Washington (1945)
New Hampshire (1919)   Wisconsin (1919)
New Jersey (1919)   Wyoming (1929)
New Mexico(1959)

Conflicts among Jurisdictions

Despite the adoption by so many jurisdictions of The Uniform Act, there remains a substantial conflict among the states, not only between those who have adopted the act and those who have not, but among the adopting states. This requires an examination of the annotations to the act in each state where it has been adopted and to the case law of jurisdictions where it has not.

A conspicuous example of such conflict is provided by the question of whether a legatee under a will may defeat the claims of his creditors by renouncing his legacy. Some states have held that a person cannot be compelled to take property against his will. The right of renunciation has, however, been denied where there has been a long delay before renouncing; where there has been collusion between the debtor and those benefiting by the disclaimer; and where the donee has caused his creditors to rely upon his apparent acceptance.[3]

The majority of courts has been reluctant to restrict the power of a devisee or legatee to renounce the bequest, at least if he acts without undue delay. In the case cited it was held that under the Uniform Act the creditor need not have reduced his claim to judgment and obtained a lien on the debtor's property or an execution returned unsatisfied in order to attack a fraudulent conveyance. This has been similarly held in other jurisdictions where the act has been adopted as well as in an ever-increasing number of states where the act has not been adopted.

The Creditor's Search for Remedy

A convenient example of the status of a creditor seeking to enforce the remedies afforded it by The Uniform Fraudulent Conveyances Act is that of a surety who has bonded a contractor and assumed, of course, the risk of incurring liability should its principal default on its obligations. This risk is vitiated, in part, by the common-law right of reimbursement against the principal as to losses sustained on the principal's behalf. In addition, the common practice among compensated sureties is to obtain a written agreement of

[3]*In re Kalt's Estate*, 16 Cal. 2d 807, 198 P.2d.

indemnification from the principal as a precondition of the delivery of its bond. The hypothetical problem posed in our example of this situation may be phrased as follows: If the principal, anticipating a default, should dispose of its assets to prevent a possible execution on same by a surety armed with an indemnification agreement, does the surety have a remedy?

The Creditor's Status under the Act

Sureties were regarded as creditors under the common law. The United States Supreme Court was called upon to decide whether a surety was included under the term "creditor" in federal bankruptcy legislation.[4] In determining Congress' intent the Court looked to the common law's treatment of sureties as creditors. The Court found that the common law regarded sureties as creditors and said:

> Under the common law rule a creditor having only a contingent claim, such as was that of petitioner at the time respondent made the transfer in question, is protected against fraudulent conveyance. And the petitioner, from the time that it became surety on Mogliani's bond, was entitled as a creditor under the agreement to invoke that rule.

The Uniform Act, in § 1, defines a creditor as "a person having any claim, whether matured or unmatured, liquidated or unliquidated, absolute, fixed or contingent." Sureties have frequently been included within this statutory definition also. A surety who had bonded a general construction contractor sought to have certain of its principal's transfers set aside as violations of the Uniform Fraudulent Conveyance Act as incorporated in the Maryland code.[5] The Court made it very clear that the surety had "the standing of a creditor to maintain this action."

Necessity of Judgment

Some older cases had held that before seeking to set aside a fraudulent conveyance a creditor had to have obtained judgment against the debtor.[6] The language of the Uniform Fraudulent Conveyance Act, describing a *creditor* as "a person having any claim, whether matured or unmatured, liquidated or unliquidated, absolute, fixed or contingent" and a *debt* as including "any legal liability, whether matured or unmatured, liquidated or unliquidated, absolute, fixed or contingent," would seem to defeat any such rule.

However, even after the passage of the Uniform Act, some courts continued to insist that a judgment was a necessary prerequisite to an action to set aside a fraudulent transfer.[7] Perhaps the leading case repudiating such a view is *American Surety Co. v. Conner,* in which the opinion was written by Judge Cardozo.[8] In that case, Conner, a bank employee, had embezzled money over a

---

[4]*American Sur. Co. v. Marotta,* 287 U.S. 513 (1933).
[5]*F. S. Bowen Elec. Co. v. United States Fid. & Guar. Co.,* 256 F.2d 46 (4th Cir., 1958).
[6]*Ellis v. Southwestern Land Co.,* 108 Wis. 313, 84 N.W. 417 (1900).
[7]*Gross v. Pennsylvania Mort. & Loan Co.,* 104 N.J. Eq., 439 A. 323 (1929).
[8]*American Sur. Co. v. Conner,* 251 N.Y. 1, 166 N.E. 783 (1929).

long period of time. He also during this time married a woman who relied on his promise to secure her financially with land and jewelry. Later, Connor's thievery was discovered and his wife successfully sued to annul the marriage. The surety on Conner's Fidelity bond which had paid for his employer's loss resulting from the embezzlement, sought to recover the land and jewelry given by Conner to his wife, claiming it was a fraudulent transfer.

The question was presented whether a judgment was needed before the fraudulent transfer could be attacked. The Court held that the effect of the then recently enacted Uniform Act was to terminate "the ancient rule whereby a judgment and a lien were essential preliminaries to equitable relief against a fraudulent conveyance." The Court added that it was the aim of the act that "the path is to be cleared of harassing impediments to the swift pursuit of justice." No doubt was left after this decision that a creditor might maintain a suit in equity to annul a fraudulent conveyance, though the debt had not matured.

Under the Federal Rules of Civil Procedure, it is explicitly stated that there is no need to have obtained a judgment before seeking to set aside a fraudulent transfer: "In particular, a plaintiff may state a claim for money and a claim to have set aside a conveyance fraudulent as to him, without first having obtained a judgment establishing the claim for money."[9]

As set forth above, the modern business man is left in doubt as to the role he is to assume in the extension of credit, whether in a specific transaction or by establishment of an "open account," and is well advised to scrutinize the actions of any given debtor toward those of his assets collateralizing indebtedness with the act and its remedies in mind.

PROBLEMS PERTAINING TO BONDING COMPANIES AND FRAUDULENT CONVEYANCES

Need for Surety to Have Performed Surety Obligation

A more perplexing question within our specific example is whether a surety has actually to have been called on to meet his obligations and to have expended money before he can act to set aside fraudulent conveyances by his principal. Can a surety whose principal has not yet defaulted but who is fearful of such a default seek to set aside his principal's fraudulent conveyance when he has not yet paid any money under his surety obligation?

Before the Uniform Act was passed the majority view was that a surety in such a position could not set aside fraudulent conveyances, although some states did take the opposite view.[10]

In accord with the majority view was the case of *Ellis v. Southwestern Land Co.* cited previously. The plaintiff in that case was a surety on an undertaking to pay the costs of an appeal and damages if the lower court judgment was affirmed. Shortly thereafter his principal conveyed all his property to a corporation. The

[9]F.R.C.P. 18(b).
[10]71 A.L.R. 354.

plaintiff sued to have the conveyance set aside as fraudulent before having paid any money out on the bond.

The Court ruled that the plaintiff could not obtain the relief he sought. The Court said: "Plaintiff is a mere surety. He has paid no part of the judgment against him. He may never do so. It may be collected from the principal or from some one of the other parties who signed the undertaking. At law he would have no standing in court until he paid the debt."

One commentator suggested the anomalous result of such reasoning: "Though such a holding . . . may be justified in legal theory, certain it is that the surety is denied protection when he needs it the most."[11]

The Uniform Act, Article 1, as noted earlier, describes a creditor as a person "having any claim, whether . . . fixed or contingent" and a debt as "any legal liability, whether . . . fixed or contingent." Such language would seem to include a surety whose obligation is contingent, dependent on his principal's performing his obligation. Unfortunately there seem to be few cases in recent years on the question. A Tennessee court did say that "by reason of this statute (the Uniform Act) a surety may bring an action to set aside a fraudulent conveyance of his principal before any loss incurred or payment made.[12] The remark does not constitute a controlling precedent, however, because the sureties in the case had paid their obligation and taken a judgment over against the principal. The Tennessee court did not have before it a factual situation on which to base a definitive ruling.

The problem of the surety in this context, and the possible relief afforded to such problem by the provisions of the act, should be kept in mind by the general commercial creditor. The act's language appears to encourage a broad conceptual approach to both the debt and the standing of a creditor, and against its background the aggressive pursuit of remedies by creditors is encouraged.

Alternative Remedies for the Surety

Exoneration   Glenn, in his treatise, *Fraudulent Conveyances and Preferences*,[13] noted that the surety's rights prior to actual loss were disputed. He was of the view that a surety should not be able to set aside fraudulent conveyances until he had paid his surety obligation. He thought that the surety had another adequate remedy. A surety may seek *exoneration* from his principal when the time for the principal to meet his obligation has come. And in extreme cases, where the surety fears his principal will dispose of his assets so as to be unable to meet his not-yet-due obligation, the surety may seek injunctive relief. Exoneration refers to the act by which a surety implements the application of any fund controlled by its principal to the payment of those claims for which the surety has issued its bond.

---

[11]40 Yale L.J. 485–486 (1930).
[12]*McDonald v. Baldwin*, 24 Tenn. App. 670, 148 S.W.2d 385 (Ct. App. Tenn. Mid. Sect., 1940).
[13]*Glenn, "Fraudulent Conveyances and Preferences,"* § 93(d) (1940).

An example of the remedy is found in *Morley Construction Co. v. Maryland Casualty Co.,*[14] where the court granted exoneration. The surety brought an action against its principal, alleging that the principal, unless restrained, would "convert or conceal its funds" and be unable to meet its obligations, causing the surety an "irreparable loss." The surety said that unless its principal were enjoined from withdrawing and disbursing its funds and the bank enjoined from permitting any withdrawal, it would suffer such a loss. The surety asked the court to direct the principal to exonerate the surety.

Quia timet   The court noted that the complaint partook of "the nature of a bill *quia timet."* Such bills are ordinarily applied to "prevent wrongs or anticipated mischiefs, and not merely to redress them when done." The relief given depends upon the circumstances. It could be the appointment of a receiver, an order to pay a fund into court, directing money to be paid or the issuance of an injunction. The court also said that the surety is not required to pay the debt before calling for exoneration.

Surety's right to set aside fraudulent conveyances made before performance of surety obligation   If a surety has performed his obligation as surety he may certainly move to set aside his principal's fraudulent conveyances made while he was surety but before he had to perform his obligations as such. For the general commercial creditor, a scrutiny of such transactions is always in order, with particular emphasis on transfers of the debtor which precede maturation of the indebtedness in question but have affected the capacity of the debtor to meet his obligations.

What conveyances are fraudulent under the Uniform Fraudulent Conveyances Act   Section 4 of the Uniform Act states: "Every conveyance made and every obligation incurred by a person who is or will be thereby rendered insolvent is fraudulent as to creditors without regard to his actual intent if the conveyance made or the obligation is incurred without a fair consideration."

The test under this section thus turns on the questions of whether the transfer was made for fair consideration and whether the debtor is insolvent after the transaction. Intent is not taken into account; if the conveyance meets the criteria established, it is fraudulent despite the lack of any fraudulent intent. "A conveyance by an insolvent is fraudulent without regard to intent if it is without fair consideration."[15]

Section 4, unlike some other sections of the act, does not extend its protection to future creditors but only to creditors at the time of the transaction.

Section 7 of the Uniform Act, however, states: "Every conveyance made and every obligation incurred with actual intent, as distinguished from intent presumed in law, to hinder, delay, or defraud either present or future creditors, is fraudulent as to both present and future creditors."

It should be noted that there is no question of fair consideration or insolvency raised in this section. Anyone, no matter how solvent, who seeks to

---

[14]90 F.2d 976 (8th Cir., 1937).
[15]*Douglas v. First Nat'l Realty Corp.,* 351 F.Supp. 1142 (D.C., 1972).

prevent or even delay his creditor's collection of a debt by means of a conveyance runs afoul of this section. In *Pattison v. Pattison*,[16] a judgment debtor for $1,000 held over $100,000 in property in Canada. He conveyed his house in the United States to his sister to prevent execution on it. The court found that this was a fraudulent conveyance despite the debtor's legal solvency because of the purpose of the transfer.

Elements of the two previously mentioned sections are combined in §6 of the Uniform Fraudulent Conveyances Act. It states: "Every conveyance made and every obligation incurred without fair consideration when the person entering into the obligation intends or believes that he will incur debts beyond his ability to pay as they mature, is fraudulent as to both present and future creditors."

This section does require a lack of fair consideration but does not demand an actual intent to "hinder, delay, or defraud"; an intent or even a belief on the part of the debtor that he will incur debts which he will not be able to pay as they mature is sufficient. Both present and future creditors are protected by this section.

In *N. Erlanger, Blumgart & Co. v. Keehn*,[17] a man deeded his home to his wife three months before he personally guaranteed the debts of the corporation he owned. Some time later a judgment was obtained against him based on his guarantee. The court in denying a motion to dismiss an action brought by the creditors to set aside the conveyance, said that while the conveyance was made before the man became a debtor, the transfer was possibly fraudulent under §§ 6 and 7 of the Uniform Act. The conveyance was made by a person about to incur debts who might well have intended or believed these debts to be beyond his ability to pay. And he well might have intended to "hinder, delay, or defraud" his future creditors by this transfer.

Section 5 of the Uniform Act would also seem to have occasional possible application to sureties of contractors. It states:

> Every conveyance made without fair consideration when the person making it is engaged or is about to engage in a business or transaction for which the property remaining in his hands after the conveyance is an unreasonably small capital, is fraudulent as to creditors and as to other persons who become creditors during the continuance of such business or transaction without regard to his actual intent.

However, it is expected that sureties are careful about investigating the contractors they bond. Contractors, requiring the bonding, will not seek to dispose of their assets prior to investigation by the surety. Thus the provisions making transactions fraudulent as to future conveyances will probably not be of as much use to construction sureties as those concerning transfers by present creditors. But indemnitors, who are often principals of the bonded contractor, might anticipate their indemnity status and undertake conveyances which are fraudulent as to a future creditor.

---

[16]301 N.Y. 65, 92 N.E.2d 890 (1950).
[17]19 Misc.2d 1017 191 N.Y.S.2d 51 (1959).

Clearly, the opposite side of the coin sets forth some clear guidelines for contractors and their principals as to those transfers of corporate or personal assets which may face challenge from a surety, whether in its role as indemnitee under a written agreement or in accord with principles of common-law contribution. Since the task of undertaking certain major jobs may require new combinations of capital created by asset pledges or transfers, participating contractor-principals must exercise certain self-policing techniques with a view toward potential subsequent challenges to their property conveyances, transfers, or gifts.

Often, many transactions are undertaken for tax purposes (whether personal income or estate). Without disputing the value, and even necessity, of such deals, a contractor-principal should be wary of excessively enthusiastic short-term planning that may encourage legal interference from a present or future creditor.

Creditor's remedies under the Uniform Fraudulent Conveyances Act   When a creditor's claim has matured, he may with regard to a fraudulent transfer under § 9 of the Uniform Fraudulent Conveyances Act:

> a. Have the conveyance set aside or obligation annuled to the extent necessary to satisfy his claim, or
> b. Disregard the conveyance and attach a levy execution upon the property conveyed.

Such a creditor may not act against "a purchaser for fair consideration without knowledge of the fraud at the time of the purchase" or one deriving title from such a purchaser.

If the creditor's claim has not matured, §10 of the Uniform Fraudulent Conveyances Act allows the following remedies against a fraudulent transfer:

> a. Restrain the defendant from disposing of his property,
> b. Appoint a receiver to take charge of the property,
> c. Set aside the conveyance or annul the obligation, or
> d. Make any order which the circumstances of the case may require.

TRANSFERS UNDER THE BANKRUPTCY ACT

Another entire dimension of the treatment of acts purporting to transfer title to property in situations which may compromise the rights of creditors of the transferor arises in the bankruptcy courts. In these forums, the search for methods to identify, control, and distribute the assets of the bankrupt, and to determine priorities for such distribution among competing creditors has led to the adoption and subsequent refinements of the Bankruptcy Act, 11 U.S.C. 1, et seq.

A main objective of the Bankruptcy Act is to ensure equality of distribution of assets among creditors. Sections 1–72 deal with distribution of the bankrupt's nonexempt assets that are free, that is, unencumbered, among the unsecured or general creditors, some of whom may be entitled to priority in such distribution. The act fixes the time of deciding when the rights and positions are established of creditors and debtors as of the date when the petition is filed, whether voluntary or involuntary. Upon adjudication of bankruptcy, the trustee acquires title to the nonexempt property of the debtor and is empowered to challenge transfers or transactions which occurred prior to the date of filing in accord with various statutory guidelines.

Intent is substantially less of a factor in the Trustee's examination and challenge of various preferential transfers in the bankruptcy context than it is in the general context of fraudulent conveyances. The policing of a debtor's transfers by various creditors in *anticipation* of a failure by him to properly secure the repayment of an indebtedness places a grave burden on the judiciary to prevent unwarranted interference in the debtor's rights of alienation, and control over his personal assets.

The thorough examination of intent, whether by direct evidence thereof or as inferred from the context of a particular transaction, embodies this judicial caution in the application of creditor remedies. Even the broad provisions of the Uniform Fraudulent Conveyances Act have not entirely vitiated this tension between debtor's rights and creditor's remedies.

The Bankruptcy Act, however, represents a substantially different context alike for the debtor and creditor. Whether voluntarily, or involuntarily, the debtor's entire commercial life and all his nonexempt assets are within the purview of the court. The debtor, of course, receives the substantial protection of the court and the opportunity to renew his personal and commercial life without the burdens of untenable indebtedness, His mistakes are in substantial measure relieved by his discharge.

In exchange for this protection the bankrupt turns over his residual and nonexempt estate to the court which, with the aid of the trustee, attempts to effect a distribution of assets in conformity with both valid and recognized liens on specific assets for the secured creditors and a policy emphasis on preserving the general estate in order to increase the possible return to those unsecured creditors. The interests of the debtor are not here paramount and, in the transactions scrutinized by the trustee, the focus of concern is competing creditors' priorities rather than the intent of the debtor.

Preferences

Preferences are a category of transfers undertaken by a debtor which by statutory definition set forth in § 60a(1) of the Bankruptcy Act are subject to the challenge of the trustee. The effect of a preference is that such a transfer will enable a creditor to obtain a greater percentage of his debt than some other creditor of the same class.

A preference within the provisions of the act is voidable only and not void and may be avoided only at the insistence of the trustee in bankruptcy.

The essential elements of a voidable preference may be set forth as follows:

> A transfer of any of the debtor's property or money to or for the benefit of a creditor, for or on account of an antecedent debt, or made or suffered by the

debtor while insolvent, within four months of bankruptcy, or, as sometimes stated, within four months of the filing of the bankruptcy petition, the effect of which is to enable the creditor to obtain a greater percentage of his debt than other creditors of the same class, the creditor receiving which or for whose benefit the transfer is made has, at such time, knowledge or reasonable cause to believe that the debtor is insolvent.

For example, if the bankrupt were to pay a lien creditor, while insolvent, within four months of the date of filing, the effect would be a preference if the lien holder had reason to believe the bankrupt was insolvent. In this case the lien holder would, through such payments, be receiving a larger share than others in the same class, and the trustee could have the payments set aside. Note that this would not be the case if payment was made to a creditor with a security interest, or mortgage, because such payment would not diminish the estate available to unsecured creditors. The specific rights of such creditors in definite collateral have the effect of removing these secured creditors (to the extent sums owing them are fully secured) from the general creditor class.

Section 60*a* provides that a transfer of an interest in real estate shall not be deemed made until "so far perfected that no subsequent bona fide purchasers from the debtor could create rights in such property superior to the rights of the transferee."

Any mortgage lender should promptly record, as transfers are deemed made as of the date of recording, and if a lender fails to record until within four months of filing of the petition, the mortgage or deed of trust embodying the lien may be deemed as given for or on account of an antecedent debt.

Of course, a transfer of an asset for a fair present consideration cannot be set aside as a preference, even if within four months of filing and even though the purchaser or lender knew of the debtor's insolvency. A contrary rule would prevent the debtor's attempts to work out of his difficulty.

Lienors as purchasers from the transferee of the debtor must pay a fair consideration. Where such a purchaser or lienor has given less than such value, he shall nevertheless have a lien upon such property but only to the extent of the consideration actually given by him. In short, while the trustee may not recover the property from an innocent third-party purchaser or lienor, he may seek to get the true value from such preferred creditor.

Fraudulent Transfers

Sections 70*c* and *e* of the Bankruptcy Act provide the Trustee of the bankrupt estate with broad powers related to his standing to dispute transactions of the debtor. The Trustee is empowered to avoid any transfer by the bankrupt which a creditor could have avoided, except as against a bona fide holder for value prior to the date of adjudication of bankruptcy. The trustee can proceed under any law which enables creditors to avoid transfers made or allowed by the bankrupt. He may proceed under § 67*d*, which is the Bankruptcy Act's version of the Uniform Fraudulent Conveyances Act discussed above. Sections 67*d*, 2*a*, *b*, *c* and *d* contain the provisions applicable in bankruptcy that are similar to Uniform Fraudulent Conveyances Act, § 4, 5, 6, and 7.

Section 67d (3) provides that a transfer is deemed a fraudulent conveyance, even though given for a present consideration, when the parties know that the consideration is to be used to prefer some third party in contemplation of bankruptcy or liquidation. The necessary elements are:

1. That the debtor has made a transfer of his property or incurred an obligation

2. That the debtor was insolvent at the time or as a result of the transfer or obligation

3. That the transfer or obligation became effective within four months of the filing of the petition initiating a proceeding under the Bankruptcy Act

4. That the transaction must have been entered into in contemplation of the filing of such a petition or in contemplation of liquidation of all or the greater portion of the debtor's property

5. That the transaction must have been entered into with the intent to use the consideration obtained to enable a creditor of the debtor to obtain a greater percentage of his debt than some other creditor of the same class

6. That the transferee or obligee must, at the time of the transaction, know or believe that the debtor intends to make such use of the consideration

The defense, of course, is that the transferee is a bona fide purchaser, without knowledge of the intent of the debtor. Section 67d(6) protects a bona fide purchaser, lienor, or obligee for a present, fair equivalent value from an avoidance by the trustee, if guiltless of actual fraudulent intent. He may retain the property, lien, or other security interest, as security for repayment. And this is so even if he has parted with less than fair value for it.

Liens Acquired through Process

Attachments, garnishments, and judgment liens obtained within four months before the filing of a petition in bankruptcy are deemed null and void by § 67a if the debtor was insolvent at the time the lien was perfected. The rationale of this section is to minimize the effects of a "race" to conclude debt collection or other litigation among creditors prior to the filing of a bankruptcy petition. The policy emphasis rests on affording the broadest possible relief to creditors generally once the debtor is effectively insolvent in accord with the basis of the credit relationship as established prior to that insolvency. With this analysis in mind it is not surprising that provision is made in § 67a that all such liens are reinstated with the same effect as if never nullified *if* there is neither a final adjudication of bankruptcy of the debtor nor the confirmation of any arrangement or plan under the act.

It is noteworthy that liens arising by operation of law are exempt from the impact of § 67a and that "statutory liens in favor of employees, contractors, mechanics, or any other class of persons" are acknowledged as valid in § 67b of the Bankruptcy Act. In addition, statutory liens for taxes and debts of the United States or any state or subdivision are recognized as valid.

Chapter **50**

Bankruptcy Proceedings and Other Solutions Available to a Financially Distressed Enterprise

ALEXANDER B. ADELMAN, ESQ.
Partner, Adelman and Lavine, Philadelphia, Pennsylvania

MELVIN LASHNER, ESQ.
Partner, Adelman and Lavine, Philadelphia, Pennsylvania

The Federal Bankruptcy Act and state insolvency laws have as their stated purpose the recognition of the beneficial effects of rehabilitating an honest debtor. These laws also determine the distribution of the assets of a debtor upon liquidation if rehabilitation is not possible, and provide for the honest debtor's discharge of his debts.[1]

These laws were enacted to aid a building contractor experiencing financial difficulties as well as to help any other manufacturing, wholesale, or retail debtor although the problems involved in building construction can be quite different from those of other businesses. The building contractor should consider these laws as a respectable alternative to closing his doors when financial difficulties arise. The sooner the principals of a financially distressed building enterprise recognize that they need specialized legal help, the more chance there is for rehabilitation. This discussion is specifically designed to be of help to the building contractor so that he may understand what is involved in bankruptcy and other insolvency proceedings and to dispel some of the fears and misconceptions that may have arisen in his mind regarding these remedial statutes.

RECOGNIZING THE PROBLEM

How a Contractor Can Determine When Bankruptcy Proceedings Are Indicated

Financial troubles are an accumulation of a great many factors and reflect serious deficiencies in the running of a business, These deficiencies are usually translated into a lack of available cash to meet current operating expenses. The following actions taken by the principals of the debtor or by third parties who deal with the building contractor, when occurring in combinations, should be indications to the building contractor that financial problems are serious and that immediate steps should be taken to avoid collapse:

1. Banks refuse to grant loans.
2. Principals of the company fail to deposit taxes when payrolls are met.
3. Private lenders refuse to grant loans.
4. Principals refuse to advance additional capital.
5. Accounts receivable withhold payments.
6. Subcontractors refuse to work for lack of payment.
7. Suits are instituted by subcontractors and suppliers.
8. Work at job sites halt.
9. Notices are sent to bonding companies by subcontractors.
10. Bonding companies take over jobs.
11. Sheriff sales are listed by judgment creditors.
12. Bank accounts are attached.
13. Banks set off bank accounts against loans.
14. United States government files liens and levies for past taxes.
15. Removal of equipment by secured creditors.
16. Removal of supplies and equipment by unsecured creditors.

[1]Bankruptcy Act, Chap. III, § 14, 11 U.S.C. § 32.

Usually many of the above actions occur within a relatively short period of time, and the business deteriorates in proportion to the extent that immediate action is delayed. Before too many of these actions encroach on the effective operation of the business, a lawyer should be consulted as to the many procedures available to help a financially troubled enterprise.

What Information Is Required by the Attorney

An attorney will require certain information to help him in determining whether court proceedings are indicated. Recent financial statements which include the last available balance sheet and the most recent profit-and-loss statement are essential. It will be helpful if the attorney is supplied with a list of all the tangible assets of the company and their values together with a complete list of the current accounts receivable. In addition to the above information, the attorney should have an in-depth analysis of each construction project presently in progress together with a realistic appraisal of whether or not that project should be continued or abandoned because of a poor profit position.

In compiling the list of assets, bonded jobs must be kept separate from unbonded jobs. Creditors on bonded jobs are not subject to a settlement, either court-imposed or out-of-court, because of the liability of the bonding company for payment of those debts. If a bankruptcy proceeding results, courts have held that the bonding company has a prior right (over the trustee in bankruptcy) to the funds due the contractor if the bonding company has paid the debts for labor and materials of the contractor on that job.[2] State courts have held similarly in cases involving state insolvency proceedings.[3]

In addition to the above information, a list of creditors with full addresses and amounts due is required. The list of creditors should be broken down into creditors on bonded jobs and creditors on unbonded jobs for the reasons stated above.

After compiling and evaluating the above information, a decision must be made whether or not to continue the enterprise. A decision to continue the enterprise through legal proceedings means a drain on the principals' financial and emotional resources. The alternative is to abandon the enterprise and to allow the sale of the assets with the proceeds being distributed to creditors according to applicable law. With all the above information on which to base a decision and after a conference with the principals involved in the enterprise, an attorney can make a reasonably accurate recommendation as to what procedure is best to choose to reach the ends desired by the contractor client.

PROCEEDINGS UNDER THE FEDERAL BANKRUPTCY ACT

Once a decision is made to salvage a financially distressed enterprise, the procedure used is a petition under Chapter X, XI, or XII of the Bankruptcy Act. No attempt will be made here to discuss the various differences of these

---

[2] *Pearlman v. Reliance Ins. Co.,* 371 U.S. 132 (1962).
[3] *Jacobs v. Northeastern Corp.,* Appellant., 416 Pa. 417, 206 A.2d 49 (1965).

alternatives as that would involve a complex discussion of the Bankruptcy Act, and it is best left to legal counsel with expertise to decide which chapter to use.[4] The object of all the proceedings is the same: to save the enterprise with the consent of the creditors.

Personal Strain on Principals

If a decision has been made to attempt to salvage the financially distressed enterprise through bankruptcy proceedings, the principals of that enterprise must be prepared to make substantial financial, emotional, and personal sacrifices. Upon the filing of the petition there will be an immediate reduction in the amount of money that the principals will be able to take as salaries, which salaries must be approved by the Bankruptcy Court. During the course of the bankruptcy proceedings, operating capital may be necessary and the principals themselves may be required to go to their individual resources in order to keep the enterprise operative.

In addition to the running of the company, the principals will be involved in lengthy and time-consuming court proceedings and will probably be involved also in negotiations with financial sources to assist in funding a plan with creditors; all of which may compel the principals to spend longer working days than they had previously experienced.

The additional time needed to attempt to save a financially distressed business and the myriad of problems involved in rehabilitating a financially distressed enterprise place a heavy emotional strain on the principals, who must devote almost their full waking hours for the duration of the proceedings to the business. The outcome of the proceedings may be in doubt until the final order of confirmation is signed and, thus, the emotional strain endures throughout the entire proceeding.

If the financially distressed enterprise is worth saving and if the enterprise is able to be successfully rehabilitated, it will be, at least, in a great part due to the time and efforts expended by the principals in accomplishing this result, thus making worthwhile the time, effort, and emotional strain of all involved.

Advantages to Filing

In those cases where the principals desire the financially distressed enterprise to continue operations, there are several immediate advantages that accrue with the filing of a bankruptcy petition. A petition filed under Chapter X, XI, or XII of the Bankruptcy Act will allow a business enterprise to continue in operation during the proceedings. The immediate advantages of filing such a petition can be summarized as follows:

1. An immediate stay is in effect, thus preventing any sale or lien or any further action against any of the assets of the enterprise.[5]

---

[4]Chapters I through VII of the Bankruptcy Act pertain to straight bankruptcies; Chapter VIII with Reorganization of Railroads in Interstate Commerce; Chapter IX with Municipalities; Chapter X with Corporate Reorganization; Chapter XI with Arrangements with Unsecured Creditors; Chapter XII with Real Estate Arrangements.

[5]Bankruptcy Rules, Rule 11–44.

2. No further proceedings can be instituted against the enterprise in state courts, and all the work involved in defense of creditors' actions is focused in the bankruptcy court.

3. Unprofitable contracts can be rejected.

4. All creditors know that they must wait for any payment so that all funds can be conserved for the operation of the business.

5. A recalcitrant creditor can be forced to accept a plan offering less than full payment of his debt provided a majority of creditors, in number and amount, accept the plan and the plan is found, by the court, to be in the best interests of creditors.[6]

6. Operating funds may become available from banks, private sources, or from the principals themselves because these new funds are not subject to the payment of monies due to pre-petition creditors.

7. Subcontractors and suppliers are more confident that they will be paid for work done and materials delivered, and work at job sites usually resumes.

8. Bank accounts can be used to meet payroll without fear of attachment.

9. Bonded jobs can be turned over to bonding companies and removed from the proceedings promptly.

10. If there is a liquidation, all unsecured creditors are paid equally.[7]

Disadvantages to Filing

Some of the disadvantages of filing a petition under any of the above-mentioned chapters are:

1. If satisfactory arrangements are not made with the creditors pursuant to the Bankruptcy Act, the business enterprise will cease to operate and there will be an adjudication in bankruptcy and a liquidation of all assets.

2. Control of the business may be placed in the hands of an independent third party such as a receiver or trustee appointed by the court.

3. Additional expenses are incurred that may not be involved in an out-of-court arrangement, including counsel fees, receiver's fees, trustee's fees, accountants' fees, and court expenses.

4. The Bankruptcy Act delineates the many steps necessary to bring an enterprise out of such a proceeding, and these steps—which must be followed precisely—are time-consuming and expensive.

Operation of the Enterprise

With the filing of the petition, the business enterprise is placed under the control of the bankruptcy court. The bankruptcy court will decide whether the principals of the distressed enterprise called the *debtor* will continue to make the operating decisions or whether a trustee or receiver will so do.

By filing the petition, the debtor has in fact turned over all of its assets to the bankruptcy court's control for the benefit of its creditors. In order to regain

---

[6]Bankruptcy Act, Chapter XI, Article IX, Confirmation of Arrangement, § 362 (1), 11 U.S.C. § 762.

[7]Some creditors are given priority of payment under the Bankruptcy Act such as wage claimants, tax claimants, and landlords.

control of these assets, the debtor must file a plan of payment called the *plan* that is acceptable to the majority in number and majority in dollar amount of its creditors.

The Plan

The main thrust of a bankruptcy proceeding where the financially troubled enterprise is to be rehabilitated is the formation of an acceptable plan. The continued operation of the business, which is paramount in the principals' minds, is really of secondary consideration in the bankruptcy proceedings.

The plan is of primary importance. It must be constructed in such a way, and presented to creditors in such a manner, that it can be funded, thus allowing the enterprise to continue thereafter, revitalized, although probably smaller in scale than was the case before the filing of the petition.

Information Dissemination

In order for the creditors to make a reasonable decision on the plan as filed by the debtor or by the trustee appointed by the court, the creditors must have sufficient information to make that decision. The Bankruptcy Act provides for full and complete disclosure of all pertinent facts by the debtor. The debtor must file with its petition, or shortly thereafter, complete answers to various questions about its operation for the last two years, including the location of its books and records. These answers are called the *statement of affairs*. At this time, the debtor must also file a complete list of all its assets, stating in detail their location and valuation. In addition, names and addresses of all creditors— secured, unsecured, tax, and other priority creditors—must be listed with the amount of their indebtedness. It is from this list that notices are sent to all creditors of all hearings in the proceedings. These lists are called the *schedules*.

Subsequent to receiving this information, the court will probably appoint an independent accountant to audit the debtor's books and records and to prepare a financial statement as of the date the petition was filed. This audit may be intense enough to uncover a great deal of information that would be helpful to creditors making a decision as to whether the debtor is an honest or a dishonest contractor. The accountant will also prepare monthly operating statements so that the creditors will have specific information to determine if the debtor is dissipating the creditors' assets during the operation in the proceedings or whether the debtor is holding its own in the operation. This information is important to creditors because these proceedings are usually prolonged and losses in operation will diminish the return available to creditors if liquidation results.

In addition to these written reports and statements, the principals of the debtor will be interrogated about the operation at a first meeting of creditors during an open court hearing at which time the principals will be asked to describe why the operation was not a successful one, how they plan to operate the enterprise during these proceedings so that it will be more profitable, and other relevant questions that apply to this particular enterprise.

Based upon all the reports and testimony elicited, creditors are required to make a determination whether the plan offered by the debtor is acceptable.

The Negotiation of the Plan

If the operations of the business during the bankruptcy proceedings are going well, and if financing for a plan appears likely, negotiations start in earnest between the debtor and the creditors' committee. The object is to propose a plan which the creditors' committee believes would provide for the creditors more money than would be provided by a liquidation of the debtor's assets, still leaving the debtor sufficient funds to operate a successful, if smaller, enterprise after the proceeding concludes.

Most or all the facts necessary for such a decision will have become available to creditors by this time through interrogation of the principals of the debtor, through accounting reports, and through an examination of the debtor's assets. The creditors will be able to evaluate the proposals contained in the debtor's plan since they are usually knowledgeable in the building trades, and therefore know the value of the assets of the debtor in liquidation.

There is usually some difference of opinion between the debtor and the creditors' committee as to what that figure should be, but if enough information has been generated during the proceedings, and if the creditors have determined that the debtor is an honest debtor worthy of their help in being rehabilitated, the debtor should be able to negotiate an acceptable plan. Such a plan would probably be accepted by the creditors because, though their return will be less than the full amount of the debt, it will be greater than that which they would have received in liquidation.

When the acceptable figure is reached, the debtor will file the plan with the court and the creditors' committee will solicit and file enough acceptances to allow approval of the plan at a special hearing arranged by the court after notice to creditors.

Each creditor who has filed a claim is entitled to vote, and any creditor that does not file an acceptance is deemed to have voted against the plan. Since the creditors' committee has determined that the acceptance of the plan will provide more money at an earlier date for creditors than a liquidation would provide, the creditors' committee is usually successful in the solicitation of a favorable vote. The plan is usually approved if all parties work together to get sufficient acceptances.

Confirmation of the Plan

The debtor then must conclude financing that will provide for the payment of administration expenses, taxes, other priority claims and the agreed amount that was provided for unsecured creditors. If there is a deferred payment provided in the plan, the debtor will usually be required to provide security to the creditors for payment of that deferred amount, and the debtor must arrange for this security. The court is informed when the funds are available, and the court will set a hearing date for confirmation of the plan.

The court will confirm a plan of arrangement if it is satisfied that all the proceedings have been in compliance with the provisions of Chapter XI of the Bankruptcy Act, that the plan filed and approved by creditors is in the best interest of creditors, that the plan can be carried out by the debtor and is feasible, and that the debtor was not guilty of acts or failed to perform any duties which would bar the discharge of a bankrupt.[8] At confirmation any creditor who believes the plan is defective for any of the above reasons can, after filing written objections to the plan, produce evidence to the court in support of his contention, but lacking such attack, the court will usually confirm a plan that the debtor has submitted and that the creditors have accepted.[9] At that hearing, the court considers all requests for fees claimed by the attorneys, accountants, creditors' committee, receiver or trustee, and other parties who have helped to bring about a successful proceeding.

When the appeal period has expired, the order entered by the court will become final and distribution will be made. At this point, the debtor is out of the court proceedings; all unsecured debts will be discharged; and the debtor will be free to operate without the surveillance of the court.

STATE INSOLVENCY PROCEEDINGS AND OTHER AVAILABLE PROCEDURES

Preliminary Statement

State insolvency laws and various other procedures outside of the Federal Bankruptcy Act can be used by attorneys for solutions to specific problems but do not provide a procedure for complete rehabilitation of a financially distressed debtor as does the Federal Bankruptcy Act. The most widely used procedures by attorneys are state court insolvency proceedings, assignments for the benefit of creditors and common-law settlements.

These procedures have one basic flaw. Any recalcitrant creditor, joining with two other creditors, and who for one reason or another does not trust the procedure chosen by debtor's attorney may file an involuntary petition in bankruptcy against the debtor. In this petition, the creditors would cite certain acts necessarily involved in the above-stated procedures as an act of bankruptcy.[10]

This action by a creditor will force the debtor to proceed under the Federal Bankruptcy Act, and in response to such an action by a creditor, the debtor may find himself involved in an expensive bankruptcy proceeding that he did not contemplate. This action by these creditors may result in all creditors obtaining a dividend lower than that which these creditors could have obtained in the state proceeding or in the out-of-court proceedings, for state proceedings are less expensive, usually less complicated, and usually involve less delay than federal bankruptcy proceedings. The lower expense notwithstanding, creditors often are suspicious of any procedures other than those of the Federal Bankruptcy Act and often choose to force the insolvent debtor to comply with all the requirements of the Federal Bankruptcy Act.

State Insolvency Laws

The insolvency laws of the various states seldom provide an opportunity for complete rehabilitation. These state statutes are usually limited to providing a

---

[8]Bankruptcy Act, Chapter XI, Article IX, Confirmation of Arrangement, § 361-67, 11 U.S.C. 761–767.

[9]Bankruptcy Act, Chapter XI, Article IX, § 366, 11 U.S.C. 766.

[10]Bankruptcy Act, Chapter III, § 3; 11 U.S.C. § 21(a).

method for liquidation of the debtor's assets under state court supervision and a schedule for distribution of the proceeds of the sale of these assets to creditors in these proceedings.[11] The state statutes which set forth the procedures to be followed for liquidation and distribution of assets often follow the Federal Bankruptcy Act but are lacking because they do not provide the debtor a complete release from all liability. In addition, the state statutes, although they set forth a procedure to obtain information from the debtor, do not set up the special machinery by way of available court time to enforce the dissemination of information throughout the proceeding that is necessary for creditors to make important decisions about the proceedings or that is necessary for the ferreting out of assets that may be concealed by the debtor. This failure to supply information often leaves creditors with a feeling that all the assets of the debtor have not been accounted for and often results in dissatisfaction on the part of the creditors with this procedure. As a result, state insolvency statutes have not given to debtors or to creditors a reasonable alternative to the Federal Bankruptcy Act and these procedures have fallen into disuse from a lack of confidence by debtor and creditors.

Assignment for the Benefit of Creditors

Another procedure for liquidation of debtor's assets is an assignment for the benefit of creditors. This is a written document that transfers all right, title and interest in debtor's assets to an assignee who will take charge of the assets, sell them and make distribution to creditors. The assignee may record the assignment as required by some state statutes[12] but most often will not involve himself with any court proceedings. An assignment for the benefit of creditors oftentimes is a satisfactory way of liquidating the assets of an insolvent debtor. If the assignee is experienced, and a proper liquidation of assets occurs, creditors may obtain a substantially larger distribution from an assignment than they could from a liquidation under the state insolvency laws or the Federal Bankruptcy Act. The distribution to creditors under an assignment procedure not only is larger, but it usually is distributed to creditors in a much shorter time than a distribution in a state or a federal bankruptcy liquidation. An assignee with experience in the field oftentimes relies on the help of the creditors to obtain the highest possible sale price for the debtor's assets. The creditors usually have much more control in the liquidation of the assets in an assignment than they would have in a bankruptcy proceeding. State law sometimes provides for a recording of the assignment document and/or a procedure for distribution of assets if a problem develops in the course of the liquidation of assets under an assignment.[13] The satisfaction that results from a speedy distribution of a relatively substantial dividend usually leaves creditors with a feeling that the insolvent debtor did everything possible to ensure creditors as fair a liquidation as could be had from the debtor's assets. If the debtor is free of any improper conduct, this procedure often works out quite satisfactorily.

---

[11]*See e.g.,* Purdon's Penna. Stat. Anno., 39 P.S. §§ 1-327.
[12]Purdon's Penna. Stat. Anno., 39 P.S. § 191.
[13]*See e.g.,* Purdon's Penna. Stat. Anno., 39 P.S. §§ 191–216.

Common-Law Settlement

A common-law settlement has a great deal to recommend it provided creditors are cooperative. It is a procedure which does not involve state or federal law and provides for a meeting between the debtor and his creditors. At this meeting, negotiations start for the payment of less than the full amount of the debtor's indebtedness to its creditors. This procedure has many advantages. The first advantage is that the debtor can stay in business and continue operations unencumbered by substantial costs incurred in a bankruptcy proceeding. In addition, if a good creditors' committee is formed, the debtor can expect help from the creditors' committee both in the operation of its business and in the solicitation of acceptances. The one disadvantage of this procedure is that recalcitrant creditors cannot be compelled to accept the plan submitted by the debtor even if a majority of creditors accept this plan. Recalcitrant creditors can combine to file an involuntary petition in bankruptcy or individually can institute suit against the debtor in the state court. These creditors who do not accept the debtor's plan must be handled individually, and if there are a great many recalcitrant creditors, the out-of-court settlement will not be effective. By dealing with each individual creditor, the debtor may end up paying a substantially higher figure than he might have paid even with the added costs of a bankruptcy proceeding, thus possibly causing a collapse of the business enterprise.

Creditors can expect a fairly substantial distribution in a common-law settlement provided that a creditors' committee can produce enough acceptances to ensure that the debtor will not have to deal with many recalcitrant creditors. An active creditors' committee and an honest debtor can produce a larger payment to creditors without the substantial costs of a bankruptcy proceeding in a common-law settlement, and this particular proceeding should be favored by creditors. Creditors working with a vigorous creditors' committee are usually ensured of a large and prompt dividend through this procedure.

CONCLUSION

The Federal Bankruptcy Act provides a complete and substantial remedy to debtors who want to rehabilitate their business or to liquidate their business if rehabilitation is not possible. The state court and common-law settlement procedures have advantages and defects that make them appropriate in special cases, but these procedures are not appropriate for every insolvent debtor. An attorney should be consulted to discuss with the debtor whether common law, state, or federal proceedings should be used in the particular situation that is unique to the debtor. Creditors should rely on an active and vigorous creditors' committee to protect their rights, and if the debtor and creditors' committee work together, the business enterprise can be saved or can be liquidated with the highest possible distribution to creditors. Cooperation and not contest is the watchword in all the procedures, and cooperation works to everyone's benefit in these difficult situations.

Chapter 51

Entitlement to Retained Percentages

ALEXANDER M. HERON, ESQ.
Partner, Pope, Ballard & Loos, Washington, D.C.

INTRODUCTION

Retained percentages are those portions of the contract price which, under the contract provisions, are withheld for the security of the owner or, similarly under subcontracts, for the security of the general contractor. One of the forms of contract giving rise to much of the law in this field is United States government Standard Form 23A and its predecessors which constitute the general provisions of construction contracts for government work. These conditions provide that in making progress payments, 10 percent of the estimated amount of the payment shall be retained until final completion and acceptance of the contract work. However, any time after 50 percent of the work has been completed and satisfactory progress is being made, the contracting officer may authorize any of the remaining progress payments to be made in full. This form of contract also provides that whenever the work is substantially complete, if the contracting officer considers the amount retained to be in excess of an amount adequate for the protection of the government, he may, at his discretion, release to the contractor all or a portion of the excess amount. The general provisions further provide that upon the completion and acceptance of each separate building or public work or other division of the contract on which the price is stated separately in the contract, payment may be made without retention of a percentage. It is under government contracts that most of the litigation on this subject has developed, although the rules developed there may be applied with equal reason to private contracts having comparable provisions and the security of performance and payment bonds.

The American Institute of Architects' Standard Form of Agreement Between Owner and Contractor, AIA Document A101, 1967 Edition, provides in Article 6 that progress payments shall be made to the contractor on account of the contract sum based upon such percentage of the portion of the contract sum allocable to labor, materials, and equipment incorporated in the work together with such percentage of the portion of the contract sum allocable to materials and equipment stored at the site as may be agreed upon by the parties. Final payment, consisting of the entire unpaid balance of the contract sum which includes retained percentages, shall be paid in a designated number of days after substantial completion of the work unless otherwise stipulated.

The general conditions of the American Institute of Architects, AIA Document A201, 1970 Edition, provide in Article 9.7.3 that the retained percentage shall not be payable until the contractor submits to the architects certain required details including assurance that payment has been made for all labor and material used in connection with the work, the consent of the surety, and other data establishing payment or satisfaction of all obligations in connection with the work including liens. Article 9.7.4 provides that, if after substantial completion of the work, final completion is materially delayed without the fault of the contractor, the owner shall make payment of the balance due for that portion of the work fully completed and accepted. That Article further provides that, if the remaining balance of the work not then fully completed or corrected is less than the retainage and if bonds have been furnished, the written consent of the surety to the payment of the balance due for that portion of the work fully completed and accepted shall be submitted by the contractor to the architect prior to the certification of payment. Such payment shall then be made without constituting a waiver.

In other instances the retained percentage provisions may vary widely depending upon the terms of the agreement between the contractor and the owner. In any case the retained percentages are created by the contract terms and exist only because the parties have agreed upon that method of payment. In this discussion we are concerned only with situations where there has been a failure or breach, usually by the general contractor, as a result of which the work has not been finished or furnishers of labor and material have not been paid and as a consequence claims have arisen which the parties seek to satisfy out of the remaining contract funds.

The use of the retained percentage device has covered a long span of years. It received the attention of the Supreme Court in the landmark case of *Prairie State National Bank* v. *United States*,[1] which involved a contest over the right to the retainages coming before the court for determination in 1896. The contract

---

[1]*Prairie State Nat'l Bank v. United States,* 164 U.S. 227 (1896).

in that case, executed in 1888, provided for a retention of 10 percent of the monthly payment to be withheld by the government until the acceptance of the work.

Similar provisions are found in widely used forms of subcontracts authorizing the general contractor to withhold retainage from the subcontractor in a manner similar to the withholding by the owner from the general contractor. Thus, ultimately, the burden of the withholding may and frequently does fall on the subcontractors.

The rules of law which control this subject represent the application of principles of equity developed over some centuries. In their application to these problems it will be seen that the law which has been developed in this area had its origin at the end of the nineteenth century. It has developed steadily since that time by judicial decisions to the point where these doctrines are well established.

RIGHTS OF THE OWNER

Since the retained sum is provided by contract and remains in the hands of the owner until such time as all conditions of the contract relating to its release have been fulfilled, the owner's right to this fund is paramount to the rights of all other claimants. In other words, the work must have been completed to the point of acceptability, and the contractor must have satisfied the owner and the architect that all requirements imposed by the agreement on the contractor have been either fulfilled or waived by the owner before the latter will be required to release the retainages.

In the absence of the completion of the contract, the owner is entitled to withhold the retained fund, and if it becomes necessary for him to complete or to correct failures on the part of the contractor, the completion costs and all other costs and damages arising from default by the contractor may be charged against the retained funds. After that point the interest of the owner in the retained fund will have terminated and the interests of the materialmen, trustee in bankruptcy, the contractor, and the surety become the subject of consideration depending upon the factual situation out of which the claims of each have developed. But the owner is entitled to insist upon full compliance with the terms of his agreement with the contractor before any other claims to the retained funds can be recognized.

In addition, the owner may offset against the contract funds remaining in his hands, any unrelated claims which he may have against the contractor,[2] subject, however, to this limitation: if the surety completes the work, it is entitled to demand of the owner so much of the remaining contract funds as will reimburse it for its cost of completion.[3] That is because, had the owner completed

---

[2] *United States v. Munsey Trust Co.,* 332 U.S. 234 (1947).

[3] *Aetna Cas. & Sur. Co. v. United States,* 435 F.2d 1082 (1970). *See also Trinity Univ. Ins. Co. v. United States,* 382 F.2d 317 (1967), *cert. denied,* 390 U.S. 906 (1968). *Security Ins. Co. v. United States,* 428 F.2d 838, 192 Ct. Cl. 754 (1970).

the work, it would have been obliged to use the remaining funds for this purpose, and the surety is entitled to make the same use of them. This limitation does not apply to instances where the surety's claim is based upon payment to suppliers of labor and material to the contractor. In that case the owner's right to set off unrelated indebtednesses of the contractor will prevail.

RIGHTS OF THE MATERIALMEN

The rights of the materialmen to participate in distribution of the retained percentages are interwoven with the rights of the surety on the contractor's labor-and-material payment bond. The cases which have given rise to the application of equitable principles and to the marshalling and distribution of the retained percentages have arisen primarily under government or state contracts although there is no reason why, in parallel cases, the same principles should not apply to private construction contracts as well. In the public work sector the statutory bonds provide almost invariably for completion of the construction work as well as for payment to furnishers of labor and material. In the case of construction of public works there is no right of mechanic's lien in the usual sense, but the courts have recognized an equitable lien or equitable interest in the contract balances in favor of the furnishers of labor and material whose claims remain unpaid. Where the amount of the payment bond was insufficient to pay all suppliers, the courts have held the remaining contract funds to be subject to the prior claim of the suppliers even where the surety had paid the full penalty of its bond.[4] The surety's claim was subordinate and secondary to the claims of the labor and material furnishers. The surety was not allowed to compete with the obligees of its payment bond in a contest for the contract funds. Similarly, where the surety had become insolvent and was unable to pay the suppliers, the court held that the receiver for the surety could not maintain a claim to the funds against the suppliers who were awarded the contract balances.[5] There is no real reason why the same rules should not be applicable in cases of private construction where the bond given by the contractor secures payment to furnishers of labor and material even though the suppliers may have mechanic's lien rights in addition to their bond rights. Where, however, the contractor's bond on private work does not provide for payment to labor and material suppliers, it is improbable that the suppliers will have anything more than a right of mechanic's lien. However, if only a performance bond is written, but the private contract contains a provision requiring the contractor to furnish a lien-free project, the performance bond, in effect, may be considered a labor-and-material payment bond by indirection. In the absence of a labor-and-material payment provision in the bond, the surety which may be called on to complete or answer in damages will be entitled to credit for the retained percentages or contract funds remaining in the hands of the owner. It is the presence of the bond with its consequences that gives rise

[4]*American Sur. Co. v. Westinghouse Elec. Mfg. Co.,* 296 U.S. 133 (1935).
[5]*Philadelphia Nat'l Bank v. McKinlay,* 72 F.2d 89 (1934).

to the application of the legal principles which have created the rights with which we are here concerned.

RIGHTS OF THE TRUSTEE OF BANKRUPT

Where the contractor has become bankrupt in the course of his work and has defaulted in the performance of his contract, the owner is entitled to obtain completion of the work and to charge the cost of completion against the retained percentages as well as any other unexpended contract funds in his hands. If the owner should not complete but enter into a contract with the surety for completion, the surety may successfully maintain its right to the retainages and contract funds under its completion contract to the extent necessary to reimburse it in full for the cost to which it has been put. In such case the surety succeeds to the owner's position and will be entitled to enforce all the rights which the owner has. If payment of labor and material is required by the bond, the surety still remains liable to suppliers and may add that liability to its completion costs as the basis of its claim against the retained percentages.

However, in instances where the work has been completed by a contractor who is adjudicated bankrupt following completion, the contract funds will be awarded to the trustee in bankruptcy of the contractor.[6] This does not mean that the bankrupt estate or the contractor's general creditors will have the benefit of those funds. The surety's paramount interest will be recognized in the bankruptcy court.[7] It will be entitled to have the retained percentages and contract balances held as a special fund to which it has a prior claim limited only by such instances in which the material furnishers for some reason still remain unpaid. In that case the claims of the suppliers are superior to the claim of the surety.[8]

RIGHTS OF THE CONTRACTOR

The contractor's right to the retainages is dependent upon full performance of the contract by him. That performance includes also, under the usual provisions of most standard contract forms, payment to furnishers of labor and material, evidence of which can be demanded by the owner under the contract terms. If the contractor should succeed in obtaining the retainages without having paid the labor and material suppliers for which his surety would be liable, both the surety and the suppliers would be entitled to seize the contract funds in a court proceeding provided they remain in an identifiable form. The latter is unlikely, however, the probability being that the contractor would have disposed of the funds promptly upon their receipt so that they could no longer be followed. Where the contractor has failed to complete and failed to pay labor

---

[6]*American Sur. Co. v. Owens,* 66 F.2d 190 (1933). *See also Pearlman v. Reliance Ins. Co.,* 371 U.S. 132, 139 (1962).

[7]*Pearlman v. Reliance Ins. Co.,* 371 U.S. 132 (1962).

[8]*American Sur. Co. v. Westinghouse Elec. Mfg. Co., supra* note 4.

and material suppliers as required by his bond, his claim is subordinate to the claims of all other parties involved.

RIGHTS OF THE SURETY

It has been pointed out before that the right of the surety on the performance and payment bond to the retainages or the balance of the contract funds is interwoven with the rights of the furnishers of labor and material. The fact is that in the situations with which we are concerned, that is, default in performance of a contract and default in payment of furnishers of labor and material, the surety is normally the most active party in pursuing the contract fund. It is usually the surety which takes steps to impound the retainages and contract balances. The owner does not need to take steps of this kind since the funds are in his hands and he is in a position to fully protect his interests. The labor and material furnishers rarely feel the need to take such steps since they may look to the payment provisions of the bond and can insist upon payment of their claims by the surety.

The decision of the Supreme Court in *Prairie State National Bank v. United States,*[9] forms the basis in American jurisprudence for treating retained percentages as a special fund for the indemnity of interested parties. In the *Prairie State National Bank* case, a bank undertook to lend money to the contractor for use in the performance of its contract with the United States. The contractor defaulted, and the surety completed the work. The bank, which had previously obtained a power of attorney with a direction that payment under the contract be sent to it, contended that it had an equitable lien upon the retained percentages remaining in the hands of the United States. The surety which had completed the work also claimed the retained percentages. The Court held that the surety's right to the retainages was superior to that of the bank. It pointed out that had the United States, the owner, been obliged to complete the work, it would have been entitled to use the contract funds remaining in its hands for that purpose. The surety was entitled to insist that those funds be used for that purpose. Consequently, when the surety undertook the burden of completion, it succeeded to the rights of the United States under the equitable doctrine of subrogation, whereby the law recognizes one person as having succeeded to the rights of another person, or as having stepped into the shoes of the other person by performing an obligation owed by that person to another. The Court in *Prairie State National Bank* relied on English cases including one decided in 1838[10] in which the surety was released from its completion bond by reason of the owner's having failed to retain the agreed percentages—in that case, one-fourth of each payment—until completion of the whole work.

The decision in the *Prairie State National Bank* case was followed by *Henningsen v. United States Fidelity & Guaranty Co.*[11] In that case Henningsen's contract to

---

[9]*Prairie State Nat'l Bank v. United States, supra* note 1.
[10]*Calvert v. London Dock Co.,* 2 Keen 638 (1838).
[11]*Henningsen v. U.S. Fid. & Guar. Co.,* 208 U.S. 404 (1908).

construct certain buildings for the United States was secured by a performance and labor-and-material payment bond taken pursuant to the statute which preceded the Miller Act. On completion of the work there remained unpaid claims for labor and materials in excess of the bond penalty. The surety responded by paying the full amount of its bond. That amount was inadequate to pay all claimants. A bank which had lent money to the contractor in the course of the performance of the work and which had taken an assignment of the payments to be received under the contract made claim to the contract balances remaining in the hands of the United States.

The Court followed the principles laid down in the *Prairie State National Bank* case and held that the surety which had paid claims of laborers and material-men was also subrogated to the rights of the United States and that the surety was entitled to reimbursement for the amounts which it had paid. This decision was premised in part upon the fact that the surety's bond put it under legal obligation to pay the furnishers of labor and material and having responded to that obligation, was entitled to stand in the shoes of the United States when it sought reimbursement. In this case a portion of the withheld contract payments was paid direct to creditors, that amount being credited to the penalty of the bond. The surety paid the balance thus paying furnishers of labor and material in full.

Where a general contractor under a government contract had defaulted in the performance of his work and the owner, after having procured completion, still held in its hands an unexpended balance of the original contract price, the surety on the labor-and-material payment bond, having paid about $350,000 of the contractor's debts, claimed the remaining funds. It was held that the surety under these circumstances had a prior claim to the fund. The Court also held that the owner had a right to use the retained funds to pay the laborers and materialmen, that the latter had a right to be paid out of the fund, and that the surety which paid the laborers and materialmen was entitled to the benefits of those rights to the extent necessary to reimburse it.[12] The Court reaffirmed the body of law on this subject which had developed since the *Prairie State National Bank* case.

In another case the contractor failed after completing the work, and the surety paid the full amount of its bond into court for distribution among furnishers of labor and material. The amount of the bond was inadequate to pay all of the labor and material furnishers in full. In addition an unexpended balance still remained in the contract. That was paid over to the contractor's trustee in bankruptcy. It was claimed both by the furnishers of labor and material and the surety. The Court held that the laborers and materialmen had claims superior to those of the surety and that until they had been paid in full, the surety would not be permitted to exercise its otherwise well-established rights of subrogation. This result was reached on the basis of comparative equities, that is, the surety having agreed to pay the claims of the labor and material suppliers and, although having done so to the limit of its responsibility,

---

[12] *Pearlman v. Reliance Ins. Co., supra* note 7.

was still not permitted to compete with them in the distribution of funds flowing from the contract.[13] A surety liable only for part of the debt does not become subrogated to the collateral or to the remedies available to the creditor unless he pays the whole debt or unless it is otherwise satisfied.

Where the owner was given notice by the surety that there were outstanding unpaid claims of subcontractors, but the owner—the United States—ignored the notice and proceeded to make additional payments to the contractor's assignee over the surety's objection, the owner was required to pay to the surety the amounts which it wrongfully paid to the assignee.[14] The decision in this case allowed recovery by the surety of amounts which constituted progress payments and expressly recognized that the rules of equity which impress a special lien or something akin thereto upon the fund are applicable to any contract balances which may remain in the owner's hands whether they constitute retained percentages or progress payments.[15]

From what has been said here it will be noted that the doctrines which have been developed in the law arise in cases where bonds have been given by the contractor and sureties have been involved. These decisions are the result of cases where sureties have almost invariably brought suit. But the principal beneficiaries of these rules have been the furnishers of labor and material, since the rights of sureties are conditioned upon full payment of the latter and unless they are paid the contract funds will be first awarded to them.

[13]*American Sur. Co. v. Westinghouse Elec. Mfg. Co., supra* note 4.

[14]*Great Am. Ins. Co. v. United States,* 492 F.2d 821 (1974). *See also Argonaut Ins. Co. v. United States,* 434 F.2d 1362, 193 Ct. Cl. 483 (1970). *National Sur. Corp. v. United States,* 133 F. Supp. 381, 132 Ct. Cl. 724, *cert. denied,* 350 U.S. 902 (1955). *Continental Cas. Co. v. United States,* 169 F. Supp. 945, 145 Ct. Cl. 99 (1959).

[15]*Argonaut Ins. Co. v. United States, supra* note 14. *See also Framingham Trust Co. v. Gould-National Batteries, Inc.,* 427 F.2d 856 (1970). *National Shawmut Bank v. New Amsterdam Cas. Co.,* 411 F.2d 843 (1969). *In re Dutcher Constr. Corp.,* 378 F.2d 866 (1967). *Reliance Ins. Co. v. Alaska State Housing Auth.,* 323 F. Supp. 1370 (1971). *National Sur. Corp. v. United States,* 319 F. Supp. 45 (1970).

Part Twelve

Estate Planning

Chapter **52**

Estate Planning Problems Relating to Contractors

MARK I. SOLOMON, C.L.U.
CMS Companies, Philadelphia, Pennsylvania

PAUL SILBERBERG, J.D., C.L.U.
CMS Companies, Philadelphia, Pennsylvania

This chapter focuses on those estate planning problems which are unique to the contractor who owns his own business, and it discusses in detail methods for dealing with these problems.

RETAIN OR DISPOSE

The first question which must be answered by the business owner is whether his business should be retained or disposed of upon his death. This is a particularly important question for the contractor since his business will invariably be the largest single asset in his estate and many times will comprise the bulk of his estate. In view of this, the decision which is reached regarding this asset will usually dictate the disposition of the balance of the estate.

Factors which would weigh in favor of retaining the business are:

- Is there successor management within the family unit? If not, is there a qualified manager who can replace the principal and will be satisfied to stay with the company as a minority stockholder or as an employee?

- Is there sufficient liquidity in the estate to meet its obligations?

- Does the surviving spouse have sufficient income so that she is not dependent on the ability of the company to provide her with a salary or with dividends?

Contracting companies, unlike many others, are usually dependent upon the skills of one or two key people. The ability to bid a job and bid it right, the ability to motivate employees, to complete the job at the right cost, to know where to purchase supplies, to maintain relationships with other contractors—all these are qualities not easily transferred. Every reader knows of a successful contracting firm wherein the principal died and his widow, son, or daughter retained the business, only to lose everything because he or she did not have the business acumen to operate the company successfully. The knowledge, respect, contacts, or trust of the employees and suppliers needed to make it work were lacking.

If there are any cardinal rules in this area, the first would be that the business owner should not plan on retaining the business if there is no qualified successor management within the family. If children or grandchildren are not actively employed in the business, chances are that the business should be disposed of upon death. The batting average in those situations where the principal has retained the business for the family and has lacked successor management within the family may be adequate for the major leagues, but they are not good enough when the principal asset of one's estate is at risk.

A similar situation which produces a high risk would be the situation when there are young children who are in school and a key employee is asked to run the company upon the death of the business owner. Although in some circumstances a key employee may assume the management of the company upon the death of the principal, run it successfully, and continue to distribute profits to the family of the deceased, these are few and far between. The more common situation is for a key employee to realize that he or she has the ability to handle the company single-handedly and that the profits which are being shared with the family can be his or hers alone.

It is the authors' experience that the key employee will either leave after a year or two, or will negotiate the purchase of the business from the heirs. The price received by the family in this case is usually far less than would have been received had a buyout been negotiated during the life of the principal to take effect upon death. The key employee simply comes to realize that the company has little value without his or her efforts and ability.

In summary, unless there is active and able management within the family, the business should be disposed of.

Retention of the Business

If there is some successor within the family who could manage the business, a number of other estate planning questions must be considered. Primarily, is there:

1. Enough cash to meet federal and local estate taxes, as well as probate and administration expenses?

2. Sufficient income for the spouse of the deceased so that she does not have to rely on the future success of the company?

Meeting Estate Clearance Costs

Too many estates have been forced to liquidate the business interest because the estate did not have sufficient cash to meet its liabilities.

In an effort to ease the burden on the estate, Congress enacted § 303 of the Internal Revenue Code. Normally, if less than all the shares of stock owned by a business owner are sold to the corporation, the proceeds of the sale are treated as a dividend and taxed as ordinary income. Section 303 provides an exception to this rule and permits a corporation to purchase sufficient stock from the estate to pay federal and local estate and inheritance taxes, as well as probate, administration costs, and funeral expenses. In order to qualify, the value of the stock must be equal to at least 50 percent of the adjusted gross estate. Prior to the 1976 Tax Reform Act there was a more liberal qualification test for 303.

The contractor who is contemplating the use of § 303 has a unique problem because of the nature of his business. Most contractors must be extremely protective of their balance sheet and its ratios because of the importance of bonding. If a large block of stock is purchased by the corporation, cash is moved off the balance sheet and is replaced by treasury stock. Thus, the current ratios would be reduced since current assets will be diminished and current liabilities will remain unaffected.

As a result, contractors should insure this liability by having the corporation purchase life insurance of which it is the owner and beneficiary. Upon death, the corporation will receive the proceeds income tax free and use them to purchase stock from the estate. As a result, the corporation can absorb the estate clearance costs without adversely affecting the balance sheet and the estate will have the liquidity it needs.

CREATING INCOME FOR THE WIDOW

Many business owners think that their widow will be able to draw the same salary that the principal did during his lifetime; this is not so. The Internal Revenue Service will only permit the corporation to deduct compensation if it is reasonable. It is usually difficult to prove that the widow is making a contribution to the company commensurate with her compensation. As a result, the corporation may lose all or part of its deduction.

Equally important is the corporation's continued ability to pay a large salary or dividends to the widow. Between the reduction in profits due to the loss of the principal and the increased compensation which needs to be paid to the successor management, little may be left for the widow.

There are several methods of solving this particular problem. The simplest is for the business owner to make certain that he has sufficient nonbusiness assets which can be invested to produce an income for his widow independent of the business. If the business succeeds and there is a surplus, the corporation can declare dividends; however, the basic necessities of the family will not be jeopardized by the inability of the company to pay dividends.

Widow's Income: Group Insurance

If the contractor does not have sufficient liquid assets outside his business, he should consider increasing his personal life insurance. Normally, this is unattractive since the individual must pay the premiums with his personal after-tax dollars. However, recent changes in state laws have removed many limitations on the amounts of group insurance so that it is now possible to purchase substantial amounts of group insurance on the principal on a most favorable basis. Furthermore, the federal government permits supplemental group insurance for one class of employees. For example, all officers could receive five times salary as a group insurance benefit without increasing the group insurance on other employees if the overall plan is based on criteria which preclude individual selection. A number of practitioners feel that the group insurance on the president's life alone could be increased without increasing group insurance on any other employee of the company as long as the overall group plan is reasonable.

The attractiveness of this approach is not only that the insurance is purchased at a discount due to the purchasing power of a group but more importantly that premiums are deductible to the corporation. Furthermore, the insured need not report as income any part of the premium for the first $50,000 of such coverage (base amount plus supplemental group insurance) and the amount which need be reported on amounts in excess of $50,000 is based on a government table[1] which is substantially less than the premium. For example, the premium at age 60 would be $2,378 per year for $100,000 of insurance, yet the amount which need be reported as income would be only $978. Thus, the employee could receive $100,000 of insurance at a personal cost of $489 if he is in a 50 percent tax bracket (the first $50,000 is tax-free and reportable income of $19.56 per $1,000 equals $978 on the next $50,000, costing $489 in additional taxes).

Widow's Income: Split-Dollar Insurance

If a group insurance plan cannot be designed to fully satisfy the principal's need for an independent source of income for his widow, the principal could enter into a *split-dollar agreement* with the corporation. Structured as an employee benefit to help the key executive obtain personal life insurance protection, the corporation would advance all or a portion of the premium each

---

[1] Income Tax Regulations § 1.79-3 *d* (2).

year which it could treat as an interest-free loan to the executive. Upon death, the corporation could recoup its cumulative premium outlay, with or without a factor for interest. The balance of the proceeds would be available for the widow's income needs.

The insured must report income as recipient of the economic benefit provided by the corporation under the split-dollar agreement. The economic benefit is measured by a separate government table[2] which lists the reportable income per $1,000 of protection. This table is different and somewhat higher than the Table I rates published for group insurance, and there is no $50,000 exemption as there is for group insurance. For illustrative purposes, the rate is $20.73 per $1,000 at age 60, so a person insured for $100,000 would report $2,073 as income for the year, costing $1,037 in additional taxes assuming a 50 percent bracket.

Widow's Income: Deferred Compensation

Another attractive alternative is for the corporation to enter into an agreement with the business owner during his lifetime, whereby the corporation would provide a widow's pension beginning upon the death of the owner. Under this concept, the corporation would agree to provide a benefit for a period of years or for the widow's lifetime. The payments made by the corporation should be deductible if the benefit is deemed reasonable. The widow would be required to report the benefit as income for tax purposes.

In order to ensure the corporation of the necessary cash, it is common for this type of agreement to be funded by a corporate-owned life insurance policy. Upon death, the corporation would receive a tax-free lump-sum death benefit which could be disbursed to the widow over a period of years.

The only weakness to this plan is that the widow becomes a general creditor of the corporation, and the corporation must, therefore, be solvent throughout the payout period in order for her to receive her payments. Even if the obligation is insured, the widow has no assurance of receiving the promised benefit since the insurance proceeds must become a general asset of the corporation.

DISPOSITION OF THE BUSINESS

We have taken the position that, if there is no successor within the family to manage the business, it is usually advisable for the contractor to plan on disposing of his business interests at death. While it is possible to leave the details of this decision to the executor, it is not recommended. The executor does not possess the necessary background or knowledge to operate the business successfully, and finding a willing buyer during the probate period is a difficult, if not impossible, task. Even if a willing buyer is found, the buyer often lacks the necessary funds. Furthermore, the buyer knows that the executor must sell and as a result it is rare that the estate will realize the going-concern

[2]Revenue Rul. 55-747, 1955-2 CB 228; Rev. Rul. 66-110, 1961-1 CB 12.

value of the company. If a buyer cannot be found or mutually agreeable terms cannot be reached, the executor will be forced to liquidate the business. Used equipment and machinery will bring but a fraction of their true value at an auction. The estate could consider itself fortunate to realize twenty cents on the dollar if this course of action need be followed.

A better approach would be for the business owner during his lifetime to arrange for the sale of his business upon death. The most logical purchaser would be partners of the principal or trusted employees. Under the terms of such an agreement, the price could be established and revised each year. Furthermore, terms could be arranged under which the purchase price would be paid. If the principal is in good health, insurance can be purchased to fund the buy-sell agreement since this step will assure the business owner that upon death his estate will receive the agreed-upon price in cash. The only drawback to this arrangement is that the employee or partner may not be able to absorb the premium burden from his after-tax income. If this is the case, one possible solution would be for the corporation to lend the prospective buyer all or a portion of the premium each year pursuant to a split-dollar agreement, as described previously. Upon death, the corporation could recoup its cumulative outlay, with or without a factor for the use of money. The balance of the proceeds would be paid to the owner of the policy, who would use the funds to purchase stock from the estate.

In order to assure the business owner that the proceeds are used by the employees for their intended purpose, a trust could be drawn which would receive the proceeds, exchange them for the stock, and then distribute cash to the estate and stock to the employee. This approach gives both the business owner and the employee what each needs: for the principal—cash for his business; for the employee—capital with which to purchase the business.

PLANNING THE ESTATE

Once plans have been formulated for the retention or disposition of the business interests, the job of the estate planner is greatly simplified and certain estate tax savings devices such as the marital deduction can be applied.

The marital deduction permits an individual to leave the greater of $250,000 or one-half of his adjusted gross estate to his surviving spouse without federal estate taxation upon his death.[3] The assets in the marital share will be subject to estate taxation at the spouse's subsequent death. However, a number of purposes are often served by use of the marital deduction. First, it defers taxation on a substantial portion of the estate, which in itself is a valuable result. Second, any assets in the marital estate which are consumed by the surviving spouse during her lifetime will escape estate taxation altogether. Third, since the estate tax is a progressive tax, splitting a larger estate into two smaller estates can result in tax savings.

[3]Effective 1/1/77.

To qualify for the marital deduction, the assets can either be left outright to the surviving spouse or left in trust. If a marital trust is used, the spouse must have the power to appoint the ultimate beneficiaries of the trust.

Tax savings can also be generated by proper planning for the remaining nonmarital portion of the estate. Any assets above the marital share which are left to the surviving spouse will be subject to estate taxation both at the business owner's death and then again at the spouse's subsequent death, assuming of course that the owner predeceases the spouse. By leaving these assets in a residuary trust for the ultimate benefit of his children, the assets will not be taxed at his wife's death. It is still possible to allow the widow to use the income from the residuary trust for the remainder of her lifetime, thus delaying transfer of the property to the children until sometime after the surviving spouse dies without causing the assets to be included in the spouse's estate.

The selection of which assets to place in the marital and the residuary trusts can be extremely important to the successful evolvement of the estate plan. The contractor should be acutely aware of the potential consequences of leaving company stock to the marital trust.

This problem can arise when the contractor decides to retain the business for the benefit of those children who represent active management. If, in the interest of utilizing the marital deduction, the contractor leaves stock to the marital trust, this division of ownership between the inactive spouse and the active children can be the seed for future family discord. For example, the surviving spouse might desire dividend income whereas the active children would prefer to withdraw their incomes as salaries—deductible to the corporation—and utilize profits for replacement of machinery or business expansion.

Another potential problem should be recognized when stock is left to the marital trust in that the surviving spouse could remarry and the company stock could ultimately be left to the second husband or come under his control indirectly via his influence on his wife.

To sum up, when the decision has been made to retain the business for the benefit of active children, it is generally wise not to leave company stock to the surviving spouse, either outright or in the marital trust. The stock is usually non–income producing and nonmarketable, so that it does not represent an independent, secure source of income for the widow. Furthermore, it may encourage family disputes and may subject the company to the influence of an outsider if the widow remarries.

If company stock makes up the bulk of the contractor's estate so that to maximize the marital deduction it appears that he must leave some of the stock to the marital share, the contractor could plan to have the active children purchase sufficient stock from his estate so that none of the stock is allocated to the marital share. The purchase may be prearranged pursuant to a buy-sell agreement. If funding is required, the contractor and the active children should consider some sort of life insurance arrangement. For example, the children could purchase a life insurance policy on their father's life, using corporate dollars under a split-dollar agreement. At death the proceeds payable to the children can be used to purchase stock from the estate, thereby providing sufficient cash for the marital share and ensuring that all the company stock will be owned by the active children.

PROBLEM OF FUTURE GROWTH

Freezing the Estate

Once the contractor has reached the basic decisions regarding retention or disposition of his company and has made plans to pay the estate clearance costs and provide an adequate income for his widow, the question often arises: "As my company continues to grow, how can I put a ceiling on my estate tax liability?"

An interesting technique is to recapitalize the company, replacing the existing stock with two classes: *preferred stock* with a fixed price representing the bulk of the current company value and *common stock* with a relatively low current value.

The business owner can retain the preferred stock and give away or sell the common. Once he no longer owns the common and retains only the preferred, he has frozen the value of his estate as far as his company is concerned. The future growth of his company will be reflected in the common stock, which will no longer be an asset of his estate.

The right to vote can be given either to the preferred or to the common.

Reducing the Estate: Gifts

If the business owner is concerned with reducing his estate, he may want to embark on a gift program.

There is a $3,000 annual exclusion, which allows a donor to give up to $3,000 per year to as many different individuals as he chooses. Since a spouse may also join in the annual exclusion, the contractor and his wife may give up to $6,000 per annum per donee without taxation. If, for example, there are three children in the family, joint gifts of $6,000 may be made to each child each year, allowing gifts of $18,000 per year free of gift taxation.

Valuation of the contractor's business will be a major issue in his estate plan. An arm's-length buy-sell agreement can be used to determine a value which the Internal Revenue Service will probably accept for estate tax purposes. However, this advantage is not available to the business owner who plans to retain the company for his family. A buy-sell agreement between a father and his children holds little weight with the IRS in determining the value of the company for estate tax purposes.

Valuation of a closely held company is a complicated and ambiguous subject, beyond the scope of this chapter. Suffice it to say that the IRS looks at a variety of factors including book value, history of earnings, and valuation of similar companies. The final valuation for estate tax purposes often results in a compromise from negotiations between the estate—arguing for a low value to minimize estate taxes—and the IRS, which invariably argues the opposite.

A gift program is sometimes advised as a method to help accumulate evidence to establish a value for the company. If the IRS accepts gift tax returns over a period of years which specify the value of the company stock, some practitioners feel that this makes it more difficult for the IRS to later repudiate itself and argue for a significantly higher value. However, it should be emphasized that the gift valuation is not binding on the IRS for estate tax purposes.

When contemplating a significant gift program, the business owner should be strongly advised that the gifts are absolute and irrevocable. This is especially meaningful in an everchanging world. Large gift programs should not be considered until the business owner has sufficient assets to provide both him and his spouse with a comfortable and independent base of security which will withstand the impact of inflation and other changes in the economy. It is unwise to let the tax tail wag the dog. Embarking on a significant gift program to save estate taxes should be done with the utmost caution.

RECENT CHANGES IN THE TAX LAW

The Tax Reform Act of 1976 made sweeping changes in the income, estate, and gift tax laws. The impact of these changes is still being analyzed, and it will be some time before Treasury Regulations, IRS Rulings, and court decisions will be available to further guide the contractor and his professional advisors in the estate planning process. Outlined below are some of the major changes which affect the business owner's estate planning.

The gift tax used to be less than the estate tax. A unified transfer tax-rate schedule has been adopted. This will deter major gift-giving programs. For amounts above the annual exclusions, gifts are a means of avoiding taxes on the future growth of the asset. This advantage must be weighed against the payment of the tax at the time of the gift rather than deferral of the tax until death, plus the loss of the use of the funds required to pay the tax.

Under the old law there was a $30,000 lifetime exemption for gifts and a $60,000 estate tax exemption. These exemptions have been replaced by a unified credit, which will be phased in over a five-year period beginning in 1977. In 1977 the unified credit is equivalent to a gift or estate exemption of $120,000, which increases to $175,000 by 1981.

The marital deduction was changed from one-half of the adjusted gross estate to the *greater* of $250,000 or one-half of the adjusted gross estate.

These changes will benefit individuals with estates of less than $500,000. For example, if the adjusted gross estate is $400,000, the businessowner formerly was allowed a $200,000 marital deduction and a $60,000 estate tax exemption, resulting in a taxable estate of $140,000. Now he is allowed a marital deduction of $250,000 and by 1979 the unified credit will reduce the taxable estate to zero.

It is important to have wills reviewed, since some of the benefits under the new law can be lost without proper action.

The old law allowed qualifying estates to extend payment of the tax over 10 years. To qualify, the value of the closely held business had to be at least 35 percent of the adjusted gross estate or 50 percent of the taxable estate. The interest rate fluctuates and is currently 7 percent. This provision has been retained in the new law.

In addition to the 10-year extension, if the closely held business interest constitutes at least 65 percent of the adjusted gross estate the executor can now elect to stretch tax payments over 15 years. No tax (only interest) must be paid during the first 5 years, and thereafter the tax is payable in equal installments over 10 years. Interest is 4 percent on the first $1 million of qualifying property.

One of the most significant "loopholes" that was closed was the loss of the stepup in basis at the date of death. If the businessowner originally invested $10 for each share in his company and during his lifetime he sold his stock for $100, the $90 gain would be taxable income, probably subject to the capital-gain rates. Under the old law if the businessowner held his stock until death, the basis was "stepped-up" to the value at death, that is, $100. Sale of the stock after his death would mean avoidance of income taxation on the $90 gain. The new law discontinues the stepup in basis so that appreciation since December 31, 1976, is subject to income taxation.

A grandfather clause protects most of the gain prior to 1977. All future appreciation will be subject to income taxation at the time of a sale, which tax is in addition to the unified estate and gift tax.

SUMMARY

The most basic question to be answered by the contractor in planning his estate is whether his business should be retained or disposed of upon his death. As a general rule, unless there is active and able management within the family, the business should be disposed of. In that event it is wise to make plans while the contractor is still active, such as to enter into a buy-sell agreement with a partner or with a key employee.

If the business is to be retained, plans should be made to provide sufficient liquidity to pay the estate clearance costs and to provide a surviving spouse with an independent source of income. Company stock should be left in the hands of the active children and other property should be used to provide for any inactive children and to fund the marital trust. If necessary, plans should be made for the active children to purchase enough stock from the estate so that company stock need not be used to maximize the marital deduction.

A preferred recapitalization can be used to freeze the value of the contractor's estate, since future growth of the company will accrue to the common stock which can be given or sold to the children. A modest gift program may be used to reduce some of the tax impact on the estate and especially to take advantage of annual exclusions. However, only those with very large estates should consider a more ambitious gift program, and even then only after a careful analysis of the economics which will account for the loss of the use of the funds required to pay the current gift tax.

Finally, estate planning is a process more than an end result. Circumstances change, and it is wise to periodically review the overall estate plan to redefine objectives and then to make certain that the plan most efficiently accomplishes the desired results.

Index